1809: Thunder on the Danube

1809

Thunder on the Danube: Napoleon's Defeat of the Habsburgs

VOLUME III: WAGRAM AND ZNAIM

JOHN H. GILL

FRONTLINE BOOKS, LONDON

This volume is dedicated to

David G. Chandler
(1934–2004)

For help along the way

FRONTLINE BOOKS, LONDON

1809 Thunder on the Danube: Napoleon's Defeat of the Habsburgs, Vol III

This edition published in 2010 by Frontline Books, an imprint of
Pen and Sword Books Ltd, 47 Church Street, Barnsley, S. Yorkshire, S70 2AS
www.frontline-books.com

Copyright © John H. Gill, 2010

ISBN: 978-1-84832-547-0

For more information on our books, please visit
www.frontline-books.com,
email info@frontline-books.com or write to us at the above address.

Typeset by JCS Publishing Services Ltd, www.jcs-publishing.co.uk
Printed and bound in Great Britain by MPG Books Limited

Contents

Key to Map Symbols

John H. Gill © 2008, all rights reserved

Stars indicate fortresses, forts, and blockhouses: ★

Units types are indicated by the following symbols. As in the text, units known by their proprietors' or commanders' names are printed in italics.

Sample cavalry unit: Austrian *Liechtenstein* Hussars No. 7 = *Liechtenstein*

Sample infantry unit: Austrian *Hiller* Infantry No. 2 = *Hiller*

Sample artillery (all sides):

Nationality is shown by colour: white for Austrians, black for French, and grey for Napoleon's German allies.

Bavarian 3rd Division = **3 Div**   **French 1st Cavalry Division =** **1**

Austrian movements (advance and retreat) are shown with dashed lines, while those of the French and allied German troops are solid.

Austrian movement = ‑ ‑ ‑ ‑ ‑►   **Allied movement =**

Where helpful for clarity, the following units size symbols have been used.

Regiment

Battalion or Squadron

Company

Maps and Tables

MAPS

TABLES

Illustrations

Except where noted, all illustrations are from the author's collection. ASKB is the Anne S. K. Browne Collection where the curator, Mr Peter Harrington, has repeatedly earned my special appreciation for his courtesy, knowledge, and helpfulness.

The illustrations appear between pages 266 and 267.

Acknowledgements

As always, there are many people to thank for bringing a project such as this to fruition. In order of chapters, I should start with two friends who helped me with Russian (locating sources and translating): Dr Alexander Mikaberidze and Yuri Zhukov. Likewise, many years ago a co-worker named Michael Marczek provided invaluable assistance with several important Polish sources; more recently Richard and Jola Kraemer swam upstream through the turbid waters of archaic Polish to elucidate a number of key points; Andrzej Kosim has also been extremely helpful. In the Hungarian arena, I am especially grateful (again) to Herr Ferdi Wöber, who has brought a tremendous amount of material to light relating to the campaign in Magyar lands; he was a good walking companion in Papa and drove me around the field at Raab. Furthermore, he, Robert Ouvrard, and Martina Kurz are to be thanked for arranging a superb symposium in June 2009 for the bicentennial anniversary of 1809. Dr Jozsef Zachar and Istvan Nagy have also provided very helpful material on Hungarian matters; it is with great regret that I note Dr Zachar's passing in late 2009. Vlado Brnardic has been cheerfully supportive for Croatia; Mag Christa Herzog-Tschinder located wonderful data on Styria; and Dr Frederick Schnied helped with Wagram. For Wagram, I owe an especially large debt to Mag Michael Wenzel, the world expert on that complex struggle. The staff of the Kriegsarchiv in Vienna, especially Dr Otto Kellner, deserve special thanks for courtesy and reliability. Further north, Dr Thomas Hemmann has again been very generous with his assistance, as has Uwe Wild, while Mark van Hattem, Bas de Groot, and Geert van Uythoven have uncovered and supplied all manner of recondite Netherlandish material (Go, Orange!). Similarly, P. B. Krieger Thomsen in Denmark thoughtfully provided an English translation of his excellent article on the Danes at Stralsund. Among Italian friends, I am especially indebted to Ciro Paoletti and Virgilio Ilari. In the United States, Dr Sam A. Mustafa, who knows more about Schill than Schill probably knew, kindly donated suggestions and detailed notes, just as Dr Michael F. Pavkovic was a reliable source for sound editorial advice. Peter Harrington, curator of the Anne S. K. Brown Collection, has once again been more than invaluable in helping me in my quest for uncommon images. Errors are my own, but all of these people and others unnamed have been extraordinarily helpful.

My thanks also go to my friends on the Frontline team: Michael Leventhal, Deborah Hercun, and editor Jessica Cuthbert-Smith (who has kindly stuck with me through this long campaign). I hope Kate Baker, who did so much to put the first two volumes into print, is enjoying her new adventures. Warm thanks, as well, to Lionel Leventhal and Greenhill Books for friendship, courtesy, and assistance over almost two decades.

Most important of all has been the unstinting support of my family, Anne Rieman, Grant Gill, and Hunter Gill. Anne put me on the road to 1809 in the late 1980s and has accompanied me to associated battlefields, libraries, and archives ever since. She and the two sons who have joined us along the way have consistently demonstrated amazing patience. Whether tolerating my odd hours or reading and re-reading draft chapters or engaging in discussions of everything from nineteenth century European politics to illustration layouts, they have been an invaluable part of this lengthy process—and always with a smile. Additionally, my father, Herbert J. Gill, read the manuscript with thorough care, offering helpful suggestions. Without their backing none of this would have been possible. I can only hope that these few words will convey some glimmer of the gratitude they deserve.

Preface

Welcome to the third volume of this study of the 1809 war between Napoleonic France and Habsburg Austria. Those who have delved into the first two volumes will have recognised that this is essentially a 'traditional' campaign narrative focused on military operations within their diplomatic-strategic context. War, after all, is fundamentally about combat and solid battle narrative is indispensable to expanded analysis. In the present case, I hope that the history offered in this study will be useful for other scholarship by offering a fresh perspective that is comprehensive in sourcing and approach. In the first instance, I trust that these volumes will make some relatively recondite material accessible to the English-language readership for the first time. Second, I have made a particular effort to cover the entire war, addressing the subsidiary campaigns (Italy, Poland, Hungary, etc) as thoroughly as possible within the constraints of space. Napoleon, Charles, Franz, and the rulers of other concerned states certainly had all of these 'lesser' theatres of war very much in mind as they crafted their strategies and policies at the time. Unfortunately, there were simply not enough pages to detail the conflict in some areas, such as combat in the Tyrol and insurrections in Germany, and I must ask readers to refer to my *With Eagles to Glory* for specifics on some of these actions.

Those who have perused the first two books will also have noted that this work is aimed at several audiences. The first of these is the scholarly community. As mentioned above, it is hoped that this study will serve as a foundation or touchstone for others examining this rich period of history. Whether the reader is interested in Stadion's efforts to reform the Habsburg state, French domestic politics, the manifold transitions emerging in Germany, or popular images and experiences of combat, the war of 1809 provides an ineluctable backdrop, if not an essential component of analysis, relating to the period. Furthermore, within the larger framework of global military history, this conflict is a turning point in France's military fortunes under Napoleon and, in the view of one scholar, represents the world's first 'modern war' within what another describes as the first 'total war'.[1] The second major audience is what one may loosely term the 'interested public': enthusiasts who may be 'amateur' in the sense of working outside academe and perhaps lacking formal historical training, but who are often sedulous researchers and keen observers dedicated to accuracy and detail.[2] It is hoped that these individuals will find some useful material here for the furtherance of their pursuits. Moreover, it is important to link these two audiences. On the one hand, those in the 'interested public' are urged to explore the perspectives and depth proffered by historians writing in the 'non-traditional' mode (broadly, the so-called 'new military history') on topics that are beyond the scope of this study. I have attempted to suggest some pointers in the notes for further reading in at least some areas. At the same time, this war offers the scholarly community a coherent body of data to mine for further research. I have expended many words on side campaigns and much space on orders of battle, not only because these are intrinsically interesting (as I find them) and relatively unexplored regions, but also because they offer crucial data if we want to assess the actions of the various antagonists in this conflict. Rather than simply stating that 'Napoleon secured his flanks' or that he had so many thousand men at Wagram, it is important to understand *how* and *with what forces* he secured his flanks and what *other* forces were available but not employed in any given battle or foray. One might think of this as a question of 'asset distribution'. In other words, commanders and monarchs had certain assets and resources, how they chose to distribute them gives us a view into their thinking, their priorities, their capabilities, and limitations. Thorough research into orders of battle therefore not only allows us to assess troop numbers, quality, and organisation at a given battle, but also underwrites a more strategic view of the commander's or ruler's situation by painting an holistic picture of *all* his available assets and how he distributed them to achieve his objectives.[3] Wagram is a grand example of this phenomenon as Napoleon took risks on all other fronts in order to bring every possible bayonet and sabre to bear on the principal focus of his attention: the Austrian Hauptarmee.

This work, then, is a starting point, a foundation, it cannot—even in three volumes!—cover all dimensions of this complex struggle, and much of the further work must be left to others to expand our horizons and increase the depth of our understanding of this central conflict in the Napoleonic epoch. There are a host of under-researched areas related to 1809 to investigate. These include the Landwehr (operational/organisational history, motivations, socio-political-economic impact, popular imagery, etc),[4] a good, modern biography of Kaiser Franz II/I, the Russian role (including the tsar's relations with his generals), dynastic politics within the House of Habsburg, and many more. In the meantime, I hope you enjoy reading this study as much as I have enjoyed preparing it, and I look forward to seeing you in the archives as we continue our exploration of this pivotal year.

Conventions

ON ORTHOGRAPHY

There are no simple, easy answers when it comes to presenting names and titles from a variety of foreign languages (even if one discards 'Charles' for a more Germanic variant, one has to decide between 'Carl' and 'Karl'). Except for the most prominent individuals, therefore, I have used spellings and titles from their original languages or those most often encountered in contemporary sources. Thus 'Archduke Charles' for 'Erzherzog Carl' (or 'Karl'), but 'Kaiser Franz I' rather than 'Emperor Francis I' (recall that, as noted in Volume I, he had been 'Franz II' until 1806, when he laid aside the title of Holy Roman Emperor). This is all in an effort to retain the flavour of the age and remind us of the variety of nations involved in the war, while keeping things familiar for an English-language readership. Similarly, the titles 'tsar', 'Kaiser', and 'emperor' have been employed to make it easier to distinguish between Alexander, Franz, and Napoleon when these monarchs are not addressed by name. As for spellings of names, I have generally taken these from *Krieg 1809* and Wurzbach for Austrians and from Six, Pigeard, and Quintin on the French side (see Bibliography for details).

As this account moves away from Germany and Austria into other lands, the situation becomes more complex. Readers should note that for simplicity I have avoided the various accent marks that provide nuance to Polish, Hungarian, Czech, Slovak, and the southern Slavic languages (eg Generals Dabrowski and Zajaczek rather than Dombrowski and Zayonczek). As in the previous volumes, I have generally retained contemporaneous German spellings of place names for populated places and geographic features in the Habsburg Empire (Lemberg rather than Leopol, Lvov, or L'viv). For Russian personal names, I have used the transliterations in Alexander Mikaberidze's valuable volume on Russian generals of the era.

OTHER CONVENTIONS

As in the first two volumes, the following conventions apply here:

- French, German, and Austrian ranks and noble titles are preserved in so far as this is feasible (a table relates these to current US and British ranks and lists abbreviations);
- 'Ligne' and 'Léger' refer respectively to French line and light infantry;
- Austrian regiments are designated by the titles derived from their *Inhaber* ('patrons' or 'proprietors') rather than their numbers;
- Units known by the names of their *Inhaber* or their commanders are presented in italics (Württemberg Oberst Karl von Neuffer commanded Jäger-Bataillon *von Neuffer*);
- Arabic numerals indicate French corps d'armée (Davout's 3rd Corps) and Roman numerals are used for the Austrians (Bellegarde's I Corps) as a device to help differentiate between them in the text;
- Battalions or squadrons of a regiment are designated by Roman numerals (II/*Jordis* indicates the 2nd Battalion of *Jordis* Infantry Regiment No. 59);
- 'Rheinbund' refers to the Confederation of the Rhine;
- 'Allied' and 'Allies', when capitalised, refer to the French and their German confederates, while 'German' refers to the host of small states between the Rhine and the Prussian border;
- In most cases, modern German/Austrian, Italian, Polish, and other spellings have been used for geographical names so the reader can locate these on a present-day map or road sign; however, contemporary Austrian names have been retained for many terrain features and towns in the Czech Republic, Slovakia, and Hungary;

All dates are according to the Gregorian calendar (rather than Julian).

Table of Comparative Military Ranks and German Noble Titles

Austrian and German Ranks (Abbreviation)	French Ranks (Abbreviation)	Modern British or U.S. Equivalents
Feldmarschall (FM)	(no equivalent rank)	Field Marshal or General
Feldzeugmeister (FZM) or General der Kavallerie (GdK)	(no equivalent rank)	Lieutenant General
Feldmarschall-Leutnant (FML) or General-Leutnant (GL)	Général de Division (GD)	Major General
General-Major (GM)	Général de Brigade (GB)	Brigadier General
[staff] Oberst	Adjutant-Commandant	[staff] Colonel
Oberst	Colonel	Colonel
Oberst-Leutnant (OTL)	Major	Lieutenant Colonel
Major (MAJ)	Chef de Bataillon or Chef d'Escadron	Major
Stabs-Hauptmann	Adjoint	[staff] Captain
Hauptmann, Rittmeister (cavalry), or Kapitän	Capitaine	Captain
Oberleutnant (OLT) or Premierleutnant (PLT)	Lieutenant	Lieutenant, First Lieutenant
Leutnant	Sous-Lieutenant	Subaltern, Second Lieutenant

Notes:

    a All comparisons are approximate, protocol and functions could vary widely.

    b The rank of Feldmarschall-Leutnant was unique to the Austrian military (the Germans used General-Leutnant), but Feldzeugmeister, General der Kavallerie (or Infanterie), and Feldmarschall were occasionally used by Napoleon's German allies.

    c In the French Army, the title 'Major Général' indicated a function rather than a rank and was unique to Berthier. Similarly, the title 'Generalissimus' was unique to Archduke Charles. Technically, the French title of 'Marshal' was also an appointment rather than a rank.

GERMAN NOBLE TITLES

German (Abbreviation)	English
Erzherzog (EH)	archduke
Freiherr	baron
Fürst	prince
Graf	count
Grossherzog	grand duke
Herzog	duke
Kaiser	emperor
Kaiserin	empress
Kronprinz	crown prince

Note: the prefix 'Erb-' was sometimes used to indicate an hereditary title (Erbgrossherzog).

Prologue

It is probable that I will soon recall you to finish all of this with a grand
battle.

Emperor Napoleon to Marshal Davout, 21 June 1809[1]

The war in the Danube valley, the principal theatre of operations, divides
conveniently into three broad phases interrupted by one extended pause.
The first volume of this series covered the opening campaign of the war:
Austria's April 1809 invasion of Bavaria and its rapid repulse as Napoleon
arrived on the scene from Paris to assume command of his scattered forces.
The second phase, the French offensive into Austria, culminating in the
great bloodletting at Aspern–Essling on 21–2 May, was the focus of the
second volume. That tome also described the invasion of Italy by Archduke
Johann, followed by his withdrawal and the energetic pursuit conducted by
Napoleon's stepson, Viceroy Eugene.

We now come to the third phase of the war along the Danube. In terms of
the narrative, it is late May 1809, and a six-week pause ensues as both sides
assess the struggle at Aspern and decide on their next moves. The pause
affords us an opportunity to step back in time to April and catch up on the
combat in the other theatres of this vast conflict. Though subsidiary to the
Danube, these other arenas were important to Napoleon and the Habsburg
leadership as they made decisions on strategy, diplomacy, and resource
allocation. The first of these, Poland, was critical to Austrian political-military
calculations as a field where Austria might gain a quick victory and cajole
or compromise Prussia into joining the war. It was also the stage on which
Russia would play a carefully ambiguous role, doing irreparable damage to
the Franco-Russian alliance but also generating enormous anxiety in the
Habsburg court. We pick up the second theatre, Hungary, in late May, as
Eugene turns his Army of Italy east to seek out and neutralise Johann at the
Battle of Raab on the anniversary of Marengo. Dalmatia, Croatia, and Styria

provide the third theatre, the southern strategic flank for both sides. Going back again to April, the narrative follows the abortive Austrian invasion of Dalmatia and the subsequent French advance through Croatia to a struggle for the Styrian capital, Graz, in late June. Though not 'southern' per se, this section also covers the fighting in the Tyrol as it was intimately connected with Styria and other events on this flank.

These excursions bring the story back to the Danube, in the warm, pleasant days of late June 1809. They thereby lay the groundwork for an examination of French and Austrian strategy as Napoleon focuses all of his terrifying energy on accomplishing a second crossing of the great river, and Austrian counsels drift in endless, bitter, fruitless debate concerning their courses of action. On 4 July, Napoleon, taking the decision from their hands, strikes across the Danube on a wild night of thunder and storm, a true 'night out of Macbeth'.[2] His assault opens the Battle of Wagram, a contest of epic proportions. Only Leipzig, the 'Battle of Nations' in October 1813, would exceed it in scale and scope. The French gain a victory, but it is not sufficiently overwhelming to bring an immediate end to the war. Napoleon must thus pursue Archduke Charles to one final confrontation outside the medieval walled city of Znaim in Moravia. Here, savage fighting and cunning diplomacy intersect amid another violent thunderstorm to bring an armistice that sets the two sides on the road to peace.

The final phase of the war along the Danube from Wagram to Znaim thus forms the core of this volume. This central thread, however, is surrounded by a welter of smaller but strategically important secondary combats. From the North Sea to the Adriatic, from one of Britain's greatest amphibious invasions to hopelessly rash forays by exhilarated German patriots and vicious guerrilla warfare among the beautiful vales of the Tyrol, these flanking actions create the context for the central campaign. This, then, is the story of the final phases of the 1809 war, a titanic battle, a surprising armistice, a strict peace, and a host of contributory struggles at the mid-point of Napoleon's imperial career. From this point forward, his star began to falter, while those of his foes started to strengthen individually as they gradually coalesced into combinations that were beyond even his powers to oppose.

PART I

Clearing the Strategic Flanks

CHAPTER I

War Along the Vistula

Poland was the second most important theatre of operations in the initial stages of Austrian planning for war in 1809.[1] Although it had slipped to third place in March as Italy assumed greater prominence, Poland remained a key element in Austria's strategy, from both a military and a political standpoint. On the military side, a Habsburg invasion force was to 'drive on Warsaw with overwhelming strength', knocking the Poles out of the war and thus removing a potential threat to the Austrian strategic rear before turning west to join the Hauptarmee in central Germany.[2] Politically, Vienna hoped to purchase Prussia's participation in the conflict by offering King Friedrich Wilhelm III captured Polish territory, including Warsaw. It was further hoped that the Austrian advance would drive Polish troops onto Prussian lands, provoking a confrontation and perhaps forcing the reluctant Prussian monarch to ally himself with Austria.[3] Alternatively, parts of Poland might be offered to the tsar to keep Russia out of the war. Finally, a resounding Habsburg victory could be expected to dampen any insurrectionary thinking among the discontented ethnic Poles of Austrian Galicia. With these goals in mind, Charles's instructions to GdK Archduke Ferdinand Karl Josef d'Este, the commander of VII Corps, stressed speed, surprise, and the importance of making an impression on 'public opinion'. Apparently concerned that Ferdinand would dissipate his strength by making unnecessary detachments, the Generalissimus enjoined him to keep his force together and to conduct his operations 'with such vigour that nothing can resist you; the enemy's embarrassment must be exploited and he must be left no time to recover until Your Grace is assured of his harmlessness.'[4] These words, written on 28 March, resonate with irony, given the debilities that the Main Army would display in precisely these areas during the campaign in Bavaria.

Ferdinand, his family displaced from northern Italy, was fired by a sense of injustice and had been a passionate proponent of war with France, earning the nickname 'war trumpet' for his determined advocacy.[5] He was approaching his twenty-eighth birthday in April 1809 and had previously participated in combat during the 1799 and 1800 campaigns in Germany with varying fortunes, including the cataclysm at Hohenlinden. In 1805, newly promoted to General der Kavallerie, he had been the nominal commander of the Habsburg army that invaded Bavaria, but escaped the ignominy of capture by fleeing to Bohemia before the surrender at Ulm. He later had the better of Wrede in a series of minor engagements near Iglau.[6] Young, ambitious, and sure of himself, his desire for military glory may have been further piqued, as Pelet suggests, by the residual taint of the flight from Ulm (deserved or not).[7] He certainly regarded the Poles as second-rate foes who would be easily vanquished, and he looked forward to taking his corps west to engage the 'real' enemy in the principal theatre of operations.[8] This corps, with some 24,040 infantry and 5,750 cavalry, was structured like its fellows within the Hauptarmee but, owing to its independent mission and the open terrain in which it was to operate, it had twice as much light horse (four instead of two regiments) and its own miniature cavalry reserve of two cuirassier regiments.[9] It was also assigned a large artillery component of ninety-four guns, though only seventy-six of these were on hand at the start of hostilities. In general, VII Corps was superior to its Polish adversaries in training and experience, but some infantry regiments had a high proportion of brand-new inductees and several were recruited wholly or partially from ethnic Poles of Galicia.[10] Many of these men were unwilling subjects of the Habsburg crown and clearly preferred the cause of independence espoused by their brothers in the Duchy of Warsaw. Their sympathies and restiveness demanded special vigilance on the part of their commanders and in several instances led to serious desertion problems. In addition to Ferdinand's field formations, approximately 7,600 to 8,000 men were available to defend Austrian Galicia in the army's rear. This small force, under the orders of FML Fürst Friedrich Carl Wilhelm Hohenlohe-Ingelfingen, was composed almost entirely of depot troops—raw recruits who were only beginning to learn how to handle their muskets and manoeuvre in formation. Further second-line forces (ten Landwehr battalions) were designated to garrison Krakow, a critical supply base and fortress guarding the entry to Moravia.

Though the Austrians enjoyed broad advantages in training, experience, and numbers, VII Corps lacked a bridging train.[11] This would prove a serious deficiency in a theatre dominated by the broad Vistula and intersected

by numerous smaller watercourses. Given that Sandomierz was the only fortified crossing over the Vistula between Krakow and Warsaw, 'prudence commanded him [Ferdinand] to make himself master of the Vistula,' as Polish Captain Roman Soltyk noted in his history of the war.[12] A secure crossing site with fortified bridgeheads on both banks could have been constructed before the war (albeit at the risk of provocation) as 'a pivot for his operations', to permit VII Corps to operate either west or east of the great river with equal facility.[13] Instead, Ferdinand, with no bridging equipment, found his operations confined to the western (left) bank and he only gave thought to a suitably sited and protected crossing after his opening moves had failed to produce a decisive result. For contemporaries, the triangle of Polish fortifications at Modlin, Serock, and Praga was also critical; a later observer calls them 'the strategic core' of the duchy, locations where the Poles could recruit, train, and, if necessary, recuperate in relative safety.[14] Soltyk notes that Ferdinand lacked a siege train that might have allowed him to reduce these key points and others (such as Thorn), but such an encumbrance would have been inconsistent with the need for rapid operations.[15] Furthermore, as Ferdinand did not expect serious resistance from the Poles, he did not see this lacuna as a serious matter. Indeed, he founded his strategic thinking on the assumption that the Prussians would soon join the war and mop up Polish remnants while VII Corps marched west. This notion of imminent Prussian intervention on Austria's behalf—inspired in part by the steady correspondence he maintained with Oberst Graf Goetzen, the pro-war governor of Prussian Silesia—seems to have evolved into a firm conviction in the archduke's mind, an illusion that would guide his actions in the coming weeks.[16]

On the other side of the border, the Polish army commanded by GD Prince Joseph Poniatowski was inferior to the Austrian field force in almost every respect. The disparity in numbers was especially glaring. Where Ferdinand rode at the head of 29,800 men with seventy-six guns initially (rising to ninety-four), Poniatowski had barely 14,200 men and forty-one pieces on hand at the opening of the war. This figure included a small contingent of Saxon troops who, when the war broke out, were already under orders to return to their kingdom. Apart from the Saxons, this was largely a new army as far as its soldiery was concerned, having only come into existence in the latter stages of the 1806–7 war. Additionally, it was in the middle of a major reorganisation as third battalions were being created for each infantry regiment and company strength was expanding from 95 to 140 men to conform to the French model. Beyond the small field army, Polish troops constituted major portions of the garrisons in Danzig, Stettin, and Küstrin, a requirement that deprived Poniatowski of three infantry regiments (5th, 10th, and 11th) and the 4th Chasseurs. A few of these units, along with thousands of new conscripts and volunteers, would be drawn into the fighting in Poland during the course of the conflict, and men of the 4th Chasseurs would find themselves in action against German insurgents. Furthermore, three of the duchy's infantry regiments (4th, 7th, and 9th)—one-quarter of its foot soldiers—were committed to the French adventure in Spain. These deductions left Poniatowski with a mere five regiments of Polish infantry, five of cavalry, and his Saxon contingent of two battalions and two hussar squadrons in the Warsaw area when the Austrians crossed the border. The only immediate reinforcement he could expect was the 12th Infantry in Thorn, which would hardly compensate for the impending loss of the Saxons. The Polish leadership, however, counted on nationalistic enthusiasm to increase the power and endurance of their forces. With a vision of national liberation as inspiration, they hoped to foment rebellion in Habsburg territory, raise the countryside against any Austrian invasion, and field large numbers of new formations once the campaign began.

Compared with their troops, many of the Polish generals and senior officers had amassed considerable combat experience fighting under French banners or in battle with Russia and Prussia since the early 1790s. The two most tested, competent, and popular—GD Jan Henryk Dabrowski and GD Joseph Zajaczek—however, thoroughly detested one another, and neither had much use for Poniatowski. These and other intrigues and suspicions at the top levels of the army cancelled out much of the experience that these men and their subordinates had accrued over the years and created fissures that had the potential to compound the army's other problems.[17] Moreover, the prince, 46 years old in 1809, was the son of an Austrian general and had himself served as a Habsburg officer for several years. Poniatowski had demonstrated courage, coolness, a talent for light cavalry operations, and an abiding interest in training in the course of his military apprenticeship, but this personal history left him vulnerable to malicious innuendo about confused loyalties and lingering pro-Austrian sympathies. Ferdinand certainly thought there were Habsburg attachments to exploit.[18] After leaving Habsburg service, Poniatowski was placed—more or less against his will—in command of large Polish forces during 1792 and 1794. He had not shone, so his military competence also came into question, but Napoleon had appointed him as minister of war and *de facto* army commander when the duchy was established in 1807.[19] All of these factors presented Poniatowski with daunting challenges as he tried to counter Ferdinand's invasion in 1809. Fortunately for him, what the Poles did have in good measure was dedication to their cause and country. These passions would not sustain them indefinitely and would be vulnerable to the shock of setbacks, but patriotism and zeal would form a strong foundation for future victory if the army could be relatively successful in the initial tests of combat.

The army had been organised into three divisions under Poniatowski, Dabrowski, and Zajaczek during 1808—at least in theory. In reality, the detachments to Spain, Danzig, and the Prussian fortresses made the divisional organisation irrelevant, and Poniatowski's fractious relations with his fellow generals of division promised friction, frustration, and confusion should war come. The army therefore functioned as a single unit under Poniatowski's orders, with Dabrowski and Zajaczek playing relatively minor roles. He would soon shunt both off to raise and organise new units in the hinterlands, distant from himself, each other, and the main force of the army. He thus took direct control of the principal field army with a group of energetic, skilful generals of brigade as his immediate subordinates.

The mission that this field army was to perform was relatively open. Napoleon, trusting that the threat of a Russian advance would deter Austria from invading Poland, initially believed that 'the Duchy of Warsaw is not menaced.'[20] As a consequence, Poniatowski was simply directed to concentrate his troops, cover Warsaw, foment unrest among the Poles across the border, and hold himself in readiness to enter Galicia if war broke out. The intentions behind these instructions illuminate Napoleon's clear strategic vision. Focused on the principal theatre of war, the emperor would strain every sinew to augment his own forces in the Danube valley while diminishing those of his immediate enemy. In the first instance, therefore, the Poles were to 'be a diversion and oblige the enemy to maintain numerous forces in Galicia', as far as possible from the main front. Major elements of the Polish army, however, might deploy to Saxony if the Russians held the Austrians in check as Napoleon expected.[21] Implied in these tasks was the need to deny the Austrians any major successes and to keep the Polish army in existence as a viable force.[22]

Poniatowski, however, had more ambitious plans. As an ardent patriot with considerable military experience, his interpretation and execution of Napoleon's directives were informed by a fine grasp of his strategic role in the coming war and a firm faith in 'the advantages of the offensive'. Although he mistakenly believed that the Habsburg commanders would limit themselves to a defence of Galicia, he was concerned that a serious Austrian attack would cripple the Duchy of Warsaw's ability to support its army and possibly endanger the very existence of the revived Polish state. As early as 4 February 1809, therefore, he proposed using offensive operations into Galicia to achieve two strategic objectives. First, he saw an invasion as the 'best means . . . to provide for the defence of Warsaw', as he would thereby seize the initiative from the Austrians and keep them distant from the heart of the duchy. Second, by taking the war to the enemy, he could exploit 'the attachment of the Galicians to the French cause and to their nation', raise new troops, and support his forces from the resources of the enemy's territory.[23] Politically, he could also hope that a successful advance into Galicia would set the stage for the province's subsequent incorporation into the duchy. Perfectly suited to Napoleon's intentions, Poniatowski's early proposals thus provided a well-considered foundation for Polish operations in the campaign that was about to open.

FERDINAND'S MARCH ON WARSAW

The weather that spring was as inclement in Poland as it was in Bavaria: 'a cold and raw April weather mixed with snow flurries', in the words of a Saxon hussar. 'The roads were bottomless', he continued, 'as it had alternately frozen, thawed, rained, and snowed for many days.' The region's infamous roads and tracks—'all are bad', noted Pelet—slowed everything and combined with the wretched weather to inflict wet, bone-chilling misery on the soldiers of both armies as they marched. 'A sharp wind drove the snowflakes into our faces so that one could not see ahead very well, while the horses had to wade through mud up to their knees.'[24]

Consistent with his instructions to keep his corps together and his own desire to march for Germany as soon as possible, Ferdinand's plan was to gather the main body of VII Corps at a village named Odrywol, eleven kilometres south of the Pilica River in order to open hostilities with a rapid strike to Warsaw via Nowe Miasto. At the same time, a detached brigade under GM Johann von Branowaczky was to capture or blockade the little fortress at Czestochowa, far to the south-west, before joining the corps.[25] All

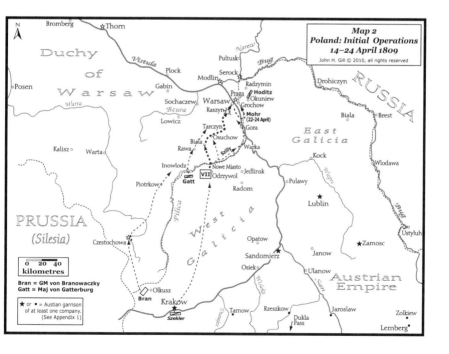

of this action was to take place west of the Vistula, only two squadrons of *Kaiser* Hussars were left on the east (right) bank under Major Friedrich Graf von Hoditz to observe the Poles. Apparently, neither Charles nor Ferdinand saw any usefulness in having a significant force on the far side of the river.[26] Ferdinand was supposed to initiate his offensive on the same day as the other Habsburg forces (10 April), but the combination of vile weather and poor roads retarded the assembly of his corps. When the last units finally dragged themselves into their soggy bivouacs around Odrywol on 13 April, therefore, Ferdinand was already three days behind schedule. The men were exhausted, and Ferdinand felt he had no choice but to grant them the 14th to recover from their exertions. Writing to Charles that night he explained the delay, but exuded optimism: 'From the spirit that fills the entire army corps, I foresee great success.'[27]

The following morning, once he got the corps moving, he passed over the Pilica at Nowe Miasto and headed for Biala with the main body, while three squadrons of *Kaiser* Chevaulegers covered his flanks and Rittmeister Anton Szilly rode towards the Vistula along the north bank of the Pilica with his squadron of *Palatinal* Hussars.[28] Branowaczky, also delayed, had dutifully marched for Czestochowa on the 14th, while the *Szekler* Hussars, still awaiting their last two squadrons, apparently remained in Krakow. Ferdinand had Warsaw in his sights as the initial goal of his advance but, knowing almost nothing about Polish dispositions or intentions, he feared that the Poles and their Saxon allies would retreat west towards Saxony on learning of his approach. He thus inclined slightly towards his left (west) to keep the Poles from escaping.[29] The archduke and his staff expected no serious opposition and thought that their reconnaissances would discover the Polish defenders somewhere along the Bzura.[30] Issuing a fruitless proclamation to the Polish people (his promises to restore the previous order could only promote Polish resistance), Ferdinand and his men pushed ahead.[31]

The Poles were surprised by the Austrian invasion. With the excellent intelligence available, Poniatowski was well aware that Ferdinand was approaching the border, and he reported on 12 April that 'the movements of the Austrian troops in Galicia have assumed a more serious character.' The prince, however, decided that estimates placing Ferdinand's strength at 30,000 were nothing more than 'fanfaronades and menaces'. Assessing Austrian numbers at between 15,000 and 18,000, he concluded that the 'corps that will operate along the Pilica is more likely to observe our movements than to affect the invasion of the duchy that has been rumoured for so long'. His confidence notwithstanding, Poniatowski took some precautions. Most of the army had been cantoned in and around Warsaw/Praga, Modlin, and Serock, but on 12 April he had pushed a detachment forward to Raszyn (3rd Infantry with four guns), brought two battalions to Warsaw from Serock and Modlin (I/6th and I/8th respectively), called 12th Infantry down from Thorn, and moved the cavalry closer to the Austrian border. On the morning of 15 April, learning that Ferdinand had actually crossed the border in force, he hastened to collect his small command at Raszyn, some fifteen kilometres south-west of Warsaw. Urged by his aggressive instincts, he considered advancing to meet the enemy the following day, but his artillery chief and trusted adviser, French GB Jean Baptiste Pelletier, dissuaded him by pointing out that reliable intelligence now placed Ferdinand's strength at 26,000– 30,000, double the number of available Poles and Saxons. The prince thus remained at Raszyn to await developments while covering the capital.[32]

In the meantime the Austrians advanced, and by evening on 16 April, VII Corps had reached Biala. Here the archduke received a message from Major Josef Graf Gatterburg commanding two *Kaiser* Hussar squadrons that were scouring the countryside on the Austrian left. Gatterburg, writing from Rawa, reported the surprising intelligence that 'the enemy army has posted itself before Warsaw and the Bzura is entirely unoccupied.'[33] This was welcome news indeed at VII Corps headquarters. 'Heaven grant that they [the Poles] accept battle before Warsaw,' wrote corps chief of staff Oberst Franz Brusch von Neuburg as the whitecoats turned towards Tarczyn on 17 April.[34] The opposing cavalries clashed briefly on the 17th, but the affair was minor. GB Aleksander Rozniecki, commanding the Polish screening forces, characterised the action and the spirit of the young Polish troopers: 'Nothing much is happening, a few killed, a few wounded, but carrying the fight to the enemy has spread extreme joy throughout our squadrons.'[35] In general, however, the Poles remained elusive, and as his corps settled in around Tarczyn on the night of 18/19 April, Ferdinand still had no solid information on Poniatowski's whereabouts.

The Battle of Raszyn (19 April)[36]

The Polish prince had assembled his small army in an excellent position along the Mrowa stream at Raszyn some twenty kilometres north of Ferdinand's headquarters. Poniatowski knew that the odds were against him, but he did not believe he could give up Warsaw without a fight and wanted to prove that the Poles were prepared to defend their homeland. Moreover, a retreat without battle was likely to demoralise the army and give his personal rivals ammunition to accuse him of cowardice, incompetence, or latent Austrian sympathies. To improve his army's chances and offset his adversary's advantages in numbers and experience, he decided to stand on the defensive behind the barrier of the Mrowa. This was a small watercourse, but its banks were exceedingly marshy and recent rains had rendered the low ground almost impassable to formed bodies of troops. In the area of the battlefield, bridges afforded unhindered crossing at only three points: the villages of Michalowice, Raszyn, and Jaworow. The roads leading to these bridges, however, were carried over the marshes on narrow dykes and thus easily covered by the fire of infantry and guns posted on the heights north of the stream. The villages themselves formed excellent strongpoints and essentially defined the major elements of the Polish army: GB Lukasz Bieganski on the right at Michalowice (3rd Infantry, four guns); GB Ludwik Kamieniecki on the left at Jaworow (II/1, II/8, six guns); and 2nd Infantry with the infantry and artillery of GM Ludwig von Dyherrn's Saxon contingent occupied the centre around Raszyn. Poniatowski placed an advanced force under GB Michal Sokolnicki (I/1, I/6, I/8, six guns) at Falenty across the Mrowa and kept the Polish 1st Chasseurs, a squadron of Saxon hussars and five horse guns in reserve two kilometres north of Raszyn. The other Saxon hussar squadron and the elite company of 5th Chasseurs (ie a half-squadron) were stationed to guard the extreme right flank near Blonie, while a battalion (II/6) and two guns were held at Wola.[37] Finally, GB Rozniecki deployed a screening force of several cavalry regiments and four horse guns to cover the main position: 3rd and 6th Uhlans were on the right with vedettes at Nadarzyn; two squadrons of 2nd Uhlans were near an isolated inn; and the third 2nd Uhlans squadron was apparently north of the Mrowa (probably on the left flank). In all, this gave the Polish-Saxon force a mere 9,418 infantry, 3,180 cavalry, and forty-one guns.[38] Two Polish regiments were missing from the order of battle. The 5th Chasseurs, in the rear at Praga, would be called up to cover Poniatowski's far left during the battle, but would not participate in any fighting. The 12th Infantry (1,100 strong) was marching south from Thorn but would not reach the Warsaw area until 20 April.

Ferdinand, despite his many detachments, would bring a considerably larger force to the battle: a total of some 23,350 infantry and cavalry supported by sixty-six guns. Curiously, owing to the extensive detachments and the absence of the *Szekler* Hussars, the Austrians and Poles would have approximately the same amount of cavalry on the field that day (3,057 to 3,180). Though desiring a battle, the archduke did not expect one as he pushed

Hussars were to clear the way for an advance against the Polish left by GM von Civilart's brigade, assisted by GM Franz Freiherr Pflacher's. Mohr's infantry (*Vukassovich*) would conduct a supporting attack against Falenty while the two Grenz battalions protected the right flank and Schauroth the left. GM Leopold Freiherr von Trautenberg's brigade (just clearing the woods south of Janczewice) and the heavy cavalry would form the reserve.[42] It was a fairly straightforward operation, but all these arrangements took time to co-ordinate, and it was 3 p.m. before *Vukassovich* and the Grenzer started north towards their objectives.

Unopposed, the two *Wallach* battalions had soon completed their mission, occupying Dawidy to protect the Austrian flank from a non-existent threat. The men of *Vukassovich*, however, found themselves embroiled in a prolonged and vicious fight as they advanced on Falenty. Connected to Raszyn only via a narrow causeway through the marshes, the village jutted out from Poniatowski's main position like a veritable redoubt

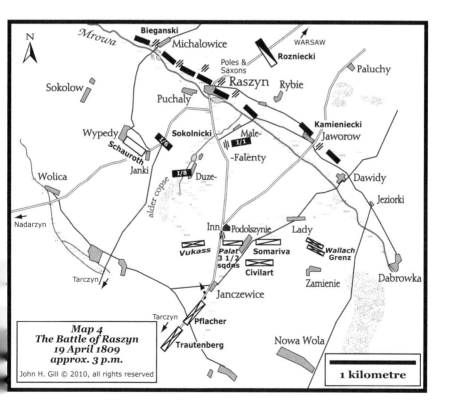

Map 4
The Battle of Raszyn
19 April 1809
approx. 3 p.m.

1 kilometre

and Sokolnicki's men had busily fortified it during the morning, dismantling fences and overturning wagons to create crude breastworks. Falenty and a small copse of alders immediately to its south were entrusted to the fusiliers of I/8 and four guns; I/1 was in a supporting position just behind the village. The former battalion's voltigeurs lined the causeway and nestled themselves among the bushes edging the marsh. Sokolnicki held one additional battalion (I/6) and two guns west of Falenty on the Nadarzyn road to protect his right flank. Trusting to Austrian lethargy, Poniatowski did not expect a serious engagement before 20 April and thus left his subordinate in this hazardously exposed position.

Across the rolling terrain to the south-east, however, Oberstleutnant Ludwig Freiherr Gabelkoven, the new commander of *Vukassovich*, was marching his regiment past Ferdinand's command post and forming it for the attack. In skirmish order, the two companies of the 3rd Battalion led the way (the other four companies were with Schauroth); they were supported by the 2nd Battalion, while the 1st Battalion followed as regimental reserve. The Polish artillery at Falenty, its fire reinforced by the two pieces that had been with I/6 and three horse guns hurried up from the reserve and played among the white-coated ranks, but the Austrians persevered and drove into the alder copse. Hand-to-hand combat swayed back and forth for a time, but the veterans of *Vukassovich* eventually pushed the inexperienced Poles out of the woods and back towards the village. The Polish battalion was wavering when Poniatowski galloped up from Raszyn and led I/1 forward in a spirited counter-attack that brought the woods once more under Polish control. *Vukassovich* recoiled but was quickly rallied by its officers and took up a position a few hundred paces south-east of the copse.

In the short lull that now ensued, Ferdinand noticed Austrian hussars and infantry from Schauroth's small command to his left near Janki. Schauroth had swung west from Lazy towards the Dyrdy woods after separating from the archduke at around 1 p.m. Charged with shielding the Austrian left, his men pushed through the forest and on to Wolica, following the cavalry of the Polish screening force as it withdrew to the north. When Poniatowski pulled Rozniecki's regiments back behind the Mrowa to join his reserve, Schauroth took the opportunity to move his men forwards to the Wypedy–Janki line, a perfect location from which to support a renewed assault on the Falenty wood. Schauroth soon had in his hands a note from the archduke directing just that and two of the III/*Vukassovich* companies were sent to hit the Poles from the west while the bulk of the regiment undertook another effort from the east and south.

This time, Gabelkoven chose a different tactic, sending eight companies against the copse (2nd Battalion and the two companies of the 3rd) while the 1st Battalion conducted a simultaneous assault against the village itself with three batteries in support. The combined attack succeeded. Struck from all directions by a total of ten companies, the inexperienced Poles in the copse and village put up a courageous struggle but could not hold. Fighting desperately from every house and barricade, Sokolnicki's troops maintained their cohesion long enough for most of their artillery to escape but then cracked and withdrew into Raszyn in disorder. A dismounted howitzer and a gun were left in the hands of the victorious Austrians.[43] It was about 5 p.m.

Meanwhile, Ferdinand's intended main attack had run into trouble. The three and one-half squadrons of *Palatinal* Hussars that were supposed to clear Jaworow for the following infantry found it difficult even to approach the swollen Mrowa. The first obstacle was a line of Polish horse (probably the two squadrons of 2nd Uhlans) immediately south of the stream. Austrian trumpeters sounded the charge and the hussars started forward to brush aside the Poles, but the uhlans suddenly filed off to the right to unmask a battery that at once opened fire. The hussars, foundering in waterlogged ground that they had neglected to examine in advance, suffered under a peppering of Polish canister as they tried to extricate themselves from their predicament. Many hussars had to dismount to pull their mounts out of the mud. The *Somariva* Cuirassiers, attempting to gain the Polish left and succour their comrades, were also caught in a treacherous mire and had to retreat out of range in disorderly haste. The Austrian advance only resumed when a cavalry battery pulled up and compelled the Polish guns to retire across the stream. Slowly picking their way past ponds, bogs, and brooks, the troopers of *Palatinal* finally reached the stream at about 4 p.m., only to discover that the withdrawing Poles had removed the bridge and all local bridging material. Moreover, the normal banks of the Mrowa were completely flooded. Cavalry operations under these conditions were clearly pointless and Ferdinand impatiently ordered Civalart to get his infantry across the obstruction without delay. Confounded by difficult terrain and Polish bullets, however, the Habsburg foot soldiers had no better luck than their mounted brethren and the archduke's main attack soon dissolved into a time-consuming (and ultimately fruitless) search for bridging materials. Pflacher's men, also ordered to Jaworow, merely ended up waiting in the meadows south of the Mrowa. A wider flanking manoeuvre via Dawidy was deemed inadvisable given the lateness of the hour.

Back in the centre, the Austrians pursued their advantage and pressed into Raszyn itself, but fire from the Saxon guns brought their advance to a halt and a sudden counter-attack by Dyherrn's infantry hit them in the left flank and threw them back across the Mrowa. With his attention focused on getting Civilart's men across at Jaworow, however, Ferdinand was unaware of the reverse at Raszyn. He believed *Vukassovich* had broken through and he was concerned that the regiment would be left behind when Civilart and Pflacher advanced. He therefore sent Hauptmann Renner of his staff to Gabelkoven with instructions to initiate the 'pursuit' of the presumably defeated Polish centre. Reaching the scene, Renner immediately recognised his chief's misconception and on his own initiative ordered I/*Weidenfeld* from Pflacher's brigade to support *Vukassovich* at Raszyn. The assault was thus renewed at about 7 p.m. After a bitter house-to-house struggle, the Poles again lost Raszyn, and I/*Weidenfeld* apparently advanced in the twilight to push the Saxons out of a wood north of the town. The engagement came to a close at about 9 p.m., the Austrians withdrawing into and behind Raszyn, the Poles and Saxons maintaining their positions to the north. A battalion from *Davidovich*, sent by Ferdinand to reinforce the centre in the early evening, did not become involved in the combat. As night closed over the field a small portion of VII Corps had thus sufficed to create a serious dent in Poniatowski's front.

Poniatowski held a council of war at 10 p.m. to determine whether his force could undertake another battle. His young army had fought well in its first engagement, but the cost had been high: approximately 1,400 were dead, wounded, or missing (including 300 Saxon casualties).[44] At the time the meeting was called there were probably some hundreds more who had been knocked loose from their units and were straggling about the area between Raszyn and Warsaw. Given time, most of these would return to the ranks, but they were lost for the next day or two. To make matters worse, Poniatowski learned during this nocturnal conclave that Dyherrn, bound by orders he had received on 15 April, planned to depart for Saxony immediately. Considering the loss of Dyherrn's troops on top of Polish casualties and the battered state of his army, Poniatowski decided to retreat on Warsaw during the night.

The Poles were fortunate that Ferdinand had been incapable of exploiting his large numerical superiority during the day. His troops came into action late and—except in the centre—ineffectually, there was no real effort to outflank the Poles or pressure their wings, and there was no pursuit. The archduke thus allowed the moment and the enemy to slip away. The men of VII Corps seem to have recognised at once that they had squandered a superb opportunity to inflict a potentially mortal wound on their foe and blame seems to have heaped up quietly at the door of the man who had drafted the battle plan, Oberst Brusch, Ferdinand's chief of staff.[45] None of these Austrian recriminations, of course, altered Poniatowski's immediate situation: he had no choice but rapid withdrawal under cover of darkness.

To Poniatowski's surprise, Ferdinand now granted a further reprieve. Austrian losses at Raszyn had been considerably lower than those suffered by the Poles—a total of between 400 and 600 (over 250 from *Vukassovich*)—and the archduke still had a chance to catch the nascent Polish army around Warsaw and crush it before it could solidify. Ferdinand, however, was eager to hand Warsaw to the Prussians, cut loose from the Vistula, and march to the principal theatre of war in Germany. He had no interest in a potentially lengthy siege or costly assault. He therefore decided to offer Poniatowski a negotiated convention to occupy Warsaw without a fight, thus speeding up his operations while sparing both the city and his army. He also hoped that this ostensibly magnanimous gesture would turn Polish hearts against the French. He therefore entered into negotiations with Poniatowski regarding the fate of Warsaw. In two personal meetings on 20 and 21 April, the archduke and the prince worked out an arrangement, and by 5 p.m. on 23 April the Poles had evacuated their capital with all of their men, guns, stores, munitions, and anything else they could move. In a subsequent convention, the two sides agreed that Austrian guns in Warsaw would not fire on the Praga bridgehead and the Poles in the bridgehead fortifications would not bombard the city.[46] These conditions concluded and implemented, Ferdinand peacefully occupied Warsaw on the evening of the 23rd. He had already written to Friedrich Wilhelm of Prussia, apprising the neutral monarch of his instructions 'to transfer and hand over the duchy to Your Majesty as soon as Your Majesty should find yourself moved to accept the recommendations made by His Majesty the Kaiser to make common cause with Austria against the common foe and towards the final liberation of Europe.'[47]

Ferdinand's seeming victory, however, was hollow. Possession of Warsaw proffered some advantages but had little real significance as long as the Polish army was at large. Although Dyherrn duly departed for Saxony, the Poles, shaken and vulnerable but hardly destroyed, withdrew to Modlin and Serock to recuperate. Ferdinand let them go. He thus lost his best opportunity to break his enemy as Charles had intended. Poniatowski, anguished at giving up the city, feared that he had 'signed away my honour', but Pelletier reassured him: the Austrians, he realised, 'would see a great part of their force paralysed by the occupation of Warsaw'.[48] Moreover, the Poles remained determined despite the defeat at Raszyn and the loss of

Warsaw. They had fought doggedly, they retained their 'limitless confidence' in Napoleon and the popular Poniatowski, and, thanks to good leadership, they quickly regained their morale; they would soon be back.[49] 'The success of Raszyn', notes an Austrian historian, 'drained away to nothing.'[50]

THE INVASION FLOUNDERS

Ferdinand, having allowed the Polish army to escape and having denied himself direct offensive options against Praga, was not quite sure what to do next. Warsaw was in Austrian hands, but the archduke found himself, as GD Pelletier had predicted, paralysed by his possession of the Polish capital. He could not abandon his conquest without serious repercussions, but the need to protect it tied down a significant portion of his corps. Moreover, he could not move before the Prussian monarch replied to his offer of 22 April. In the meantime, he found himself hedged about by an aggressive and hostile population. A cavalry officer scouting towards Kalisz, for example, reported that he 'found nothing but the unanimous desire to take up arms against the Austrian troops.'[51] 'The people and the nobles are both inclined against us,' noted a staff officer, 'they see in us the destroyers of their supposed existence, so they hate us and would let no opportunity pass to do us harm.'[52] After considering his options, Ferdinand decided to shift the bulk of his corps to the east bank of the Vistula in an effort to inflict further damage on the Poles. He thus set his engineers to work constructing a bridge at Gora and ordered GM Mohr to cross with the advance guard brigade to remove the annoyance at Praga.[53] This was risky in the extreme as the lack of a bridging train imposed lengthy delays on spanning the river and Mohr, with only some 5,000 men and fourteen guns (five battalions, six squadrons, two batteries), would be isolated in the face of numerically superior Polish forces.[54] Mohr shipped his brigade across on boats during the 22nd, and by 24 April he had ringed Praga with hussar pickets and *1st Wallach*; he posted *Vukassovich* to support the blockade and placed *2nd Wallach* at Radzymin to tie in with Major von Hoditz.[55]

Engagement at Grochow (25 April)[56]

Poniatowski reacted promptly to Mohr's presence on the right bank. He had withdrawn to Modlin and Serock and revived the army's spirits in the short period following Raszyn. Thanks to the incorporation of numerous

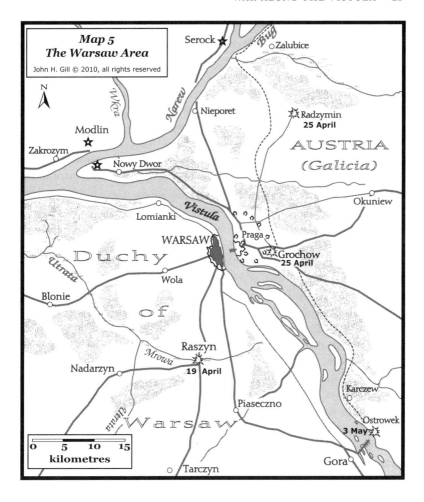

Map 5
The Warsaw Area

replacements and the arrival of 12th Infantry, he now had approximately 10,400 infantry in thirteen battalions, fifteen large cavalry squadrons with 3,750 troopers in the saddle, and thirty-two pieces in six batteries.[57] Taking about half of this force, he formed three attack columns, crossed the Narew during the night of 24/25 April, and advanced on Mohr's positions. The Poles, however, did not know if the Austrians had a bridge over the Vistula and could not believe that Ferdinand would be so imprudent as to place a small detachment across the river on its own. Several key Polish generals, worried by this uncertainty, the inexperience of the army, and its recent defeat, thus advised against this bold plan.[58] Accordingly, Poniatowski moved cautiously, treating the advance as a reconnaissance in force rather than a fully fledged offensive.[59]

Led by GB Sokolnicki, the first, or left, column, was composed of 12th Infantry, 2nd Uhlans, two companies of 2nd Infantry, and two guns (perhaps 1,800 infantry and 750 cavalry). The men had made a long march from Modlin via Nowy Dwor, but Sokolnicki attacked with vigour when he came upon 1st Wallach, a battery, a hussar division, and three guns covering the blockade east of the Praga fortifications late on the afternoon of 25 April. The Poles dislodged the Grenzer after a short, intense fight and Sokolnicki granted his soldiers a much-needed rest before pressing on towards Mohr's main position at Grochow, about one kilometre further south. The Polish general had sent a small detachment (an uhlan squadron and a voltigeur company from 12th Infantry) to swing around the Austrian flank, and he apparently hoped that this pause would also allow time for his surprise to take effect. Though there was no sign of his flanking force, the energetic Sokolnicki advanced once his men had recovered somewhat from their exertions during the night and morning. Mohr, with four battalions, four squadrons, and two batteries, enjoyed a considerable superiority in numbers, especially in artillery, but Sokolnicki, deploying his cavalry on the left, infantry on the right, and his two guns on the road in the centre, attacked without hesitation. As Colonel Jan Weysenhoff the commander of 12th Infantry remarked, 'in a fight with a superior foe . . . one's only salvation is audacity.'[60] The impetuous assault was initially successful: the Poles had thrown back the Austrian hussars, captured two guns, and were threatening the village when a counter-attack by III/Vukassovich restored the Austrian line and reclaimed the guns. The combat swayed back and forth until well into the night, with neither side gaining a significant advantage before darkness and exhaustion brought the engagement to a close. The fighting was clearly visible from Warsaw and local citizens (as well as Austrian officers) crowded terraces and other vantage points to watch the action. The obvious progress of Polish arms as the firing line moved south generated obvious enthusiasm among the anxious Poles, further diminishing Austrian hopes of gaining any significant popular support.

To the east, Colonel Julian Sierawski and the third Polish column (II/6th Infantry, two squadrons of 3rd Uhlans, two guns) had seized Radzymin after a brisk morning fight with 2nd Wallach and a platoon of hussars. Arriving near the town at midnight from Serock, Sierawski conducted a thorough reconnaissance and attacked as soon as he heard Sokolnicki's guns. Steady Austrian fire threw the overeager 3rd Uhlans into confused flight when they tried to pursue, but the Poles coolly maintained themselves in Radzymin and soon forced the Austrians to retreat towards Okuniew. By 11 a.m., when GD Dabrowski arrived with the reserve (5th Chasseurs and 6th Uhlans), the skirmish was over. The second column consisted of GB Michal Ignacy Kamienski with 1st Chasseurs and the other squadron of 3rd Uhlans. Riding in the centre, Kamienski's troopers did not engage in any fighting, but cut off and captured 183 Grenzer who were trying to make their way from Radzymin to Okuniew. More of *2nd Wallach* might have fallen into captivity if two *Kaiser* hussars, familiar with the local area from previous postings, had not led the Grenz battalion to safety.[61]

The fighting at Grochow and Radzymin cost Mohr's force some 400 casualties, including a surprising number of prisoners and missing (238); Polish losses were probably similar in killed and wounded (150–200).[62] Both sides retired the following day. Mohr gathered in Major von Hoditz's hussars (who had not been engaged) and fell back to Karczew on learning that Polish troops were approaching Okuniew, while Poniatowski, worried that powerful Habsburg forces might be lurking on the east bank and uncertain about Russian intentions, returned to the banks of the Narew south of Serock.[63] The Austrians were thus able to march unmolested when additional action by the Poles might have resulted in the destruction of Mohr's brigade. The material gains of this Polish foray were therefore limited, but there was a clear sense of success: the blockade of Praga had been broken and the enemy had been forced to retreat. Though Poniatowski was superior to Mohr in total numbers, the actual troops engaged were nearly equal at Radzymin, and Sokolnicki was numerically inferior at Grochow, especially in guns. Not only had the Poles prevailed in these circumstances, but Sokolnicki's men had done so under the eyes of their compatriots watching from the very porches of the capital across the river, 'redoubling their ardour to respond to the attention of their countrymen'.[64] Poniatowski's understandable sense of caution may have reduced the scope of this little victory, but the Poles had deployed an admirable degree of audacity at the tactical level. They would soon do so at the operational level as well.

Gora and Galicia

The engagement at Grochow awakened Ferdinand to the risks inherent in leaving Mohr isolated on the far side of the Vistula, but also inspired him to throw the bulk of his corps across the river as quickly as possible to trap and crush Poniatowski's growing army. He sent Schauroth to Gora on 26 April with Trautenberg's infantry and GM Gabriel Geringer's horsemen, telling his chief engineer: 'I must repeat that a bridge over the Vistula at Gora is more urgent for me with every passing hour and that I must have one whatever the sacrifice.'[65] Mohr's brigade could not be left in its vulnerable position on the far bank pending completion of the bridge, so his command was rowed back across the river, its transfer undisturbed by the cautious Poniatowski. By the 29th, the only Austrians remaining on the right bank were Hoditz's two squadrons at Karczew and two battalions of *Baillet* Infantry with three guns near the village of Ostrowek opposite Gora. These men, assigned to construct a bridgehead on the eastern shore, struggled to create useful fortifications from the sandy soil while watching the painful progress of bridge construction. Progress was slow indeed. With no bridge train and a frustrating scarcity of local building materials, the Austrian engineers found spanning the 285-metre wide Vistula almost impossible. By 3 May, however, they had come within reasonable sight of finishing their task, and Ferdinand hopefully brought the bulk of his corps south from Warsaw with plans of crossing on the 4th.

Ferdinand left GM von Branowaczky in charge at Warsaw and the surrounding area with two infantry regiments and thirteen cavalry squadrons. Branowaczky had arrived in Nadarzyn from the fortified cloister at Czestochowa on 27 April with I/*1st Szekler* Grenzer, five squadrons of *Kaiser* Chevaulegers, and half of his 3-pounder battery. To the archduke's intense annoyance, Branowaczky had failed in his mission to capture or even effectively blockade Czestochowa. Initially all had proceeded according to plan. His brigade had crossed the border on 14 April and duly reached the little fortress on the 18th. Branowaczky, however, quickly concluded that Czestochowa could not be taken by sudden assault, and the Polish commander declined to surrender. Faced with this conundrum, Branowaczky, having made no serious attempt to seize the fortress, departed for Warsaw with his entire brigade on 20 April. The following day, perhaps pricked by his conscience, he deposited two squadrons of *Kaiser* at Plawno—a full day's march from Czestochowa—to somehow observe the Polish garrison from a distance of thirty kilometres. He then continued on his way, dropping off a squadron and a company at Piotrkow. This tepid performance left both the minor military goal of neutralising Czestochowa and the major political goal of impressing the Prussians unaccomplished. Seven days later, while marching to Warsaw, Branowaczky received an angry missive from Ferdinand. 'I cannot approve of the measures taken against Czestochowa,'

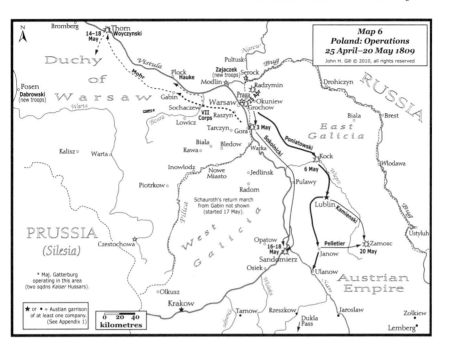

Map 6
Poland: Operations
25 April–20 May 1809

wrote the archduke. 'You are too distant to achieve the goal I had in mind.'[66] Reacting to his commander's ire, Branowaczky sent Oberst Johann Gramont von Linthal back to Czestochowa with I/2nd Szekler, four 3-pounders, and two howitzers to invest and perhaps capture the fort.[67] With his brigade much reduced and his mission unfulfilled, Branowaczky thus reached Nadarzyn on the 27th, where he remained until called to Warsaw on 3 May.[68]

While Branowaczky's men were marching hither and thither about the Polish countryside, Poniatowski was moving. Despite the success at Grochow, he acted with great caution until he could ascertain Austrian strength on the east bank of the river. As Ferdinand's predicament became apparent, however, the prince grew bolder. 'The movements of the enemy . . . visibly indicate his uncertainty and his lack of desire to undertake any important operations,' he wrote on 29 April, 'I will profit from this state of affairs by carrying a part of my force into Galicia.'[69] This sense of decision and determination in Polish headquarters coincided with news of an Austrian threat and vulnerability. The threat was the bridge slowly but surely inching its way across the Vistula at Gora; the vulnerability was the isolated bridgehead at Ostrowek. Poniatowski had been moving south along the river in a tentative fashion, Sokolnicki leading the vanguard.[70] The advance, albeit careful, forced Hoditz to vacate Karczew and retire to Kock on the Wieprz. By 1 May, the Poles were near the village of Ostrowek and the bridgehead opposite Gora. Diligent reconnaissance by Colonel Kazimierz Turno of the 5th Chasseurs revealed that the enemy garrison numbered only some 2,000 men with three guns, and that the defences were sketchy at best. It was also clear, however, that the bridge was nearly complete.[71] 'There is not a moment to lose, we can ruin all of the enemy's projects on the right bank of the Vistula,' scribbled Turno at midnight on the night of 1/2 May, 'but a delay of a few hours will be irreparable.'[72] Poniatowski acted immediately: 'Not wanting to allow time to finish this [bridging] operation, already far advanced . . . I gave the order to attack.'[73]

Sokolnicki reached Ostrowek at 7.30 p.m. on 2 May and sent an officer to summon the Austrian commander to surrender. The Polish officer, pretending not to speak German, learned that the bridge was still incomplete by listening to the injudicious Austrians and brought back this critical piece of intelligence when he returned with the obligatory refusal from Schauroth. Sokolnicki, actively assisted by Pelletier, recognised that he had to strike at once and set about preparing a night assault. He had six guns and approximately 5,100 men in 6th and 12th Infantry, three companies of 8th Infantry, and 5th Chasseurs. Of these, he committed some 2,500 to the storm: nineteen infantry companies and a squadron of chasseurs.[74] His opponents were 1,630 men of *Baillet* Infantry No. 63 under their colonel, Oberst Josef Czerwinka, supported by three 3-pounders.[75] Sokolnicki, having organised his men into four storm columns and two reserve columns, launched the assault sometime between midnight and 2 a.m. on 3 May to the sound of the 6th Infantry's massed drums rolling out across the inky night. Whether the Poles charged the breastworks five times as Ferdinand claimed in his report is not clear, but 'desperate' fighting raged in the darkness, often 'with bayonets and musket butts', according to Czerwinka.[76] Both sides displayed equal valour, but Sokolnicki finally led one of the reserve columns (the fusiliers of I/6) forward to clinch a tidy victory, and the Poles 'had the honour of greeting the dawn . . . from the top of the trenches.'[77] A Polish chasseur seized an Austrian who tried to escape with *Baillet*'s standard, and Turno's horsemen intercepted and sank a large boat full of fleeing whitecoats, capturing the lot. In all, the Austrians lost 530 men dead, wounded, or missing, and an additional 1,103 officers and men captured, including Oberst Czerwinka. The three guns were also left in Polish hands. Polish sources give Sokolnicki's

the bayonet' in a bold assault by Rozniecki's infantry around 1 a.m. on 18 May after an hour-long fight.[90] Most of the troops defending the bridge-head (the three *Wallach* companies and the *Stain* companies) escaped across the river and even managed to destroy the bridge, but Eggermann could see no utility in further resistance.[91] He and Sokolnicki (who wanted a quick end to the siege) signed a convention that morning and the Austrians marched out with their arms and field artillery on 19 May. The battle claimed between 150 and 200 Polish casualties (more than 100 from the 12th Infantry) and 185 Austrians (mostly from the Grenzer charged with holding the bridgehead); additionally, 802 of the ethnic Poles in the Austrian ranks deserted as the garrison withdrew, bringing total Austrian losses to nearly 1,000.[92] Sokolnicki, elated at his victory, was convinced that the conquest of Sandomierz and its bridgehead 'will force the enemy to evacuate all of our duchy and assures our possession of the two Galicias'. He urged Poniatowski to use the place as 'the central point, the pivot, of our future operations' and to drive north towards Radom or even Krakow.[93]

As Eggermann's men were marching away from Sandomierz, another Austrian garrison was about to fall into Polish hands. Poniatowski had charged Kamienski and Pelletier with seizing the critical fortress of Zamosc, portal to East (or Old) Galicia. Kamienski arrived before the fortress walls on 15 May with his three squadrons, but could do little beyond preventing inundation of the marshy terrain around the town and issuing a futile surrender demand until Pelletier arrived on the 18th with infantry and a small battery. Taking command, Pelletier spent the 19th reconnoitring and gathering materials for an assault with the willing assistance of local citizens. Among these were the district commissioner, who provided key advice on the state of the town's defences, and a group of enthusiastic volunteers with hunting pieces who spent the day sniping at Habsburg troops on the walls (including a septuagenarian who wanted 'the pleasure of killing a few Austrians').[94] Following thorough preparations, five attack columns—perhaps 2,000 men—advanced in silence at 1 a.m. on 20 May. Austrian vigilance was patchy and the two columns charged with storming the walls were able to place ladders against their target bastions without being noticed. When the first grenadier ordered to climb up refused, his company commander, a captain named Daine, ran him through with his sword. The next man in line clambered up with alacrity, followed by the single-minded Daine and the rest of the company. The Austrians, taken by surprise, fled the walls, allowing Daine and the other assault parties to open the town's gates. Cheering Poles were soon storming into Zamosc, including Captain Soltyk, who led his twenty horse artillerymen on an impromptu mounted charge. By 4 a.m., the fighting had ceased, leaving the Poles with some 2,600 prisoners and forty captured artillery pieces at a cost of forty-seven killed and wounded.[95] Poniatowski could justly praise 'the most brilliant manner' in which the troops conducted the attack and the superb leadership provided by Pelletier.[96]

In three weeks, therefore, Poniatowski had completely turned the tables on Ferdinand, displaying a rare combination of audacity, caution, and strategic insight in the process. 'Profiting from the enemy's inaction,' as he told Berthier, he had recognised his opportunity and had moved expeditiously to exploit it. He now had to choose between striking north, as Sokolnicki proposed, and continuing the advance into the inviting expanses of Galicia. He selected the latter course. Mystified by Ferdinand's behaviour ('who has taken a position on the Bzura for reasons we cannot fully understand') and very conscious of his small army's numerical inferiority, he was unwilling to commit himself across the Vistula.[97] He was also profoundly sceptical of the tsar's intentions—'I do not know how far I may count on the Russians'— and worried about the large Russian army looming in the east.[98] His central position on the right bank of the Vistula at its confluence with the San, on the other hand, would allow him to operate in any direction as the evolving situation demanded. He therefore remained in place, seizing the moment to push small detachments deep into Galicia, liberating the province and shielding his left flank while taking full advantage of the region's extensive resources, especially in willing manpower. At the same time, on his strategic right, Dabrowski and Zajaczek continued to generate new forces while protecting the heart of the duchy from Austrian depredations and keeping a wary eye on the Russians.

Fruitless Foray: Ferdinand's Turn to Thorn

While Poniatowski drove south, Ferdinand was marching in the opposite direction. Frustrated in his attempt to pass the Vistula at Gora, he had decided to strike north. He hoped thereby to accomplish three objectives. First, by posing a threat to Polish magazines, depots, and recruiting grounds, he might draw Poniatowski north as well, effectively forcing the Poles to abandon any deeper thrust into Galicia. Second, and probably more important in his mind, a move north would bring him closer to Prussia, increasing the pressure on Friedrich Wilhelm to join the war against Napoleon. Third, he wanted to disperse the new Polish units forming in the central districts of the duchy, scattering them before they could become a serious threat. He was destined, however, to be disappointed on all three counts.

Ferdinand moved quickly. Detaching the lone remaining battalion of *Baillet* to Nowe Miasto and dispatching *1st Wallach* Grenzer to reinforce the garrisons in Zamosc and Sandomierz, he collected the bulk of his corps at Piaseczno on 4 May and marched north the following day to arrive on the Bzura at Sochaczew on the 8th. Left behind in Warsaw were four battalions and the *Szekler* Hussars under Schauroth and a lone squadron of *Palatinal* at Gora.[99] Aiming to cut the connection between Thorn and Posen, Ferdinand sent Mohr downriver to Thorn on 9 May and shifted his main body to Gabin on the 10th.[100] Mohr, with six battalions, five squadrons, and twelve guns arrived opposite Thorn during the night of 14/15 May,[101] and successfully stormed the west bank bridgehead the following morning with two battalions of *Vukassovich* (probably 1,200–1,400 men) against approximately 1,000 Poles of III/11th Infantry. The victory came at the cost of eighty-one men, but the dead included Ferdinand's chief of staff, Oberst Brusch, who led his old regiment (*Vukassovich*) from the front and is alleged to have sought death to expiate his failures earlier in the campaign.[102] The Poles lost 250 men and two or three guns, but most escaped, blowing up the bridge in their retreat and thereby denying the Austrians the opportunity of operating on the eastern shore.[103] Mohr bombarded Thorn for three days in a vain attempt to induce capitulation, but the Polish governor, GB Stanislaw Woyczynski, flamboyantly refused and the only result was misfortune inflicted upon the city's inhabitants.[104]

While Mohr was banging on Thorn's gates, Ferdinand received a polite but definite demurral from the Prussian king and learned that Poniatowski, far from being distracted, was still pushing into Galicia. The first of these dashed his principal hopes for the entire campaign and seems to have left him temporarily bereft of ideas. The second piece of news, however, was a threat that the archduke could not ignore. Moreover, he was becoming frustrated with the nature of the war, feeling himself badgered on all sides without being able to come to grips with the enemy. 'I must completely surround myself with detachments in order to secure all communications,' he wrote on 11 May. 'These people disperse themselves at once if they see a body of our troops, but fall on isolated groups.'[105] At the same time, he did not want to give up any of his gains. The result was half-measures that brought further dispersal of VII Corps: Schauroth was sent to Sandomierz via Nowe Miasto at all speed with five battalions and thirteen squadrons on

17 May to defeat in detail a supposedly scattered enemy who 'cannot match us in numbers, much less in skill'.[106] Four of the *Baillet* companies at Nowe Miasto were bundled into wagons and, along with a squadron of *Kaiser* Hussars, rushed off to strengthen Sandomierz, but, as we have seen, it was already too late to save the fortress.[107] Ferdinand also ordered Mohr west towards the Warta to disrupt thousands of new Polish troops forming under Dabrowski around Posen and Kalisz. Mohr marched off on 19 May with his five line infantry battalions and two chevaulegers squadrons, leaving his Grenzer, three squadrons, and four guns to watch Thorn.[108] For the moment, the archduke remained at Gabin with his 'main body' (now reduced to ten battalions and thirteen squadrons). 'The Vistula, that separated us from the enemy, chained us to the necessity of doing nothing,' wrote the new corps chief of staff, Major Theodor Graf Baillet Latour, 'much time thus passed that was irrevocably lost.'[109]

Ferdinand, however, was also nervous about Krakow, as the Landwehr troops that were to form its garrison had not yet arrived. He therefore reinforced the city with four companies, two and one-half squadrons, and seven guns from the Czestochowa blockade (17 May); only two companies, a half-squadron, and two pieces remained behind at the little fortress. The commander of this miniature force, however, feeling quite alone in a hostile countryside, finally ended this mismanaged enterprise on his own accord on the 19th and marched off towards Krakow.[110]

News of the fall of Sandomierz overturned all of Ferdinand's plans. Poniatowski's advances, already worrisome, were now dire and Schauroth's command might be too small to counter the main Polish army, even though Ferdinand continued to enjoin Schauroth to attack the supposedly dispersed and inferior enemy. Moreover, he received a letter from Charles telling him not to leave the Polish theatre and re-emphasising the need to neutralise the Poles and secure Galicia.[111] On 22 May, therefore, Ferdinand recalled Mohr to the Bzura, placed FML Ludwig Ferdinand Mondet in charge of the forces around Warsaw, and headed south himself with eight battalions, fourteen squadrons, and four and one-half batteries. By 26 May Schauroth had arrived outside Sandomierz, Mohr was back on the Bzura at Lowicz, Mondet held Warsaw with Civilart's brigade, and Ferdinand's main body was at Gora, heading for Warka on the Pilica. The Thorn expedition had been a distracting failure, but the archduke remained hopeful that Sandomierz would fall quickly and that he and Schauroth, operating on both banks of the Vistula, would be able to throw the Poles beyond Lublin without losing his hold on Warsaw.[112]

Austria Abandons Warsaw

Ferdinand, driving his main body south to counter Poniatowski, also found himself under pressure from the north. West of the Vistula, this pressure took the form of Dabrowski, carefully following Mohr's withdrawal with 7,200 men and eight guns. GB Maurycy Hauke, marching on Sochaczew from Plock, added another 1,600 or so infantry.[113] At the same time, Zajaczek assembled some 4,500 fresh recruits and twelve pieces on the east bank opposite Warsaw and threatened to cross the river should Austrian vigilance relax. Continual ambuscades along the river and sharp skirmishes among the forests and villages punctuated the movements of the armies.[114] Despite the rawness of these new Polish levies, the Poles often had the best of this miniature encounters and the archduke had to respond, dividing his forces and diverting his attention from Poniatowski's main army. Reading exaggerated reports that Dabrowski had 20,000 men, he rode north from Warka on 27 May with his staff, while his column continued towards Sandomierz under GM Sebastien Freiherr Speth von Zwiefalten. By the time Ferdinand arrived, Dabrowski had crossed the Bzura (1 June) and reached Rawa. Dabrowski retired when the archduke led part of Mondet's command to confront the Poles on the 2nd, but with Warsaw endangered from both east and west, Ferdinand realised he could no longer hold the city. Mondet thus evacuated the duchy's capital on the night of 1/2 June and marched to Bledow to cover the approaches to the Pilica, while the archduke returned to the south to see if he could recover Habsburg fortunes at Sandomierz.[115]

As Ferdinand indulged in his risky foray to Thorn and endured the subsequent retreat, Poniatowski was making progress in East Galicia. With the capture of Sandomierz and Zamosc, he gathered most of his little army between the San and the Vistula with headquarters at Trzesn. Small detachments, however, garnered major gains to the south-east. Rozniecki (2nd and 5th Cavalry, four companies of 8th Infantry, four guns) surprised the *Czartoryski* and *Bellegarde* Depot Divisions at Jaroslaw on 25 May, capturing 920 men and large stores of munitions before turning east for Lemberg with the two cavalry elite companies.[116] Trotting into Lemberg on the 28th, he was 'received with enthusiasm' and found that GB Kamienski had occupied the town without resistance on the 23rd with two squadrons of 6th Uhlans and one of 3rd Uhlans (Hohenlohe had pulled out the previous day to withdraw to the Dnestr).[117] The arrival of regular Polish troops and generals ignited the populace. 'The whole country was in motion, and the

insurrection extended from the Dnestr to the Zbrucz [Russian frontier],'
wrote Soltyk, 'Wherever detachments of Polish cavalry appeared, the
population rushed to arms.'[118] Tiny Polish detachments and local volunteers
even pushed towards the borders with Hungary. Rozniecki announced that
he was taking control of Galicia in the name of the French emperor and
instructed local authorities to replace Austrian emblems with French eagles;
this was an effort to mollify the Russians, who feared the resurrection of a
major Polish state. As Galician notables set about raising troops, Rozniecki
and Kamienski rode off to rejoin Poniatowski on the San. They left only
one regular unit behind, the squadron of 3rd Uhlans, perhaps 200 to 250
men. This small force, however, was commanded by the extraordinarily able
and audacious Chef d'Escadron Piotr Strzyzowski and would soon have an
impact in East Galicia far in excess of its small size.[119]

These myriad movements created a confusing tableau, but the upshot
was clear: all of the Austrian marches were south, out of the territory they
had conquered and away from the heart of the duchy. The Poles, on the
other hand, were either regaining lost ground or pushing into Habsburg
lands to great popular acclamation. Moreover, while the Poles were elated,
their surprising successes spread gloom and confusion among Habsburg
officers and officials. Observing retreating columns of troops and civilians
in northern Hungary during late May, an Austrian officer recorded, 'I
encountered many imperial district and commissary officials, especially
those from West Galicia, as well as many depot companies hurrying to
Hungary with their war chests and accompanying this flight in a sort of
terreur panique.'[120]

In summary, the two armies faced each other in three general combat
zones as June began. The principal forces of both sides were in the centre
around Sandomierz: Ferdinand with about half of his corps north of town
and Poniatowski with almost all of his regulars either within the walls or
encamped to the south between the San and Vistula. On the northern edge
of the theatre, a host of new Polish levies under Dabrowski, Hauke, and
Zajaczek confronted Mondet (with approximately one-third of VII Corps)
between the Pilica and Warsaw. To the south-east, Hohenlohe had retreated
behind the Dnestr with his three depleted brigades of depot troops.[121]
Opposing him at present was Strzyzowski's lone squadron, but the Polish
authorities in Galicia were busy organising three new regiments of infantry
and five of cavalry. Concerned for the safety of Hungary's northern borders,
the Austrians were also trying to mobilise a brigade of Insurrection troops
at Kaschau. Finally, Ferdinand had an additional force of second-line troops

(ten Landwehr battalions and several depot companies) with a few regulars under FML von Eggermann in and around Krakow.

These dispositions clearly demonstrate that Ferdinand had failed in all of his objectives. Austrian forces still outnumbered the Poles, but he had neither neutralised the Polish army, nor acquired the duchy's resources, nor prompted Prussian intervention, nor squelched domestic rebellion. In part because he continued to disparage his opponents, he had dissipated his strength and momentum so that his troops now found themselves scattered about in a 'land where hearts, homes, purses, and barns were as far as possible closed against them'.[122] 'This war at all points—harassing me with far-flung detachments in conjunction with the local population, threatening all communications and depots, but then evading every earnest attack—hinders me greatly in covering a land as large as Galicia is, with no fortified places and divided by the Vistula,' he lamented to Charles.[123] He was frustrated and annoyed, reacting to events rather than setting the direction of the war, but he remained determined to come to grips with the main enemy army, convinced he could crush the Poles in an open engagement.

Poniatowski, on the other hand, had seized the initiative and conducted a brilliant campaign of manoeuvre, eventually forcing Ferdinand to abandon Warsaw and most of the duchy. He had accomplished this while keeping his own army intact and he was now industriously augmenting his strength with each passing day. He was thus entirely justified in the satisfaction he displayed in his 31 May report to Berthier: 'If, according to the instructions of H. M. the Emperor, the purpose of our operations was to occupy and hold in check an enemy corps equal in force to our own, we may felicitate ourselves in having achieved it.'[124] This notion of tying down an equivalent number of Austrians while preserving his own forces and divining Russian intentions seems to have dominated his operational thinking for the next several weeks as the campaign entered a new phase.

JUNE 1809: FERDINAND TAKES THE INITIATIVE

The first two weeks of June brought more rapid manoeuvres and sharp actions, overlaid now with an increasingly dense layer of three-way diplomacy, uncertainty, and chicanery. On the Austrian side, Ferdinand strove to restore Habsburg fortunes and redeem his own reputation by taking the initiative against Poniatowski's main force. The Polish prince, on the other hand, after his burst of activity in May, lapsed into a relatively passive stance as he waited

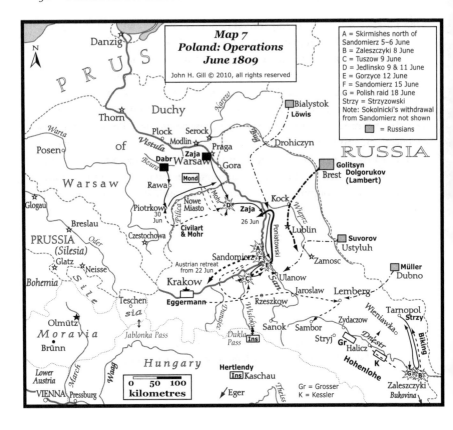

Map 7
Poland: Operations
June 1809

John H. Gill © 2010, all rights reserved

A = Skirmishes north of
Sandomierz 5–6 June
B = Zaleszczyki 8 June
C = Tuszow 9 June
D = Jedlinsko 9 & 11 June
E = Gorzyce 12 June
F = Sandomierz 15 June
G = Polish raid 18 June
Strzy = Strzyzowski
Note: Sokolnicki's withdrawal
from Sandomierz not shown
= Russians

Gr = Grosser
K = Kessler

Ferdinand's Southern Offensive

Schauroth, as noted above, arrived north of Sandomierz on 26 May and tried to press close to the walls the following day, only to be shoved back by a vigorous Polish sortie.[125] Sokolnicki, commanding a garrison of 5,000 to 6,000 men (approximately half of the Polish army) in this crucial city, had almost as many troops as Schauroth and was determined to maintain an active defence (see Appendix 1). Having ascertained that Sokolnicki's energetic Poles had repaired the fortifications and were in no mood to capitulate to

for military affairs to mature and political events to clarify. Finally, a third force now entered the field: a powerful Russian corps whose actions, however ambiguous, would have a profound effect on the outcome of the campaign.

Schauroth's small force, Ferdinand had to abandon his optimistic plans of crossing the Vistula north of Sandomierz. He decided instead to mask the fortress on its northern side and surround it by striking at Poniatowski south of the Vistula. When GM von Speth and the VII Corps main body reached Opatow on 2 June, therefore, they relieved Schauroth's outposts so that the latter could march upstream to cross the Vistula at Opatowiec in accordance with the archduke's new plan.[126] To increase the pressure on Poniatowski and cover Schauroth's right flank, Ferdinand's concept called for Eggermann to advance from Krakow to Lemberg with a 'division' of perhaps 3,000 to 4,000 men (mostly Landwehr and depot troops) while Hohenlohe's ad hoc force attempted to move on the same destination from the Dnestr.

Table 1: VII Corps Main Body, 5–17 June 1809

Date	North of the Vistula (Sandomierz)	South of the Vistula (Wisloka and San)	Detached (San)
5 June	Ferdinand	Schauroth	
	Davidovich Infantry (3)	*Strauch* Infantry (3)	
	Weidenfeld Infantry (3)	III/*Baillet* Infantry (four cies)	
	III/*Kottulinsky* (1)	I/*1st Wallach* Grenz (three cies)	
	Somariva Cuirassiers (6)	I/*1st Szekler* Grenz (1)	
	Szekler Hussars (7)	*Lothringen* Cuirassiers (6)	
	Palatinal Hussars (1)	*Kaiser* Hussars No. 1 (6)	
		2nd West Galician (four cies)	
11 June	Geringer	Ferdinand (as above)*	Piccard/Hoditz
	Davidovich Infantry (3)	*Lothringen* Cuirassiers (5)	*Lothringen* Cuirassiers (1)
	I/*Weidenfeld* (1)	*Kaiser* Hussars No. 1 (3)	*Kaiser* Hussars No. 1 (3)
	Szekler Hussars (7)	I/*1st Szekler* Grenz (two cies)	I/*1st Szekler* Grenz (four cies)
		II and III/*Weidenfeld* (2)	
		III/*Kottulinsky* (part—see text)	
		Somariva Cuirassiers (6)	
		Palatinal Hussars (1)	
		Kaiser Chevaulegers (1)	

Table 1 (continued)

15 June Geringer	Ferdinand (as above)*	Piccard/Hoditz
Davidovich Infantry (3)	*Lothringen* Cuirassiers (3)	*Lothringen* Cuirassiers (3)
I/*Weidenfeld* (1)		*Kaiser* Hussars No. 1 (3)
Szekler Hussars (7)		I/*1st Szekler* Grenz (four cies)
Strauch Infantry (3)	(- *Strauch* Infantry)	
III/*Baillet* Infantry (four cies)	(- III/*Baillet* Infantry)	
17 June Ferdinand	Trautenberg	Hoditz (to Eggermann)
Strauch Infantry (3)	*Kaiser* Hussars No. 1 (4)	*Kaiser* Hussars No. 1 (2)
Davidovich Infantry (3)	I/*1st Szekler* Grenz (1)	
Weidenfeld Infantry (3)	I/*1st Wallach* Grenz (three cies)	
III/*Kottulinsky* (1)		
III/*Baillet* Infantry (four cies)		
Somariva Cuirassiers (6)		
Lothringen Cuirassiers (6)		
Szekler Hussars (7)		
Palatinal Hussars (1)		
Kaiser Chevaulegers (1)		
2nd West Galician (four cies)		

Notes: Only changes to preceding orders of battle are shown (indicated by asterisk*).
cies = companies
Numbers in parentheses show battalions or squadrons.

Schauroth marched for Opatowiec as directed and crossed the great river on 5 June, heading for the Wisloka. That day also saw the Austrians edge closer to Sandomierz, clashing with a reconnaissance force that Sokolnicki had pushed out from the city to locate the enemy.[127] The fighting was indecisive, but left the Poles feeling confident and the Austrians cautious, sentiments that gained strength when Sokolnicki's well-posted men repulsed an Austrian probing attack on 6 June. In the meantime, however, Ferdinand had concluded that Schauroth's force would be too weak to tackle expected Polish resistance. He therefore departed Opatow himself on 6 June with three

The question that immediately arises, however, is why Poniatowski accepted battle with his army divided and his back to a river in the first place. Why not simply withdraw behind the San? The Austrians were certainly surprised by this decision.[135] Soltyk calls his position 'strange' and explains it by noting that Poniatowski had hoped Russian assistance would allow him to maintain part of his army on the west bank of the San to succour Sandomierz and threaten Ferdinand from multiple directions.[136] The Russian 9th Infantry Division, commanded by Lieutenant General Prince Arkadii Aleksandrovich Suvorov, had indeed arrived east of the San on the Polish left during the evening of 11 June and the two sides were in close contact. Poniatowski promptly requested Suvorov's help on the night of the 11th, 'As it is possible that the attack will be serious tomorrow', but Suvorov and his subordinates cited incapacity, lack of mutual trust, and other excuses to deny any assistance.[137] When battle came, they 'did not budge', as Soltyk noted.[138]

Without Russian support, Poniatowski could not remain west of the river. He therefore retired to the eastern bank on the night of 13/14 June and a lull descended along the San for several days. In the meantime, action again erupted at Sandomierz. With the city now hemmed in from north and south, Ferdinand was determined to seize it quickly. He therefore sent *Strauch* Infantry (three battalions), III/*Baillet* (four companies), four 12-pounders, and four howitzers to the north bank to reinforce Geringer with orders to storm Sandomierz. Geringer duly organised an assault for the night of 14/15 June, opening with an artillery barrage at 11 p.m. and launching four attack columns at 1 a.m. The assault was a bloody failure. Losing 1,400 casualties (724 from *Davidovich*, which bore the bulk of the fighting), the Austrians were repulsed at every point. Polish losses came to 404. Ferdinand blamed feeble artillery preparation and poor infantry tactics for the disaster, and Geringer attempted to exculpate himself by citing the strength of the fortress as repaired by the Poles during their four-week occupation. Clearly, however, a key factor was the stout defence offered by the Polish garrison, tactically adept and inspired by Sokolnicki's leadership. Geringer could only report rather lamely that 'Despite the greatest exertions of bravery and disregard for all danger and for the murderous fire, it was not possible to penetrate into the city . . . at 6 a.m., I therefore ordered all four columns to withdraw out of cannon range.'[139] The defeat of the Austrian attack, however, could not alter Sokolnicki's impossible position. Surrounded with no hope of relief and facing a vastly superior enemy, he chose to preserve his command for the future rather than sacrifice it in a fruitless siege. Negotiating generous terms and dragging the discussions out as long as feasible, he arranged for the last of his unbowed troops to depart on the morning of 19 June. Retaining his arms, standards, field pieces, and the Austrian deserters who had joined Polish ranks, Sokolnicki and his men marched for the Pilica escorted by I/*Davidovich* and two squadrons of *Szekler* Hussars. Forty-eight hours after crossing the river back into the duchy, they would once again be free to participate in the campaign. The Austrians took immediate possession of Sandomierz.

Mondet and Mohr versus Zajaczek and Dabrowski

While Ferdinand and Poniatowski were sparring around Sandomierz, Mondet was contending with advances by Zajaczek and Dabrowski north of the Pilica. As we have seen, Mondet's division, under the archduke's personal command, had driven off Dabrowski's advance towards Rawa without a fight on 2 June. Ferdinand departed for Sandomierz at once, leaving behind instructions for Mondet 'to oppose and beat back every further advance on the left bank of the Vistula towards the Pilica'. He hoped thereby to 'gain time to open my operations around Sandomierz and to drive the enemy out of Galicia by my advance on both banks of the Vistula'.[140] To execute this mission, Mondet had evacuated Warsaw as ordered and retired to Bledow with a detachment posted in and around Rawa, while Major Gatterburg conducted raids and reconnaissance patrols off to the north-west with four squadrons and two guns.[141] Under a constant nattering of skirmishes, Mondet remained in these general locations from 4 until 7 June.

Zajaczek, having occupied Warsaw, marched for the Pilica, arriving at Warka on 7 June, where he was joined by Hauke. He then pushed south through great forests towards Jedlinsk in the hope of manoeuvring Mondet out of his position north of the Pilica.[142] Mondet was indeed alarmed by the appearance of a major Polish force in his right rear, and responded by dispatching Mohr with two battalions of *Vukassovich*, half 2nd *Wallach* Grenzer, and five squadrons of *Palatinal* to protect a large magazine that the Austrians had established at Radom. Mohr marched via Jedlinsk, deposited a detachment there to secure the bridge over the Radomka River (four *Vukassovich* companies and a squadron), and reached Radom on 9 June. That same day, however, Zajaczek arrived at Jedlinsk from the north and threw Mohr's detachment out of the village in a sharp skirmish that cost the Austrians 162 men.[143] Zajaczek felt quite pleased with his advance thus far, explaining to Poniatowski that he had occupied a position 'susceptible to a fine defence'.[144]

Mondet, on the other hand, could not allow Zajaczek to remain in this 'very fine' position. He collected his division at Przytyk on the 10th and advanced from the west the following day while Mohr pushed north from Radom with most of his command. The cavalry leading Mondet's column soon ran into the Polish advance guard, posted some eleven kilometres west of Jedlinsk under GB Hauke. The Polish brigadier, threatened by swarms of Habsburg horse against which he had little defence, sent an urgent call for help as his troops retreated in disorder. Zajaczek, who apparently did not expect to encounter Mondet's entire division, left III/3rd Infantry, two companies, and a gun at Jedlinsk, and rushed to his subordinate's assistance. In the intense battle that ensued, Mondet enjoyed a slight superiority in overall numbers, but significant advantages in cavalry and artillery. These advantages soon told. Although the green Polish infantry performed well under heavy artillery fire and repeated cavalry attacks, the Polish horse was driven from the field, and a combined charge by *Kaiser* Hussars and Chevaulegers finally broke one battalion when a hussar corporal leaped his mount into the Polish ranks (at the cost of his horse's life and his own). This incident alone left 500 prisoners in Habsburg hands.[145] Zajaczek, exerting himself to the utmost, brought his division off the field without losing cohesion and was able to retain his hold on Jedlinsk as night fell, but there was no disguising the defeat. Mohr's efforts to force the Radomka and cut off the Polish retreat, on the other hand, failed against an able defence conducted by III/3rd Infantry. Although the resistance offered by this battalion and several others provided some conciliation, the day had been a serious setback for the Poles. Losses numbered over 1,000, as compared to at most 500, and perhaps as few as 200, Austrian casualties. The disorganised Poles beat a hasty retreat towards the Vistula.

Zajaczek had 'imprudently' exited the forests from which he could have menaced Mondet with relative impunity and had taken his force into open country where Austrian advantages were most pronounced. He had risked his entire command on the day of battle, and was lucky to avoid destruction during his retreat as he now found himself trapped between the enemy and the unbridged Vistula.[146] Arriving opposite Pulawy on 14 June, he discovered Russian Lieutenant General Fedor von Löwis's 10th Division on the far shore. Löwis, however, refused pleas for assistance and several days passed before Zajaczek could arrange a means of crossing the great river. He and his men were most fortunate that Mondet was slow to act and left Mohr to conduct the pursuit alone. Too weak to do more than harass Zajaczek, Mohr returned to Radom on 15 June. Zajaczek was thus allowed to escape, but the victorious Mondet soon found himself facing a new threat.

This new danger arose from Dabrowski's action. Although criticised for not co-ordinating his movements with Zajaczek's, Dabrowski had departed Lowicz on 10 June to reach Rawa on the 11th as the guns were rolling at Jedlinsk; he had even pushed a small advance guard as far as Nowe Miasto. He turned the following day to occupy Piotrkow on 16 June, but his advance guard (a squadron of newly raised cavalry and a company of volunteer chasseurs) played havoc with Austrian patrols south of the Pilica.[147] Beyond these annoying clashes, Dabrowski's move to Piotrkow represented an intolerable threat to Krakow and, on 15 June, Mondet sent Civilart's brigade with the three squadrons of *Kaiser* Chevaulegers to Konskie to join the two chevaulegers squadrons already operating near the town. The archduke was even more alarmed than Mondet when he learned of the potential danger to his lines of communications. Telling Mondet that 'the principal purpose of your operations must be the prevention of any enemy undertaking towards Krakow,' he ordered Mondet to leave a garrison in Radom, shift west to protect Krakow, and, if possible, defeat Dabrowski.[148] Mondet complied, moving his main body to Konskie. Mohr, depositing III/*Vukassovich* and two *Palatinal* squadrons in Radom, joined him, but departed almost at once. Crossing the Pilica at Przedborz on 25 June, he reached Piotrkow on the last day of the month. Mondet arrived by a more direct route on 1 July. The Austrians endured almost daily skirmishes with Dabrowski's patrols or local insurgents, but neither Mohr nor Mondet had a major encounter.

While the Austrians were vainly seeking a major action, Dabrowski easily slipped away. Departing Piotrkow on 19 June, he marched down the Pilica, his advance guard chasing off an Austrian detachment to occupy Nowe Miasto on the 24th.

ENTER THE RUSSIANS

In addition to the manoeuvres, battles, sieges, and skirmishes outlined above, June introduced a further political-military complication into the campaign: the Russian army. In accordance with the understanding he had signed with Napoleon at Erfurt in October 1808, Tsar Alexander had mobilised an army on his borders with the Duchy of Warsaw and Austrian Galicia. This was potentially a powerful force, amounting to between 40,000 and 50,000 infantry and cavalry in three (later four) infantry divisions and two cavalry corps with a rich supply of guns. Command, however, was placed in the hands of General of Infantry Prince Sergey Golitsyn who, in the words of one historian, 'could not pass as a great warrior, even among the "salons" of St Petersburg, but who would show himself to be a most agile diplomat.'[149] Golitsyn, brought out of retirement for the posting, was considered sickly, slow, and inept. GD Caulaincourt, the French ambassador, described him as 'an aged man and one of the most mediocre generals of Catherine II's reign.'[150] He was widely known to harbour anti-French attitudes. Moreover, the general sympathies of the officer corps, like those of the empire's social and political elites, lay with Austria. Compounding these background factors, the entire process of assembling Golitsyn's corps and putting it in motion proceeded at a glacial pace. Although the tsar had promised in April that his troops would be ready forty-eight hours after the start of hostilities, Golitsyn only received his orders on 18 May—three weeks after news of the war reached St Petersburg—and a further two weeks passed before his columns actually crossed the border into Galicia.[151] French questions and complaints evoked only excuses and equivocations, leading Napoleon to tell Savary in early June 'It is no alliance that I have there.'[152]

The Circumstances Demand Armies

The degree to which Golitsyn's torpor derived from his imperial master's intentions as opposed to his own inclinations is not clear. A German officer in St Petersburg voiced the common belief when he described Golitsyn's orders as 'so constrained that the Austrians have nothing to fear from this side', and the French and Poles, of course, drew the conclusion that Alexander was reneging on the Erfurt agreement, betraying his ally.[153] On the other hand, Alexander, when he tired of exculpating Golitsyn's inaction, would express regret that he could not 'beyond a certain point, change the old routines of the Seven Years War', and his letters to the general contain apparently pointed prods to action: 'I order you, on receipt [of this letter], not to lose any time, not even a few hours, to cross the border and proceed along the route designated to you, if only with a regiment or battalion.'[154] But Alexander had made a secret agreement with Austria to avoid mutual hostilities before the war: he did not relieve Golitsyn once war began, and his subsequent enjoinders did not elicit noticeably greater operational vigour.

All of this suggests that Alexander was struggling to advance his interests in a complex triangular game. On one side was France with its swift and terrible warrior-emperor. The tsar certainly wanted to adhere to the *letter* of the Erfurt protocol with Napoleon—'As to my co-operation, you may count on it, it will be open and complete'—and seems to have endorsed at least something of the treaty's spirit.[155] On the other side, Alexander did not want to pursue his alliance with Napoleon at the price of permanent damage to his relations with Austria. In his eyes, Austria had itself to blame for its misfortunes ('They will pay dearly for their folly and boasting . . . What fanfaronades!'), but he had no interest in participating in the destruction of the Habsburg monarchy, 'a calamity for Europe', and worked hard to avoid such a disastrous outcome.[156] Moreover, he had no desire to violate his secret understanding with Austria to retard the entry of his troops into Galicia and 'to avoid every collision and every act of hostility' with Austrian troops.[157] There was a third facet to his interests in this war as well: Poland. Russian policy was adamantly opposed to the resurrection of a Polish political entity, the tsar warning that some of Poniatowski's proclamations were 'a little too Polish' and Foreign Minister Rumiantsev declaiming that Russia should 'renounce' its alliance with France and 'sacrifice to the last man before suffering an augmentation of the Polish domain, as that would threaten our existence'.[158] At the same time, St Petersburg was by no means averse to creating conditions that might conduce to Russian acquisition of historically Polish territory at some future date.[159] Such acquisitions, of course, could only come at Austria's expense. This foreign policy consideration also had critical internal implications, as the tsar was determined to subdue any hint of rebellion or tendency towards independence among his own ethnic Polish subjects. At a different level, he also had to balance his foreign policy with the sentiments of the empire's elites, that is, not going so far towards meeting Napoleon's expectations that he would utterly alienate strong domestic factions that completely despised the French emperor. All of these external and internal factors would be evident in Russian action and inaction during the coming weeks as Golitsyn's army made its deliberate way into Galicia.

Neither the Poles nor the Austrians quite knew what to expect of the Russians. Poniatowski hoped for genuine assistance, but was wary, repeatedly expressing his uncertainty in correspondence with Napoleon and Berthier. Several incidents during May confirmed the Poles' worst suspicions. The most egregious came early in the month, when Polish cavalry patrols intercepted a letter from Lieutenant General Andrey Gorchakov, commander of the 18th Division cantoned near Brest, to Archduke Ferdinand; in it, Gorchakov congratulated the Austrians on the victory at Raszyn and expressed the hope that Austrian and Russian forces would soon collaborate in combat. The incriminating letter, forwarded to Napoleon and from him through Caulaincourt to the tsar, prompted an outburst of ire from the Russian emperor. He directed Golitsyn to demand from Gorchakov immediately a most detailed answer as to 'how he could have had the audacity, if this is true, to receive correspondence not only from the archduke . . . and this is even more important, on what basis did he dare to respond to the archduke and specifically in the manner described?'[160] Gorchakov was removed from command and replaced by Lieutenant General Vasily Dolgorukov.[161] Though Golitsyn wrote to Poniatowski in excruciatingly polite terms—'Rest assured, my prince, in the sincerity and eagerness that I will demonstrate to have the pleasure of fighting by your side as soon as possible, and to prove to you that the honour of a true Russian consists in executing the sacred will of his sovereign'—it is hardly surprising that the Polish commander remained decidedly suspicious.[162] The French were no less dubious and, ultimately, deeply disappointed. Writing to Caulaincort at Napoleon's behest on 2 June, Foreign Minister Champagny remarked sardonically: 'Compliments and phrases are not armies; the circumstances demand armies.'[163]

As Champagny's letter was making its way to St Petersburg, however, the Russian army was finally on the march. Starting on 3 June, the Russians advanced along four routes. In the north, Löwis and his 10th Division marched from the Bialystok area through Drohiczyn to reach the Vistula at Pulawy by the 10th. Suvorov, departing his assembly area near Ustyluh, arrived on the San near Ulanow during 11 June with 9th Division's advance guard. As we have seen, neither of these officers made any concrete move to assist nearby Polish forces. Nor did Golitsyn offer any help. Marching between Löwis and Suvorov, he moved slowly west from Brest through Kock with his headquarters and the 18th Division (formerly Gorchakov's), to arrive in Lublin on 10 June. A fourth column composed of the 1st and 2nd Cavalry Corps under overall command of Lieutenant General Peter Müller-Zakomelsky entered Galicia from Dubno but did not reach its destination, Lemberg, until 26 June. An additional division, the 24th under Lieutenant General Dmitri Dokhturov, remained inside Russian territory for the time being.

Perfidious Inaction

Though their intentions were ambiguous, the arrival of the Russians had a dramatic effect on political-military dynamics in Galicia. Habsburg cavalry exchanged a few blows with Cossacks on 14 June east of Ulanow in a case of mistaken identity (the tsar related this to Caulaincort as an 'engagement'), but Ferdinand reiterated strict orders to avoid any hostilities and the Russians, eager to eschew conflict with their supposed enemy, excused the incident. Lively, cordial interaction was soon the norm between Austrians and Russians on the San. At the same time, the Russians would not operate as Austrian allies, and expressed their intention to advance according to their instructions.[164] As Ferdinand explained to Charles, 'The Russian generals, all the officers, and soldiers of their army loudly declare themselves our friends and enemies of the French; they treat the Poles very badly and hold them in contempt; still the Russians say: we must follow the orders of our emperor.'[165]

The presence of the 30,000 or so Russian troops between Pulawy and Ulanow thus stymied Ferdinand's offensive plans and, as Charles noted, their further advance spoiled the successful capture of Sandomierz.[166] Moreover, the Habsburg hierarchy deeply mistrusted the Russians and had no desire to see any more of Galicia come under the tsar's sway. The Austrian leadership also feared a threat to the monarchy's strategic rear through Teschen and Hungary; there were even worries that the large Russian army facing the Turks on the lower Danube might enter Bukovina.[167] They hoped that Ferdinand would convince the Russians to stop at the San or, at a minimum, that he would delay Russian movement west as long as possible. Ferdinand, however, had few realistic options to preclude Russian progress. He could neither attack Golitsyn's men, nor ask for free passage to engage the Poles, nor offer effective opposition once the Russians decided to advance.[168] He could, however, negotiate. He was unable to persuade the Russians to halt on the San, but, in a series of clandestine exchanges, he reached an arrangement with Golitsyn whereby the Russians would advance slowly, would not cross the Vistula, and would go no farther west than the Wisloka.[169] Satisfied that he had delayed the Russians, he therefore abandoned his plans of taking the offensive towards Lublin and withdrew the bulk of his army north of the Vistula. By 17 June, as Sokolnicki dragged out his departure from Sandomierz, Ferdinand had assembled the main body of his corps at Opatow. Here he stayed for several days while his men and local labourers demolished the Sandomierz fortifications. This task accomplished, he turned west towards Staszow on 22 June, hoping that his main body and Mondet's division could manoeuvre to maintain control over the West Galician districts north of the Vistula and the conquered portions of the duchy as far north as Piotrkow.[170] He left a small screening force south of the Vistula under Trautenberg to observe the Russians, but the two sides courteously exchanged march plans and took every measure to avoid friction when the Russians crossed the San on

21 June.[171] Six days of sluggish marching brought Golitsyn and his corps to the Wisloka on the 27th.

   Poniatowski, 'chained' to his position on the San, was also negotiating with Golitsyn.[172] Incensed that Russia's 'perfidious inaction' hobbled all his offensive plans and precluded relief of Sandomierz, Poniatowski gave up on the idea of combined operations with Golitsyn's corps.[173] Frictions and frustrations mounted daily as he endeavoured to get his putative allies to advance across the San in a genuine offensive. 'I cannot decide', he wrote, 'whether it is the enemy or the ally that should be feared most.'[174] With Ferdinand moving north of the Vistula, however, he felt he had to follow. He thus came to an agreement with Golitsyn that the Poles would operate on the left (north) bank of the river while the Russians advanced along the right (south) bank. Zajaczek had joined the prince on 19 June after crossing the Vistula at Pulawy, so Poniatowski now had some 12,000 men at his disposal. He reorganised his small army into an infantry division (Zajaczek) and a cavalry division (Rozniecki), sent a squadron of 1st Chasseurs to reinforce Strzyzowski at Tarnopol (the Russians would not permit him to leave the entire regiment), and turned north on 22 June, the same day that Ferdinand was leaving Opatow. Reaching Pulawy on 24 June, the Poles immediately began constructing a bridge across the Vistula. Two days later, they were across the river, poised to advance.

Lemberg and the Dnestr

Small clashes and tangled politics also characterised activity at the southern end of the theatre. Eggermann had marched for Lemberg to support Ferdinand's planned offensive towards Lublin, passing through Rzeszow on 14 June, while a small detachment of Hungarian Insurrection troops pushed its way through a hostile population from the Dukla Pass towards Sanok.[175] Eggermann, joined on 16 June by Major von Hoditz's two hussar squadrons, arrived in Lemberg on the 21st without major incident. The Polish authorities and militia fled, but Major General Müller's two Russian cavalry corps soon appeared outside the city, so Eggermann's stay was brief. The two sides effected an amicable handover and, by 27 June, Eggermann was retiring towards Sambor, untroubled by the Russians (who might have easily cut off and swallowed up his small command). Poniatowski lamented that the Habsburg commander had found safety in 'the same lethargy and the same connivance' as prevailed along the San.[176]

Hohenlohe was also to serve as an adjunct to Ferdinand's planned offensive. First, however, his scattered troops had to repel audacious advances by Chef d'Escadron Strzyzowski with his squadron of 3rd Uhlans and large numbers of militia and armed citizenry. Strzyzowski, leaving Lemberg late in May, had occupied Tarnopol and then pushed Austrian GM Anton Bicking von Sobinak's outposts back towards the Dnestr in a series of miniature skirmishes between 2 and 7 June. He arrived before Zaleszczyki on 8 June, but found the defences too strong and withdrew after some probing attacks. For the next ten days, he collected new strength from the surrounding countryside including, much to the alarm of the Russians, 400 armed and mounted ethnic Poles from Russian Podolia. By 18 June, he had the 250 troopers of his squadron, 400 mounted volunteers, 300 volunteer foot chasseurs, and some 4,000 armed peasants. Although many of the latter were equipped with scythes, pikes, and other agricultural implements, he felt himself strong enough to try the defences again. A daring flank diversion across the Dnestr on Bicking's left certainly alarmed the Austrians, but the attack on the east bank failed as Strzyzowski's levies soon 'lost their composure and scattered in all directions'.[177] The Polish commander was undaunted, but he learned during the night that Eggermann was approaching Lemberg and thus saw no option but retreat to Tarnopol. Followed by Bicking, he withdrew in good order, reached Tarnopol on 27 June, and began gathering forces for a new advance.[178]

Late June Lull

Drawing together these various operational strands reveals a curious overall picture as June edges towards its end. Poniatowski (including Zajaczek) is west of the Vistula opposite Pulawy with the main Polish force. A few days' march to the north, Dabrowski and Sokolnicki are waiting on the Pilica, the former at Nowe Miasto, the latter—now free to participate in combat—near the confluence of the Pilica and Vistula. Ferdinand has concluded that retreat is his only option and is making his way towards Krakow from Staszow, while Mohr and Mondet are about to enter Piotrkow in their fruitless hunt for Dabrowski—as we have seen, they occupy the town on 30 June and 1 July respectively. The entire countryside is alive with enthusiastic Polish insurgents, depriving the Austrians of intelligence and instilling in them a pervasive sense of uncertainty. Polish advances and Austrian retreats had encouraged large numbers of Ferdinand's ethnic Polish troops to desert, many defecting to Poniatowski's forces.[179] Golitsyn and the main Russian force are on the Wisloka, their further intentions unknown. Finally, in East Galicia, Müller's Russians have taken Eggermann's place in Lemberg, while the latter marches for the Dukla Pass. Hohenlohe, however, is still on the cautious offensive, his main body having crossed the Dnestr near Halicz and Bicking still following Strzyzowski to Tarnopol. For the moment a lull in fighting—though not in military diplomacy—thus prevailed in Poland as all three sides attempted to balance their actions along the Vistula with operations on the Danube.

It is useful to pause at this point and cast our eyes from the Vistula back to the banks of the Danube, where the Hauptarmee has been basking in the glow of the victory of Aspern, but has done nothing to exploit its success. At the same time, south and east of Vienna, Viceroy Eugene has just visited a severe humiliation upon a hapless Habsburg general and is on the verge of invading Hungary.

Before leaving the waters of the Vistula, however, several observations are in order. First, though seemingly remote from the main arena of combat—and often neglected for its remoteness—the Polish theatre was a key piece in the mosaic of politics, strategy, and battle in 1809. On the political side, though Prussian officers continued to press for intervention, Ferdinand's failure was an important element in King Friedrich Wilhelm's decision to hold his realm aloof from the war. Strategically, the numerically inferior Polish forces kept VII Corps from marching to the principal theatre of operations, demanded the diversion of secondary forces (Landwehr and Insurrection), deprived the Habsburg monarchy of significant resources (especially Galician recruiting grounds), and posed a threat to Moravia and Hungary in the Hauptarmee's strategic rear. There was also a psychological dimension as Ferdinand's failings contributed to the general sense of defeat and discouragement on the Austrian side. Second, Poniatowski's ability to turn the tables on the Austrians, despite the many disadvantages under which he laboured, draws our attention to the prince's military talents. He certainly made mistakes, but he also demonstrated impressive skills: combining caution and audacity in operations with deft management of difficult subordinates, organisational skill in raising new troops, and an invaluable ability to motivate the young Polish soldiers. Third, the tsar's soldiers played a central role in the Polish campaign. It was a role, however, that pleased neither of the other two belligerents. The Poles and French were disgusted by the delay, equivocation, and prevarication they encountered, while the Austrians could never truly trust the Russians despite the web of clandestine contacts. The Russian generals in the field may have even frustrated their tsar, introducing an additional layer of torpor that went well beyond Alexander's intentions. At a minimum, this ambivalent army behaved like an armed neutral with its own agenda, not as a stalwart Austrian ally with Habsburg interests at heart. Though the Russians exasperated the Poles, therefore, the consequences of their involvement were far more negative for Austria than for Napoleon and Poniatowski. Golitsyn's presence not only thwarted Ferdinand's June offensive, but his march west, albeit slow and well advertised, forced the Habsburg leaders to look over their strategic shoulders as they struggled with the monarchy's multiple challenges on the Danube. The complications and uncertainties inherent in the Russian advance will gain greater salience as we examine Austria's strategic situation in late June, because the Kaiser, Charles, and Stadion are about to be confronted with another calamity, this time in the pleasant green fields of Hungary.

CHAPTER 2

On Hungary's Endless Plains

Volume II of this work left Viceroy Eugene de Beauharnais's Army of Italy and Archduke Johann's Army of Inner Austria among the crags and forests of Styria. Eugene, having broken FML Johann Jellacic's division at St Michael on 25 May, has affected his union with Napoleon and is preparing for new missions with confidence. The bulk of his army is encamped about Bruck an der Mur. To the south, Grouchy and MacDonald are at Marburg (Maribor), Lamarque has reached Gonobitz (Sovenske Konjice), and Rusca has his small division at Spittal with outposts as far as the Sachsenburg fortress.[1] Spirits are high and the army feels well rewarded by Napoleon's warm words of praise in a 27 May proclamation. Johann's situation, on the other hand, is rather grim. His headquarters and one fragment of his army are in Graz along with the shaken fugitives from the St Michael disaster—in all about 10,000 men. Other shards of the Army of Inner Austria find themselves in Pettau (FML Albert Gyulai) and east of Laibach (Ljubljana) in Croatia (FML Ignaz Gyulai with 15,500 men). FML Chasteler has some 9,300 men in the Tyrol (not counting local insurgents), but Innsbruck has fallen and he is virtually isolated. The Austrian invasion of Dalmatia has collapsed and GM von Stoichevich's defeated division is retreating to Croatia, allowing GD Marmont to march for Laibach and points north. Ignaz Gyulai is attempting to muster the Croatian Insurrection (11,300), while Hungarian Insurrection troops assemble near Raab (Györ) under Archduke Joseph's instructions.[2] Now, with May concluding and June blossoming ahead of them, these two armies are on the verge of exchanging the mountains of Styria for the verdant plains of Hungary.

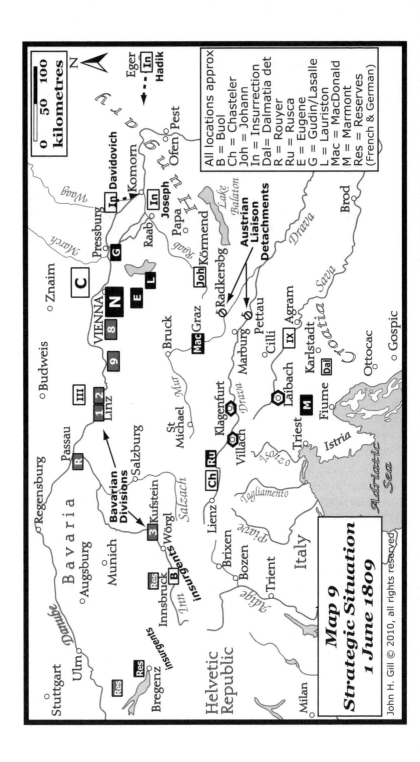

Map 9
Strategic Situation
1 June 1809

All locations approx
B = Buol
Ch = Chasteler
Joh = Johann
In = Insurrection
Dal = Dalmatia det
R = Rouyer
Ru = Rusca
E = Eugene
G = Gudin/Lasalle
L = Lauriston
Mac = MacDonald
M = Marmont
Res = Reserves
(French & German)

Austrian
Liaison
Detachments

0   50   100
kilometres

N

INTO HUNGARY

Johann could not stay in Graz. Though he yearned to operate independently (preferably in conjunction with the Hungarian Insurrection) and to 'force Napoleon to make detachments', Jellacic's defeat, Eugene's advance beyond Bruck, and the arrival in Marburg of Grouchy and MacDonald all made his present position untenable.[3] A detachment of Austrian light troops threw a French outpost out of Frohnleiten north of Graz on 27 May, but steady skirmishing and destroyed bridges to the south only imposed slight delays on Grouchy.[4] By the 29th, his surging, well-directed advance had brought his command to the outskirts of Graz; MacDonald was at Wildon only kilometres down the road.[5] Leaving a detachment of 913 in the city's citadel under Major Franz von Hackher, Johann pulled out that evening, marching east for Körmend and Hungary.

Table 2: Graz Citadel Garrison, 29 May 1809

Commander: Major von Hackher	
de Vaux depot	237
Lusignan depot	166
Strassaldo depot	263
1st Graz Landwehr	105
3rd Graz Landwehr	73
Engineer officers and miners	21
Artillery	48
Total	913

Source: Tepperberg, *Grazer Schlossberg 1809*, p. 62.

Johann and Charles at Odds Over Strategy

On 1 June Johann was in Körmend on the Raab (Raba) River. The French had done nothing to disturb his retreat. Parts of Albert Gyulai's detachment, marching from Pettau (Ptuj), had united with the archduke at St Gotthard (Szentgotthard) on 30 May and the *Hohenlohe* Dragoons (five squadrons) had arrived from Ignaz Gyulai to give Johann a total of 19,500 infantry and 2,200 horse. An additional 1,770 cavalry came in the form of two Insurrection hussar regiments under GM Janos Andrassy. Posted in Körmend and north along the Raab, the Hungarian troopers bolstered the

Army of Inner Austria's weak mounted arm and provided a valuable link to
the Insurrection corps that Archduke Joseph was slowly assembling around
the small fortress of Raab on the Danube.[6] Organisationally, Johann retained
command of Chasteler (still being called VIII Corps) and Ignaz Gyulai (IX
Corps), but neither of those corps retained much of its original composition.
Likewise, the force under Johann's immediate orders, though still burdened
with its weighty title, resembled a corps rather than an army. Among other
changes, Albert Gyulai, having reported himself ill, vanished from the scene
for the remainder of the war.[7] With no corps echelon in his principal field
force, Johann assumed this role and issued orders directly to his subordinate
division and brigades from this point onwards.

Table 3: Albert Gyulai's Detachment, Late May 1809

Joined Johann at St Gotthard	
Franz Jellacic Infantry	3
Strassaldo Infantry	2
Ogulin Grenz	2
Detached to Ignaz Gyulai	
Reisky Infantry	2
Remained at Pettau	
Ott Hussars	2
Marburg Landwehr (remnants)	2

Notes: All battalions very weak, especially Landwehr.
F Jellacic reduced to two battalions after joining Johann.
Source: Johann, Feldszugserzählungen, p. 131.

Under no immediate pressure from the enemy and feeling stronger with
these reinforcements, Johann's spirits revived and he began to consider
offensive operations as his army enjoyed several days of welcome rest. The
nature and direction of Johann's future operations, however, created an
acrimonious exchange of proposals, counter-proposals, orders, and objections
between Johann and his elder brothers, Charles and Franz. The crux of the
debate was whether the Army of Inner Austria should immediately join the
Hauptarmee on the Danube or whether it should remain south of the river
and continue to operate independently.

Johann quickly discovered that his conception of the empire's future
strategy clashed with the plans his brother the Generalissimus was
formulating. Charles, vacillating between offensive and defensive plans in the

wake of the victory at Aspern, wanted to have as many troops as possible at hand when he next confronted the French emperor. It is likely that the vivid memory of Aspern influenced his thinking, as that battle, though a victory, had been a very near-run contest against an outnumbered Napoleon. Charles became especially concerned in early June, when intelligence led him to believe that Napoleon had already gathered superior numbers and was preparing to attack, presumably on 14 June, the anniversary of Marengo. Charles also proceeded from two underlying assumptions about Johann and his army. First, based on Johann's glum reports from Graz, he believed that the Army of Inner Austria, battered and scattered, was nothing more than a 'detachment', too weak to operate on its own.[8] Second, he was convinced that Johann habitually split his command, dispersing his power and wasting forces in detachments; ironically, of course, this proclivity was not limited to Johann. Charles also wanted to rein in his somewhat wilful and—from his perspective—overly independent younger brother. Johann's prolonged stay in Körmend seems to have been a significant irritant and his younger brother's communications probably were interpreted in army headquarters as efforts to delay union with the Hauptarmee. In Charles's mind, these considerations and assumptions pointed to one conclusion: Johann must move north at once, cross the Danube (preferably at Medve near Raab), and march to Pressburg, where he would be in a position to support the Main Army either in offence or defence.

Johann, on the other hand, was passionately opposed to his brother's plan. He was convinced that his own presence in Inner Austria (Styria, Carinthia, Carniola) would compel Napoleon to detach significant forces, thus weakening the French and affording Charles an opportunity to strike. He proffered several proposals, including offensives towards Wiener-Neustadt, Ödenburg (Sopron), or Bruck, but his favoured idea was to launch a sudden attack on the isolated MacDonald, then combine with Ignaz Gyulai to defeat Marmont in the south, before returning to the north with as many as 50,000 men to take on Eugene. Underestimation of French strength contributed to his thinking. He gradually learned that the viceroy was on the verge of entering Hungary from Ödenburg, but believed the enemy had only 18,000 men when the actual figure was twice that number.[9] In his view, therefore, 'the march behind the Danube could only be detrimental', abandoning the resources of Inner Austria, Hungary, and Croatia (Charles saw Bohemia and Moravia as more vital to the empire), leaving Chasteler and Ignaz Gyulai to their own fates, and doing nothing to impede the junction of all Napoleon's forces around Vienna.

Of course, as with Charles, other factors were also at work in Johann's calculations. First of all, he placed a high value on his independence and broad authority. He had no interest in seeing his freedom curtailed by drawing closer to the Main Army. Second, and just as important, he was deeply bitter about what he saw as the Main Army's inaction after Aspern. His fury and frustration breathes through his contemporary correspondence and subsequent memoirs. 'The army on the Danube was victorious, but to what end?' he wrote to Kaiserin Maria Ludovica, 'Has this river been crossed, is Vienna in our hands, is Napoleon withdrawing?' 'Without these', he continued in exasperation, 'everything is useless, pointless . . . everything now stands as before.'[10] 'Without investigating whether or not the Austrian side could exploit this victory [Aspern], the concept in the Main Army showed much indecision,' he recorded in his memoir of the war. 'The orders that the archduke [Johann] received and His Majesty's correspondence prove this; one generally heard that something would be undertaken, but never what would be undertaken; anyone would easily recognise that every delay was a great gain for Napoleon.'[11] For him, therefore, acceding to Charles's wishes was tantamount to accepting a badly flawed strategy. He wanted no part of it.

In the end, Johann had no choice. He waited in Körmend until 7 June, hoping that Charles would change his mind as soon as he understood that the Army of Inner Austria was once more in 'battle-ready condition'.[12] The Generalissimus, however, saw in his brother's urgent importunities only disobedience, naiveté, and a ruinous tendency towards a brittle cordon defence—in other words, a thin line of forces that would defend nothing by trying to defend everything. Johann made a final appeal to Kaiser Franz on 6 June, writing that he was certain that the advantages of his plan 'would not escape' the Kaiser's insight and concluding with a blunt, almost insubordinate challenge: 'I await Your will, if more favourable orders do not come from the Generalissimus, there are moments when one must take things upon himself.'[13]

In the event, Johann did not wait for an answer to his 6 June letter. Overwhelmed by impatience and full of bitter disgust ('the Hauptarmee has little desire to act'), he took his army north-east down the Raab on the 7th, 'after I had waited in vain for an answer to the recommendations I had made'.[14] He told Joseph that he did not want to cross the Danube 'under any circumstances' and was secretly pleased that a lack of bridging material made passage over the river difficult if not impossible.[15] He seems to have flirted with insubordination, but followed his orders, he later recorded, after he saw that the Main Army's 'prolonged hesitation had already allowed the opportune moment to pass.'[16] His immediate task, however, was clear: unite with Joseph at Raab. Reinforced, refurbished, and somewhat refreshed after its extended stay in Körmend, the Army of Inner Austria therefore departed on 7 June, marching north-east via Baltavar to arrive in Tuskevar on the 9th. Here Johann granted his men another rest day before continuing their trek to Raab and the Danube.

Lacking the Most Basic Necessities

Awaiting Johann in Hungary were the troops of the Hungarian Noble Insurrection. This curious and complex institution, relic of a bygone age, was founded on the feudal premise that the Hungarian magnates owed military service to Franz as the reigning King of Hungary.[17] Once called to duty, contingents were raised locally and formed into infantry battalions (six companies) and cavalry regiments (six squadrons) on a regional basis.[18] Foot and horse alike were clad in the blue hussar-style uniforms traditional to Hungary and all came under the command of Archduke Joseph, the palatine, or viceroy, of that kingdom. In terms of command, therefore, the Insurrection did not fall directly under Charles's orders; he could only issue requests through Franz or 'invite' Joseph to act. Command, however, was the least of the Insurrection's handicaps. Everything was in short supply: weapons, equipment, troops, qualified officers, and, most of all, training and experience. Almost none of the men called to arms on 11 April had any military background whatsoever, and the Habsburg hierarchy refused to allow line officers or non-commissioned officers to be seconded to Insurrection units as cadres.[19] Nor, of course, had the Insurrection troops ever had any opportunity to exercise together as battalions or regiments, let alone as a whole corps. Many appeared at their mustering places in civilian clothes armed with their personal sabres.[20] One staff officer, observing the units assembling near Raab in early May noted 'the troops were tyros; the infantry . . . barely organised, without clothing and equipment, with the greater part of the muskets in poor condition; furthermore, without flints and ammunition, therefore the infantry could not be used for anything, not even for picket duty.'[21] A colonel described the cavalry as 'a heap of men who did not know how to ride, mounted on horses that had never been ridden'.[22] Another officer, lamenting 'the total absence of training' and 'the small number of experienced officers', recorded that 'Some of the cavalry . . . has neither pistols nor sabres; the harness is in most cases in the most miserable condition; men and horses are recruits.' 'Things were far worse with the infantry,' he remarked, 'only a small portion organised into companies and battalions; unarmed; the weapons of those who were armed mostly useless; lacking any knowledge of military duties and drill; most with no sense of subordination; almost no experienced officers.'[23] Poor discipline and inexperience not only made the troops skittish on outpost duty, it also 'led to continual shooting' in Insurrection bivouacs, so that 'one could not ride safely into camp by day or night.'[24] Furthermore, weak discipline, lack of cooking gear, and poor logistical arrangements contributed to desertion— as men were released into villages to find food—as well as plundering and abuse of the local population.[25] In one officer's words, the institution was 'a body without a soul, struggling with the absence of the most basic necessities . . . no wonder that these defenders of the Fatherland, on top of everything else, abandoned themselves to excesses.'[26] Archduke Joseph, their commander, praised their 'fine appearance, obedience, and aptitude', but worried that 'this untrained, and still totally inexperienced force' would fall into disorder 'at the initial impact' unless given adequate support and time to prepare.[27] Time, however, was short. Most of the contingents were not scheduled to assemble until mid-May, that is, around the time Johann's army was reeling back from the defeat at Tarvis. Most were still in remote districts 'busy with the selection of officers and administration of oaths when the enemy neared the borders.'[28] Although three more weeks would elapse before the French crossed into Hungary in strength, this would not suffice to correct the Insurrection's deficiencies in training, equipment, organisation, and discipline.[29]

The situation facing Habsburg leaders in Hungary was thus dire in mid-May, and FML Daniel Freiherr Mecséry, arriving in Raab on the 17th as commander of the Insurrection's Trans-Danubian District, had to cope with the daunting tasks of gathering and preparing his scanty and untrained force while fending off French forays from the direction of Vienna. A combination of misleading 'intelligence' planted with locals and brash displays of troops helped to confuse the enemy (Montbrun's cavalry screen) and masked the Insurrection's weaknesses.[30] The Insurrection's task was made easier because the French were equally thin on the ground and Napoleon was focused on his upcoming Danube crossing, leading to Aspern–Essling; Montbrun and other French commanders were therefore disinclined to undertake major operations. Most of May thus passed in nervous observation of Montbrun's outposts and in daily alarms as the inexperienced Insurrection troopers reacted to every French patrol, real or imagined. By the end of the month,

Mecséry had two battalions and eight squadrons posted in and around Raab with vedettes on the highway leading north-west towards Vienna; four other squadrons patrolled the Kleine Schütt island between the main channel of the Danube and its smaller southern arm.[31]

The old walled town of Raab played an important role in the campaign. A fortress in its own right, albeit somewhat decrepit, it was not only a key pillar for the assembly of the Insurrection, but also important to both sides as a gateway to Hungary, dominating the principal Vienna–Pest highway and serving as a pivot for operations by either army. Hoping to enhance its inherent strength and provide a secure base for the Insurrection to form, the Habsburg authorities employed numerous peasants in the construction of an entrenched camp just west of town that would accommodate a garrison of 5,000.

South of Raab and the busily digging workers, Mecséry had the rest of his men (three battalions, five companies, two and one-third cavalry

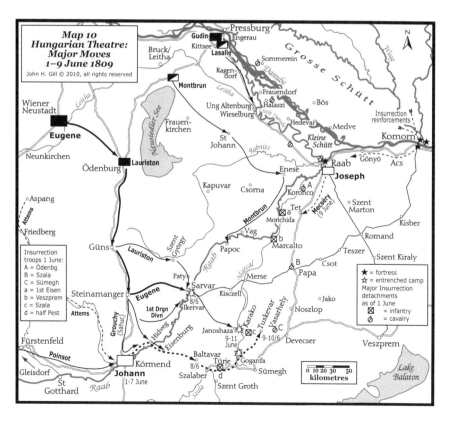

Map 10
Hungarian Theatre:
Major Moves
1–9 June 1809
John H. Gill © 2010, all rights reserved

regiments) stretched along the Raab and Marcal rivers from Csanak to Karako.[32] Additionally, the two best cavalry regiments (Veszprem and Pest), the most ready of the infantry (half of Pest Infantry No. 2), and two batteries of 3-pounders had been sent towards Körmend under GM Andrassy to establish contact with Johann.[33] More Insurrection troops were on the way. As the success at Aspern had removed the threat of French action north of the Danube, on 30 May septuagenarian FZM Paul Baron Davidovich was ordered to bring the remainder of his command (Cis-Danubian District) to Raab.[34] Likewise, Eggermann's advance into Galicia diminished the threat from Poland, allowing FML Andras Graf Hadik to march south with most of the units from the Trans-Theiss District. Additionally, after repeated proddings from the Kaiser, Joseph reluctantly transferred his headquarters from Pest to Raab on 2 June.[35] Substantial reinforcements and the archduke himself were thus en route to Raab as June began, albeit, as Joseph noted, 'neither properly assembled, nor equipped and organised'.[36]

Whatever their state of preparedness, by 10 June, as Johann's whitecoats were resting in Tuskevar, Andrassy's blue-clad Insurrection hussars were already in action against probing French along the Raab and Marcal Rivers.

Eugene's Advance

The French lost track of Johann for about a week after his departure from Graz. On 4 June, Napoleon therefore ordered Eugene to pursue the retreating Austrians and 'attempt to damage Prince Johann' while not taking himself too far from Vienna.[37] Eugene, who had collected his army around Wiener Neustadt, marched at once for Ödenburg with Grenier, Grouchy (commanding 1st Dragoon Division and Sahuc's light horse), and the Royal Guard; Baraguey d'Hilliers and the two division of the Left Wing followed over the coming days. The emperor bolstered the Army of Italy by attaching Lauriston's ad hoc command. Consisting of the Baden Brigade and Colbert's light cavalry, Lauriston's 'division' had been guarding the army's flank at Ödenburg since 29 May with a forward detachment at Güns (Köszeg) from 2 June and patrols as far as Steinamanger (Szombathely). Napoleon also added Montbrun's cavalry 'division' (actually just Jacquinot's brigade of three regiments) to Eugene's order of battle. Montbrun, advancing from Bruck an der Leitha, was to screen Eugene's left as the viceroy sought to come to grips with Johann. MacDonald at Graz with his two infantry divisions, Pully's dragoons, and 6th Hussars, constituted Eugene's extreme

Table 4: MacDonald's Wing, 5–12 June 1809

In Hungary: GD MacDonald
Advance Guard: GB Poinsot

23rd Dragoons	4
29th Dragoons	2
92nd Ligne (II, III)	2
Three battalions from Lamarque	3
2 x 3-pdrs	

Division: GD Lamarque (GB Alméras, GB Huard)

18th Léger (III, IV)	2
13th Ligne	4
23rd Ligne (III, IV)	2
29th Ligne	4
10 guns	

(All battalions shown, not clear which were detached to Poinsot)

2nd Dragoon Division: GD Pully

28th Dragoons	3
29th Dragoons	2
4 guns	

At Graz: GD Broussier

9th Ligne	4
84th Ligne	4
92nd Ligne (I, IV)	2
6th Hussars	4
23rd Dragoons	(1 company)
12 guns	

the intentions of our Brother the Archduke Charles, I can only urge you to follow with due obedience the orders of the Generalissimus in this as in all future cases.'[47] These imperial words could temporarily settle the issue, but irritation, impatience, and suspicion remained very close to the surface on both sides.

While this operational debate boiled and the principal armies tramped across the Hungarian plains, the slightly more distant forces were also on the move. From Graz, MacDonald formed an advance guard of five battalions, six dragoon squadrons, and two guns under GB Poinsot at Gleisdorf on

5 June.[48] This force occupied Fürstenfeld on the 8th and rode into Körmend the following day. MacDonald himself departed Graz on 9 June, leaving Broussier and 6th Hussars to prosecute the investment of the town's citadel.[49] Marching via Körmend (10th), MacDonald reached Vasarhely on the 11th with Lamarque's and Pully's divisions. On the Austrian side, Mecséry moved south from Raab on 9 June to assemble a force of five Insurrection battalions, eight squadrons, and a cavalry battery at Tet in anticipation of Johann's arrival. On the way, he acquired some 100 troopers from the reserve squadrons of the *Liechtenstein* and *Kienmayer* Hussars in an effort to provide more experienced role models for his Insurrection cavalrymen. Mecséry's command was to guard the Raab crossings and cover Johann's withdrawal while Joseph remained at Raab with the other available Insurrection elements.[50] To the south, septuagenarian Oberst Attems was posted at the south-western end of Lake Balaton on the 12th with a small command based on remnants of Breuner's battalion and the *Frimont* Hussars Reserve Squadron. Attems had retired from Aspang during early June and reached Körmend on the 9th; he now served as a link in the thin chain of detachments connecting Johann in Hungary to Ignaz Gyulai in Croatia.

12 June: Engagement at Papa

The morning of 12 June found Johann's army encamped around Papa, facing south towards Tuskevar and preparing to continue its withdrawal north. Eugene, on the other hand, having been unable to snare the Austrians on the 11th, was directing his entire force on the small town in the hope of bringing on a battle. This required hard riding and marching on the part of Grouchy's and Grenier's men from Karako, while Eugene pushed Montbrun and the Badeners across numerous small watercourses towards Papa from Merse and called up Baraguey d'Hilliers, the dragoons, and the Guard from across the Marcal. The viceroy himself reached Papa in the morning and could see that he had the entire Habsburg force to his front. By noon, he could clearly perceive preparations for an imminent departure, but he hesitated to engage with the limited troops at his disposal and awaited the arrival of Grenier from the south and Baraguey d'Hilliers from the west. Grenier, however, could not arrive before 2 p.m., so the fight that ensued became a rear guard action rather than the fully fledged battle that Eugene had hoped to initiate. The morning thus passed with skirmishing, artillery duels, and cavalry affairs

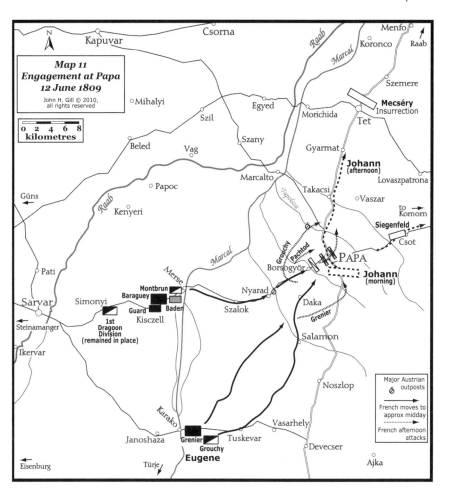

Map 11
Engagement at Papa
12 June 1809

in which the French claimed more than 150 prisoners. It all seemed fairly routine and insignificant to Johann as he headed north.[51]

The bulk of Johann's command was on its way north towards Tet before the French infantry was on the scene. The archduke, however, sent a detachment under Oberst Franz Anton von Siegenfeld through Csot towards Teszer to protect the road to Komorn and left a rear guard at Papa to cover his withdrawal.[52] This rear guard was composed of *Joseph* and *Ott* Hussars, *Allvintzi* Infantry, *1st Banal* Grenzer, Veszprem, Pest, and Sümegh Insurrection Hussars as well as several guns under the command, as usual, of FML Frimont. Frimont deployed the cavalry south-west of the town, supported by III/*Allvintzi*, and placed the rest of the infantry north of Papa to cover the eventual withdrawal. They were soon busily engaged. As Johann's whitecoats trudged north and scattered skirmish fire snapped in the air to the west, GM Ettingshausen, several other officers, and Jozsef Magyarasz, the town priest, climbed up into the church tower to observe the rills, woods, and pleasant flat meadows around Papa. With his telescope, Ettingshausen 'could clearly descry every movement of the approaching enemy'. 'I saw the enemy masses assemble themselves, step forth, and advance against our rear guard; our troops pulled back in fine order, fighting, towards Papa and through the town, it was a splendid piece of theatre, even though it could not be very welcome as we had to withdraw.'[53] Pastor Magyarasz saw that Johann's army 'stood on the road towards Raab and gave the impression that they were preparing for battle, but after two cannon shots were heard, they retired in the direction of Raab; in the meantime, the Insurrection troops fled towards Csot.'[54]

The struggle that Ettingshausen and his companions watched with such interest began at around 2 p.m. as Eugene saw Seras's division appear on the French right. Directing Grenier to outflank Papa on its southern side and sending Grouchy with Colbert and two of Sahuc's regiments to swing north of the town, the viceroy ordered Montbrun, supported by the Badeners and Sahuc's other two chasseur regiments, to 'open a passage' by attacking straight ahead and holding nothing back.[55] An initial charge, executed by 1st Chasseurs, was repulsed, but a second attack by 2nd Chasseurs and 7th Hussars 'was so impetuous that our troops entered Papa pell-mell with the enemy'.[56] Jogging forwards alongside Montbrun's troopers, the Baden infantry rushed into Papa on the heels of the fleeing Austrians. Although their ranks were thinned by heat casualties, the perspiring Germans hastened through the town: 'We followed the cavalry at a dead run. Discarded muskets, sabretaches, dead and wounded men and horses marked the bloody way.'[57] Surgeon Meier noted that there were 'many dead and badly wounded Austrians, most with sabre cuts'.[58] From the perspective of the residents, of course, the results were terrifying: 'One can imagine how the victorious enemy overwhelmed the inhabitants and robbed as much as they could,' recalled a local citizen with horror. 'After two frightful hours, the drums rolled and the houses were saved from the enemy.'[59]

With the town in French hands, Eugene ordered Grenier to turn north and join the mounted regiments on the road to Tet, in what Ettingshausen termed 'a splendid manoeuvre', but the two French divisions contributed little to the pursuit.[60] Likewise, Pachtod's division arrived too late to take part in the fighting and Severoli, much to the frustration of many French officers, deployed his division into line early in the action and lost an hour ploying back into column when it came time to advance; he too played no role in the combat.[61] Just as embarrassing was a failure in staff work that left 1st Dragoon Division with no orders; it remained west of the Marcal throughout the day. The pursuit, therefore, was conducted almost exclusively by the light cavalry under Montbrun and Grouchy. The latter had crossed the Tapolcza stream west of Papa, but had not been able to outflank the Austrian positions on the low hills north of town. Now, supported by the Baden light guns and the Jäger Battalion voltigeurs, the light horse regiments pressed after the retiring Austrians as afternoon turned to evening. The skirmishers, spreading out across the bright summer fields, were quickly joined by the horse guns, rattling up and unlimbering at speed to silence the enemy pieces, the Baden Brigade's journal keeper proudly recording that, 'As usual, our artillery fired with great skill and it soon succeeded in dislodging the much stronger enemy battery.'[62] Indeed, the Baden artillery earned French accolades for its professional performance. Among other actions, well-aimed Baden shots discomfited the Szala Insurrection cavalry as it crossed a stream near Takacsi: when a few rounds killed two or three horses, the regiment fell into confusion and rode off in great haste.[63] The pursuit continued until nightfall but the French halted with their main body no further than Takacsi. The Austrians bivouacked at Tet and Gyarmat.

The day had been a partial success for the French. On the negative side of the ledger, the engagement had been a relatively small affair and Johann had escaped.[64] He and his army remained a menace and would be reinforced by uniting with Joseph's Insurrection corps within the next two days. Weak staff work had left the dragoons idle and Severoli's obduracy delayed the arrival of the Italian division. Nonetheless, the French had inflicted more than 600 casualties (mostly prisoners from Insurrection units) for a loss of 200 of their own and had maintained the pressure on Johann. More important, Eugene had now united his own army and caught up with his quarry. It would be difficult for Johann to evade combat again. Furthermore, the skirmishes over the past several days sustained the French psychological edge, the advantage of the pursuer over the pursued. This constituted further proof for the viceroy and his men that they could and would defeat the whitecoats once they were brought to bay. At 8 p.m. that night, Eugene wrote to Napoleon: 'Tomorrow at five in the morning, we will put ourselves in motion to march to Raab.'[65]

THE BATTLE OF RAAB

Joseph had mounted a carriage and driven to Tet on the afternoon of 12 June. His diary entry for the day offers an interesting perspective on the appearance of Johann's corps as the troops passed before him in review that day 'cheering continually': 'Cavalry very weak, especially the cuirassiers [sic] and dragoons, but look relat[ively] good. My regiment looks good and is relat[ively] strong, *Ott* Hussars too, but indifferent in appearance. Infantry, other than *Esterhazy*, *Allvintzi*, and the grenadiers, weak, ragged, many recruits. Landwehr battalion miserably clothed, untrained personnel, have never stood firm before the enemy.'[66]

In addition to these troubling images of the appearance of Johann's regulars and Landwehr, Joseph had witnessed further evidence of the Insurrection's frailties that morning as disorganised, dispirited Neograd Hussars appeared in Raab from the Kleine Schütt. These were the remnants of two squadrons that had 'dissolved themselves' following a failed attempt to probe Allied troops crossing onto the island near Frauendorf (Dunakiliti) in which the Hungarian commander had been killed.[67] This was French cavalry (8th Hussars) and Hessian infantry from Lasalle's command south-east of Pressburg, and we shall take up their story later on, but it is important to keep in mind that Joseph had to worry about French troops coming from the west as well as Eugene's men approaching from the south. French cavalry had been alarming his raw troops for the past two weeks with increasing frequency and the danger on this western flank was never far from his mind. Likewise, both Joseph and Johann were anxious for the safety of the roads to Komorn. As there were no other Danube bridges in the vicinity, their communications and line of retreat—should it prove necessary—ran through this city, and they kept an understandably careful watch on the roads leading in that direction from the Vasarhely area where MacDonald was known to have arrived.

Johann and Joseph met in Tet that evening. Johann seems to have had little concern about the enemy. He considered the French pursuit feeble and believed that Eugene had displayed only '2,500 horse and three battalions of infantry' at Papa.[68] He and his chief of staff, the recently promoted GM Laval Graf Nugent von Westenrath, had concluded that the French had only 12,000 in the immediate area and were confident that they would be able to take the offensive once the junction with the Insurrection corps had been achieved. The brothers deferred detailed discussion of future operations until the following day, but reached several important agreements that would be significant in the fighting during the next two days. In the first place, to stiffen the inexperienced Insurrection troops, the two archdukes decided to amalgamate their respective forces by incorporating Insurrection brigades into regular divisions. Second, they agreed to share command. This doubtless seemed a comfortable, fraternal proposition, but it left the two staffs in confusion (which chief of staff held predominance?) and was surely curious, given the imminent intermingling of subordinate units.[69] Third, the brothers agreed that Johann would march north towards Raab on the morning of the 13th to occupy a position along the Csanak Heights, a prominent ridge that runs generally north-west to south-east approximately five kilometres south of Raab. Once united, Nugent would collaborate with FML Moritz Graf Gomez von Parientos, Joseph's chief of staff, to draft a plan for the next few days. At least, that was the general agreement Joseph and his staff thought they had reached when the archduke climbed into his carriage at 10 p.m. that night for the drive back to Raab. Although an accident en route delayed his return until 1.30 a.m. on the 13th, Joseph immediately called for Gomez and instructed his staff to reconnoitre what they termed 'an interim position' along the Csanak Heights at first light.[70] As we shall see, either Johann never accepted this general outline in the first place or he and Nugent decided to ignore it as they issued their orders for 13 June.[71]

13 June: Introductory Engagement

Expecting Johann's corps to arrive in the early afternoon, Joseph and his staff were surprised when an officer dashed into headquarters between 6 and 7 a.m. to announce that Johann's men were already at hand. Surprise turned to astonished dismay when it became clear that Johann's troops were not occupying the Csanak position, but were marching straight towards the Raab suburbs. Urgent pleas by Joseph's staff officers regarding the importance of the ground between Csanak and Gyirmot were in vain. Johann and Nugent arrived at Joseph's quarters an hour later. According to Insurrection officers, Nugent believed the corps was too exhausted to stay in Tet, even though it was under little immediate pressure from the French.[72] Placing Ettingshausen in charge of the rear guard, therefore, Johann and Nugent put their columns on the road shortly after midnight and marched for Raab with no heed for the agreement that the Insurrection staff thought had been reached. Furthermore, Johann and Nugent neglected either to inform Joseph or to reconnoitre bivouacs, so considerable consternation and confusion arose as the arriving troops were shunted off to hastily selected sites with no plan for whether or how they would be employed that day or the next. Given the composition and intentions of Ettingshausen's force, observed a frustrated member of Joseph's staff, 'there could be no doubt that the rear guard would be pressed that very day and that the enemy would become master of the neglected heights.'[73]

Ettingshausen and his rear guard began their withdrawal from the Tet area at 3 a.m. and made a fairly uneventful march to Menfo, where they arrived

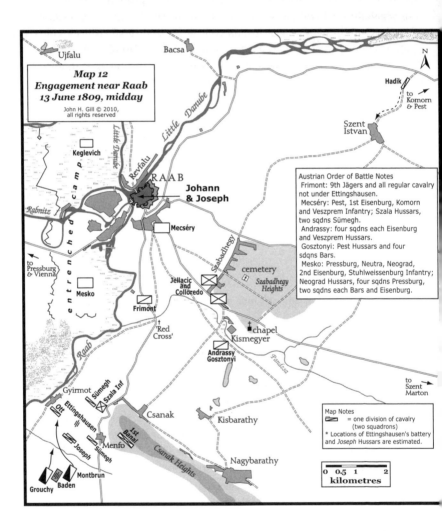

Map 12
Engagement near Raab
13 June 1809, midday
John H. Gill © 2010,
all rights reserved

Austrian Order of Battle Notes
Frimont: 9th Jägers and all regular cavalry not under Ettingshausen.
Mecséry: Pest, 1st Eisenburg, Komorn and Veszprem Infantry; Szala Hussars, two sqdns Sümegh.
Andrassy: four sqdns each Eisenburg and Veszprem Hussars.
Gosztonyi: Pest Hussars and four sdqns Bars.
Mesko: Pressburg, Neutra, Neograd, 2nd Eisenburg, Stuhlweissenburg Infantry; Neograd Hussars, four sqdns Pressburg, two sqdns each Bars and Eisenburg.

Map Notes
▭ = one division of cavalry
(two squadrons)
* Locations of Ettingshausen's battery and *Joseph* Hussars are estimated.

0 0.5 1 2
kilometres

around 11 a.m., delayed more by stoppages in Johann's column than by the French. Receiving orders to deploy on a low rise between the Raab River and the Csanak Heights, he arrayed his command—a process that was 'slow and difficult' owing to the 'totally untrained' Insurrection troops—with the *Ott* Hussars on the right at Gyirmot, the Grenzer on the vineyard-covered Csanak Heights on the left, and the Sümegh Hussars and Szala Infantry in the centre near Menfo.[74] By this time, Ettingshausen's *Joseph* Hussars were already clashing with Eugene's vanguard and the worried general was looking towards Raab, hoping to see reinforcements marching up in response to his reports of contact. But the road to his rear was empty. To Ettingshausen's exasperation, the courier who was supposed to deliver orders to Frimont to support the advance guard brought his message to Ettingshausen instead and had to make a hasty ride back towards Raab to locate the intended recipient. In the meantime, Ettingshausen employed his artillery liberally, withdrew the Szala Infantry ('that I could not expose to any attack'), and hoped for the best.[75]

Table 5: Austrian Rear Guard, 13 June 1809

GM Ettingshausen

1st *Banal* Grenz Regiment No. 10 (11 companies)	1,500
EH Josef Hussars No. 2 (4 squadrons)	300
Ott Hussars No. 5 (2 squadrons)	100–150
Sümegh Hussars (2 divisions)	800
Szala Insurrection Infantry No. 8	1,000
1 x cavalry battery	

All strengths approximate.

As Ettingshausen's anxieties were mounting, the archdukes and their staffs were sitting down to lunch. So far, the retreat had gone smoothly, though its haste meant that the troops were now planting their camps south of Raab and on the heights around Szabadhegy 'without orders and without destinations'.[76] Neither Johann, nor Joseph, nor their respective chiefs of staff had a plan for the immediate future and Joseph suggested they reconnoitre the terrain at once to array the troops and establish a coherent order of battle. Nugent and Johann, however, saw no need for hurry and wanted to grant their men time to rest and eat before making further movements. It was therefore decided that the two archdukes would take lunch while Nugent and Gomez worked out a scheme to amalgamate their two corps. While they were at table, however, the dull sound of cannon fire rumbled up from the south with increasing fury as Ettingshausen fell back before the French advance guard. Riding hurriedly out of Raab, the brothers were horrified to see that French cavalry had already advanced into the low ground north of the Csanak Heights and were approaching the Pandzsa stream. These were the ten light horse regiments under Montbrun (Jacquinot and Colbert) and Grouchy (Sahuc), in all approximately 5,600 troopers supported by the four guns of the Baden light battery. Montbrun, approaching Ettingshausen's position late in the morning, had not wanted to tangle with the Grenzer among the Csanak vineyards, and aimed his opening blow against the Austrian right near Gyirmot, but the Austrians withdrew without awaiting a charge. The French thus gained access to the lush rolling meadows between Csanak and the Pandzsa, where the archdukes and their suites saw them as they rushed from their midday repast. It was approximately 2 p.m. and Lörincs Hohenegger, the town priest of Raab, remembered the 'ferocious action' that flared between the mounted arms of the two armies. 'A crowd of people streamed out of the city gates; they wanted to witness this rare and bloody scene,' he wrote. 'The sun shone brightly and hot, the flashing sabres could be seen, it seemed from such a distance like flashes of lightning and the thunder of the cannon could also be heard.'[77]

It was instantly clear to the French that they had brought the main Habsburg army to bay. Eugene, up with his advance guard, ordered Grouchy (on the left along the river) and Montbrun (in the open ground on the right) to occupy the enemy's attention and prevent any significant advance, thereby allowing time for his hastening infantry to secure possession of the Csanak Heights.[78] Grouchy's four regiments reached the Pandzsa and even ventured across, but took fire from artillery in the entrenched camp to the west and came under attack by Austrian regular cavalry under Frimont. They gradually fell back. Montbrun, on the French right, was also forced to retire. Pressured by Andrassy's and Gosztonyi's Insurrection brigades at 3 p.m., he withdrew as far as Gyirmot. The Baden battery, having exhausted its ammunition, also pulled out, leaving the French with no artillery for a time. Instructed by Eugene to prevent enemy occupation of the critical heights, Montbrun stood his ground, suffering heavily from Austrian artillery fire while manoeuvring to repel cavalry forays. Fortunately for the French, Durutte's sweating foot soldiers and two batteries (Lieutenant Noël's and one of the Guard) arrived in time to blunt the Hungarian cavalry's advance and seize the high ground. Although swirling cavalry clashes and punishing artillery fire criss-crossed the low ground until nearly 8 p.m., the French would not be dislodged.

Indeed, once the French infantry and guns were in place, the Austrian commanders made no serious attempt to evict them. Whether through the army's disorganisation or misperception of the situation on the part of the Habsburg leadership, the Austrian infantry was not engaged. Colloredo's foot soldiers moved forward in masses to the vicinity of the Kismegyer farmstead, but they halted there and received no orders to continue their advance. Archduke Joseph was left to lament 'we brought the infantry up too late and failed to regain the Csanak Heights.'[79] The French compounded Joseph's frustration by capturing two companies from Pest Infantry No. 2 (507 men) who had been forgotten during the withdrawal and were tidily wrapped up by Grouchy's troopers near Gyirmot as they tried to slip back to Austrian lines.[80] Other than these unfortunate companies, Austrian losses in the confused fighting probably came to something over 400. French casualties were probably around 200 to 300.[81] For their 'first time in a serious fight against cavalry', the Insurrection horsemen, 'exhibited much spirit', but their many deficiencies in training and equipment were also evident and they showed themselves easily disconcerted by artillery fire.[82] Furthermore, their élan sometimes manifested itself in foolhardy behaviour: 'many of these drunken daredevils hacked their way individually into the rank and file of entire divisions where they found their deaths.'[83]

The day's outcome largely favoured the French. Eugene reported that it had been 'very glorious for our mounted troops', who 'manoeuvred with sangfroid under the enemy's fire for many hours and showed great intrepidity in the actual charges that occurred'. This excellent performance gained him a clear picture of the Austrian army and, above all, preserved French possession of the Csanak Heights. 'These dominate the entire area,' he wrote Napoleon that night, 'and will facilitate our operations on the morrow.' Although he did not know 'the intentions of the enemy', the viceroy also had a clear sense of his own mission: 'If he remains in position near Raab, we will attack tomorrow; if he retires on Komorn as his dispositions lead one to believe, we will pursue him in that direction.'[84] The archdukes, on the other hand, had neither a clear picture of enemy strength and locations nor any coherent sense of mission. A council of war late that night confirmed the amalgamation of the two corps and the joint command to be exercised by the two brothers. It did not, however, resolve the confusion between the two archducal staffs or result in any conclusions about forthcoming operations. The two chiefs of staff were supposed to work out a plan during the night but Nugent went to bed and Gomez was left to take a few peripheral steps within the bounds of his own authority. 'One should know', recorded an

Insurrection officer,'that he [Joseph] pressed for a disposition very earnestly, but the chief of the Insurrection General Staff, FML Gomez, a fragile old man of 70, was incapable and Archduke Johann's [chief of staff], General Nugent, to whom everything was handed, could not be moved.'[85] Discussions may have been overshadowed by recriminations over the loss of the Csanak Heights and there was certainly friction between Nugent and Gomez.[86] 'Peculiar relationship,' complained Joseph. 'Jealousy of both, laziness of Nugent and his nonchalance.' Indeed, writing in his diary, the Palatine expressed contempt for his brother's chief of staff: 'never gave a definitive opinion, always said one may do this, one may do that, decided nothing easily, changed his opinion every quarter hour.' In the end: 'no disposition was written for any situation.'[87]

Adding to the tension on the Habsburg side that night were two new instructions that had arrived during the day. The first of these, from Franz, directed Joseph to turn over command to Johann and report in person to the Kaiser at Wolkersdorf near Wagram. Neither of Franz's brothers found this prospect appealing. Johann declined to accept command, and Joseph fumed that he would 'rather resign completely than lay down command.'[88] Although, as we have seen, the two brothers reached an amicable agreement, this was a farrago for the staffs, and the entire situation generated unnecessary turmoil and ill will. The second letter came from Charles. Among other tasks, Johann was to strengthen the fortifications at Raab and Komorn, retain control of the Kleine Schütt, make preparations to capture and hold Ungarisch-Altenburg, send patrols as far out as possible, and maintain his main body (including Insurrection) at Raab to attack the enemy if a favourable opportunity arose. Additionally, Johann was to detach 4,000 regulars, 4,000 Landwehr, 200 cavalry, and twenty-four guns through the Grosse Schütt to Pressburg to relieve GM Bianchi so that the latter could join the Hauptarmee.[89] These impracticable instructions, outdated before they arrived, provoked incredulous exasperation in Johann, bolstering his conviction that the Main Army's headquarters was both impervious to reason and out of touch with the situation on the ground.[90] This order, he later wrote, 'is just all too clear proof of how puffed up some were from the success at Aspern and what sort of things some demanded of others without themselves contributing'. 'The dispatch of the troops', he concluded gloomily, 'was hindered by the enemy, who were close at our heels.'[91]

Evidence of the enemy's proximity and activity came from the picket lines around midnight as Eugene's men surprised outposts of the Szala Hussars—'the French fired a volley at our brigade, our horses and our men fled in terror,' noted Rittmeister Karoly Hertelendy.[92] The Insurrection troops tried to restore the situation with a counter-charge, but were repulsed and uneasy calm descended upon the darkened field. Other than this momentary combat, all was quiet. 'Between the two lines of glowing camp fires', remembered Hochenegger, 'all was black obscurity and deep silence, and this silence prophesied gloomily that thousands would die in this area come the morning. This vista was simultaneously horrifying and beautiful.'[93]

Around one of those campfires sat Léon Michel Routier and his comrades of 102nd Ligne. 'Everything announced a general and decisive battle for the morrow: each prepared himself with cheerfulness. Marauding had been so fruitful that our camp was full of excellent wine and comestibles of every sort, so we found ourselves perfectly disposed to thrash the combined gentlemen of Austria and Hungary.'[94]

14 June, Morning: Certain Presages of Victory

The ground over which the coming battle would be fought was bounded on the southern side by the Csanak Heights that had figured so prominently in the combat on 13 June. Essentially a low but relatively steep crest rising to slightly over 200 metres in the immediate vicinity of the battlefield, this vineyard-covered ridge dominated the local area, affording excellent visibility over the Austrian positions to the north, while limiting what the Habsburg commanders could see, and offering tactical advantages should the French need to fall back on the defensive. Five kilometres away to the north, across gently undulating fields of grain, Johann and Joseph benefited from a piece of high ground near Szabadhegy. Also obstructed with vineyards over much of its eastern face, it was only some 130 metres high, but it stood out from the surrounding terrain and offered good observation to the south, particularly from a projecting knoll surmounted by a small chapel. The real strength of the Austrian position, however, derived from the Pandzsa stream that flowed through the field in a sharply cut bed sometimes as much one to one and a half metres deep and bordered in many places by marshy ground.[95] Four bridges provided passage over the Pandzsa and its soggy marge, all of which were intact on the day of battle. Flowing into the Pandzsa just south-east from Kismegyer was a tiny watercourse called the Viczay that could inconvenience inexperienced cavalry and would thus have some influence on the day's events. At the centre of the line was a walled farmstead with a stout three-storey grange similar in characteristics to the famous granary at

Essling. Called Kismegyer, this miniature fortress with its granary citadel would become the focus of much of the struggle. The land became hillier and more rugged on the eastern fringe of the field, but to the north it fell away from the Szabadhegy hill towards the Little Danube in an open rolling plain. Here lay the main highway from Pressburg to Komorn, the Habsburg line of communications and prospective route of retreat. The Raab closed the battlefield on its western side, but across the river lay the entrenched camp where the Austrians had been digging away industriously since mid-May. Though the entrenchments were designed to protect its garrison against attack from Vienna, it was practically invulnerable behind the shield of the Raab. Finally, the fortress of Raab, at the confluence of the Rabnitz (Rabca), Raab, and Little Danube, sheltered a small garrison, but would play only a minor role in the battle that was about to erupt.

At 9 a.m. on 14 June, the two archdukes and their staffs rode out and took their breakfast on the small chapel knoll above Kismegyer. An 'order of battle' had been drafted during the night to amalgamate the two corps, but no orders had been issued for attack or defence. Johann wanted to attack what he believed to be a numerically inferior French force on the Csanak Heights, or at a minimum launch a powerful reconnaissance to determine French strength, and the prospect of such an operation occasioned lengthy deliberations among the officers on the hillside. Johann, however, believed he needed more time to organise and prepare the army. He decided to wait until the 15th.[96] Meanwhile, the troops went about cooking their morning meals and slowly began to assemble according to the new order of battle. This arrangement placed the army's 8,770 cavalry on the open terrain on the flanks: Mecséry with *Joseph* Hussars, *Ott* Hussars, and most of the Insurrection squadrons on the left; and Frimont on the right along the Raab with a mixed force of regular cavalry and Insurrection. Johann commanded in the centre, concentrating his 24,210 infantry there to take advantage of the farmstead and the Szabadhegy Heights, each division in two lines: Jellacic centre-right from the stone bridge towards Kismegyer, Colloredo in and behind Kismegyer. The farmstead itself was garrisoned by 2nd Graz Landwehr and three companies of *Strassaldo*. Colloredo later added two companies of *St Julien* for a total of 872 men under Major Johann Ludwig Hummel, the 65-year-old commander of the Graz battalion.[97] Behind the centre, the infantry reserve was arrayed on the heights, likewise in two lines. Most of the Austrian artillery was dispersed across the front in battery packets or arrayed on the Szabadhegy Heights, but the twelve guns that made up the reserve artillery were left in the rear near Raab and played no

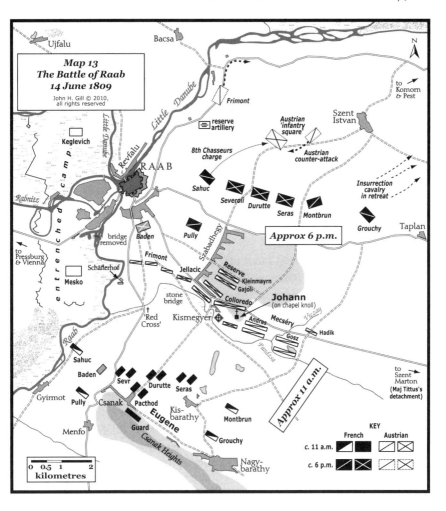

Map 13
The Battle of Raab
14 June 1809
John H. Gill © 2010,
all rights reserved

role in the battle. Other than the 'order of battle' and placement of the troops on the ground, no general disposition or orders were distributed, specifically no instructions were issued on where the army should rally in case retreat became necessary.

The Austrian position was moderately strong, but its left was 'in the air' and the Habsburg generals were concerned that they would be turned on that flank or that some significant French force such as MacDonald would threaten their line of retreat by marching directly on Komorn. Siegenfeld's detachment of two Grenz battalions, a division of *Blankenstein* Hussars, two Insurrection squadrons, and two guns (1,445 total) was therefore stationed at Romand to guard the far left flank and a squadron of Veszprem Hussars (160 men) sat at Kisber on the Veszprem–Komorn highway.[98] A battalion (II/*Esterhazy*, mostly recruits) and a squadron of Pest Hussars (150 men) were placed on the high ground beyond the left wing near Szent Marton under Major Franz von Tittus of *Esterhazy*. The largest detachment, however, was the garrison of 5,285 and ten guns in the entrenched camp south-west of Raab. This division-sized force was under GM Mesko— whom we last saw conducting rear guard actions under Hiller in the Danube valley—and was large enough to have an influence on the outcome of the battle. Although he was given no specific instructions for the coming engagement, Mesko's standing orders included directions to retire over the Raab in case of battle.[99]

The marching, waiting, and shuffling around required to settle the army into these positions occasioned a great deal of confusion, exacerbated by belated delivery of rations and largely vain efforts to issue a free portion of wine to the troops. Logistical arrangements for the Insurrection in particular had been poor all along (the institution did not fit into Habsburg wartime bureaucracy) and both man and horse had gone for many days without proper food and drink. As morning pushed on towards noon and these dispositions were being completed, many men were still awaiting their official rations, or had gone off in search of their own. They would have to postpone their meals, however, for at around this time the Austrian officers on the knoll noticed that 'multiple columns' of French troops were advancing from the Csanak Heights: 'they deployed upon reaching their positions . . . and after completing their deployment, seemed to await in silence the signal to attack.'[100]

Excitement electrified officers and men on the French side of the field. Eugene was acutely conscious that 14 June was the anniversary of Napoleon's great victories at Marengo (1800) and Friedland (1807). He wanted to celebrate the occasion with a battlefield success of his own. 'The army seemed to divine the thoughts of the general in chief,' recorded GB Vaudoncourt. 'The troops were animated with that ardour and that confidence that are certain presages of victory.'[101] 'Cries of enthusiasm resounded, followed at once by the sound of the drums and the bands of the entire army,' remembered Pierre Auvray of the 23rd Dragoons, and Lieutenant Barat of 52nd Ligne recalled that 'the sound of the guns exhilarated our brave men with joy to be going into combat at last.'[102] Marching over the Csanak ridge and unfolding onto the gentle fields were the 29,000 infantry and 10,000 cavalry of the Army of Italy, supported by approximately fifty-six guns.[103] After conducting a dawn reconnaissance of the battlefield, the viceroy planned to use his army to fight an 'oblique battle', that is, holding back his centre and left while advancing with his right to push the Austrians away from their line of retreat towards Komorn.[104] Like Johann, he placed the bulk of his cavalry on the wings: Montbrun and Grouchy on the right with eight guns facing Mecséry, and Sahuc's four regiments on the left supported by Lauriston's Baden Brigade and the recently arrived dragoons of General Pully's division. Eugene's plan placed the greatest burden on the infantry in the centre, with Seras, the rightmost division, slated to lead the main attack, followed in sequence by Durutte (centre) and Severoli (left). Pachtod would serve as immediate reserve and the Guard, as usual, provided a reserve of last resort. The viceroy could also take assurance from the proximity of Lamarque's division. That general, with 7,000 infantry and twelve guns, would be on hand by late afternoon as an ultimate reserve should the battle turn against the French. Not counting Lamarque, it is useful to note that the forces available to the opposing commanders were equal: 40,000 Austrian/Insurrection against 40,100 French/Italian/Baden troops. Johann, however, having chosen to detach 7,040 men to his extreme flanks, found himself at a numerical disadvantage.[105] Moreover, Eugene had a superior number of guns and enjoyed a considerable advantage in troop quality as one-third of Johann's army actually on the field (roughly 10,520 of 32,980) was composed of Insurrection troops with their manifold deficiencies in training and equipment. Another 4,600 were Landwehr and many of the regular regiments had recently incorporated numerous untrained recruits.[106] These factors were about to manifest themselves in painful fashion along the banks of the little Pandzsa brook.

14 June, Afternoon: Granddaughter to Marengo

The weather that morning was 'superb', and at 11.30 a.m. Montbrun moved forward, his light troopers masking the French infantry 'advancing majest-ically in columns' to the rear.[107] He quickly cleared away several Austrian squadrons south of the Pandzsa as well as a four-gun battery that had boldly rushed out to shell the approaching French; unfortunately, Colbert's men on the left, especially 9th Hussars, had to endure a terrific volume of musketry and cannon fire as they neared Kismegyer.[108] With the arrival of Seras's foot soldiers, however, the relieved cavalrymen swung swiftly to their right to unmask the infantry and turn their attention to their primary mission: the defeat of the Austrian left wing.

The Austrian officers who were assembled near the chapel could clearly see the French advance and immediately recognised the danger to their vulnerable left flank. As drums rattled, calling the troops to arms, Nugent enquired about the strength of the left wing (strangely, he did not seem to know), but took no action himself. Joseph and his staff, however, though not specifically ordered to do so, hastily called Hadik forward from Szent Ivan and dispatched a courier to Mesko with instructions to send three cavalry divisions (five and one-half squadrons) to reinforce the left. In the meantime, Austrian gunners hurried to their pieces, French batteries jangled into position, and the French infantry prepared to attack.[109]

Eugene's plan was already changing from an echeloned, 'oblique' attack to a general 'parallel' advance by the entire battle line. Several factors contributed to this alteration. In the first place, his intended scheme was in some disarray because his lead division (Seras) had been delayed and Durutte's division came into line first to the left of Kismegyer. Second, the French were surprised by the strength of the Kismegyer strongpoint. Taken under heavy fire by the farm's garrison and neighbouring units of Colloredo's command, Seras stalled temporarily, but Durutte advanced towards Szabadhegy with three battalions (two of 60th, and II/62nd Ligne) while pushing 23rd Léger towards Kismegyer to cover his right flank. Third, Montbrun was experiencing considerable difficulty crossing the Pandzsa on the right owing to the stream and its boggy bed. With his intended thrust on the right retarded and wary of drawing troops from his left to reinforce the right, Eugene thus decided for a general attack all along the line.

As Baraguey d'Hilliers brought the French left forward, the centre and right were already heavily engaged. Between 1.30 p.m. and 2 p.m., Durutte succeeded in forcing his way across the Pandzsa and throwing the Austrian defenders back into Szabadhegy. Shortly thereafter, 3rd Italian Line of Severoli's division reached the Pandzsa and advanced on both sides of the stone bridge against terrible fire. Seras, however, was stymied in his efforts to capture Kismegyer. Hummel's Landwehr and the five companies of regulars had barricaded the farmstead's four gates, crenellated its three-metre high walls, and built ad hoc firing platforms for themselves by laying boards on top of barrels.[110] Encouraged by their robust fortress and Hummel's energetic leadership, the Austrian defenders let loose a torrent of fire that broke the French assaults despite great courage on the part of Seras's troops.

It was approximately 2.30 p.m., and, as Seras was recoiling from Kismegyer, Durutte and Severoli were also in retreat. A vicious Austrian counter-attack from Szabadhegy pushed Durutte's three French battalions across the Pandzsa, while the *1st Banal* Grenzer hurled Severoli's Italians back with heavy losses; the 1st Battalion's Grenadier Company alone lost sixty men in a matter of minutes. With these well-executed ripostes, the Austrians were able to re-occupy their original defensive line sometime after 3 p.m.

These French setbacks, however, were only the prelude to more intense fighting. The 1st Italian Line, sent to replace the disordered 3rd, carried the stone bridge in an impetuous attack and forced the Grenzer back towards Szabadhegy. Colonel Carlo Zucchi, the 1st's commander, allowed the fugitives to pass through his ranks and ordered his drummers to beat the charge: 'without losing time in firing their muskets, my brave soldiers leaped to the assault.'[111] Simultaneously, the other two battalions of 62nd Ligne, ordered forward by Grenier to succour Durutte, splashed through the Pandzsa to regain a French foothold on the north side of the stream and support Severoli's flank. Though Kismegyer's defenders continued to frustrate Seras's valiant men, these successes by Severoli and Durutte gave Eugene a significant advantage on his left flank. A new Austrian counter-attack might have forced the French back over the Pandzsa, but, unfortunately for Johann and Joseph, the enemy's drive over the stream on their right coincided with a disaster on their left.

While the infantry fights were in progress in the centre and on the French left, the decisive action of the battle was occurring on the French right. Montbrun had repelled several attempts by *Ott* and *Joseph* Hussars to hinder his march towards the southernmost bridge, and, supported by Grouchy, had managed to get his hussar and chasseur regiments across the Pandzsa after considerable delay. Though the French found passage over the small bridge and marshy ground difficult, they 'soon noticed uncertainty in his [the enemy's] movements and wavering in his ranks.'[112] The firm demeanour and steady advance of Montbrun's squadrons induced some of this shakiness, but the Insurrection troopers found the French artillery fire especially unsettling and increasingly hard to bear. Mecséry tried to wheel his command into line facing south-east in order to take the French in the flank, but this manoeuvre was too much for the anxious and inexperienced Insurrection regiments. Chaos ensued, exacerbated by some units having to negotiate the inconvenient Viczay brook. Additional confusion arose as Mecséry attempted to detach several squadrons to close the gap that his shift had created between his line and the infantry around Kismegyer. Hungarian officers begged Mecséry to charge before the rain of French shot and shell broke the tenuous coherence of their squadrons, but the attack collapsed almost as soon as it began. 'Our little horses could not budge the enemy's large horses and our horses were furthermore inexperienced,' recorded the Pest Regiment's war diary. 'Although our people displayed great courage, the larger part of the soldiers were untrained, they had seen neither enemy nor combat before; thus transpired here as before that the greater strength, the better weapons, knowledge, and experience of the enemy accomplished victories, while our people fell into confusion.'[113] This sequence of events broke the Austrian left. Although parts of the Pest Hussars and some other elements held together, the bulk of Mecséry's squadrons, unnerved by French artillery and tangled by their efforts to manoeuvre, dissolved and fled to the north-east in the greatest disorder. The enemy 'dispersed with an ease that astonished us', remembered Lieutenant Noël.[114] Hadik's squadrons, too, disintegrated as their fellows tumbled into them and French shells crashed among their ranks. 'A shell exploding nearby made the horses wild, the animals tore the front line apart,' wrote an officer of the Heves Hussars, 'the regiment was carried away by the fugitives.'[115] Eugene, observing the rout of the Austrian cavalry, directed Grouchy to pursue Mecséry and ordered Montbrun to pivot to the north towards the Szabadhegy Heights and the intact Habsburg centre.

Along the Raab on the extreme French left, Sahuc and Lauriston had been advancing cautiously, skirmishing and exchanging artillery fire with Frimont's troops. This tentative engagement contrasted sharply with the furious fight for Szabadhegy. 'The combat in the centre was the hardest,' recorded Pastor Hohenegger from his vantage point in Raab, 'in part this area was illuminated by flames of the burning village of Szabadhegy.'[116] Johann, reacting to the threat to the village, drew *Allvintzi* from his reserve and launched a powerful counter-attack that once again threw Severoli and Durutte beyond the Pandzsa. Severoli and Durutte committed 112th and 102nd Ligne respectively to restore the fight and seize part of Szabadhegy, but the injection of more whitecoats threw most of 112th Ligne and 1st Italian Line into disorder, and the Allies were only able to retain a tenuous grip on the edge of the town.

While the struggle for Szabadhegy roared, Seras took advantage of the Austrian cavalry's flight to press his assault on Kismegyer. The disappearance of his left wing forced Johann to pull his infantry and guns back onto the heights and exposed the south-eastern face of the farmstead to Seras's attentions. Valentin's advance north of Kismegyer also helped to isolate the defenders, though it cost him a wound and brought the death of the 23rd's colonel. To exploit the situation, Seras swung GB Jean Claude Moreau's brigade around to attack from the south-east while GB Roussel charged from the front. Once again, great gallantry could not overcome the stubborn resistance offered by Hummel and his garrison of regulars and Graz Landwehr. Though some French broke into the compound, they were evicted in brutal hand-to-hand combat and fell back with a loss of nearly 700 dead and wounded. Seras, however, was as determined as the defenders. He renewed the assault and this time succeeded. By now, the garrison was short of ammunition, water, and bandages, French shot had knocked down much of the wall, and most of the buildings in the compound were on fire. Nonetheless, Hummel belied his years by inspiring his men to fierce resistance, and the grenadiers of the 106th faced a ferocious fight of bayonets and musket butts as their sappers smashed in one of the gates. The end, however, was no longer in doubt. A courier from Johann bearing orders to withdraw was dispatched too late and could no longer reach the doomed garrison. Surrounded and exhausted, the remnants of Hummel's command fled to the granary, but were soon forced to surrender, some of the prisoners falling under the blows of the enraged attackers. Their tenacious stand earned the 2nd Graz Landwehr honest praise from their foes and an honoured place in Habsburg military legendry, but came at the cost of three-quarters of its men dead or wounded; the five regular companies suffered equally severe casualties with a total loss of 686 out of the 872-man garrison. Seras, on the other hand, was now free to turn towards the heights beyond the farm.

Despite their losses and the shocks to their cohesion, the French and Italian divisions thus far engaged remained viable combat organisations. Eugene, seeing that Severoli had been roughly handled, ordered part of Pachtod's division forward from the reserve and rode to the left to rally the troops. By the time he arrived, however, Severoli and Durutte had 'rallied with an astonishing promptitude' and were ready to continue the attack.[117] Surging forwards, they entered Szabadhegy and mounted the heights, supported by Pachtod, just as Seras was pushing up the slope above Kismegyer. Seras exchanged blasts of musketry with Johann's reserve on top of the hill, but with Durutte threatening their right and Severoli outflanking them through Szabadhegy, the Austrians soon withdrew. On the French left, Sahuc and Lauriston also received orders to advance and press the enemy's withdrawal

Indeed, Johann had ordered a general retreat at around 5 p.m. even before Kismegyer fell. His left had vanished, his right was compromised, and his centre was under extreme pressure, leaving him little alternative if he wanted to preserve the retreat route to Komorn upon which his corps and Joseph's Hungarians depended. Most of the Austrian left 'hurried away in confusion at the gallop'.[118] A few units and groups rallied thanks to the exertions of Joseph and his officers, but many, especially from the Insurrection, fled east at speed, spreading panic as they went. 'We were turned, fell into confusion, some regiments fled, others had to retreat', noted Joseph. 'Towards 6 p.m. general rout and confusion.'[119] As no preparations for defence had been made and no rally point designated, troops retreated towards Komorn 'by instinct' and, by the following day, some fugitives had ridden as far as Ofen (Buda), over 150 kilometres away.[120] The retreat proceeded with much greater order in the centre and right, but even here there were desperate scenes. 'We saw how the infantry in the centre ran from the direction of Kismegyer–Szabad-hegy, leaving their packs, the clothing, their muskets behind', observed an Szala Hussars officer, and Joseph commented that some of the Landwehr threw down muskets and fled.[121] Frimont was heavily engaged by Sahuc's squadrons and lost two of his guns before he could escape. Johann, form-ing his infantry in masses to cross the open country north of Szabadhegy, was also under pressure, endeavouring to hold his exhausted men together as they slowly marched towards the Komorn highway. The squadron and a half of Pressburg Hussars that had been called to the field from Mesko's command arrived belatedly and, thanks to the quality of their mounts, were lucky to dash through the French in the confusion to join the main body in its retreat. As for Mesko and the bulk of his force, they had played no role in the battle—he neither received instructions from the archdukes nor acted on his own—and now found themselves in a forlorn state. Dismantling the bridge that connected the encampment to the battlefield as the retreat swept past, the division remained a distant and ineffectual witness to the defeat.[122]

Fortunately for Johann and Joseph, the French pursuit lacked vigour. Austrian officers were almost unanimous is citing an absence of aggressiveness on the part of their foe and expressing astonishment that the French had lost a superb opportunity. Colonel Zucchi agreed that 'a great mistake' had been made.[123] On the left, the Badeners peeled off to blockade Raab and some of Sahuc's men followed Frimont, but Pully was hardly employed at all. Likewise, Grouchy on the right did not display much energy in pressing the shaken Insurrection cavalry. In the centre, Eugene could see the bulk of Johann's infantry retiring to the north in what the French called 'a grand square'. To engage them, the viceroy placed Montbrun on the right and Sahuc on the left with his infantry in between. But the infantry seems to have had little contact after the Austrians evacuated the Szabadhegy Heights, little use was made of the artillery, and Montbrun's weary troopers apparently shadowed Johann's masses rather than attacking them. Periodic forays by Austrian and Insurrection cavalry and the relatively orderly nature of the withdrawal seem to have held most of the French at bay. The 8th Chasseurs were an exception. Acting on its own initiative, the regiment charged into part of the retreating column, was repulsed, charged again, shattered the Austrian 'square', and forced nearly 1,000 men to lay down their arms. 'We only met a feeble resistance,' wrote trumpeter Chevillet, 'the enemy was breached and we penetrated their flank at the first shock; then that mass found itself in extreme confusion, unable to deploy, all dispersed and took to their heels in an instant.'[124] Sahuc inexplicably delayed in supporting the attack, however, and many of the whitecoats had snatched up their muskets and partly reformed before he launched the rest of his squadrons. 'Never have I seen such a melee,' recalled J. L. Henckens of the 6th Chasseurs, 'nearly all who were in front of us were killed or taken prisoner.'[125] Nevertheless, most French participants felt that a golden moment had been squandered. The bitterly disappointed 8th had to be satisfied with a few hundred prisoners, regimental pride assuaged somewhat by the inclusion of GM Marziani in the haul of captives. Occasional skirmishing continued as the French followed their adversaries east into the falling night, but there were no major clashes and the Austrians escaped towards Acs as darkness covered the plains. 'We took ourselves through Gönyö in the direction of Acs with bitter hearts and for days without anything to eat or drink,' recorded a discouraged officer of the Szala Hussars.[126]

How does one explain the tentative pursuit? Montbrun reportedly told Austrian officers after the war that the French horses were exhausted, certainly a reasonable assumption given the activities of the previous several days, especially 13 June. He also suggested that the French were concerned about Austrian forces of unknown size lurking off on their right flank— evidently the detachment at Szent Marton.[127] It is also possible that the viceroy, having achieved an unquestionable victory, did not want to press his luck. However justifiable such excuses might be, it seems clear that there is less room for such considerations after Raab as compared to the Battle on the Piave, and that a bit more exertion on the part of Eugene's horse would have reaped significant rewards in prisoners and dealt a perhaps irremediable blow to Johann's corps and the nascent Insurrection.[128]

If not as great as it might have been, there was no doubt that Eugene had added another victory to his record of success since leaving the Adige. Nor was it an easy triumph. French losses of some 3,000 testify to the tenacity of Austrian resistance despite the many deficiencies of the amalgamated army. 'The field of battle, not very extensive, was heaped with cadavers, the wounded and the dying, the cries of these unfortunates brought tears to our eyes,' wrote Dragoon Auvray, and Rittmeister Hertelendy recorded that, 'French and Hungarian dead were to be seen, one could hear the screaming and wailing of the wounded, here and there curses; I saw dreadfully smashed, mutilated bodies of men and horses.'[129] The viceroy himself led from the front. Indeed, by the end of the day, he had only one unwounded officer left on his staff and had to turn to his Mameluke, Petrus, to carry orders (until Petrus too was wounded). Losses on the Austrian side, however, were far higher. Johann's regulars and Landwehr suffered 6,254 casualties, including some 2,400 prisoners, while the Insurrection corps lost more than 4,100 for a total cost of over 10,300 men during 13 and 14 June. *Strassaldo* took the highest percentage of casualties (64 per cent), but several other regular regiments lost nearly half their number, and the Pest Infantry was reduced to a tiny cadre. Some 80 per cent of the Insurrection losses were listed as missing, leaving many units at half strength or less, a situation that still had not corrected itself a week later.[130]

The defeat at Raab sparked bitter recriminations and accusations in the Habsburg camp. Johann immediately blamed the Insurrection for 'running away at the first cannon shot', while Insurrection officers constructed a case for laying the defeat at Nugent's feet.[131] Joseph asserted that the *Ott* Hussars had set a bad example for the Insurrection on the left by dashing off in disorder.[132] In truth, there was plenty of blame to share. The Insurrection troops were indeed a weak link in the combined force, but this was neither surprising nor unknown to Johann or other Habsburg commanders. Given the greenness of the raw material, the lack of equipment, the absence of reform, and what even Johann acknowledged as 'step-child treatment' over the decades, there were clearly severe limits regarding what could be expected of the institution in this early stage of its formation.[133] On the other hand, even filtering out some exaggeration and vitriol, the criticism of Nugent seems warranted. Joseph, who was quite objective in assessing the quality of the Insurrection troops, commented in his diary that Johann's chief of staff 'lost his head' at the crisis of the battle and 'gave no orders', leaving the various components of the army to sort out their actions individually.[134]

Assessed afresh, it seems clear that the resilient core of regulars, some of the Landwehr (notably the Graz battalions), and a few elements of the Insurrection performed well, and that Johann deserves credit for giving Eugene a tough fight. Vaudoncourt, in fact, wrote that the Austrians 'fought with more obstinacy than they had shown in the rest of the campaign'.[135] Johann also conducted the retreat with as much order as possible, though it is important to restate that the French pursuit was hardly 'all-out'. At the same time, there is good reason to question Johann's selection of the Szabadhegy position and the easy abandonment of the Csanak Heights. The Csanak ridge was not perfect and the Szabadhegy had its strengths, but halting along the Csanak would have granted Johann a solid defensive position with a better anchor for his left flank. The Pandzsa–Szabadhegy line would then have been available as a fallback if necessary. Moreover, the Csanak Heights may have afforded Johann the visibility to gain a better appreciation of the strength of Eugene's army. This is important because underestimation of the enemy seems to have been a major factor in the defeat, fostering false assumptions about the danger that the army faced and—once again—leading Habsburg commanders to conclude that they could take their time in selecting their future course of action. As with Hiller in Upper Austria, it is also remarkable that Johann—and, to a lesser extent, Joseph—remained largely ignorant of Eugene's movements and strength, even though the two sides had been manoeuvring on Habsburg territory for two weeks. The battle and its immediately ancillary events also suggest that there is reason to question whether Johann granted Nugent an unusual degree of independent authority over those several days. Johann, unlike many other Austrian commanders, routinely kept most authority and responsibility in his own hands. Between 12 and 14 June, however, Insurrection officers, including Archduke Joseph, repeatedly cited Nugent's laxity and indecisiveness as the cause for the army's conspicuous misfortunes. In part, the sharp condemnations of Nugent probably stem from reluctance on the part of officers writing in 1810 to criticise a Habsburg archduke. However, the consistency of these statements at least offers an opening for further investigation concerning whether Johann, angry and under stress, might have deviated from his own pattern of behaviour and handed considerable power to Nugent for these three crucial days.[136]

The reaction on the French side, of course, was quite different. 'Sire, I hasten to report to Your Majesty that I gave battle to Prince Johann today and that I had the good fortune to win,' wrote Eugene on the evening of the 14th. 'It was the anniversary of such a splendid day that no harm could come to us.'[137] As discussed above, a bit more energy might have garnered even greater results, but the outcome was still significant.[138] From a tactical and material perspective, Johann's main body had been badly battered and the Insurrection temporarily stunned; both corps had suffered heavy losses and would have no choice but to retreat across the Danube as quickly as possible. Operationally, Eugene could not prevent the Austrians crossing at Komorn as Napoleon had wished (the emperor did not know there was a bridge at Komorn), but the south bank of the Danube would soon be cleared of major Austrian forces, removing any serious threat to Napoleon's strategic right flank. Additionally, the victory placed Raab at Eugene's mercy.[139] Barring some extraordinary Austrian effort, the little fortress would fall in short order, further weakening the Habsburg presence on the south bank while affording the French a strong anchor for their own flank. Eugene's triumph also had a psychological benefit. In the wake of Aspern–Essling it dampened Austrian spirits and provided a welcome boost to French morale.[140] Napoleon quickly exploited the psychological value by ordering the batteries near Vienna to fire a celebratory 100-gun salute, by issuing a special order of the day in honour of the 'dazzling victory', and by focusing the bulk of the army's Nineteenth Bulletin on Raab.[141] On a more personal level, he sent letters to Josephine and Auguste Amélie, the viceroy's wife, to inform them of the victory and wrote to congratulate Eugene: 'My son, I felicitate you on the Battle of Raab, it is a granddaughter of Marengo and Friedland . . . Express my satisfaction to the army.'[142]

CONCLUSION IN HUNGARY

Late on the night of 14/15 June, Joseph and Johann arrived in Acs on the Komorn road after a long, wearying ride. 'Crowd of fugitives, impossibility of halting same,' noted Joseph in his diary.[143] He continued the next day: 'Disorder in which the army found itself. Departing at 3 a.m., view of the bivouac behind Acs and the entire road to Komorn, all covered with men, wounded, stragglers, guns, vehicles.' This gloomy cavalcade, followed rather than truly pursued by the French, trudged across the Danube at Komorn that day and settled in on the north bank to recuperate. Other than the garrison of the Komorn bridgehead and Mesko's brigade in the entrenched camp, the south shore of the great river was now swept clean of organised Austrian units. The region abounded, however, in small bands of Insurrection troops attempting to make their ways back to their home districts. Many had been on outpost or patrol duty when the retreat was ordered and had been forgotten by their regiments, other were simply flotsam from the battle, some seeking their units, more seeking to evade further service. Armed and sowing wild rumours, these men caused great distress for local people and major headaches for district authorities.[144] En route from Pest to Szent Istvan, a brigade of Theiss district infantry (3,922 men) encountered some of these stragglers many kilometres from the battlefield, and became so alarmed by their stories, that the entire brigade hastened back to its starting point in disorder.[145] These men were among those whom Joseph had in mind when he noted that as far away as Pest 'several thousand Insurrection fugitives who created disturbances and excesses' had to be disarmed.[146]

That afternoon, certainly a low point in the Army of Inner Austria's fortunes, Johann received a visit from the Hauptarmee's chief of staff, GM von Wimpffen. Their discussions did not go well: 'Never will I forget Wimpffen's inflated self-importance; this otherwise sensible man was lost in arrogance and a sense of superiority, he thought of himself as the victor of Aspern and treated all others as mere mortals who were far below the horizon of his ideas and accomplishments, dispensed advice, and suggested schemes that in truth would have hardly been feasible even with a fresh army.' Wimpffen's brief sojourn in Komorn, therefore, only exacerbated tensions between Johann and Charles, deepening Johann's disgust at the Main Army's 'inactivity after Aspern' and validating in his mind the conviction that he was the victim of impossible demands completely detached from reality.[147] Furthermore, Johann suspected that Grünne and others officers in army headquarters were attempting to undermine him and the other archdukes. Ludwig and Maximilian had already been pushed aside, he wrote on 21 June, and Charles was being manipulated by those around him.[148] For his part, Wimpffen doubtless returned to Wagram with a reconfirmed sense of Johann's obtuseness and recalcitrance, while Charles wrote that 'the Archduke Johann's corps has fallen into decay in nearly all aspects of organisation and duty.'[149]

Fortunately for the Habsburgs, there was also a bright side to Raab's aftermath. Mesko, though he had remained an inert observer to the combat, was determined 'not to be caught' in his isolated entrenchments and marched out along the west bank of the Raab on 15 June.[150] The French, missing an opportunity, largely ignored him and, crossing the Raab near Vag that night, he headed for the south-western end of Lake Balaton. Along the way, he had a successful encounter with a surprised French prisoner convoy on the 16th near Kisczell (Celldomolk). This little engagement resulted in the capture of nearly 200 French prisoners and the release of a group of 440 Austrians, including Hummel and many of the Graz Landwehr men who had defended Kismegyer with such determination.[151] Although reduced by desertion en route, Mesko linked up with the detachment under Oberst Attems near

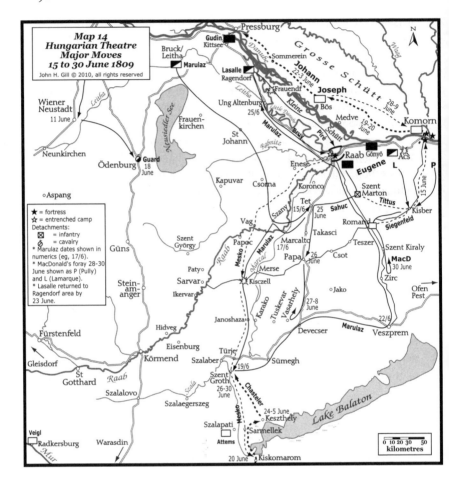

Map 14
Hungarian Theatre
Major Moves
15 to 30 June 1809
John H. Gill © 2010, all rights reserved

Sarmellek on the 18th and, by 20 June, his brigade was at Kiskomarom in contact with Chasteler. Another Insurrection detachment from the entrenched camp was equally fortunate. Forgotten in the confusion, a half-squadron of Pressburg Hussars slipped away between the Raab and the Marcal, captured thirty-one French and seven wagons north of Takacsi in an ambush, and rode triumphantly into Pest on 18 June with their trophies.

A foray from the Komorn bridgehead on 16 June also garnered trophies for the Insurrection. Launched at Wimpffen's recommendation, a reconnaissance detachment of some 2,000 Insurrection horsemen and a division of *Hohenlohe* Dragoons surprised Montbrun's command near Acs just as night was falling, and 'succeeded marvellously' in discomfiting and temporarily scattering the French.[152] Montbrun and Jacquinot were caught up in the scuffle and both lost their hats in escaping the confused melee. The Hungarians withdrew during the night and the French resumed their previous positions, but the two *chapeaux* were gone, proudly displayed by the Insurrection troopers on their return to Komorn.[153]

Reconnaissances, sporadic skirmishes, and abortive French efforts to destroy the Komorn bridge continued south of the Danube through to the end of the month, but Johann with the bulk of his force and Joseph with thirty-eight squadrons and two cavalry batteries departed for Bös (Gabcikovo) at midnight on 18/19 June.[154] Johann's instructions were to garrison Komorn, hold the Grosse Schütt, raise the siege of Raab, establish a crossing point at Ungarisch-Altenburg (Mosonmagyarovar), and relieve Bianchi's force at Pressburg. Johann saw all of this as 'military twaddle', but reached Bös on the 20th and continued west after two days to arrive in Pressburg on the 23rd. Joseph, reinforced by *1st Banal* Grenzer, remained in the Grosse Schütt. A few regular battalions and Landwehr left behind by Johann garrisoned Komorn, while Davidovich worked on training and disciplining the Insurrection infantry nearby.[155] To the annoyance of Franz and Charles, nothing useful was done to relieve Raab, Johann complaining about the lack of bridging material (a deficiency Franz found incomprehensible).[156]

Lasalle and Marulaz in Hungary

The afternoon of his arrival in Pressburg, Johann learned that Raab had fallen after stout but vain resistance. Lauriston's Badeners had sealed the southern approaches to the town immediately after the battle on the 14th, and Lasalle's command appeared on the 15th and 16th to complete the encirclement. Lasalle, as mentioned earlier, was part of the force blockading Pressburg under Davout's orders. With two light cavalry brigades, some Hessian infantry, and two guns, his principal task was guarding Davout's Hungarian flank, while Montbrun covered the gap towards the Neusiedler See on Lasalle's right. As Eugene pushed into Hungary and Montbrun moved to join him, Lasalle also advanced. As we have seen, 8th Hussars of Piré's brigade, supported by two companies of Hessian light infantry, crossed onto the Kleine Schütt near Frauendorf on 12 June and overthrew a division of Insurrection hussars in a short engagement. Piré probed forward on the island while Lasalle's other brigade (Bruyère) advanced along the Pressburg–Raab highway and tried to maintain contact with French forces on its right. The two brigades and their Hessian infantry had edged up to the outskirts of Raab by the 15th and, reinforced by two battalions of 85th Ligne, they closed the ring around the town the following day.[157] The arrival of these forces doomed the garrison. Lauriston, in overall command of the operation, initiated the formal siege procedures common to the day with the digging of trenches and the construction of batteries. Although heavy guns and ammunition were in short supply, on 19 June he opened a bombardment that soon left much of the town in flames. After eight days of waiting in vain for relief, the garrison commander, Oberst Mihaly Pechy, capitulated on 22 June. His 2,000 men marched off into captivity and the French occupied the little fortress on the 23rd.

In addition to Lasalle, other French forces also ventured towards Hungary during the second half of June. Napoleon sent 100 Polish Chevaulegers of his Guard to Ödenburg to watch that approach and, on 9 June, directed GD Marulaz to cover the yawning gap that was developing on Lasalle's right as Eugene and Montbrun passed over the Raab. Though titled a 'division' and comprised of five light cavalry regiments, Marulaz's command numbered only some 1,177 troopers.[158] Nonetheless, he moved with boldness and alacrity, reaching Tet by nightfall on 15 June while scouting to the west towards Csorna and Szany. Late on the 17th, he received orders from Eugene

Table 6: Lasalle's Division, 16 June 1809

GB Piré	
8th Hussars (4)	500
16th Chasseurs (4)	441
GB Bruyère	
13th Chasseurs (3)	485
24th Chasseurs (3)	288
Maj Gall (Hessians)	
Leib-Garde Fusiliers (1)	489
1st Leib Fusiliers (2 companies)	249
Combined Schützen	117
II & III 85th Ligne (2)	1,377
Two guns	

Strengths as of 15 June (85th), 19 June (Hessians), and 1 July (cavalry).

to pursue Mesko (the viceroy had learned of Mesko's escape from an intrepid and intelligent non-commissioned officer the previous day) and immediately set out after his quarry.[159] The result was a long, exhausting ride in the rain. 'Marching night and day, pursuing partisans,' wrote trooper Wilhelmus Kenis of 3rd Chasseurs. 'We had no rest and were therefore so exhausted that we were almost unable to perform our duties properly.'[160] Arriving near Szent Groth on 19 June, French troopers captured some men from Chasteler's command and Marulaz wisely decided it would be 'imprudent' to press his advance any further, 'with men and horses that were extremely fatigued on very poor roads and in rainy weather', through terrain that was decidedly unsuited to cavalry and against a vastly superior enemy.[161] Turning about, the division rode through the dank night to reach Sümegh at 5 a.m. on 20 June. New orders from Eugene took Marulaz and his men to Veszprem on the 22nd to press requisitions, but he was called to Raab almost at once. Arriving on 24 June, he was sent on to Ungarisch-Altenburg the following day, his brief Hungarian adventure at an end.

As June closed, the war, like Marulaz, was moving away from Hungary. Johann was at Pressburg, trying to enhance the bridgehead on the far side of the Danube and under pressure from Davout (see below). As for Joseph, once Raab had fallen, there was little reason to remain at Bös, but he busied himself pressing the training of the 'now somewhat intimidated and weakened' Insurrection troopers.[162] He received a surprise visit from Kaiser Franz on 27 June, held a review that went off 'astonishingly well', and returned to Komorn the following day, leaving ten Insurrection squadrons, Komorn Insurrection Infantry No. 7, and several Grenz battalions in the Grosse Schütt to guard the river line.[163] A few Insurrection troops were north along the Galician border and Duka was at Pest with some from the Theiss districts, but almost all of the Hungarian militia was thus assembled around Komorn, training, preparing, and sending patrols south towards Lake Balaton to prevent French incursions towards Ofen. Chasteler had reached Kiskomarom from the Tyrol on 20 June and, united with Attems and Mesko, had cautiously advanced to Szent Groth by the 26th; here he remained until the end of the month. We shall take up Chasteler's march from the Tyrol in Chapter 3, but for the moment, his presence is only significant in that it occasioned a foray to Zirc by MacDonald (with Lamarque and Pully) from 28 to 30 June, while Sahuc moved through Szent Marton—just as Marulaz was riding in the opposite direction—to Papa and briefly sent a brigade as far as Vasarhely. None of these moves provoked combat, but the sudden appearance of the French did induce caution in Chasteler's thinking.

Furthermore, exaggerated and belated reports of MacDonald's foray led senior Habsburg leaders to think that major elements of the Army of Italy were still in Hungary, when almost all of Eugene's troops were actually en route to Lobau Island as part of Napoleon's general concentration in the buildup to Wagram.

For his part, MacDonald was soon satisfied that the Austrians did not pose a major threat. He withdrew to Szent Kiraly on the last day of the month, while Sahuc recalled his brigade. Of Eugene's other troops, Lasalle and Lauriston departed for Pressburg as soon as Raab had fallen (23 and 24 June respectively), and Grenier's two divisions shifted to the Kleine Schütt on the 23rd to discourage any Austrian adventurism. The other pieces of the Army of Italy, now simply 'another corps of the Army of Germany' as far as Napoleon was concerned, remained in their encampments around Raab, waiting for the call to march for Vienna.[164]

THE BRIDGEHEAD AT PRESSBURG

One final piece of Hungarian theatre remained to be played out as the focus of war shifted north to the Marchfeld. While Eugene and Johann operated between the Raab and the Danube, elements of the Hauptarmee faced a division of Davout's 3rd Corps and affiliated cavalry opposite Pressburg. Pressburg in 1809 was important politically as the traditional coronation city for the Habsburg kings of Hungary and militarily as the first point south of Vienna where road networks and a large ferry service (capable of transporting 500 men at a time) afforded both sides an existing passage over the Danube. The goals of the two commanders, however, were different. Napoleon, focused on crossing onto the Marchfeld from Lobau, was content to expunge any Austrian presence from south of the river, thus removing a potential threat to his right flank. Charles, on the other hand, needed a large and secure bridgehead on the right (south) bank to facilitate offensive operations without the delay and risk inherent in conducting an opposed crossing of an unbridged river.

Unfortunately for Charles, the bridgehead available in May and June 1809 was entirely inadequate for offensive purposes. Austrian engineers had indeed supervised construction of a fortified bridgehead starting on 9 May, but the resultant works, confined to a semi-detached island, were far too small to support a serious offensive. Johann scornfully remarked that it was 'completely inappropriate . . . and constructed as if one had wanted to limit one's self to enclosing the city of Pressburg's promenade'.[165] Moreover, the defences were vulnerable to enfilade fire and the cramped space within the walls meant that almost any iron that landed inside would hit someone or something of value. The location of the defences also meant that the French could contain them with relative ease, especially as the village of Engerau was outside the entrenchments and thereby provided a pillar for French forces. These deficiencies mattered little when GM Hoffmeister brought his small brigade to Pressburg on 18 May as his mission was merely to deny the French access to the northern shore. In the wake of Aspern, however, as Charles was examining offensive options, the limitations of the bridgehead were a serious disadvantage to any operation downstream from Vienna.

After Aspern, activity intensified at Pressburg. The Austrians had neglected to undertake any modification of the bridgehead between 20 and 26 May, but became alarmed when light cavalry from GD Lasalle's division appeared at Hainburg on the 26th.[166] Lasalle opposite Pressburg and Montbrun near Bruck were to cover Vienna while the French army recuperated from Aspern. Lasalle's arrival generated urgent reports from Hoffmeister and led Charles to detach a brigade each of regulars and Landwehr under GM Bianchi to the city on 29–30 May. Bianchi occupied Engerau but did not fortify it, and began to organise work parties to improve the extant defences. This in turn generated reports from Lasalle, whose outposts spotted Austrian engineer officers and 'an assemblage of peasants equipped with shovels and picks'.[167]

Table 7: Bianchi at Pressburg, 28 May 1809

Brigade: GM Bianchi	
Gyulai Infantry No. 60 (2)	1,265
Duka Infantry No. 39 (2)	914
Brigade: GM Sinzendorf	
2nd UMB Landwehr (1)	640
2nd OMB Landwehr (1)	435
4th OMB Landwehr (1)	538
1st OWW Landwehr (1)	460
Brigade: GM Hoffmeister	
Beaulieu Infantry No. 58 (2)	1,420
O'Reilly Chevaulegers No. 3 (7)	870
Artillery: 4 x 12-pdrs, 16 x 6-pdrs, 7 x howitzers	

Source: Schikofsky, p. 178.

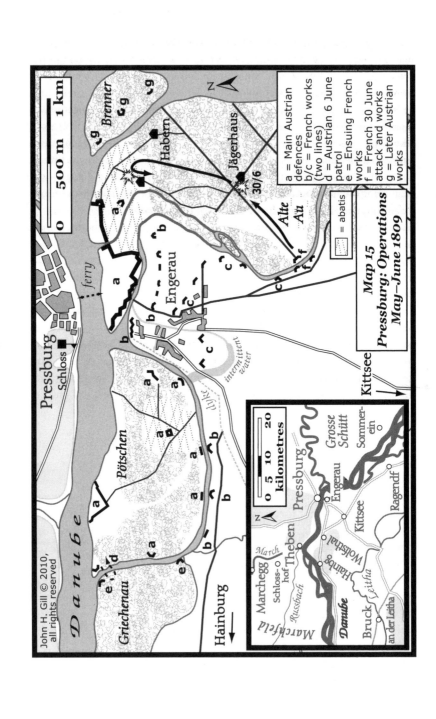

Map 15
Pressburg: Operations
May–June 1809

a = Main Austrian defences
b/c = French works (two lines)
d = Austrian 6 June patrol
e = Ensuing French works
f = French 30 June attack and works
g = Later Austrian works

⬚ = abatis

Pressburg
Schloss
ferry

D a n u b e

Brener
Habern
Jägerhaus
30/6
Alte Au

Engerau

intermittent water

dyke

Pötschen

Griechenau

Hainburg

Kittsee

500 m   1 km

0

Marchfeld
Marchegg
March
Schloss-hof
Russbach
Theben
Pressburg
Engerau
Grosse Schütt
Sommer-ein
Kittsee
Hainburg
Wolfsthal
Danube
Leitha
Bruck an der Leitha
Ragendf

0 5 10 20
kilometres

N

Lasalle's detailed reports and other intelligence led Napoleon to send orders for Davout to take a division and 'remove the bridgehead the enemy has commenced on the right bank'.[168] The marshal selected Gudin's 3rd Division for this task, and three of its regiments (12th, 21st, 85th) duly marched for Hainburg on the 31st.[169] Supervised by Davout, Lasalle launched an attack— or, more accurately, a reconnaissance in force—on 1 June with 8th Hussars, 16th Chasseurs, a battalion and a half of Hessian light infantry, and four guns supported by 85th Ligne. The advance, though 'rapid and brave', began far too late in the day (7.45 p.m.) and in too little strength (only the 970 Hessian infantry were engaged) to seize and retain possession of the village.[170] The defending battalion (II/*Gyulai*), reinforced by three additional companies (two of *Duka*, one of 2nd Unter Manhartsberg (UMB) Landwehr), soon succeeded in evicting the bold Hessians. Although firing lasted until 10 p.m. that night, the French and Hessians garnered little additional knowledge of the Austrian forces and could not maintain the foothold they had gained. The foray cost the Allies seventy-four men, the Austrians ninety-six.

Davout made a more concerted and effective effort on 3 June. Supported by three of Lasalle's light regiments, the Hessians and 12th Ligne attacked at around 4 p.m. Bianchi had concluded that Engerau could not be defended against the weight of Gudin's division and had ordered its garrison (*Beaulieu*) to withdraw to the bridgehead. Unfortunately for the Austrians, the 2nd Battalion never received this order and 117 of its men were captured when the Allies stormed the village. Efforts to breach the bridgehead, however, failed. The French and Hessians displayed conspicuous courage and skilled, gallant leadership in three determined assaults, but they could not overcome terrain difficulties (the arm of the Danube that served as the bridgehead's moat), flanking fire from guns on Pötschen Island, and fierce Austrian resistance. Firing continued well into the night, but the French had to content themselves with ownership of Engerau and a tight noose around the bridgehead. This came at a cost of some 700–800 Allied casualties, including the much-admired GB Claude Petit, as compared to Bianchi's claim of only 373 dead, wounded, and prisoners.[171] Though the bridgehead remained in Habsburg hands, the prompt French action effectively eliminated Austrian offensive options via Pressburg by containing the Austrian lodgement on the south bank before Bianchi could expand the entrenchments to encompass Engerau.

With Gudin covering Pressburg and Eugene entering Hungary, French dispositions changed. Lasalle, no longer needed at the bridgehead, shifted south to Ragendorf and Ungarisch-Altenburg, while Montbrun rode off to join Lauriston and Eugene, as we have discussed. Marulaz replaced Montbrun on Lasalle's right flank.[172] With his two light brigades and his Hessian detachment, Lasalle scattered the Insurrection hussars on the Kleine Schütt on 12 June and moved to complete the encirclement of Raab after Eugene's victory on the 14th, returning to Altenburg after the fall of the little fortress eight days later.[173] Marulaz, meanwhile, had departed on his expedition into the depths of Hungary, returning to Lasalle's command on the 25th. The end of the month thus found Lasalle once again between Ragendorf and Ungarisch-Altenburg with Marulaz covering his right flank to the Neusiedler See.

At the Pressburg bridgehead, a situation of stalemate ensued after the 3 June attack. Illustrating the bridgehead's vulnerabilities, a mere cannonade on the 4th caused ninety Austrian casualties, but sporadic combat activity consisted mostly of sniping and patrol raids as the French constructed their own entrenchments to enclose the Austrian position. A French mortar bombardment from 14 to 16 June killed or wounded another thirty-one Austrians before the mortars were diverted to Raab, and a raid by 600 Austrians opposite Theben upstream from Pressburg generated a flurry of alarm on the night of 20/21 June. This latter attack, carried out by the newly arrived brigade of GM Josef Weiss von Finkenau, revived Napoleon's interest in eradicating the bridgehead, but otherwise all proceeded with a certain dull siege monotony until the end of the month.[174] Even Johann's arrival on the 23rd with the bulk of his remaining regulars did not occasion any substantial change in the operational situation from the Austrian perspective. The presence of Johann's corps did bring an alteration in the local order of battle: all of Bianchi's troops were replaced by the archduke's men and returned to their corps in the Hauptarmee.[175] Bianchi, however, remained behind to command a brigade under Johann.[176]

Napoleon, alerted by the 20/21 June raid, had received intelligence indicating that the Austrians were planning a crossing. Johann's appearance at Pressburg, and his decision to initiate construction of a boat bridge only confirmed a conclusion the French emperor had already reached: he would have to pre-empt the Austrian move. On 23 June, he therefore ordered Davout to prepare for a bombardment of Pressburg: the marshal was to threaten to open fire if the Austrians did not evacuate the bridgehead. From Napoleon's point of view, this action would not only forestall a possible threat to his southern flank, it would also serve to distract Austrian attention from Lobau Island and his own upcoming attack. Reinforced with mortars and howitzers from the siege of Raab, Davout issued an ultimatum on 26 June, received the obligatory rebuff and commenced firing that evening. The bombardment, interrupted by two more exchanges of summonses and rejections between the local commanders, continued until 9 p.m. on 28 June, destroying many building outright and starting fires that consumed many more. The local inhabitants were terrified and even Kaiser Franz, stopping in Pressburg on the 26th en route to inspect Joseph's Insurrection troops in Bös, was inconvenienced when two shells hit the palace where he was lodged. 'All bedlam broke loose,' recorded the city's chief rabbi. 'Deafening blasts rattled windows and shook solid structures, causing bricks and roof tiles to come crashing to the ground . . . Panic-stricken men and women, carrying their valuables in bundles on their backs, ran around in a daze, seeking shelter in underground basements.'[177] In the end, 120 houses were destroyed and many others badly damaged in the shelling, but the city retained its spirit and the Habsburg generals did not relent. Local commanders, however, claiming inadequate resources and formidable French defences, did nothing to relieve the bombardment, and bridge construction was halted on the 28th at Charles's orders.[178]

One further engagement occurred at Pressburg in June as Davout launched a detachment into the Alten Au on the 30th. In a brilliant action, Colonel Pierre Decouz of 21st Ligne threw a party of volunteers across the narrow watercourse in boats at 1 a.m. to secure the crossing, rapidly constructed a bridge, and advanced against the surprised Austrian defenders (a weak battalion of St Julien, two Grenz companies, two 3-pounders) as dawn was breaking.[179] Overwhelmed, the Austrians fell back to their prepared defences, losing both guns, 217 prisoners, and many dead and wounded in the process. Among the prisoners were the mortally wounded colonel of St Julien and an important general staff Hauptmann who proved a talkative captive. French casualties were forty-seven, but they were satisfied with eliminating the Alten Au as a possible flanking threat against the French entrenchments and did not press their advantage.[180] The end of June thus saw Johann and Bianchi still in possession of the imperfect Engerau bridgehead, but well contained and unable to exploit their foothold on the south bank against the encircling French forces. This represented a partial success for both sides, but one that largely favoured Napoleon as the danger to his right flank was minimised. Furthermore, the lure of Pressburg would ultimately tie down far more Austrian troops than French.

CHAPTER 3

The Southern Flanks: Dalmatia, Styria, and the Tyrol

Connected to Johann's operations were those on the far southern flank. Here, Austrian attention was initially focused on an incursion into Dalmatia in conjunction with the invasion of Italy. As Habsburg troops recoiled on all fronts, however, Johann's two most important subordinates became FML Chasteler in the Tyrol and FML Ignaz Gyulai in Croatia. The former was principally concerned with escaping the Tyrol to rejoin the main forces, while the latter was broadly charged with protecting Croatia, distracting French reinforcements, disturbing Napoleon's lines of communications, and keeping a seaport open to permit the transfer of subsidies from Great Britain. Additionally, as the Ban (Viceroy) of Croatia, Gyulai was to hasten the organisation of that province's Insurrection troops (these would soon constitute 45 per cent of his command).

French operations in the south were also a component of Napoleon's grand design as the war moved from Italy and Dalmatia into Styria and Hungary. Where the Austrians tended to disperse their power, however, the emperor concentrated his forces and was quite prepared to take risks in doing so. Other than maintaining a modestly secure line of communications with Italy, his sole goal was to gather as many of his men as possible at Vienna in preparation for the great battle he expected when he essayed a second crossing of the Danube. Above all, this meant bringing GD Marmont's veteran Army of Dalmatia north to participate in the coming struggle.[1]

DALMATIAN DIVERSIONS

As with Poland, we must now look back to April and describe the events in Dalmatia, on the far southern flank of the principal armies, to set the strategic context for the next clash on the Danube. Here in Dalmatia, as in Italy, Habsburg ambitions exceeded available resources. Chosen to command was 56-year-old GM von Stoichevich, who had spent almost his entire career in Grenz regiments, but had an otherwise unremarkable military record. Stoichevich had two main tasks. The first was to protect Johann's left flank and rear so the archduke could conduct the invasion of Italy unhindered. This implied containing Marmont and was essential to any Austrian war planning in 1809. The second mission, however, was the actual conquest of Dalmatia, a goal well beyond Stoichevich's means, but typical of optimistic Austrian thinking in the period leading up to the war. As a corollary to these tasks, Stoichevich was to foment unrest in French Dalmatia and, as in the Tyrol, Habsburg officials had conducted clandestine negotiations with various Dalmatian notables before the war to pave the way for pro-Habsburg rebellions. Like the invasion of the Quarnero Archipelago and a planned expedition by the 4th Garrison Battalion, the 4th Massal Insurrection, and some volunteers from Zengg (Senj) to the area south of Spalato (Split), these operations were intended to secure the coastline for Austria, to divert Marmont's troops, and to facilitate Austrian entry into the province. To this end, GM L'Espine and the minute Austrian fleet were to support Stoichevich. The navy, however, small and badly neglected, committed most of its meagre resources to the conquest of the Quarnero Islands and provided little direct support to Stoichevich.[2]

The brigade at Stoichevich's disposal did not offer much cause for confidence. Of his 8,000 men, only the two battalions of the *Licca* Grenz Regiment No. 1 (approximately 2,550 men) and the lone squadron of *Hohenzollern* Chevaulegers (110 men) were regulars. The remainder of his infantry were four Grenz reserve battalions, men with only minimal training and lacking much field equipment. Moreover, like the Landwehr, they were closely attached to the region and, in Johann's opinion, 'only to be employed in the vicinity of their hearths.'[3] Stoichevich appealed for more troops, especially regular infantry and cavalry, but the only response was a commitment to send three ad hoc composite battalions, made up of three companies each from Land-battalions (or Landwehr) of various Grenz regiments.[4] These troops, late in arriving, were truly pitiable. Many of the men were over- or under-age, uniforms were scarce, as many as two-thirds of the muskets were unusable,

and such basics as shoes and cartridge boxes were notable by their absence. They were more a logistical burden than a combat bonus for Stoichevich's small command. Only an over-reliance on assistance from local rebels can explain the belief among some Habsburg officers that troops of this quality would be able to overcome a numerically superior force of French veterans.

Marmont faced many problems, but troop quality was not one of them. The 'Army of Dalmatia', though small, was largely composed of experienced, well-trained, well-commanded soldiers from reliable regiments: 'the best troops of France', in Napoleon's words.[5] Even if such imperial epigrams were more intended as motivational leadership techniques than genuine assessments of troop quality, Marmont's men clearly constituted a tough, dependable force. The army's commander, Marmont, was an intelligent, competent general and capable administrator who had already led a corps on relatively independent operations and who had been managing affairs in Dalmatia for nearly three years. On the other hand, he was completely isolated and faced the daunting task of simultaneously quelling potential unrest among an often hostile population, establishing robust garrisons in key cities to maintain a French foothold in the absence of his field army, and preparing a mobile force to operate in conjunction with Eugene. Napoleon wanted him to occupy a force at least equal to his own and to 'effect his junction as soon as possible' with the Army of Italy.[6] With operations outside Dalmatia his clear priority, he assigned slightly more than 11,000 of his 14,000 troops to two divisions assembling in the northern portion of the province, collected 2,000 of the small local horses to transport supplies, created an irregular corps of 1,000 'Dalmatian Pandours' to guard his supply trains, and organised four battalions of national guards to supplement the 2,700 regulars allotted to garrison duties. Through these careful measures, by the end of March, his troops 'were assembled on the frontier and ready to march'.[7] His actions, however, would be contingent on the situation in Italy; despite difficult communications, he would have to monitor Eugene's situation carefully to avoid being caught between two fires in a premature advance north.

The French, like the Austrians, also looked for unconventional assistance to distract their opponents. At Marmont's suggestion, the French consul in Bosnia helped instigate raids from Ottoman territory into vulnerable parts of Austrian Croatia that the Turks had ceded to the Habsburgs in the Treaty of Sistova in 1791. Although the French helped to spark these attacks, the French consul commented that 'the Ottoman Croats do not need our money to hate the Austrians', and the raiders rampaged through the border area, pillaging and burning with abandon.[8] In periods of peace, armed Grenzer would have been on hand to repel such incursions, but the war had removed most of the armed men to distant fields and Stoichevich had to detach several companies to reinforce the border defences. In addition to drawing away precious manpower, these raids sapped the morale of Stoichevich's Grenzer, causing them to fear for the safety of their families and property while they waited in Gracac for the regular war to begin. These worries would lead to considerable desertion as the war moved away from these border regions.[9]

The topography and climate of Dalmatia and southern Croatia complicated operations for both generals. A wild, raw, mountainous land, the terrain
over which the campaign would be fought was in places heavily forested,
in others bleak and craggy. Inhabited by rugged peoples of independent
disposition, it was a harsh and impoverished region, subject to extremes
of climate. Though an ideal home to darkly romantic tales of banditry and
vendetta, the primitive infrastructure and subsistence agriculture imposed
severe limitations on commanders charged with conducting—and logistically
supporting—regular military operations with fairly significant forces.
Marmont had established major magazines at Knin and Zara (Zadar), but
Stoichevich, though he had a small magazine at Gospic, had to rely on the
main depot in Karlstadt (Karlovac) for many of his supplies.

In addition to imposing logistical constraints, the terrain dictated where
most of the fighting would occur. The Licca (Lika) valley where Stoichevich
had concentrated his command was separated from Dalmatia by the
formidable Velebit range. Although there were several passes across this
obstacle (Stoichevich built blockhouses to secure them), they were hardly
suitable for swift movement by major forces. The principal access for either
side was therefore the rugged but relatively passable gap formed by the
Zrmanja River north-west of Knin.

April: Austrian Advance

Johann, recognising the challenges of terrain and climate that Stoichevich
faced, had granted his subordinate free rein to select the best date for the
invasion of Dalmatia, 'as it would take some time for the enemy to learn' that
the war had begun.[10] More than two weeks after the Army of Inner Austria
had entered Italy, however, Stoichevich and his brigade were still in Gracac
on the Habsburg side of the border, their advance impeded by foul weather,
logistical difficulties, and hopes that additional reinforcements (at least all
of the Land-battalions) would arrive. These problems were real enough,
but, in the words of one contemporary officer: 'Time passed and with it the
favourable moment for an offensive operation.'[11] Johann gradually became
annoyed that 'this general had delayed for a long time.'[12] As April drew to
a close, however, Stoichevich received reliable intelligence that Marmont
was contemplating an early attack. In the hope of forestalling his adversary
and occupying what he assessed to be a better defensive position along the
Zrmanja, he decided to advance on 26 April.[13]

Following a plan drafted by his chief of staff, Hauptmann Johann Hrabovsky von Hrabova, Stoichevich ordered his brigade forward along the entire length of the border. On his right, two columns (one battalion each) crossed the Velebit range to seize the principal bridges over the Zrmanja at Obrovac, Zegar (Kastel Zegarski), and Ervenik, while a third column probed south from Starigrad to unsettle the French near Zara.[14] Zegar and Ervenik fell to the Ottocac Reserve Battalion on the first day, but the Ogulin Reserve Battalion's initial attacks on Obrovac failed and the Grenzer only captured the town on the 27th. Meanwhile, Stoichevich pushed his main body (cavalry, artillery, and the three *Licca* battalions) through the Zrmanja defile to seize a key bridge over the river at Kravibrod and tie in with the troops at Ervenik. Hrabovsky's plan also included a bold advance on the Austrian left, where two *Szulin* companies, the mounted Serezaner, and a band of Dalmatian volunteers swept through Golubic and past Knin to attack and disperse one of Marmont's Pandour battalions at Vrbnik on 28 April.

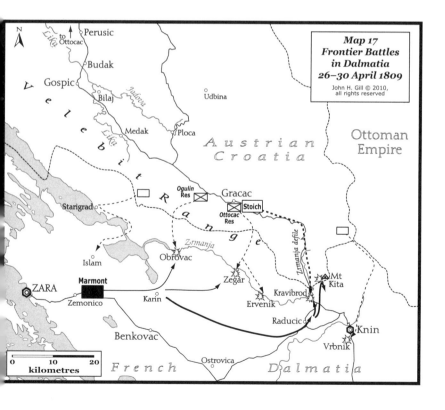

Where all of the Austrian advances succeeded, Marmont's counter-attacks failed. Efforts to dislodge the Grenzer along the Zrmanja on 28 and 29 April collapsed, in one case at the cost of 150 prisoners when men of 18th Léger charged into Obrovac, only to be cut off and forced to surrender. A more serious French attack on 30 April also came to naught. Attempting to seize the Kravibrod bridge and Zrmanja defile, Marmont's men stormed and briefly held the bridge, but were eventually repulsed by I/*Licca* in a wild hand-to-hand fight. Likewise, a turning movement around Mount Kita by the voltigeurs of 8th Léger supported by a battalion of 11th Ligne was blunted when Hrabovsky led two *Licca* battalions against the French left. The advance stalled and Marmont called off the entire enterprise. He might have renewed his efforts the following day had news of the defeat at Sacile not arrived that evening. With Eugene in retreat, however, he had to heed the call of 'reserve and prudence'.[15] Covered by a furious storm of snow, hail, and rain, the French left a rear guard at Knin and retired towards Benkovac.[16] The Austrians, out of ammunition, short of food, and daunted by the weather, were content to conserve the positions they had won.

May: French Counter-Stroke

A week passed without any major action by either party. Stoichevich worried about the threat that Ottoman raiding parties posed to his line of communications through Gospic, while Marmont coped with domestic disobedience and the possibility of widespread insurrection. Both waited for news from Italy. Meanwhile, along the coast, Croatian Insurrection troops (4th Massal from Crikvenica) and volunteers had captured Veglia (Krk), Cherso (Cres), and Lussin (Losinj) in the Quarnero Islands between 6 and 11 May with assistance from the Royal Navy's *Spartan* under Captain Brenton (as related in Volume II). Additionally, elements of the 4th Garrison Battalion from Zengg occupied Arbe (Rab) and Pago (Pag) without resistance on 9 and 11 May respectively.[17] Further south, *Amphion* (32, Captain William Hoste), supported by some Austrian sloops, opened an ineffectual bombardment of Zara on 8 May, but soon settled into patrolling the entrance to the harbour.[18]

As *Amphion* was shelling Zara, Stoichevich finally held a council of war on 8 May and decided to attack. The Austrian commander was again anxious to pre-empt an impending French advance and ordered his brigade to march that very evening despite a ferocious rainstorm. The offensive, however,

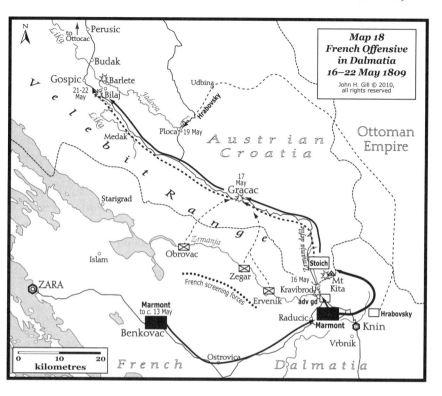

Map 18
French Offensive
in Dalmatia
16–22 May 1809

was short lived. The Austrians surprised and dispersed a French outpost at Raducic at 5 a.m. on the 9th, but Stoichevich, yielding to exaggerated reports of French strength and other worries, turned his sodden battalions around and returned to his starting positions later that day.

Marmont was indeed planning an attack. Having received word on 11 May that the Army of Italy was advancing from the Adige and learning later of Napoleon's success in Bavaria, Marmont set his own command in motion and, by the 14th, he was in position near Knin in contact with Stoichevich's outposts in the Zrmanja defile. After a day of skirmishing, Marmont launched his attack on 16 May. Stoichevich, reinforced by the two *Banal* Grenz Reserve Battalions[19] and the bulk of the three (albeit dubious) Land-battalions, now probably outnumbered Marmont, but he had dispersed his men all along the frontier while the French were concentrated with their right (Clauzel) on Knin and their left (Montrichard) facing the Kravibrod bridge. Marmont employed the same stratagem as on 30 April—attacking the Austrian left to lever the defenders out of the defile—but this time he committed more troops and swung his flanking force farther to the east. He was completely successful. While Montrichard's division occupied Stoichevich's attention at the Kravibrod bridge, Clauzel's 8th Léger and 23rd Ligne evicted the Austrian defenders from the Mount Kita position and pursued them to the north. The defence of the Zrmanja valley was now compromised. Stoichevich, noticing the French advance too late, had few reserves available. Nonetheless, he personally led two companies up the steep slopes from the valley floor in an effort to repair the situation. Marmont, however, had brought 11th Ligne and his chasseurs up onto the plateau and these fell on Stoichevich's panting men as the unsuspecting Grenzer arrived on the high ground. Charged by the chasseurs, the Grenzer were gripped by a 'terrified panic' and broke, leaving hundreds of prisoners in French hands as they fled.[20] The prisoners included the unfortunate Stoichevich, an 'old man, simply clad, who seemed dumbfounded'.[21] Oberst Matthias Freiherr Rebrovic von Razboj of the *Licca* Grenzer quickly assumed command in Stoichevich's stead and managed to extricate the shaken brigade from its difficult predicament with little further loss. The damage, however, was severe enough: casualties came to 1,000, and several companies from the Austrian left were temporarily cut off and forced to retreat through Turkish territory under Hrabovsky.[22] French losses are not known but seem to have been far fewer. Rebrovic retired to an entrenched position in the pass leading north from the Zrmanja valley during the night.

Marmont hastened to follow the retreating Grenzer and the two sides clashed again on 17 May. The French outflanked the entrenched position in the pass, but Rebrovic posted his available troops in the relatively open ground east of Gracac and prepared to give battle. He blocked the south-eastern entrance to the valley with the *2nd Banal* Reserve Battalion supported by the *Licca* Grenzer with the *Ottocac* Reserve Battalion and a Land-battalion in reserve. The *Szulin* Reserve Battalion guarded the left flank against a possible outflanking move, while three companies and the Dalmatian volunteers held the right with the *Licca* Reserves on the far right on top of the Velebit ridge. Though he would have preferred to continue his retreat, he needed to gain time to withdraw the rest of his troops from the far side of the Velebit and to evacuate the small magazine from Gracac to Gospic.

Marmont, leading his advance guard (three battalions), appeared at 4 p.m. and soon pushed the *2nd Banal* Reserves back, but the *Licca* Grenzer, ensconced among the limestone outcroppings and other terrain irregularities of this karstic region, brought the French advance to a halt in the centre. French efforts to drive in the Austrian right also came to nothing and the

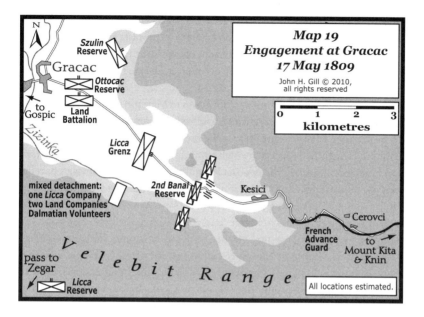

contest developed into an exchange of thrust and counter-thrust as afternoon turned to evening and evening to night. Both sides laboured under serious liabilities. The Grenzer, having not eaten for thirty-six hours and discouraged by the previous day's defeat, were in a fairly enervated condition; the French were strung out on the mountain trails, and parts of the army were delayed in trying to outflank Rebrovic. Nonetheless, both armies fought with extreme ferocity. 'We killed, wounded, and captured one another in hand-to-hand combat until eleven o'clock at night,' reported Rebrovic.[23] Illuminated by a brilliant moon, the struggle raged in the eerie silver-grey light, but neither could gain a decisive advantage and combat came to a close through mutual exhaustion. Despite their fury, each army only lost some 300 men in the seven-hour engagement; on the French side, these included Marmont, who took a slight wound from a ball in the chest, and Colonel Jean Frédéric Minal of 23rd Ligne, put out of action with seven bayonet wounds.[24]

Although the Grenzer had fought with great bravery and the encounter ended as a stalemate, it was quite clear that Rebrovic could not stay at Gracac. His men were hungry and exhausted, he still had no word from many of the detachments on his right, and reports indicated French forces would be positioned to outflank him on the left the following day. At 3 a.m. on 18 May, once the moon was down, he carefully and successfully withdrew towards Gospic. Marmont did not follow. Needing time to unite his corps, bring up his artillery, replenish ammunition, resupply victuals, remove prisoners, and evacuate his wounded, he granted his men a forty-eight-hour rest before resuming his advance.

Rebrovic collected his troops at Gospic on 19 May and used the brief respite to good advantage, resting, refitting, and resupplying his weary brigade. To his great relief, Hauptmann Hrabovsky rode in late that night to report that he had successfully returned through Ottoman territory with the troops that had been missing since the Mount Kita battle—having accumulated many stragglers and fugitives, these amounted to the equivalent of seven companies. Hrabovsky had left his weary men at Ploca and went to Gospic in person to report to Rebrovic. The latter was also hoping that the 4th Garrison Battalion would soon arrive. He had ordered it to join the brigade from Zengg after the defeat at Mount Kita, but instead of the battalion, a courier came in from FML Ignaz Gyulai bearing orders for the garrison troops to return to Zengg and calling the two *Banal* Grenz battalions to Laibach at once. Rebrovic lost the garrison battalion (the courier had encountered it en route and sent it back), but in view of the imminent battle, he retained the two Grenz battalions in contravention to Gyulai's insistent orders.[25]

21–22 May: Engagement at Gospic

After this brief interlude, the campaign resumed with great violence on the same two days that the main armies were contesting the field at Aspern–Essling. Marmont marched north from Gracac on 20 May, but found that the countryside had risen against him. 'We marched slowly, fifteen to sixteen hours a day, ceaselessly harassed by peasants whose numbers increased as we advanced,' recalled a soldier of the 81st.[26] Pushing out the Austrian advance guard, Marmont reached Medak that evening and found Rebrovic at Gospic the following day.

The terrain south of Gospic was open but irregular, dominated by the Licca and Jadova rivers; these, flowing through narrow channels, were steeply banked, and unfordable along most of their lengths. The other rivers, though smaller, were equally difficult and the valley was enclosed on both sides by rugged ranges that made outflanking too slow and difficult to contemplate. Marmont would have to fight Rebrovic where he found him. Rebrovic, having destroyed the bridges at Barlete and Ribnik, deployed almost his entire force

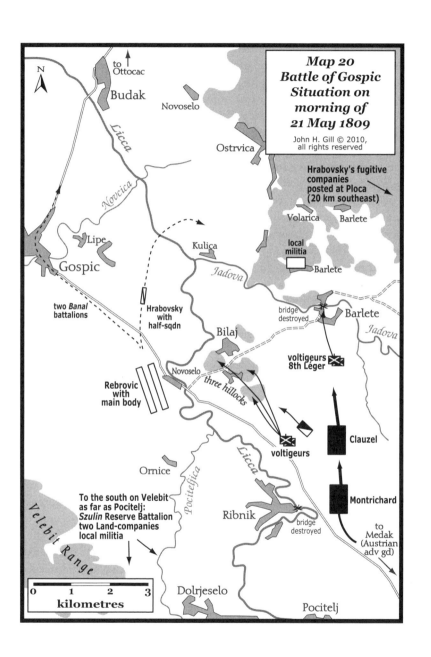

N

to
Ottocac

Budak

Novoselo

Licca

Ostrvica

Novcica

Hrabovsky's fugitive
companies
posted at Ploca
(20 km southeast)

Volarica   Barlete

Lipe

Kulica

local
militia

Barlete

Gospic

Jadova

two *Banal*
battalions

Hrabovsky
with
half-sqdn

Bilaj

bridge
destroyed

Barlete

Jadova

voltigeurs
8th Léger

Novoselo

three hillocks

Rebrovic
with
main body

voltigeurs

Clauzel

Ornice

Licca

Montrichard

Pociteljica

To the south on Velebit
as far as Pocitelj:
Szulin Reserve Battalion
two Land-companies
local militia

Ribnik

bridge
destroyed

to
Medak
(Austrian
adv gd)

Velebit Range

0   1   2   3
kilometres

Dolrjeselo

Pocitelj

west of the Licca opposite Bilaj where the main road crosses the river. This latter bridge he left intact with the notion that he could use it to attack Marmont should an opportunity present itself. He must have concluded that the threat of such a cross-river attack and the destruction of the Barlete span would suffice to protect his vulnerable left flank, because the only forces he posted there were some 700 armed citizens of the local militia in the hills behind the town. Similarly, he seems to have relied on the Licca to protect his right as there was no substantial force at Ribnik and only the *Szulin* Reserve Battalion with two Land-companies and some more militia were on this flank—mostly to observe passages over the Velebit Range. Hrabovsky's fugitive companies were also beyond reach. The Hauptmann had personally joined Rebrovic, but the troops he had led from Knin stayed at Ploca, twenty kilometres beyond the left flank. Though he seemed confident in his plan, as morning light fell into the Licca valley, Rebrovic discovered that it was largely unworkable.

Marmont, examining the field, assessed that following the main road would require his little army to make three river crossing against an enemy he believed superior in numbers: first over the Licca at Bilaj, next over the Novocica, then across the Licca again. He decided to bypass Gospic by crossing the Jadova and driving directly on Budak, thereby forcing Rebrovic to retreat. Arriving from Medak early on the 21st, therefore, he sent 8th Léger's two voltigeur companies to secure a passage over the Jadova at Barlete and directed both divisions to follow.[27] Two other voltigeur companies and the chasseurs would shield his flank at Bilaj where three hillocks provided a perfect defensive position for the French light troops.

The men of 8th Léger quickly found a ford, crossed the Jadova, established a lodgement, and began repairing the bridge with doors, planks, and other material from Barlete. French howitzer fire drove off the militia as Clauzel's division (reinforced by I/81st) approached the crossing.[28] Watching the French manoeuvre unfold from across the Licca, Rebrovic and Hrabovsky immediately recognised their danger and hurried to react. Rebrovic ordered the two *Banal* Reserve Battalions to reinforce the left and began arranging his main body to cross the Licca according to his concept plan. Hrabovsky, however, saw that both moves would consume close to two hours: the main body would have to compress into march columns, cross the Bilaj bridge, and redeploy into attack formation, while the *Banal* Reserves would only be able to pass the Licca via the Budak bridge. He therefore received permission to lead a half-squadron of *Hohenzollern* Chevaulegers to delay the French expansion from Barlete. This plan succeeded—at least in preventing the

French drive against the Austrian left. Although 8th Léger seized the hills north of the Jadova, Hrabovsky and the chevaulegers held them at bay long enough for the *Banal* Grenzer to arrive. At the same time, Rebrovic's move forced Marmont to divert his entire corps towards the centre.

Rebrovic, once across the Licca, formed his troops into three attack columns, each aimed at one of the hillocks. As he succeeded in chasing the tenacious voltigeurs off the central hillock, however, Rebrovic was shocked to see Marmont marching to the attack, Montrichard's regiments in the lead. Hastily posting two 3-pounders on this knoll, Rebrovic rode to his left column to bring up some infantry supports, but events moved too fast for him. Marmont, personally leading Montrichard's division because that general, 'without lacking personal bravery, lost all of his intelligence in situations of danger', ordered 18th Léger to attack the central Austrian column that had already ventured beyond the hillocks.[29] In an 'extremely brilliant' charge, the 18th overthrew the Austrian column and captured the middle hillock with the two Austrian guns.[30] The 5th Ligne on the left and 79th on the right enjoyed similar success against the other columns, and the arrival of I/81st and a battalion of 11th Ligne sealed the fate of the Austrian attack. After heavy fighting, heavy casualties, and great courage by both sides, Rebrovic was thrown back across the Licca with loss. The Austrian 6-pounders on the west bank, however, played upon the French with deadly effect as the combat devolved into a standoff across the bridge.

While the main action was unfolding in the centre, 8th Léger skirmished with Hrabovsky south of Ostrvica. Though reinforced by 11th Ligne as the fighting in the centre died down, the French could make little progress.[31] The firing, however, continued until well after dark so that the hills 'sparkling with flashes, seemed to be on fire'.[32]

The day thus ended in stalemate. Both sides, however, were convinced that the battle would be renewed in the morning and both were in somewhat desperate straits. Rebrovic, under pressure from Gyulai's staff officer and the stern wording of the order—'send back the two battalions without any argument'—to give up the two *Banal* battalions upon which he had been relying, felt the need to act.[33] Moreover, he regarded the first day with some satisfaction and hoped to attack again if an opportunity arose. Marmont was in 'a critical position'. His army was running short of food and ammunition, encumbered with nearly 800 wounded, and surrounded by an aggressively hostile armed populace. Furthermore, in his estimation, the obstinate defence offered by the enemy 'from every position' indicated to him that significant Austrian reinforcements were near at hand.[34] He thus saw the coming day in 'do-or-die' terms. If he could not compel Rebrovic to withdraw, he might be forced to retreat himself, with the loss of his guns and wounded.

The second day of battle did not meet either commander's hopes fully. Marmont planned to throw the bulk of his corps against the weak Austrian left on the far side of the Jadova in a surprise attack, but Rebrovic learned of this intention through spies and shifted the *Ottocac* Reserve Battalion, a Land-battalion, and five guns to Hrabovsky during the night. As a result, the fighting on the 22nd, though bitter, led to no decisive outcome. The five French regiments on this wing could not dislodge the Grenzer and the local militia. At the same time, the three *Licca* battalions, Dalmatian volunteers, and two guns under Rebrovic in the centre were hardly the force to launch a major Austrian counter-attack.[35] Indeed, Rebrovic, though faced only by 18th Léger and 79th Ligne across the Licca, believed the French stronger than they were and decided he could neither attack nor weaken himself further by sending assistance to Hrabovsky. The second day thus also ended in deadlock. With Hrabovsky reporting his troops incapable of further combat and considering the impending loss of the two *Banal* battalions, Rebrovic saw no choice but withdrawal. He pulled out during the night, the exhausted French happy to see him depart.

Both sides paid heavily for their ferocity during the engagement at Gospic. The Austrians lost at least 1,030 and French casualties were probably similar.[36] Additionally, two generals of brigade (Louis Soyez and Jean Launay) were badly wounded.[37] Especially painful on the French side was the pitiable state of the wounded who had to be carried about from place to place for many days.

Though the battle was a tactical draw, the operational result favoured the French. Marmont, no longer isolated in Dalmatia, was now free to recuperate, resupply, and march north towards Eugene. Despite the tenacity shown by what should have been second-rate Grenz units and determined leadership on the parts of Rebrovic and Hrabovsky, he had decisively repulsed the Austrian enterprise in Dalmatia. Stoichevich comes off less well as a commander. He had a nearly impossible task with the resources he had been given, but his handling of the campaign, after a bold beginning, was tentative and confused. Marmont's operational freedom and the defeat of the Dalmatian invasion, however, were not the only negative consequences for Austria. In retreating out of the Licca region, Rebrovic found his brigade melting away. Not only the local militia and the Dalmatian volunteers, but the regular, reserve, and Land-battalions suffered from heavy desertion as soldiers left the ranks both from general discouragement and, more specifically, to protect their families and homes from the depredations of Ottoman raiders.[38] 'The Licca men gradually began to flee to their homes,' noted a staff officer.[39] It was thus a much-weakened command that Rebrovic led north on 23 May.

Marmont Marches North

Marmont occupied Gospic on 23 May and turned to pursue Rebrovic towards Ottocac the following day. Respective advance and rear guards clashed briefly that afternoon about twenty kilometres south of Ottocac and, on the 25th, Marmont caught up with the retreating Austrians. In a rapid and daring march, he slipped past the Austrian rear guard with GB Alexis Joseph Delzons's brigade (8th Léger, 23rd Ligne) and surprised Rebrovic near Zutalovka. He could see 'seven or eight thousand men with artillery and baggage' from his position on a ridge above the main road and attacked at once. The alarmed Rebrovic hastened to get his guns and trains across the pass to Brinje and rode off to collect the 4th Garrison Battalion from its position near Zengg. Meanwhile, a desperate defence by the *Ottocac* Reserve Battalion held off the French, Delzons fell wounded with a luckily non-fatal ball to the head, and Montrichard dallied.[40] Marmont was furious: 'that miserable Montrichard could never march or finish anything ... without his incredible incapacity a brilliant success would have finished the campaign in a most dazzling manner.'[41]

Rebrovic had escaped, but he could not stay in Brinje without reinforcement. Massive desertion had set in as the brigade left the Licca region. 'Some 1,500 men of the Licca deserted at once and only some sixty men and the remaining officers stayed behind,' recorded Hrabovsky. 'The men of Ottocac, Ogulin and more also began to desert.'[42] His command dwindling despite the addition of the garrison battalion (soon called to Karlstadt), Rebrovic continued his march in accordance with insistent orders from the General Command in Karlstadt, reaching Verbovsko (Vrbovsko) on 30 May. Kengyel's brigade of Insurrection troops had briefly occupied Verbovsko, but had been called back to Karlstadt to protect that city's resources and to move the raw Insurrection soldiers out of harm's way.[43] The sad remains of Rebrovic's brigade, however, were now under GM von Munkacsy. He had arrived the previous day to replace Rebrovic, who seems to have been unfairly blamed for the outcome of the campaign.[44] Returned to his regiment, Rebrovic was sent back to the Licca to replenish his depleted ranks.

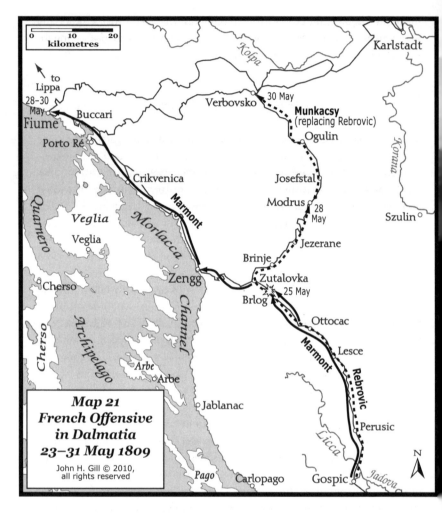

Map 21
French Offensive
in Dalmatia
23–31 May 1809

John H. Gill © 2010,
all rights reserved

When Rebrovic turned north-east from Zutalovka, Marmont headed west, setting out for Zengg at dawn on the 26th: 'That day was one of the most fatiguing that we had had along the way, not ceasing to march until ten o'clock at night with an abundant rain and, what's more, obliged to bivouac atop rocks or on the highway.'[45] The men were 'pallid, staggering, and near to expiring from fatigue and hunger' when they entered Zengg that night, but Marmont demanded one more march from his 'small army with the sacred fire that nothing could extinguish', and the troops arrived in Fiume (Rijeka) on 28 May to enjoy several days of well-deserved rest.[46] Wounded

Generals Launay and Soyez as well as several hundred other officers and men remained here to recuperate, and Marmont wrote to Eugene asking for several generals of brigade. On 31 May, as the Austrian brigade was restoring itself in Verbovsko, he marched on to Lippa (Lipa) and, by 3 June, the Army of Dalmatia was in Laibach.

THE TYROL: ROBBERY, MURDER, PLUNDERING

Marmont's arrival in Laibach tied him to another thread in the complex history of operations behind Napoleon's strategic rear: combat in the Tyrol and the escape of FML Chasteler's command.

May in the Mountains

We last saw Chasteler hastening north from Rovereto on the night of 29/30 April, his unexpected departure occasioned by the reverses in Bavaria and the imminent threat of a Bavarian invasion of the Tyrol up the Inn valley. Arriving in Innsbruck on 3 May, he could do nothing to prevent the fall of Salzburg (30 April), but Lefebvre and his Bavarian 7th Corps remained quiescent after their success at Salzburg and Chasteler had time to array his forces and consider other actions. For defensive measures, he assigned GM Ignaz Buol von Berenburg responsibility for the key passes to the north and placed GM Fenner in charge of the blockade of Kufstein and the border towards Salzburg. Their commands were very small, however, and they could only pursue their missions with active support from the armed population. To the south, GM Marchal remained around Trient to guard the Adige (Etsch) valley and GM Schmidt, detached from Johann's main body, arrived in Toblach on 10 May with his rather enervated brigade to hold the Pustertal, a vital link in Chasteler's line of communications.[47] Chasteler himself remained in Innsbruck with the bulk of his force, capable, he believed, of responding to a threat from any direction. Offensively, his presence in Innsbruck helped inspire bold Tyrolians to launch numerous raids into unprotected Bavaria, some as deep as Kempten (4 May) and Memmingen (11 May). In the south, unrest fomented by Austrian agents in the Valtellina and Valcamonica regions of Italy burst into armed rebellion in early May, but prompt action by GB Pietro Domenico Polfranceschi in Milan with several hundred depot soldiers, gendarmes, and national guardsmen supported by two cannon swiftly contained this uprising.

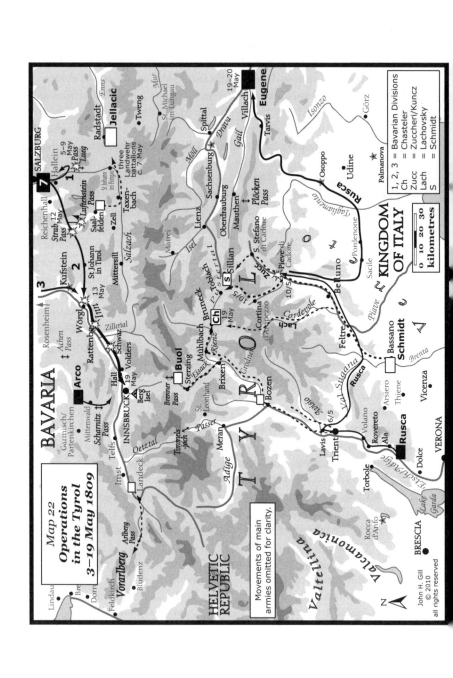

Map 22
Operations
in the Tyrol
3–19 May 1809

BAVARIA

HELVETIC
REPUBLIC

TYROL

KINGDOM OF ITALY

1, 2, 3 = Bavarian Divisions
Ch = Chasteler
Zucc = Zuccheri/Kuncz
Lach = Lachovsky
S = Schmidt

0 10 20 30
kilometres

Movements of main
armies omitted for clarity.

Lindau
Bregenz
Dornbirn
Feldkirch
Bludenz
Arlberg Pass
Vorarlberg
Landeck
Imst
Telfs
Oetztal
Timmelsjoch
Meran
Passer
Adige
Scharnitz Pass
Garmisch/Partenkirchen
Mittenwald
INNSBRUCK
Hall
Berg Isel
19 May
Volders
Arco
Rosenheim
Achen Pass
Wörgl
13 May
Rattenberg
Schwaz
Zillertal
Kufstein
St Johann in Tirol
Mittersill
Salzach
Strub Pass 12 May
Reichenhall
SALZBURG
7
1
Hallein
5–9 May
Luftstein Pass
Luftstein Pass
Luog
Radstadt
Jellacic
Tweng
St. Michael im Lungau
Enns
Mur
three
Landwehr battalions
c. 7 May
St Johann im Pongau
Saalfelden
Zell
Taxenbach
Mur
2
3
St. Leonhard
Sterzing
Brenner Pass
Buol
Mühlbach
Eisack
Brixen
Rienz
Ch
19 May
Gröden
Cortina d'Ampezzo
Bruneck
Rienz
Pustertal
Toblach
S
Innichen
Sillian
10/5
Drau
S. Stefano di Cadore
Zucc
10/5
Pieve di Cadore
Lach
Cordevole
Lienz
Isel
Matrei
Möll
Sachsenburg
Spittal
Drava
Oberdrauburg
Mauthen
Plöcken Pass
Gail
Villach
Eugene
19–20 May
Tarvis
Isonzo
Görz
Udine
Osoppo
Palmanova
Tagliamento
Pordenone
Sacile
Belluno
Feltre
Piave
Rusca
Bassano
Schmidt
Brenta
Val Sugana
Rusca
Arsiero
Thiene
Vicenza
VERONA
Lavis
Trient
Bozen
6/5
Avisio
Volano
Rovereto
Ala
Dolce
Etsch/Adige
Rusca
Torbole
Lake Garda
Rocca d'Anfo
Valcamonica
Valtellina
BRESCIA
Etsch/Adige
N

Violent unrest that combined anti-government protests with criminal activity also flared in the Veneto region and much of north-east Italy in what one author termed 'political brigandage'. This reached its high point in July and led to severe repressive measures. As in Valtellina and Valcamonica, however, local authorities employed domestic security forces to cope with these disturbances; almost no regular troops were diverted (Map 22).[48] To the west, however, a more dangerous and durable insurrection erupted in Vorarlberg. Chasteler had sent a tiny detachment of regulars across the Arlberg Pass in late April to offer a token of Habsburg support and now hoped to stoke the fires of rebellion by dispatching a second force on 8 May (see Chapter 4).[49] Meanwhile, Tyrolian insurgents, supported by Austrian regulars, fended off an attempt by Bavarian GL Deroy to relieve Kufstein, and Jellacic (still in the mountains south of Salzburg at that time) held the Lueg Pass against repeated Bavarian assaults.[50]

These clashes were preludes to a major Bavarian offensive into the Tyrol. Napoleon, in driving for Vienna, had left most of Lefebvre's 7th Corps in Salzburg to fortify the city, neutralise Jellacic, watch Chasteler, and recuperate from its strenuous marches. Wrede's 2nd Division was posted at Strasswalchen to form a link to the main army. The emperor, however, grew annoyed at the failure to relieve Kufstein and the persistence of the uprising; he soon had Berthier prepare orders for Lefebvre to 'march yourself with all your forces to eliminate the rebels, burn the villages in revolt, and execute all the rebels you take'.[51] Lefebvre responded at once, and Wrede, recalled from Strasswalchen, departed Salzburg on 10 May. The Bavarians fought a tough two-day battle against one of Fenner's detachments and a determined band of Tyrolians, but forced the Strub Pass and arrived in Ellmau on the 12th. The same day, Deroy, who had retired to Rosenheim after the failed attempt to reach Kufstein, advanced south along the Inn to relieve the fortress and approach Wrede. From the Inn to the west, however, there were almost no men available to defend Bavaria's long southern border. To contain the Tyrolian raiders, therefore, a weak brigade of depot troops and volunteers was formed under Oberst Maximilian Graf Arco near Benediktbeuren, and Napoleon directed GD Beaumont to Augsburg to organise ad hoc columns of second-line French and Allied troops.[52]

13 May: Engagement at Wörgl

Chasteler reacted quickly to the Bavarian threat from the Strub Pass. When a courier from Fenner arrived in Innsbruck on the morning of 11 May with news of Wrede's advance, the Austrian commander marched at once with his entire reserve: 3,870 men in two weak battalions of *Lusignan*, four Landwehr battalions, one and one-half chevauleger squadrons, and ten guns.[53] To speed his movement, he placed II/*Lusignan* aboard boats and shipped it down the river ahead of the marching column. Reaching Wörgl on the morning of 12 May, the battalion pressed ahead to Söll to support Fenner's tiny command west of Ellmau. Chasteler arrived in Wörgl on the evening of the 12th. Along the way, he had deposited 1st Klagenfurt at Rattenberg and had detached 2nd Villach to the north bank of the Inn, so the infantry he had available in Wörgl and Söll constituted a mere two regular and two Landwehr battalions.[54] Oberstleutnant Reissenfels, who had been conducting the blockade of Kufstein, also reached Wörgl that afternoon, but Chasteler had him retrace his steps to hinder Deroy's approach.[55] Chasteler also called on Jellacic for support. The latter still held the passes south of Salzburg with his headquarters at Radstadt, but he moved sluggishly, and poor co-ordination between the two Habsburg generals hampered effective response to the Bavarian advance.[56] Nonetheless, Chasteler planned to attack the following morning, believing that 'the courage and the good morale of the ever-increasing Landsturm' (Tyrolian militia) in conjunction with his regulars would suffice to repel the Bavarians. He seems to have badly underestimated the Bavarian force while overestimating the number of Tyrolians who would answer his belated call to arms. As darkness fell, the Austrians could clearly see 'the burning villages between Waidring and Ellmau that reddened the distant horizon this night', and 'showed all too well the footsteps of the Bavarians'. For the overconfident Chasteler, the enemy could not be allowed to spread 'fire and destruction' into the heart of the Tyrol without a fight.[57] 'I want to try my luck in Bavaria,' he wrote that evening.[58]

Dawn, however, brought a grim revelation for the Austrians. Wrede and his 6,400 men were up and moving early, and 'at daybreak . . . the steady approach of heavy cannon fire from Ellmau announced the enemy's attack.'[59] Breaking camp before 5 a.m., Chasteler hurried towards Söll and took up a position just east of the village. Wrede's advance guard (6th Light, I/3, 13th Infantry, 3rd Chevaulegers, mounted battery), however, drove in Fenner's small force, captured one of Chasteler's guns, and levered his main body out of its position at Söll. Badly outnumbered—only some 300 Tyrolian Schützen and a few local Landsturm had appeared to support the whitecoats—the Austrians fell back steadily. By late morning, unrelenting Bavarian pressure had pushed Chasteler as far as the highway bridge over the Brixentaler Ache. The intervention of I/*Lusignan* briefly stemmed the retreat here, but the Bavarians were soon across the stream, deploying in the open ground to attack the Austrians near Wörgl. Combat in the flat river valley greatly favoured the Bavarians with their superiorities in cavalry and artillery, arms that the Tyrolians especially feared and Chasteler could not match. Ill-disciplined and poorly led, the local insurgents 'scattered themselves on the slopes to the south and fired ineffectually at the Bavarians who were out of range in the Wörgl lowlands'.[60] While the local Schützen banged away harmlessly from the hillsides, three squadrons of the Bavarian 3rd Chevaulegers charged Chasteler's guns. Lefebvre, leading 13th Infantry up in support, shouted 'Bravo!' as he watched the Bavarian horse capture all nine of the Habsburg pieces—including two of the guns that the Austro-Tyrolians had seized in April. The Bavarian cavalry attack also cut off much of the Austrian infantry, forcing many to surrender and some 500 to flee south into the mountains; approximately 300 of these under Oberst Ruiz of *Lusignan* later linked up with Jellacic and some rejoined Chasteler after adventurous treks through the Alpine terrain, but all were effectively out of action for days to come. The brilliant charge secured twenty-seven caissons and much of Chasteler's war chest as well.

Chasteler's catastrophe, however, was not yet over. The Bavarian cavalry, though numbering fewer than 650 sabres, seemed to be everywhere, 'an overpowering, surging stream that could not be held back'.[61] The 1st Klagenfurt, which had come up from Rattenberg by mistake, was caught up in the confusion and Chasteler himself barely escaped capture. As one observer recorded: 'On the afternoon of the 13th, the rapid flight of military

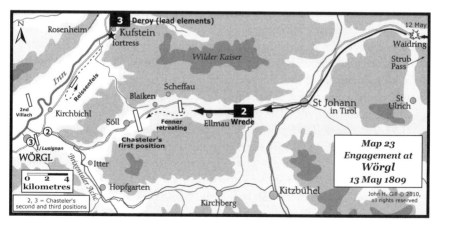

Map 23
Engagement at
Wörgl
13 May 1809

John H. Gill © 2010,
all rights reserved

wagons told us that the Austrians had lost their cannon and had turned their backs on the enemy, indeed the fleeing Chasteler himself hurried past in the night to be abused by the mob in Hall and even threatened with death.'[62] With no formed troops in the rear to retard Wrede, retreat and pursuit continued until nightfall, the Bavarians stopping at Rattenberg while Austrian officers attempted to rally elements of Chasteler's force and some Tyrolians at the Volders bridge ten kilometres east of Innsbruck. The organised regulars immediately available, however, numbered only some 100 men from *Lusignan*, forty chevaulegers, and a lone 3-pounder.[63]

In addition to the loss of all Chasteler's guns, by the end of the day, at least 607 Austrian regulars had been taken prisoner along with an unknown number of Tyrolians (Wrede claimed a total of 2,000 regulars and insurgents in his report). Another 500 or so were clambering over the crags south of the Inn, and it seems likely that a minimum of 300 were killed and wounded. Some 35 per cent of the regulars whom Chasteler had taken into the fight that morning were thus out of action as the sun went down. Bavarian losses totalled 191.[64] 'It was stupidity to get involved in a fight with so few forces,' wrote a disgusted Johann. 'He dispersed everything and continued to draw up projects that were mere fantasies.'[65]

The Bavarians resumed a slow advance up the Inn valley on 14 May with Wrede's division south of the river and Deroy's division to the north. Reissenfels was fortunate to escape to Volders, where he joined an ever-growing crowd of Tyrolians and fugitive soldiers. By the afternoon of the 14th, Buol had arrived from Scharnitz and the volatile mob of insurgents— many inspired by alcohol as well as patriotism—had ballooned to 12,000– 13,000. Buol, hoping to protect Innsbruck, sent Oberstleutnant Taxis to Schwaz early on 15 May with about 500 regulars, two guns, and several Tyrolian companies. This force fought a brutal engagement with Wrede that afternoon as the Bavarians, constantly harassed by insurgents, cautiously advanced up the Inn. The vicious combat featured dreadful atrocities by both sides and concluded with the town being utterly consumed by fire. 'Schwaz was entirely devastated today,' noted Franz Joseph Hausmann of 7th Line in his march journal.[66] The outcome, however, was never really in doubt; Bavarian occupation of ruined Schwaz finally cleared the way to Innsbruck, which Lefebvre and his men occupied without resistance on 19 May.

The 13th of May, the day that Napoleon entered Vienna, was thus an equally disastrous day for Habsburg fortunes in the Tyrol. From a tactical operational standpoint, not only was Chasteler's reserve temporarily shattered, but 'all Tyrol was now more threatened than ever and from different directions; the greater part of the lower Inn valley in the hands of a cruel enemy and even the capital, Innsbruck, abandoned.'[67] At the strategic level, the Bavarians at one stroke had removed the threat to their southern border and to Napoleon's line of communications; all of this accomplished within the course of a week. Chasteler's ability to remain in the Tyrol at all was questionable, and soon made even more dubious by the Army of Inner Austria's defeat at Tarvis and retreat to Graz. Moreover, the debacle at Wörgl led to bitter recriminations between the Tyrolian insurgents and Habsburg regulars. The regulars felt that the insurgents, unruly, unreliable, difficult to command, and frequently intoxicated, had left them to face the numerically superior Bavarians alone: 'where one had counted on thousands, barely hundreds appeared.'[68] 'The day at Wörgl had demonstrated satisfactorily that one could not always count on the popular masses, even the most enthusiastic, who . . . often acting autonomously, withdrew when they should have held their ground and held their ground when they should have withdrawn.'[69] The Tyrolians, on the other hand, found Chasteler's tactical dispositions dangerously faulty and feared that he would lead them into disaster or abandon them at some critical juncture: 'The inflamed and suspicious population, cursing almost insanely against the Austrian military as well as against the leaders in Innsbruck and Hall, began to seize couriers and letters and shouted that the fatherland was betrayed.'[70] The verbal and physical abuse of Chasteler by enraged and often inebriated locals as he fled up the Inn valley that night was thus representative of a broad sentiment.[71] Indeed, Buol was only able to withdraw to the Brenner on the night of 16/17 May by employing a ruse to fool his putative allies after they—'the greater part very drunk'—had threatened to oppose his departure with force.[72]

In addition to Austro-Tyrolian friction, the war in the Tyrol was distinguished by its great brutality. As in most insurgencies, both rebels and regulars quickly descended into barbarous behaviour. The Bavarian troops tended to view the Tyrolians as disobedient subjects of a beloved monarch who employed cunning but dishonourable tactics (firing from concealed positions in forests or mountains, rolling boulders and trees down on hapless soldiers in constricted gorges, etc), and whose womenfolk and children joined in the fighting.[73] 'In Schwaz there was shooting at the division from the houses and windows,' recorded Hausmann. 'Wherever the slightest resistance was encountered, everything was devastated and burned down.'[74] Moreover, the Tyrolian raids into Bavaria had mostly been little more than plundering expeditions that left behind destruction and deep anger. For their part, most Tyrolians resented Bavarian rule, rejoiced at their liberation in April, and were firmly determined to resist the return of what they saw as a foreign power. The result was a cycle of ferocious inhumanity as Bavarians burned and looted villages while Tyrolians murdered isolated soldiers. 'Everything is given up to the greatest mischief on both sides,' wrote a Bavarian soldier, 'robbery, murder, plundering'.[75] And a civilian official with Deroy's division cogently observed: 'The Tyrolians are said to have treated our soldiers cruelly; but our side is no less hard. In general the mutual bitterness is great, and I fear behaviour in the Tyrol will become frightful and hardly to be mitigated through orders.'[76]

25–30 May: Indecisive Battle, Bavarian Retreat

While the Bavarians blazed a slow, harsh path to Innsbruck, Chasteler dithered. Disheartened and uncertain after the defeat at Wörgl and the abuse he had suffered at the hands of his erstwhile Tyrolian allies, he fled towards the Brenner Pass, but could not reach an operational decision. During 15–16 May, he seemed to change his mind every few hours, sending five different and contradictory orders to the baffled Buol in the space of those two days.[77] Chasteler was a veteran of many engagements and had been wounded thirteen times in Habsburg service, but he lost his composure entirely on the night of the 18th when he learned that Napoleon had declared him an outlaw and condemned him to death for the supposed murder of several hundred French and Bavarian prisoners after Bisson's surrender on 13 April.[78] Orders from Johann did not help as they left the conduct of future operations to Chasteler's discretion and thus only served to increase the pressure on a harried general who knew little of the war outside the Tyrol. Several days of oscillation between dejection and elation ensued, during which the exhausted Chasteler—who was probably suffering from combat stress—temporarily turned over command to Buol while the Austrian troops marched and counter-marched back and forth across the mountainous countryside to no useful effect. Resuming active command on 21 May after this brief interregnum, Chasteler finally decided leave the Tyrol. By the 25th, he and the bulk of his command were encamped along the Drava between Lienz and the fortress of Sachsenburg. Left behind was Buol with most of his men at the Brenner Pass and a detachment at Bozen under Leiningen to guard the southern approaches (see Table 8).

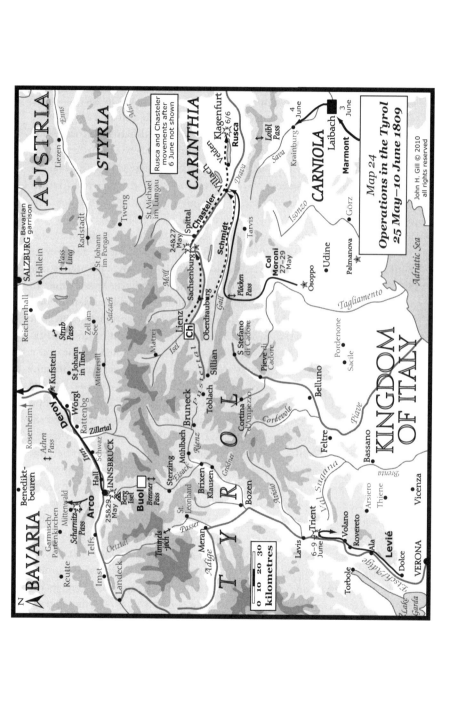

Map 24

*Operations in the Tyrol
25 May–10 June 1809*

John H. Gill © 2010
all rights reserved

Rusca and Chasteler
movements after
6 June not shown

The Tyrolian leaders had rightly regarded all of Chasteler's indecision as evidence of Austrian operational confusion and believed it confirmed their suspicions that the Habsburg generals were both untrustworthy and cowardly.[79] Although infuriated by Chasteler's imminent departure, there was little they could do to stop him. They could, however, act on their own. Committed to ridding their land of the hated Bavarians and inspired by the innkeeper Andreas Hofer, they would strike with surprising swiftness and success.

Unrelated events conspired to favour the Tyrolians. Even before the re-occupation of Innsbruck, Napoleon had instructed Lefebvre to return to Salzburg with Wrede to defeat and pursue Jellacic; Deroy alone, he optimistically assessed, would suffice to pacify the Tyrol.[80] Lefebvre, despite being on the scene, also misread the situation, happily reporting on 21 May 'the complete submission of the Tyrol following our victories and the severe punishments that have been administered'.[81] With Arco occupying the Scharnitz Pass on the 22nd to open a second line of communications to Innsbruck, the French marshal thus felt confident enough to depart with Wrede for Salzburg on the 23rd. He had occupied Innsbruck for only four days. Now in receipt of new orders to protect the army's line of communications in the Danube valley, Lefebvre picked up 1st Division in Salzburg and marched for Linz. As indicated by these orders, Napoleon shared his subordinate's rosy view of the Tyrol's supposed submission, writing on 24 May to Bernadotte that 'the duke Danzig has taken Innsbruck. The insurrection in that direction is therefore finished and there is no longer any need for concern.'[82] The Tyrolians had other ideas.

Deroy, isolated and vulnerable in Innsbruck, did not know it yet, but Andreas Hofer and other Tyrolian leaders had been planning an attack despite Chasteler's departure. They were thus delighted to see Wrede, 'the Angel of Death', march away and, with support from some of Buol's whitecoats, they struck on 25 May.[83] The ensuing struggle was indecisive, as was a subsequent engagement fought on the 29th. Known as the Second and Third Battles of Berg Isel (for a hill south of Innsbruck that figured prominently in the fighting), the combat in both cases was ferocious and costly, but neither side could gain a decisive advantage even though the Bavarians were outnumbered by more than two to one on each day. Deroy's situation, however, was hopeless. Surrounded in the centre of a hostile land at the end of an impossible supply line, he had no choice but retreat and slipped away quietly on the night of 29/30 May. By nightfall on the last day of May, he had retired safely to Kufstein; two days later he withdrew to Rosenheim. Also on 29 May, Tyrolian insurgents evicted Arco from his positions south of the Scharnitz Pass, so the end of May saw the Tyrol once again free of Allied troops and Bavaria once more open to predatory incursions from across the Alps.[84] Kufstein once again stood as Bavaria's lone outpost in the rebellious region.

Chasteler's Escape

As the Tyrolians, with limited help from Austrian regulars, were ejecting the Bavarians from the Inn valley, Chasteler was attempting to rejoin Johann. His path through the Drava valley, however, was blocked by GD Rusca and his little division of French and Italian troops.

Rusca, charged with protecting the Army of Italy's line of communications and observing Chasteler, was in Spittal. He had spent the first three weeks of May making a long march from Trient through the southern crags of the Alps to guard Viceroy Eugene's strategic left flank. His appearance near the Pustertal caused no little anxiety for Chasteler, but Rusca, fearful of being cut off and annihilated in the mountains, was concerned about his own command's safety and eventually headed down the Piave valley to join Eugene via Tarvis. Reaching Spittal on 23 May, he sent the Istrian Battalion and two guns to take Sachsenburg, where skirmishes flared on the 24th and 26th.[85] The Istrians performed well, but in both cases reinforcements from Chasteler arrived just in time to prevent Rusca from seizing the fortress.[86]

While Rusca was marching through Tarvis, another Allied force was making its appearance in the vicinity. This was a flanking column of two battalions (II/Dalmatia and four companies of 3rd Italian Light from Palmanova), numbering approximately 900–1,000 men under Colonel Angelo Moroni of the Dalmatian Regiment. Forcing its way through the Plöcken Pass on 27 May, Moroni's detachment caused wild rumours and panic among the Tyrolians and Landwehr. GM Schmidt in Oberdrauburg accepted the rumours as fact and had all of the bridges between Oberdrauburg and Sachsenburg destroyed as a precaution. Common sense soon returned, but the damage had been done and Chasteler, delayed by the need to repair these bridges, would not be able to enter Spittal until 2 June.[87] The Dalmatian battalion, oblivious to its effect on Habsburg morale, reached Villach on 29 May, and pressed on to join the Army of Italy near Raab late on 14 June.[88] The Italians returned to Palmanova. Rusca, with at most 4,538 infantry and cavalry—almost all of them recruits—to execute his expansive mission, was doubtless sorry to see these potential reinforcements depart.[89]

Rusca soon learned that Chasteler was approaching. Believing himself badly outnumbered and fearing an outflanking move through the Gail valley, he began withdrawing, first towards Villach (1 June) and then to Klagenfurt. He arrived at the latter town on 4 June after an indecisive skirmish en route. Pugnacious and energetic, he spent the following day bolstering its defences, collecting all the grain and forage from the surrounding area, and writing to Marmont to request support. 'If I were strong, I would attack; but in the state in which I find myself, I cannot do this without danger,' he told Marmont, 'I will stay in Klagenfurt and defend myself.'[90] He planned a most active defence. Chasteler, on the other hand, only wanted to escape. To do so, however, he would have to fight his way out past Klagenfurt.

Klagenfurt in 1809 was a small walled town, square in outline, with a gate on each face. Situated in a fairly broad valley encircled by rugged hills, it was an important crossroads for north–south as well as east–west traffic. Chasteler was relying on the east–west highway, but did not want to delay his march or run the risk of a serious engagement. He therefore planned to mask the town, essentially locking Rusca inside its walls, while his corps and its baggage slipped south to regain the Völkermarkt road and continue their withdrawal. In the pre-dawn hours of 6 June Chasteler set his plan in motion, posting an advance guard detachment on the far side of the town beyond the Glan (under Major Vinzenz Lachovsky of *Hohenzollern*) and blocking each of the four gates with a company of I/*Hohenlohe-Bartenstein*. Chasteler had intercepted some of the correspondence between Rusca and Marmont, so he detached the battalion's other two companies and most of his pioneers to the south to burn the Drava bridge and watch the road over the Loibl Pass from Laibach. He positioned the rest of his command farther back from the town walls to ensure safe passage for the trains: II/*Hohenlohe-Bartenstein*, most of the Landwehr, two and one-half squadrons, and two 3-pounders to the sector south-east of Klagenfurt; GM Schmidt to the south-west with nine companies, a half-squadron and two 3-pounders; finally, *Johann Jellacic* with a squadron and three 3-pounders held the Kalvarienberg under Anton von Volkmann, now promoted to Oberst. It is not clear why Chasteler chose to assign such a large force to the strong position on the Kalvarienberg (sixteen companies) while leaving Schmidt with only nine companies in the open terrain to the south-west.

This bright, clear June day began badly for the Austrians. In a series of sudden, violent attacks, Rusca surprised and dispersed three of the four companies guarding the town gates; the Lais Schützen, local boys from

Table 8: Chasteler at Klagenfurt, 6 June 1809

Advance Guard: Maj Lachovsky

2nd Banal	(3 companies)
Hohenzollern Chevaulegers	(1)
9th Jägers	(1 company)
two small Landwehr detachments	

Main body: GM Fenner, GM Marcal

Hohenlohe-Bartenstein	(1 ⅔)
Hohenzollern Chevaulegers	(2)
1st Villach Landwehr	(1)
2nd Bruck Landwehr	(1)
1st, 2nd 3rd Klagenfurt Landwehr	(3)
2 x 6-pdrs, 2 x 3-pdrs, 1 x howitzer	

Oberst von Volkmann

Johann Jellacic	(2 ⅔)
Hohenzollern Chevaulegers	(1)
3 x 3-pdrs	

GM Schmidt

I/*Franz Karl*	(1)
2nd Banal	(4 companies)
Lais Schützen	(1 company)
Hohenzollern Chevaulegers	(½)
2 x 3-pdrs	

Detached to south

I/*Hohenlohe-Bartenstein*	(2 companies)

Baggage guard

2nd Banal	(2 companies)

Klagenfurt, scattered and fled.[91] Subsequent attacks shattered I/*Franz Karl* and the Grenzer of Schmidt's command. The tall crops on the flat ground around the town contributed to the surprise of the Austrian troops as they hampered visibility and command. Rusca, in contrast, had mounted a tower in Klagenfurt that afforded him a splendid view of the field, but forced him to resort to the unusual command and control expedient of dropping his instructions to waiting orderlies in small packets weighted with stones.[92] Despite this peculiar technique, Rusca's opening attacks had been tremendously successful. At least 390 whitecoats had been captured and an

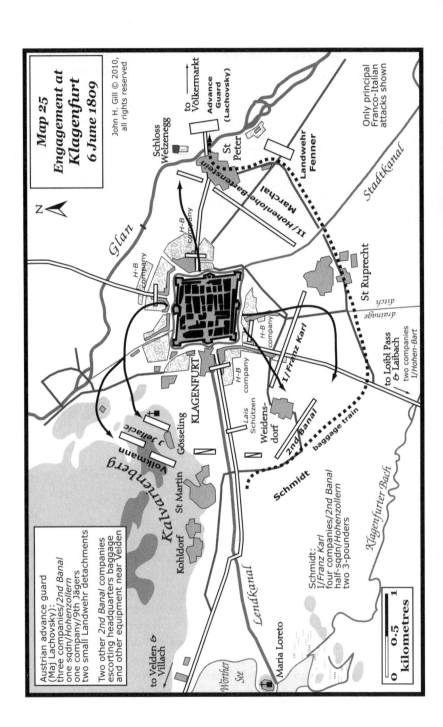

Map 25
Engagement at Klagenfurt
6 June 1809

Only principal
Franco-Italian
attacks shown

N

to
Völkermarkt

Advance
Guard (Lachovsky)

St Peter

Landwehr
Fenner

Schloss
Welzenegg

II / Hohenlohe Bartenstein

Marchal

Stadtkanal

Glan

H–B company

H–B company

St Ruprecht

drainage ditch

I / Franz Karl

to Loibl Pass
& Laibach

two companies
I/Hohen-Bart

H–B company

KLAGENFURT

H–B company

Gösseling

Lais
Schützen

Weidens-
dorf

2nd Banal

baggage train

J Jellacic

Volkmann

St Martin

Schmidt

Kalvarienberg

Kohldorf

Klagenfurter Bach

Schmidt:
I/Franz Karl
four companies/2nd Banal
half-sqdn/Hohenzollern
two 3-pounders

Lendkanal

to Velden &
Villach

Wörther
See

Maria Loreto

0   0.5   1
kilometres

Austrian advance guard
(Maj Lachovsky):
three companies/2nd Banal
one sqdn/Hohenzollern
one company/9th Jägers
two small Landwehr detachments

Two other 2nd Banal companies
escorting headquarters baggage
and other equipment near Velden

enormous gap now yawned between Schmidt and the Austrian right flank near St Peter as the Habsburg commanders attempted to rally their men. Fortunately for the Austrians, the position guns and most of the baggage train had passed St Ruprecht by 9 a.m. and trundled off to safety across the Glan. Schmidt, however, now made several decisions that ruined his career. Apparently suffering from a severe migraine that made it almost impossible for him to mount his horse, he first sent the shaken remnants of *Franz Karl* (perhaps 150 men) to join Volkmann on the heights. Then, sometime in the early afternoon, he decided that Volkmann had been outflanked and ordered his Grenzer as well as Volkmann to retreat to Velden. By 2 p.m., his small force had departed the battlefield. Meeting up with two additional companies of *2nd Banal* that he had left in Villach to guard some of the headquarters wagons and other baggage, he ordered a retreat to the Tyrol and vanished from Chasteler's knowledge for days to come.

Volkmann, who had wisely chosen not to obey Schmidt's repeated calls to retreat, now found himself the object of Rusca's attention. With the enemy largely cleared from the southern portion of the field, Rusca had decided to throw Volkmann's men off the Kalvarienberg from which they could dominate Klagenfurt. The French and Italian recruits displayed great courage and surprising steadfastness, but Volkmann skilfully employed his regiment, his guns, and the small band of *Franz Karl* men to repel every attempted assault. As dusk fell, he was still in possession of the heights. Having saved Austrian honour through his sturdy performance, he slipped away during the night to rejoin Chasteler on the Völkermarkt road on 7 June.

The day's results were mixed. Chasteler had escaped with all of his guns, most of his baggage, and the bulk of his troops (approximately 5,000 infantry and 350 cavalry); he was free to continue his retreat.[93] On 15 June he was in Warasdin (Varazdin), and by the 26th, as we have seen, he was united with Mesko at Szent Groth west of Lake Balaton. On the other hand, his command had been very roughly handled. Rusca and his small division of recruits, though outnumbered, had exacted a considerable price from their foe for the passage. Thanks to his own energy and cunning, combined with the valour of his men, he had surprised the Austrians and inflicted 830 casualties.[94] Another 800 or so were now trapped in the Tyrol with GM Schmidt, essentially lost to the army for the remainder of active combat operations. On top of this, 'the Landwehr had largely disintegrated.'[95] French and Italian losses were small in comparison, totalling about 340 men.[96] Marmont might have intervened to do even more harm to the Austrians, but did not learn of Chasteler's movements in time to act effectively.[97]

Table 9: Chasteler's Command, 25 June 1809

GM Fenner
 Oberst von Volkmann
  Johann Jellacic (2 ⅔)
  Franz Karl (1)
  Artillery: 4 x 6-pdrs, 2 x howitzers
 Oberst Auracher
  9th Jägers and Lais Schützen (2 companies)
  Two Landwehr battalions (2)
GM Marchal
 Oberst Mumb
  Hohenlohe-Bartenstein (1 ⅓)
  Hohenzollern Chevaulegers (5)
  Artillery: 4 x 3-pdrs
 Oberst Attems
  1st UMB Landwehr (1)
  Frimont Hussars (1)
  Composite Croat Company (1 company)
  Artillery: 2 x 3-pdrs
 Major Veigl (not listed in source)
  Hohenlohe Dragoons (1)
  Det/*Ott* Hussars
  St Georg Grenzer (1 company)
GM Mesko
 GM Keglevich
  Pressburg Insurrection Infantry No. 1 (1)
  Neutra Insurrection Infantry No. 3 (1)
  Neograd Insurrection Infantry No. 4 (1)
  Bars (Neograd?) Insurrection Hussars (2)
  Other Insurrection Hussars (½)
 Oberst Esterhazy
  2nd Eisenburg Insurrection Infantry No. 6 (1)
  Stuhlweissenburg Insurrection Infantry No. 10 (⅓)
  Pressburg Insurrection Hussars (2)
  Szala Insurrection Hussars (¼)
 Artillery: 3 x 6-pdrs, 2 x howitzers, 2 x 3-pdrs

The identity of Insurrection Hussars is unclear.
Source: Order of Battle, 25 June 1809, KAFA, Kart. 1437.

Table 10: Buol's Command, 10 June 1809

*GM Buol (northern Tyrol)

Lusignan (3)	1,566
De Vaux (1)	546
Salzburg Jägers (1)	234
9th Jägers (2 companies)	120
Hohenzollern Chevaulegers (2)	119
Artillery and train	81
4 x 3-pdrs, 3 x 6-pdrs	

*Oberstlt Leinigen (Trient)

Hohenlohe-Bartenstein (3 1/2 companies)	484
9th Jägers (3 companies)	150
Hohenzollern Chevaulegers (1)	46

Rittmeister Bannizza (southeast of Sillian)

2nd Banal (1 company)	120
Hohenzollern Chevaulegers	12

Major Triangi (Oberdrauburg area)

3rd Inner Austrian Volunteers (1)	320
I/*Johann Jellacic* (2 companies)	150
2nd Banal (1 company)	110
Hohenzollern Chevaulegers	12

GM Schmidt (en route to Lienz)

1st Banal (1 company)	120
2nd Banal (2 companies)	450
I/*Franz Karl* (3 companies)	210
Hohenzollern Chevaulegers/Staff Dragoons	36
Staff Infantry	20
O'Reilly Chevaulegers (since Strub Pass)	8

Rittmeister Esch (Vorarlberg)

Lusignan (1 company)	150
Escaped Prisoners of War	100
Hohenzollern Chevaulegers	30
(4th Company/9th Jägers	130)

*Indicates troops under Buol as of 25 May (at Brenner Pass and Bozen respectively on that date).

Note: escaped prisoners (Selbstranzionierte) were men who had freed themselves and made their way to the Tyrol. 9th Jägers are not listed in source (see Chapter 4).

Source: 'Summarischer Ausweis', 16 June 1809, KAFA, Kart. 1437.

Rusca remained in Klagenfurt for the next several weeks. With a detachment in Villach under GB Antonio Bertoletti (IV/67th Ligne, 1st Italian Light), he coped with small insurgent forays, held the Austrian troops in the Tyrol in check, and secured the Army of Italy's line of communications. The unfortunate GM Schmidt, whose performance in the war had hardly been stellar, would later be subjected to a military court of inquiry for his behaviour on 6 June. Distraught, he took his own life before the proceedings concluded.

Chasteler's departure left GM Buol in the Tyrol with approximately 4,910 regulars. Most of these were posted between Innsbruck and the Brenner under Buol's personal command, but Oberstleutnant Leiningen had 680 in southern Tyrol at Trient (which he had re-occupied on 27 May), 530 men garrisoned at Sachsenburg, and, in between, there were detachments totalling some 820 in the Pustertal. There was also GM Schmidt. Though Chasteler's staff was still listing the location of his 840 fugitives as 'God knows where' as of 12 June, he eventually reached Lienz, where he stayed for the remainder of the month.[98] An additional 400 or so men were in the Vorarlberg for a grand total of 5,320. Buol's men and their Tyrolian confederates, however, now cut off from the rest of the empire, suffered from serious shortages of powder, lead, money, and food, so that Buol regarded Schmidt's men as just so many 'useless but hungry mouths in a period of daily increasing scarcity'.[99] Thousands of fugitives from the other Habsburg armies only exacerbated the tenuous logistical situation.

Fortunately for Buol, the level of combat in June was low. Deroy had retired to Rosenheim on 2 June, falling back from there on the 6th to establish a screen of trained veterans south of Munich in support of the second-line troops along the border with the Tyrol. With Deroy out of the way, the Tyrolians renewed the blockade of Kufstein and eagerly launched numerous incursions into Bavaria for money, food, and other booty, with some assistance from Austrian regulars. This menace generated anxiety among Bavarians and French alike. 'Fear and consternation reign in the capital,' wrote GD Adrien du Bosc, Comte Dutaillis from Munich, but the insurgent raiding parties had no staying power and the growing collection of French and Bavarian reserves sufficed to hold them in check.[100]

A series of raids and threats of raids from both sides also kept tension alive in the south. Leiningen's small command, for example, raided Bassano on the 3rd, causing some alarm among Italian authorities. The Italians responded by sending Colonel Joseph Levié with two battalions of his 3rd Italian Line, some mounted gendarmes, and three guns up the Adige to repel

Leiningen. Levié succeeded in capturing Trient on 6 June, but Leiningen secured himself in the town's citadel and would not be dislodged. Early on the morning of 9 June, over 1,000 Tyrolians descended on Trient from the north and, abetted by a sally from the citadel, sent Levié reeling back down the Adige.[101] The Italians retired to Ala, but as in Germany, the Austro-Tyrolian forays into northern Italy elicited only a minimal reaction from Napoleon's subordinates at the strategic level. The emperor saw such stabs as nuisances and was content to contain them with second-line forces; no regulars would be detached from the main army. When an Austrian raiding party from near Sillian occupied Belluno on 13 June, for example, the threat posed by depot troops, gendarmes, and other armed servants of the Italian state forced a hasty withdrawal after two days. Following this momentary excitement, the situation along the Tyrol's southern borders largely subsided into a watchful quiet for the remainder of the month.

DEFENDING CROATIA TO THE UTTERMOST

Although external raids, logistical problems, and internal administration absorbed the attention of most Tyrolians during June, some rebel leaders and Austrian officers began to consider how they might both end their isolation and profit by the successes they had achieved. Many of the schemes they concocted can only be described as wildly unrealistic (such as collaborating with Schill's band), but the one upon which they focused and the one that appeared to them most feasible involved co-operation with FML Ignaz Gyulai and the IX Corps troops in Croatia. This notion seemed to acquire increasing relevance in their minds as the month progressed, but in the end the Tyrolians and their Habsburg adherents would be bitterly disappointed.[102]

My Naked Army

As Chasteler exits our accelerating drama, FML Ignaz Gyulai marches in. When the Army of Inner Austria left Italy in mid-May, Archduke Johann dispatched Gyulai to Croatia to assume command of a congeries of units: broken regular battalions, dwindling Landwehr, and the as-yet unformed Croatian Insurrection. Within the general task of 'defending Croatia to the uttermost', he was to hold the Isonzo and cover Trieste, falling back via Präwald (Razdrto) towards Laibach if necessary. Johann also gave him authority over Stoichevich, the navy, and the Carniola Landwehr as well as the local Grenz troops and militia.[103] All of this sounded like a lot more than it was. Gyulai arrived in Laibach on 16 May, but as we have seen in Volume II of this study, the available troops were completely inadequate for these demanding missions. By 23 May, Präwald and Laibach had fallen to MacDonald, and Rebrovic was retreating from Dalmatia with his rapidly eroding brigade.[104] Other than some fugitive *Szulin* Grenzer who had escaped the surrender of Laibach, Gyulai had a mere 4,340 regular infantry and 1,120 cavalry.[105] His only hope of new troops lay in the Croatian Insurrection. He thus sent his division-sized 'corps' to Neustadtl (Novo Mesto), placed an advance guard at Weixelburg (Visnja Gora), left GM Gavassini in charge, and rode off to hurry the organisation of the Insurrection, fortunate that French intentions lay to the north.

Like Hungary, Croatia enjoyed certain political privileges in exchange for providing a 'Noble Insurrection' in cases of imperial emergency. As in Hungary, however, this institution was riddled with flaws. Although more than 11,000 were gathered by the end of May, equipment of all types was in short supply, and 'this respectable number was comprised of untrained, mostly raw, peasants, only a small number of their officers had any previous service.'[106] Discipline was also a problem. Drunken Insurrectionists in Agram (Zagreb), fearing they would be incorporated into regular regiments, mutinied and personally defied Gyulai even after he had struck one of their number with his sword.[107] 'Force had to be used to form them,' remembered Johann, 'and the Ban even had to send regular troops out after the mutineers.'[108] The quality of Gyulai's command was further compromised by the inclusion of numerous reserve and Land-battalions from the Grenz districts. In the words of a 30 May inspection report: 'These troops more resemble a wild horde. They have neither undergarments nor shoes. Many stand naked in the remnants of their clothing . . . Most are boys who barely reach the muzzles of their old and heavy muskets . . . Among the infantry most of the muskets are faulty—and poor—and there are at most two officers per company and these mostly anxious invalids.'[109]

The flimsy Carniola Landwehr battalions had simply evaporated by the end of May; the remnants were disarmed and sent home, leaving only a small Jäger battalion drawn from Triest men who volunteered to stay with the army.[110] Even Gyulai's regulars posed problems.[111] Many had been badly shaken by the army's reverses and a large percentage were brand new recruits from depot companies. Given these daunting deficiencies, it is hardly surprising that Gyulai complained to Archduke Johann. 'My naked army', he wrote on 15 June, 'consists in the most part of reserves, mobilised citizens, and escaped prisoners of war.'[112] Nor is it surprising that Gyulai had been largely inactive since his departure from Italy in mid-May. Consumed with what he perceived as the vital mission of protecting Croatia and preserving an outlet to the sea (in the hope of English subsidies), he had held his weak command well east of Laibach while waiting for the Croatian Insurrection to achieve some level of organisation.

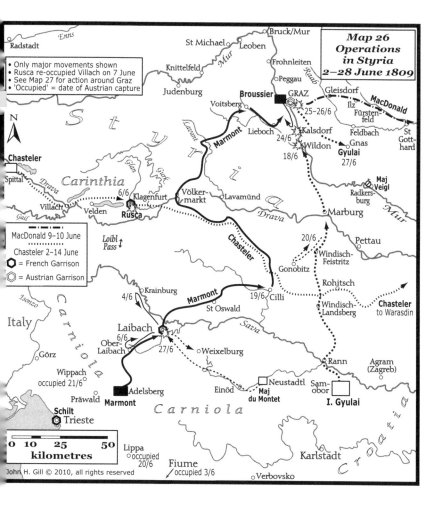

Map 26
Operations
in Styria
2–28 June 1809

- Only major movements shown
- Rusca re-occupied Villach on 7 June
- See Map 27 for action around Graz
- 'Occupied' = date of Austrian capture

MacDonald 9–10 June

Chasteler 2–14 June

⬡ = French Garrison
◎ = Austrian Garrison

Towards the end of May, hoping to take advantage of the victory at Aspern, Gyulai considered a surprise attack on Laibach or a strike against Marmont at Fiume. News of Marmont's march on Laibach, however, scotched his plans and he remained in Neustadl, worried that Marmont might advance to threaten Agram and uncertain of his own next move. A courier bearing an urgent plea from Chasteler arrived on 4 June to shift his attention to the north. He thus marched via Rann (Brezice) to reach Windisch-Landsberg (Podcetrtek) on 6 June, but his move was too late to assist Chasteler's escape and, although the two generals conferred at Rohitsch (Rogatec) on the 10th, their operations lacked any real coherence. Indeed, Gyulai, hoping that Chasteler's regulars would bolster his hotchpotch force, was disappointed when the latter marched on to Hungary in accordance with Johann's orders.

Gyulai remained generally in the vicinity of Landsberg with his advance guard at Windisch-Feistritz (Slovenska Bistrica) until 12 June, when somewhat confusing orders from Johann called for him to tie down Marmont and yet simultaneously be close enough to Hungary to support Johann in a manoeuvre against Eugene. Gyulai decided that Marburg offered the best central location to facilitate these missions and by 15 June he had cautiously moved his main body to billets in and around the town. He hoped that his presence would suffice to daunt the French, and wanted to avoid any action that might dispel 'the nimbus of empty power' created by the size of his force.[113] He seems to have given no thought to the Tyrol, but anxieties about his rear tugged at his mind. Continuing raids from Ottoman territory absorbed much of his time and eventually diverted most of the 5,000 Slavonian Insurrection troops to the Turkish border. He also worried about the safety of Agram and left behind Major du Montet with a small detachment to cover the city and harass the French in Laibach. Maintaining access to the Adriatic to secure future English subsidies was another high priority. The occupation of Fiume by a squadron of Banderial Hussars on 3 June helped ensure the link to the sea and resulted in the capture of the two French generals of brigade who had been left in the city to recover from wounds received in the Dalmatian campaign. The way was thereby cleared for *Leonidas* and *Mercury* to deliver the first British subsidies, some £250,000 in silver, to Zengg on 14 June. Finally, Gyulai and other Habsburg leaders thought about Dalmatia, and GM Peter von Knesevich was placed in command of a small brigade at Gospic with an eye towards reconquering the province. While Napoleon would soon strip his rear areas of almost all troops, therefore, the Austrians left significant numbers (albeit often militia or raw recruits) in distant parts of the empire, far from the principal theatre of war.

13–26 June: Blockade and Battle at Graz

As Gyulai carefully edged towards Marburg, he kept one eye on Laibach and the other on Graz. MacDonald and Grouchy had occupied the latter city on 31 May, but Grouchy soon departed and, by 9 June, MacDonald too was gone, leaving only Broussier's infantry division and 6th Hussars behind to blockade and, it was hoped, capture the Graz fortress. This fortress, the Schlossberg, was strong, but there were too few men (913) and cannon (18) to defend it. The garrison commandant, however, was an energetic and determined engineer major named Hackher who had no intention of surrendering his charge. Luckily for Hackher, Broussier lacked almost everything he would have needed for a proper siege, being weak in infantry and having only eight 6-pounders and four field howitzers for artillery. He also lacked time to exhaust the garrison's food supply. His only hope was to intimidate the commandant into capitulating, a tactic to which Hackher would not yield. With the few howitzers at his disposal, Broussier bombarded the fortress from 13 to 20 June and launched seven forays towards its walls. As one observant citizen noted, however, 'the French would not undertake a serious assault because they were too weak to sacrifice so many men,' and these 'assaults' seem to have been designed to exhaust the defenders' ammunition and morale rather than with any real hope of taking the place by storm.[114] Whether earnest or not, none of these efforts succeeded and Hackher remained as defiant as ever when bivouac fires to the south intimated the approach of Austrian relief forces on the night of 17/18 June.[115] Broussier therefore ceased the bombardment around midnight on the night of 20/21 June and retired to Gösting, some five kilometres north of Graz.

Broussier was right to be concerned: Gyulai was indeed approaching, albeit cautiously. The 6th Hussars, charged with guarding the route from Marburg, had allowed themselves to be surprised by the Austrian advance guard and lost sixty men to *Frimont* Hussars in a skirmish on 18 June, but Gyulai did not press his advantage.[116] Broussier, on the other hand, thinking it better to attack than be attacked, moved south to Wildon on the 21st and skirmished inconclusively with the Austrian advance guard. With no information whatsoever on Marmont's whereabouts, however, the French general was understandably unwilling to confront what he knew to be a vastly superior enemy force. He thus pulled back to Graz during the night of 22/23 June and resumed his blockade of the Schlossberg. This second 'blockade', however, lasted for little more than twenty-four hours before Broussier again withdrew to Gösting around 11 a.m. on the 24th.[117]

On arriving in Gösting, Broussier learned that Marmont had reached Voitsberg, only some forty kilometres by road from Graz. He therefore decided to make a diversion in Marmont's favour by attacking the Austrian advance posts on the west (right) bank of the Mur. At 4 p.m., he advanced to the south, driving back the *Frimont* and Banderial Hussars 'under the eyes of the inhabitants of Graz who had gathered in the fortress and the most elevated houses of the city to witness the spectacle'.[118] The Austrians attempted to defend Kalsdorf, but Broussier's blood was up. Although it was 9 p.m. and light was fading fast, he sent his lead regiment, 9th Ligne, forward. The regiment not only gained the village in its first rush, but broke the Massal Insurrection battalion on the far side and repelled a cavalry counter-attack. Watching the wild flight of the Insurrection infantry towards Wildon as the combat closed at 10.30 p.m., Broussier generously praised the 9th for 'its intrepidity, its silence, and its sangfroid' in the attack, but he drew rather exaggerated conclusions about the quality of Gyulai's corps that, to him, had just been soundly defeated by a lone regiment.[119]

Having chastened Gyulai, Broussier decided to retire again to Gösting and marched his division back north at 3 a.m. on 25 June. Here he received, twelve hours later, an order from Marmont. The latter had departed Laibach on the 17th in response to orders to march for Graz via Marburg. He had reached Cilli (Celje) two days later and approached Marburg, but Gyulai had withdrawn behind the Drava, and Marmont thought it imprudent to attempt an opposed river crossing. He thus turned north-west and passed over the Drava at Völkermarkt on the 22nd to arrive at Voitsberg on 24 June with Clauzel's division. Montrichard with the rear guard was a day's march behind, owing, in Marmont's words, to his 'incredible ineptitude'.[120] As Marmont berated Montrichard, Napoleon (through Berthier) excoriated Marmont for 'resting tranquilly' too long in Laibach, for moving too slowly (he had expected Marmont to reach Graz on 23 or 24 June), for failing to intercept Chasteler, and for appearing to require specific orders before acting.[121] Preparing to cross the Danube, Napoleon was counting on Marmont to dispose of Gyulai. As he told Eugene, 'It will not be possible for me to make the movement I am considering if the enemy is not distanced from that flank.'[122] From Napoleon's perspective, Marmont was offering excuses rather than seeing to the swift completion of this important task, and orders from Vienna took on an increasingly stiff tone. Under this barrage of pointed promptings, Marmont wrote to Broussier on the 25th, directing him to march south past Graz along the west bank of the Mur the following day so that the two forces could attack

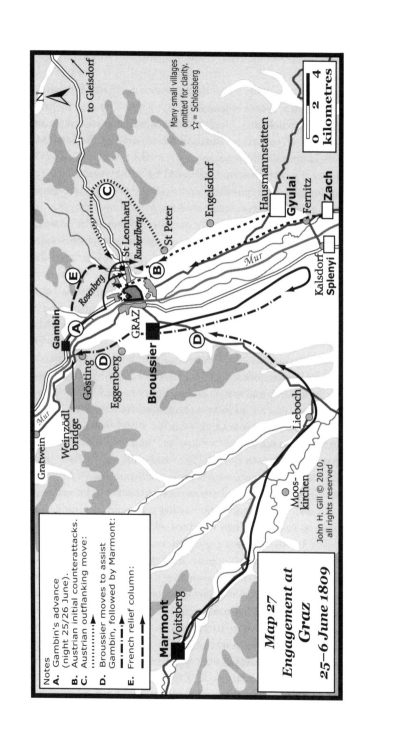

N

to Gleisdorf

Many small villages
omitted for clarity.
☆ = Schlossberg

Engelsdorf

Hausmannstätten

Gyulai

Fernitz

Zach

St Peter

St Leonhard
Ruckerlberg

B

C

E

Rosenberg

Mur

Kalsdorf
Splenyi

A

Gambin

GRAZ

Gösting

D

Eggenberg

D

Broussier

Weinzödl
bridge

Gratwein

Mur

Lieboch

Moos-
kirchen

John H. Gill © 2010,
all rights reserved

Marmont
Voitsberg

kilometres
0   2   4

Notes
A. Gambin's advance
    (night 25/26 June).
B. Austrian initial counterattacks.
C. Austrian outflanking move: ....
D. Broussier moves to assist
    Gambin, followed by Marmont: ·—·—·
E. French relief column: ·–·–·

Map 27
Engagement at
Graz
25–6 June 1809

Gyulai's men at Wildon. This set the stage for an epic small-scale struggle on 26 June.

Broussier set off at 8 p.m. on the 25th with six battalions, ten guns, and his cavalry. He left three companies of 9th Ligne to guard the bridge near Gösting and dispatched Colonel Jean Hugues Gambin to re-occupy Graz and chase off the '150 hussars and as many Croats' that he believed to be in the city.[123] Gambin would have only the 1st and 2nd Battalions of his 84th Ligne and two 3-pounders, and he would be on his own on the far side of a swift, unfordable river, but there seemed little danger, given the prevailing French appreciation of the situation.

There were indeed few Austrian troops in Graz when Broussier issued his orders (three Insurrection companies, two squadrons each of *Savoy*, *Frimont*, and *Banderial*). Most of Gyulai's men, however, were just a few kilometres to the south between St Peter and Fernitz, on the eastern side of the Mur; only Splenyi and the advance guard were on the western bank. Additionally, Munkacsy's brigade arrived to camp outside the city at around the time Gambin was crossing the river, and III/*Franz Karl* soon joined Munkacsy's Grenzer and Insurrection troops. There were thus some 5,000 Habsburg infantry and cavalry in and immediately outside Graz when Gambin encountered Croatian pickets north of the city with the 1,340 men of his two battalions between 10 and 11 p.m. on the night of 25/26 June.

What ensued was an unusual night action. As Munkacsy's brigade was alerted and pushed out from Graz, Gambin found that he could no longer proceed directly towards the Schlossberg and city as he had intended. He thus turned east into the hills and made his way to St Leonhard and the Ruckerlberg by dawn under continual skirmishing.[124] Approaching St Leonhard, the French ran into heavy fire from an unknown number of enemy who were ensconced in the walled cemetery adjacent to the town's church, but Gambin skilfully surrounded it and launched a successful bayonet attack. 'The enemy, seeing themselves so closely pressed, gave themselves up as prisoners because they thought we outnumbered them . . . those who were outside the suburb took flight, those in the church tower surrendered as well.'[125] Having captured some 400 Croatians and locked them in the church, Gambin cleared the rest of the village and threw Munkacsy's disordered men back towards Graz by 4 a.m. on the 26th. While the French industriously readied the village and their other positions for defence, Gyulai responded with half-measures. The first counter-attack came at around 9 a.m. as III/*Franz Karl* advanced directly on St Leonhard and the two Personal Insurrection battalions attempted to outflank Gambin by taking the Rosenberg. Although they successfully mounted the slopes, the attack dissolved almost at once. 'Other than 103 men, they dispersed at the first enemy volley and left their standard behind . . . part fled to Radkersburg, others as far as Croatia,' recorded the IX Corps operations journal, concluding with marvellous understatement: 'thus nothing decisive was achieved'.[126]

Gambin occupied an extensive position for his two battalions—the Ruckerlberg, St Leonhard, and part of the valley marked by 'the billowing powder smoke from the gardens, hedges, and houses'—but his men exhibited the talent for village fighting that characterised French troops of the era.[127] 'The sly French slipped into the houses and fired out of the roofs and windows,' noted a local citizen.[128] Disregarding the constant pressure, the men of the 84th were in good spirits: 'we kept up a bold front despite our extremely small numbers,' recalled a sergeant.[129] They soon found their ammunition running low, however, and many made short forays to seize cartridges from hapless Croats who ventured too near the French positions. The early part of the afternoon passed in this sort of indecisive combat, but between 3 and 4 p.m., Gyulai—who seems to have believed he was facing Broussier's entire division—finally organised a serious assault. Kalnassy led the various elements of *Simbschen* and *St Julien* against the Ruckerlberg while a knowledgeable local guided two Grenz battalions on a long swing to the east to outflank Gambin. Several attacks were required to dislodge the tenacious French, but the weight of numbers and French exhaustion finally made the difference. Gambin and his men, who had now been in action more or less continuously for at least seventeen hours, resisted fiercely, lost both of their guns, recovered one, and nearly lost an eagle before being forced to retreat around 5 p.m.[130] The Austrians, in addition to gaining a 3-pounder and some prisoners, also managed to free 300 of their own from the St Leonhard church.

Fortunately for Gambin and his weary troops, help was on the way. Broussier had heard the steady musketry as he marched past Graz during the night, but had continued on to his rendezvous with Marmont at Lieboch as ordered. When the two generals met at 8 a.m., Marmont wanted to await the arrival of Montrichard, but sent Broussier back at once to rescue the isolated 84th. Broussier reached Gösting at approximately 1 p.m., where he learned that the three companies of 9th Ligne he had left there had successfully repulsed weak Austrian probes towards the vital bridge. Some time elapsed before the entire division was on hand, but at around 3 p.m., Broussier sent III/84th and the two battalions of 92nd Ligne to disengage Gambin; he soon followed with two battalions of the 9th, leaving one battalion of the latter regiment, the artillery, and the cavalry at Gösting.[131] This move was both timely and successful. The leading three battalions appeared north of St Leonhard between 5 and 6 p.m., and advanced immediately, first halting and then throwing back Gyulai's columns. Gambin's men joyously embraced their comrades of the 84th and joined in a final spoiling attack around 7 p.m., before the entire force turned about and retreated to the north-east to make its way back to Gösting. The Austrians did not pursue.

The results of this curious engagement largely favoured the French. Although the Schlossberg had been resupplied and the Austrians held the field, Broussier and Marmont were now united and—most important from the French perspective—the road to Vienna remained open. The Austrians also seem to have suffered considerably heavier casualties. Gyulai reported a total of 975 dead, wounded, and captured in addition to 667 missing (though many of the latter later returned to the ranks). Broussier's claim of 278 casualties from the 84th and another nineteen from the 92nd may be low, but it seems unlikely that the total approached the Austrian figure. Moreover, the French by no means felt defeated. On the contrary, Marmont planned to attack on the 27th and everyone, from common soldier to general, regarded the day as a great triumph of French arms. Napoleon, when he learned of the affair, berated his generals for their actions—'Marmont manoeuvred quite badly; Broussier, even worse'—but could not praise the 84th enough. 'The regiment covered itself with glory,' he told Eugene, and 'found in its courage the means to compensate for the poor movements that had been made'.[132] The 84th soon became one of the few regiments to have the right to display a special motto on its standard in recognition of its stalwart performance against great odds: 'un contre dix' ('one against ten').[133] Gyulai, on the other hand, found himself besieged by fears: Marmont might attack, Eugene might move south from Raab, French reserves might come up from Italy, south-western Hungary was threatened. Most of all, he seems to have been anxious about 'the unreliability of our troops' and believed that his orders stipulated that he not involve himself in 'uncertain combat'.[134] Deciding that he had accomplished his 'assigned goal' by revictualling Graz, he withdrew towards Gnas during the night.[135] He thereby incurred the wrath of his superior, Archduke Johann, for being 'slow, uncertain about losing people, not thwarting the enemy's designs'. 'This entire operation remains inexplicable,' concluded the archduke.[136]

The citizens of Graz were as confused as Johann as they peered out in the dawn's light on the morning of the 27th: 'how astounded were they that as early as 3 a.m. not one of the Austrians was to be seen in the city or in their entire vicinity. Everyone struggled to decipher this odd development, but no one succeeded in grasping this military measure.'[137] The French re-occupied the city the same day, Marmont's men coming in 'like hungry wolves' and plundering the poor inhabitants 'who had already suffered much the previous day from the French and the Croats.'[138] Marmont, in a rather dilatory 'pursuit' of the enemy, sent Clauzel's division to Feldbach on the 29th to worry Gyulai, but new orders soon called him to Vienna. By the morning of 2 July, the French combat troops, parks, and wounded had vanished on the road north to Wagram.[139]

On 1 July almost all French forces were thus departing Styria for Vienna. Only Rusca was left behind with his small division at Klagenfurt and Villach. He, too, would soon shift north. For the Austrians, Gyulai and his corps in and around Gnas constituted the principal force south of the Danube. To the east, Chasteler was at Szent Groth; he was now united with Mesko and had patrols reaching out towards Güns and Sarvar. He was to serve as what Johann called an 'intermediary corps' between Pressburg and Gyulai.[140] Further south, Major du Montet had surprised the Laibach garrison on the night of 27/28 June and captured 150 prisoners, but could not take the citadel and had to withdraw.[141] Habsburg troops also had the best of several other small encounters in Croatia, regaining some towns in the process (see Map 26). Furthermore, they retained access to the Adriatic through control of Fiume and other coastal areas. Austro-Tyrolian forces also dominated the Tyrol, and the region's borders were illuminated by the fires of raids and rebellions.

Napoleon, however, knew that the war would be decided on the Danube. Lack of troops may have forced a temporary evacuation of the Tyrol, but this was a threat that could be contained by second-line troops. Likewise, although Marmont's lassitude may have cost the French opportunities to inflict debilitating blows on Chasteler and Gyulai, both were effectively neutralised for the short term. Neither they nor the troublesome mountaineers would be in a position to interfere with the sanguinary contest about to explode on the Marchfeld.

CHAPTER 4

A Month of Preparation

The struggles in Poland, Hungary, and Inner Austria framed the strategic thinking of the political-military leaders on both banks of the Danube. Though we must treat each of these sets of operations sequentially in our narrative, these battlefield developments, of course, occurred simultaneously and thus shaped the environment in which the two sides considered their options in the aftermath of Aspern. So we must now return to the banks of the Danube between the Marchfeld and Vienna, where the warm June days are wearing away towards July.

I Will Risk Nothing

The success at Aspern immediately rekindled a heated strategic debate in Habsburg leadership circles. Kaiser Franz had sent FML Ferdinand von Bubna to congratulate Charles on the evening of the battle, with the words: 'Tell my brother I will thank him again tomorrow in person for the victory he has won, but he should not grant them [the French] a reprieve, rather fall upon them again soon.'[1] On 23 May, however, the morning after the battle, the Austrians were as shocked and bloodied as the enemy, as stunned by their accomplishment as the French were by their repulse. Hiller pressed repeatedly and passionately for an immediate exploitation, but Charles limited his response to tentative orders for IV and VI Corps to harass the French crowded on Lobau Island.[2] The force Rosenberg was to employ, however, was almost ludicrously inadequate: one infantry brigade, 100 cavalry, and a few guns. Hiller and Klenau were to provide support. Nothing came of this. Indeed the 'attack' never actually took place because a reconnaissance by

Rosenberg's subordinates immediately reported insurmountable difficulties.[3] Charles blamed exhaustion, empty ammunition caissons, burned-out artillery pieces, the turbulence of the Stadtler Arm, and lack of bridging material for the tepid effort.[4] These explanations satisfied most observers for a time, but as the days lengthened and turned into weeks, criticism of the Generalissimus and his staff mounted swiftly, both in volume and vitriol. 'The stagnation since 22 May seems inexplicable to me,' noted an Austrian sympathiser in his diary in mid-June. 'It seems the Archduke Charles has no other result from the battle of the 22nd than to have 25,000 men fewer.'[5]

As we have seen, Charles's imperial brothers Joseph and Johann were among the most scathing, scornfully complaining about the 'weighty army' that 'rested unmoving on its laurels.'[6] Maria Ludovica shared Johann's 'dark mood', lamented that 'till now nothing has happened', and blamed Charles for being 'naturally weak . . . too weak to act appropriately, ashamed to have failed'.[7] Baldacci, one of the Kaiser's intimate circle, had blithely remarked that 'The Emperor Napoleon is a wretched person and a completely ordinary, ignorant general, who would certainly have been destroyed long before if Archduke Charles were not an even less competent leader.'[8] Perhaps the most influential and vociferous voice at court, however, was Stadion. Among other things, the foreign minister, whose understanding of military issues was hazy at best, laid the responsibility for the defeat at Raab on Charles. 'If one follows a system of temporisation, as the Archduke Charles is doing, one must at least demand of him that he possess enough intelligence to protect the troops from misfortunes and, in this case [Raab], he could have done so were he not so miserly with troops in every place where he does not command in person.'[9]

Combined with his long-standing mistrust of Charles (and many others in the army), Stadion, in the wake of Aspern, returned to the unfounded optimism that had characterised his thinking before the war.[10] He blamed the army for the monarchy's current predicament, but expressed his conviction that the situation in mid-1809 was retrievable if sufficient 'decisiveness and activity' were displayed: 'We cannot allow ourselves to stand by and watch as one province after another falls into the enemy's hands, while we await the accidents of the future without acting.' He continued to rely on his perception of the 'hatred' Germans felt towards Napoleon and how a 'fortunate blow' would 'set in motion a great part of the forces that stand ready for us'. He further asserted that the war in Spain, forthcoming Anglo-Sicilian landings in southern Italy, a British invasion of northern Germany (that he claimed was a promised certainty), upcoming Austrian diversionary incursions from

Bohemia, and Tyrolian raids into Bavaria would, at a minimum, limit the reinforcements that Napoleon could expect to receive. Venturing into the military realm, he airily proposed exploiting these 'likely and eventually forthcoming foreign diversions in northern Germany and Italy' through 'the somewhat active and skilful employment and combined movements of our various armies.'[11]

On the diplomatic front, Stadion reinvigorated his previous schemes and contacts vis-à-vis the major concerned powers. In Russia's case, he sent GM Josef Stutterheim to Tsar Alexander with a letter from Kaiser Franz expressing the latter's 'astonishment' that Russian forces seemed to be behaving as enemies, and urging Alexander to 'cease an unfortunate complication' that could injure the interests of both empires.[12] At the same time, Stadion attempted to foment unrest on Russia's southern frontiers.[13] He also complained bitterly that Great Britain, despite being at war with Russia, was not employing its fleets in the Baltic and the Black Seas with sufficient vigour to 'give even the least disquiet to Russia.' 'You cannot,' he told the Austrian ambassador in London, 'speak too strongly with Mr Canning on the object of this despatch.'[14] His ire with the Court of St James, however, was not restricted to its supposed lethargy against Russia. He also derided 'the insufficiency, or better said, the nullity of military succour' from Britain and the 'very discouraging parsimony' regarding the financial means for subsidies that were 'not only onerous, but nearly illusory.'[15]

While imploring Russia for peace and Britain for activity (against both Napoleon and the tsar), Stadion again invested his greatest hopes in Prussia. The arrival in the Austrian court at Wolkersdorf of Wilhelm Friedrich, the Prince of Orange, seemed to justify Stadion's optimism. The prince, a cousin of Prussian King Friedrich Wilhelm III, brought assurances that seemed to confirm Prussia's entry into the war as an Austrian ally within a matter of weeks.[16] Several hectic days of consultations with Stadion and Charles ensued, military information was exchanged, the prince and his adjutant were taken into Austrian service—partly as a public display of putative Austro-Prussian collaboration—and an emissary was readied for dispatch to the Prussian court in Königsberg. The chosen envoy was newly promoted Oberst August Freiherr von Steigentesch, whom we last saw leading the 2nd Vienna Volunteers out of Bavaria. Carrying letters from Franz, Charles, and Orange, he was sent publicly and in full uniform with the expressed intent of 'compromising' the Prussian monarch and 'forcing' his kingdom into action.[17] Steigentesch reached Königsberg on 15 June and soon learned that either the Prince of Orange had exceeded his brief or Friedrich Wilhelm III had changed his mind.[18] 'I was received like a dog at a garden party,' he reported of his audience with Friedrich Wilhelm.[19] The king dismissed Orange's letter as coming from 'one of those passionate gentlemen', then, on asking Steigentesch the purpose of his mission, almost immediately answered himself: 'I know it already, most likely that I should have the honour of being destroyed along with Austria.' After several days of disheartening calls and audiences, Steigentesch departed Königsberg on 23 June with nothing to show for his travels. Not only was the mission a failure, but the blatant attempt to compromise Prussia aroused Friedrich Wilhelm's fury and introduced a new tension into the sensitive Austro-Prussian relationship, dampening any hope of near-future military co-operation.[20]

Charles was decidedly less sanguine than Stadion. Where the foreign minister descried advantages that were largely imaginary and refused to countenance any cessation of hostilities that would require Austria to lose territory, the Generalissimus was convinced that Austria's only hope lay in concluding peace as quickly as feasible. 'Since the Battle of Regensburg and above all since that of Aspern, I continually preach peace, peace, peace, better to sacrifice a few things than lose everything,' he wrote on 23 June.[21] Charles's thinking was founded on the key assumptions that Aspern had chastened Napoleon and that the French emperor would treat with his Austrian counterpart as long as the latter had a viable army in the field. Conversely, Napoleon would have no reason to negotiate if that army, 'the sole army remaining to our emperor', were destroyed. His underlying conviction thus remained that endangering the army would endanger the continued existence of the state and the dynasty.[22] Often 'distressed and dejected', he knew that many at court opposed this approach, and he expended much of his energy fending off suggestions for offensive action rather than investigating how these actions might have been realised.[23] Unwavering in his assessment of the army's strategic options, however, he persisted in his view, despite the mounting chorus of criticism.

One concern upon which Charles and Stadion agreed was the importance of Russia. Neither placed much hope in Josef Stutterheim's mission to the tsar, and both were deeply alarmed by the Russian occupation of Galicia and Golitsyn's steady, if outwardly cordial, advance west from the San. As Wimpffen expressed in a 20 June memorandum, Austria felt pinched between 'the two colossi pressing towards their mid-point', and, vastly overestimating the degree of Franco-Russian co-operation, even feared that Napoleon might be prodding the Russians towards the Austrian rear and holding back on crossing the Danube a second time to allow the Russians to penetrate more deeply into Habsburg territory.[24] A sense of indignation at having been betrayed and deep suspicion of the tsar's motives heightened this military danger: once lost to the Russians, territory might be impossible to recover. As Franz told Ferdinand, 'the words of the Russian generals may not be quite open and their friendly declarations may not be entirely genuine,' so that they 'could avoid opposition through courteous declarations and place themselves in possession of the greater part of the province without any effort.'[25] Charles was especially concerned for the safety of Teschen and dismayed that the successful capture of Sandomierz had been 'spoiled by the further advances of the Russians.'[26] At the same time, Austria was poorly positioned to offer active opposition to creeping Russian encroachments. The Austrian leadership thus directed Ferdinand 'to gain time' and to suppress the Poles, but 'to carefully avoid collisions with the Russians.'[27] Stadion even authorised Stutterheim to use 'pecuniary means' to influence the Russians commanders.[28] Beyond this general agreement on the significance of the Russian threat, however, the appearance of Golitsyn's corps only occasioned more friction among the senior Austrian leaders. As the desire and pressure to do *something* mounted during June, Stadion and others, frustrated by Charles's inactivity, came to the conclusion that the Russians were a target of opportunity. By the end of the month, they had concocted a plan and acquired Franz's concurrence. Ferdinand, suitably reinforced from the torpid Main Army, was to be given the military weight to use 'an appropriately serious tone' with the Russians and, if necessary, to attack and defeat them.[29] 'The more forbearance and pliability I showed', grumbled Franz, 'the more the pushiness [of the Russians] increased.'[30] Enough was enough—now it was time to act. On 2 July, Charles received an imperial order to detach 12,000–15,000 men to Poland 'as rapidly as possible', as long as he did not plan to undertake something himself within the next several days. Charles found these notions ridiculous: 'No one had the courage to order me to conduct an offensive operation, but I have the order to reinforce our former army of Galicia with 12,000 to 15,000 men. One imagines that the news of the arrival of these reinforcements will stop the Russians!'[31]

Napoleon would have been sardonically amused had he known of these Austrian anxieties and the resultant instructions to the army. For him, as we have seen, Russian inaction was a bitter disappointment, and he had Champagny send a private letter to Caulaincourt in St Petersburg outlining his thoughts. 'The emperor no longer believes in the alliance with Russia,' wrote the foreign minister, directing Caulaincourt to maintain all proper outward appearances so that neither the Russians nor others in Europe would detect the schism Napoleon perceived.[32] To his intimates, however, Napoleon was clear, telling GD Savary in early June: 'I have been duped.'[33] He would project a cordial façade and highlight the threat of Russian advances publicly, but his thinking had undergone an important shift.[34] The Austrians, of course, knew nothing of Napoleon's change of heart vis-à-vis Tsar Alexander. Allowing themselves to be overwhelmed by impatience with the monarchy's situation and resentment towards the army, Stadion and others at court thus impelled Franz to sign the orders detaching a significant body of men to reinforce Ferdinand. As we shall see, this was not the only scheme for detachments foisted upon Charles as June became July. Fortunately for the Generalissimus and the Habsburg dynasty, Napoleon intervened before any of these orders or insinuations could be put into effect.

Consideration of such wild schemes illuminates the profound sense of frustration engendered by Austria's strategic predicament. Habsburg military options were indeed limited. As Hiller had advocated, there may have been a fleeting opportunity immediately after Aspern, but once this had been lost, there were only three realistic offensive possibilities: Krems, Tulln, or Pressburg. Charles, with the greatest reluctance, did issue a 'disposition' on 30 May for a crossing at Pressburg.[35] In another example of the Austrian system's lethargy, a week had already passed since Aspern–Essling, and several more days would have been required to implement these orders.[36] Davout's arrival at Engerau, however, scotched this plan almost before it had been signed. Charles was doubtless deeply relieved. Operating from the assumption that he was badly outnumbered, he saw little to recommend an offensive in any of these locations. He calculated that it would take at least four days to bridge and begin crossing the Danube, and—at least at Krems and Pressburg—the terrain on the south bank offered the French defensive advantages. Most importantly, he estimated that Napoleon would need only two days to cross the Stadtler Arm and be in the Austrian rear on the north bank of the great river. The Hauptarmee might then find itself caught straddling the river with substantial forces trapped on the south bank, while Napoleon was positioned to threaten the roads to Bohemia and Moravia, vital links that the Habsburg commander 'could never lay open to an enemy invasion.'[37] Moreover, Charles knew his army was clumsy in the attack, and he had just witnessed Napoleon fail in the execution of an opposed river crossing. If the great 'Emperor of Battles' and his 'victory-accustomed army' had been repulsed under similar circumstances, reasoned Charles, how could the much less agile Habsburg host and its stultified leadership hope to do better? Weighing all these disadvantages and uncertainties, the archduke concluded that a combination of defence and delay was the best, indeed the only, suitable strategy; a Danube crossing would be 'a gamble where all probability is against success'.[38] 'As for me, my plan is fixed and is that of Fabius against Hannibal,' he noted in a private letter, 'I will risk nothing, as the forces at my disposal are the last remaining to the state.'[39]

In all of this assessing and reassessing, one does not have to look hard to detect Napoleon's psychological domination of his opponent. Charles and his staff ignored all of the difficulties facing the French emperor, and saw him leaping on their flanks and rear at a moment's notice should the Hauptarmee attempt to slip off to its left or right.[40] This psychological ascendancy manifested itself in Charles's distinct aversion to an offensive stroke. 'If ordered, I will pass the Danube, but I believe I will be beaten and he [Franz] and his ministers will pay dearly for their arrogance and impatience,' he told he adoptive uncle. 'If we win a battle the profit will not be very great, if we lose one, all is lost; and is not the latter possibility the more probable if we have to cross the river in the presence of or near an enemy army?'[41] At the same time, he retained confidence in his army's defensive capabilities: 'If the enemy crosses over the Danube, we will probably defeat him.'[42] Given these assumptions, it is hardly surprising that Charles remained north of the Danube, handed the initiative to Napoleon, and waited to see what his foe would do. Still, the French were mystified. 'In the entire French army, accustomed to regard a great battle as the introduction rather than the last act of a grand drama, there was only one opinion concerning the omission we so condemned,' wrote a Saxon officer. 'It was considered incomprehensible.'[43]

With court and headquarters entangled in dispute and indecision at the strategic level, Austrian military operations languished. Charles withdrew most of the army from the river's edge on 25 May to spare the men the pestilential miasma created by the thousands of human and equine corpses that littered the Aspern–Essling battlefield. The I, II, IV, and Reserve Corps thus encamped north and west of the Russbach, while VI Corps and a large 'Advance Guard' under Klenau guarded the banks of the Danube. The Generalissimus left V Corps to watch the river on his right, but called in Kolowrat with most of III Corps and III/*Froon* from Bohemia. He also brought III/*Reuss-Greitz*, the *Blankenstein* Hussars division, and some other small detachments from the Army of Inner Austria, ordered Johann to Pressburg to have him closer at hand, and had a bridgehead built at Marchegg. Furthermore, the army absorbed numerous replacements and incorporated twenty-one Landwehr and volunteer battalions, brigading these in most cases with regular regiments to increase the manpower of the line brigades while lending steadiness to the inexperienced Landwehr units.[44] Charles also had some indifferent earthworks constructed between Stadtlau and Enzersdorf, but largely ignored the eastern face of Lobau Island and did nothing to fortify the army's position in depth.[45] Other than these activities, the pleasant weeks of early summer passed in twice-daily drill, some large formation manoeuvres, and periodic alarms as the Austrians reacted to their own anxieties and imprecise intelligence on the French. Nothing happened, however, and the army spent most of its time with the quotidian business of drilling, digging, and waiting. In his training circulars, Charles stressed the utility of the battalion mass as the basic infantry formation (revealing the continued worry about the superiority of the French mounted arm) with perhaps a 'light chain of skirmishers' if facing enemy infantry. He also instructed his subordinates to keep their artillery in batteries and concentrate its firepower while retaining a suitable ammunition reserve.[46] He seems to have been satisfied with the response to this training, and, by the end of June, claimed he was 'very content with the appearance and spirit of the troops, as well as with their discipline'.[47] Absent from the comfortable monotony of this routine, however, was any thought of disturbing the French in their assiduous efforts to turn Lobau into an unassailable fortress, arsenal, and assembly area.[48]

The Danube No Longer Exists for the French Army

Napoleon, unlike Charles, was his own master. He commanded all the resources of the state and his strategy was firmly fixed on setting the conditions for a new crossing of the Danube to bring the Austrian Hauptarmee to battle and destroy it.

In the first place, he transformed Lobau Island into a vast encampment criss-crossed with orderly roads and equipped with powder magazines, bakeries, food stores, and a hospital. Workshops of every description sprang up to craft the numerous bridges and boats he would need to carry the army across the Stadtler Arm. 'The island of Lobau presented a truly extraordinary sight owing to all the activity; one could say that a city totally dedicated to the works of military industry had appeared as if by enchantment.'[49] The many roads were even illuminated at night by street lamps that reminded the men of Paris. Second, he saw to the island's defence. 'The emperor,' noted one officer, 'profiting from the sort of suspension of hostilities that had occurred since the Battle of Essling, covered the island with fortifications.'[50] He had removed all of the wounded and most of the army as soon as possible after

Aspern, leaving Massena's 4th Corps with responsibility for its defence and organisation. As June progressed, he bolstered the defences by constructing fourteen batteries and arming them with 109 guns and mortars, many of siege calibre; these would not only serve to protect Lobau, they would also support the assault crossing by beating down Austrian artillery and destroying enemy entrenchments.

Third, Napoleon connected Lobau and its associated islands to the south bank by two stout bridges (one of boats, the other on pilings) to the Schneidergrund and three from that island to the Lobgrund. These were protected by an *estacade*, a row of pilings rammed into the Danube's bed to ward off the boats, floating mills, and debris that had repeatedly broken his bridge during Aspern–Essling. Upstream from the *estacade*, French engineers even tried to employ a great chain from Vienna's arsenal that had last been used during the Turkish siege more than a century and a half earlier.[51] The crossings were further fortified with multiple redoubts, redans, and entrenchments that soon arose on the Schneidergrund, on the southern fringe of Lobau, and even on the south bank. Erected under the overall guidance of GD Bertrand, the entire enterprise was a remarkable feat of military engineering that absorbed vast amounts of material and manpower as well as 4,000 wagons and most of the artillery's horses. Wood was plentiful, but cordage and anchors were scarce. The French stripped the region's churches and mills to provide the requisite rope, and scoured as far as Pressburg and Raab for anchors, but still had to resort to all manner of improvisation to fulfil needs that seemed to expand every day. The results of all this effort left a profound impression on contemporaries. A Saxon officer, for example, examining 'the great pier bridge', observed that it 'lacked nothing in sturdiness ... indeed, colourfully painted and equipped with lanterns as it was, it could be called elegant'.[52] Major Vladimir Ivanovich Baron Löwenstern, a former Russian officer who had attached himself to Napoleon's court, commented that 'the preparations that were made were as gigantic as the enterprise itself'.[53] Adding to the requirements, Napoleon created a riverine flotilla under Capitaine de Vaisseau Pierre Baste, newly arrived with two battalions of naval troops. Consisting of ten gunboats and twenty armed pinnaces, the flotilla was intended to intercept destructive material drifting downriver, but also played a useful role in reconnoitring and alarming Austrian pickets on the river's many islands.[54] The flotilla, although innovative and intriguing, was a mere caparison for the true accomplishment: the completion of the bridges. Napoleon could announce with justified pride that 'The Danube no longer exists for the French army: General Count Bertrand has executed works that excite astonishment and inspire admiration.' Comparing the spans with those of Trajan and Caesar, he added: 'The works on the Danube are the finest works of campaign ever constructed.'[55]

But the bridges over the principal channel of the Danube were only one part of the engineering marvel under construction on Lobau Island that summer. Napoleon's plan for the upcoming crossing called for carrying his army across the eastern portion of the Stadtler Arm south of Gross-Enzersdorf. He would then turn north and advance into the Marchfeld with a force of unprecedented size, outflanking the Aspern–Essling line and compelling Charles to accept battle. This concept demanded boats to transfer an adequate advance force across the arm in the initial stages of the assault and, far more challenging from a technical standpoint, a set of partly prefabricated bridges to support a rapid crossing by thousands of men and horses, along with hundreds of guns and other vehicles. The first step was to connect Lobau to the various islands in the Stadtler Arm, as these would serve as posts for batteries and as launching pads for future bridges onto the Marchfeld. Named after French generals to minimise confusion, these islands were, from left to right: St Hilaire (actually a group of islands), the Mühl-Haufen (Ile du Moulin or later Bessières), Espagne, Pouzet, Lannes, and Alexandre. Additionally, Lobau itself was renamed Ile Napoléon. The Mühl-Haufen and Pouzet (Flösserstatt-Haufen) were in Austrian hands, but the French had occupied the others shortly after Aspern, tied them

Table 11: French Danube Flotilla, 26 June 1809

Vessel	Number	Armament	Crew
Marengo	1	3 x 3-pdrs	30
Lodi	2	1 x 4-pdr	25
Jena	3	1 x 6-pdr	30
Montebello	4	4 x 8-pdr	50
St Hilaire	5	1 x howitzer, 3 x 6-pdrs	40
Eckmuhl	6	1 x 6-pdr	30
Montenotte	7	1 x 6-pdr	30
Dego	8	1 x 6-pdr	30
Rivoli	9	3 x 3-pdrs	30
Arcole	10	1 x 3-pdr	25

Twenty smaller armed boats also patrolled the river.

Source: Buat, vol. II, p. 407.

to Lobau with bridges, and busily fortified them with artillery batteries as June progressed. To make the jump across the arm from the eastern face of Lobau, Napoleon ordered the preparation of four bridges that could be emplaced in a relatively short time between Ile Alexandre and the point where the Stadtler Arm spilled out into the Danube. All of these represented significant challenges, but one, an articulated, 'single-piece' structure, was a technical masterpiece that was intended to float down from its concealed construction site behind Ile Alexandre and snap into place in a matter of minutes. Conducted behind a screen of trees, all of the work involved in assembling these bridges, though noisy, was invisible to the Austrian pickets across the water and offered no hint as to the intended points of attack.[56]

The contrast with his Habsburg opponents is striking. Where the French built their own boats and bridges, the Austrians complained that none were to be found. Where the French stripped Vienna's arsenals of heavy cannon to arm the batteries on Lobau Island, the Austrians never made a serious effort to bring down any of the siege pieces from the Bohemian and Moravian fortresses to buttress the firepower of their defences. Nor did they endeavour to capture any of the French-held islands in the Stadtler Arm. Had Charles exerted the energy to place a combination of siege guns, field guns, howitzers, and mortars in well-protected, carefully sited batteries along the banks of the Stadtler Arm and on several of these islands, it is difficult to see how the French could have continued to maintain themselves on Lobau, let alone engage in their massive construction projects.[57]

Beyond the immediate environs of Vienna, Napoleon's priorities were rebuilding his army, removing threats to his flanks, drawing as many troops as possible to the intended crossing area, and securing his line of communications back to France. The six-week pause between Aspern and Wagram made the first of these tasks relatively straightforward. Replacements were incorporated (at least 32,705 of all arms), equipment repaired and replaced, horses procured, and ammunition restocked.[58] Everyone rested and, if rations were not as regular as might have been desired, the troops were soon in fine spirits. Napoleon reviewed many, if not most of the regiments and the replacement detachments personally, distributing rewards, examining equipment, questioning soldiers, testing officers. One Guard artillery officer was astonished to be quizzed about a particular 12-pounder whose deficiencies Napoleon had noted during some previous review.[59] 'Every day I presented the battalions or march regiments,' remembered GD Dumas. 'The emperor reviewed them with minute attention and indicated to me their destination and that of the young officers who had come from the schools.'[60]

The heavy losses among senior generals at Aspern necessitated some organisational shifts, the most prominent being the elevation of Oudinot to command 2nd Corps. At the division level, GD Charles Louis Dieudonné Grandjean took the much-lamented St Hilaire's post, Jean Toussaint Arrighi de Casanova replaced Espagne, Jacques Pierre Puthod assumed Demont's command, and Bernard Frère received Claparède's division. To address the numerical superiority of the Austrian artillery at Aspern and the qualitative decline evident in some of the French infantry, Napoleon returned to the old practice of issuing cannon to the infantry regiments. This expedient was not an ideal solution but it was cheaper and, above all, faster than creating new artillery batteries to increase the army's overall complement of guns. Following a series of decrees in late May and early June, each infantry regiment or demi-brigade of the 2nd, 3rd, and 4th Corps was to form an artillery detachment to man two small guns (3- or 4-pounders) drawn from the seemingly inexhaustible Viennese arsenals.[61] This measure added sixty-six pieces to the army's artillery, an arm Napoleon augmented further by enlarging the Guard artillery to sixty guns and by increasing the batteries assigned to the corps as much as time and resources would allow.[62] These tasks, and innumerable others, fell to the army's new artillery chief, GD Jean Ambroise Baston, Comte de Lariboisière, who replaced Songis after illness forced the latter to return to Paris.

While Charles temporised, vacillated, considered, and reconsidered; while the Habsburg court pursued military fantasies; Napoleon deployed the full range of his personal energy, military talent, and imperial authority. Moreover, he transmitted this impulse to all ranks, creating a level of earnest industry on the French side of the Danube that was enormous, focused, and all-encompassing. 'The emperor worked continuously and everyone followed his example,' commented Savary, while Löwenstern observed that 'the activity deployed for this enterprise surpassed anything that one could imagine.'[63] Or, as a French civilian official noted in his diary on 12 June: 'His Majesty works a great deal. I believe he is preparing a dance for the Austrians the likes of which they have never seen before.'[64]

Securing the Line of Communications

We have seen the importance the emperor attached to clearing his strategic right flank and ensuring that the Armies of Italy and Dalmatia were available for the next major battle. He also took careful steps to protect his strategic left while simultaneously positioning additional troops within marching distance of Lobau. This entailed a steady eastward shift of the German units stationed in the Danube valley during June. Leaving Rouyer's Rheinbund division at Passau to anchor one end of the river line, he pulled Marshal Lefebvre out of the Tyrol with the 1st and 2nd Bavarian Divisions to garrison Linz and the area as far east as Ybbs (thus leaving Deroy isolated at Innsbruck); Vandamme's Württemberg contingent picked up the chain at Melk and covered the river all the way to Vienna. This was a thin shield indeed, so Napoleon posted the Saxons of Bernadotte's 9th Corps around St Pölten, where they could serve as a general reserve, but would also be close enough to participate in the coming engagement. Furthermore, he had in mind the notion of bringing Wrede's 2nd Division from Linz in time for the battle, a desire that would lead to an epic march on the part of the Bavarians. Smaller units also joined the host around Vienna. In addition to the two naval battalions, the Nassauers of Rouyer's 2nd Rheinbund Regiment were brought in to strengthen Vienna's garrison, while the yellow-coated men of the Neuchâtel Battalion (from Berthier's principality) and the 1st Provisional Chasseurs were incorporated into Imperial Headquarters. These carefully conceived strategic arrangements frequently meant long marches and privations for the men involved, as Lieutenant Alexis Mathieu of the Naval Artificer Battalion wrote in a letter home on reaching Vienna: 'From Passau to here we have experienced what it means to be at war, we considered ourselves lucky after making ten or even twelve leagues to have a morsel of biscuit and some fresh straw so we would not have to sleep on the earth.'[65]

These movements were also, of course, related to securing the line of communications back to Strasbourg. Both sides continually tested and harassed each other along the great river. The Saxons, for instance, were mortified to lose sixty-two prisoners to an Austrian raiding party in Amstetten on the night of 31 May/1 June when the officer in charge of the advance guard neglected basic security measures. Additionally, bands of angry Austrian civilians sometimes attacked foraging detachments and quartering parties, inciting vengeful reprisals by the Allied troops. 'When we came to the farmhouses, we found there murdered Saxons buried in straw or dung with their clothing and weapons,' wrote Private Christian Friedrich Frenzel of *Prinz Maximillian* Infantry. 'The peasants and inhabitants had done that. Revenge ignited the farmsteads.'[66] Cross-river raids, ambuscades, cannonades, patrols, and alarms thus punctuated the daily routine. Both sides, however, were thin on the ground, and all of this activity distracted neither Napoleon nor Charles from his principal concern—though the

Austrians seem to have entertained exaggerated estimates of the potential threat posed by the French and their allies.[67]

Napoleon's line of communications, however, extended far beyond Passau, and he instituted comprehensive arrangements to protect his vital link to Strasbourg. The threats to this long lifeline were potentially significant. Napoleon's German allies were not only vulnerable to raids from Tyrolian and Vorarlberg insurgents, but Austrian regulars could launch forays from Bohemia, Prussia might join the conflict (though Napoleon considered this unlikely), and Britain might land troops in Holland or northern Germany. Furthermore, these exogeneous forces might ignite rebellion inside the Rheinbund states. The emperor was cognisant of these dangers, but considered them manageable and was determined not to divert major regular forces to combat them. He would meet the twin challenges of raids and rebellions with a combination of second-line troops and deception.

The forces available in Germany by late May were a variegated lot.[68] In the north, GM Johann von Ewald commanded an independent brigade of Danish troops on that kingdom's southern border between Hamburg and Lübeck, while the Dutch and Westphalian divisions of King Jerome Bonaparte's 10th Corps were scattered in posts from the North Sea to Kassel and Magdeburg. Jerome was also responsible for the fortress garrisons in Prussia and the untried Mecklenburg and Oldenburg contingents. Most of the Saxon troops left behind in that kingdom after the departure of 9th Corps would soon come under his orders as well. Farther west, Marshal Kellermann had the 'Corps d'Observation de l'Elbe' at Hanau and GD Beaumont was assembling his reserve division at Augsburg to support the units that Bavaria, Baden, and Württemberg had committed to defending their southern borders against the depredations of Tyrolian and Vorarlberg raiders.

Though they might have seemed impressive on paper, all of these formations suffered from potentially debilitating weaknesses in quantity and quality. In terms of numbers, there were simply not enough men under arms. Even with their full complements of troops, Kellermann, Jerome, Beaumont, and other commanders would have difficulty accomplishing their missions if especially grave challenges developed, particularly if those challenges arose simultaneously. Moreover, weeks would pass before these forces attained their assigned strengths. Despite continuous effort, for instance, by early June, Kellermann could only muster 8,400 of his 14,000 men.[69] Similarly, Beaumont, with 6,300 rather than the 10,000 Napoleon had expected, complained to Berthier: 'Your Grace . . . believes me much stronger than I am.'[70] Likewise, Danzig and the other eastern fortresses had far too few men for proper garrisons.[71] Problems with numbers were compounded by serious questions of quality. With the exception of the Dutch and a few German regiments, all of Napoleon's line of communications troops were inexperienced conscripts. Many of Kellermann's were recruits of the rawest variety. Formed into new units with too few officers, they were 'far from having the cohesion or capacity to face the enemy', and had to learn the most fundamental basics of soldiering.[72] Additionally, Napoleon was concerned about the loyalty of some of his German troops and repeatedly adjured his subordinates to monitor the behaviour of certain allied contingents.[73]

To intimidate potential troublemakers and to mask the weaknesses of his reserve forces Napoleon relied heavily on deception. He instructed his subordinates to exaggerate the number of available troops, and he equipped the higher commands with exalted titles, such as 'Army of the Reserve' and 'Army of Observation of the Elbe' when the actual sizes of these formations warranted at best the designation 'corps'. In addition to employing gossip and rumour, newspapers carried stories of these forces every few days to keep them in the public eye.[74] In at least some cases, these measures were effective. The frustrated Oberst von Steigentesch, for example, complained that the Prussians talked of Kellermann, 'a spectre before whom all quake', as if he 'were already in Berlin or advancing on the Oder'. They credited him with a powerful force and feared he was in Erfurt, perhaps already united with Westphalian, Dutch, and Danish troops to pose a direct threat to their unhappy kingdom.[75]

Raids and Rebellions

Though the quality of Napoleon's reserve formations was questionable, some of them had already seen action by the time Steigentesch was making his lugubrious reports.

The first challenge in central Germany came before the war had even begun. An angry and hot-headed former Prussian officer named Friedrich von Katte, inspired by covert contacts with the Tugendbund (the League of Virtue, a pan-German nationalist movement), hoped to capture the fortress of Magdeburg by surprise to spark 'a general explosion'.[76] He crossed the Elbe at Havelberg on 2 April and led approximately 300 followers towards the city the next evening, but was intercepted by a patrol of Westphalian National Guards. His band dispersed after a brief scuffle, and Katte, pursued by Prussian authorities, fled to Bohemia where he would later join the Duke of Brunswick's free-corps.

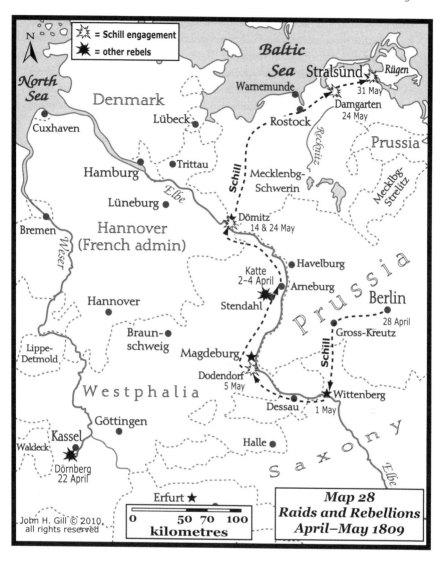

Map 28
Raids and Rebellions
April–May 1809

More serious, but equally ineffectual, was an abortive anti-Westphalian uprising instigated by Oberst Wilhelm Freiherr von Dörnberg, the commander of the Westphalian Garde-Jäger Battalion. Dörnberg was also a member of the Tugendbund and, hoping for assistance from Prussian and Austrian forces, he assembled a broad-based group of dissidents from within Westphalian society. Beyond a vague notion of seizing King Jerome and his French generals, however, the group's plans were nebulous and their organisation patchy. When Dörnberg and his fellow conspirators called the people of Hesse to arms on the morning of 22 April (as Napoleon was marching to roll up Rosenberg's IV Corps at Eggmühl), some 4,000–5,000 prospective insurrectionists assembled south of Kassel, while 1,200 collected to the west, and another 4,000 or so gathered north-west of the capital. Fortunately for Jerome, his newly constructed army remained loyal. Some individuals defected, but the majority of the officers reaffirmed their oaths to the king and faithfully led detachments against the rebels on the morning of the 23rd. The flightiness of the rebels was a further boon: many slipped away after the first flush of excitement had dissipated. The band from the south, rowdy, undisciplined, inebriated, and more or less led by Dörnberg himself, 'came up the highway in dense bunches, not ordered but wildly disorganised, screaming, and yelling and firing their guns in the air'. One volley sufficed to disperse this 'mob' and 'sabring cavalry completed the defeat'.[77] The other two groups of would-be rebels suffered similar fates, and by evening the attempt had collapsed. Dörnberg fled to Bohemia disguised in an old coat borrowed from a friend.[78]

The most renowned episode in central Germany during 1809 was the ride of Prussian Major Ferdinand von Schill. Schill had acquired celebrity status for his role in the defence of Kolberg in 1807, a time when Prussia was desperate for heroes. Fervidly patriotic, excitable, and prone to wishful thinking, he seems to have succumbed to the thrill of popular adulation. No doubt the promptings of eager Tugendbund conspirators—'bold hot-heads ... who overestimated the power of his name', said a friend—and the thrum of expectation that pervaded the air in Berlin in early 1809 fired his imagination as well.[79] Enclosed within a hothouse of anti-French sentiment, corresponding with Katte and Dörnberg, and drawing on his own experience as a reckless partisan raider in 1807, Schill became convinced that all Germany was yearning to rise against Napoleon and that his own talisman name was the banner to which all would rally. News of the Austrian invasion of Bavaria brought emotions to a feverish pitch. Schill decided to act.

Schill commanded the 2nd Brandenburg Hussars garrisoned in Berlin. On 28 April, he led his regiment out of the Prussian capital on the pretext of conducting manoeuvres. Once safely outside the city, he announced to his men, as one officer remembered, that 'The moment has arrived, the favourable time, where they could avenge the fatherland's oppression and shame against the hated foe.' 'The Austrians have already won a victory,' he assured them, and 'Westphalia would be ready to rise up as soon as liberators show

Table 12: Schill's Command, 31 May 1809

In Stralsund	1,490 total
Infantry battalion (4 companies)	300
Rügen Landwehr (battalion)	300
2nd Brandenburg Hussars (4 squadrons)	350
Mounted Jäger (1 squadron)	80
Uhlans (three squadrons)	200
Artillery	60
Former Swedish soldiers (assisting artillery)	200

On Rügen Island
400 poorly armed, poorly organised infantry

Other
A lieutenant and 40 cavalry, detached from Dömitz, escaped to Prussia.
Approximately 270 men sailed to Prussia from Warnemünde.
Another 80 or so were captured by Danes while trying to flee to Sweden.

Source: Ollech, vol. I, p. 36.

themselves.'[80] Most of the troopers received their commander's passionate words with enthusiasm and the regiment set off on what became a long and fateful ride. From his contacts with Katte, Dörnberg, and a host of other disgruntled Westphalians, Schill concluded that the new kingdom was ripe for rebellion and he made for Magdeburg to ignite what he believed to be the dry tinder of patriotic anger. He quickly learned, however, that GD Claude Michaud, the French commandant of the fortress, was aware of his march and had blocked passage of the river. Forced to detour, Schill and his men passed the Elbe at Wittenberg on 1 May but had to hasten out of Saxony with the *Zastrow* Cuirassiers at their heels. They received a warmer reception in Dessau and headed for Magdeburg, collecting a few recruits and confiscating some horses and cash on the way. They encountered a small force sent by Michaud at Dodendorf on 5 May and won a tactical victory over the mixed French and Westphalian detachment. Schill's losses, however, were more than he could afford (eighty-two out of a total of between 550 and 650), especially as the countryside was not rising spontaneously and Magdeburg, a powerful fortress, was clearly alert to his presence. Moreover, he now knew that Dörnberg had failed, that the Austrians had suffered a defeat in Bavaria, and that the Prussian government was demanding his immediate return for appropriate punishment.[81] With these considerations in mind, he bypassed Magdeburg and took his band to Arneburg, where he arrived on 8 May. He spent nearly a week there, resting, recruiting, patrolling, organising, and arguing with some of his officers over the band's next moves.

When Schill finally departed on the 13th, he had a considerably larger force. The new recruits included serving regulars (such as an entire Prussian light infantry company that had deserted to join him) and some veterans, but too many were ne'er-do-wells, 'people of most dubious morality', in the words of one officer.[82] 'Thrown together indiscriminately from all the nations of Europe—even prisons—the majority [of the newcomers] knew no other purpose than robbery and plunder,' so that, for many observers, the command more resembled a collection of bandits than the advance guard of a liberating army.[83] Nonetheless, Schill captured the little Mecklenburg-Schwerin fortress of Dömitz on 14 May, spending several more days there in organising and deliberating before striking north for Stralsund on the 18th.[84] Leaving about 400 men to hold Dömitz, he intimidated his way into Rostock (22 May), scattered the Mecklenburg-Schwerin troops who tried to block his passage of the Recknitz at Damgarten (24 May), and overwhelmed the small French garrison of Stralsund on the 25th.[85] Determined to turn the city into 'a second Saragossa', he recruited more men, made some efforts to improve Stralsund's defences, wrote to Archduke Charles for help, and vainly attempted to contact the Royal Navy.[86]

Schill's march triggered a storm of panic in Kassel, especially because Jerome and his officials initially took at face value Schill's brash claim to be the vanguard of an army of 13,000, or even 30,000, commanded by the venerable Marshal Blücher himself. The conviction that 'such hostilities could not be committed without at least the tacit consent' of the Prussian government heightened the anxiety in the Westphalian court and convinced many that larger Prussian forces *must* be looming on the far side of the Elbe.[87] Jerome immediately appealed to Kellermann for assistance and the optical telegraph was soon busy transmitting messages to Clarke, the Minister of War in Paris, and through him to the emperor.[88] It was mid-May and Napoleon was in Vienna, focused on getting his army across the Danube in what would become the prelude to the Battle of Aspern. He had no patience for this nonsense out of Germany. Clarke's preliminary orders to begin moving troops and calling out the National Guards thus earned everyone a stiff imperial rebuke. 'The idea that Prussia would declare war is folly,' he wrote, adding that Kellermann 'will not dispose of a single battalion without my orders if it is not for the defence of Mainz or of my frontiers'.[89] Furthermore he reiterated that Kellermann, on threat of relief from command, was to divert to his own corps nothing that was destined for the main army, 'neither troops, nor artillery, nor military equipment'.[90] Jerome would have to rely on his own resources.

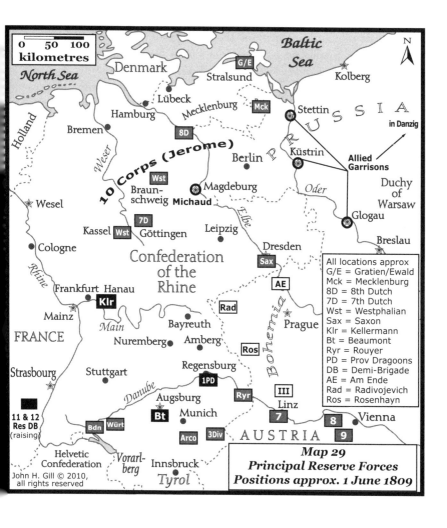

Map 29
*Principal Reserve Forces
Positions approx. 1 June 1809*

All locations approx
G/E = Gratien/Ewald
Mck = Mecklenburg
8D = 8th Dutch
7D = 7th Dutch
Wst = Westphalian
Sax = Saxon
Klr = Kellermann
Bt = Beaumont
Ryr = Rouyer
PD = Prov Dragoons
DB = Demi-Brigade
AE = Am Ende
Rad = Radivojevich
Ros = Rosenhayn

These resources proved more than enough, given the size of Schill's band and the meagre response he received from various German populations who might greet him with cheers, but seldom joined his ranks. While sending part of his Guard to Halle, Jerome, in his capacity as 10th Corps commander, called GD Gratien's Dutch division down from Hamburg. Gratien initially swung south to Göttingen to protect Kassel, but as the situation clarified and the actual menace posed by Schill's men assumed more reasonable proportions, he turned north-east in pursuit of the raiders, reaching the Elbe opposite Dömitz on 18 May. The 8th Infantry remained behind there with GB Philippe de Rivet, Comte d'Albignac and a Westphalian brigade, while Gratien marched on Lüneburg with the bulk of the division (7th Infantry and the foot battery were left in Göttingen).[91] Meanwhile, Ewald had received orders from his king 'to treat the Schill corps as enemies' and 'to support our allies'.[92] He began co-ordinating with Gratien at once, and the two generals met at Trittau, near where Ewald had concentrated his brigade on 24 May. That same day, as Schill was defeating the Mecklenburgers at Damgarten, d'Albignac opened a bombardment of Dömitz and sent the Grenadier Company of II/8th across the Elbe in boats; the Schill detachment in the little fortress wisely decided to withdraw and, barely escaping the pursuing Dutch, reached Rostock on the evening of the 25th.[93] Schill's adventure, however, was about to end. Although d'Albignac remained at Dömitz, Gratien and Ewald marched quickly towards Stralsund, arriving outside the city on the morning of 31 May with a combined strength of some 5,270 infantry and cavalry. Gratien successfully deceived Schill concerning the point of attack, but the assaulting units—6th and 9th Dutch Infantry and II/Oldenborg—had to charge three times before the defenders broke.'As we had orders to give no quarter', wrote a grenadier of I/9, 'all those in front of us were either sabred or shot so that we were forced to climb over the bodies of the dead and wounded who were piled on top of one another.'[94] Bursting into the city, the Dutch and Danes prevailed in a short, bitter street fight, killing 300–400 of Schill's men and capturing 568 for a loss of 68 Danes and 173 Dutch. Schill himself was among the dead. 'Stralsund has been taken by storm,' reported Ewald, 'the work of an hour and a half was hard, the misfortune of the city is great, Schill is dead, we had tough fighting in all the streets, which are covered with dead.'[95] 'Schill is dead and well dead,' wrote Gratien to Jerome.[96] Although 400–500 of the 'Schill'schen' escaped to Prussia to join 270 of their comrades who had fled by boat, the revolt was thus extinguished. 'The grand plan that he intended to execute with success exceeded his powers,' noted one of his men.[97] As Schill's spirit rode off into history and German national mythology, however, Gratien and Ewald marched back west to attend to more practical and immediate problems.[98]

Bohemia: Meaningful Diversions

In addition to internal rebellions and raids from renegade Prussians, Napoleon and his allies had to contend with diversionary expeditions launched by their principal enemy, Austria. These forays were the outcome of the strategic struggle between Charles and Stadion. The minister, clinging to the hope of a massive German uprising and trying to goad the army into doing something, was an avid advocate of sending strong detachments into central Germany. The Generalissimus, focused on the Danube and hopes of negotiations, found these operations fatuous and claimed he had to be ordered twice before he would send instructions to GdK Riesch, the commandant in Bohemia.[99] The archduke's reluctance notwithstanding, orders went to Riesch in late May, and that general promptly issued his own to his two subordinates, GM Am Ende and GM Radivojevich:

> In the hope that the complete victory gained over the Emperor Napoleon on 22 May will arouse the most advantageous sensation in northern Germany and to promote this sensation even more, His Imperial Highness the Generalissimus orders the conduct of meaningful diversions towards the Kingdom of Saxony and the Principality of Bayreuth with the greatest possible exertion of all available troops and forces in Bohemia.[100]

'All available troops and forces', however, did not amount to much. Am Ende and Radivojevich had been left behind with a defensive mission of guarding Bohemia's borders as the tide of war swept down the Danube towards Vienna in late April. Each had little more than two battalions and two squadrons of regulars, supplemented by several battalions of questionable Landwehr. 'The uniforms, arms, training, and discipline of these Landwehr were only adequate for limited demands,' observed a Brunswick officer, 'I have never seen an infantry that marched more clumsily or poorly.'[101]

Am Ende was also saddled with two semi-independent free-corps. The 'Legion of Vengeance' or 'Black Corps' of the dispossessed Friedrich Wilhelm Herzog von Braunschweig-Lüneburg-Oels (Duke of Brunswick) wore black uniforms and adorned themselves with death's head symbols.

Comprising two small infantry battalions, an incomplete hussar regiment, and a battery, the legion included a number of trained professionals, but 'too many drunkards, marauders, and other do-nothings', in the words of one of their officers.[102] Discipline was lax and combat effectiveness dubious, leading Am Ende to complain that the Brunswickers were 'indulging themselves day and night' with drink, and corrupting the Austrian troops. The small collection of men supposedly serving the deposed Kurfürst Wilhelm I of Hesse-Kassel was worse. 'There is not the least subordination among the Hessians, rather a total anarchy,' wrote the exasperated Am Ende.[103] Radivojevich did not have these liabilities, but his command was even smaller: 4,400 men compared to 8,550 under Am Ende. Nor did the commanders escape contemporary censure. 'One could not have made a more unfortunate choice than this general,' remarked one of Brunswick's officers of Am Ende, while another commented that 'the general's physiognomy, his great belly, in short his entire outward appearance did not make the most favourable impression on us.'[104] One of Am Ende's staff officers lamented that 'his extreme caution, his fear of responsibility' did not suit him for independent command.[105] Stadion derided Am Ende as a cautious pedant and objected that Radivojevich, though charged with winning hearts and minds in Bayreuth, could not communicate intelligently in German.[106] Extremely restrictive orders to stay close to the Elbe and to protect Theresienstadt only heightened Am Ende's native caution.[107]

On the Saxon side of the border were feeble fortress garrisons and a tiny mobile force of depot troops (approximately 1,540 men) left behind when 9th Corps marched off to the Danube valley in mid-April. Operating from Dresden under command of the energetic, aggressive, and ambitious Oberst Johann Adolf von Thielmann, the mobile force was reinforced in April by the excellent *Zastrow* Cuirassier Regiment from Danzig—just in time to chase off Schill—and, on 14 May, GM von Dyherrn arrived at Torgau with his detachment from Poland.[108] These reinforcements were most timely because the restless Duke of Brunswick was poking at the Saxon border defences. Thielmann was equally restless and eager for glory. During a probe into Bohemia, he ambushed a Brunswick patrol near Nollendorf on 25 May (only its leader—the luckless Katte—escaped), and had the better of the Austrians in an ensuing skirmish. Violent but indecisive skirmishing also erupted at Zittau on 30 May after Brunswick's men occupied the town, but both sides withdrew the following day.[109]

This inconsequential border sparring excited new fears in Kassel as anxious Saxon couriers rode in bearing exaggerated rumours—tales including

Blücher again, with 10,000–15,000 Prussians. Campaigning did not begin in earnest, however, until 9 and 10 June when Am Ende, having cajoled most of his Landwehr into joining the expedition, crossed the border into Saxony. The Saxons, knowing themselves to be badly outnumbered, evacuated Dresden on the 10th, and the Austrians duly occupied the Saxon capital the following day. A lively skirmish flared during the night of 11/12 June when the pugnacious Thielmann sent a detachment probing back towards the city. The fighting dragged on into a daylong rear guard action as Thielmann withdrew to Wilsdruff before a mixed force of light troops led by Brunswick. To the duke's anger and disgust, Am Ende failed to provide timely support and the Saxons fell back towards Nossen with a loss of perhaps 100 men.[110] Though the day thus ended with a small success for the Austro-Brunswick troops, the simmering friction between Am Ende and Brunswick led both commanders to write to Riesch in Prague and Charles in Wagram: the duke accused the

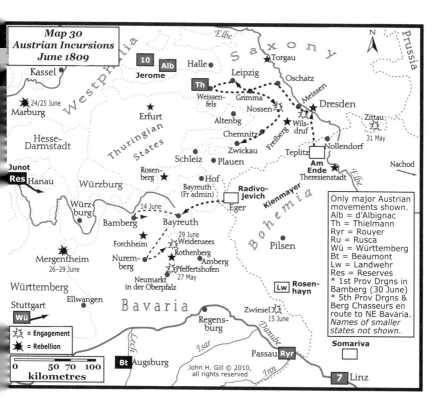

Map 30
Austrian Incursions
June 1809

Only major Austrian movements shown.
Alb = d'Albignac
Th = Thielmann
Ryr = Rouyer
Ru = Rusca
Wü = Württemberg
Bt = Beaumont
Lw = Landwehr
Res = Reserves
* 1st Prov Drgns in Bamberg (30 June)
* 5th Prov Drgns & Berg Chasseurs en route to NE Bavaria.
Names of smaller states not shown.

= Engagement
= Rebellion

0 50 70 100
kilometres

John H. Gill © 2010,
all rights reserved

general of lethargy, while Am Ende deplored gross excesses committed by the Brunswick troops. In response, Charles sternly rebuked Brunswick for the indiscipline of 'a swarm of people who at the moment have no fatherland', and appointed a dynamic overall commander for the northern diversions.[111] This step, to remedy a lacuna from the start, sent FML Kienmayer towards Saxony to bring unity to Am Ende's and Radivojevich's operations and to exercise tighter control over the troublesome free-corps.

Riesch, meanwhile, authorised Am Ende to accede to Brunswick's insistent demand for a march on Leipzig. Brunswick had moved to Meissen with the combined advance guard on the 14th and had been fuming with impatience ever since.[112] The hesitant Am Ende finally moved on 19 June. Having deposited a substantial garrison in Dresden and covered his left with flanking detachments at Wilsdruff and Freiberg, he joined Brunswick in Meissen and marched via Oschatz and Grimma to enter Leipzig on the 22nd, after skirmishing with Thielmann's command outside the city.[113] King Friedrich August, who had removed his court to Leipzig on 13 June, fled to Frankfurt and the Saxon troops retired on Weissenfels. The Austro-Brunswick force followed on the 23rd, but soon learned that Westphalian GB d'Albignac had arrived and that both Jerome and Gratien were en route. This was too much for Am Ende. Feeling uncertain and vulnerable, he ordered a retreat. The Austro-Brunswick force thus departed Leipzig on the evening of 24 June, despite the Black Duke's strenuous protests.

The Allies were indeed approaching, albeit perhaps not as rapidly as they might have done. Mid-June found Jerome's 10th Corps quite scattered after the pursuit of Schill: the Guard in Kassel, d'Albignac in Brunswick (Braunschweig), and Gratien en route for Magdeburg. It took some time to gather all of these troops, especially given the immature state of the Westphalian army and the inexperience of many of its generals. Although the army held much promise and had withstood domestic insurrection thus far, it was still a very incomplete institution in June 1809. Many of the men were absolutely new to uniform (especially that of the freshly baked kingdom), many officers were unqualified, staff work was often shoddy in the extreme, essentials such as flints and kettles were in short supply, and Jerome, though not lacking talents, tended towards indolence and inattention. He was not the man to take the army in hand and lead it firmly but carefully on its first campaign. Nonetheless, the very size of the forces descending on Am Ende—some 13,440 infantry and cavalry all told—made 10th Corps formidable, and d'Albignac marched with credible celerity—eighty kilometres in three days—to join Thielmann at Weissenfels on 23 June. The two now set out to pursue the retiring Austrians and caught up with Am Ende near Nossen on the 27th. Although the Allies (after clumsy Westphalian deployment) seemed prepared to attack, d'Albignac received orders to await Gratien, and the potential engagement devolved into a long, but inconsequential, cannonade.[114]

Kienmayer arrived that night in Austrian headquarters with the 3rd Tscha-slau and a new plan. While Am Ende withdrew to Dresden and protected the approaches to Theresienstadt, Kienmayer would take half of the command to Bayreuth to threaten Napoleon's line of communications. This division of the invading force took place on 28 June and, unhindered by the Allies, the Austrians and their confederates marched off to the west and south to arrive in Zwickau on 1 July. Am Ende did not believe he could defend Dresden and retired to Nollendorf (Naklerov), leaving the city open for Jerome. The Westphalian king, with his army and his travelling court, had made a grand entrance into Leipzig on 26 June and could not resist repeating the performance with extra flourishes as he rode into the Saxon capital on 1 July. Thielmann had entered the previous evening to 'the loudest and most indubitable jubilation of the people', but Am Ende was left undisturbed and Kienmayer's column was not pursued.[115] Only the two cuirassier regiments and two French infantry companies were sent west and these turned north to Leipzig on reaching Altenburg.[116] Leaving Jerome and his cavalcade of soldiers, comedians, courtesans, and courtiers to enjoy the splendours of Dresden, we must now turn our attention to FML Radivojevich and his incursion into Bayreuth.

Radivojevich had departed Eger on 9 June and entered Bayreuth on the 13th.[117] A former Prussian territory, the principality and its eponymous capital had been under direct French administration since 1806, and the populace generally welcomed the Austrians. 'We have been received in Bayreuth with open arms', wrote Radivojevich to Am Ende, 'and I cannot praise enough the good spirit of the entire population.'[118] Ensconcing himself in the city, Radivojevich issued stirring proclamations, developed an active propaganda machine, and launched raids into Bavarian territory. One raiding party burned Bamberg on 14 June, while the largest of these—two battalions, seventy uhlans, two guns—entered Nuremberg on the 26th, causing great alarm for the Bavarian authorities. The Austrians, however, evacuated the city on the night of 27/28 June on learning that GD Jean Delaroche was approaching from Regensburg with a column comprising 1st Provisional Dragoons, 225 Bavarian depot infantry, and a cannon.[119] The Austrians foiled Delaroche's attempt to ambush them near Weidensees on the morning of the 29th, but lost both of their guns in the process.[120] They returned to Bayreuth on 30 June, while the French and Bavarians retired to Forchheim. As their detachments wandered the countryside, the Austrians also endeavoured to raise a volunteer 'Franconian Legion' from the supposedly sympathetic inhabitants of Bayreuth. This effort, enthusiastically pursued by Major Johann Karl Georg von Nostitz-Jänckendorf (an expatriate Prussian officer), met with indifferent success: only eighty-six volunteers were recruited during the first eight days in Bayreuth and the 'legion' never numbered more than 500 men.[121]

The Allied reaction to Radivojevich's incursion was fourfold. First, based on Bavarian fortresses and depots in the area, local French and Bavaria troops marched out to contain the Austrian raiders. In addition to Delaroche's intervention, garrisons from Forchheim and Rosenberg operated east of Bamberg for a few days, squabbling with Austrian patrols before returning to their fortresses on the 21st. Second, King Max Josef ordered the establishment of a northern border brigade on 25 June. This was part of a new plan that evolved during June to bolster Bavaria's home defence forces in the face of the threats from its southern, and now from its eastern frontiers. Comprehensive directives thus called for accelerating the formation of the six reserve battalions ordered in April and for the creation of six more to bring the total to twelve.[122] Third, Württemberg was also threatened by Radivojevich's appearance in Bayreuth, and King Friedrich pulled together an observation corps of 4,285 at Ellwangen to shield the eastern borders of his realm. As we shall see, this contributed to the resurgence of the Vorarlberg rebellion. Finally, the French reserve corps slowly collecting around Hanau received orders to march east. The corps was now under GD Jean-Andoche Junot, who arrived in Hanau on 26 June (Kellermann was shifted to command several administrative 'military divisions' in eastern France). Junot found only one division (GD Olivier Rivaud de la Raffinière's) even remotely ready for combat, but he moved out promptly on the 28th with Rivaud's two brigades, 6th Provisional Dragoons, and twelve guns, in all some 5,500 men. This force reached Würzburg on 2 July. By this time, Delaroche was in Bamberg (from 30 June) with 1st Provisional Dragoons and 200 Bavarians; he also had 5th Provisional Dragoons in Forchheim, and had ordered the Berg Chasseur Regiment to ride to Nuremberg. Though King Friedrich refused his requests for assistance, Junot was thus beginning to assemble a sizeable command in eastern Bavaria as June closed.[123]

Further south, Landwehr under Oberst Gustav von Rosenhayn connected Radivojevich to the Habsburg forces observing Linz.[124] Though their mission was primarily defensive, they several times sallied out of Bohemia to unsettle the Bavarians and to menace Passau, a key link in Napoleon's supply chain. Dupas, the senior local commander, responded by dispatching a company of Weimar light infantry from the 4th Rheinbund (120 men), a company

Table 13: Württemberg Observation Corps, Late June/Early July 1809

Crown Prince Friedrich Wilhelm
1st Brigade: GM Prinz Paul

Horse Guards	(4)	458
Foot Guards	(1)	623
Prinz Friedrich Infantry Regiment	(2)	1,212
Artillery: 3 x 6-pdrs, 1 x howitzer		
2nd Brigade: GM von Scheler		
1st Depot Battalion Boxberg	(1)	648
2nd Depot Battalion Berndes	(1)	682
Land-Battalion Stuttgart	(1)	(in rear)
Land-Battalion Heilbronn	(1)	662
Artillery: 3 x 6-pdrs, 1 x howitzer		
Total		4,285

Assembled around Ellwangen, strengths as of 4 July.

Source: HStAS, E270aBü99 and 113, E270bBü69.

of Bavarians (102 men), and twenty-one French hussars to Zwiesel on 8 June. In a minute but sparkling little action, this tiny detachment defeated a foray by some 620 Landwehr on the 15th. This small success sufficed to chastise Rosenhayn and, other than some skirmishing on 26 June, the Allied detachment was untroubled to the end of the month. By then, GD François Bourcier had replaced Dupas, and the garrison had been strengthened by the arrival of three squadrons of 5th Provisional Dragoons.[125]

In all of this activity, however, Napoleon permitted no diversion of regulars. With the exception of the Berg cavalry, none of the line troops destined for the main army around Vienna would be distracted by the Austrian incursions. 'Do not forget', Berthier told Junot, 'that *the most important objective to fulfil* is not to derange the emperor's combinations.'[126]

Fighting in the Vorarlberg

Junot was annoyed that Württemberg's King Friedrich would not supply any troops for the march on Bayreuth, but the corpulent monarch had concerns of his own, and those emanated principally from the south, not the east. Moreover, this danger, the rebellion in the Vorarlberg, threatened not just Württemberg, but Bavaria, Baden, and indeed Napoleon's line of communications back to Strasbourg.

The Vorarlberg, like the Tyrol, had come under Bavarian rule following the Treaty of Pressburg in 1805. Like their Tyrolian cousins, the inhabitants resented Bavarian control and, prompted by Habsburg agents and the Tyrolian example, they took up arms in late April 1809. The arrival of a minuscule Austrian detachment (twenty chevaulegers and 104 infantry) in Feldkirch on 25 April helped spur the rebellion. These Habsburg troops were joined by a second detachment on 12 May (fifteen chevaulegers, 230 infantry, one 3-pounder) and a third group on the 14th (twenty-one chevaulegers, some

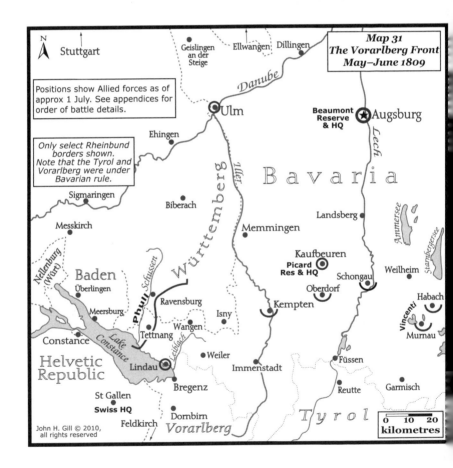

130 men of 9th Jägers).[127] As in the Tyrol, the local populace would do most of the fighting, but the arrival of the Austrians seemed to promise great things. Combined with local grievances, Tyrolian successes (real and imagined), and thrilling rumours of distant triumphs (the ubiquitous Blücher made an obligatory appearance at the head of 40,000 men), these few whitecoats helped transform simmering anger into active rebellion.[128] Assiduously assessing all this from Stuttgart, King Friedrich observed that 'the grand lies spread by the court in Vienna have plunged them [the Vorarlbergers] into a state of delusion and frenzy,' but, he believed, 'their awakening will be cruel.'[129]

The campaign in the Vorarlberg may be divided into three phases. The first, from late April to mid-May, encompassed the outbreak of the rebellion and initial attacks into Bavaria, Württemberg, and Baden. It concluded with a gradual ebbing of the insurgent tide after the fall of Innsbruck to Lefebvre's 7th Corps on 19 May. The second phase lasted from late May through late July and featured a revived insurgency returning to the offensive, just as many of the Allied troops were called away to counter other dangers. This led to a general Allied withdrawal and a series of small defensive engagements north of Lake Constance. Finally, in late July, the Allies launched a series of co-ordinated drives into the region in concert with the second offensive into the Tyrol; these had quashed the rebellion by early August.[130] There was also a curious external political-military dimension to the conflict as the Swiss, keen to protect their borders and assert their neutrality, mobilised 5,000 men under General Nikolaus Rudolf von Wattenwyl in late April. Later reinforced by an additional 2,000 and some artillery, these men guarded the jagged border with the Tyrol and the Vorarlberg but never faced a real test.[131]

From the Allied perspective, the burden of combat, patrolling, and garrison duty fell most heavily on the Württemberg and Baden contingents, backed by a small force of second-line French troops. These circumstances presented serious obstacles to effective co-operation. Although the Vorarlberg was Bavarian land, that kingdom's military resources were fully absorbed along the Danube, in the Tyrol, and elsewhere. The crowned heads of both Württemberg and Baden, however, were deeply suspicious of Bavaria and disinclined to dedicate troops to assist their brother prince. Friedrich, for instance, indignantly expostulated to Napoleon at employing 'my troops to re-conquer his lands while leaving my own exposed to the atrocious brigandage of these insurgents.'[132] They also mistrusted one another, Baden being particularly anxious that Württemberg's domineering king would exploit military necessity to occupy and lay claim to Baden lands. At the same time, both rulers worried about the loyalty of the southern districts of their own monarchies. Recent acquisitions, these areas had previously been under Habsburg rule and were considered susceptible to subversion that might quickly spread across the newly drawn borders. 'I fear the most unfortunate consequences,' wrote Max Josef, 'above all in the area of Swabia where the inhabitants of Bavaria as well as Württemberg and the Grand Duchy of Baden ask nothing more than to revolt.'[133] Domestic security concerns as well as pressure from Napoleon thus pushed King Friedrich of Württemberg and Grand Duke Karl Friedrich of Baden to commit substantial portions of their small military establishments to contain the Vorarlberg revolt and quell any rebellious tendencies among their new subjects. An additional complication arose because the units sent to the Vorarlberg were not technically part of either state's obligation to the Rheinbund, indeed they exceeded the formal treaty requirements. The French had only a tenuous claim to issue them orders, and initially at least, Baden was wary of placing its troops under Württemberg generals. Command and control in this intricate, delicate multinational environment thus posed daunting challenges and only the emperor's overriding presence, Beaumont's diplomatic skills, and the common threat allowed the uncertain structure to function at all.[134]

Although there were no battles on the scale of those in the Tyrol, the Vorarlberg insurrection was alarming for the south German princes. In the almost total absence of Bavarian troops, the rebels quickly gained control of the province, occupied Lindau, and began bold raids into neighbouring territories. In the most daring of these, 375 insurgents sailed across Lake Constance on 13 May and struck north to capture a large Bavarian wagon train near Messkirch, some twenty-five kilometres beyond the lake.

Allied troops were already on the way when this embarrassment occurred. Württemberg GM Ludwig von Koseritz arrived in Ravensburg on 4 May with *Franquemont* Infantry and four guns, but this small force, reluctantly turned over to French command, marched off to Kempten in Bavaria on the 15th to join Beaumont's division. The French general arrived in Augsburg on 12 May to assume control (more or less) of operations along the Tyrol/Vorarlberg border and to watch the frontier as far as Bohemia. Three of his provisional dragoon regiments (2nd, 3rd, 4th) had been in the city since the 8th; the other two (1st, 5th) rode in on the 18th. Beaumont employed these to garrison Augsburg (to which Napoleon attached great importance) and to bolster the southern defences. King Friedrich, meanwhile, had to find troops to cover his own borders and sent GM Johann Georg Graf von Scheler to Lake Constance with a weak brigade.[135] The Württembergers reached their destination on 18 May and a tiny Baden detachment arrived in Ueberlingen on the 19th.[136] Where the Badeners technically came under Beaumont's orders, as a practical matter they had to operate in conjunction with, and usually under, their Württemberg allies. Scheler, on the other hand, was only to accept direction from his king and was specifically prohibited from exerting himself to reconquer Bavarian territory.[137] To the east, GB Joseph Picard, one of Beaumont's subordinates, had pushed south from Augsburg, occupying Memmingen and Kempten with an ad hoc brigade.[138] From here, he posted detachments further south and sent Colonel François Grouvel with 4th Provisional Dragoons, 100 French infantry, and fifty Württemberg Jäger to hold Bregenz. By 25 May, therefore, a cordon of Allied troops stretched from Füssen–Immenstadt–Weiler (Picard), through Lindau and Tettnang (Württemberg), to Constance (Baden), with Grouvel at Bregenz and Dornbirn.

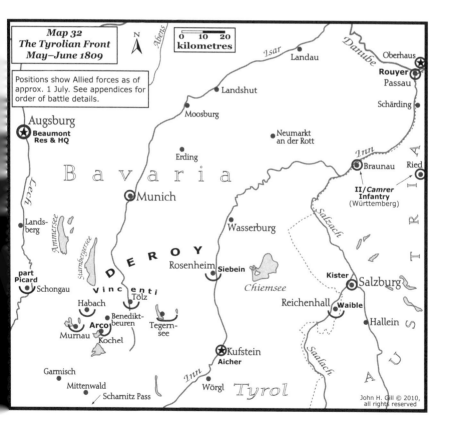

The general structure of defences along the Tyrol/Vorarlberg border during June thus consisted of three sub-sectors. In the east, generally from the Saalach to the Lech, was GL Deroy's division with Arco's brigade and an ever-growing number of Bavarian reserve units. Beaumont's men comprised the centre from the Lech to around Isny: two or three provisional dragoon regiments, the recovering 65th Ligne, and a congeries of French and Bavarian second-line troops. On the right were the Württemberg, Baden, and French troops north of Lake Constance, the latter two assigned to Beaumont, while the Württembergers jealously guarded their independence.

The Tyrolian defeats, their own setbacks, lack of equipment, and a paucity of leadership and organisation combined to subdue the Vorarlberg insurgents at this point. The senior Austrian officer, convinced all was lost, fled to Switzerland. Two other Austrian officers, equally disheartened, decided to attempt a breakout to Bohemia. With thirty-seven chevaulegers and about 100 men of 9th Jägers, they headed north, evading a Württemberg pursuit force and escaping an unexpected scuffle with some determined Bavarian depot troops. Beaumont, however, set Colonel Marie-Antoine de Reiset on their trail with 1st Provisional Dragoons. Reiset, marching 'day and night', caught and dispersed the little band at Pfeffertshofen on 27 May. About half fell into Reiset's hands immediately, the rest scattered into the countryside only to be snatched up by another of his squadrons.[139] The few survivors joined thousands of former Habsburg soldiers—deserters, marauders, escaped prisoners of war, and everything in between—roaming the southern Confederation states. Most were prisoners who had slipped away during the march to Strasbourg because 'the number of soldiers who escort the columns is absolutely insufficient to keep an eye on them,' and 'the evasions thus multiply to disturbing proportions.'[140] Authorities in one town on the shores of Lake Constance claimed that they had shipped 2,136 escaped Austrian prisoners across the lake between 16 May and 27 June alone.[141] Many of these men gradually made their way back to Habsburg domains to rejoin the ranks in the Tyrol or Vorarlberg, but whether dedicated soldiers trying to regain their units or individuals of less savoury disposition, all were a great burden to local populations and a dire worry for the Rheinbund princes. Indeed, a major reason for placing a small Baden garrison in Constance was to inhibit the transit of these fugitives, and some of the Baden reinforcements designated for the Vorarlberg front were diverted to march through remote portions of the duchy in order to suppress roving bands of Austrian soldiers and assert the crown's authority.

The second phase of the Vorarlberg campaign began as May neared its end. Grouvel had noted that the population, inspired by the reviving Tyrolian insurgency, news of Aspern, and all manner of wildly optimistic rumours—the Austrians had outflanked Napoleon on the Danube! Napoleon's brother was captured in Spain!—was becoming restive.[142] He requested reinforcements from Picard and Scheler and, thus strengthened, attempted to learn more through a reconnaissance to the south on 29 May. This, however, turned into a miniature disaster. Encountering overwhelming numbers of armed militia, he was forced to retreat, abandoning Dornbirn and Bregenz in the process. Leaving a garrison in Lindau, the entire border corps withdrew behind the Schussen River. Casualties only came to fifty-five men wounded or taken prisoner, but the skirmish and the ignominious Allied retreat boosted insurgent spirits on the very day that the Bavarians and Tyrolians were grappling with one another at Berg Isel.

Friedrich was furious at the embarrassment of Dornbirn and ordered GL Friedrich von Phull south with additional forces on 6 June.[143] Baden and French reinforcements also arrived, but the insurgents repelled an Allied reconnaissance in force along the Loiblach on 13 June and, by 20 June, the Allied line was once again behind the Schussen.[144] Further east, Vorarlbergers, in sketchy co-operation with Tyrolians, attempted to seize Kempten on the 19th.[145] These attacks proved abortive, but did prevent Picard from venturing any further south towards the mountains.

The Austrian incursion into Bayreuth caused Friedrich to shift a substantial portion of his border force to Ellwangen to face this new menace. Their departure on 28 June coincided with the withdrawal of most of the French infantry, leaving Phull with insufficient strength to conduct offensive operations, even had he so desired. The latter part of June thus passed in constant patrols, alarms, and minor encounters capped with a rebel success when a small flotilla captured the tiny Baden garrison in Constance (thirty-eight men) in a surprise attack on the 29th. Diversionary probes by insurgents at Lindau and along the Schussen were easily repulsed, but this combined enemy effort highlighted the vulnerabilities of the Allied position and the weakness of the defence forces.[146] These actions also excited fears that the Vorarlbergers would conduct landings along the lake's northern shore and spark rebellion in the dubious southern districts of Baden and Württemberg.

As if to demonstrate that such fears were not unrealistic, a violent uprising flared in the former lands of the Teutonic Order near Mergentheim (Bad Mergentheim) on 26 June. Mergentheim had previously been ruled by Habsburg Archduke Anton Viktor as head of the order, but Napoleon had dissolved the order and granted the territory to Friedrich on 24 April 1809. Friedrich was not the monarch to tolerate any defiance and Scheler, leading a punitive column of 2,700 men, stormed the city and crushed the revolt on the 29th.[147] An outburst in Westphalian Marburg was even more ephemeral. Launched on the night of 24/25 June by a septuagenarian former Oberst named Andreas Emmerich, it only attracted about four dozen supporters and, confronted by the tiny local garrison, it had collapsed by morning. Even the normally anxious Westphalian court seems to have reacted with equanimity.[148]

As June ended, therefore, Napoleon's line of communications through Germany remained intact and relatively free. Despite alarms and excursions, his defensive system of second-line troops and deception sufficed to withstand both internal rebellion and external incursion, while the presence of his principal army at Vienna prevented his Habsburg adversaries from detaching any substantial regular forces to support these raids and insurrections. The situation was by no means ideal: the Tyrol and the Vorarlberg had been lost and their insurgents posed a real threat to his communications and to the adjacent states of his Rheinbund allies; and detachments of Austrian regulars and Landwehr roamed about in Saxony and Bayreuth. From Napoleon's vantage point, however, adequate reserves were en route to counter or at least contain all of these dangers. Furthermore, from a temporal perspective, he knew that his rear area security system would not have to sustain these pressures for very much longer. Austrian leaders and pan-German patriots might express passionate optimism about the—largely illusory—potential for rebellion inherent in the situation, but Napoleon could view all of these challenges as manageable. He knew that, within a matter of days, the great armament he was assembling on the banks of the Danube would pass over the mighty river for a second time to open what he confidently expected would be the final phase of this unwanted war. 'It is here that all will be decided,' he wrote to Friedrich on 24 June. 'Everything is proceeding to my satisfaction.'[149]

PART II

Wagram, Znaim, and Peace

CHAPTER 5

Wagram

Scanning the strategic horizon as June slipped into its final days, the objective eye would discern that conditions did not favour Austria. The outlook was not entirely grim, but, as Charles noted, 'None of the assumptions that supported and justified the decision for war has been met.'[1] Prussia had just reaffirmed its intention to remain aloof, there was no evidence of cracks in the Rheinbund, and Germany had not risen in revolt—indeed, all the sparks of rebellion north of the Danube had been quickly stamped out. Kienmayer's troops in Bayreuth and Saxony did pose a distant danger to Napoleon's lines of communication, but Junot was en route to contain the former, and Jerome's arrival—albeit laboured and often clumsy—had sufficed to check the latter. Moreover, Jerome was now poised to present a threat to Bohemia. Great Britain had provided an initial tranche of subsidies, but there was no indication that significant military action (as desperately desired by the Habsburg court) was in the offing. Russia had formally joined Napoleon as promised and Golitsyn's corps, though not actively hostile, was steadily pressing its advantages against the cornered Archduke Ferdinand. Johann and Joseph, battered at Raab, had been forced north of the Danube and the Pressburg bridgehead was tightly enclosed by the vigilant Davout. The Dalmatiain enterprise had failed and Marmont had reached Graz to hold Gyulai in check. The only bright spots from the Austrian perspective were the successes gained by the Tyrolian and Vorarlberg insurgents. In the absence of regular troops, however, these were largely self-limited by their ties to their respective homelands, while the hotchpotch collections of second-line units that Napoleon had cobbled together were proving adequate to curtail their marauding.

Operationally, the end of June found the Austrian forces deployed in a huge arc from Somariva north of Linz, through Schustekh and the rest of V

Corps at Krems and the Danube bend, to the Hauptarmee on the Marchfeld, and Johann at Pressburg. By the 28th, Archduke Joseph had retired to Komorn, leaving only the thinnest of screens connecting his Insurrection corps to his brother's troops. Chasteler stood at Szent Groth on Joseph's left, but neither he nor the archduke demonstrated much enterprise. Farther south, the chastened Gyulai awaited an opportunity to move against Graz again, while GM von Knesevich slowly assembled a small brigade in distant Croatia. The French and their confederates occupied the interior of this arc, with Rouyer, Lefebvre, and Vandamme covering the Danube from Passau to Vienna, Davout at Pressburg, and Eugene at Raab. Broussier and Marmont were still in Styria with Rusca's tiny division in Carinthia protecting communications to Italy. The French side of this tableau, however, was about to change with terrifying and decisive rapidity.

An Accelerating Storm[2]

As work on the Lobau bridges and fortifications neared completion, Napoleon considered the timing of his new offensive. By 29 June, he had selected 4 July as the day on which the entire army was to be assembled on or near Lobau. Such a massive concentration would be impossible to conceal and the assault would probably be launched on the 5th so as not to afford the Austrians time to exploit opportunities on the weakened French flanks.[3] Beyond issues of his own readiness (bridges, batteries, troops on hand, and so on), the emperor had two immediate operational concerns. First, he wanted to deceive Charles regarding the intended crossing point. Second, he was keen to be sure the Austrians did not slip away—either to conduct a crossing of their own elsewhere or to evade the coming struggle entirely. In particular, he was concerned that Charles might be planning to cross the Danube at Komorn and offer battle in Hungary, a move that would delay the decisive victory Napoleon needed to bring the war to a successful conclusion quickly.[4] To forestall any Habsburg action and lock the Hauptarmee in place, he therefore ordered Massena to seize a bridgehead in the Mühlau—the same area where the French had crossed prior to Aspern—on 30 June. In addition to focusing Austrian attention away from the true assault site on the eastern edge of Lobau, this operation would serve as a reconnaissance in force, allowing Napoleon to assess the enemy's strength and gauge Charles's intentions. Under cover of the Lobau batteries, Ledru's brigade of Legrand's division crossed over the Stadtler Arm in boats that afternoon. The enemy was overwhelmed in a moment,' wrote Chef de Bataillon Charles Louis Gueheneuc of 26th Léger.[5] Engineers threw a bridge across the arm with practised efficiency and, by 5 p.m., the French were once more established on the Marchfeld. As Legrand's infantry gathered up prisoners and chased off the surviving Austrians, French engineers and sappers immediately busied themselves repairing the fortifications left over from May and constructing a new line of redoubts to protect the bridgehead.

The Austrians, impressed by the tremendous energy of the French and unnerved at the power of the supporting batteries on Lobau, barely reacted to the incursion, and their rapid withdrawal confirmed Napoleon in his disdain for his opponent. When one of Massena's adjutants reported Legrand's success, the assembled officers at imperial headquarters were surprised by news 'that no one had expected'. 'Those gentlemen over there do not know how to make war,' Napoleon told the adjutant. 'The activity of the French always confounds them.'[6] The image this left with the emperor was evident in letters written late that night and early the following morning: 'At the first cannon shot, the enemy disappeared and retired behind the Essling redoubts' in response to the French demonstration, he told Eugene.[7] Napoleon was correct in his assessment of both the Austrian lassitude that allowed them to be surprised by Legrand's assault despite six weeks of watching Lobau Island, and in his conclusion that the Habsburg host lacked the speed and agility of the French and their allies. As would be demonstrated in the coming days, however, these shrewd judgements did *not* mean that the Austrians were entirely unskilled or that they were in any way deficient in dogged courage and endurance when facing situations that fell within the compass of their understanding of warfare. The resilience of his adversaries would soon give Napoleon cause to rethink his assumptions, but Austrian behaviour thus far seemed consistent with established patterns. His concern during the first four days of July 1809, however, was completely different: 'Our sole fear', he wrote, 'is that the enemy will not stand and fight.'[8]

Napoleon need not have worried: the last thing Charles wanted was to depart the Marchfeld. Unbeknown to the French emperor, Legrand's sudden crossing had stopped an Austrian plan to take the offensive across the Danube at Krems. Starting on 26 June, Charles had reluctantly yielded to pressure from the court and issued a series of orders for the army to move towards Krems on 1 July.[9] Doubtless relieved that Napoleon's advance provided an unassailable excuse to cancel an operation he considered intolerably risky, Charles instead deployed the Hauptarmee into a position behind Aspern and Essling during the early hours of 1 July to be ready for a

French advance, even though the observation post on the Bisamberg noted no significant movement onto Lobau from the south bank.[10] Indeed, the day passed quietly, the thousands of whitecoats waiting passively under the bright summer skies. Nonetheless, it was clear to the archduke that a major French operation was brewing. What he did not know was the purpose of the Mühlau crossing. 'Is this a demonstration or does he want to crush us with the superiority and calibre of his artillery, to dislodge us at that point and then debouch, this is what I do not know,' he wrote on 3 July.[11] Furthermore, army headquarters persisted in worrying that Napoleon might cross at other sites. What if the activity on Lobau was just a feint to disguise a main attack at Nussdorf, Orth, or Fischamend? What if the French launched multiple simultaneous crossings? These imaginings loomed over Habsburg thinking to 6 July, diverting forces that might otherwise have joined the army for the Battle of Wagram.[12]

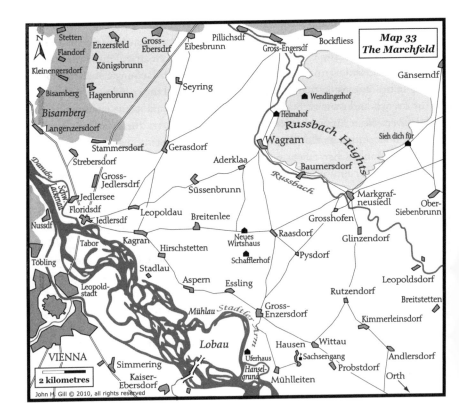

Map 33
The Marchfeld

Though Charles was convinced that the long-awaited French offensive was finally about to begin, this conclusion was by no mean obvious to the leaders and advisers at the imperial court in Wolkersdorf. Frustrated by the Hauptarmee's long period of inactivity and anxious about Russian advances in Galicia, on 2 July Franz dispatched the letter discussed in the previous chapter instructing Charles to detach up to 15,000 men to support Ferdinand in Poland, 'if you do not intend to undertake something here within the next several days'.[13] In other words, rather than accepting the burden of decision himself as reigning monarch, Franz was passing the responsibility to his brother. Charles regarded this pusillanimous note with something close to contempt, but he was able to dissuade his brother from this folly—at least there is no evidence of orders being prepared for this course of action.

As this imperial missive was making its way to the Generalissimus, Napoleon was increasing the pressure on his adversary. The emperor had moved his personal headquarters onto Lobau on 1 July and noted with satisfaction that Legrand's advance had provoked the desired reaction: 'the army of Prince Charles is all here in battle order,' he told Eugene in the early hours of the 2nd.[14] Starting around 8 a.m. that morning, a tremendous bombardment from the Lobau guns covered the Austrian entrenchments between Essling and Gross-Enzersdorf with a hail of iron, causing 300 casualties among Klenau's Advance Guard and severely damaging several of the works. A significant number of balls and shells even fell among the II Corps troops behind Essling. The cannonade provided cover for Pelet to lead 600 voltigeurs from Boudet's division to seize the Mühl-Haufen, or Ile du Moulin, just downstream from the Mühlau. The small garrison of Grenzer was captured or killed despite the proximity of infantry and artillery supports, a feat both sides considered a significant accomplishment for a small detachment in the face of considerable firepower from the northern bank.[15] The pontooneers earned special praise for constructing a significant bridge in two hours, despite heavy fire.[16] With the bridge complete, Pelet's men hastened to install an eight-gun battery on the island. Napoleon, who personally observed this miniature operation, was very pleased. 'You see quite well,' he told Massena, 'that nothing is impossible with such troops.'[17] Meanwhile, a second bridge was constructed to link the original Mühlau bridgehead with Lobau. Additionally, French guns bombarded the islands near Stadlau and the Danube flotilla successfully landed 500 men on the Schierling-Grund south-west of Aspern. These actions, large and small, were designed to increase the level of visible activity on the western and northern fringes of Lobau away from the intended crossing point on the island's eastern face. Similarly, the only notable French action on 3 July was the establishment of a small lodgement with a redoubt (Redoute Petit) on the northern bank of the Stadtler Arm opposite the Mühl-Haufen; a bridge was constructed the following day to connect it to the island.[18] Napoleon, 'who attached great importance' to this island, personally toured it on the 3rd in Massena's company.[19] Unfortunately for the latter, his horse fell as he was examining the island, causing a painful injury that prevented him from riding. Not to be deterred, the marshal arranged for a coach to carry him about as he attended to his duties. Still suffering from the fall, he would use this unusual means of transport during the coming battle as well.

On the Austrian side of the river, the day represented an odd combination of operational reconsiderations and chimerical hopes. The reconsiderations arose because Charles had no firm plan in mind for how to oppose Napoleon's offensive. Despite six weeks of repose to analyse his options, he was still undecided on the basic question of whether to fight the coming battle close to the Danube or to await the French in positions along the Bisamberg and Russbach Heights. In Habsburg thinking, the former was associated with allowing part, but not all, of the French army to cross onto the Marchfeld. Fundamentally, it represented a refighting of Aspern–Essling, but posed serious disadvantages should retreat become necessary, as the Austrian army would have to conduct a lengthy withdrawal across open fields in the presence of the numerous French horse. Additionally, much of the terrain near Lobau was cut up, wooded, and irregular—especially on the Austrian left where the French would actually cross—and Charles knew all too well which army was better suited to such conditions.[20] The second option, favoured by Wimpffen and probably Grünne, was based on good defensive positions and protected the roads to Bohemia and Moravia. Moreover, whether the French chose to attack the Bisamberg or Russbach Heights, the Austrians should be able to strike the enemy flank from the other position. This could lead to a more decisive outcome, as the enemy would be vulnerable to defeat and a potentially devastating retreat to the Danube.[21] On the other hand, Charles did not have enough men to occupy both positions (the Bisamberg and Russbach Heights) with adequate numbers and nothing had been done to enhance either. Accepting this option also entailed placing the troops along the river (VI Corps and the Advance Guard) in a perilous situation, potentially too far from support and facing a decidedly superior foe.

Vacillation between these two courses of action during June, complicated by periodic mental excursions to review true offensive operations, only produced half-measures—weak fortifications near Lobau, no works on the heights, no serious effort to reinforce the defences with fortress guns from arsenals in Bohemia/Moravia, and so on—and left the Generalissimus without a comprehensive plan when the ineluctable French crossing finally unfolded. What all this meant on the ground was that Charles implemented a plan that had been made on 5 June and deployed the army towards Lobau after Legrand's crossing on the 30th, but quickly revised his thinking when he witnessed the strength of the French artillery during the 2 July bombardment.[22] 'It is not my intention to give a defensive battle close to the banks of the Danube where I risk everything and the enemy, with his solid position thanks to batteries of siege guns, risks nothing,' he wrote.[23] On 3 July, therefore, most of the Hauptarmee returned to its previous stations on the slopes of the Bisamberg and above the Russbach stream, leaving VI Corps and the Advance Guard to watch the French on Lobau. The only gesture towards strengthening the army's defences consisted of vague instructions to Rosenberg to supplement his position on the left flank with 'several independent redoubts'. The lone remotely offensive move was a decision to have the VI Corps artillery shell Lobau during the night of 4/5 July. With only field artillery at hand, feebly supplemented by a lone 12-pounder battery, this notion hardly promised much in the way of results.[24] The Hauptarmee thus again indulged in half-measures.

External considerations compounded Charles's local operational problems. For one thing, the court, despite the looming menace immanent in all of the French activity from 30 June to 3 July, still persisted in seeing threats and opportunities in secondary and tertiary theatres. Based on erroneous information from Joseph about MacDonald's movements in Hungary in a report, for instance, Franz and his advisers concluded that 'the enemy is sending a significant number of troops to the rear that can only be directed against FML Chasteler and the Ban [of Croatia, Ignaz Gyulai].' The Kaiser thought to perceive 'possibilities for our own operations' in this incorrect intelligence—MacDonald had already departed—and believed it merited Charles's 'special attention'.[25] The archduke ignored this goad, but other stimuli elicited a serious reaction. Incredible as it seems, army headquarters prepared a comprehensive set of orders early on 4 July detaching nineteen battalions (9,500 men) and 'a proportionate number of guns' to reinforce Kienmayer in Germany. This corps was to assemble at Bockfliess under FML Hohenlohe on the 5th and march for Bohemia the following day.[26] It is not clear whether this plan was prompted by demands from the court or fears that setbacks in Saxony had created a threat to Bohemia—perhaps some combination of both.[27] Recent reports from the Bisamberg observation post indicated little unusual French activity and probably contributed to the idea that such detachments might be made safely, but we are still left with a bizarre situation where Austrian diversionary actions in Germany, far from distracting Napoleon, were on the verge of inducing a substantial weakening of the Hauptarmee on the eve of the war's decisive battle. These orders, of course, were never issued and the troops never left their bivouacs, but nothing better illustrates the strategic-operational confusion and delusion in the Habsburg court and army headquarters.

While the Austrian leadership was weighing these military factors, a political development sparked Charles's hopes that the monarchy might still find a negotiated settlement to the conflict. From the Austrian perspective, there seemed some glimmer of an opening in French behaviour since Aspern. The tone of Napoleon's pronouncements seemed more respectful (in particular, hints of expunging the Habsburg monarchy dwindled), Berthier responded quickly and courteously to complaints about the shelling of Pressburg, and for several days he had been in correspondence with Wimpffen regarding a possible prisoner exchange. This interaction resulted in an agreement on 3 July that FML Weissenwolff should present himself to the French outposts the following morning to be granted an audience with Napoleon for further discussion of the potential exchange. Charles, and even Franz, seem to have attached no little hope to Weissenwolff's mission, but the guidance the general received was 'vague' and he was in any case pursuing a chimera.[28] Napoleon believed he could not conclude the war without a major victory and his orders for the crossing had already been issued on the night of the 2nd. All was in readiness, the crossing would begin on the night of the 4th as scheduled. Weissenwolff would thus watch the coming battle unfold from the French side of the Danube. Across the silent river, FML d'Aspre felt the sense of foreboding. 'We are coming to the denouement,' he wrote to a friend the night before the battle.[29]

The Concentration is General

By the time Weissenwolff was reporting to the French outposts on the morning of 4 July, Napoleon's preparations were entering their final stages. A blizzard of orders had flown out of imperial headquarters for the past few days, calling the army to concentrate on Lobau. Formations from as far away as Hungary (Eugene), Graz (Marmont and Broussier), and Linz (Wrede's Bavarian division) were ordered to Kaiser-Ebersdorf by forced marches. The bare minimum was to be left to hold the flanks and lines of communications. 'I count on attacking the enemy on the 5th,' the emperor had written Davout on 29 June, 'the concentration is general.'[30]

To delay Austrian detection of the coming attack, the assembly of the army on Lobau proceeded incrementally in its initial stages. The Baden brigade rejoined 4th Corps on 30 June and two of Oudinot's divisions crossed over during the night of 1/2 July. Two nights later (3/4 July), the Guard and the white-coated Saxons of Bernadotte's 9th Corps made their way onto the island. Gazing about in amazement, one of them commented: 'It is impossible to paint a picture that would represent what Lobau looked like: troops of every arm from many nations and peoples in the diversity and variety of their uniforms and weapons; the crowding together of all these in a small area; the astonishing quantity of available munitions; the earthworks, partly still under construction, partly completed and occupied with troops and guns.' 'All this', he concluded, 'afforded the most imposing sight.'[31] The transfer had been conducted with 'great order and celerity', reported GD Dumas the following morning.[32] These moves, conducted at night by units close to Vienna, went largely unnoticed by the Austrian observation posts in Gross-Enzersdorf and on the Bisamberg. As the day of battle approached, however, Napoleon abandoned stealth for speed. Confident in the zeal of his commanders, the experience of his staff officers, and the marching capacity of his troops, as well as in his own abilities, the emperor could wait until almost the last minute to assemble his army for what he hoped would be the war's decisive battle. It was only on the morning of 4 July, therefore, that Austrian officers on the Bisamberg and others south along the Danube, reported heavy columns of infantry, cavalry, and guns darkening the roads from Hungary. 'It is reported from the observation post on the Bisamberg that since 4 a.m. columns of enemy infantry and cavalry with artillery have been marching onto Lobau, and all intelligence agrees that the enemy is gathering his entire strength at Kaiser-Ebersdorf,' wrote Charles to Hiller at 9 a.m. on the 4th.[33] That evening he informed Johann that, 'The movement of troops through Fischamend toward Schwechat and likewise from Bruck an der Leitha in that direction went on all day today. It is Marshal Davout and the viceroy.'[34]

The bulk of the Allied army was indeed on the march. Starting in the late afternoon with Lasalle and Marulaz, an endless stream of men, horses, guns, and other vehicles crowded the bridges and their approaches.[35] 'Everything in and around Kaiser-Ebersdorf was so jammed full with newly arrived troops that one could hardly set one's foot on the earth,' wrote a frustrated

Table 14: Troop Arrivals and Actions on Lobau, June/July 1809

In place: 4th Corps, incl. 23rd Chasseurs, 3rd Baden Inf

30 June
+ Baden brigade (1st and 2nd Inf, Jägers) from Pressburg
+ Legrand seizes Mühlau bridgehead

Night of 1/2 July
+ 2nd Corps: Tharreau and Grandjean (evening)

2 July
+ French seizure of Mühl-Haufen (*Ile du Moulin*)

3 July
+ French lodgement opposite Mühl-Haufen (*Redoute Petit*)

Night of 3/4 July
+ Imperial Guard
+ 9th Corps

4 July (afternoon/evening)
+ Lasalle/Marulaz (incl. Hessian infantry detachment)
+ 3rd Corps
+ Frère's division/2nd Corps
+ Grand bombardment and crossing begin

5 July
+ Crossing continues, seizure of *Ile Pouzet*
+ Army of Italy (*c.*1 a.m.)
+ Heavy cavalry divisions (*c.*5 a.m.)
+ Broussier from Graz (*c.*3 p.m.)
+ Pachtod from Hungary (late afternoon/evening)
+ Marmont from Graz (late afternoon/evening)

6 July
+ Wrede (from Schönbrunn, *c.*10 a.m.)

Note: dates/times indicate arrival on Lobau, not on Marchfeld.

Saxon, trying to reach his brigade.[36] But this colossal and incredibly complex move occurred with only minor hitches, and Paulin remembered that all were 'silent and impatient' as they approached the bridges. 'At last, on the night of 4 to 5 July, all the troops started off and executed the movements as they had been ordered,' he continued. 'Measures of every sort had been taken to avoid disorder and assure the march of the troops.'[37] As midnight came, 3rd Corps and the final division of 2nd (Frère) were on Lobau; the

Army of Italy and the heavy cavalry were at Kaiser-Ebersdorf, awaiting their turn. One march away were Marmont, Broussier, and Pachtod to the south and Wrede at Schönbrunn. All was thus assembled and, with a shattering cannonade under a violent storm, the crossing had begun.

The rapidity and success of these marches led the admiring Pelet to write, 'At that moment strategy acquired the precision and regularity of tactics.'[38] Doubtless, all was not as smooth and orderly as Pelet suggested, but the staff work was impressive for the era and the marching often astonishing. Broussier and Marmont from Graz, and Wrede from Linz, all covered approximately 200 kilometres in four days, moving mostly at night to minimise heat casualties—two months after the battle that had destroyed it, Wrede's troops still shuddered to pass through the charred carnage of Ebelsberg.[39] The long distances involved and congestion at the bridges meant that these formations and Pachtod's division did not arrive on Lobau until late on the 5th or early on the 6th, but many of Eugene's men marched more than 100 kilometres over three days to reach their assembly areas on the island exactly on time. They joined an increasing crowd of soldiers and a growing hum of excitement. As his regiment approached Ebersdorf, for example, trooper Kenis of 3rd Chasseurs recalled, 'we saw squadrons and battalions approaching from all sides to assemble at the same point, so that we could guess that something was up.'[40]

Napoleon's will infused the army with urgency and expectation. Movements were to be made by forced marches, adequate rations for man and horse were to be carried, and commanders were enjoined to 'take all measures so that not a single man is left in the rear, and that absolutely nothing is forgotten.'[41] At the same time, the corps were to strip themselves to the bare minimum, 'you will leave or send to Schönbrunn all lame horses, unnecessary baggage, women, and in general all encumbrances and everything that cannot fight.'[42] This impulse of excitement communicated itself down into the ranks: 'Vienna was overflowing with soldiers; the tumult and expectation, that pervaded the suburbs and hinted at something great, cannot be described,' wrote a Saxon.[43] Another who sensed that great things were in motion was Christian Schaller, a Bavarian artillery corporal whose battery was attached to Wrede's division for the march to Wagram:

On the 1st of July, Wrede's division departed from Linz for Vienna on His Majesty the Emperor's orders. I had the good fortune to find myself with it. The hope of taking part in the most remarkable day of this campaign lent wings to our steps. A divisional order from GL Freiherr von Wrede, that encouraged us to steadfast endurance of the march's burdens and expressed the confidence His Majesty the Emperor had in us, had the desired effect. We competed with one another in exhibiting our indifference to rest.[44]

Sous-Lieutenant Barat of 52nd Ligne in the Army of Italy recalled that he and his colleagues were 'thrilled to be under his orders', and, that 'each of us was happy, now united with the Grande Armée [sic], finally to fight under the eyes of the emperor.' 'The troops were in the best disposition,' wrote Capitaine d'Espinchal of 5th Hussars, 'the enthusiasm and ardour had reached a point of exaltation that promised the most happy success.'[45] Those whose duties kept them on the south bank looked on with envy.[46]

The sentiments expressed by these soldiers reflect the general confidence the army had in its commander.[47] Indeed, the build-up period prior to Wagram furnishes another example of Napoleon's dominance of the military art during his era. While Charles temporised, vacillated, considered, and reconsidered, while the Habsburg court pursued military fantasies, Napoleon deployed the full range of his individual energy, military talent, and imperial authority.[48] In part, his seemingly boundless activity was an inherent component of his character, but he had also learned from the experience of Aspern and was a determined to exert every effort, exploit every moment to ensure a secure passage this time. As Marmont noted when he reported to his master on 5 July: 'I found him in all his military grandeur. If he had opened the campaign with few troops and feeble means, the resources of his spirit and the energy of his will had created for him immense forces . . . Napoleon had profited from the lesson he had received . . . that vast island of Lobau represented the greatest military population that one could ever think to see united at the same point.'[49] His capacity for detail and personal involvement in every aspect of the gigantic enterprise seemed infinite. 'He held frequent reviews and visited the banks of the Danube every day to reconnoitre, as much as the area allowed him, the position of the enemy,' remembered Colonel Berthezène of 10th Léger. 'Many times he was seen on the lower part of the island, hidden in a soldier's greatcoat with a musket on his arm, placing himself in the picket line in order to make his observations more easily.'[50] Whether tasting the soup of a surprised Baden squad, insisting on adequate wine rations for the troops on the island, or inspecting the numerous engineering projects, he made his presence and direct concern felt across Lobau and throughout the army. 'The emperor himself came to examine the work,' wrote engineer Capitaine Paulin. 'He sat on a block of wood, gave his ideas, and spoke familiarly and cheerily with each of us.'[51] His army responded to this familiar yet demanding style of leadership and he, confident in them and in their officers, knew he had in hand an instrument upon which he could rely. This mutual confidence between leader and led was now about to undergo a most sanguinary test. 'This splendid movement, cunningly hidden from the enemy, was completed and the concentration of the army was accomplished,' wrote Berthezène. 'Nothing remained but to debouch from Lobau Island onto the left bank.'[52]

Achieving this concentration of power, of course, meant that only a thin shell of troops was left along Napoleon's immediate flanks. In general this consisted of strongpoints connected by frequent patrols. Rouyer still held the fortified bridgehead complex at Passau, but with Wrede's departure, Lefebvre was left with only the Bavarian 1st Division at Linz (3rd Division received orders to march to Linz, but could not arrive until after Wagram). On Lefebvre's right, Vandamme's Württembergers had to extend their line all the way to Vienna to cover areas previously held by other corps. South of the city, Baraguey d'Hilliers was to watch Johann at Pressburg and cover the gap as far as the Neusiedler See with Severoli's division and an ad hoc cavalry brigade under GB Nicholas Marin Thiry.[53] More than seventy kilometres away, aristocratic old GD Louis Comte de Narbonne-Lara commanded the small and uncomfortably isolated garrison left in Raab. Additionally, 6th Hussars were in Wiener-Neustadt, a detachment of Polish Chevaulegers of the Guard operated out of Ödenburg, and Marmont's two battalions of 18th Léger awaited the arrival of a munitions convoy in Bruck an der Mur. GD Rusca also had a role to play in Napoleon's grand scheme.[54] Leaving GB Bertoletti in Klagenfurt with his three Italian battalions, he marched north for the Semmering Pass with the remaining infantry—barely a regiment, let alone a brigade or division—and had reached Judenburg by 4 July. We shall return to his perils and adventures later in the narrative.

Unlike Napoleon, Charles did not call in additional outlying forces before 4 July. His army had been concentrated since early June with the arrival of III Corps, and, with the exception of Reuss, Johann, and Chasteler, there were few trained regulars left to add to the Hauptarmee on the Marchfeld. Moreover, he had elected to place himself on the strategic defensive, so he was largely in a reactive mode; that is, he would have to wait for Napoleon to move before issuing his own orders. He was unwilling, for example, to relieve Reuss of his Danube observation mission or to withdraw Johann from Pressburg before he was absolutely certain of Napoleon's intentions.[55] His indecision compounded this strategic problem. Unsure of whether to fight the French on the riverbank or await them on the heights to the rear, he could not decide what to do with Johann. On 30 June, he seemed inclined to use Johann and Joseph in a diversionary advance on the south bank of the Danube. Reversing himself on the morning of 1 July in reaction to his brother's worries about being unable to hold the Engerau bridgehead, Charles authorised Johann to withdraw from the works on the south bank if he could do so with little loss. By evening, however, he had apparently concluded that Legrand's 30 June crossing was a feint and responded by ordering Johann to 'occupy the enemy by every possible means'.[56] In addition to Johann, the Austrians clung to the hope of distracting Napoleon with other detachments as well, such as Chasteler, Gyulai, and Kienmayer. Given the quality of the Landwehr and Insurrection troops that made up many of the forces on the strategic flanks, this approach was perhaps unavoidable: such formations were unlikely to fare well against Napoleon's French and German veterans in an open battle. However, the Habsburg leaders clung to a strategy that only had at best slim chances of success. They thereby compounded the weakness created by their fear of multiple French river crossings and only succeeded in distracting themselves more than their adversary. All of this meant that on 4 July, as the French were beginning to cross the Stadtler Arm, the closest Austrian reinforcements were at best approximately one and a half to two days' march away: Johann at Pressburg (forty-five kilometres) and Schustekh of Reuss's corps at Krems (sixty kilometres). Furthermore, the forces that had even the remotest possibility of distracting the French (Joseph at Komorn, combined with Chasteler) could not have been in a position to do so for several days—plus at least two days to draft and dispatch any such instructions. In other words, the Hauptarmee was on its own—certainly for the first day of battle and possibly for any subsequent combat as well—against the full might of whatever force Napoleon had assembled.

The army at Charles's disposal was nonetheless considerable, and, as we have seen, with his 3 July 'Disposition' he had chosen to array the majority of his forces either behind the Russbach or on the eastern slopes of the Bisamberg. From left to right, this order placed IV Corps at Markgrafneusiedl, II Corps behind Baumersdorf (now Parbasdorf), I Corps around Wagram, the Grenadiers at Gerasdorf, and III Corps in the rear around Hagenbrunn. Liechtenstein's reserve cavalry was to occupy 'its old bivouacs' in the general square formed by Süssenbrunn, Breitenlee, Raasdorf, and Aderklaa. Here they could stand in readiness, awaiting events beyond the range of the massive artillery concentration on Lobau.[57]

The Generalissimus, of course, could not leave the river front completely devoid of troops. Awaiting the French along the Danube, therefore, were the

Hauptarmee's VI Corps and Advance Guard. The first of these was now under FML Klenau. Hiller, claiming illness but also deeply indignant at being endlessly vexed by army headquarters, had asked to be relieved on the morning of the 4th.[58] Permission granted, he had departed to take the waters at a spa, and Klenau had shifted from the Advance Guard to VI Corps. Klenau, a cavalryman of 52, already had thirty-four years of service to his credit, winning renown against the Turks and against Revolutionary and Imperial France in both Germany and Italy. He had started the 1809 war as the advance guard commander in II Corps, had been given command of an ephemeral 'Advance Guard' just before Aspern, and had overseen the larger and more balanced Advance Guard since 23 May. On Klenau's left was the Advance Guard, now commanded by FML Nordmann. Nordmann was a 50-year-old Alsatian who had begun his military career in the French cavalry, became an émigré in 1793, and fought against the Revolution before accepting a Habsburg commission in 1798. His experience in Austrian service included campaigns in Germany and Italy prior to crossing the Inn in April 1809 as commander of Hiller's advance guard. Promoted to FML after Aspern, he now found himself in charge of what would be the crucial sector in the opening phases of the war's greatest conflagration.

Both VI Corps and the Advance Guard were under Klenau's general orders. The former had 17,600 infantry and cavalry supported by fifty-six guns to cover the Austrian right from the twisting branches of the Danube near Aspern up to and including Essling, while the latter, with some 13,800 men and thirty-four pieces, was responsible for the left wing from Essling to the confluence of the Stadtler Arm and the Danube. Both were disposed in entrenchments that had been constructed since late May, but these were weakly armed and neither properly constructed nor sited to the best advantage. They did buttress defences between Aspern and Essling, especially given the inherent strength of the villages, but the new fortifications petered out on the Austrian left to a few weak and isolated flèches. They excited only derision from some officers, and Charles's orders to strengthen them—issued on the afternoon of 2 July because 'the right flank in front of Aspern is not sufficiently secure'—could not possibly have been carried out to any significant degree.[59] Furthermore, the fact that such instructions were being issued on 2 July suggests that no one on the Habsburg side had paid adequate attention to this question during the six-week hiatus in operations.

The mission assigned to Klenau was challenging. On the one hand, he was not to defend his positions to the last man, on the other, he was not to leave 'a position from which much damage can be done to the enemy' without offering 'adequate' resistance. The Generalissimus relied on Klenau's 'insight and renowned courage' to execute this difficult task.[60] Once retreat became necessary, Klenau was to conduct an 'eccentric' withdrawal, that is, the two elements of his command were to diverge, with VI Corps retiring on the right towards Stammersdorf, while Nordmann fell back to Glinzendorf on the extreme left wing. Liechtenstein's cavalry was to screen these moves and discourage French pursuit. Still unsure of French intentions, the Austrians thus watched the masses of troops making their way to Lobau as the hours of 4 July turned to evening. FML Schwarzenberg, newly returned from his mission to the tsar, wrote to his wife: 'Great events are awaited, and it seems to me much blood will flow in the coming days, God grant that it is not in vain.'[61] He and his colleagues would not have long to wonder.

A *Night Out of* Macbeth

Napoleon's plan for the crossing was outlined in detailed instructions issued on 2 July and supplemented by numerous other directives over the following two days. The basic concept was portrayed with exemplary clarity: 'In general, we will conduct a movement by the right, pivoting on Enzersdorf, to envelope the entire system of the enemy.' Oudinot would open the ball on the French right, launching an assault crossing of the lower Stadtler Arm onto the Hanselgrund under cover of a massive bombardment by the Lobau guns and supported by Capitaine Baste with eight of his gunboats. Oudinot's men would screen the construction of the initial bridges and would carry with them materials to throw two spans over the small Steigbügel Arm to facilitate their advance on Mühlleiten and Sachsengang. A third small bridge would be floated up the watercourse from Lobau. In addition, Baste would assist Oudinot's advance by capturing the Rohrhaufen on 2nd Corps' right flank. Massena would come next, crossing upstream on the left, seizing Ile Pouzet and driving methodically on Enzersdorf to form the anchor upon which the rest of the army would turn as it crossed during the early morning hours of 5 July. Davout would follow Massena and these three corps—4th, 2nd, and 3rd from left to right—would comprise Napoleon's first line 'as quickly as possible' on the north bank. Bernadotte's Saxons, the Guard, and the Army of Italy would cross next, to form the second line; the third line would consist of the Cavalry Reserve. The emperor optimisticaly planned for Marmont and Wrede to join the Guard as part of the general reserve—as we have seen, however, they did not arrive in time to participate on the first day. GD Jean

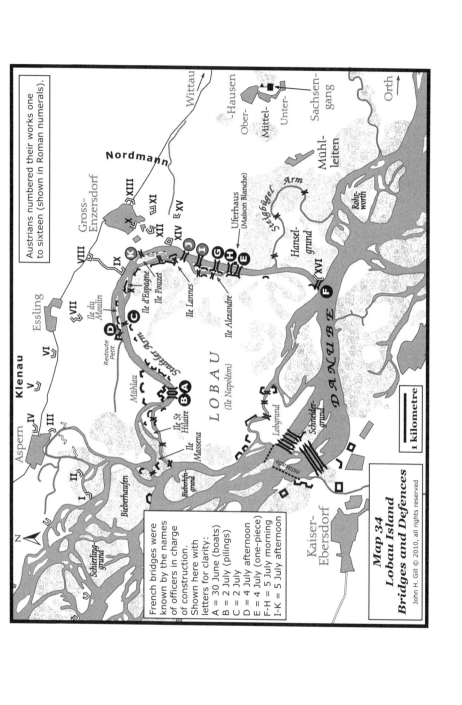

Austrians numbered their works one
to sixteen (shown in Roman numerals).

Wittau

Nordmann

Gross-
Enzersdorf

Essling

Klenau

Aspern

-Hausen
Ober-
Mittel-
Unter-
Sachsen-
gang

Orth

Mühl-
leiten

Uferhaus
(Maison Blanche)

Steigbügel Arm

Hansel-
grund

Rohr-
wörth

Ile d'Espagne
Ile Pouzet

Ile du
Moulin

Ile Lannes

Ile Alexandre

Redoute
Petit

Städtler Arm

Mühlau

LOBAU
(Ile Napoléon)

Ile St
Hilaire

Ile
Masséna

Bieberhaufen

DANUBE

Lobgrund

Schneider-
grund

Stadler Arm

Schütte-
grund

Kaiser-
Ebersdorf

N

French bridges were
known by the names
of officers in charge
of construction.
Shown here with
letters for clarity:
A = 30 June (boats)
B = 2 July (pilings)
C = 2 July
D = 4 July afternoon
E = 4 July (one-piece)
F-H = 5 July morning
I-K = 5 July afternoon

1 kilometre

Map 34
Lobau Island
Bridges and Defences

Reynier was charged with the defence of Lobau with the 109 artillery pieces, 3rd Baden Infantry, two Saxon battalions, two of Oudinot's battalions, and Berthier's battalion of yellow-clad Neuchâtel infantry.[62] The plan called for a remarkable degree of precision and co-ordination—especially during a night operation—but Napoleon was confident that midday on 5 July would see the bulk of his army across the Stadtler Arm and prepared to advance.[63]

The weather, however, threatened to confound Napoleon's meticulous plans. 'After midday, threatening thunderheads piled themselves up; the heavens clouded over more thickly; day was almost transformed into night; the thunder rolled in the distance, and individual, heavy rain drops fell.' This afternoon thunderstorm temporarily blinded the Austrian observation post on the Bisamberg, but it was merely the prelude to an evening deluge of extraordinary duration and power. As evening fell, 'the storm clouds, driven by a strong wind, came on and halted angrily over our heads; suddenly the rain flowed down in streams,' wrote a Saxon.[64] 'It grew dark so that one could not see one's neighbours,' recalled another. 'Suddenly bolt after bolt flashed on the water, and the lightning did not let up.'[65] The skies seemed to burst. 'Rain and hail fell alternately in powerful streams so that the vedettes could hardly stay atop their horses', and vision was reduced to a minimum as recorded in the Austrian Advance Guard's journal.[66] 'Flashes of lightning and claps of thunder rapidly succeeded each other, the clouds were rent asunder, and a downpour of rain of extraordinary violence' crashed down upon both armies.[67]

To this swelling scene of natural ferocity was soon added all the sound and fury mankind could muster.[68] At 9 p.m., 1,500 men of Conroux's brigade launched themselves into the Stadtler Arm aboard a small flotilla of rafts, escorted by Capitaine Baste's eight gunboats.[69] Concealed by the double obscurity of night and storm, they reached the Hanselgrund at about 9.30, but the Austrians noticed them almost at once and started firing. Baste replied with his boat-mounted cannon and the French battery on Lobau opened up as well. It was the signal for a vast bombardment as French batteries all along the edge of Lobau came dreadfully alive. Those between Ile du Moulin and Ile Alexandre alone would fire 2,875 projectiles and consume more than 5,000 kilograms of powder during the next several hours. Their Austrians counterparts, already under orders to shell the island that night, soon replied.[70] 'The thunder no longer rolled, it cracked in the most terrible strikes, whose harbingers, frightful lightning bolts, illuminated the deep obscurity for a few moments,' recalled a Saxon soldier. 'Accompanying this was the thunder of the guns.' As a trooper of 11th Chasseurs wrote, 'the lightning and the cannon fire seemed to be one,' and many witnesses endeavoured to depict a singular night in which man and nature seemed to contend in manifestations of violence.[71] In Wolkersdorf, Stadion was helped to clamber on top of a barrel on a rooftop despite his gout to observe the display, and GM d'Aspre watched from Gerasdorf. 'The cannonade was furious,' he scrawled in a letter to a friend the next morning, but 'that which rendered the scene even more terrible was that it rained in torrents with the most violent wind I have ever experienced in my life; add to that the air enflamed by the reverberations of the cannon, the cries of the wounded and the dying, the caissons flying into the sky, the bombs exploding among the clouds.'[72] 'The raven-black air was criss-crossed with the fiery trails of bombs and shells that seemed to form a ceiling of flames,' wrote a Saxon Hussar officer. 'It was a horrifically beautiful night!'[73]

The Austrians suffered most from the storm of iron: 'the enemy's fire was effective, killing and wounding many men,' recorded the Advance Guard's journal. The fire also silenced many of the Nordmann's guns.[74] 'Whole clouds of balls, shells, and bombs rained on unfortunate Enzersdorf,' and the town quickly caught fire to illuminate the 'eerie night'.[75] Its flames 'carried

Table 15: Bridge Completion from Lobau to North Bank

30 June 1809
- First bridge (on boats) to Mühlau bridgehead

2 July
- Bridge to Ile du Moulin
- Second bridge (on pilings) to Mühlau bridgehead

4 July
- Bridge from Ile du Moulin to north bank (time uncertain)
- One-piece bridge (by midnight)

5 July
- Stadtler Arm mouth (1.30 a.m.)
- From Ile Alexandre (2 a.m.)
- South end of Ile Alexandre (5.30 a.m.)
- From Ile Alexandre (11.30 a.m.)
- From Ile Lannes (2 p.m.)
- To and from Ile Pouzet (5 p.m., possibly as late as 9 p.m.)

All times approximate.

a lugubrious clarity to certain parts of that imposing scene, even into the interior of our batteries,' wrote Pelet.[76] But shot and shell also fell among the Allied troops waiting on Lobau. 'The bullets decapitated the trees,' observed trooper Joseph Abbeel of the 2nd Carabiniers, and the 1st Saxon Grenadiers took numerous casualties from falling branches. Other Saxon infantry made a bizarrely comic picture as they hid behind trees, sometimes nine deep in the lee of a single trunk.[77] Some of their countrymen were lucky to escape unscathed when an Austrian ball smashed the kettle in which they were trying to prepare a simple meal.[78] Oddly, a few soldiers such as young Sergeant Nicholas Louis Planat de la Faye of the Guard artillery 'slept profoundly' despite the 'cannonade that went on all night' and 'the appalling thunderstorm'; others, like the Bavarians near Schönbrunn, could find no rest in flooded bivouacs. 'The constant soaking and the cold, strong wind in July was very burdensome—I froze in the night like a wet dog,' recorded one.[79] Such vignettes aside, most men were awed by the scene about them. Some discovered a weird splendour, as GM d'Aspre recounted in a letter the following day: 'The rain, the thunder, the wind, all that added to the most severe cannonade made a spectacle of horrible beauty.'[80] For many others, the night approached their vision of the end of the world: 'The storm from above and the enemy cannon fire, it seemed as if the Judgment Day had arrived.'[81] For a literary Saxon, the drama could only be described as 'a night out of *Macbeth*'.[82] Indeed, no one who experienced the night of 4/5 July on the banks of the Danube ever forgot it. 'It is thirty-seven years now since that awful day, and yet the grand scene still rises vividly before me,' remembered Colonel Lejeune.[83]

All this turbulent drama of man and nature did not, however, impede the attack. 'The French army bore all of this with courage and patience,' noted Löwenstern as he watched the operation unfurl itself during the fearful night.[84] Above all, Napoleon never wavered. Officers had approached him at nightfall suggesting postponement of the crossing because of the shocking weather, but the emperor rejected this advice out of hand and appeared all over the island as he oversaw the execution of his carefully crafted plans.[85] 'Napoleon, now on horseback, now on foot, directed that beautiful and vast operation,' wrote Colonel Pelleport, and GD Savary, remarked on the importance of his example: 'the storm was so violent that no one would have worked if he had not been there.'[86] Similarly, a Saxon soldier recalled that 'the emperor directed everything himself; neither the rain that fell in streams, nor the difficulty of the flooded terrain, nor the enemy's fire hindered him from showing himself everywhere at once and personally seeing to the punctual and rapid execution of his orders.'[87] 'The emperor was at our head, on foot and in the most abominable weather one could possibly see,' scribbled a young lieutenant of 3rd Léger to his mother.[88] Though intensely active and decisive, Napoleon remained composed, waiting calmly or issuing demanding, laconic orders as the situation required. Lejeune was startled as 'a flash suddenly revealed to me when I least expected it that I was standing side by side with the emperor, whose profile with the little hat and the grey cloak stood out for a moment.'[89] Capitaine Paulin, sent by Bertrand to report that the one-piece bridge had been completed, recorded that he found Napoleon 'not far away, sitting on a hummock, completely soaked from the rain'.[90] On the other hand, as dawn arrived and the crossing seemed to be proceeding too slowly, he ordered the construction of three more bridges, one each from Ile Alexandre, Ile Lannes, and Ile Pouzet. The would only be completed later in the day and would prove rather superfluous, but the army's ability to react successfully to major requirements such as this on short notice is a small indication of its ardour, adaptability, and professional competence.[91] In the meantime, the crossing proceeded swiftly, with a minimum of resistance and friction.

5 JULY: THE BATTLE OF WAGRAM—FIRST DAY[92]

Between 9.30 and 11 p.m., Oudinot's men landed on the far bank and chased off one and one-half companies of 1st Jägers in Redoubt No. XVI to secure the Hanselgrund, capturing three 3-pounders in the process. The Jägers 'hardly had time to fire two salvoes' from their small cannon before retreating.[93] Steadily reinforced, 2nd Corps began forming itself into three lines for an advance on Mühlleiten, while sappers hastened to finish the little bridges over the Steigbügel Arm and other workers struggled to construct ad hoc fortifications to protect the crossing sites. Capitaine Baste, once 2nd Corps was beginning to disembark, shifted to the main channel of the Danube and 'pursued the enemy from island to island' as far as Orth.[94] On Oudinot's left, Massena had by now seized a lodgement as well. Some 1,500 men from Boudet's division, led by one of his promising staff officers, Colonel Charles Escorches de Sainte-Croix, made the assault crossing, followed quickly by Molitor, Carra Saint-Cyr, and the light cavalry of Marulaz and Lasalle. As the first troops disembarked, their rafts and boats were immediately rigged up as ferries to expedite the passage. Although the one-piece bridge snapped into place as designed within five minutes shortly before midnight, most of the troops from both corps were transported by these means initially.[95] As the wild morning wore on, however, the other three bridges were completed and the pace of crossing accelerated. 'The French infantry crossed the bridges at a run and the cavalry and artillery followed with order and celerity,' remarked a watching Saxon gunner.[96] By 6 a.m., 2nd Corps minus Colbert, 4th Corps minus Legrand, and Friant's division of 3rd Corps were on the north bank. Indeed, they were already on the move. Tharreau, leading Oudinot's corps, crossed the Steigbügel, pushed through Mühlleiten, and arrived outside Hausen (Oberhausen) at 8 a.m. The defenders in this sector (south of the Uferhaus or 'Maison Blanche') were the 1st Jägers. Faced with an enemy whose numbers 'increased from minute to minute', the battalion fell back steadily on Hausen, but two of its five companies became lost in the confusion and ended up with the Hauptarmee's left wing at Markgrafneusiedl, ten kilometres away.[97] The remaining three companies— too few to hold Hausen—quickly retreated into a two-storey Schloss, or manor, called Sachsengang. This miniature fortress was already occupied by three companies of 7th Jägers, but the outlook was bleak. 'I climbed into the manor's tower to get an overview of our situation and saw unfortunately that we were in the middle of an enemy mass of incalculable size,' wrote Unterleutnant Wilhelm Reiche. 'Far and wide there was nothing to be seen of our army.'[98] The Austrian officers twice refused offers to surrender, but Tharreau brought up his howitzers and 'after a few volleys, ceased fire, presuming with reason, that the commandant of the chateau, attacked by artillery and superior forces, would show himself disposed to capitulate.'[99] This proved true, but several hours apparently passed before the Jägers gave up. Some 800 went into captivity and Tharreau's men occupied the manor.[100] Despite this annoyance, by 9 a.m., Oudinot was able to turn north and bring his corps into line with Massena's. Behind him, Davout's men were marching to the east to assume their position towards Wittau on the army's right flank. Aggressive French light cavalry had already cleared a path for Davout. Charging and breaking some of GM Franz Freiherr von Frelich's hussars as the Austrians, coming from picket duty near Orth, attempted to form on Nordmann's left, the French troopers pursued their quarry toward Rutzendorf.

Massena's chief obstacle was Gross-Enzersdorf. A walled town with a boggy ditch and redans at each of its gates, Enzersdorf was a formidable post. The burning village was defended by I/*Bellegarde* with several other battalions in support, but Carra Saint-Cyr sent swarms of skirmishers forward and Sainte-Croix stormed in from the south at the head of 46th

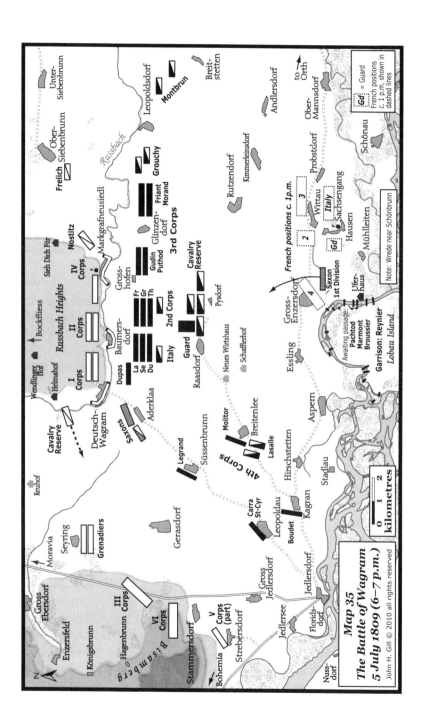

Map 35
The Battle of Wagram
5 July 1809 (6–7 p.m.)

French positions c. 1p.m.

Gd = Guard

French positions
c. 1 p.m. shown in
dashed lines

Note: Wede near Schönbrunn

Ligne. At the same moment, parts of II/*Bellegarde* and III/*Chasteler* were entering from the north to relieve the garrison, which had suffered heavy casualties and exhausted much of its ammunition. In a vicious street fight, the French destroyed the defenders, capturing at least 300 men from *Bellegarde* and most of III/*Chasteler*. The rest of the whitecoats fled in disorder, leaving Enzersdorf firmly in French hands.[101] This success deprived the Austrians of the last strongpoint on their left flank and positioned the French to envelope the remaining entrenchments towards Essling and Aspern. Massena's advance also isolated the company of *Wallach-Illyria* Grenzer on Ile Pouzet, leaving these hapless men no choice but to surrender.

It was now approximately 10 a.m. and a pause ensued as Napoleon waited for the rest of his available forces to cross and occupy their designated posts in the growing battle line. Legrand had returned stealthily from Mühlau, marched through Lobau, and crossed the Stadtler Arm 'in dense masses and with such tumultuous urgency that those in the rear shoved those ahead as if they were afraid they would come too late for the bloody party'.[102] Legrand came up behind 4th Corps between 8 and 9 a.m., but the army's second line (9th Corps, the Guard, the Army of Italy) was only beginning to make its way on to the Marchfeld between 9 and 10. This brief respite gives us an opportunity to review the Austrian reaction to the French offensive thus far.

Many factors hampered the Austrian commanders as they tried to respond to the French assault. Chief among these were the obscurity of night and storm, the surprising location of Napoleon's main attack, the unanticipated speed of the crossing and bridging operations, and the ferocious cannonade. Moreover, most Austrians seem to have concluded that the French would not attempt a crossing under such miserable weather and many of the 1st Jäger's pickets seem to have been more interested in seeking shelter than watching the Stadtler Arm.[103] Baste and his sailors were thus able to approach undetected. Once the mighty bombardment opened, the defenders suffered horrific losses and the Advance Guard found that the fire raking the level ground south of Enzersdorf was so terrible that the area could not be traversed safely. The 1st Jägers were thus effectively cut off and Nordmann had to send hussars scouting into the darkness to gain an idea of what was happening on his left flank. These troopers quickly brought back the alarming news that the French were already swarming over the meadows below the Uferhaus, the Jägers were retiring, and the Grenzer were retreating on Enzersdorf. 'Only a few people came back' from the latter battalion, which also lost its colonel and all of its other senior officers.[104]

The Jägers were left entirely to their own devices. 'My left wing has been completely outflanked by the enemy and is in continuous retreat, the advance troops have disintegrated, and my situation is serious,' reported Nordmann at 10 a.m., 'I need immediate reinforcement to change things around.'[105] With Enzersdorf lost, he fell back to a position approximately two kilometres north of the blackened town. His weak left was in danger, he could expect no support, and all units were reporting heavy casualties, but he was still tied to VI Corps at Redoubt No. VIII between Enzersdorf and Essling.[106] Other than cannon fire, Klenau had thus far escaped serious action, his men being largely observers to the devastation visited upon the Advance Guard.[107]

The odd Habsburg dispositions that made the left wing so vulnerable also contributed to the French achieving a quick foothold and expanding rapidly. The Habsburg leaders completely underestimated Napoleon's ability to place an enormous number of men and guns on the north bank in a remarkably short period of time.[108] Klenau, who had reported at 6 a.m. that he did not think a major attack was underway, was shocked two hours later to find that 'the enemy, following his crossing, has outflanked FML Nordmann's left wing with inexpressibly astonishing rapidity.'[109] The Austrians were thus faced with a situation that was evolving much faster than expected and were very relieved—at least temporarily—when the French paused in their floodtide advance. 'Other than some weak skirmishing, all is quiet,' reported Nordmann.[110]

Nordmann, though feeling unsupported, was not entirely without assistance. Rosenberg sent Radetzky (now an FML) with six squadrons of *Ferdinand* Hussars and a cavalry half-battery to buttress Nordmann's left flank. The regiment's other two squadrons and another cavalry half-battery rode towards Rutzendorf, where the 1st *EH Carl* Legion helped hold off the French light cavalry that had been pursuing the hapless Frelich. The 2nd Moravian Volunteers were deposited in Glinzendorf as an additional support. Meanwhile, Liechtenstein's Cavalry Reserve deployed as well: Roussel d'Hurbal's brigade (*Albert* and *EH Franz* Cuirassiers) at Neues Wirtshaus, the other four cuirassier regiments at Raasdorf, and the light cavalry and dragoons towards Pysdorf.[111] Liechtenstein, endeavouring to prevent the probing French horse from outflanking his troopers or Nordmann's men on their left, kept edging east to keep pace with the enemy. Although neither side risked a melee, both employed their artillery liberally, a circumstance that largely worked to the detriment of the outgunned Austrians. The after-action report of the Reserve Cavalry, for instance, described 'an extraordinarily heavy cannon and canister fire' that 'caused our cavalry extremely heavy losses.'[112]

Curiously, Charles had not yet ridden to the front. Only at 11.30 a.m. did he depart Wagram and then to ride to Markgrafneusiedl, not to Klenau or Nordmann. Wimpffen did visit Klenau, but it is not clear how much he learned. Indeed, the Generalissimus and his advisers seem to have had no idea that Napoleon had brought an immense force to the north bank of the Danube; they thus remained comfortable in the 'illusion' that the day would pass in limited engagements between the respective advance guards.[113] Charles did, however, send a message to Johann. The previous night, as numerous reports depicting the increasing French strength on Lobau came in, he had finally ordered Johann to depart Pressburg. 'It will come to a great battle here on the Marchfeld that will decide the fate of our house,' he had told his younger brother. 'Your Grace will certainly wish to take part.' Johann was to leave Bianchi with 'very few troops and some guns' at Pressburg and make plans 'immediately upon receipt of this' to march with 'all possible available troops'. Now, at 5.30 a.m. on the 5th, Charles wrote again, instructing his brother 'above all to establish a close connection with the left wing of the army at Markgrafneusiedl'. Johann was to rest for three hours in Marchegg before continuing his march to Untersiebenbrunn.[114] At the same time, Charles also issued instructions for the corps along the Russbach to construct redoubts and to repair some earthworks near Baumersdorf; the grenadiers were to strengthen the defences of Gerasdorf; and 'a few redoubts' were to be built near Stammersdorf.[115] It is difficult to take such orders seriously. Either Charles believed he would have sufficient time to complete these works, or he was grasping at straws now that the great confrontation was at hand. In the absence of tools, time, and urgency, neither these fortifications, nor those Rosenberg had been ordered to construct on 3 July, achieved any degree of readiness. They would have no noticeable influence on the storm of violence that was about to explode across the Marchfeld.

An Extraordinarily Beautiful Sight: The French Advance

The Marchfeld upon which the coming struggle would be fought was a broad and almost entirely flat expanse of rich farmland on the left bank of the Danube. Although dotted with small villages and occasionally offering shallow declivities and folds in the terrain that might benefit units at the low tactical level, this vast plain between the Bisamberg and the March River was otherwise nearly featureless. The plateau that bounded the Marchfeld to the north, however, would play an important role in the battle. Known as the Russbach Heights, it rose only a few metres (no more than ten at its highest point) above the farmland to the south, but the flatness of the surrounding terrain made this topographically minor feature tactically significant. Its southern face was steep enough to make the climb challenging for horsemen, but it levelled out to near imperceptibility on its eastern front north of a farmstead called Sieh-Dich-Für. This, the Austrian left flank, was 'the weakest side of the position, its true key'.[116] A small stream, the Russbach, flowed below the escarpment like a narrow moat. The Russbach was only two to three metres wide, but it flowed in a sharply cut channel a metre deep and was bordered by boggy ground in some places. Edged with willows, it was a troublesome obstacle for infantry, but very difficult for cavalry, and impassable for artillery between Wagram and Markgrafneusiedl, except where there were bridges.[117] Below the latter village, on the other hand, it was passable for all arms 'with little difficulty and little preparation'.[118] Three villages formed potential bastions for a defence of the heights: Wagram, Baumersdorf, and Markgrafneusiedl. This last, lying in the low ground at the base of the rise, was particularly noteworthy for an old stone defensive tower perched on the slope above the town. During 5 July, the Austrians hastily and belatedly attempted to improve the dilapidated encircling wall around this square tower and took some steps to place all three villages in a state of defence, but there was no time to bolster the natural strength of the position with manmade works in any appreciable way.[119] Unintended obstacles for both sides were the hutments, pits, ditches, and other camp obstructions that encumbered the top of the plateau owing to the Hauptarmee having bivouacked there for nearly six weeks.[120] These were not decisive, but they hindered movement—especially for mounted troops— and would provide some shelter for skirmishers for both armies during the fighting on the evening of 5 July. In sum, 'our position was one of the best one could find,' as one Landwehr battalion commander stated, having the additional advantage 'that one could distinguish all the movements of the enemy' from the top of the escarpment.[121]

Ten kilometres away, between Enzersdorf and Wittau, the Allied army was preparing to set out across the seemingly endless expanse of the Marchfeld. 'A bright and glorious summer's day had succeeded the awful night of storm,' and at least 137,000 troops now stood neatly ordered, silent, rank upon rank, their bayonets, sabres, and accoutrements glittering in the brilliant sun.[122] 'It was an extraordinarily beautiful sight,' wrote GM Karl von Nagel of the Hessian brigade.[123] It was also an extraordinary accomplishment. In approximately fifteen hours—half of that in darkness and under a tremendous storm—Napoleon had brought a gigantic army across a significant body of water (the Stadtler Arm) and, pushing aside light resistance, had arrayed his force in a position to outflank the enemy's initial defences. It was the largest force he had ever commanded on a single field. Now it was time to move. At 12.30, he issued orders for a general advance and, at approximately 1 p.m., the great mass of men, horses, and guns rolled forth across the fields, marching through 'wheat up to the shoulders of the infantrymen'.[124]

The first French line, consisting of Massena, Oudinot, and Davout, stretched from Enzersdorf and the Stadtler Arm bend on the left to Wittau and Probstdorf on the right; Montbrun was posted towards Kimmerleinsdorf (now Franzensdorf). Lasalle (including Marulaz) rode in front of Oudinot and Davout initially, and, as mentioned above, had been checked in his attempt to capture Rutzendorf. As the afternoon wore on, however, Colbert arrived at approximately 3 p.m., allowing Lasalle to shift west and rejoin 4th Corps. Similarly, Grouchy at first took a position south of Pysdorf with the Army of Italy's two dragoon divisions, but swung far to the right as the advance began, riding towards Leopoldsdorf (or Loibersdorf) to protect the army's flank in co-operation with Montbrun's light horse. Davout, 'certain that the army of Archduke Johann was destined to manoeuvre against the French extreme right', especially instructed Montbrun to reconnoitre 'in the direction of Marchegg to discover the movements of the army at Pressburg'.[125] His infantry, however, preceded by thirty guns, marched on Glinzendorf with Gudin and Friant in the lead, followed by Puthod to Gudin's left rear and Morand echeloned to Friant's right rear.[126] Oudinot's destination was Grosshofen. Likewise leading with artillery, he arranged his three divisions one behind the other: Frère, Grandjean, and Tharreau. On the left, Massena pivoted on Enzersdorf and headed west with Boudet along the Stadtler Arm, Carra Saint-Cyr in the centre, and Legrand on the right; Molitor trailed behind and to the right of Legrand to form a link with Oudinot. As the left and right wings pushed towards their objectives, they diverged, creating a gap in the centre into which Napoleon deployed 9th Corps, followed by the Army of Italy.

Other than some cavalry skirmishing and considerable artillery fire, the French flanking corps steadily drove the whitecoats back with manoeuvre and weight of numbers. 'This first affair was solely an artillery affair,' noted one of Davout's officers. 'The enemy did not engage any of his masses and always held himself at a great distance.'[127] In the centre, however, Dupas and the Saxons had to clear their path with force. Dupas's men had been inspired by a rousing speech from Bernadotte before they set off. 'Soldiers!' the marshal had shouted, 'Do you want to earn laurels too? Hurry or you will be too late!' 'These words were received with enthusiasm', recalled Hauptmann Carl August Schneider of the attached *Metzsch* Schützen Battalion, 'and the march began with boundless exhilaration.'[128] Advancing to the right and considerably ahead of the rest of 9th Corps, Dupas received orders directly from Napoleon that conflicted with those from Bernadotte. To the marshal's annoyance, the general wisely decided to obey his emperor's instructions and, confusion notwithstanding, had easily captured Raasdorf from the shaken remnants of *Chasteler* and *Wallach-Illyria* by about 3.30 p.m. One battalion, I/5th Léger, sufficed for this task.[129] Dupas then turned north to shield Oudinot's left until the Army of Italy could arrive.

In the meantime, Bernadotte was collecting other causes for grievance. The *Prinz Johann* Chevaulegers had been detached to Oudinot early in the day, apparently without Bernadotte's knowledge, and now he was ordered to leave the 1st Saxon Division and a battery at Enzersdorf to guard the bridges. This was only a temporary measure, but it rankled and compounded the *de facto* detachment of Dupas, leaving the marshal with only his Advance Guard and GL Georg von Polenz's 2nd Division to conduct his advance in the centre. Delays in getting all of the Saxon artillery across the Stadtler Arm meant that this force consisted of a mere six battalions, sixteen squadrons, and eight guns as it made its way across the wheat fields south of Raasdorf. Nonetheless, his horsemen were adequate to overthrow the opposition Liechtenstein offered. This came in the form of GM Roussel d'Hurbal's brigade of cuirassiers (*Erzherzog Franz, Herzog Albert*), deployed west of Raasdorf near the Neues Wirtshaus. Worried that the Austrian heavies represented a danger to the left flank of his infantry, Bernadotte sent his chief of staff, GB Maurice Etienne Gérard, to remove the threat. The Saxon contingent's chief of staff, Oberst Karl von Gersdorff, rode up at almost the same moment with the same mission. Approached by the Saxon Hussars and *Prinz Clemens* Chevaulegers, the Austrians easily repelled an impetuous but ill-advised charge by the latter regiment, but the rest of the Saxon horse, called forward by Gersdorff, was soon on the scene. Roussel's men, who had successfully turned back *Prinz Clemens* by receiving that charge at the halt, elected to repeat this tactic and waited motionless instead of counter-charging as most cavalry experts of the day recommended. The result was defeat for the white-coated troopers as the Saxon Hussars turned their left flank and the Saxon heavy squadrons slammed into their ranks from the front. The Austrians 'fled as fast as their horses would carry them in greatest disorder' after a swirling melee, and the Saxons rode back exultantly to reform near Raasdorf, receiving well-earned praise from Bernadotte for their performance.[130]

One of the Saxon Hussar squadrons did not take part in the fight with the Austrian cuirassiers. Taken under fire by infantry on their right flank as they advanced, the Saxons coolly wheeled and charged the foot soldiers, scattering them and seizing a flag, along with many prisoners. Napoleon rewarded the Saxon troopers with gold and warm accolades, telling them that 'he cherished this outstanding regiment as one of the bravest in his army.'[131] With the Saxon horse having cleared the way, Bernadotte continued his advance, stopping just beyond Aderklaa with his infantry on the right and his cavalry on his fairly unsupported left flank. Here, loosely connected to Dupas on his right and Massena on his left, he awaited the arrival of his 1st Division from Enzersdorf.

It was now between 6 and 7 p.m. and the Allied army was arrayed in a wide arc with Montbrun towards Breitstetten, and Grouchy near Leopoldsdorf, Davout on either side of Glinzendorf, Oudinot and Eugene south of Baumersdorf, Dupas slightly left and ahead of the Army of Italy, Bernadotte north of Aderklaa, and Massena stretched in a thin cordon from Süssenbrunn (Legrand), to Breitenlee (Molitor and cavalry), Leopoldau (Carra Saint-Cyr), and Kagran (Boudet). The Guard was in reserve near Raasdorf, where the Cavalry Reserve was also beginning to arrive. On the opposite side of the field, Klenau had retired to the Bisamberg Heights above Stammersdorf with moderate losses, joining Kolowrat and the Grenadiers on the slopes respectively north-west and north of Gerasdorf. Most of the Reserve Cavalry was assembled between Gerasdorf and Wagram. Wagram, the pivot of Charles's position, was held by I Corps, as were the adjoining heights, with II Corps on its left above Baumersdorf, and IV Corps stationed on the extreme left around Markgrafneusiedl. FML Johann Nepomuk Graf Nostitz-Reineck was also posted here with his division of the Cavalry Reserve to buttress Rosenberg on this vulnerable flank. Additionally, the shaken remnants of the Advance Guard were incorporated into IV Corps. Nordmann's command, however, was in tatters; many of its guns had been dismounted during the past twenty hours of battle, and its strength had been reduced to 6,200 infantry and 1,100 cavalry.[132]

With the long day drawing to a close, most men on both sides were certain there would be no more combat before the following morning. Enervated by hours of marching and fighting under the hot July sun and what had been for many a sleepless, rain-soaked night, they were hoping for a drink, a meal, and a rest to ready themselves for the coming dawn. Napoleon, however, had other ideas.

Some Music Before Night

Napoleon was uncertain as evening fell. He was determined to destroy Charles's army as rapidly as possible, but the weak resistance during his march across the Marchfeld and the gradual evaporation of gunfire as night came on suggested that the force to his front might be nothing more than a strong rear guard. Personal observation disclosed little as the trees along the Russbach and the steep escarpment hid the strength of the enemy on the plateau.[133] To clarify the situation, he thus decided to conduct a large-scale reconnaissance in force against the Russbach position.[134] If the Austrians were planning a withdrawal, this might lock them in place. If they were planning to stand, he would gain an appreciation of the enemy's strength, dispositions, and morale. Information from scouts confirmed that Johann had not moved from Pressburg, so there was nothing to fear on his right flank.[135] He decided to act. Calling Colonel Alexander Girardin, Berthier's first aide-de-camp, Napoleon said 'Go and tell Oudinot that I hear nothing; let him push forward a little and give us some music before night.'[136] Other staff officers were sent dashing off to Bernadotte, Eugene, and Davout. GD Honoré Reille, carrying the instructions for the viceroy, encountered Dupas after delivering his orders to Eugene, and told Dupas to join in what he described as a '*coup de main*'—a sudden, surprise assault.[137] By approximately 7.30 p.m., therefore, all of the Allied commanders along the Russbach had orders to advance despite the lateness of the hour. The available evidence does not indicate that Napoleon intended a full-scale assault, but 'events sometimes display a vitality of their own', and a number of factors would soon conspire to take matters out of his hands.[138]

The evening attack on the Russbach Heights can be considered as four different thrusts, related to one another and partly overlapping in execution, but unco-ordinated and separated by time: Oudinot, Dupas/Eugene, Davout, and Bernadotte. Though crippled in their potential by debilitating flaws, the surprising aspect of these disjointed operations is that they came very close to dramatic success at several points.

Oudinot, closest to Napoleon's headquarters and most prepared, made the first advance at approximately 7.30 p.m., sending Frère's division against Baumersdorf and the segment of the Russbach to the east. Frère's opponents were 8th Jägers, 2nd *EH Carl* Legion, and several companies of *Frelich* Infantry supported by artillery firing over the heads of the men in the village and the Jägers skirmishing along the Russbach.[139] Led by the resolute and energetic GM Ignaz von Hardegg, the Habsburg troops yielded nothing.

The Jägers were forced out of their posts along the brook, but the French attack, poorly organised and unsupported, blundered into a vicious crossfire and quickly stalled. The artillery fire 'put some hundred of our men out of action, including three officers', wrote Chef de Bataillon Castillon of IV/76. 'My horse was killed, my shako pierced, and my rolled greatcoat riddled with bullets.'[140] Frère retired in disorder.

Oudinot responded to this check by calling on two of the most renowned regiments of Grandjean's division: 57th Ligne and 10th Léger. 'This attack was no better co-ordinated than the preceding one, but the troops were better and showed the favourable results that could have been obtained had it been calculated with sagacity and executed with a greater number of men,' wrote the bitter Colonel Berthezène of 10th Léger.[141] These deficiencies notwithstanding, 57th Ligne drove into the village, while 10th Léger crossed the Russbach just to the east and stormed the heights beyond. Hardegg, whose conduct garnered sincere praise from his foes, was equal to the threat posed by the famous 57th.[142] 'The fighting in the village amongst the flames was murderous,' but Hardegg, supported by III/*Rohan*, III/*Frelich*, and II/*d'Aspre*, clung to enough of burning Baumersdorf to frustrate the French attack and deny access to the two small bridges over the Russbach.[143] The 10th Léger, meanwhile, faced challenges of its own. Although its intrepid advance gained it a foothold on the heights, it was halted by GM Wenzel von Buresch's brigade (*Zach* and I/*Josef Colloredo*) to its front, and then taken under fire on its right flank by the 2nd and 3rd Battalions of *Hiller*, and, from its left, by some of the Jägers who had retreated from the Russbach. Under extreme pressure, the regiment collapsed when Hohenzollern, seizing the right moment, led the *Vincent* Chevaulegers in a successful charge. Recoiling down the slope, the 10th uncovered the rear of the 57th in Baumersdorf, causing that regiment to retreat in confusion. 'Night having arrived, it was no longer possible to continue the attack with success,' was Oudinot's understated summary, and his corps 'took position in three lines' just south of the little town.[144] Berthezène recorded in disgust that his regiment 'had pointlessly lost the greater part of its strength'. His men were just as angry: 'Ah! If St Hilaire were alive, things would have come out differently!'[145] The Austrians had suffered too, with 8th Jägers, for example, reduced by nearly one-third.[146] Content to have repelled the ferocious assault, they only pursued far enough to re-occupy their previous positions, and fighting on this part of the battle line faded into silence. Hardegg was awarded the Commander's Cross of the Order of Maria Theresa for his superb performance.[147]

Overlapping with Oudinot's failed effort was a bold advance and near success between Baumersdorf and Wagram. Though generally considered one event—and certainly experienced as such by the Austrian defenders—this attack actually consisted of two simultaneous, but unco-ordinated, advances by Dupas and the Army of Italy; indeed, Dupas became involved through Reille's initiative, not through any plan of Napoleon's. The emperor's planning did, however, cover the provision of additional artillery support and the twenty-four guns of the Guard horse artillery thundered up to unlimber to Dupas's left front. These, along with Dupas's own batteries and some from Eugene, opened a heavy fire on the heights. The artillery bombardment was brief, and Dupas advanced almost at once 'with enthusiasm and under cries of "Vive l'Empereur"'.[148] It was about 8 p.m. The lack of preparation became immediately evident: with only some thirty minutes elapsing between receipt of orders from Reille and his advance, Dupas had no time to conduct a reconnaissance, and his men were thus surprised to stumble upon the Russbach as they attempted to charge the heights. Despite considerable confusion, the infantry got itself across, quickly reorganised, and resumed their attack, but Dupas was troubled that his artillery could not follow in support.[149] Coming up behind Dupas, the Army of Italy's lead division encountered the same unpleasant surprise. As Eugene's frustrated cavalry and artillery searched in vain for a crossing, however, the infantry—Lamarque's division with MacDonald at its head—passed over the brook 'under a most violent fire of canister and musketry'.[150]

By sheer good fortune, the French attack struck exactly on the seam between the Austrian I and II Corps, and at a spot where a shallow draw afforded somewhat easier access to the plateau. Furthermore, the clouds of smoke from the guns and Baumersdorf, combined with the deepening twilight, made it difficult for the Habsburg soldiers to detect the danger until the French were upon them. Dupas swung to the left and MacDonald led seven of Lamarque's battalions up on the right, leaving four in reserve on the low ground. The leading units gained footholds on the heights with astonishing speed despite heavy enemy fire. 'The French climbed the heights with a truly remarkable boldness,' wrote one Austrian soldier.[151] Austrian skirmishers were nested in the pits that had served as barracks for the past six weeks, but the French overthrew these quickly and charged the Habsburg masses beyond 'in a spontaneous movement by the entire division'.[152] The sudden, violent appearance of the French infantry shocked the Austrians, for they abandoned many guns, several masses (or squares) recoiled in disorder, hundreds of men laid down their arms, and triumphant French troops seized as many as five standards. Both Bellegarde and Hohenzollern had their corps in two lines, the first of which absorbed the impact of the spirited French attack. Bellegarde's left flank regiment, *Vogelsang,* 'was rolled up after brief resistance', dragging III/*EH Rainer* with it as it broke and fled.[153] In the confusion, men of the second line (*Argenteau* and 4th *EH Carl* Legion) 'lost their composure' and fired on *Vogelsang,* and the panicked fugitives spread disorder as they streamed to the rear.'[154] The second line fell back under this pressure, II/*Argenteau* disintegrating in the process. On the other side of the French penetration, the II Corps Landwehr that had been posted near the mouth of the draw seems to have taken to its heels, while I/*Rohan,* endeavouring to counter-attack from Hohenzollern's second line, was carried away by fleeing soldiers.

The French and Saxons were surprised by their unexpected achievement. Hauptmann Schneider of the *Metzsch* Schützen wrote: 'we took eighteen guns, that is, we went right through them, there were no crews, no teams.'[155] 'The frontal attack having succeeded beyond all our hopes,' reported MacDonald, 'we pursued the fugitives.'[156] Attempting to capitalise on their momentary advantage, the French generals called for reinforcements. Lamarque's four reserve battalions arrived at once and Grenier was crossing the Russbach with his two infantry divisions, but artillery and cavalry were stymied by the stream, and the French infantry was left to face the Hauptarmee unsupported.

The remainder of this confused and hard-fought action is difficult to untangle in detail, but the general outlines are clear enough. Dupas and Lamarque were close to cracking the Austrian centre. Several Austrian battalions had broken and fled, others were badly shaken, and the French had gathered up large batches of prisoners as well as a number of flags. Though the French hold on the plateau was tenuous, Charles faced a crisis. Riding to the scene of potential disaster, he inspired, cajoled, or beat men back into the ranks, using the flat of his sword so often that it eventually snapped in his hand.[157] Bellegarde likewise displayed great personal bravery and tactical leadership in this critical moment. Stabilising the line and organising counter-attacks, both men were in considerable danger. Bellegarde escaped unscathed, but Charles took a grazing wound and was nearly captured while rallying *Vogelsang.* Regimental officers were also crucial in holding their men to their duty. Oberst Joseph von Schäffer, for instance, rallied *Argenteau* and led it back into action with the 4th Legion, while Major Jakob Fromm speedily took command of *Erbach* when that regiment's colonel fell. Thanks to such leadership, the Austrians were able to stem the threatening tide of dissolution.

The struggle, however, was by no means over. Durutte seems to have come up on the plateau and the battle swayed back and forth with tremendous ferocity. At some point in the swirl of combat, Hohenzollern, riding up from the French right, charged in with the *Vincent* Chevaulegers (and probably with *Klenau* Chevaulegers), only to be undone by Sahuc, who had managed to appear with at least part of his division.[158] The 9th Chasseurs captured a standard from III/*Argenteau* in a bold charge, but were thrown back by four squadrons of *Hessen-Homburg* in a wild fight.[159] 'I have never seen such carnage,' related Chevillet of the 8th, 'the field was covered with dead.'[160] The cavalry melee seems to have granted the Austrian infantry time to restore itself, but Charles was disgusted by what he saw as much 'dashing about in the greatest confusion' on the part of *Hessen-Homburg*.[161] Using their superior numbers, the Habsburg commanders slowly gained the upper hand and forced the French back to the bivouac pits near the edge of the plateau. Here the French and Saxons dug in their toes and clung to their gains, but a series of disasters were about to undo all they had achieved through their skill and gallantry. Ever-increasing billows of powder smoke and the growing darkness hampered leaders in their efforts to exercise some kind of control over the struggle and, significantly, made distinguishing between friend and foe extraordinarily difficult.

In the first of several 'friendly fire' incidents that night, Seras's men loosed a volley at Dupas's Saxons when the fighting was at its highest pitch. The Saxons were in the centre of Dupas's line engaged to their front, according to Dupas, when Seras's division came up from behind and, discerning what they thought was an enemy line ahead of them, opened fire on their white-coated allies. The result was chaos. The Saxons retreated in disorder, while Seras's men, still formed in closed columns, believed themselves under attack; they fell into confusion and tumbled back across the Russbach.[162] The French attack did not collapse at once, but this self-inflicted wound proved a harbinger of defeat. The units remaining on the plateau were in disarray and unsupported, night was falling fast, and Austrian counter-attacks were mounting. Some of the shattered and shaken Habsburg battalions were returning to the fight and Charles brought III/*Kolowrat* over from Bellegarde's right to help hold the line. The Austrian cavalry seems to have returned to the fray, while the *Erbach* Infantry conducted such a successful advance that Charles authorised the regiment to use the 'Grenadier March' ever after as a special mark of honour. Struck from both flanks and fired on by their own comrades, 'the greatest confusion' quickly spread within the French ranks, and the entire force, 'without being repelled, spontaneously abandoned a position it had taken with such heroic courage.'[163] Lamarque and some others may have regained the heights in places for a few moments, but the cause was lost. Leaving behind most of their many prisoners and four of the five captured flags, the men fled to the rear, 'harassed by fatigue, desperate, and covered with wounds and blood', despite valiant efforts of the officers to rally them.[164]

The calamity in the French centre did not end with the panicked retreat across the Russbach. It was now very late, perhaps 10.30 p.m., and completely dark as French commanders tried to use Sahuc's cavalry and possibly the nearby Saxon *Prinz Johann* Chevaulegers to stem the rout—attached to Oudinot in the morning, the regiment seems to have come under Dupas's command in the afternoon. Pounding up out of the gloom, however, the friendly cavalry only increased the disorder, as the fleeing infantry, believing they were under attack by Austrian horsemen, dispersed in all directions.[165] In addition to suffering heavy casualties in the attack, therefore, the formations involved were knocked all apart. Scattered over the battlefield, most of the men recovered their composure when they came upon the Guard in the darkness, but some fled as far as the Danube bridges.

A sense of order would only be restored late that night, but even then some individuals utilised the darkness to escape further duty. Though most units had reassembled themselves by dawn, many remained seriously damaged. In the Army of Italy, Grenier, Seras, Sahuc, and GD Martin Vignolle, Eugene's chief of staff, were all wounded, the colonel of the 13th Ligne killed, four regiments had nearly 30 per cent of their officers dead or wounded, and 106th Ligne lost an eagle to III/*Argenteau*.[166] Dupas reported that the *Radeloff* Grenadiers had 'disappeared', the *Metzsch* Schützen were reduced to forty-three men, and he could only collect 'two small battalions' from his entire division.[167] Many of these soldiers, of course, had simply become separated from their battalions and lost their way in the night. Hauptmann Albrecht von Metzsch and some 300 of his men, for example, spent the night somewhere between Dupas and 9th Corps. Nonetheless, the absence of these and many others left large gaps in the ranks and fractured unit cohesion. Still, losses were not as bad as they first seemed, and many men also retained their spirit despite the repulse and the casualties.[168] Coming upon Colonel Pierre Billard of the 29th in the darkness, Eugene expressed delight on finding his subordinate unhurt. 'I had been given the sad news that your regiment had been entirely destroyed and that you were numbered among the wounded,' he exclaimed. 'No,' replied the colonel, 'and I hope the feeble debris of the 29th and I will take our revenge tomorrow.'[169]

At approximately the same time that Dupas's men were falling back in disorder from the Russbach Heights, Davout's corps was returning to its bivouacs. Davout's advance had been minimal. Sceptical of the entire enterprise, he seems to have endeavoured without success to dissuade Napoleon from accepting the erroneous conclusions of some imperial staff officers that the Austrians had evacuated Markgrafneusiedl and were in retreat. Unable to convince his master, he limited his efforts, moving to threaten the Austrian left without committing his command to an irrevocable assault. In the words of his corps' account: 'The Marshal Duke of Auerstädt left his infantry in position before Glinzendorf and advanced forty guns towards Markgrafneusiedl supported by a strong line of skirmishers in an attempt to chase the enemy from the village by sustained fire.'[170] He reinforced the menace by sending Morand and Friant across the Russbach, while his light cavalry manoeuvred near Leopoldsdorf. Although the French artillery fire inflicted many casualties on Rosenberg's men, the bombardment and the threat of a bayonet attack only 'seemed to instil courage in the Austrians.'[171] As had been clear from the start, the Austrians had no intention of abandoning their position, and Davout recalled his troops south of the Russbach around 10 p.m. to rest and re-arm for the coming day's trials. Thus ended the third French thrust this night.

The final act in this four-part drama was played out between Aderklaa and Wagram, where Bernadotte was to seize the latter village with his Saxon troops. Bernadotte, as usual, was disgruntled. He had protested at being placed in command of foreign troops as soon as he received his orders in March and never ceased complaining about them. Since crossing the Danube, he had given up two battalions to the Lobau garrison, had lost control of the *Prinz Johann* Chevaulegers, and had just seen his two French regiments and two more Saxon battalions pulled away; his 1st Division had not yet arrived from guarding the bridges, and much of his artillery was not up. Now he was to storm an enemy-held village at the close of day according to the instructions he was given at around 7.30 p.m. Whether owing to his pique at perceived slights and infringements on his prerogatives or to some other combination of factors, he delayed his attack and did not employ due diligence in its preparation. On the other hand, his task was daunting and, until 1st Division arrived, he had only his 2nd Division and cavalry at hand, perhaps 7,700 infantry and cavalry with a mere eight guns. With no other Allied troops within supporting distance—Dupas was already charging the heights—an immediate attack could be considered rash. Bernadotte waited.

Though Bernadotte may be excused for awaiting the arrival of 1st Division, he thereby missed an opportunity to strike at Wagram while the crisis on Bellegarde's left burned hottest. Dupas, it seems, had even pushed some men up the town's eastern fringes. He might also have, like Davout, chosen a more circumspect approach and limited himself to a cannonade and some menacing manoeuvres to test the enemy's will. Instead, he sent GM Karl von Lecoq's three line battalions directly at Wagram at about 9 p.m., when things were already turning against the French on the Russbach Heights. Lecoq faced poor odds. Oberst Ernst von Oberdorf of *Reuss-Plauen* held Wagram with two battalions of his regiment and 2nd Jägers along the Russbach, his 3rd Battalion in reserve in the town, and I/*Anton Mittrowsky* on his immediate right behind the brook, making at least 5,300 men against 2,500 Saxons.[172] A feeble artillery preparation only managed to set the village on fire and the Austrian Jägers took a heavy toll of Saxon skirmishers in an extended firefight, but Lecoq seized the south-western edge of Wagram and several times pushed as far as the market square before being brought to a halt. All tactical order was lost as the Saxons waded the muddy Russbach and became embroiled in vicious street fighting. Both Lecoq and Oberdorf were wounded, but the Saxons could make no further progress and GL von Zezschwitz sent GM Heinrich von Zeschau forward with his brigade and the *Prinz Maximilian* Battalion to relieve Lecoq's exhausted men.[173] This effort, too, soon stalled, degenerating into a murderous exchange of musketry among the smoke, flames, and ruins. 'Deutsch-Wagram, which lay before us, was also burning,' wrote Unterleutnant Carl Kaendler, 'we tried twice to take it by storm but were received with such a monstrous cross-fire of balls, shells, and canister that we could not . . . the fire continued with unbelievable furore until around 11 p.m.'[174] Bernadotte now made one last attack, ordering GM Valentin von Hartitzsch to advance with his two grenadier battalions and the *Egidy* Schützen.[175] No one told Hartitzsch that his countrymen were ahead of him as he marched off into the darkness and, crossing the Russbach, his men opened fire when white-coated forms seemed to charge against them from the burning village. In the confusion of darkness, combat, tactical disarray, and the ghastly light cast by the flames, the grenadiers and Schützen fired several volleys at fellow Saxons before their officers discovered the deadly error and stopped the shooting. By then the damage had been done. Hartitzsch fell mortally wounded, and the Saxons in Wagram, thinking themselves outflanked, fled in panic, crashing into Hartitzsch's brigade as they routed. A simultaneous Austrian counter-attack by I/*Anton Mittrowsky* from the west and III/*Reuss-Plauen* (assisted by 200 volunteers from II/*Anton Mittrowsky*) from the east cleared out the remaining Saxons.[176] By 11 p.m. Wagram was again firmly in Habsburg hands.

Covered by the last two untouched infantry battalions (*Prinz Friedrich* and *Prinz Anton*), the battered Saxon brigades withdrew in disorder to bivouac in a large square near Aderklaa. The effort to storm Wagram had cost the corps dearly. The *König* and *Low* Battalions had each lost 50 per cent of their strength, most of the others engaged were reduced by 30 per cent, one brigadier was badly wounded, another was dying, and many other senior officers were down. The confused fighting and the 'fratricide', combined with the eventual repulse and flight, also had a negative impact on Saxon morale. Furthermore, Bernadotte's spectacular failure at Wagram that night increased the friction between him and Napoleon. The indignant marshal, convinced that his enemies in imperial headquarters had deprived him of support (especially Dupas), made dark hints about Berthier's treachery and spouted supercilious criticisms of Napoleon's tactical decisions. These remarks, reported to the emperor, left Napoleon 'in no mood to make allowance for any shortcomings' on the part of Bernadotte or his corps the following day.[177]

Courage and Intrepidity

The 5th of July thus concluded with mixed results. On the one hand, Napoleon had brought more than 150,000 men across the Danube in the space of twenty-four hours along with thousands of horses, 400 guns, and countless other vehicles. This was an astonishing achievement by any standard, perhaps unprecedented in military history. Pachtod's division would cross at 11 p.m. that night, Marmont was on Lobau along with Broussier's division, and Wrede's Bavarians were nearby. The emperor had thus surprised his foes (and some of his own officers) and was positioned for the decisive battle he so earnestly sought. At the same time, the results of the evening attacks were dismal and reflected poorly on most of the senior French commanders, Napoleon included. Starting at the top of the command chain, Napoleon's worry that Charles might slip away is entirely understandable, and a reconnaissance in force was a reasonable means both to determine Habsburg intentions and, if necessary, to hold the Hauptarmee in place. The execution of this plan, however, was execrable. If Napoleon's aim was a probe of limited scope, as seems most likely, he did not communicate this clearly to his subordinates. The lapse here certainly can be attributed to him directly, but perhaps as well to the senior staff officers who may have over-interpreted his orders as they delivered them. On the other hand, if he had intended a powerful assault, he had invested too little effort in coordinating its various parts.

Whatever the case, it is evident that Oudinot, Dupas, Eugene, and Bernadotte each believed he was to conduct a full-scale assault. Davout proved the prudent exception, fulfilling the letter of his instructions without hurling his corps into an all-out attack with little preparation and only two hours or so of daylight remaining. Apart from Davout's performance, execution at the corps level was also badly flawed. Eugene, MacDonald, and Dupas can be excused as they had almost no time to reconnoitre or ready themselves, but Oudinot and Bernadotte discredited themselves in their management of their separate attacks. Oudinot seems to have allowed Frère's advance to dribble away without an earnest push, while he should have either supported the 10th and 57th fully or, better yet, have restrained their attacks in the first place. Bernadotte's performance was lacklustre at best, showing little tactical finesse. In addition to delaying and thereby missing an opportunity to strike while I Corps was engaged in a near life-or-death struggle with Dupas and the Army of Italy, he made no effort to synchronise his attacks or to outflank the defenders: the Saxon brigades were thrown against Wagram piecemeal and defeated in detail.[178] In short, the evening attacks were hastily conceived and, in two cases, poorly executed. Though he now knew that the Austrians were in place and meant to fight, the lack of clarity in planning and absence of oversight in direction meant that Napoleon had purchased this information at a very high price indeed.

The surprising aspect of the French evening attacks is that they twice made significant gains and at one point had the prospect of achieving a true breakthrough. The failure of 10th Léger's attack was inevitable given the lack of support and the overwhelming odds, but the fact that this lone regiment was able to mount the heights at all is remarkable.[179] Likewise, Dupas and Eugene attained stunning success in their hurriedly assembled assaults. Some additional support and a modicum of co-ordination, especially with Oudinot to capture Baumersdorf, might have left the French in possession of a firm foothold on the plateau that night. Officers and men showed themselves both motivated and tactically skilful. As Austrian reports acknowledge, many Habsburg battalions folded and fled under the initial shock of the unexpected attack. Thanks to the exertions of Charles, Bellegarde, Hohenzollern, and regimental officers, the two Austrian corps were able to recover and repel the assault, but it is worth noting how close it came to success, despite all of the deficiencies in preparation and difficulties of terrain. It is also useful to keep in mind that the panic and disorderly retreat occurred in the dark. It seems very likely that these troops would have conducted themselves better and rallied more rapidly had they suffered this severe setback during daylight. Considering that two of these divisions were the same ones who readily reassembled and repeatedly conducted determined attacks at Raab only three weeks earlier, there is every reason to conclude that they would have exhibited similar mettle had they been able to see their officers and eagles, had conditions allowed them to distinguish friend from foe. This is not to argue that the quality of French infantry had not declined since 1805 or 1806. The erosion was evident. Situations such as this ill-considered evening attack, however, do suggest that the degradation was not as severe nor as precipitous as is often depicted and alerts us to the importance of nuance in assessing combat performance in 1809. Dupas was not merely bragging when he wrote, 'I praise the courage and intrepidity the officers and men displayed during a struggle as unequal as it was memorable and glorious for the division.'[180]

On the Austrian side of the field, officers seem to have perceived more synergy in the French attack than actually existed. Given the strain that the evening's fighting had placed on the Hauptarmee, this was not a surprising interpretation, indeed, the Austrians had good reason to be pleased with the outcome of the day's events. There were, however, troubling signs as well. The severe losses suffered by the Advance Guard for one, but some of the Landwehr had shown itself quite flighty during the evening battles, and there was as yet no word from Johann. In addition to the Advance Guard, losses had been heavy among the engaged units of I and II Corps; three of the five brigade commanders in I Corps, for example, were out of action as well as several regimental colonels. These considerations do not seem to have bothered any of the Hauptarmee's senior commanders or staff. When Rosenberg expressed concern about being outflanked, Wimpffen dismissed the idea of a French manoeuvre against the Austrian left as 'silly' and improbable, while Charles commented that Johann had been summoned for exactly this purpose.[181]

The Night of 5/6 July

The night of 5/6 July was unseasonably cold, strangely quiet, and 'completely clear.'[182] 'Other than a few musket shots here and there, all became silent, fading into and swallowed up by the obscurity,' wrote Paulin. 'Bivouac fires were rare as there was little wood and, as the temperature had been very high during the day, it seemed we could pass the summer night under the beautiful stars without a fire,' he continued. 'But I have never experienced such piquant cold.'[183] Artillery Lieutenant Noël, who regretted 'that unfortunate attack that made us lose several hundred men for no purpose', also felt the cold and fell asleep under a caisson, 'rolled up in my mantle', while Capitaine Maurice de Tascher and fellow officers of the 12th Chasseurs, 'passed the night in the wheat, the reins on our arms'.[184] It was also oddly still and Chef d'Escadron Boulart of the Guard horse artillery remembered that 'there was so little breeze that the powder smoke remained stationary and suspended above the ground for a long time, surrounding us like a thick fog,' after the fighting on the heights came to a close.[185]

As the officers and men of both armies marvelled at the cool night and tried to stay warm, their commanders were plotting the next day's actions. Charles and his advisers decided on a bold offensive strategy. During the afternoon, the archduke had considered a plan to unite all of his forces on the Russbach Heights on the 6th, and may have had an appropriate 'disposition' drafted.[186] As night fell and he returned to his headquarters, he changed his mind and composed a new plan for a general attack all along his line. The speed of the French crossing had left the Hauptarmee effectively divided into two wings—one on the Bisamberg, the other along the Russbach—and Charles had done nothing to draw the corps on the Bisamberg closer to the rest of the army during the day.[187] As it was now no longer feasible to unite the army on the heights, Charles saw a surprise attack as 'the only conclusion that could avail a weaker party against a stronger in completely open terrain', something his key staff officers seem to have preferred all along.[188] The 'disposition' for the morning thus directed his improvised right wing to advance almost due south-east: Klenau along the Danube, Kolowrat through Leopoldau on Breitenlee, the Grenadiers on Süssenbrunn.[189] Bellegarde was to retain his position on the heights with part of his corps, but would pivot the rest on Wagram to capture Aderklaa and form the left flank of the attack. Liechtenstein's cavalry would cover the gap between the Grenadiers and I Corps. All corps were expected to be in position at 4 a.m. on 6 July. Hohenzollern's mission was initially defensive, but he and the rest of I Corps were to be prepared to join the general advance as the situation permitted.[190] Rosenberg, on the other hand, was ordered to attack at 4 a.m. in concert with the right wing. Nothing had been heard from Johann, but it was hoped that he would arrive to support the left flank. At 2 a.m., Charles sent his brother another note, informing him of the coming attack and urging him 'not to rest in Marchegg, rather to exert every effort to be able to participate in the battle'.[191]

Rosenberg's role is one of the lingering controversies regarding this attack plan. Did Charles imagine a double envelopment? Was IV Corps only to provide a diversionary feint? There is no clear answer, but it seems most likely that the army leadership, counting on Johann's arrival, saw Rosenberg as a secondary attack that would stress the French line and perhaps pre-empt the threat to their own left—as they had witnessed in Davout's manoeuvres the preceding evening. Rosenberg's task was not the only dubious point in the 'disposition'. Among other things, it did not state the purpose of the attack. The 'operations journal' (composed months later) stated the advance was 'to cut his [the enemy's] communications with Lobau', but the actual 'disposition' merely assigned tasks and starting hours without outlining an overall goal.[192] This lacuna left the army conducting an 'artless' general attack 'with no finesse and no deeper aims'.[193] The unwieldy deployment of the army in two tenuously connected wings has already been mentioned, and even Charles acknowledged that his line was 'too extended to be powerful'.[194] Most striking, however, is the fact that there was no reserve. Kolowrat was to leave a brigade on the Bisamberg, but he elected to satisfy this order with two or three battalions and a half-battery.[195] Moreover, a lone brigade would hardly have constituted an army-level reserve in any case. This deficiency was probably unavoidable, given the army's size relative to the enormous scope of the Marchfeld and the awkward positions in which it found itself on the evening of the 5th. Nonetheless, the lack of a reserve meant that almost the entire army was committed from the start of the day and Charles would have little means of influencing the battle once it began. Unlike Napoleon, Charles was operating on exterior lines and would have difficulty recovering should events take an adverse turn.[196] Nor did he call in any of V Corps. It was too late to bring the entire corps to the field, but GM Johann von Neustädtler's brigade (3,400 men) was readily available. Given the importance of the coming contest, one might have expected the Generalissimus to call on all resources. Instead, the brigade remained near Strebersdorf and took no part in the battle.[197]

The most critical flaw, however, was in timing. Although Wimpffen deserves credit for the rapid conception and drafting of the 'disposition', he completely failed in thinking through the practical sequence required to set the army in motion: orders delivery by courier, issuance of instructions by subordinate commanders, co-ordination among subordinates, assembling the troops, and movement of formations into attack positions. As a result of this unforgivable lapse on the part of the chief of staff, the corps commanders could not possibly meet the prescribed timelines. Kolowrat and Klenau, who were to march at 1 a.m., did not receive their copies of the 'disposition' until 2 a.m. and 2.15 a.m. respectively. Inexplicably, even Rosenberg, though much closer to headquarters, did not have his copy in hand until 2 a.m. Furthermore, Wimpffen apparently believed the Grenadiers were at Gerasdorf when they were actually around Seyring and would thus require an additional hour or so to get into position.[198] The Hauptarmee's plan, then, though not bad under the circumstances, suffered from several potentially fatal disabilities. Above all, the timing error meant that it could not be implemented properly. It was out of date before it left headquarters. 'The failure', Radetzky noted bitterly, 'was in the calculation of time.'[199] Come the dawn, the army, poorly co-ordinated, would lurch into action in disjointed thrusts, weaker than it need have been and lacking a reserve for contingencies.

Napoleon, as was his custom, did not fix upon a definitive plan of operations. Relying on the competence of his subordinates, the agility of his army, and the incisive dexterity of his own thinking, he drew his forces closer together to await whatever opportunities might come with the dawn. It seems likely he envisaged a well-orchestrated frontal attack on the Austrian centre (such as had almost succeeded by accident that evening) that would break the enemy army in two and deprive it of its retreat routes to both Bohemia and Hungary. But there was time to consider the details in the morning light. For the moment, the key was to have the army concentrated and able to operate in any direction.[200] Massena was therefore to march at 2 a.m. and assemble near Aderklaa with most of his corps, while Davout would slide to his left, closer to Grosshofen. Pachtod and Broussier were to rejoin Eugene, while Marmont supplemented the Guard in reserve (he arrived at around 2 a.m.). All of the corps in the centre—Oudinot, Eugene, Bernadotte—were to retain their positions and, in order to avoid the previous evening's disorder, were 'to contract their outposts and not to engage in any attack until the enemy should have made some movements and manifested his intentions.'[201] Napoleon made his headquarters amid this great mass totalling some 161,000 infantry and cavalry with more than 450 guns. Wrede, who eagerly reported to the emperor on the night of 5 July, only received his orders at 1 a.m. He was to place his division at Enzersdorf, a position from which it could either support the army's centre or counter Johann—whose strength Napoleon overestimated—should he approach from Pressburg. Only Boudet remained on the left flank along the Danube 'to cover and defend as necessary' Aspern and the Lobau bridges.[202] The emperor knew that V Corps was on the Bisamberg and that VI Corps had just retired in that direction. He did not know that III Corps and the Grenadiers were also on his left. He logically judged that Charles would most likely concentrate on the Russbach Heights, 'the most advantageous of all', and 'if there were any movement towards counter-attack to fear, it would be on our right, where Prince Johann would arrive, where the terrain was more open and more favourable; nothing seemed to call our attention to our left.'[203] In other words, Napoleon's analysis led him to the conclusion that the Austrians would implement exactly the sort of plan that Charles seems to have developed in the late afternoon. Boudet's lonesome position on the far French left, therefore, was not an expression of the emperor's disdain for the enemy or exaggerated faith in his own troops, though he was certainly capable of such sentiments. Rather, Boudet was extra insurance against what Napoleon assessed to be an unlikely outcome.[204] In the event, the archduke would surprise the emperor, but the French dispositions would provide the flexibility that Napoleon needed to adapt to this unforeseen circumstance.

6 JULY: THE BATTLE OF WAGRAM — SECOND DAY

The twenty-six or so hours from the beginning of the French crossing to midnight on 5/6 July had been a gruelling trial for both armies. Storm, tension, heat, long waits in the sun, and the sudden shock of battle had left many men exhausted. Clean water was scarce and few had had proper sustenance. Saxon Leutnant Larisch paid a soldier three twenty-crown pieces for half a flask of water 'and never had a draught refreshed me so much'. Sergeant Louis Frèche of IV/24th Léger could not get a sip for any price: 'The batteries tormented us a lot, but thirst and hunger were our greatest afflictions.'[205] The fighting, though often furious, had been concentrated in certain places, and only parts of each host had been heavily engaged. However intense, it was but a violent prelude to the brutal bloodletting both sides were about to experience.

Rosenberg: Advance and Recall

At 4 a.m. on 6 July, Capitaine Chlapowski and other staff officers were 'reclining on the ground like ancient Romans' and enjoying 'a feast worthy of Paris', courtesy of imperial headquarters, when they heard 'a heavy artillery bombardment' begin not far away. Mounting up as the sun rose, he and his companions stared about in awe. 'The most beautiful sight I have ever seen in my life then unfurled before our eyes,' he recalled. 'Within a radius of about a mile, we could see the entire Austrian army, with its right flank anchored on the Danube, and its left extending beyond Wagram, as well as our own army with its left at Aspern and the rest of the line running parallel with the enemy.' Similarly, Parquin of the 20th Chasseurs remembered that 'the dawn, as it broke on the horizon, revealed a forest of bayonets which shone from all points of the plain as they reflected the sun's light in a thousand different directions. From afar could be heard the beat of drums.' Other musicians also began playing to wake their regiments, but 'soon they were all drowned out by the roar the cannon.'[206]

The action that disturbed Chlapowski and his fellow diners was occasioned by Rosenberg's advance. Having received the 'disposition' at 2 a.m., he dutifully launched his attack at 4 a.m. as prescribed. To do so, he returned to standard Austrian practice and formed his corps into three 'columns', each with its own advance guard. He directed the first (eleven battalions, four squadrons) on Grosshofen and the second (twenty-one battalions, four squadrons) to Glinzendorf, while the third (forty-two and one-half squadrons) trotted towards Leopoldsdorf and the far left flank. Three of the former Advance Guard regiments remained behind at Markgrafneusiedl with the position batteries.[207] By 5 a.m., French skirmishers had been pushed back from the Russbach, and the two advance guards were preparing to storm Glinzendorf (I/*Stain* and 2nd Moravian Volunteers) on the left and Grosshofen on the right (1st *EH Carl* Legion). In an advance conducted with great determination, the right column gained a foothold on the edge of Grosshofen against Puthod, but the rest of IV Corps' efforts were barely under way when orders arrived stating that 'the attack should not proceed too rapidly'. These were soon superseded by new instructions for IV Corps to 'cease all offensive operations and restrict itself to defence of the position' around Markgrafneusiedl. With casualties of more than 1,000 men and many of his guns out of action, Rosenberg turned about, his attack having accomplished nothing beyond weakening his corps and shaking its morale.[208] 'That was the result of the attack by the Austrian gentlemen,' remarked one of Puthod's officers.[209] This was 'the first bad symptom of the ultimate issue of the battle', noted a German volunteer in *Deutschmeister*. 'The enemy saw the advantage to be gained and was not slow to profit by it.'[210] By approximately 6 a.m., IV Corps had returned to the heights.[211]

Hearing Rosenberg's guns, Napoleon assumed they signalled Johann's arrival and took himself immediately towards his right flank, ordering the

Guard infantry and artillery as well as Nansouty's and Arrighi's cuirassier divisions to follow. By the time he reached Davout, this brief episode was already coming to an end and he quickly perceived that the threat was receding. He also learned that Johann was nowhere to be seen and he had a chance to ascertain for himself the vulnerability of the Austrian left flank. He ordered the Guard to return to its reserve position; but, not to miss an opportunity, he had the two cavalry divisions send their horse batteries to the Austrian flanks to rake the retreating whitecoats with a devastating enfilade fire.[212] As the battered Austrians retired to their former positions, Napoleon ordered Nansouty back to the reserve, but he left Arrighi with Davout and remained for a time with the marshal, discussing the strike against Rosenberg.[213] Although the emperor wanted an assault 'at once', Davout proposed taking two hours to restock his ammunition and manoeuvre across the Russbach as he had the previous evening. 'The marshal promised that, at that time, he would attack vigorously in a manner that would produce the greatest results.'[214] Napoleon assented and was about to return to the centre to decide how he could engage the entire army in capitalising on Davout's turning movement when news came from his left. 'General Reille arrived from Massena's corps at that moment and announced to us that things were going badly on that front, that all the effort of the Austrian army was directed at that point, and that there was not a minute to lose in taking ourselves there.'[215]

Aderklaa: Crises in the Centre

Bellegarde, like Rosenberg, set his troops in motion according to the disposition's timetable. Indeed, he was somewhat early, and probing troopers from *Klenau* Chevaulegers of GM Karl von Stutterheim's advance guard were already reporting at 4 a.m. that the only enemy in Aderklaa were miserable groups of wounded Saxons. Happily surprised by this good fortune, Bellegarde hastened to occupy the village with 2nd Jägers, supported by the rest of Stutterheim's infantry (4th *EH Carl*, III/*Kolowrat*), while two batteries unlimbered to the right of Aderklaa under the protection of six chevauleger squadrons. The other two squadrons rode off in search of the Grenadier Corps that was supposed to be coming up on Bellegarde's right. Until the grenadiers arrived, I Corps would have to postpone further advance, so Bellegarde deployed the remainder of his attack force between Aderklaa and Wagram in two lines: *Reuss-Plauen*, *Kolowrat* (I, II), and *Rainer* in the first, supported by *A. Mittrowsky* and *Erbach*. Left behind on the heights were the regiments that had suffered most on 5 July: *Vogelsang* and *Argenteau*, along with 1st Hradisch Landwehr. These came under the command of FML Dedovich, who, having recovered from his Aspern wound, had reported to Charles at 4 a.m. 'in order to participate in the coming battle'.[216]

Where were the Saxons? During the early morning hours, without informing anyone, Bernadotte had irresponsibly withdrawn his shaken corps from its exposed position at the hinge between the army's left wing and centre. Several factors contributed to the marshal's decision: instructions to close up on Eugene, worry about his weakness in infantry, and concern for the state of Saxon morale after the disconcerting experiences of the previous evening. At dawn, 9th Corps, totalling about 6,000 Saxon infantry still with the colours, found itself arrayed in the open fields some 1,000 metres south-east of Aderklaa. Anticipating Massena's imminent arrival, however, Bernadotte slid to the right between 6 and 6.30 a.m, placing his cavalry on his right and Dupas's depleted 'division' behind the Saxons. To mitigate the vicious artillery crossfire from the Russbach Heights and Aderklaa, he refused both flanks and brought his own guns forward. The result was a ferocious mutual cannonade that ripped ghastly holes in the white-coated ranks on both sides. This was the state of affairs when new forces joined the fray at approximately 7.30 a.m.

At that hour, the two divisions of Austrian grenadiers appeared on Bellegarde's right, their approach covered by the *Knesevich* Dragoons. As with I Corps, the grenadiers now had to wait as III Corps was still not in position on *their* right for the intended grand advance. Their arrival, however, proved most fortunate for Charles as Massena's corps was now coming into view south-east of Aderklaa.

In accordance with his orders, Massena had begun shifting his somewhat scattered corps towards Wagram in the pre-dawn hours that morning. Legrand and Carra Saint-Cyr had been delayed by disengaging themselves from Austrian advance troops (Grenadiers and III Corps respectively), so Molitor arrived first on Bernadotte's left flank. The rest of 4th Corps, with Lasalle shielding its left rear, was soon on hand, however, and so was the emperor. Napoleon had ridden along the centre of his line, discussing his plan to assault the heights with his commanders and inspiring his troops. As one colonel described the scene, 'The emperor coursed along the front of the line of battle at the gallop, his arm extended towards the Wagram heights, showing all the army the position it would take, the spectacle was magnificent, I do not think one could see a more beautiful military tableau'.[217]

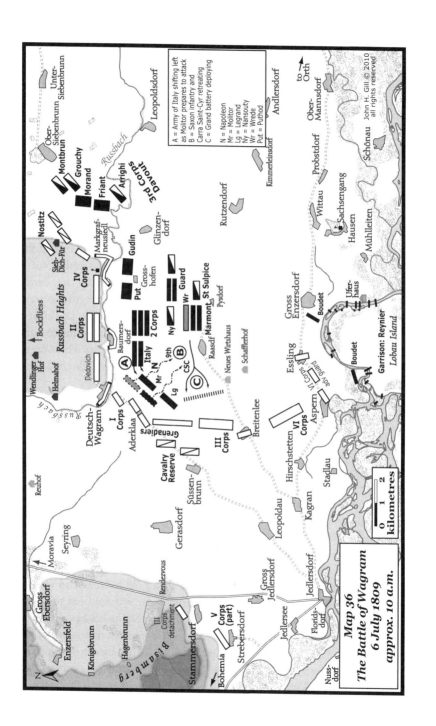

Map 36
The Battle of Wagram
6 July 1809
approx. 10 a.m.

A = Army of Italy shifting left
as Molitor prepares to attack
B = Saxon infantry and
Carra Saint-Cyr retreating
C = Grand battery deploying

N = Napoleon
Mr = Molitor
Lg = Legrand
Ny = Nansouty
Wr = Wrede
Put = Puthod

kilometres
0   1   2

'The young army, so ardent and so susceptible to enthusiasm, responded with acclamations and demanded the order to attack,' wrote Pelet. Napoleon, 'stopping for a few moments with the marshal', ordered Massena to retake Aderklaa and returned to the centre.[218]

Massena selected Carra Saint-Cyr's division to conduct the attack, but the general dallied, trying to devise a way to turn the strong Austrian defence. During this brief interval, as the French infantry slowly approached its objective and came under fire from the Austrian battery near Aderklaa, Marulaz seized an opportunity to charge the Habsburg guns. In a sudden rush, the French horsemen were upon the hapless gunners, many of whom cut the traces of their battery horses and fled. Liechtenstein, whose Cavalry Reserve was now on the scene, recognised the danger and sent four squadrons of *Kronprinz* Cuirassiers to the rescue. These, however, like the rest of the mounted reserve, were behind the grenadiers and had to make their way forward before coming into action. Nor were they up to the task when they arrived, and Liechtenstein personally dashed up just in time to rally the wavering cuirassiers. The *Rosenberg* Chevaulegers and *Albert* Cuirassiers soon joined the melee, while FML Moritz Liechtenstein brought GM Karl von Kroyher's brigade up in support. The weight of numbers drove the French back and, succoured by Bruyère's brigade, Marulaz retired with only two cannon as trophies for his brilliant feat.[219]

Massena had by now lost patience with Carra Saint-Cyr's delay in assaulting Aderklaa. In one of the oddest scenes in military history, the marshal had his carriage with its team of shimmering white horses driven forward among Carra Saint-Cyr's battalions and told the general, 'Enter the village, my friend, and slaughter those beggars!'[220] Attacking with great élan, the 24th Léger on the left and 4th Ligne on the right rapidly cleared Aderklaa of Jägers and legion men, creating a momentary crisis for I Corps. The fleeing defenders carried away both battalions of *A. Mittrowsky* as well as the *Scharlach* Grenadiers who were rushing up in a vain effort to counter-attack. A 'panicked terror' spread through Bellegarde's first line like wildfire, and the corps teetered on the verge of collapse. As on the previous evening, Charles and Bellegarde personally intervened to hold formations together and, with 'extraordinary exertion and energy', order was restored.[221] In the meantime, the impetuosity of the attacking French regiments had exceeded their wisdom. Thrusting beyond the confines of Aderklaa, they came under harrowing fire and were driven back in disorder as Liechtenstein sent Habsburg horsemen against the 24th Léger, d'Aspre threw the other three grenadier battalions of GM Franz Baron Merville's brigade into the fray, and

Bellegarde committed the untouched III/*Kolowrat*. 'We found ourselves cut off and enveloped . . . the shock became terrible and very murderous,' wrote Colonel Louis Léger Boyeldieu of 4th Ligne. 'The fighting was hand to hand and those few who could escape only did so with incredible effort.'[222] Boyeldieu fell wounded and captive, the 4th lost an eagle, the 24th likewise lost its colonel and its eagle, and both regiments dissolved in the greatest disorder. The 24th suffered most, being reduced to little more than battalion strength in the space of a few minutes. With the Hessian brigade on the right and 46th Ligne committed from Carra Saint-Cyr's reserve, however, the furious fighting continued and the village changed hands several times in a short period. The Austrians ended up in control of smouldering Aderklaa, but timely intervention by Saxon cavalry halted Liechtenstein's tentative attempts at pursuit of the disorganised French and Hessians. Combat also flared between Aderklaa and Wagram as Bernadotte endeavoured to support Carra Saint-Cyr by sending Dupas's 'division' and three Saxon battalions into the gap between the two towns. Counter-attacked and swamped by fire, this foray soon came to an end, the pursuing Austrians repelled by Bernadotte leading another charge of Saxon horse.

Where Charles had coped with a crisis in I Corps a short time earlier, Napoleon now faced a potential fiasco. It was about 9 a.m., Carra Saint-Cyr's division was wrecked and the Saxon infantry had collapsed, his centre was a mass of disordered, terrified fugitives, and the Austrian offensive was looming beyond his weak left. Even parts of Legrand's division had been disrupted by the confusion as fugitives streamed through its ranks. Moreover, Kolowrat's corps was now presenting a new threat as it deployed near Breitenlee. Massena and his staff 'were surrounded with dead and dying' and Saxon refugees jostled the marshal's carriage in their hurry to escape.[223] Fortunately for the French, the Austrians did nothing to exploit this opportunity.

The emperor, however, retained his composure. In his estimation, Davout's drive would compromise the Hauptarmee and nullify any Austrian attack against his own left before it posed a vital threat. Riding to the centre with a heavy cavalry division in tow, he joined Massena in the carriage, helped calm some of the panic, and issued new orders to account for the evolving situation.[224] The Saxon infantry was shattered beyond repair and Massena needed time to reorganise his shaken troops, but Molitor was available and Napoleon ordered him to seize Aderklaa as the pivot around which the battle would now turn. The 2nd Léger, 16th Ligne, and a battalion of the 67th successfully stormed the village despite fierce resistance, while the 37th and the other battalion of the 67th guarded their left against Liechtenstein's menacing horsemen. Despite this small victory, the French situation was tenuous and, other than Molitor and Legrand, the only intact formation on Napoleon's left was the cuirassier division (which he had posted opposite Breitenlee). Kolowrat was in Breitenlee, Klenau had occupied Aspern, and, to make matters worse, Molitor could not maintain his hold on Aderklaa. Sometime between 10.30 and 11 a.m., Molitor evacuated the town under intolerable pressure after displaying 'valiant determination' against 'all the efforts of the enemy army'.[225] Charles, for his part, entrusted the defence of Aderklaa to d'Aspre's division of grenadiers and several battalions of I Corps, all under the nominal direction of his youngest brother, Ludwig. This left Legrand's division a rather isolated bastion and the principal target for the attentions of the Austrian gunners. 'Death rolled through our ranks,' noted the Badeners.[226] Kapitän Karl von Freydorf, the highly respected commander of the Baden foot battery, was one of the victims, his right foot carried away by a ball as his guns were being withdrawn. Rescued by loyal gunners at the height of the Austrian attack, he added to his renown by smoking his pipe as surgeons amputated his leg.[227] While Freydorf's men faithfully bore their leader from the field in the centre, significant developments were taking place towards the Danube.

Advance on Aspern: Klenau Stalls

The greatest burden of the Austrian offensive fell on Klenau and Kolowrat. As the tense contest for Aderklaa was raging, they had finally brought their two corps into the tactical picture. Massena and his staff could see 'strong enemy columns set themselves in motion near Stammersdorf, their bayonet points sparkling in the sun.'[228] Kolowrat had reached Breitenlee in time to tie down Legrand, and one of his batteries poured a heavy fire into Carra Saint-Cyr's left flank as the French formed to assault Aderklaa. Like the grenadiers to his left, however, Kolowrat then had to halt to give Klenau time to catch up. Now, with Bellegarde and d'Aspre consolidating their success at Aderklaa, III Corps resumed its methodical, rather plodding advance, its right flank on the Breitenlee–Raasdorf road, its left tied to the grenadiers east of Süssenbrunn. Unfortunately for Charles, the Hauptarmee and his plan were already reaching their limits. His right wing—his main effort—was too weak for the terrain it was to cover, and the gap between Süssenbrunn and Aderklaa (more than two and half kilometres) had to be filled with Prochaska's lone grenadier division deployed in a single line of battalion masses. Liechtenstein's horse stood to the rear in support, and

Charles did not dare shift them elsewhere, despite the aggressive prince's suggestion that he ride to assist Rosenberg. Nor did the Generalissimus have an independent reserve to exploit the chaos in Napoleon's left-centre. Almost the entire army was now engaged. With few exceptions, it would have to fight out the rest of the battle where it was.

On the other hand, a tremendous opportunity had opened in front of the Austrians. Klenau marched slowly but steadily via Leopoldau and Kagran, FML Ludwig Graf von Wallmoden-Gimborn and the *Liechtenstein* Hussars covering his left flank towards Breitenlee and tying him to Kolowrat. He encountered Boudet's outposts between Hirschstetten and Aspern. Though outnumbered almost four to one and completely lacking cavalry, Boudet put up stiff resistance, but a series of mistakes and misunderstandings left his artillery vulnerable and beyond supporting distance of the nearest infantry.[229] Moreover, through no fault of his own, his right flank was completely open. As Klenau's advance guard pushed ahead and his main body began deploying east of Hirschstetten, elements of the *Liechtenstein* Hussars swung towards Aspern and, 'charging brusquely', took Boudet's battery in the flank, capturing nine of the twelve pieces.[230] A dismounted howitzer also fell into Austrian hands. Shocked by the loss of his artillery and overwhelmed by superior enemy numbers, Boudet fell back in haste, part of his division retiring into the Mühlau bridgehead, part towards Enzersdorf.[231] VI Corps undertook a few probes towards the bridgehead and engaged the 3rd Baden Line, but lack of initiative and galling fire from the Lobau guns dissuaded Klenau from any further action in that direction. Nonetheless, between 10 and 11 a.m., VI Corps was able to occupy 'Aspern and all the entrenchments up to and near Essling along with this village' with its advance guard, while 'the main body remained arrayed in battalion masses between Aspern and Breitenlee, and awaited developments in the centre.'[232]

Combat in the Centre: A Most Terrible Fire

While Klenau waited, Napoleon acted. The scene in the French left-centre was grim: Bernadotte's corps had been shattered and its wreckage had to be withdrawn from the field, Carra Saint-Cyr's division was a shambles, Legrand and Molitor had taken serious casualties and were under heavy pressure, Boudet, having lost his guns, had retreated towards Lobau, allowing Klenau to push into the French rear. Although the emperor's situation was dire, he reacted coolly and promptly with a series of bold and astonishing decisions.

For many on or approaching the battlefield, the outlook was black indeed. The men of Wrede's division, dressed in parade uniforms and 'marching towards Lobau Island as rapidly as possible', came upon foreboding sights near the bridges where, 'left of the road, wounded Saxons already constituted a solid line ... blood flowed and dripped under the attached wagons.' The field on this hot and cloudless day offered hellish scenes as 'the wounded sought to shield themselves behind shocks of corn, but that offered no safety, and large patches of standing grain were in flames.' Likewise, 'all of the villages that fell between the lines stood in flames.'[233] 'Overall, the first sight of the battlefield ... was not cheery,' noted a Bavarian cavalry lieutenant.[234] The Bavarians had assumed their post behind the French Guard between 8 and 9 a.m. Now Napoleon sent word to them that 'the battle was decided and won.' 'Although the unconstrained advance of the Austrians on our left in no way gave the impression of a victorious battle,' continued the lieutenant, 'there was no one who doubted these words, and all looked forward to the coming events with joy and on all sides expressed the desire to participate actively soon.'[235] Similarly, a veteran musician of the 93rd Ligne, departing Lobau for the battlefield during the mid-morning, recorded his sense of confidence despite the terror that gripped rear area soldiers and civilian camp followers.

Towards nine o'clock, we headed off to rejoin our regiment, when we encountered a mass of fugitives debouching from the bridges and crying 'Retreat, retreat'. There was soon a general panic on the entire island of Lobau. The *cantinières*, the musicians, the medical orderlies, the whole crowd of non-combatants, the herd of beef cattle, the logistical personnel, the ambulances, and all such had taken itself off in disorder from the direction of the bridges on the right bank [of the Stadtler Arm].

He concluded, however, with a sensible and nonchalant appraisal: 'As for me, I was not too frightened as, hearing the cannon growling two or three leagues from us, it seemed to me improbable that the army was in retreat.'[236]

If Napoleon was perturbed, he gave no sign of it. He remained focused on the decisive aspects of the battle as it had now developed: Davout's progress and a new plan he had quickly crafted to penetrate the Austrian centre. Davout, outflanking Rosenberg, would stretch and stress the Hauptarmee, forcing Charles to commit all his forces and thereby weaken the hinge of the enemy line between Aderklaa and Breitenlee.[237] The emperor selected this spot for his own main attack, this to be conducted by MacDonald's wing of the Army of Italy. As he arranged his forces for this central thrust, however, he had to buttress his left sufficiently to gain time for his deployments. Rather than draw on his infantry reserves to bolster this flank with a 'passive barrier', Napoleon solved his tactical problem by employing troops already in contact, strengthened by horse and guns from the reserve to launch an 'energetic offensive'.[238] First, Massena, reinforced by St Sulpice's cuirassiers, would reorder his corps, turn it ninety degrees to the left, conduct a flank march across the front of the Austrian right wing, and drive Klenau away from Lobau. The Army of Italy would likewise wheel ninety degrees to its left and shift to the space opposite Süssenbrunn in preparation for the grand assault against Charles's centre, while Bessières brought up Nansouty and the Guard cavalry in support. For the moment, the infantry reserves remained in the centre 'like a dark storm cloud' in the words of an officer on the Austrian staff.[239] When the time was right, however, Wrede and the Guard infantry would follow the central attack, and Marmont would move towards Wagram to close the gap between Eugene's right and Oudinot's left. Oudinot would limit himself to continuing the ongoing cannonade for the moment, but would assault the Russbach Heights as soon as he saw that Davout had driven Rosenberg back onto the plateau. Dupas's remnants and the Saxon cavalry, on the other hand, were withdrawn to Raasdorf to serve as a rallying point for the rest of the broken 9th Corps. The stalwart Saxon gunners, however, remained in place until mid-afternoon, when the battle effectively passed them by; some of the Saxon horse may have stayed to cover the guns.[240] The rest of the Saxons had vanished and, at some point in this kaleidoscope of motion, Napoleon encountered Bernadotte and apparently exchanged harsh words with the errant and argumentative marshal.[241] Finally, to cover Massena's audacious flank march and prepare the way for the central attack, Napoleon ordered the formation of a grand battery between Aderklaa and Breitenlee. Lauriston, entrusted with command of this massive undertaking, would assemble the Guard's sixty guns with approximately forty from the Army of Italy and the Bavarian 12-pounder battery for a total of at least 100 pieces. All of this astounding activity, of course, was to occur simultaneously. The depth of mind—thinking several steps ahead of the enemy—and the facility of imagination necessary to conceive of this vast operation on the spot were remarkable enough, but the superb leadership on the part of his subordinates and the tactical competence of his army complemented Napoleon's personal qualities. The emperor could issue his intricate instructions with confidence.

The breathtaking scope, complexity, and audacity of these operations left contemporaries in awe. The grand battery excited particular attention and admiration. 'All was serious, imposing, solemn on that vast theatre,' wrote

Chef de Bataillon Boulart of the Guard artillery, then 'all of a sudden, a great agitation manifested itself near us; the drum, the trumpet were heard; in less than a minute everyone was at his post; the entire Guard, formed in a single mass, departs and moves to its left . . . the artillery at the gallop and in the lead.'[242] 'By 10.30, the sixty pieces of the Guard, to which were united numerous line batteries, were all in action and opened a most terrible fire on the enemy.'[243] 'There are the flageolets!' remarked nearby Guard infantrymen as they watched the batteries dashing into action, 'The music will soon be complete!'[244] What the Austrians could see and experience was 'a monstrous amount of artillery' delivering a 'most effective and murderous fire.' 'One could not speak of batteries,' wrote one officer, 'because the entire front seemed to be one deployed battery.'[245] The impact was harrowing: 'Shot upon shot knocked man and horse out of the ranks and files,' in the words of the Cavalry Reserve account. 'One may aver without exaggeration that it would be difficult to find an example of such sustained, heavy cannon fire in military history.' 'The troops endured this murderous fire with admirable resolution,' recorded the Grenadier Corps, though 'some masses were soon surrounded with mangled corpses.'[246] Although the concentrated hail of French shot, shell, and canister caused numerous casualties and disabled many Austrian guns, the return fire was also deadly. The enemy artillery, observed Boulart, 'did us great harm and carried away men and horses every instant'.[247] At length, the Guard artillery commanders—all of whom were wounded—had to call for Guard infantry volunteers to keep the pieces blazing. The men responded with enthusiasm, but their zeal cost some their limbs or lives.[248] The batteries on the left suffered most, especially when they attempted to advance, but those on the right (twelve 12-pounders) near Aderklaa were so close to the Austrian lines that most of enemy shot went the over the heads of the sweating French gunners. 'I have never gone into battery so close to the enemy', reported their commander, 'and never lost fewer men than at Wagram.'[249]

While the artillery opened its monumental bombardment, Bessières covered MacDonald's deployment for the great attack. At the head of Nansouty's regiments, the marshal charged III Corps and the thin line of Grenadier battalions with enough success to remove any thought of further advance from the minds of the Habsburg generals. 'The earth shook under our feet,' wrote Guardsman Coignet as the iron horsemen thundered past, and bystanders called out, 'Bravo! There are our brave cuirassiers! The affair will soon be over!'[250] But the Austrian battalion commanders held their men together despite mounting casualties, and Liechtenstein's counterattacks eventually forced the French squadrons to retire.[251] Unfortunately for

Napoleon, Bessières fell wounded during one of these charges, depriving the emperor of an overall cavalry commander. As at Aspern, however, Napoleon's purpose was not to break the Austrian line, but to keep the whitecoats at bay so his tactical combinations could ripen.

To the right of the grand battery, one key element of Napoleon's scheme was unfolding as the Army of Italy, led by MacDonald's wing, slowly came into position. Fortunately for Napoleon, Eugene had turned MacDonald's two divisions (Broussier and Lamarque) to the left to create a new flank when Bernadotte's corps collapsed. Shifting the entire army from the Russbach to its new dispensation opposite Süssenbrunn, however, was a lengthy process and some staff officers became anxious, wondering at Napoleon's apparent inaction. The emperor, mounted on his horse Euphrates, waited stoically on a low rise in the angle where the army's left wing and centre met, east of Aderklaa. 'That angle was a veritable bullet trap,' observed the worried Savary as he rode along with his impassive master.'I allowed myself to think about how the bullets passed by him . . . every instant I expected to see him fall.' When a staff officer's shako was knocked away by a ball, the emperor smiled and commented dryly, 'It's a good thing you are not taller!' Showing himself to Broussier's and Lamarque's men to inspire them, making small adjustments to his instructions, Napoleon, above all, watched the progress of Davout's firing line as measured by its relationship to the tower at Markgrafneusiedl.[252]

The other key element of Napoleon's left wing was the intrepid Massena. With Lannes gone and Davout on the right flank, no other marshal could have been entrusted with such a difficult mission in such trying circumstances. 'The thunder of the cannon resembled a whirlwind,' wrote one of his Hessian officers, 'all was fire and smoke.'[253] Massena, however, was master of the moment. Issuing orders from his carriage, he turned 4th Corps to its left and marched behind the grand battery, headed almost due south for Essling. His light cavalry led the move, followed by Legrand, Carra Saint-Cyr's much reduced division, and Molitor, with St Sulpice on the left flank.[254] His artillery leap-frogged along the route of march on the right to counter the Austrian guns. This audacious flank march was executed under dreadful artillery fire and the constant threat of enemy cavalry, but the corps conducted itself in exemplary fashion. To maintain discipline among his own ranks and to exert a psychological influence on the Austrians, for instance, Colonel Toussaint Campi of 26th Léger had his men slow their march to an ordinary pace, despite the many dangers.[255] 'The cannonade we had to endure is beyond all description,' recorded Oberstleutnant von Franken in the Baden brigade's war diary,'eight to ten soldiers were often knocked down by a single cannon ball, but the men held their places.'[256]

As Massena was marching, he sent staff officers to Napoleon with the ominous news that Boudet had lost his guns and withdrawn into the Mühlau bridgehead.'The cannon you hear to the rear are those of the Austrians,' stated one of these officers, but the emperor did not respond for several moments. Then, seeing that Davout's firing line had passed the Markgrafneusiedl tower, he turned to the startled officer:'Ride to Massena and tell him to attack and that the battle is won at all points!'[257] As the young officer galloped away, Napoleon had others spread the same message throughout the army. These officers also carried orders for MacDonald to advance against the Austrian centre, for Oudinot to assault the heights around Baumersdorf, and for Davout to press his attacks. It was now shortly after noon.[258]

Davout versus Rosenberg: The Battle Was Lost

Despite the drama of the action in the centre, the decisive action of the day unfolded on the extreme eastern edge of the battle line, where Davout and Rosenberg fought for control of Markgrafneusiedl and the heights above it.

Davout prepared his attack carefully, a process that took some time as he shifted Morand and Friant across the Russbach with the cavalry to assume the positions they had occupied the previous evening. Montbrun and Grouchy, on the extreme right with some 6,000 light cavalry and dragoons, drove Frelich's weak detachment back towards the fringe of the heights.[259] Next to them was Morand's 1st Division, assigned to assault the plateau about one kilometre north of Markgrafneusiedl. On his left was Friant, but Morand's dispositions blocked an immediate advance by his 2nd Division, so he deployed his guns and seven attached 12-pounders on his left to support the advance. Arrighi's cuirassiers were also across the stream (just south of Friant), while Gudin and Puthod remained south of the Russbach, prepared to storm the village and the adjoining heights.[260] It was not until 10 a.m. that all were in position and Davout felt ready. At that hour, perhaps spurred by a peremptory query from the emperor, he set the corps in motion.[261] In all, Davout had approximately 32,000 infantry, 7,900 attached cavalry, and 100 guns to overthrow the 22,000 infantry, 5,200 horsemen, and sixty pieces under Rosenberg's command.

Following the abortive dawn advance, Rosenberg had returned his corps to its previous positions defending Markgrafneusiedl and the heights towards Baumersdorf. He had placed only cavalry on his left: Frelich with the remains of the *Stipsicz* and Primatial Insurrection Hussars near Obersiebenbrunn and the rest on and below the plateau about one kilometre from Markgrafneusiedl. Failing to anticipate Davout's outflanking move, Rosenberg now hastily shifted Mayer's brigade to the heights north of the village as he watched the long lines of French troops unfolding in the low ground north of the Russbach. His corps was thus arrayed with the cavalry on the far left, Mayer on the heights facing east, GM Josef Freiherr Weiss's brigade and Provenchères's two battalions in and on both sides of Markgrafneusiedl; GM Robert Freiherr Swinburne's and GM Phillip Landgraf von Hessen-Homburg's brigades took up the line on the right to tie in with II Corps.[262] The only reserve was Riese's weak brigade, a collection of regulars and Landwehr from the former Advance Guard that had been severely depleted in the fighting on 5 July. Furthermore, Rosenberg's artillery situation was serious. French gunnery during the morning dismounted so many of his guns that 'the complete extinguishing of artillery fire before Markgrafneusiedl allowed the enemy to move to his planned attack.'[263]

Morand opened the attack on the French right, advancing against Mayer's brigade with 17th Ligne and 13th Léger in the lead. A difficult fight ensued in which Mayer counter-attacked and disordered the 17th, only to be thrown back by GB Gilly with 15th Léger and 33rd Ligne from Friant's division. Habsburg cavalry attacks against Morand's right delayed, but could not halt, the steady progress of the powerful French assault. Nordmann, Mayer, GM Peter Vécsey, and Oberstleutnant O'Brien were all wounded, the mortally injured Nordmann falling into the hands of Friant's men as they joined the attack on the slopes.

As Morand and Friant were striving to master the heights, Montbrun and Grouchy were duelling with the Habsburg horse near Sieh-Dich-Für. In a typically tangled mounted action, 7th Hussars launched a sudden charge to overthrow *Blankenstein* in the Austrian first line, but were driven off and pursued at speed by O'Reilly Chevaulegers, *Hohenzollern* Cuirassiers, and part of *Riesch* Dragoons. The Austrian horsemen overwhelmed Jacquinot's two chasseur regiments (the 1st foolishly received the charge at the halt), but were themselves undone by 1st Dragoon Division and 11th Chasseurs in a charge 'pressed home and made with rare unity'.[264] Montbrun especially praised the 11th for capturing sixty-five troops of O'Reilly and the regimental commander, Oberst Sardagna.[265] Jacquinot's troopers also returned to the attack to 'take a long and vigorous revenge' against their assailants. 'This cavalry-to-cavalry combat was magnificent!' exclaimed a trooper of 2nd

244 ~ THUNDER ON THE DANUBE

Chasseurs as he attempted to describe the confusion and exhilaration of the fighting.[266] Austrian dragoons eventually stemmed Grouchy's pursuit, but the Habsburg cavalry, weakened, disordered, and exhausted, could no longer prevent the French from continually outflanking Rosenberg's left.

Meanwhile, a vicious struggle was underway for Markgrafneusiedl itself. Puthod's men, to Rosenberg's surprise and annoyance, quickly secured the open ground west of the village, but French efforts to press ahead among the burning houses and up the slopes stalled. Similarly, Gudin's attempts to enter from the east did not succeed at first. Before long, however, the French were in control of the blackened town; the Austrians troops in the low ground to the north only escaped because a courageous Landwehr lieutenant led his company of 1st Iglau in a desperate charge to hold off Gudin's attack. The carnage in this 'terrible affair' was appalling. 'The enemy defended himself valiantly and did us horrible damage,' wrote Capitaine Coudreux several days later, 'the field of battle was covered with our dead and his: one battalion of General Desailly's brigade found itself with a single officer; the balls rained on our ranks.'[267] 'I had never fired so many rounds,' said a soldier of 7th Léger, 'my musket was so hot I could not use it.'[268] The fighting, however, moved inexorably onto the plateau. The Austrians in the angle were caught in a ferocious crossfire, the improvised redoubt around the tower fell to Gudin, and Puthod's battalions scaled the heights west of Markgrafneusiedl. Rosenberg's line bent but did not break. Davout brought Arrighi's cuirassiers up to the plateau in an effort to capitalise on the enemy's distress, but the heavy troopers found the ground encumbered by ditches, pits, huts, and other bivouac debris, some of it in flames. Despite great élan and exertions, they could not conduct effective charges and tumbled back down the slopes in disarray. At Arrighi's request, Davout sent the division off to his right to join Grouchy.[269] This, however, was an inconsequential setback; the success of Davout's cavalry on the right wing and the firm foothold his infantry and artillery now had on the plateau were the keys to victory. With the fall of the tower Radetzky noted glumly, 'the battle was lost'.[270]

Austrian efforts to retrieve their deteriorating situation were ineffectual. Charles had now arrived, bringing with him from II Corps the *Hohenzollern* Cuirassiers, the four wayward squadrons of *Hessen-Homburg*, and *Frelich* Infantry, as well as 1st and 3rd Brünn Landwehr. These helped stabilise the line, but, as the commander of the 3rd Brünn noted, 'it was too late . . . we only served to protect the rallying and retreat of the troops in front of us.'[271] Attempts to counter-attack were 'mowed down' by a storm of French musketry and cannon fire; retreat was the only viable option.[272]

Covered by the reinforcements from II Corps, the battered whitecoats began withdrawing to the north-west at around 1 p.m. It had taken Davout approximately three hours to bring about Rosenberg's defeat. Although the Austrians did not rout, their cohesion eroded badly as they pulled back under baleful fire. Furthermore, with Rosenberg's retreat Davout was squarely on Hohenzollern's flank, ideally located for his artillery to pour a terrible enfilade fire on the Austrian troops above Baumersdorf. Watching in dismay, Major Valentini observed that 'the dreadful effect of the ricochet fire from these guns that hurled their shot along the entire front at short range manifested itself, causing thereby significant devastation in the masses and a negative impact on the composure of the troops.'[273]

Davout's victory decided the day. Napoleon, astride Euphrates on the small hummock east of Aderklaa, had been observing 3rd Corps' progress closely and knew that Charles's position was fatally compromised. 'You see that Davout will again win the battle for me,' he told his staff.[274] Indeed, by this time, the Generalissimus had lost the initiative. His army's ponderous offensive had ground to a halt and he increasingly found himself simply responding to French moves. Now, as Charles was attempting to stem the tide of collapse on the Austrian left, Napoleon unleashed the rest of his army in the centre.

MacDonald's Attack: Into the Volcano

Napoleon's attack on the Austrian centre was a complex undertaking. Because he entrusted GD MacDonald with command of the principal thrust, it is often known as 'MacDonald's column' or, more accurately, 'MacDonald's square', but it contained many moving parts, not all of which would work together in harmony when they were needed.

The heart of the attack was MacDonald's wing of the Army of Italy: Broussier's newly arrived division along with Lamarque's depleted brigades. Napoleon added Seras as well, that division now under GB Moreau in place of its wounded commander. Keenly aware of the urgency of the situation, MacDonald arranged his force as carefully as time allowed, placing Broussier on the right and Lamarque on the left, followed by Moreau/Seras in reserve for a total of approximately 11,000 infantry.[275] Each of the leading divisions had two rows of four battalions deployed in line at its front, with the remaining battalions (four for Broussier, eight for Lamarque) in columns of division behind these lines.[276] This made a large, hollow square, albeit with the rear face only covered in the initial stages by a regiment of carabiniers in their tall bearskin caps.[277] Moreau followed, not as part of the square per se, but as a separate formation for MacDonald to inject into the fighting, as he judged appropriate. Some writers have cited this formation as an example of tactical crudeness, claiming it was only adopted because the quality of the French soldiers was too poor to permit anything more sophisticated. This overstates the case. Some of the formations adopted may have lacked finesse, but from their performance through the campaign—including the rather remarkable change of orientation they had just completed in shifting from the Russbach position—there can be no doubt that the soldiers and officers of the Army of Italy were quite capable of complex manoeuvres. Their continued actions up until nightfall, despite appalling casualties, are further testament to their tactical skill. MacDonald (and Napoleon) might have preferred to take more time to prepare with a series of sequenced actions, but they believed: that the time was right to start the attack; that the grand battery had weakened the Austrian centre sufficiently; and that adequate support was at hand in the cavalry attached to MacDonald. The size of the square was a drawback in that it made a fine artillery target, but it was hollow, not solid like a true 'column' or an Austrian 'mass'. Nor was it as inflexible as commonly portrayed, something the Habsburg squadrons learned when they attempted to penetrate its ranks and were stopped cold by well-delivered musketry. For all the controversy, therefore, the formation MacDonald chose, while not ideal, was suited to tactical conditions where he would have to advance quickly and powerfully, contend with threats from three sides, and fend off the numerous and courageous enemy cavalry.[278]

MacDonald's artillery had been detached to the grand battery, but Nansouty's division and the Guard cavalry were supposed to accompany him on his left and right flanks respectively to exploit any openings in the Austrian line. This mounted component of the attack, however, would prove tardy and poorly co-ordinated, and at first MacDonald had only four squadrons of cuirassiers at the left rear of his great square—the carabiniers arrived shortly thereafter. Simultaneously, Durutte, Pachtod, and GB François Joseph Gérard (commanding Sahuc's horse) were hurrying towards MacDonald's flanks, creating a panorama of movement that could not escape Austrian notice.

The grand battery continued to thunder as MacDonald led his 'terrible mass' forward across the burning plain sometime after noon.[279] His objective was the bell tower of Süssenbrunn, just behind the seam between d'Aspre's Grenadiers and Kolowrat's III Corps. Giving 'the entire army a spectacle

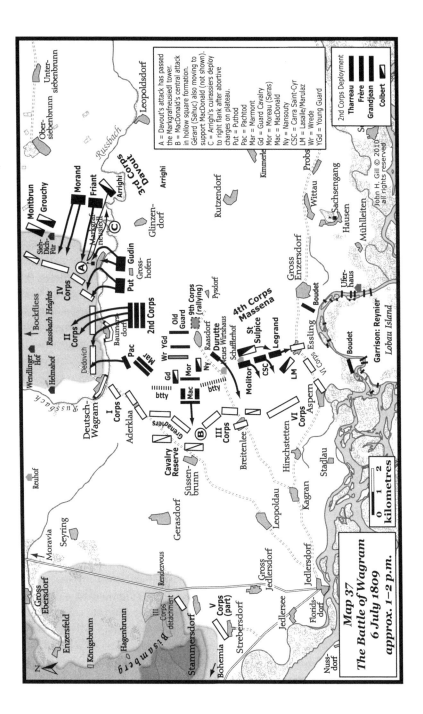

Map 37
The Battle of Wagram
6 July 1809
approx. 1–2 p.m.

A = Davout's attack has passed
the Markgrafneusiedl tower.
B = MacDonald's central attack
in hollow square formation.
Gérard (Sahuc) also moving to
support MacDonald (not shown).
C = Arrighi's cuirassiers deploy
to right flank after abortive
charges on plateau.

Put = Puthod
Pac = Pacthod
Mar = Marmont
Gd = Guard Cavalry
Mor = Moreau (Seras)
Mac = MacDonald
Ny = Nansouty
CSC = Carra Saint-Cyr
LM = Lasalle/Marulaz
Wr = Wrede
YGd = Young Guard

2nd Corps Deployment
Tharreau
Frère
Grandjean
Colbert

kilometres
0   1   2

of admirable courage', he advanced, 'conducting his divisions under a rain of canister and bullets . . . without displaying the least disorder'.[280] The Austrians, however, having observed the preparations on the French side of the field, were ready when MacDonald began to roll forward. The Grenadiers refused their right flank, while Kolowrat pulled back his left, creating between them a funnel into which MacDonald's square marched. It was 'a volcano' of lead and iron.[281] 'The spot where we were in line and particularly the places where we were formed in squares, men were left in heaps,' noted Lieutenant Lacorde of the 84th in his journal, 'it was an appalling spectacle.'[282] Despite the heavy fire and rapidly mounting casualties, the soldiers of the Army of Italy persevered, calmly repelling attempted charges by Austrian horse, blazing away with a 'rolling fire of musketry', and closing ranks as their comrades fell. MacDonald was well short of his objective, however, when he felt he could proceed no further. He was isolated, far in advance of the army, and surrounded on three sides by the enemy, but he perceived an opportunity and called for reinforcements. To his right, he saw 'twenty-five to thirty abandoned artillery pieces', to his left, a scene 'of even greater confusion', but his orders to launch the accompanying cavalry met with aggravating and, to him, incomprehensible delay. Nansouty on the left took a painfully long time to charge and, when he did, the favourable moment had passed. The heavy troopers recoiled with loss. On the right, the Guard horse was equally slow. GD Walther reported to MacDonald with all courtesy, but rather officiously asserted that he could not attack without specific orders from Bessières—now wounded and off the field—or the emperor himself. MacDonald was understandably wroth. Eventually, the two light regiments of the Guard, the Chasseurs and Polish Chevaulegers, did charge, but here too the opportune instant had slipped away.[283] The Guard Dragoons, attached Italian Guard cavalry, and Grenadiers-à-Cheval, also close by, never got into the fight at all. 'That immense and superb cavalry did not take a single prisoner,' wrote the disgusted Savary. 'They have never done anything like this to me,' exclaimed Napoleon. 'They will cause this day to end without results.'[284] It was now about 2 p.m.

While MacDonald's men were enduring their brutal trial by fire, Napoleon was pushing other formations into action. On MacDonald's right, Pachtod's division attacked towards Wagram, while Durutte advanced on the left, aiming for Breitenlee. Behind came Wrede and GB F. J. Gérard with Sahuc's light cavalry. Additionally, Napoleon ordered GD Reille to manoeuvre the Young Guard to support MacDonald. 'Do not risk anything, as all I have remaining with me are the two regiments of the Old Guard,' he told the general. This was something of an exaggeration as Marmont's small corps, deployed opposite Wagram, was out of cannon range and unengaged, but he doubtless expected Reille to understand the need to balance prudence with aggressiveness.[285]

General Offensive: Success Was No Longer In Doubt

MacDonald's attack did not occur in isolation. Fighting now raged all along the line as conditions matured and Napoleon's orders for a general offensive reached their intended recipients. The French advance broadly coincided with Austrian withdrawal. Charles was with II Corps.[286] He had personally witnessed the defeat of his left wing, the troops around him were in considerable disarray, and he could clearly seeing large masses of French reserves around Raasdorf; it was probably evident that his right wing was stalled, if not in retreat. He thus knew that his army was potentially compromised. With no reserves of his own to alter the flow of the battle, he could only hope for Johann's appearance. Around 2 p.m. this illusion was dashed when a courier returned with a message from the younger archduke. Johann, writing from Marchegg at 10.30 a.m., announced that he would march as soon as his artillery arrived, pledging to be on the road no later than 1 p.m. with hopes of arriving at Leopoldsdorf no later than 5 p.m.[287] This was far too late in Charles's estimation; his army could not sustain the fight where it was for another three to four hours. Around 2.30 p.m., he issued a disposition for a phased withdrawal.

The French were already validating Charles's analysis as the Habsburg staff officers hastened to finish the new disposition. Towards the Danube, Legrand's division, leading 4th Corps, reached Essling and his two French regiments successfully stormed the Austrian entrenchments. The other two divisions closed up, wheeled to the right, and began a methodical advance between Breitenlee and Hirschstetten. Legrand, 'greeted with a heavy cannonade', likewise turned west, and Massena called up Boudet to add his reformed regiments to the line.[288] The general direction of advance was towards Leopoldau, with Boudet along the Danube headed for Kagran, Marulaz and Lasalle on Boudet's right, then Legrand, Carra Saint-Cyr, and Molitor in the centre and St Sulpice on the right. Although the infantry was largely unengaged after evicting the whitecoats from Essling and Aspern, the artillery chased Klenau's troops, and the light cavalry was extremely active. With support from St Sulpice's heavies, Lasalle and Marulaz continually harassed and charged the retiring Austrians. A minuscule portion of V Corps entered the fray at this stage as a division of *EH Carl* Uhlans and a cavalry half-battery intervened to rescue a Landwehr battalion from capture.[289] Otherwise, all of the pressure was on Klenau's men. As VI Corps officers recorded of the afternoon: 'Amidst incessant engagements, the corps reached the heights of Stammersdorf at nightfall and were arrayed in order of battle.'[290] Those 'incessant engagements' included a French attack on Leopoldau as evening came on. The defenders, I and II/*Duka*, resisted firmly and withdrew successfully, but the 3rd Battalion was 'utterly destroyed' by rampaging French cavalry as it tried to retreat from its reserve position behind the village.[291] It was apparently during this engagement (between 7 and 8 p.m.), that Lasalle was killed by a bullet to the head.[292] The quintessential hussar, his death was another great loss for the French army. Marulaz took command of the two divisions at once and fired the spirit of the flagging troopers with a rousing call to the 8th Hussars, his old regiment. Joined by the chasseur regiments, his squadrons threw themselves on the nearby Austrian cavalry at around 8 p.m. in a final charge. It was his last contribution to the campaign. With his horse killed (the twenty-sixth over his career) and himself wounded (his nineteenth wound), he painfully held himself in the saddle until night before turning over command to GB Bruyère and retiring from the field.

While these human dramas were playing themselves out, Durutte, on Massena's right, occupied Breitenlee during the afternoon. He encountered stiffening resistance from III Corps as he pushed beyond the village, but the Austrians were already withdrawing in accordance with Charles's orders, so the French more followed than pursued their adversaries to end the day north of Leopoldau.[293]

MacDonald, his formation drastically reduced, resumed his advance as Wrede came up on his right.[294] Wrede had received his orders directly from Napoleon: 'Now I unleash you; you see MacDonald's awkward position. March! Relieve his corps, attack the enemy; in short, act as you think best!'[295] Arriving between 2 and 3 p.m., the Bavarian cavalry leaped into action at once and the infantry deployed with skill, but with MacDonald's artillery still in the rear, the thirty Bavarian guns were especially welcome. Joined by those 6-pounders of the Guard still mobile, the Bavarians soon found themselves in an extended duel with the Austrian batteries on the Bisamberg. With Wrede, the Guard light cavalry, Gérard's horsemen, some guard artillery, and his own remnants, MacDonald finally levered the Austrians out of Süssenbrunn by outflanking the village to the north. Wrede was wounded, his place taken by GM Minucci, but the advance continued with MacDonald repeating his outflanking manoeuvre at Gerasdorf. As the Austrians evacuated the village, he noted that their infantry was withdrawing in disorder and launched the two Guard light regiments in a series of vigorous charges. These led to a great turmoil of cavalry west of Gerasdorf as the sun edged towards the horizon. The French and Polish troopers captured several guns and some prisoners, but could not break the Austrian masses on the slopes to the west, nor could they overcome the Habsburg horse despite repeated and valiant efforts. The Polish Guardsmen grappled with the *Schwarzenberg* Uhlans at some point in these see-saw clashes, and some of the Poles seized lances from their opponents. Using these traditionally Polish weapons to good effect against their former owners, the Poles thus set their regiment on a path of transition from chevaulegers to lancers. As for the Young Guard infantry, Reille had already turned these regiments back towards Süssenbrunn on learning that outriders from Archduke Johann's corps had reached the eastern edge of the battlefield. 'They established themselves around the village,' to be prepared to respond 'in case of some mishap'.[296]

On the far French right, Davout continued to press relentlessly ahead. 'The entire success of the skilful manoeuvre executed by the corps . . . was no longer in doubt,' recorded the 3rd Corps report. 'All the troops were perfectly established on the plateau, covered by Montbrun and Grouchy . . . all that remained was to push the enemy with vigour so as not to allow him time to recover. The retreat of the enemy's extreme left was so pronounced that his line already had the form of a right angle.'[297] Gudin, though hampered by the Austrian encampment, drove along the edge of the heights straight at the point where Hohenzollern had had to bend his line back as Rosenberg retreated. Puthod advanced on Gudin's left, while Friant and Morand and the cavalry kept stretching the end of the enemy's line, attempting to envelope his left completely. 'We pushed them, we pressed them at all points, and only night halted our victorious pursuit,' wrote the 12th Chasseurs' Capitaine Tascher.[298] Tascher may have embellished a bit, but Rosenberg, though he maintained order in his ranks, had no choice but steady retreat to the range of hills north of Bockfliess. In closing actions here, Montbrun charged Austrian infantry masses to hurry their departure and two battalions of 108th Ligne, storming into Bockfliess, killed or captured several hundred inebriated whitecoats.[299]

Davout's progress was the signal for Oudinot to attack. With Hohenzollern's line unhinged by Rosenberg's predicament and weakened by the detachments he had sent to support IV Corps, the outcome was predictable, but the fighting was fierce. 'One fought now only for one's life,' remembered Leutnant Veigl of 8th Jägers, 'no longer for victory.'[300] Tharreau on the left, Grandjean in the centre, and Frère on the right made 'a rapid and vigourous' attack 'led by a swarm of skirmishers'. Scaling the heights, they forced the Austrians back towards Helmahof.[301] Hohenzollern, under a vicious crossfire (*Rohan* lost eighteen men to a single howitzer shell), had no choice but rapid withdrawal. 'It was very difficult to keep the troops in any sort of order,' he reported.[302] To make matters worse for Austrian II Corps, Pachtod's relatively fresh division, supported by the Guard 12-pounders, crossed the muddy Russbach 'with great daring' and clambered up the heights east of Wagram on Tharreau's left, more or less simultaneous with Oudinot's attack. Having dashed up the slope 'under a terrible fire and in disorder', the regiments had to reform behind their skirmishers and under a 'hail of bullets'. Pachtod, fortunate to have Lieutenant Noël's battery at hand, forced the Austrians out of Wagram and jeopardised Hohenzollern's rear. Despite severe casualties, his division pursued Bellegarde's retreating troops beyond the town, only halting when confronted by threatening ranks of Habsburg heavy cavalry towards the Bisamberg.[303]

While Pachtod headed towards Seyring, 2nd Corps advanced steadily, its pace increasing as Oudinot was finally able to get his artillery and cavalry on the plateau. Colbert's brigade had spent three or four hours standing in support of the grand battery when it was called forward at around 2 p.m. to join Oudinot on the plateau. Galloping past the mounted ranks, Oudinot called out to Chef d'Escadron Pierre Labiffe of the 7th Chasseurs, 'Make ready, Labiffe, you are going to charge', and the brigade now struck at the retreating Austrians repeatedly. Hohenzollern, as we have seen, was barely holding his corps together, and crossing the Russbach near Helmahof disrupted the Austrian masses. This offered Colbert several opportunities. The 7th Chasseurs 'charged resolutely, but at one hundred paces a terrible volley from the square facing it caused the most fearful confusion in the ranks of this regiment'. Though Colbert was badly wounded in the process, 9th Hussars and 20th Chasseurs had better luck, breaking a battalion of *Zedtwitz* and demolishing III/*Rohan* as these regiments fell into disorder while attempting to escape into the low ground near the brook. As the French cavalry was recovering, the last Habsburg formations made their way across the Russbach around 3.30 p.m., and fighting on this portion of the dreadful field slowly faded into silence.[304]

On the opposite end of the vast canvas of battle, Johann's advance guard made a belated appearance at Untersiebenbrunn between 4 and 5 p.m. The sight of Austrian cavalry patrols occasioned wild panic among the stragglers and baggage' in the French rear, and these rushed madly for the Lobau bridges. 'The disorder was complete,' wrote Löwenstern. 'One saw nothing but smoke and dust; one heard nothing but shrieks and disorder.' 'Later we learned that some lancers [sic] from the army of Archduke Johann had appeared on the plain and caused this pandemonium.'[305] Johann's scouts do not seem to have noticed this rumour-fed bedlam. For them, the gruesome battlefield was ominous, the situation dangerously unclear. They spotted French cavalry pickets and knew there was a strong detachment in Obersiebenbrunn, but it was obvious that the battle had moved far to the west, where 'dull, distant shots could still be heard'.[306] With his own staff officers unable to get through to Charles, and hearing no word from headquarters, Johann decided 'there was nothing more to do', and withdrew. He cynically but correctly concluded that his late arrival would be cited as the cause for the lost battle and returned to Marchegg at nightfall.[307]

The commotion created by this panic sparked a momentary uproar in imperial headquarters, rousing Napoleon from his tent and leading most officers to conclude that Johann had at last arrived. The Guard speedily formed 'a forest of iron' around the emperor, and staff officers flew off into the gloom to reconnoitre. They soon discovered that Austrian cavalry patrols had alarmed noncombatants in the army's rear to generate the 'horrible spectacle'. These were indeed scouts from Johann's command, but one of Napoleon's officers, Chef de Escadron Henri Amédée Mercure de Turenne, soon returned to report, 'There are not thirty thousand there, rather ten thousand, I have seen them.' Relieved that Johann was retiring rather than attacking and that his force was much smaller than had been assessed, Napoleon and his staff returned to their repose after about an hour of watchfulness.[308]

What had happened to Johann? Johann's absence is one of the enduring controversies of the battle and basically revolves around three questions: Could Charles have recalled him sooner? Could Johann have arrived in time? Would his arrival have produced a different outcome? The first submits to a fairly straightforward answer. Charles should have ordered Johann to the Marchfeld sooner than the message he sent at 7 p.m. on 4 July, as he watched the obvious French build-up on Lobau that day. Even a few hours might have made a difference. As it was, the courier, delayed by night and the furious storm, took an unusually long time to deliver the first message, so Johann did not have it in his headquarters until 6 a.m. on 5 July. The larger problem, however, was that Charles had vacillated during the opening days of July, his thinking blurred by poor intelligence—erroneous reporting from Joseph and others that powerful elements of the Army of Italy were still in Hungary, for instance—by fatuous hopes of distracting the French at Pressburg, and by indecision regarding the kind of battle he wanted to fight on the Marchfeld.[309] As we have seen, he first ordered Johann to evacuate the Engerau bridgehead and then told his brother to launch a diversionary attack. Johann understandably found these rapid shifts confusing, and confirmatory of his scornful views regarding Charles's advisers, but the notion of a diversion accorded very well with his own predilections.

This brings us to the question of whether he could have marched earlier. As directed and as he desired, Johann was making preparations to attack Severoli's men at Engerau on 5 July. He postponed his foray owing to the dreadful weather—the French, of course, did not—but claimed that the placement of troops for the attack left his corps straddling the Danube and his men unprepared to march north. He also argued that he had to call in outposts and detachments from all along the river. Moreover, the troops were weary, wet, and hungry; they had to rest and eat before they marched. Lastly, he wanted to wait until nightfall to conceal his move from Severoli's observation posts. These answers seem evasive, equivocal, insufficient to explain a delay of eighteen to nineteen hours between receipt of an important directive and departure of the advance guard. A number of objections may be raised: most of the troops that went to the Hauptarmee were not the ones across the river on 5 July, Johann might have moved without calling in every remote outpost, he might have injected a sense of urgency into the preparations, the risk of the enemy learning about the move was worth taking. Indeed, the urgency of the situation, that Charles stated could decide the fate of the House of Habsburg, seemed to demand something more than routine activity; one might consider Massena's march from Augsburg in April under hideous weather, for example. Instead, Johann did not even bother to answer the first missive from the Generalissimus—an astounding, almost unforgivable lapse. At a minimum, he should have informed Charles of his difficulties and likely earliest arrival time. Whether from lethargy or discontent stemming from previous frictions with headquarters, he did not. If GM Bianchi's impressions are correct, Johann did not even hasten to inform his chief of staff, Nugent, so that key individual did not learn of the first note until 2 p.m. on 5 July.[310] There is evidence from an Insurrection staff officer that Johann's senior officers spent their time on 5 July deliberating, debating, and disputing rather than acting.[311] Johann certainly had legitimate concerns regarding the readiness of his small corps, but we have no indication that he applied any particular dynamism or interest to ensure that a cohesive body of as many men as possible were on the road as soon as possible to answer the call of duty in the climactic battle of this war. Instead, his first elements did not march until sometime between midnight and 1 a.m. on the night of 5/6 July. One might also question if he could not have marched faster. A contemporary Austrian staff officer, comparing the excuses Johann offered with the performances of Davout and Wrede, excoriated the archduke and his commanders for a dearth of activity, boldness, decision, and speed.[312] Similarly, Rosenberg's son, riding with Johann as a courier, lamented what he characterised as a cautious, slow move from Marchegg to the battlefield.[313] Again, a few hours might have made the difference.

Would the difference of a few hours have made a difference in the battle's result? That is, could Johann have changed the outcome of the battle by arriving substantially earlier on 6 July with 10,000–13,000 men? It seems highly unlikely.[314] In war, as in most other human endeavours, chance and unanticipated developments can never be discounted, but the probability is very low that Johann's corps could have transformed Wagram into a Habsburg victory. Napoleon was well aware of the potential threat to his far right flank—indeed he credited Johann with 25,000–30,000 men, twice the actual figure—and he maintained a sizeable reserve throughout the struggle. Even if Davout's infantry is left out of the calculations, Marmont was never truly engaged, there was an abundance of cavalry on that wing, all or part of 30th Ligne seems to have been assigned to Montbrun for this purpose, the Young Guard could have been recalled, and the Old Guard was at hand. Johann, therefore, might have lessened the degree of defeat by a timely appearance, but he was hardly likely to alter to the overall outcome. The panic just decsribed among sutlers, marauders, herdsmen, skulkers, wagoners, wounded, and other rear area persons was worrisome, but it did not mean that the French army was on the verge of dissolution and only required Johann to push it over the edge. In sum, Johann's response to the summons to the field was sluggish, almost sullen; in other armies, in other circumstances, he might have been called before a court martial. He almost certainly could have marched many hours sooner, but it is very unlikely that his earlier arrival would have changed the course of events in any historically significant fashion; it is both unfair and inaccurate to lay the defeat at his doorstep.[315]

In any case, Johann, arriving belatedly, wisely retired into the deepening twilight and the hot, bloody day came to a close. The concluding clashes left the two armies arrayed across a broad, jagged front stretching twenty-two kilometres from the Danube near Strebersdorf to Gross-Schweinbarth where Radetzky commanded a hotchpotch flanking detachment for IV Corps. Most of Rosenberg's men, joined by some temporarily orphaned elements of II Corps, bivouacked from just north of Bockfliess to Gross-Ebersdorf, covering the routes to Moravia. The bulk of II Corps (approximately 10,000 men) was on the Bisamberg near Enzersfeld with the Grenadiers on their right around Hagenbrunn. The Cavalry Reserve, which Nostitz's division had rejoined, screened the area west of Seyring, while I, III, and VI Corps collected on the slopes in the vicinity of Stammersdorf. The available formations of Reuss's V Corps closed the gap between Strebersdorf and the Danube on the road to Bohemia. Charles was also near Stammersdorf, bone weary, but dictating orders to continue the retreat.

The French likewise encamped in an extended arc from the Danube to Bockfliess. Massena held the left with Boudet forward at Jedlersdorf supported by Bruyère, but most of his troops halted west of Leopoldau. The Saxons, somewhat reordered after their catastrophes, assembled east of the town. The battered Army of Italy collected itself around Gerasdorf with Wrede to their right and 2nd Corps between Wagram and Seyring. Oudinot, wounded yet again, would be rewarded for his performance with a marshal's baton. Of Davout's corps, Gudin and Puthod were around Wagram, but the rest of the infantry and his considerable cavalry stopped in the area around Bockfliess on the northern edge of the Russbach Heights. Napoleon, surrounded by the Guard and Marmont, established his headquarters east of Aderklaa near the small hillock he had used as his observation post for most of the day.

The Greatest Battle of Modern Times

As the cacophony of combat dissipated and the panic in the French rear areas settled into a chagrined murmur, the men of both sides could consider what they had experienced. Many were simply relieved to be alive and unharmed. 'God gave me the grace to survive all the battles we have had,' wrote Carabinier Henri Joseph Parteger. 'I tell you, my most dear father, that the last battle that we had on the 6th of the month of July, I had extreme good luck to survive that battle.' Parteger had had two horses killed under him during the day, the second falling to a cannon ball that tore away part of Parteger's boot and stirrup; he escaped with a minor abrasion. At the same time, many recognised that Wagram had been extraordinary, perhaps unprecedented, in its scope, scale, ferocity, and cost. 'I do not believe that, in modern times, a more terrible battle has been given,' Coëhorn told his wife in a letter two days after the great struggle. Pelet, in the history he composed more than a decade later, after all of the grand battles of that violent epoch, described Wagram as 'one of the most remarkable in ancient and modern times, by the immense works that preceded it, by the force of the armies that fought it, finally by the political and military results that followed it'. 'I have never seen so many troops,' wrote Charles on 9 July, recalling the appearance of the French army on the morning of the 6th 'in a strength that has hardly ever been assembled in a single place since ancient times.' At a simpler level, veteran François Joseph Jacquin of the 37th Ligne simply noted that he and his comrades 'had never seen such a bloody battle'.[316]

The cost in human lives was staggering. Casualty figures are always subject to controversy, and those for Wagram are complicated by the fact that in some cases each side recorded all losses suffered between 30 June and 12 July in one aggregate sum. Nevertheless, one may estimate with fair reliability that the Hauptarmee lost a grand total of approximately 38,870 in the course of these sanguinary two days. This included four generals killed (d'Aspre, Nordmann, Vukassovich, Peter Vécsey) and eleven others wounded, among whom GM von Stutterheim, the hero of Eggmühl, and FML Dedovich were prominent. Dedovich, freshly recovered from his Aspern–Essling wound, had reported to Charles early on the morning of the 6th, only to be hit again within hours of taking the field. Charles himself, of course, also suffered a minor wound on the evening of the first day. Fourth Corps and Nordmann's Advance Guard paid by far the highest price, contributing approximately one-third of the total casualties, followed by I and II Corps, fewer in VI Corps and the Grenadiers, and relatively small numbers from the Cavalry Reserve and III Corps. The four Jäger battalions (1st, 2nd, 7th, 8th), owing to their employment and a degree of bad luck, were largely wiped out, as were the three regiments of Riese's brigade. Notable as well is that some of the Landwehr battalions simply vanished, and that the majority of casualties among these units and some of the volunteers were in the 'missing' category, indicating that they dissolved during or shortly after the battle.

Figures on the French side are not as precise in all cases, but still afford a reasonable estimate of 35,060 killed, wounded, captured, and missing. Worst hit was Bernadotte's 9th Corps (including Dupas) with 40 per cent casualties after the disastrous attack on Wagram on the 5th and hours in Austrian crossfire the following day; Dupas alone lost 67 per cent. Somewhat surprising is that Oudinot's corps suffered the next largest percentage of

Table 16: Wagram: Comparative Casualty Estimates

Austrian

I Corps	6,900
II Corps	9,500
III Corps	1,900
IV Corps and Advance Guard	13,400
V Corps	10
VI Corps	2,500
Grenadiers	1,770
Cavalry Reserve	1,980
Artillery	910
Total	38,870

French

Imperial Guard	680
2nd Corps	8,670
3rd Corps (including dragoons)	6,170
4th Corps	5,210
2nd Division/7th Corps	30
9th Corps (including Dupas)	6,750
Army of Italy	6,500
Cavalry Reserve	1,050
Army of Dalmatia	(negligible)
Total	35,060

All figures estimated and rounded to nearest ten.

casualties, some 32 per cent of its starting strength. Given that only part of the corps was engaged on the evening of the 5th, this suggests that the fighting on the afternoon of 6 July was severe indeed—probably a result of heavy Austrian artillery fire after 2nd Corps crested the plateau, before its own guns were on hand. The Army of Italy also paid a fearsome toll, losing almost one-quarter of its strength. Casualties for 3rd Corps and 4th Corps, as well as 1st and 3rd Heavy Cavalry Divisions amounted to between 15 and 18 per cent each. Marmont, Wrede, and the Guard infantry took almost no casualties, but the Guard artillery lost 476 men killed or wounded and 405 draught-horses. Five generals were killed, most notably the irreplaceable Lasalle, while Bessières and thirty-six French or German generals suffered wounds of some kind. Napoleon, though constantly under fire at the apex of his line, was unscathed. The number of French prisoners is often given as 7,000 from the published Austrian 'Relation' of the battle. Buat offers a more likely figure of 3,000–4,000, but this is still a surprising number for the winning side. Similarly, in terms of battle 'trophies', the defeated Austrians claimed an edge, asserting the capture of twelve eagles or flags and twenty-one guns, compared to a French record of ten standards and twenty guns.[317]

The scene left in the wake of the battle appalled observers. Capitaine Tascher noted that some of the houses in Markgrafneusiedl 'were in flames; others were given over to pillage; the wounded, the dying were scattered among the flaming debris'. 'Many of the wretched wounded had been roasted alive when the ripening crops had been set afire,' wrote Noël. 'The villages were filled with wounded,' he commented as his battery traversed the field four days later. 'We passed a field hospital near which was a heap of limbs, arms, and legs. It is better to see such things after a battle than before.' Benevolent citizens of Vienna, who had watched the slaughter from afar with avid patriotic interest, spontaneously came out to the awful field to alleviate the suffering. Despite their generous mercy, even a month later, a Saxon gunner found the Marchfeld desolate, 'still covered in dead men and horses'. Coming upon the spot where a Landwehr battalion had stood, he found 'twenty-six corpses lying one behind the other, still in full equipment, all laid low by the same cannon ball', nearby 'thirty dead French were leaning against a wall', and there was a cuirassier pierced 'with a perfectly round hole that had exactly the diameter of a 12-pounder ball'.[318]

Like the French cuirassier, many of these dead and wounded were the victims of the powerful arrays of guns employed by both sides on 5 and 6 July. 'At Wagram I saw all the horrors of battle,' remembered a lieutenant of the 105th Ligne, 'the sustained fire of the artillery and musketry by both sides created an appalling carnage.'[319] The exact figures are murky, but the brown-coated Habsburg gunners manned nearly 400 pieces, while their French and German opponents had at least 475 on the field in addition to the 109 bristling from the parapets along Lobau Island. The French alone fired between 90,000 and 100,000 artillery rounds, 15,000 just from the Guard's pieces. In a letter to GD Songis two days after the battle, Lariboisière wrote: 'A battle so long and one in which the artillery played such a fine role has never been seen; additionally the consumption [of ammunition] and losses were prodigious … It was a cannonade such as I have never heard.'[320] Likewise, it was for Charles 'the most terrible cannon fire that I have ever heard'.[321] The sheer number of guns, howitzers, and mortars would have resulted in gargantuan casualties, but the effect was increased by the manner in which the batteries were used. The dominance exerted over the Austrian line by the Lobau guns on the 5th and the punishing impact of the grand battery the following day stand out as signs of an increasing role for artillery on the battlefield. Even setting these aside, however, tactical situations such as the angle of the French line east of Aderklaa or the bend in Rosenberg's line near Markgrafneusiedl created unforgettable crossfire opportunities that both sides eagerly exploited. The artillery's contributions were thus crucial for the two armies, as their commanders generously acknowledged. 'The artillery', announced the official Austrian account, 'has remained true to its old renown.' And Napoleon told Lariboisière: 'At Eylau, you provided me with powerful support, but today you have won the battle.'[322]

If the artillery played a singularly important role and the infantry, as usual, bore the brunt of the fighting and casualties, the cavalry also deserves a few words. As there were no grand charges of the Jena or Eylau style at Wagram, the cavalry can be overlooked in the swirl of dust and smoke in such a complex, multifaceted engagement. The most obvious cavalry action, and the most irritating to Napoleon, was the failure of the French to provide adequate, timely support to MacDonald's square. However, this represented a problem of command and control—Bessières's wound and Walther's mulish refusal to act at MacDonald's request—not an overall decline in the utility of cavalry or timorous behaviour on the part of the French squadrons. More than one French commentator lamented the absence of Murat, who might have made supreme use of several opportunities. Moreover, Napoleon had already dispersed much of his heavy reserve—Arrighi to Davout, St Sulpice to Massena—reducing the options available to his subordinates. At the grand tactical level it is worth highlighting that the French mounted arm again, as at Aspern, performed a critical role in holding off or disrupting the Austrians at several important points. In the tactical realm, the Saxon horse fended off Austrian threats in the centre at least twice, and the French cavalry certainly helped harry the Austrians off the field, destroying several battalions even if it was unable to break any of the major formations. Above all, the success that Montbrun and Grouchy achieved on the far eastern flank was fundamental to the French victory. By defeating Nostitz and the others, they protected Morand's right and inexorably forced Rosenberg to fall back or risk collapse. As such, they were a vital component of the day's eventual triumph.

The Habsburg horse also turned in a generally solid performance from the tactical perspective. The Herculean scale of the struggle obscures many smaller cavalry actions that were crucial to local sub-battles and, in the aggregate, to the larger outcome: Liechtenstein saving the guns near Aderklaa, or his eponymous hussar regiment seizing the unfortunate Boudet's pieces. The Austrian troopers served the Generalissimus well in many of these small, local encounters. Beyond small unit tactics, on the other hand, the Austrians once again proved incapable of organising and executing battle-changing mounted operations. Leadership, doctrine, entrenched attitudes, and the 6 July disposition, meant that the Habsburg troopers, for all their valour, were never united in a major force for offensive exploitation or defensive counter-attacks.

The problems that hobbled the Austrian cavalry reflected larger deficiencies in the army as a whole. As at Aspern, officers and men lacked nothing in bravery or resilience, and, as at Aspern, they could be stubborn, determined opponents when fighting under circumstances in which they felt comfortable. The tenacious defence of the Russbach Heights and Baumersdorf or the determined struggle for Aderklaa are examples of these qualities. As before, however, the army high command proved incapable of orchestrating a coherent offensive, while corps and division commanders lacked the initiative to function outside strict and detailed instructions. Klenau, considered one of the better senior leaders, thus halted after his surprising success on the morning of the 6th, Kolowrat seems to have quickly abandoned any notion of advance, and no one could move quickly enough to capitalise on the great disorder among the French opposite Aderklaa after the Saxon collapse and Carra Saint-Cyr's repulse. It is noteworthy that no advancing corps made any progress once it encountered substantial resistance. There was a 'total lack of resolution and combination', in the words of FML von Wallmoden. 'Briefly, arriving at the critical moment, there seemed to be no desire to engage in a decisive battle.' Instead, there was hesitation, resulting in 'a murderous and pointless parade'.[323] Liechtenstein, Bellegarde, and Hohenzollern stoutly defended their posts, but probably would have done no better had they been in command of VI Corps. None of these men turned in an especially distinguished performance at Wagram, yet all were promoted or decorated after the war. Only Rosenberg, who arguably did the best he could in a bad situation—made worse by the pointless order to attack on the morning of the second day—failed to earn laurels. Indeed, he was personally singled out for censure by the Kaiser. Many of these weaknesses, of course, were immanent in the Habsburg military system of the day, requiring years to change, but some originated at the top during the weeks prior to Wagram. Charles, vacillating for six weeks over the type of battle he wanted to fight, did nothing to ameliorate this situation among his senior leaders. The result was confusion about corps missions, failure to fortify the Russbach position, delay in recalling Johann, the useless sacrifice of the Advance Guard on 5 July, and awkward positioning of the army that night. Dissention and intrigue among his staff and persistent interference from the imperial court only compounded the operational paralysis.

As for Charles, he certainly exhibited great courage and local leadership, but the extent of the battle quickly exceeded his grasp. He failed to recognise the scale and threat of the French crossing until midday on the 5th, and, once his various subordinates were set in motion on the 6th, he could only alter events by personal intervention. This proved nearly impossible given the size of the field and his own limitations. The cumbersome machine rarely acted without his personal involvement and its disarticulated elements ground to a halt when left to their own devices. 'Soon each [corps] acted according to the impulsions of the moment and the circumstances that affected it most closely,' wrote Wallmoden, observing that the halt and retreat in the centre and on the right were 'more the result of instinct than of higher plans'.[324] Charles was keenly aware of the army's deficiencies in the attack but was unable to compensate for these weaknesses or adjust his plans to minimise them.

On the other hand, Charles recognised the army's sturdiness in set-piece situations on open terrain, especially when on the defensive. He could not alter the nature of the senior commanders, but the reforms he had promulgated over the preceding years and the corps structure he introduced in 1809 greatly enhanced the army's durability and resilience. These qualities made the army and its constituent components much more difficult to break.[325] An attack might stall, a retreat might be necessary, and disorder might ensue, but the attacks were earnest, the defence was tougher, and, given a chance, the army would reconstitute itself in fairly short order. In a previous conflict, for example, Habsburg troops subjected to MacDonald's or Oudinot's assaults might have routed, but not at Wagram. The whitecoats at Wagram thus were 'everywhere in retreat, but not in disarray'.[326] Durability and resilience were thus the vital factors that limited the scope of Napoleon's military success at Wagram and for the remainder of the war. 'It had been a long time since the Austrian army had presented itself in the field in such an honourable manner,' commented Colonel Berthezène, 'and that was the work of the archduke.'[327] Napoleon's inability to achieve a more dramatic victory on 5–6 July was not so much because the quality of the French troops was poor, rather that the Austrians had improved. Indeed, as one commentator argues, the Austrians probably achieved more at Wagram where they were outnumbered than they did at Aspern where they had enjoyed a dramatic quantitative advantage.[328]

Where the Austrians had improved, the French had declined. There were more conscripts in the ranks, so it could be more difficult to rally units and more men might choose to absent themselves from the line of battle if the opportunity arose—such as after a repulse on the first evening. However, it is important not to overemphasise this corrosion of the army's sharp edge. The panicked flights to the bridges after Klenau's unexpected appearance on the morning of the 6th, and the chaos that evening when foragers, pillagers, or roaming *cantinières* (the stories vary) were startled by Johann's scouts, were vexing, but in reality they amounted to momentary annoyances. Colourful images of Napoleon hastily rising from his campbed at the alarms raised in the twilight hours of 6 July are interesting and can be illuminating, but Marmont's assertion that such chaos was unknown among the armies of Austerlitz and Jena must be tempered with some nuance.[329] Certainly Napoleon responded promptly and with vigour—he had been expecting Johann all day— himself mounting up, and sending officers galloping in the direction of the clamour. This reaction was entirely logical. As he curtly told one officer, 'victory should never inspire too much confidence; and it may escape those who rely upon it implicitly.'[330] In any event, 'the inexplicable brouhaha' was of brief duration and the imperial encampment returned to normal.[331] The key is that these panics occurred not in the ranks of the combat troops, but largely among rear area personnel and camp followers, 'the equipment train, spare horses, stragglers, knaves, and all the herd of non-combatants that always pullulate in the trail of a victorious army.'[332] 'The troops remained immobile.'[333] The worst effect for those at headquarters was that several liaison officers from the tsar were present to witness this embarrassing episode. More serious were the disorderly flights by the troops attacking the heights on the evening of 5 July and by Carra Saint-Cyr's men at Aderklaa on the 6th. The first, as discussed earlier, was not as bad as it first seemed and was greatly exacerbated by the poor visibility. The second, on the other hand, occurred in broad daylight after the shock of near-encirclement and the loss of two regimental commanders. In both instances, however, veteran soldiers and experienced officers soon regrouped themselves and rejoined the fight. Carra Saint-Cyr's division, though shaken and depleted, consolidated itself within an hour or two to participate in Massena's flank march. Eugene's men probably would have collected themselves sooner had they been able to see. They certainly leaked conscripts during the night, but their evening experience did not prevent them from manoeuvring skilfully, standing firm under fire, and attacking with determination on 6 July. Moreover, there were certainly contemporaries who would have offered different views. 'Tell your son that the French are the first soldiers of the world!' wrote the wounded Coëhorn to his wife on 8 July; Sergeant Marc Desboeufs of the 81st, after wandering over to see the emperor's tent out of curiosity, wrote, 'The blood spilt during the day made no impression on me; I was filled with pride to belong to this grand army whose valour overturned empires, and the grandeur of the scene that had just taken place totally absorbed my spirit.'[334]

Though the battle was an undeniable French victory, Napoleon was feeling rather less grand than his loyal sergeant. In his mind, the results did not seem commensurate with the gargantuan preparations. According to Savary:

> The emperor was indifferently content with the Battle of Wagram; he wanted a second representation of Marengo, Austerlitz, or Jena and he had taken great care to obtain such a result; but far from this, the Austrian army was intact; it was departing to throw itself into some position that would necessitate new planning efforts to bring about an engagement followed by better results.

Napoleon may not have been entirely satisfied, but the victory so dearly purchased in this unwanted war would be enough. Charles, stunned by the magnitude of the battle, certainly entertained no illusions about the outcome: 'Prince Jean [Liechtenstein] has been sent to Napoleon to see if he can arrange something,' he wrote to his uncle. 'Was it necessary to wait until a battle had been lost?'[335]

Charles's glum but realistic assessment pointed the way to the future, and Colonel Antoine Drouot of the Guard artillery would soon be able to write that 'the brilliant results of the battles on the 5th and 6th have forced the enemy to demand a ceasefire.' There was, however, yet one more battle to fight before this new Habsburg peace initiative would bear fruit. In the meantime, the battered Austrians withdrew north into the night and the exhausted French sought sleep on the blasted, smoking field. One of the greatest battles in military history was over. 'That was the celebrated Battle of Wagram,' wrote Marmont years later, 'the greatest battle of modern times in number of men united on the same ground in the view of an observer ... one may imagine the beauty and the majesty of that spectacle.'[336]

CHAPTER 6

Znaim

It is unlikely that Charles gave much, if any, thought to renewing the battle on 7 July. Although his offensive had failed, he had successfully withdrawn his army from the field intact. It was the principal shield of the monarchy; he was not about to risk it again so soon. He thus ordered a withdrawal during the night of 6/7 July, choosing to accept the dispiriting attrition of a retreat rather than venture all in continued combat. From a new 'position', such as the hills behind the Pulkau at Jetzelsdorf, he might be able to offer battle once more. In the meantime, he hoped to put some space between himself and his adversary, and perhaps grant enough time for peace proposals to take hold. Late that night and on into the morning of the 7th, therefore, the Hauptarmee moved painfully north towards the Moravian hills. The bulk of the army (I, III, V, VI, Grenadiers, Cavalry Reserve) took the main road through Korneuburg and Stockerau to bivouac in the general area of Stockerau, but II Corps marched almost due north to Ernstbrunn, while Rosenberg headed for Mistelbach with his corps and various pieces of Hohenzollern's command that had attached themselves to him during the previous day's fighting. An officer from one of Hohenzollern's detachments described that night in his journal: 'harassed by hunger, thirst, and fatigue, and with despair in my soul, a soldier gave me a few drops of water and a morsel of commissary bread, and I slept for a few hours in a ditch bordering the road.'[1]

Napoleon was in no condition to pursue that night. The Austrians had proved determined opponents during the preceding two days and now occupied excellent defensive positions from which they could offer tenacious resistance, especially given the confusion and uncertainty inherent in night actions. He probably knew that Reuss's V Corps had not been engaged and, until the stampede to the bridges later that night, he did not know the location of Johann's corps. The most important consideration, however, was likely the army's exhaustion. Not only had the men just concluded two days of ferocious combat under blazing heat with little to eat and less to drink, most had been marching, toiling, waiting, or huddling under thunderstorms since early on the 4th. These burdens, of course, had also sapped even Napoleon's prodigious reserves of energy. 'I am so fatigued that I cannot write any more,' he told Cambacérès.[2] Furthermore, a very large proportion of the army had conducted epic forced marches to reach the Marchfeld in time for the battle and had had no opportunity to recover from those exertions. Ammunition would also have to be restocked after the enormous expenditures of the 5th and 6th. Finally, wisdom dictated that he ensure the security of Vienna and his rear area before driving north into the unknown. Rather than compromise the victory he had achieved, therefore, the emperor decided to await the dawn.[3]

EVERY NIGHT A MARCH, EVERY DAY AN ATTACK: 7–9 JULY

The dawn, however, brought little immediate clarity to the operational situation. Napoleon was up early, riding the line to assess the condition of his own army and evaluating intelligence on the enemy. Unfortunately for the French, Charles had successfully slipped away during the scant hours of darkness, leaving behind rear guards that screened the movements of his principal forces. The question for Napoleon, therefore, was which of the three principal avenues of escape Charles's main body was using: the most direct route to Prague via Horn, the highway north to Znaim, or the eastern road leading to Brünn and Olmütz.

Napoleon spent most of 7 July reordering his army on the Marchfeld, ensuring care of the wounded, arranging the security of Vienna and his southern flank, notifying the larger world of the victory at Wagram, and trying to gather intelligence on Charles's whereabouts. Measures for rear area security included rebuilding the Tabor bridge, arming and victualling Vienna as a fortress, and issuing orders for Vandamme and Reynier to focus their attentions on the south (right) bank.[4] Among other steps, Vandamme was to garrison the Kaiser-Ebersdorf bridgehead and patrol as far as Bruck an der Leitha and Ödenburg. On the Marchfeld, Napoleon visited several units, sent an officer to inspect local defences and provisions for the wounded, moved his headquarters to Wolkersdorf (he would

(Clockwise from top left)

1 **Prince Joseph Poniatowski** (1763–1813): Commanded 5th Corps in 1812 and 8th Corps in 1813. Became the only non-French Marshal of France on 16 October that year; wounded at Leipzig, he drowned trying to cross the Elster River three days later.

2 **Archduke Ferdinand d'Este** (1781–1850): Commanded an Austrian Reserve Army in 1815, but never saw combat after 1809. Later served as military commander in Hungary and Governor of Galicia.

3 **Sergey Fedorovich Golitsyn** (1749–1810): Appointed a councillor of state after the war, but died in February 1810 before assuming his new position. (ASKB)

4 **Polish Infantry**: The grenadier (right) wears a bearskin, while the fusilier (centre) and voltigeur (left) wear the *tschapka*, traditional Polish military headgear. (ASKB)

5   **Archduke Joseph** (1776–1847): Appointed Palatine of Hungary in 1795, he remained in this position for more than fifty years, winning much acclaim for his governance of the kingdom.

6   **Granary at Raab:** Similar to the famous granary as Aspern, this building is the only remaining feature of the Kismegyer walled farmstead. (Ferdi Wöber)

7   **Hungarian Insurrection troops** (*below*): Dressed in blue hussar-style uniforms, with home districts indicated by colours of shakos for hussars and collars/cuffs for infantry. (ASKB)

8   **The Battle of Raab** (14 June) (*opposite*): 2nd Graz Landwehr defends the Kismegyer farmstead against French assault as seen from the Austrian rear. The granary is on the right, with the barricaded entrance gate and improvised firing platforms in the centre, while a stall burns on the left. (ASKB)

(Clockwise from top left)

9 Peter Knesevich (c.1746–1814): Called from retirement in 1809, he led the second Austrian invasion of Dalmatia; returned to retirement after the war.

10 Auguste Frédéric Louis Viesse de Marmont (1774–1852): One of Napoleon's comrades since 1792. Made a marshal on the field at Znaim, he remained in Dalmatia until 1811; then suffered defeat at Salamanca in 1812; commanded 6th Corps in 1813–14, but surrendered his troops to the Allies in the latter year, contributing to Napoleon's downfall.

11 Serezaner: Two hundred of these irregulars were attached to each Grenz regiment. Local militia (as at Gospic) would have had a similar appearance.

12 Grenz Infantry: Grenz troops were in the process of changing from white to brown (shown here) uniform coats in 1808–9. The regiments in Galicia initially went to war with only one battalion.

(Clockwise from top)

13 **Tyrolian Rebels**: Contemporary image showing Tyrolians on outpost duty in typical local costume. (ASKB)

14 **Wilhelm von Dörnberg** (1768–1850): Served in armies of Hesse-Kassel, Netherlands, and Prussia before joining Westphalian Guard; active in Germany during 1813–14, he also fought at Waterloo as a British major general.

15 **Ferdinand von Schill** (1776–1809): Prussian cavalry officer who gained popular adulation for partisan action around Kolberg in 1807; killed at Stralsund.

16 **Andreas Hofer** (1767–1810): Born in St Leonhard in the Passeiertal, he inherited the Sandhof Inn and was thus known as the 'Sandwirth' ('Innkeeper of the Sandhof'). Helped plot and lead the Tyrolian rebellion, captured in January 1810; tried and executed in Mantua that February.

17 **Jean Andoche Junot** (1771–1813): Commanded a corps in Portugal in 1810 and the Westphalians in 1812; sent to Illyria in 1813, he became increasingly erratic and returned to Paris, where he committed suicide.

18 **Friedrich Wilhelm, Duke of Brunswick** (1771–1815): Led his 'Black Corps' in the Peninsular War; returning to Brunswick, he raised a new corps, participated in the Waterloo campaign and was killed at Quatre Bras on 16 June 1815.

19 **Austrian troops near Nuremberg** (late June): Contemporary image of uhlan and infantry officers in centre, with hussars and uhlans on left, Brunswick troops in rear, Grenzers (white coats) and Landwehr on right. (ASKB)

20 Jerome Bonaparte, King of Westphalia (1784–1860): Accompanied his army to Russia in 1812, lost his kingdom in 1813, and commanded a division at Waterloo. Played a role in French politics in the 1840s–50s and made a Marshal of France under his nephew Louis-Napoleon in 1850.

21 Louis Bonaparte, King of Holland (1778–1846): Forced from his throne by Napoleon in July 1810. Charles Louis Napoleon, his third son with Hortense de Beauharnais, would become Napoleon III.

22 7th Dutch Infantry Regiment: One of four infantry regiments in Gratien's division, a key component of Napoleon's rear-area security plans. Of the other Dutch line infantry, 3rd, 4th, and I/5th were in Holland; 2nd was in Spain. (Netherlands Legermuseum)

(*Clockwise from top left*)

23 Johann Joseph Cajetan Graf von Klenau (1755–1819): Commanded a corps in 1813–14 in Germany; corps commander again in Italy in 1815; ended his career as military commander of Moravia-Silesia.

24 Karl Philipp Fürst zu Schwarzenberg (1771–1820): Returned from his mission to the tsar before Wagram and commanded a reserve cavalry division in that battle, then the reserve corps at Znaim. Negotiated Maria Louise's marriage to Napoleon in 1810, commanded the Austrian Auxiliary Corps in 1812, and served as overall Allied commander in 1813–14 and 1815.

25 Johann Nepomuk Graf Nostitz (1768–1840): Commanded part of the reserve cavalry in 1813, and a reserve division in 1815; retired in 1821.

26 Joseph Wenzel Graf Radetzky (1766–1858): One of Austria's most celebrated generals, he was Schwarzenberg's chief of staff in 1813–14, and again in 1815; defeated Italian rebels in 1848–9; died at 91 having served five different emperors.

(Clockwise from top left)

27 **Henri Gatien, Comte Bertrand** (1773–1844): Governor in Illyria in 1811, then corps commander in 1813; accompanied Napoleon to St Helena and escorted the emperor's remains back to France in 1841.

28 **Jacques Jean Alexandre Bernard Law de Lauriston** (1766–1828): Ambassador to Russia in 1811, imperial aide-de-camp during 1812, corps commander in 1813; he sided with the Bourbons in 1814–15, became a marshal in 1823, and ended his career as a minister of state.

29 **Antoine Drouot** (1774–1847): Commanded the Guard foot artillery at Wagram and remained in key artillery, staff, and command positions through 1815. 'There are not two men in the entire world like Drouot for the artillery,' said Napoleon.

30 **Carl Philipp Freiherr von Wrede** (1767–1838): Commanded a division and later 6th Corps in 1812, then led an Austro-Bavarian corps to defeat at Hanau in 1813, where he was badly wounded; commanded Bavarian troops in 1814 and 1815, and had a major role in Bavarian politics from 1817.

31 **The bridges over the Danube's main channel**: The downstream bridge (on boats) and the upstream (on pilings) provided access from Kaiser-Ebersdorf to Lobau Island. A major military engineering accomplishment, they excited admiration from all sides, with several contemporaries describing them as 'elegant'.

32 **Charles at Wagram**: Charles threw himself into the crisis of the fighting on the evening of 5 July, suffering a minor wound and risking capture as he personally rallied I Corps.

33 **Napoleon at Wagram**: Though under heavy fire at the apex of his line for much of 6 July, Napoleon issued orders with superb composure.

34 **Friedrich Freiherr von Bianchi** (1768–1855): Commanded divisions in Russia during 1812 and Germany in 1813, then a corps in Italy in 1814; defeated Murat at Tolentino in 1815; retired in 1824.

35 **Jean Louis Ebénezer Reynier** (1771–1814): Responsible for Lobau during Wagram, Reynier was appointed to command the Saxon contingent on 9 July; he would lead Saxon troops again in 1812 and 1813 as 7th Corps of the Grande Armée.

36 **Saxon Cavalry:** The Karabinier Regiment on the left wore straw-coloured coats, while the dragoons and chevaulegers wore red. The central figure is from the *Albrecht* Chevaulegers with green distinctions. (ASKB)

37 **Guard Horse Artillery**: Four batteries of twenty-four pieces under Colonel Augustin Marie d'Aboville, who lost an arm at Wagram.

38 **Guard Foot Artillery and Train**: Six foot batteries contributed thirty-six pieces at Wagram under Colonel Drouot, who was wounded in the foot.

39 **The Grand Battery at Wagram** (6 July): Napoleon watches a horse battery gallop into action. Guard Chasseurs-à-Cheval of his escort are at lower left. (ASKB)

40 **Polish Chevaulegers of the Imperial Guard**: During the evening engagements at Wagram, some of the Polish troopers seized lances from their opponents and began their regiment's transformation from light horse to lancers.

41 **Austrian Uhlan**: One of the regiments in the melee with the French Guard was the *Schwarzenberg* Uhlans (III Corps); *EH Carl* Uhlans of V Corps also fought in the evening actions.

42 **Archduchess Marie Louise** (1791–1847): She became Napoleon's second wife in 1810 and mother of Napoleon II, the King of Rome (1811–32); became Duchess of Parma from Napoleon's first abdication until her death; married her lover, Austrian FML Adam Albert Graf von Neipperg, in 1821 (three children); third marriage to the Count of Bombelles, her grand chamberlain, in 1834.

43 **Schönbrunn Palace**: The Habsburg summer palace in Vienna and twice Napoleon's residence by conquest (1805 and 1809). Napoleon met with Liechtenstein and Bubna here, and Staps attempted to assassinate the emperor during a review in the grand courtyard.

44 **Napoleon on the second day at Wagram:** This was the image many veterans retained of 6 July. As a sceptical Saxon hussar officer remarked: 'Only now, in this eternally memorable hour, could I say that I have seen a battle!'

45 **Archduke Charles Monument, Heldenplatz, Vienna:** German historian Hans Delbrück remarked that the statue appropriately shows Charles always looking backwards. (Photo by Anne L. Rieman)

occupy the lodgings that Franz had just evacuated in haste), and appointed MacDonald a Marshal of France on the field of battle to the general acclamation of the army. 'Judge, sir, of my surprise and emotion', wrote the new marshal to his grandfather, 'as I had no reason to anticipate so speedy and unhoped-for a return to the good graces of His Majesty.'[5] News of the Austrians, however, was scarce and contradictory. Massena, probing to the west along the Danube discovered a rear guard in Korneuburg, captured the town in a bold assault by 26th Léger and the Baden Jägers, and engaged in a lively cannonade with other Austrians until dark. These actions did not provide much information, and news from Montbrun on the Brünn highway was equally unconvincing. Rather than lose any more

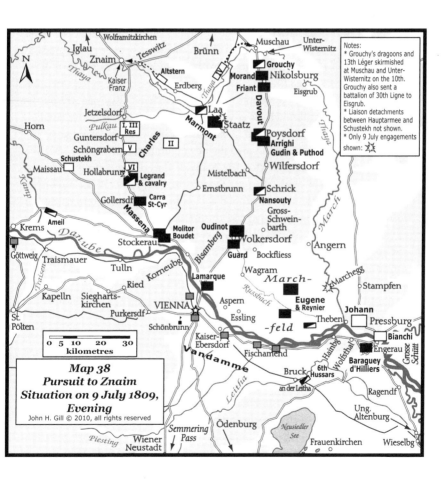

Notes:
* Grouchy's dragoons and 13th Léger skirmished at Muschau and Unter-Wisternitz on the 10th. Grouchy also sent a battalion of 30th Ligne to Eisgrub.
* Liaison detachments between Hauptarmee and Schustekh not shown.
* Only 9 July engagements shown: ⚔

Map 38
Pursuit to Znaim
Situation on 9 July 1809, Evening
John H. Gill © 2010, all rights reserved

time, Napoleon decided to launch pursuit forces in both directions. At
11 p.m., therefore, he directed Massena to advance towards Stockerau and
sent Marmont north on the Brünn road with his small corps augmented by
the Bavarian division and Montbrun, to whom he also attached Colbert's
brigade (now under Colonel Pierre Edme Gauthrin of 9th Hussars). The
rest of the army would collect itself on the Marchfeld in the centre of the
coming theatre of operations and await events.

Napoleon also made some changes to his order of battle. In addition to
Marmont's ad hoc command, Massena and Davout each retained a cuirassier
division to press the pursuit, and Davout continued to command Grouchy
in the absence of his light cavalry. The greatest changes occurred in the
Army of Italy and 9th Corps. Disappointed with Bernadotte's performance
throughout the war and weary of his constant sniping and complaining,
Napoleon was infuriated when the marshal issued a bombastic order
crediting the Saxons with standing 'as motionless as bronze' at Wagram. It
was the last straw. A 9 July letter from Berthier relieved Bernadotte from
command and directed him to report to the emperor, 'who has the intention
of giving you another command'.[6] Napoleon assigned Reynier to lead the
Saxons, no longer known as a 'corps' (the unsatisfactory Montrichard
replaced Reynier on Lobau), and placed the contingent under Eugene. The
viceroy's expanded command also included Vandamme's Württembergers
as well as his own army. Within the Army of Italy, Pully was recalled from
Davout and Gérard from Massena to provide a solid mounted component,
while Seras's division was disbanded and its battalions distributed to other
formations. Pachtod was assigned to Grenier's wing, though he was out
of action with his wound, and the Royal Guard infantry remained with
the Imperial Guard for the time being. All of this left Eugene with some
44,000 men immediately at hand. The other element of former 9th Corps,
Dupas's division, was also broken up. The 5th Léger was allotted to Boudet
and 19th Ligne to Legrand, but these weak regiments would not join
Massena until after the armistice.

Charles made good use of the respite Napoleon granted him.
Protected by Klenau's rear guard, the bulk of the Hauptarmee marched
on the Znaim highway to reach Hollabrunn–Guntersdorf on 8 July.
Kolowrat and Bellegarde moved on secondary roads slightly to the east,
while Hohenzollern—still missing the troops that had retreated with
Rosenberg—arrived in Ernstbrunn that day. For the 9th, the Main Army
would continue on these routes, aiming for the Jetzelsdorf 'position'.
Klenau at Hollabrunn would cover the withdrawal, while GM Johann

Ritter Allmeyer von Altstern took his 'brigade' (800 *Rohan* infantry, 150 *Hohenzollern* Cuirassiers, brigade battery) to protect the crossings over the Thaya (Dyje) at Laa.[7] Rosenberg, thinking he was obeying instructions, arrived in Mistelbach on the 7th and also marched to Laa on 8 July to protect the army's left flank.[8] Charles, however, clinging to outdated concepts of cordon defence, was angered because Rosenberg thereby left open the road to Brünn and Olmütz. The archduke was already annoyed with the IV Corps commander for what he perceived as a poor performance at Wagram and had issued a shocking and unseemly circular to his senior generals on 7 July, blaming 'the troops of the left wing' for the loss of the battle. He now dispatched several stiff orders to Rosenberg, making him personally responsible for the safety of Brünn and particularly Olmütz.[9] These orders would soon have significant consequences.

For flanking forces, the Generalissimus directed Schustekh, who had conducted a fairly large but inconsequential cross-Danube raid near Göttweig on 6 July, to fall back from Krems to Maissau on the Prague highway. No thought was given to calling Schustekh to the Main Army; he would be sent north towards Horn to protect against nonexistent threats. Charles informed Ferdinand and Johann of the situation, warning the former that the French might intend to threaten Olmütz or to 'effect a connection with the Russians'.[10] Johann was instructed to defend Hungary along the March River in concert with Joseph. Charles could not resist adding a concluding jab to his letter to Johann: 'It is painful for me that I must remark to Your Grace that Your Grace's earlier arrival, by a few hours and with only a few thousand men, would have been decisive for the fate of the battle.'[11]

In addition to informing his cousin and sending orders (with a sting) to his younger brother, Charles reported to his elder brother, the Kaiser. This 7 July missive gave full—and perhaps exaggerated—expression to the archduke's discouragement. He spoke of the army's 'utter exhaustion' after the battle and the 'actual dissolution' of some regiments; he hoped the enemy would not pursue, as he would only be able to offer minimal resistance. 'I cannot hide from Your Majesty that this army cannot be counted upon in its current condition. We have lost much and our loss will become endlessly heavier owing to the many sick and stragglers that fall into the enemy's hands.'[12] Hyperbole aside, Charles was disheartened by gloomy reports from his corps commanders and what he personally saw of the army's appearance. 'The enemy follows us and attacks the rear guard every evening,' he wrote to Albert on the 9th. 'The fatigue, the heat, and the disorder of every retreat mean that we have many stragglers.'[13]

Engagement at Hollabrunn—9 July

Klenau's men were still serving as rear guard when Massena reached Hollabrunn on 9 July. The marshal had seized Stockerau the previous day and headed north on the 9th with Legrand's division and his numerous cavalry in the lead. The corps, however, was strung out along the highway. Carra Saint-Cyr followed Legrand at some distance, but Massena had left Molitor and Boudet at Stockerau until he could be certain there was no danger from Krems—he sent Ameil to scout in this direction with 24th Chasseurs and the Baden Light Dragoons. Klenau had selected Hollabrunn as an excellent rear guard position and deployed his men well, but the *St Georg* Grenzer, 1st and 2nd Vienna Volunteers, and 4th UMB Landwehr could not keep Massena's men from capturing the town. Klenau, however, counter-attacked at once, and a bitter struggle for possession of Hollabrunn ensued between Legrand's battalions and Austrian troops under FML von Wallmoden and GM Andreas Mariassy. The Hungarians of *Benjovszky* and *Splenyi* fought an obstinate defence, superbly supported by parts of *Gyulai* Infantry, *Klebek* Infantry, *Blankenstein* Hussars, *Liechtenstein* Hussars, and well-posted guns on the hills north of town. The French and Baden troops were equally determined in the attack and the fighting raged into the night. Hollabrunn changed hands three times and most of it burned to the ground. In the end, this costly engagement left both sides in partial possession of the ruined town. Klenau's subordinates had served him well, delaying Massena's advance, albeit at the cost of some 900 casualties.[14] Worn out and depleted by the relentless engagements and the attrition of the marches, Klenau's exhausted VI Corps would be withdrawn from its rear guard mission and replaced by Reuss's relatively fresh V Corps that night.

A fierce rear guard action also flared on the Austrian left flank as Montbrun and the Bavarian horse clashed with Radetzky between Staatz and Laa. Behind this screen, Rosenberg departed Laa as ordered early on 9 July, losing thirty men dead to heat stroke while marching on the north bank of the Thaya towards Muschau (Musov) on the Brünn road. He left behind the orphaned detachments of II Corps to make their way back to Hohenzollern. By his obedience to instructions, however, Rosenberg left the road to Znaim and Charles's line of retreat wide open. GM von Altstern appeared as ordered, but his tiny detachment could only count itself lucky to escape when Montbrun, having chased off Radetzky's troopers, crossed the Thaya just as the Austrians were arriving. Avoiding combat, Altstern hastened for Znaim, assisted in his escape by widespread inebriation among

Marmont's troops, who had discovered the region's many wine cellars and lost no time in sampling the vintages. Though delayed by this indiscipline, the intelligence that the French collected inadvertently led to the correct conclusion and finally shed clear light on Austrian intentions. 'Rosenberg's entire corps is retiring towards Znaim,' Marmont reported.[15]

On Marmont's right, Davout advanced up the Brünn highway against almost no resistance. Besides pursuing Rosenberg, Davout had orders to assist Marmont if needed. Marmont, however, thinking he was chasing only a rear guard and possibly wanting to operate away from a senior general, told Davout that he needed no support at Laa. The marshal therefore marched ahead to bivouac for the night with his 1st and 2nd Divisions around Nikolsburg (Mikulov) and the other two at Poysdorf along with Arrighi.

This is a good point to wrap up Rosenberg's participation in the war by peering ahead twenty-four hours. Rosenberg's closest pursuers on the 9th were the dragoons and infantry of Grouchy's small command who seized Nikolsburg in a bold charge that night. The French general aimed to capture the Thaya bridge at Muschau the next day. On the morning of 10 July, however, Rosenberg's *Hessen-Homburg* Hussars managed to burn the Muschau span just as the French appeared. Grouchy, not to be denied, cleverly sent 7th Dragoons and I/13th to his right, where they seized the bridges at Unter-Wisternitz (Dolni Vestonice) in a brilliant action.[16] Rosenberg, with the Thaya breached and under repeated injunctions to protect Olmütz, had no option but continued withdrawal to the north. Meanwhile, events around Znaim were moving the war towards its climax.

Intermixed with this skein of military activity over the days after Wagram was an increasingly prominent diplomatic thread. On the morning of 9 July, as the French were pushing aside Klenau's outposts just before the engagement at Hollabrunn, an Austrian officer appeared, requesting passage for Liechtenstein to meet with Napoleon on Kaiser Franz's behalf. Annoyed at what at first seemed to be a ruse, the French eventually accepted his message and forwarded it to imperial headquarters. It was the first step in what would rapidly culminate in a ceasefire and peace.

What had happened? Between 7 and 8 July, Franz, over the objections of the war party at court, had acceded to Charles's urgings and authorised the Generalissimus to sound out Napoleon on the possibility of an armistice. This decision resulted in the delivery of the note from Klenau to Massena's pickets on the morning of the 9th. In the meantime, Franz had appointed Liechtenstein as his emissary. Liechtenstein was not only a prince and a senior general, he was also well known to Napoleon and had been entrusted wth similar diplomatic duties at the end of the 1805 war. On the morning of the 10th, Charles happily reported that Napoleon had accepted Liechtenstein as an envoy and that FML Weissenwolff, detained by the French on 4 July, had returned from Napoleon's headquarters with extravagant words of praise for the courteous treatment he had received. All of this, in Charles's view, augured well for a peace agreement. But Franz was already beginning to reconsider. Stadion had submitted his resignation on the 8th, then, on being persuaded to stay, had drafted a memorandum that promoted the notion of curtailing Charles's command responsibilities. As the court was planning to move to Hungary, the Main Army would find itself cut off from every communication', Stadion argued, so Charles should be restricted to command of the Hauptarmee alone. It was a transparent effort to ease Charles out of the Generalissimus position and vitiate his influence at court.[17] By this time, however, events were slipping beyond the grasp of Franz, Stadion, and others in the imperial entourage: Liechtenstein was already on his way to the French emperor, the armies were in motion, and Napoleon was on the move.[18] There was still one more battle to be fought.

Kaiser Franz was in Znaim on 9 July when a hussar officer interrupted the imperial lunch with the alarming news that French troops were in Erdberg (Hradek) on the road west of Laa, only some twenty kilometres from Znaim. As courtiers and footmen hurriedly packed their master's belongings, Franz hastened to inform the Generalissimus. Another note with more such intelligence soon followed. Charles, planning the defensive position near Jetzelsdorf, thus received two disturbing notes from his elder brother that evening. The information was exaggerated, probably occasioned by Montbrun's scouts (Marmont's men were in no condition to march to Znaim on 9 July), but Charles could not know that and the threat was real enough. Having chastised Rosenberg into moving north, the Generalissimus now found the Hauptarmee's rear vulnerable, Altstern's miniature force being completely inadequate to its task. With his planned position on the Pulkau outflanked, Charles immediately put the army on the road for Znaim, the Reserve Corps departing at 9 p.m., followed by III and VI Corps, with I Corps on secondary roads to the east and II Corps along the south bank of the Thaya.[19] Reuss assumed the onerous rear guard duties from Klenau's exhausted troops.

From Marmont's reports and Massena's description of the intense fighting at Hollabrunn, Napoleon had likewise come to a conclusion on the night of the 9th: Charles had taken the road to Znaim, and Marmont was in deadly danger. 'The entire enemy army is retiring on Znaim,' he wrote to Davout. 'It is therefore necessary to march in all haste to General Marmont. Everything leads to the conclusion that if there is not a serious engagement today, there will be a more serious one tomorrow.' The emperor himself would 'go towards the sound of the guns.'[20] Even with the extraordinary marching capacity of Napoleon's troops, however, much of the army's power would not be able to reach the new battlefield until the night of 11/12 July.

Before moving to this final great contest, two observations are useful. First, from a strictly defensive viewpoint, Charles had conducted a masterful retreat, holding the army together, fending off incessant French probes, and protecting his large baggage train. However, he was also excessively cautious and overly concerned with protecting everything rather than perhaps uniting his forces for a counter-attack. Instead, all actions were of 'a completely defensive character'.[21] This is understandable, given that his principal aim was preservation of the army, but it meant that he missed, and perhaps did not even detect, opportunities such as smashing the isolated Massena and Marmont before they could be reinforced. Furthermore, however well executed, it remained a retreat in the wake of a traumatic, enervating battle. Though Napoleon had not yet committed his army in a definitive direction, his pursuing corps pressed the Austrians relentlessly. 'Every night a march and every day an attack,' wrote Charles.[22] That meant that the army shed hundreds of stragglers a day, many, if not most of whom were snatched up by the pursuing French. As a result, the army would be severely diminished when it reached Znaim. Liechtenstein, for instance, stated that some of his brigades could only put 200–400 men in the saddle, and the combat strength of the entire *Rohan* Infantry Regiment was only some 800 men.[23]

Second, although Napoleon is often condemned for 'indecision' or 'inactivity' during the days immediately after Wagram, there is reason to reconsider this assumption.[24] The criticism arises from hindsight, denigrating French deployments from 7 to 9 July because they meant that Napoleon could not concentrate the bulk of his army at Znaim to defeat Charles on 10–11 July. Viewed from imperial headquarters at Wolkersdorf, however, the post-Wagram panorama looks a bit different. Napoleon had sent strong pursuit forces, Massena and Marmont, on the most likely avenues of retreat, and bolstered Marmont with Davout when erroneous reports indicated that the Hauptarmee was heading for Brünn. Choosing one path or the other too soon would have placed the force on the other route in unacceptable jeopardy. He could have moved his central reserve—Oudinot, the Guard, Nansouty— to Ernstbrunn, approximately equidistant between these two avenues, but that might have left his rear area and Vienna vulnerable to Johann, Joseph, Chasteler, and Gyulai.[25] Until he was certain of Charles's location, therefore, he wisely kept this reserve and the Army of Italy on the edges of the

Marchfeld. By the time he had solid information to commit to one course of action, it was too late to unite the army at Znaim on 10–11 July. The 'problem' with Napoleon's strategy on 7–9 July, therefore, was not imperial indecision or lassitude, but time. In some respects, he did 'miss an opportunity' to catch the weary Hauptarmee *in flagrante delicto* as it struggled to get its heavy baggage over the Thaya at Znaim, but it is hard to see how Napoleon could have justified moving any earlier than he did under the circumstances and with available intelligence. As we will see when we review his acceptance of the ceasefire, he could have assembled an overwhelming force on the field at Znaim on 12 July. Instead of fighting another battle, he opted to end the war.

THE BATTLE OF ZNAIM: 10–11 JULY[26]

The night of 9/10 July found the Hauptarmee on the road for Znaim. Altstern reached the town at 9 p.m. from Laa, leaving three squadrons of cuirassiers to watch the eastern approach. On the far left flank, Rosenberg, with the Thaya barrier breached, was preparing to continue his withdrawal towards Brünn, and to the right, Schustekh was going to march from Maissau to Horn, detaching a small force under GM Anton Graf von Hardegg to maintain contact with the Hauptarmee. Napoleon's forces were more scattered. Davout had Grouchy and two battalions of 13th Léger south of the Thaya facing Rosenberg, 1st and 2nd Divisions around Nikolsburg, and 3rd and 4th at Poysdorf with Arrighi. Montbrun had crossed the Thaya near Laa, but the bulk of Marmont's hung-over troops were still east of the river. Massena was echeloned along the Znaim highway from Hollabrunn (cavalry, Legrand) through Göllersdorf (Carra Saint-Cyr) to Stockerau (Molitor, Boudet); his flanking detachment under Ameil was just east of Krems. The Guard and 2nd Corps were still in the vicinity of Wolkersdorf, but Nansouty was posted at Schrick. With few exceptions, all of these forces were about to converge on the little Moravian town of Znaim.

The Battle of Znaim: First Day—10 July

Znaim, an ancient marketplace still encircled by a medieval wall in 1809, sits above a sharp bend in the Thaya, surrounded by rugged countryside decorated with numerous vineyards. Although much of the terrain consists of open, rolling hills dotted with villages, the Thaya flows in a very narrow valley west of town and the streams to the east wander through steep ravines; the Leschna (Leska) between Zuckerhandel (Suchohrdly) and Klein-Tesswitz (Tesswitz or Dobsice), in particular, was difficult for skirmishers and utterly impassable for formed bodies of troops. A stone bridge passed over the Thaya south of Znaim and there were two firm fords downstream, but in summer the water level was low and the river was fordable along much of its length south and east of town.[27] The highways from Nikolsburg and Laa met east of Tesswitz, forming a gap between the Thaya and a large wood called the Burgholz. The paved road to Iglau (Jihlava) and Bohemia—Charles's escape route—crossed the stone bridge south of Znaim and passed through town before turning north-west.[28] As the only realistic route for the huge, cumbersome baggage train that accompanied the Hauptarmee, the safety of this highway was one of the archduke's principal concerns in the coming battle.

Leading the Austrian march to Znaim were the *Schwarzenberg* Uhlans under GM Schneller. Marching through the night, the weary uhlans and their unfed, unwatered mounts crossed the Thaya south of Znaim on the morning of 10 July. The Grenadiers and Reserve Cavalry were right behind them. They were not a moment too soon. French cavalry patrols were already evident on the road from Laa as Schneller probed to the east, and Charles hastened to deploy the available troops to protect his army's lone route of retreat. He posted one grenadier brigade (Merville's, now under Oberstleutnant Franz Scovaud de Bastite) south of the Thaya facing Naschetitz (Naceratice), but sent the other three down the Laa highway, placing GM Karl Steyrer von Edelberg's on the hills east of the Leschna (temporarily under Schneller's command), with GM Albrecht Joseph Graf Murray's west of the stream, and GM Anton von Hammer's in reserve. Of the cavalry, four regiments under Schwarzenberg were positioned south of the Thaya with Scovaud, while the bulk of the mounted regiments went to the left flank near Kukrowitz (Kucharovice).[29] Here they were joined by the *Schwarzenberg* Uhlans as that regiment withdrew in front of increasing French pressure. Altstern's small brigade remained at Znaim.

Marmont arrived between 10 and 11 a.m. after a fast march from Laa under oppressive heat. Believing he only faced the enemy rear guard, he immediately deployed to attack: Minucci's Bavarians on the left near the river, Claparède on the right, Clauzel in reserve, and Montbrun on the outer right flank near the Burgholz. Montbrun quickly drove back the *Schwarzenberg* Uhlans and overthrew a brigade of dragoons that had come up in support. Attempting to reach the highway north of Znaim, however, the French light horse encountered five Austrian cuirassier regiments and had to curtail their advance. There was little real contact, but the French considered themselves outnumbered and retired between Winau (Unanov) and Brenditz (Primetice).

Shortly after this action, Liechtenstein received word that Napoleon had accepted him as Franz's envoy. Turning over command to Schwarzenberg, he left the battlefield and headed south for Stockerau, erroneously presumed to be the French emperor's location.

In the meantime, Montbrun's thrust had cleared a potential threat to the French infantry's right. Schneller and Steyrer were thus in trouble. They were outnumbered, the three puny 3-pounders that Steyrer had brought up were no match for the heavier Bavarian and French guns, their left was now uncovered, and no one came to their assistance. Despite dogged and prolonged resistance, therefore, it is hardly surprising that the Allies shoved the grenadiers off the hillside and stormed ahead, Delzons on the right towards Zuckerhandel and Beckers's Bavarians on the left against Tesswitz. In another of the horrendous village battles that seemed to characterise this war, the Bavarians and the Austrian grenadiers grappled over Tesswitz for two hours. Reinforced by 81st Ligne, the Allies gained control of the burning town, at least temporarily, while Clauzel's men dominated the ground above Zuckerhandel and moved on Kukrowitz. Small-scale skirmishing also crackled along the south bank of the Thaya. Marmont committed very few troops here, but worry about the security of the bridge kept significant Austrian forces tied down—none of which made any substantial effort to disturb Marmont's left across the river.[30]

Fortunately for Charles, the rest of the Hauptarmee was coming on the scene. Hohenzollern arrived to replace Scovaud in protecting the area south of the Thaya. He was soon followed by Bellegarde, but by now the stone bridge was jammed with vehicles and under fire from bold French and Bavarian skirmishers. Bellegarde therefore took advantage of the nearest ford to get most of his corps across the river and had Henneberg's brigade turn right to clear off the skirmishers and reinforce the grenadiers at Tesswitz.[31] The impulse of this reinforcement once more gave the whitecoats control of the blackened village, but Marmont counter-attacked almost immediately. Charles assigned the rest of I Corps a place on the left of the line, where they arrived just in time to secure the heights west of Kukrowitz against Clauzel's men in the village. Kolowrat's corps also used the fords, 'hurrying at double time' past Znaim to go into line north of Brenditz.[32] By the time Klenau arrived, the stone bridge was clear, but considering the state of his tattered corps, Charles assigned it a reserve role near the highway west of Brenditz.

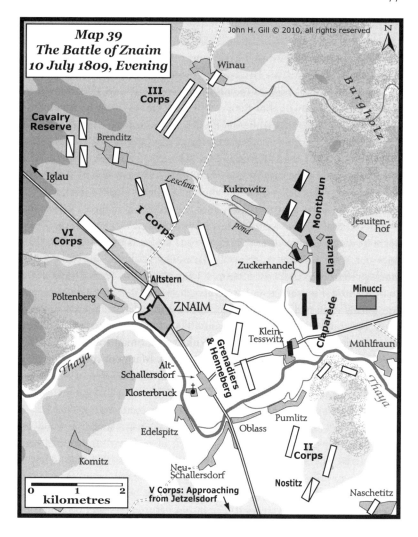

Map 39
The Battle of Znaim
10 July 1809, Evening

N

Winau

III
Corps

Cavalry
Reserve

Brenditz

Iglau

Leschna

Kukrowitz

Burgholtz

Montbrun

Jesuiten-
hof

I Corps

Pond

Clauzel

VI
Corps

Zuckerhandel

Minucci

Altstern

Pöltenberg

ZNAIM

Claparède

Klein-
Tesswitz

Mühlfraun

Thaya

Alt-
Schallersdorf

Grenadiers & Henneberg

Klosterbruck

Thaya

Edelspitz

Oblass

Pumlitz

Komitz

Neu-
Schallersdorf

Nostitz

II
Corps

Naschetitz

0   1   2
kilometres

V Corps: Approaching
from Jetzelsdorf

Night was now coming on, but the fighting for Tesswitz continued with
unabated fury. Almost all of Minucci's infantry was thrown into the dreadful
fray, supported by a gallant charge by 2nd Bavarian Chevaulegers that sent the
Kirchenbetter Grenadiers hurrying to the rear 'somewhat shaken and in some
disorder'.[33] The village, a key tactical feature on the battlefield, changed hands
many times—6th Bavarian Infantry claimed to have made six assaults—but

ended up in the hands of the Allies.[34] The fighting, however, cost Minucci's command alone some 895 casualties, making 10 July the bloodiest day for any Bavarian division during the entire war. Leaving 79th and 81st Ligne in possession of Tesswitz, the Bavarians withdrew to the heights for the night. Combat was also finishing on the northern side of the field. Charles ordered an attack on Kukrowitz, but then recalled the troops when he decided the village could not be held while the French controlled the heights. Towards sunset, Montbrun made another attempt to edge around the Austrian line. With almost all of the Hauptarmee in place, this endeavour proved futile for unsupported light cavalry, and the French troopers retired to the area between Zuckerhandel and the Burgholz as darkness cloaked the field.

As the musketry spattered away into the enfolding night, Charles could be relieved that he had secured the long and difficult defile from the Thaya north through Znaim against a dangerous and unanticipated threat. He does not seem to have recognised Marmont's weakness and would have much preferred to evacuate Znaim during the night, leaving only a rear guard behind. He learned to his dismay, however, that the army's sluggish and unruly train had become bogged down only a few kilometres north of town. He thus saw no choice: he would have to stay the night and endure whatever 11 July might bring. To gain time for the train to clear off and to grant his men some much-needed rest, he now sent Marmont a proposal for a local ceasefire, citing as rationale the fact that Liechtenstein was en route to see Napoleon.

Marmont rejected the archduke's offer out of hand, stating that he did not have the authority to agree to such arrangements and informing the Austrian envoy that his orders were 'to attack all-out', that Napoleon himself would arrive 'any instant with a good number of troops', and that he hoped tomorrow to take prisoner a large part of the Austrian army.[35] Marmont's pugnacity and canniness are evident in his reply. He could see the huge enemy force assembled around Znaim and the great, confused baggage train. He knew very well that he had placed himself in grave danger by his unsupported advance from Laa and 'acutely regretted not calling for Marshal Davout'.[36] While sending to Napoleon and Davout for help, he thus counted on the quality of his troops, listened intently for Massena's guns, and deployed brassy aggressiveness to hide his weakness. Though later criticised for his seemingly rash advance, Marmont could be justly proud of the action on 10 July. 'I think that today's affair has, at a minimum, resulted . . . in retarding his [the enemy's] march a great deal,' he told Berthier.[37]

Charles, meanwhile, had another threat to consider: Massena.

Engagement at Schöngrabern—10 July

As the Hauptarmee was assembling at Znaim and fending off the impetuous
Marmont, Massena and Reuss were engaged in an extended duel twenty-five
kilometres to the south, named for the small village of Schöngrabern.

Like Hollabrunn, Schöngrabern nestles in the pleasant valley of a small
stream that runs perpendicular to the main highway. Like Hollabrunn, it
thus formed a nearly ideal rear guard position, and here Reuss assumed these
duties as Klenau's exhausted corps marched north on the morning of 10 July.
Reuss placed 3rd Jägers in Schöngrabern, supported by two squadrons
of *Blankenstein* Hussars, and arrayed the rest of his corps (approximately
11,000 men) on the next two ridges north of the village and straddling the
road. He did not have long to wait, for Massena was hard on Klenau's heels.
Carra Saint-Cyr's division had not come up, so the French were temporarily
outnumbered, but the marshal still drove ahead with Legrand and the cavalry
when he reached Schöngrabern around 9 a.m. 'The horse artillery opened
the engagement as usual,' and Massena had the light cavalry and Baden
Jägers swing west to outflank the village, pushing aside the *Blankenstein*
Hussars and forcing the Austrian Jägers to evacuate Schöngrabern.[38] While
this was going on, Reuss received orders to leave behind a covering force and
march to Znaim at once. He assigned this covering force task—in essence,
the rear guard's rear guard—to GM Johann Graf Klebelsberg with the
Jäger battalion, *Gradiska* Grenzer, *EH Carl* Uhlans, *Blankenstein*, a cavalry
battery, and a 6-pounder foot battery, perhaps 3,500–3,700 men. Despite
his numerical inferiority and the aggressive competence of the French and
their Baden allies, Klebelsberg performed his mission with exemplary skill.
He 'withdrew the battalions, the squadrons, one after another in the finest
order,' observed Pelet.[39] Massena repeatedly outflanked Klebelsberg on
the west, but the Austrian general always escaped and these manoeuvres
accomplished his primary objective: gaining time for Reuss to depart
safely. By nightfall, Klebelsberg had retired to the daunting hills north of
the Pulkau at Jetzelsdorf and Massena's tired troops bivouacked around
Guntersdorf. Carra Saint-Cyr had arrived during the afternoon, but Molitor
was more than twenty kilometres away at Göllersdorf and Boudet remained
in Stockerau. Everyone was miserable in a driving rain.

Unlike Hollabrunn, casualties during the series of skirmishes on 10 July
were less than might have been expected, perhaps 300–400 for each side.
The French light cavalry, however, lost its third division commander when
Bruyère was wounded in the foot; Piré took his place. The Austrians, on the

other hand, lost several hundred additional men when a detachment was left behind in the retreat. Early that morning, Reuss had sent two hussar squadrons off to the west to establish contact with Schustekh, and an uhlan squadron with 4th Jägers to the east to protect that flank. In the wake of the day's fighting this latter detachment found itself cut off; it would wander furtively about the Moravian hills and forests for the next eight days.[40]

Also wandering on the night of 10/11 July, but openly and with most earnest purpose, was Prinz Johann von Liechtenstein. The prince passed safely through French lines during the day's rear guard actions, had a brief conversation with Massena, and rode on into the increasingly cloudy afternoon in search of Napoleon.

The French emperor was in Laa that evening, accompanied by the Guard cavalry and horse artillery. By dint of superb marching, 3rd Corps, Nansouty, and Arrighi were all within twelve kilometres of Napoleon. Their accomplishment, however, meant that they were still thirty-five to forty kilometres from the battlefield. Oudinot and the rest of the Guard, having not passed Staatz, were yet further back. Nonetheless, the army was gathering rapidly. Having waited for several days for the intelligence he needed, Napoleon was moving with his accustomed vigour and alacrity. At 2 a.m. he would depart for Znaim.

The Battle of Znaim: Second Day—11 July

Charles brought all of his forces north of the Thaya during the night, so that by dawn on 11 July the 64,000 men of the Hauptarmee were arrayed in a tight arc centred on Znaim.[41] Reuss was responsible for defending the Thaya south of town as far as Tesswitz and had barricaded, but not destroyed, the crucial bridge near Oblass. His cavalry, of limited utility among the gullies and vineyards, waited behind Znaim. Bellegarde's corps covered the long area from Tesswitz to Brenditz, facing east along the Leschna with a battery of 12-pounders covering the exits from the ravine and the eastward approaches to Znaim. On his left was III Corps guarding the draw south of Winau to prevent an undetected advance against Brenditz and the all-important highway. Similar concerns for the security of the road led the Generalissimus to place the Cavalry Reserve and Grenadiers on the open hillsides west of Winau and II Corps on the slopes west of Brenditz. Klenau's corps was sent back to Wolframitzkirchen (Olbramkostel) some ten kilometres north-west along the highway with an additional 9,650 men. Army headquarters was also established in Wolframitzkirchen. On the outer right flank, 3rd Jägers were posted near the Pöltenberg monastery to preclude a French crossing from that direction. Charles, principally concerned with ensuring the escape of his train and the vulnerability of the highway behind his army, thus weighted his line heavily on the left. Most of the day's action, however, would explode on the Austrian right immediately south of Znaim.

The dawn hours passed in relative quiet as the white-coated battalions and squadrons completed their moves to their new positions and Marmont awaited the arrival of reinforcements and his imperial master. As early as 6 a.m., however, French light cavalry and horse artillery appeared on the hills south of Pumlitz and Oblass, hastening the withdrawal of small Austrian detachments south of the Thaya and hindering efforts to destroy the stone bridge. Any notion of eliminating the bridge vanished as Legrand's infantry arrived between 9 and 10 a.m. Although Legrand had at most 5,000 men, Massena conducted a brief reconnaissance and attacked. A lively cannonade was soon in progress, with French and Baden guns posted near Edelspitz delivering a dreadful enfilade fire on the Austrians along the river's northern bank. The Austrians, clearly visible on the hillside, also suffered from shot and shell fired by French and Bavarian batteries near Tesswitz and Zuckerhandel.[42] Supported by this effective gunnery, clouds of Allied skirmishers waded the Thaya to drive off the defenders while others removed the barricade on the bridge despite a galling hail of bullets. With the bridge cleared, Legrand advanced in closed columns, French on the right, Badeners on the left. Before long, however, both brigades were largely dispersed in thick skirmish lines entangled in a furious firefight with Reuss's numerically superior corps. Carra Saint-Cyr and St Sulpice had now arrived, and Massena brought a regiment of cuirassiers across the river to support the infantry, there being no room for the other regiments. He also sent his light cavalry to establish contact with Marmont at Tesswitz. Resistance stiffened as Charles, concerned about Reuss's plight and the possible loss of Znaim, sent the Grenadiers to reinforce V Corps. Murray's and Scovaud's brigades hurried up in direct support, while the other two remained north of town in reserve, but Reuss, rather than using these reinforcements en masse, gradually injected them into the vicious fighting, battalion by battalion, until almost all were committed.[43] Although Legrand was now seriously outnumbered, he continued to maintain heavy pressure on his adversaries.

All of this action was clearly visible to Napoleon, who had arrived around 10 a.m. Observing the stunning panorama from beneath an oak on the heights above Zuckerhandel (forever after the 'Napoleon Oak'), his main interest was holding Charles in place until his reinforcements could arrive, but he also wanted to facilitate Massena's attack. He thus had Marmont advance against Bellegarde across the Leschna and directed Montbrun to threaten the Austrian route of retreat. In compliance with these orders, Marmont pushed forward his two French infantry divisions, but both soon stalled in the face of Austrian artillery fire and reinforcements. Clauzel on the right was halted by the Austrian battery west of Kukrowitz, and Claparède in the centre could not debouch much beyond Zuckerhandel. Similarly, Montbrun's light cavalry, taken in the flank by Bellegarde's artillery, could do little against the strong all-arms force that Charles had posted around Winau. Although none of these initial efforts reached its objective, there is a good chance that Napoleon intended nothing beyond occupying his opponent's army for the time being. Given his lack of infantry, he was probably more focused on keeping the Austrians engaged than in launching a full-scale assault before Davout and Oudinot arrived.

It was now approximately 2 p.m. Marmont had stalled, but Massena was making steady, if slow, progress. The Klosterbruck Monastery and Altschallersdorf were in Allied hands and the marshal's firing line was edging steadily closer to Znaim when three events brought a sudden, dramatic change to the battlefield. First, Reuss gave orders for a battalion of the grenadiers Charles had sent to him to counter-attack and push back the aggressive Allied skirmish line. Second, as formed Allied supports rushed to hold off the Austrian advance, they came under misdirected artillery fire from two French 12-pounders on the hills south of the Thaya. Threatened in front and fired upon by their own guns from behind, the troops began to waver. Third, nature chose this moment to intervene with a sudden thunderstorm of tremendous violence. In a flash, infantry muskets became unusable, visibility dropped to nothing, leaders' voices were drowned out, men ran for shelter, and confusion fell like a dark blanket on all sides as a deluge of heavy rain and hail plummeted down in sheets.

Oberstleutnant August Graf zu Leiningen-Westerburg, however, kept his head and exploited the moment. Ordered to clear the enemy from the highway, he had been forming his grenadier battalion for the counter-attack when the storm crashed down. He now led his grenadiers into Legrand's scattered and disordered lines with the bayonet and at the run. The grenadiers drove all before them in their wild dash towards the bridge. Other units, including two guns, spontaneously joined the impromptu charge. As Reuss reported, 'It was impossible to hold back the established reserve, everyone ran forward, though not in formation.'[44] Stunned French and Baden troops broke in all directions.

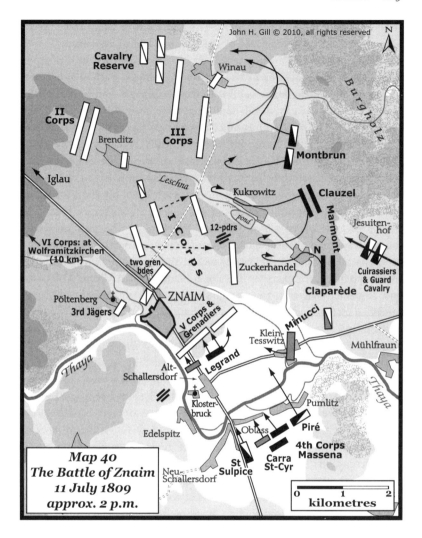

Map 40
The Battle of Znaim
11 July 1809
approx. 2 p.m.

'I shouted to my grenadiers to turn around and hurry so that we would not be caught,' wrote a Baden lieutenant. 'And then it was a headlong rush down the hill and beyond to reach the regiment.'[45] Dozens of Badeners and French, including two generals, were taken prisoner and hundreds of others were surrounded as the impetuous Leiningen thrust ahead. GB François Nicholas Fririon, Massena's chief of staff, only escaped by plunging into the now swollen Thaya. Much of the combat here was hand to hand, and Surgeon Meier noted, 'many badly injured by musket butts and bayonet stabs.'[46]

Unfortunately for the Austrians, Leiningen was not the only officer to maintain his sense of composure. Massena responded with cool decision, calling on the nearby heavy cavalry to charge. The effect was as stunning as Leiningen's attack. With GB Guiton at their head, the 10th Cuirassiers crossed the stone bridge and slammed into the unsuspecting grenadiers. The battalion disintegrated, losing 323 men as it fled. The cuirassiers swept up dozens of other prisoners, captured the two cannon, and freed most of their countrymen, including the generals, as other regiments joined the sudden onslaught.[47] 'In fifteen minutes the matter was closed', observed a Hessian watching from the south side of the Thaya, 'and a battalion of hacked up Hungarian grenadiers was brought to this bank.'[48] The iron horsemen, followed by some of the infantry, surged towards Znaim. Alert Austrians barely had time to drop the barrier pole at the town gate as the cuirassiers trotted up out of the chaos on the slopes below, but 5th Vienna Volunteers and *Lindenau* arrived in time to hold off the French attack, and Znaim remained under Austrian hands.

Although the cuirassiers could not seize Znaim, their charge gave Legrand time to bring some order to his shaken division and return to the attack, albeit only in small more-or-less independent detachments at first. Furthermore, Carra Saint-Cyr (roughly 5,000 men) was now crossing the Thaya downstream from the bridge, and Marmont had reinvigorated his attack. The French infantry on the right remained stymied by Bellegarde's defences, but the Bavarians successfully pushed waves of skirmishers up the steep vine-covered slopes north-west of Tesswitz. As afternoon melted into evening, therefore, Massena's two divisions and Minucci's men were steadily driving the Austrians back towards the town, even penetrating into the suburbs. Charles, of course, was most concerned about his left, where Montbrun posed a threat to the Austrian line of retreat.[49] 'The enemy, despite the superiority of numbers and the advantage of a fine position, was pushed back at all points,' wrote Chef de Bataillon Gueheneuc in the 26th Léger's diary.[50] All accounts highlight the bitterness of the combat at this stage, the intensity of emotion on both sides doubtless heightened by the overpowering weather, the instantaneous reversals of fortune, and a general sense that the war was reaching a climax after the titanic confrontation at Wagram and days of urgent pursuit.

At this pinnacle moment of intense exhilaration, determination, and anxiety, Austrians, French, and Germans alike were stunned when

French and Austrian staff officers rode up shouting 'Peace! Cease fire!' and announcing that a ceasefire had been concluded. It was approximately 7 p.m. It took the better part of an hour for officers to separate the fervent combatants, but as the sun was nearing the horizon, quiet settled over the field 'as if by some enchantment'.[51] Although no one quite knew it yet, the war of 1809 was over.

An Armistice Saved Us: 11–12 July[52]

The Battle of Znaim offers many curious aspects. Weather and terrain are fundamental considerations in all military operations, but here the dramatic thunderstorm, as at Teugn-Hausen on 19 April, had a rare and dramatic impact on combat. Likewise, the terrain was unusual with steep, narrow ravines, a fortified town, and fighting channelled between the Burgholz and the nearly impassable western reaches of the Thaya. The location of the highway was especially important as it forced Charles to fight almost parallel to his line of retreat. From a military leadership perspective, the battle is another example of French vivacity and aggressiveness compared to Austrian hesitancy and caution. This style of leadership paid benefits in outcomes. Though Marmont's attacks on the second day were contained, it seems likely he was restraining his advances to avoid an all-out engagement, but on the first day, he skilfully used boldness to hide his weak numbers. Perhaps Napoleon was counting on the further development of these qualities as well as his long friendship with Marmont when he elevated his comrade of many campaigns to the marshalate on 12 July. As for Massena, we see another display of energy and instinctive tactical competence resulting in another case of outnumbered French pushing Austrians back from good defensive positions as Claparède and Legrand had done at Ebelsberg on 3 May or 10th Léger had on 5 July.[53] Beyond the strictly operational realm, Znaim is also noteworthy for the intersection of the military and the political, as it is intimately linked to the process by which the armistice was signed and the war came to a close.

Prince Metternich now returns to the story. Metternich had been interned by the French in April, but was allowed to stay in Vienna, where he had much contact with Napoleon's generals and officials. Exchanged for Dodun just before Wagram, he had watched the battle from the Russbach Heights with Kaiser Franz and had travelled with the grand imperial cavalcade when it rumbled out of Wolkersdorf for Znaim on the evening of 6 July. In council with Franz and Stadion on the 7th, he relayed his impression that the French were open to a peace offer. Charles's desires on this subject were well known and, on the 8th, Franz directed the Generalissimus to send Liechtenstein to Napoleon, authorising the prince to accept any peace that guaranteed 'the perfect integrity of the monarchy'.[54] Stadion, also present at the conference on the 7th, was in temporary eclipse.

All of this resulted in Liechtenstein being on the road to Stockerau and Wolkersdorf on the afternoon of 10 July. As we have seen, the arrangements for his safe passage had been made with the French 4th Corps outposts, so he rode through Massena's lines and met briefly with the marshal before continuing south. With Napoleon on the move, however, the prince only caught up with his quarry at the imperial encampment outside Zuckerhandel after midnight on 11/12 July, unaware that Berthier and Wimpffen were meeting nearby. Napoleon received his visitor graciously, but his lengthy discourse was laced with brusque references to dismembering the Habsburg monarchy and dethroning Franz.

Moreover, by the time Liechtenstein arrived, an armistice was already nearing completion. On the afternoon of the 11th, Napoleon had decided to accept the local ceasefire proposal that Charles had offered to Marmont the previous day. It was this temporary local agreement that sent staff officers galloping into harm's way to end the ferocious fighting that evening. Berthier and Wimpffen finalised the text of a one-month suspension of arms during the night as Liechtenstein was meeting with Napoleon; Charles, without consulting Liechtenstein, accepted its harsh terms. In his words, 'an armistice concluded that evening saved us.'[55] Published on 12 July, the agreement called for Austria to pay a heavy price. Not only were the French left in possession of what they already occupied, but Austria had to evacuate much of Moravia, western Hungary (including Pressburg), the Vorarlberg, and—in the most agonising step—the Tyrol; Brünn, Graz, and Sachsenburg were all to be turned over to French garrisons. Given French military successes thus far and Austria's role as the aggressor in the conflict, these terms, though punitive, were understandable from Napoleon's perspective. Indeed, he viewed them as necessary and intentionally sought to impose the same conditions that had applied after Austerlitz.[56] In Komorn, however, where Franz had taken his court, the armistice ignited a storm of indignation and vituperation when its terms became know. Franz, as he departed Znaim on the 9th, was already falling under the sway of the war faction again. Indeed, he seems to have chosen Hungary as a destination in order to distance himself from Charles and Napoleon, thereby making any moves towards peace more difficult.

'Count Stadion assures me that the Kaiser, who has departed for Hungary, is still in the same warlike disposition,' wrote the Prince of Orange on 12 July, 'Count Stadion is totally against peace.'[57] News of the armistice thus reached Komorn at a time when discourse at court was dominated by those who favoured continuance of the war and saw Charles and his staff as defeatist and incompetent. Though Franz would grudgingly ratify the accord on 18 July as a temporary measure, he never forgave his brother.

Charles had good reasons for pursuing and accepting the armistice despite its painful conditions and the certain knowledge that it would generate a sanctimonious uproar among the members of the war faction. He was steadfast in his view that his weary army was the last guarantor of the Habsburg monarchy: as long as it remained relatively intact, the dynasty would endure.[58] He was convinced, however, that the destruction of his army would lead to the dissolution of the monarchy and the fall of the House of Habsburg. The Austrians entertained exaggerated notions of Napoleon's strength on 11 July, and the archduke, watching the steady arrival of French reinforcements and the emperor himself, was certain that another battle could only end in another defeat in an ill-conceived war.[59] An immediate armistice, on the other hand, would both preserve the army—and thus the dynasty—and cripple efforts of the war faction to continue the otiose struggle.[60] Additionally, it would freeze the Russians in place, preventing them from making any more 'friendly' acquisitions at Habsburg expense. The 12 July agreement was the result of these reasonable policy considerations.

There were also, however, several personal factors. First, Charles had opposed the timing of the war from its inception, and the progress of the conflict had reinforced his belief that Napoleon would not be defeated in 1809. Second, not only was the Austrian army reaching the end of its endurance, on a personal level Charles was physically and mentally drained by the events of the preceding seven days. All of this contributed to his gloomy conclusions: 'Without the armistice we would have been crushed.'[61] He was not entirely mistaken, but in this state of exhaustion and pessimism he overestimated French capabilities and underrated his own army's resilience.[62] Third, he could sense the storm of vindictive outrage approaching from court. Already on 9 July Franz had written denigrating the army's 'courage and good spirit . . . order and discipline', implicitly citing Charles as the source of these woes, while hinting at imminent curtailment of Charles's authorities and, as a personal affront, demanding that Charles cashier his protégé Grünne. This letter only confirmed Charles in his decision to act while he still had extensive powers as Generalissimus to present the court in general and the war party in particular with a fait accompli. He penned a lengthy justification of his decision, while privately ridiculing the vaporous plans proposed by the cabinet commanders at court, but his days as army commander were numbered.[63]

On the other side of the field, Napoleon appraised the situation differently. His divisions were also tired and, contrary to Austrian assessments, the bulk of his infantry and additional heavy cavalry (perhaps 55,000 men) was strung out along the roads to the east and south, urgently moving to join him by forced marches.[64] By afternoon on the 11th, he only had some 36,000 infantry and cavalry at hand, compared to approximately 64,000 Austrians available on the battlefield; he could not expect to gain numerical ascendancy until the following morning. The prospects for a crushing victory would then be high, but there was a good possibility that Charles would escape during the night, depriving the French of an immediate triumph and dragging the war yet further north into Bohemia. Charles did issue orders at noon for just such a shift.[65] Such a delay would strengthen the hand of Austria's war faction and could incite additional unrest in Germany, perhaps even bring Prussia into the conflict on Austria's side. For Napoleon, who above all wanted to end the war quickly, any such prolongation was highly undesirable. Acceptance of the local ceasefire, on the other hand, would cost Napoleon nothing and might nail Charles in place for the night.[66] Then, on the 12th, he would be in a position to eliminate the Austrian army if the archduke rejected his armistice terms.

In addition to these immediate military considerations, there was a larger political question with regard to the general armistice: what terms did Napoleon want to impose on Austria? If he intended to dissolve the monarchy, he would need to destroy the Austrian army utterly. If, however, he could be satisfied with a weakened but intact Habsburg realm, then an immediate cessation of hostilities was acceptable, even preferable. If the former course seemed more appropriate to Napoleon the general—and some of his marshals argued for it: the final defeat of their inveterate foe—Napoleon the statesman selected the latter.[67] He knew Russia would not tolerate the destruction of the Habsburg monarchy and he wanted no additional trouble in the east while still embroiled in Spain. Furthermore, many Austrian and French interests were compatible, and conserving the Danubian monarchy as a significant power, albeit under a French shadow, might allow Napoleon to build on these in the future. There may have been a personal aspect in Napoleon's case as well. He too was weary, and he was dissatisfied with the results of Wagram after huge expense in blood and effort to bring about this unwanted war's culminating battle.[68] Although the final shape of the desired peace was still unclear to Napoleon at this point, his military, political, and perhaps personal concerns thus made an armistice attractive. He held an impromptu council in his tent on the night of the 11th and listened attentively to various viewpoints, but terminated the discussion by stating, 'enough blood has flowed.'[69] He thereupon ordered Berthier to sign the agreement, and the active phase of the war came to a close.

Eugene and Johann Once Again: 10–18 July

Like many of the generals at Napoleon's council on the night of 11 July, many of the junior officers and soldiers were dismayed by the apparent clemency towards a foe they considered an 'irreconcilable enemy', perpetually the junction point for anti-French coalitions. The Guard Horse Grenadiers reportedly broke their sabres over their knees on hearing the news, and Colonel Berthezène recorded that 'this resolution by the emperor was poorly received by the troops,' who believed the Austrian army had 'reached a moment to be vanquished' one final time and perhaps erased entirely'.[70] If displeasing to some in the army, Napoleon's decision was made. The war thus moved to a different phase in which the principal forces watched, waited, and rebuilt themselves, while peace talks proceeded, and distant actions kept the conflict very much alive for some participants. Before shifting our gaze to these and other theatres, however, it is useful to review the final actions of the main forces in and around the Danube valley.

Napoleon, when he called Davout from Pressburg to Lobau, posted Baraguey d'Hilliers opposite the Austrian bridgehead with a thin force consisting of Severoli's infantry 'division' (3,190 men) of French, Italian, and Dalmatian troops as well as 1,300 French and German light cavalry under GB Thiry. Many of the latter were brand new to basic notions of equitation, let alone combat on horseback. Baraguey d'Hilliers thus was at a great qualitative and quantitative disadvantage when he occupied Davout's positions on 3 July, as Archduke Johann was then still in Pressburg preparing his foray across the Danube. The odds evened out when Johann was called to Wagram and left Bianchi at Pressburg with barely 2,700 infantry and 230 Insurrection hussars. Baraguey d'Hilliers, 'desiring to profit from the impression created by the defeat of the main Austrian army', attacked the bridgehead through the Alte Au on 8 July with IV/1st Ligne and I/7th Italian Line. Capturing several guns and overthrowing 2nd Ober Wienerwald (OWW) Landwehr and the regulars of *Strassaldo*, the advance made good progress until Bianchi personally restored the situation with a counter-attack by *Lusignan* and his other Landwehr battalion. Fighting went on until 8 p.m., when both sides retired with losses of between 100 and 200 each.[71]

Johann's corps returned from its march to Wagram on the evening of the 8th and into the 9th, and the archduke again made plans to attack the blockading forces. As in June, he imagined a complex operation combining his corps with Joseph, Chasteler, and Gyulai to advance on Vienna. Again, however, he had to call off his enterprise. The Hauptarmee's retreat and Eugene's pressure towards the March having made a crossing impractical and dangerous, Johann retired to Komorn, once again entrusting Bianchi with the security of the Pressburg area as far as Stampfen, albeit this time without the bridgehead. Bianchi successfully withdrew his men across the river on 11 July, fending off an attack by a battalion of the Dalmatian Regiment through the Alte Au in the process. He now faced another challenge as the Army of Italy was crossing the March.

In accordance with his orders, Eugene assembled, reorganised, and rested his army on the eastern side of the Marchfeld after Wagram for several days. Patrols became more active as Gérard and Pully returned to the army, and the Saxon cavalry supported by the *Egidy* Schützen skirmished with an Austrian rear guard detachment near Marchegg on the 9th, but the army did not make a serious move towards the March until 10 July. Although Eugene remained cautious, the Saxons crossed the March at Marchegg and advanced on Pressburg. A brief skirmish ensued between the Saxon advance guard and part of Bianchi's brigade on 13 July when the local Austrian commander, rejecting news of the armistice, rashly attacked some unsuspecting troopers of *Prinz Johann* Chevaulegers. The Saxons reacted with vengeful vigour in a well-executed counter-attack, capturing two guns, killing eighty-four Austrians, and taking another 352 prisoners, mostly from II/*Beaulieu*. The two sides sorted out their misunderstandings on the armistice and Bianchi withdrew, allowing the Saxons to take possession of Pressburg on the evening of 14 July.[72]

Although the Habsburg court now had some news of the armistice, most refused to believe it without official confirmation from Charles. Military operations thus continued for another week in a complex minuet of frenetic planning and sluggish movements. To Charles's disgust—'less talk, more action,' he commented dryly—Johann persisted in trying to implement his questionable offensive towards Vienna.[73] Marching via Komorn, he united his corps with Chasteler at Tet on the 17th and sent the combined command south with the intention of assembling all his scattered forces at Körmend. The corps had only reached Szent Groth when confirmation of the armistice arrived on 20 July and all offensive operations came to a halt.[74] The Insurrection was also to be involved in this scheme. While GM Andrassy went to hold the line along the Waag River with a detachment of 4,000 men, the bulk of Joseph's troops advanced cautiously west on 11 July to blockade Raab.[75] The Pest Hussars had even cut the road between Raab and Vienna before the terms of the armistice required Joseph to withdraw. The end of the war thus found Andrassy along the Waag in the north, Bianchi in the Great Schütt, Joseph east of Raab, and Johann in Körmend, lamenting the monarchy's fate, but still full of notions on how to resume the offensive once the armistice expired.

The other element of Johann's command was Gyulai's IX Corps. With Marmont and Broussier on the way to Wagram, Gyulai re-occupied Graz

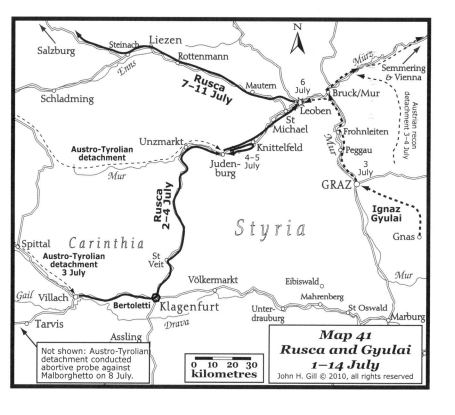

Map 41
Rusca and Gyulai
1—14 July
John H. Gill © 2010, all rights reserved

on 3 July and sent flying detachments into the Mur and Mürz valleys to trouble the French and gather information. In addition to capturing many French wounded, these small forces learned that Rusca was marching up from Villach and Klagenfurt. Rusca, ordered to hold Bruck and the Semmering Pass in the French army's rear, had departed Villach on 2 July, left Bertoletti in Klagenfurt with his Italian troops, and reached Judenburg late on 4 July with his two French battalions, the Istrians, and some cavalry, slightly over 2,200 men. The following day, however, he halted in Judenburg on learning that Gyulai was moving towards Bruck and had placed a strong detachment in Leoben under newly promoted GM Ferdinand von Fellner. Conducting a bold night attack on 6 July, Rusca surprised Fellner and routed his detachment (a battalion of *Szulin* Grenzer, a detachment of *Frimont* Hussars, one and one-half squadrons of *Savoy* Dragoons), inflicting casualties of 250 dead and wounded, while capturing an additional 396 men. Fellner, who had completely neglected security arrangements, was among those killed. This tidy success notwithstanding, Rusca could not stay in the Mur valley. Gyulai blocked his route north and mixed detachments of regulars and rebels sent by Buol from the Tyrol were now in his rear. One of these had placed itself in Judenburg, shutting off that avenue, as another occupied Villach.[76] Demonstrating initiative and stern leadership, Rusca turned his tiny 'division' around and marched for Salzburg via Rottenmann. Despite 'continual harassment' by insurgents along the way, he kept his little command together, moved with commendable rapidity, and even brought along his large haul of prisoners when he reached his destination on the 13th.[77] Gyulai, on the other hand, did not know quite what to do with his large (at least 23,000), but largely untrained and inexperienced force. In the end, he did little, and the armistice found his corps distributed along the valleys around Bruck an der Mur.

CHAPTER 7

Insurgents, Invasions, and Peace

Fighting in the central arena came to a close with the armistice of Znaim, but combat flared in some of the secondary theatres for several days, the bitter Tyrolian insurgency burned on, and Great Britain actively joined the war with a large amphibious assault, albeit very much under its own conditions. Meanwhile, French and Austrian diplomats wrangled over the peace terms, Prussia was tempted to enter the lists, and soldiers of both sides prepared for a renewal of conflict.

CONCLUDING COMBATS: POLAND, GERMANY, DALMATIA

As the main French and Austrian armies retired to cantonments to recover from the exertions of the Wagram campaign, combat between regular forces of both sides persisted in Poland, in south-central Germany, and in Dalmatia.

Eastern Ambiguities: Poles, Russians, and Austrians in Galicia

We left Prince Poniatowski at Pulawy on the west bank of the Vistula, having crossed the great river in late June with his main force (see Map 1). To his right were Sokolnicki and Dabrowski on the Pilica, to his left Golitsyn's Russians, more enemies than friends. The Russian advance to the Wisloka River, however, had made Archduke Ferdinand's position at Opatow untenable. As July began, he was retiring towards Krakow, and Eggermann was marching west from Lemberg. By the time Charles and Napoleon were confronting each other on the Marchfeld, therefore, Ferdinand had his corps arrayed in an arc east and north of Krakow, with Eggermann (including Hertlendy's small Insurrection brigade) covering the Dukla Pass and other possible entries into Hungary. Ferdinand remained intent on holding the Russians at the Wisloka by negotiations and keeping the Poles out of Krakow by force. He would be gravely disappointed in both of these desires.

Poniatowski seems to have succumbed to the charms of the society and countryside around Pulawy; he waited here for eight days before moving west again. Nonetheless, on 2 July he marched on, united with Sokolnicki and joined Dabrowski at Radom on the 4th. With about 23,000 men, he now turned towards Krakow, marching steadily if not with any special speed, and the first advance guard clash occurred near Pinczow on 9 July. Ferdinand, still disparaging his opponents, hoped to strike the Polish left from his position along the Nida, but he received new orders on the night of the 11th. With the overall Habsburg position collapsing in the wake of Wagram, he was directed to abandon Krakow, to protect Olmütz, to maintain close liaison with the Hauptarmee, and to avoid a withdrawal south where his corps was likely to be 'annihilated'.[1] Starting on 12 July, he thus contracted his defensive arc and withdrew to the west. He was determined, however, not to hand Krakow over to the Poles. He thus informed the Russians, who had by now reached the Dunajec, that they could and should occupy the city. A race for Krakow ensued, and the Austrian rear guard delayed Poniatowski's advance troops long enough for a small detachment of Cossacks and dragoons to clatter into the city late on 14 July. The Austrians marched out at 4 a.m. the following morning.

Along the way, the Russians had ridden through an Austrian camp unannounced and, mistaken for Polish uhlans, had been instantly attacked. Although a dragoon was killed and the detachment commander and several Cossacks were wounded, the commanding officer assured the apologetic Austrians that 'he would happily accept a few more sabre blows if he could thereby give the Poles a black eye'.[2] This spirit of enmity blossomed when Chef d'Escadron Wlodimir Potocki trotted up to the Krakow city gates at 6 a.m. on the 15th with a platoon of true Polish uhlans. By now, General Sievers and a larger Russian detachment had arrived, and many tense scenes played themselves out as Poles confronted Russians at the gate and in the main square. Poniatowski, riding in with his suite shortly afterwards, had to force his way physically through a line of hostile Russian hussars as Russian cannon faced Polish infantry with lowered bayonets in the main square. Entering the city hall, however, the prince decided the issue by claiming Krakow in Napoleon's name, an assertion the Russians could not counter without formally discarding the half-alliance with France. Rancorous distrust continued to characterise Russo-Polish contact until Sievers departed the city some days later. Nonetheless, the fact remained—as Poniatowski proudly noted in his report to Napoleon—that Polish forces had entered their ancient capital three months to the day after the start of the Austrian invasion.[3] News of the Znaim armistice arrived the following day and combat in this portion of Galicia came to a close.

In the distant reaches of East Galicia, however, a series of small engagements remained to be concluded. FML Maximillian Graf Merveldt, now commanding what had been Hohenlohe's composite force of depot troops, garrison units, and Bukovina mounted volunteers with exotic names ('Arnauts'), had pushed two columns across the Dnestr. The eastern column, under GM Bicking, made for Tarnopol, while GM Johann von Kessler's crossed the river at Halicz in the west. Chef d'Escadron Strzyzowski in Tarnopol, however, was not to be daunted. While energetic militia intimidated Kessler's column, Strzyzowski, reinforced by 100 men from 1st Chasseurs, aggressively attacked Bicking. With his few regulars and large numbers of militia, Strzyzowski had perhaps as many as 2,700 men, but many were of very dubious quality. Nonetheless, he manoeuvred the Austrians away from the city and energised his little force. In one bold escapade a Polish officer with twenty chasseurs temporarily captured Bicking in a daring night raid. It was only a momentary escape for the Habsburg general. Strzyzowski trapped the Austrians near Wieniawka (Chmielowka), cut them off from local water supplies for two days, and forced the despairing Bicking to surrender his 1,200 men and three guns on 18 July. Strzyzowski now pursued the retreating Kessler, but the Austrian recrossed the Dnestr and the Poles found themselves in a skirmish with Merveldt's superior forces near Mariampol on the 21st, when news of the armistice brought peace to this remote corner of the war.[4]

A combination of Polish perseverance, Russian intervention—albeit half-hearted or even hostile to the Poles—and Austrian ineptitude thus placed much of Galicia under Polish, and thereby Napoleonic, control. Poniatowski had skilfully fulfilled his mission of tying down a significant Austrian force without diverting a single soldier from the main theatre of war. Ferdinand, on the other hand, proved incapable of exploiting his initial advantages and quickly lost control of events. Instead of offering advantages, the war in Poland and the ambiguous behaviour of the Russians quickly became a major worry for Habsburg leaders. Watching helplessly as Ferdinand retreated and Golitsyn advanced, they perceived an increasing threat to the monarchy's strategic rear. This worry loomed over all decisions after Aspern;

in the prevailing atmosphere of anxiety, Austrian concerns even extended to Bukovina.[5] A theatre that had seemed to promise crucial military-political rewards thus evolved into an unanticipated source of danger and distraction.

Dalmatian Diversion

As Charles was retreating from Wagram, Austria made another stab at dominating Dalmatia (see Map 15). On the coast, GM l'Espine attempted a land attack on Trieste with support from the Royal Navy blockading force (5–8 July), but the unreliable Insurrection troops and poor Anglo-Austrian co-ordination were no match for GB Schilt's skill and determination.[6] GM von Knesevich had considerably more success with a brigade of some 3,000 men assembled from troops left behind when Ignaz Gyulai had marched north to Graz.[7] Having sent Dalmatian volunteers to foment unrest on 5 July, Knesevich gathered his command at Gracac. He advanced on the 19th, blockaded Knin, and seized Ostrovica (on 20 July); a small detachment also captured Sebenico with the help of local citizens on the 21st as the French garrison fled to the nearby fort of San Nicolo. Knesevich then took his main force to Zara, where he arrived on the 25th after skirmishing with a French supply column near Brenkovac en route (23 July). Marmont's deputy in Dalmatia, GB Jean Etienne Casimir Poitevin, Comte de Maureillan, refused a surrender demand, and intermittent fighting continued on 26–7 July as Knesevich blockaded the town, but a planned Anglo-Austrian bombardment was called off when news of the ceasefire arrived on the afternoon of the 28th. Further south, the Austrians and Dalmatian rebels occupied Trau (30 July) and Spalato (2 August) without opposition before learning of the armistice; the tiny French garrisons escaped to Klissa. In the meantime, Knesevich and Maureillan had agreed to a convention that left Zara, Knin, Klissa, and San Nicolo in French hands, but granted the Austrians control of all Dalmatia north of Spalato pending a final peace treaty. In their zone, however, the French had to repress general unrest prompted by the Austrian invasion.[8]

Thunder in Bayreuth

Returning to the northern edge of this sprawling canvas of combat, we come to the confrontation between Kienmayer and Junot in Bayreuth, with King Jerome and his Westphalian corps hovering in the background.[9]

GD Junot, charged with repelling the threat to Napoleon's line of communications through Germany, had marched rapidly from Hanau via Würzburg, picked up GB Delaroche's dragoons in Bamberg and occupied Bayreuth on 7 July. His force of some 7,090 infantry and cavalry was composed of French and Bavarian depot infantry and French provisional dragoons with sixteen guns. This was more than enough to cause GM Radivojevich to withdraw rapidly from Bayreuth on the 7th, skirmishing with Junot's dragoons as he retreated to the east. With only some 4,300 men, the nervous Radivojevich dispatched numerous messages to Kienmayer, asking for immediate help. Kienmayer was on the way. He found himself in 'a very uncomfortable situation' with Jerome on one side and Junot on the other, but he was annoyed to find that 'fourteen days to three weeks have passed and nothing of significance has been done' by Radivojevich.[10] He had brought more than 5,000 men from Saxony and was determined to defeat his two adversaries separately before they could unite. He reached Hof on 7 July as Radivojevich was retreating, and marched to his subordinate's assistance early the following morning.

Thus 8 July brought a sharp skirmish between these two odd armies in the steeply hilly and heavily wooded terrain around the village of Gefrees. The French had been pushing Radivojevich when Kienmayer arrived at around 10.30 a.m. and found that the French had neglected their left flank. Kienmayer exploited this lapse without hesitation and forced the French back, but the green troops conducted their retreat in good order. They had taken up a solid defensive position between Gefrees and Bayreuth when another of the violent thunderstorms that punctuated this war crashed down on the armies, ending combat on what had been a dreadfully hot day. The French lost 185 men in the fighting around Gefrees, the Austrians and their various allies somewhat fewer than 100 (including seven Brunswick men dead from heatstroke). Though both forces largely consisted of second-line troops, both performed well, Kienmayer praising his Landwehr and Junot his inexperienced conscripts for their steadiness and courage.

Junot, however, now lost his personal courage and retired precipitously to Amberg. Kienmayer, learning that Jerome had reached Plauen in his rear, gave up the pursuit on the 9th and turned back north to attack 10th Corps. The Westphalian king had finally marched out of Dresden on 4 July and arrived in Plauen on the 8th, too late to combine with Junot against Kienmayer. Though he had dropped off Thielmann's Saxons on departing their kingdom (Thielmann led a raid to Komotau in Bohemia on the 8th), Jerome had approximately 11,000 men and thus still enjoyed a slight numerical advantage over the Austrians; combined with Junot, the superiority could have been decisive. That was not to be tested. Junot remained inert at Amberg and Jerome did not wait for Kienmayer. The Austrians thus arrived outside Plauen on 12 July to find only a few deserters and marauders left behind. Jerome had marched north, apparently believing exaggerated reports of Kienmayer's strength and anxious about the security of his realm in the wake of wildly inflated rumours concerning a British landing on the north German coast. It was the end of combat among regular troops in Germany. News of the armistice arrived several days later and Kienmayer retired to Bohemia on Charles's orders.

Am Ende also returned to Bohemia. Advancing timidly after Jerome's departure from Dresden, Am Ende had occupied the Saxon capital from 14 to 21 July where his Landwehr made a poor impression for having an 'appearance that was hardly military'.[11] He and Thielmann exchanged many

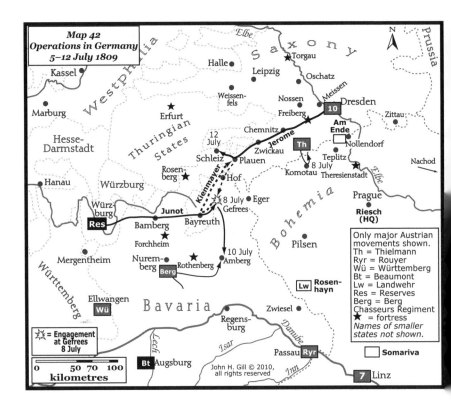

words but few bullets after the blustering Saxon colonel arrived outside the city walls on the 20th and more-or-less intimidated his way into Dresden the following day.[12]

If Am Ende was a disappointment, Charles had every reason to be pleased with Kienmayer's performance. Making good use of a classic strategy of the central position, he repulsed two enemy corps while keeping his command intact as a small, but viable, threat to Napoleon's line of communications. On the other hand, Napoleon's arrangements for rear area security also functioned as intended. Although Junot and Jerome failed to collaborate effectively and the latter's corps was hobbled by feckless leadership and amateur staff work, they sufficed to contain the Austrian incursions. Different leaders might have produced different outcomes. Had Kienmayer been in place in early June, or had Jerome and Junot demonstrated greater competence, the results might have been more dramatic. As it was, the Austrian expeditions accomplished nothing towards their primary goal of diminishing Napoleon's strength in the Danube valley.

The Black Duke's March

The armistice ended combat between regular troops, but Friedrich Wilhelm of Brunswick did not consider himself a party to the ceasefire agreement. Certain that a 'humiliating peace' would follow the armistice, the duke declared himself 'unwilling to bow before Napoleon like the other princes of Germany'; he told his officers that he intended to march north to fight for 'the freedom and independence of the German nation'. Though he was doubtless a fiery and determined individual, Friedrich Wilhelm may have been encouraged by the rumoured landing of British troops on the North Sea coast as he expressly mentioned attempting to unite with them. In any case, most of his officers and men agreed to this bold venture and the 'corps' of some 2,010 departed Zwickau for Leipzig and Westphalia on 24 July.[13]

Marching an admirable average of forty-one to forty-two kilometres per day, the Black Corps had several brushes with Saxon detachments (24/25 July), passed through Leipzig, and entered Westphalia, where they fought two sharp encounters with Jerome's troops. The first of these, on 29 July, saw the Brunswick troops overwhelm the 5th Westphalian Line at Halberstadt. The Westphalian recruits put up a stiff fight, but yielded when most of their officers were killed or captured. With 200 men dead or wounded and 1,500 taken prisoner, the 5th Line ceased to exist. Brunswick's losses came

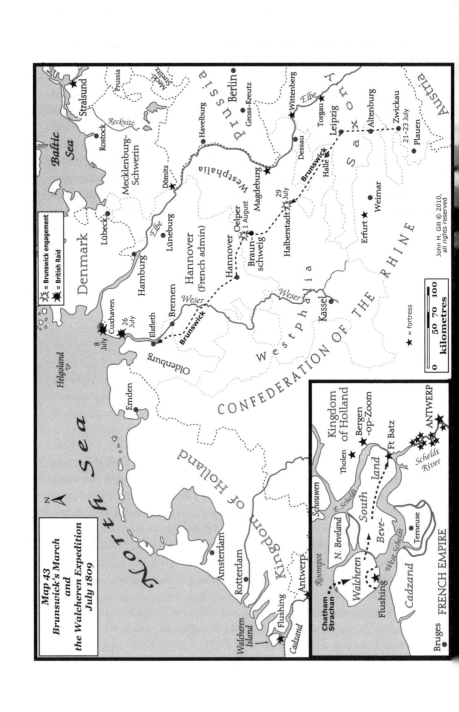

Map 43
Brunswick's March
and
the Walcheren Expedition
July 1809

North Sea

Baltic Sea

Helgoland

☆ = Brunswick engagement
✦ = British Raid

★ = fortress

0   50 70 100
kilometres

John H. Gill © 2010,
all rights reserved

Denmark

Stralsund
Rostock
Lübeck
Hamburg
Bremen
Emden

Mecklenburg-
Schwerin

Mecklenburg-
Strelitz

Prussia

Recknitz

Havelburg

Berlin
Gross-Kreutz

Dömitz

Lüneburg

Hannover
(French admin)

Hannover

Elsfleth
Cuxhaven
8 July
26 July

Oldenburg

Brunswick

Weser

Weser

Elbe

Elbe

Wittenberg

Dessau
Magdeburg

Halberstadt
29 July

Oelper
1 August

Braun-
schweig

Brunswick

Halle

Torgau
Leipzig

Altenburg
Zwickau
21-23 July
Plauen

S a x o n y

Austria

Weimar

Erfurt

Kassel

Westphalia

W e s t p h a l i a

CONFEDERATION OF THE RHINE

Kingdom of Holland

Amsterdam

Rotterdam

Antwerp

Flushing
Cadzand

Walcheren
Island

Kingdom
of Holland

Schouwen

Tholen

Bergen
-op-Zoom

Roompot

N. Beveland

E. Scheldt

South
Beve-
land

Walcheren

Flushing

Ft Batz

*Scheldt
River*

ANTWERP

Chatham
Strachan

Terneuse

West Scheldt

Cadzand

Bruges

FRENCH EMPIRE

N

to 150–200 men. Three days later at Oelper outside Brunswick, the duke's men ran into GD Jean-Jacques Reubell with about 5,000 Westphalian and Berg troops and ten guns. The ensuing skirmish was a tactical draw, but had the makings of a strategic victory for the Westphalians as they had blocked Brunswick's progress. With Gratien's Dutch division on the way, Brunswick's fate might have been sealed had Reubell demonstrated any degree of fortitude or foresight. Instead, he withdrew into the night, and the Black Corps hurried north the following day. Reubell's efforts to catch up proved fruitless, Ewald's Danish troops, like Gratien's Dutch, were too far away, and Herzog Peter Friedrich Ludwig of Oldenburg, though a Rheinbund member, moved his few troops out of the way to avoid incidents with the fleeing Brunswickers. Friedrich Wilhelm and his band easily embarked on requisitioned ships at Elsfleth in the Weser estuary on 7 August and set sail to continue their struggle against Napoleon in British service. After years of campaigning in the Iberian Peninsula, they would end their wars at Waterloo fighting against an army whose general officer ranks included the former King of Westphalia, Jerome Bonaparte. Jerome, on the other hand, came away from this concluding experience dishonoured and embarrassed. Even his attempt to arrest Reubell failed, as the general, sensing what was coming, took ship to the United States.

A MOSQUITO RAID AND A GRAND EXPEDITION

A key feature of Stadion's earliest plans for the war against Napoleon and a constant theme throughout the months of conflict was the possibility of a major British landing in Germany. Convinced that the appearance of large numbers of redcoats on German soil would rouse the population against the French, the Austrian war party and disparate German patriots used every possible avenue, contact, and connection to bring about an invasion. The authorities in London, however, had other ideas about Great Britain's interests. Although the Royal Navy would conduct several small raids during the course of the war, the major landing, when it came, would occur in Holland, not Germany.

The strategic mobility afforded by the Royal Navy made sea-based raids by parties of sailors and marines a valuable tactic, one which many captains exercised with zeal and skill in 1809. If never enough to satisfy Austrian expectations, British ships conducted several actions in the Adriatic through April and May, and began delivering the specie Austria so ardently desired in June. The Royal Navy in the Baltic, however, was focused on Russia, and the only activity on the rest of the German seaboard came from a small blockade force at the mouth of the Weser. From this flotilla, approximately 320 sailors and marines under Commander William Goate of *Mosquito* landed near Cuxhaven on 8 July, destroying a nearby coastal battery and driving off the gunners. The British remained in the vicinity off and on for nearly a month, capturing a second battery on the 26th, promoting commerce in contravention to Napoleon's Continental System, spreading exaggerated stories, and leading active social lives—for the officers, at least. Danish General von Ewald arrived with a detachment from the other side of the Elbe estuary on 1 August and forced the British to re-embark, but he could do nothing against the warships, and the British re-occupied the harbour when Ewald was called away to join the pursuit of Brunswick. The Danes returned briefly after this fruitless chase, but marched back to their homeland on 12 August, leaving the British masters of the local area until Westphalian troops appeared to take possession in early September.[14] However profitable for the local populace and satisfying for the British naval personnel involved, the principal impact of all of this coming and going was a gust of wild rumours that blew through Germany and Austria for a short time during July. Jerome, for instance, wrote to Napoleon in great worry on 17 July that 20,000–30,000 British had disembarked on the coast! Ten days later, these fears had subsided.[15] The reaction on the other side, of course, was the opposite: initial elation, followed by deep disappointment when the landings proved to be small raiding parties with no larger purpose.[16]

Walcheren Fiasco

A much larger British landing with a much larger purpose took place at the end of July in Holland on the island of Walcheren. Indeed, the invasion at Walcheren was 'incomparably the greatest armament that had ever left the shores of England', and one of the largest amphibious assaults in history up to that time.[17] Its objective, location, and timing, however, were inconsistent with Austrian interests, and its execution left long casualty lists and a legacy of failure.

For some years, senior leaders in London had proposed an attack on Antwerp as a means of removing the threat posed by French warships and naval construction facilities there. Intelligence about French naval activity at Antwerp revived discussion of such an operation in early 1809, even before Austria invaded Bavaria. Vienna's urgent requests for British support in Germany and the start of the war naturally intensified consideration of amphibious options somewhere in northern Europe during the coming summer. There were basically two courses of action: a landing on the north German coast (at the mouth of the Weser or Elbe) with the hope of sparking a German revolt against Napoleon, or a descent on Antwerp to strike a blow against French naval power. There were, however, serious drawbacks to either option. In the first place, the British army was relatively small and still recovering from the debilitating campaign in Spain and the close escape from Corunna in January 1809. A serious operation on the Continent would risk this army and be extraordinarily expensive at a time when the exchequer was under stress. The government was therefore reluctant to commit scarce resources to a major land campaign in northern Europe, especially one that had no clear objective and might entangle Britain's limited army in a campaign with no obvious end point. Moreover, the cabinet had recently decided to give priority to Portugal as the locus of Britain's overseas efforts. As a result, though official Habsburg emissaries and enthusiastic German, Prussian, and Austrian patriots of every imaginable description pressed for a landing in Germany, London would not accede to such a course of action unless a significant regular army was in the field with which British troops could co-operate.[18] This was not to be. Before Britain could begin to assemble a proper invasion force, Austria had been ejected from Germany, and Prussia, the other potential ally with a real army, refused to make an unambiguous commitment. Furthermore, the experience thus far in 1809 did not suggest that Germany was ripe for revolt. So Britain returned to the Antwerp option, an operation that offered a clear objective, a limited time commitment, and an obvious, direct benefit for British security interests. As one historian points out, in a sense Austria, by drawing off Napoleon's armies, was providing a diversion in Britain's favour, as the absence of French troops made the attack feasible in the first place.[19] The opportunity seemed too good to miss. Although many military officers suggested that the proposal would be extremely difficult to execute successfully, by early summer the plan was in motion.[20] The decision-making process, domestic political considerations, and the time required to outfit the massive invasion force, however, meant that what became known as the 'Grand Expedition' did not set sail until 28 July, more than two weeks after Charles and Napoleon had agreed to the armistice.

The invasion fleet of 616 warships and transports delivered more than 39,000 officers and men to the coast of Holland on the evening of 28 July, and landing operations on the northern side of Walcheren Island began on the 30th.[21] Rear Admiral Sir Richard Strachan served as the senior navy officer, while overall command was invested in Lieutenant General John Pitt, Second Earl of Chatham. From the outset, however, things went awry. Bad weather and command confusion led to the cancellation of a complementary landing on Cadzand on the southern side of the estuary. Leaving this in French control reduced the prospects for what was already a risky proposition. On the other hand, the Walcheren operation proceeded well, South Beveland was quickly occupied during the first few days of August, and Flushing (Vlissingen), a key fortress at the mouth of the estuary fell on 16 August after a brief siege.

The capture of Flushing, though it infuriated Napoleon, proved the last success of what became an agonisingly long campaign.[22] Roads were poor, supplies difficult to procure, and increasingly acrimonious disputes between Strachan and Chatham hindered operations. Prospects dimmed. By 5 August, Strachan was already suggesting that Antwerp was out of reach.[23] Worse, as early as 10 August, soldiers were beginning to fall ill to a 'miasmatic fever', or what was soon known as 'Walcheren fever'. This virulent mixture of ailments decimated the ranks, killing many and often leaving its survivors disabled for life.[24]

The British also had to contend with an energetic enemy. Napoleon and his brother, King Louis of Holland, had long discussed the possibility of a British attempt on Antwerp and the preparation of the 'Grand Expedition', if not its exact destination, had been public knowledge for weeks. Antwerp and Flushing were logical targets, as Louis warned on 5 July, but he could not neglect the rest of Holland's long and vulnerable coast.[25] His army, with Gratien's division in Germany and a brigade in Spain, was too small for this task. When the British arrived, therefore, 'the region was empty of troops who could have offered any resistance,' wrote a Dutch captain, 'if he [Chatham] had displayed a little more speed with his landing troops, he could have made himself master of Antwerp in every sense.'[26]

Local commanders and senior officials in Paris immediately informed Napoleon at Schönbrunn that the assault was underway, but they also took actions on their own. These decisions often earned them imperial rebukes, but within days, thousands of men in French uniforms were en route to the threatened area. Many of these might have challenged the label 'soldier', as they were often depot troops, brand-new conscripts, national guardsmen, gendarmes, naval artificers, or other men more-or-less in uniform. 'Our armed mob,' one officer called them, 'a feeble mass, incoherent and poorly disciplined . . . the national guards, sent to us from the interior, arrived without uniforms, without cartridge boxes, and most without arms.' Their numbers, on the other hand, were impressive and the Dutch Guard made a fine martial appearance: 'Every day, every night, we receive reinforcements, and finish some new entrenchment, or even arm some new battery.'[27] From a rough figure of 20,000 French and Dutch 'troops' within seventy kilometres or so of Walcheren when the British landed, the number had risen to some 46,000 by 13 August when Bernadotte arrived to take command.[28] He found a tangle of confused commanders, questionable officers, dubious troops, and unserviceable artillery, but his presence was part of a typically Napoleonic veil of deception. By granting grand titles to sketchy formations, assigning well-known marshals to lead them, and exaggerating their numbers, Napoleon hoped to discourage further British advances that would test his inferior troops in combat.[29] Orders of battle and titles changed frequently (possibly another wrinkle to the deception), but at various times four different marshals would be associated with the defence of the Scheldt, heading formations with imposing names such as 'Army of Antwerp', 'Army of the Tête des Flandres', or 'Reserve Army of the North'.[30] Locally, the French supplemented these strategic measures with tactical tricks such as displaying a sad pair of 4-pounders 'like theatre scenery' and repeatedly firing them on 15 August (Napoleon's birthday) 'to make the English [sic] believe we had an abundance of artillery and ammunition'.[31]

Troop quality was not the only problem Napoleon faced. Franco-Dutch frictions, Parisian political scheming, dissention among commanders, incompetence, and misunderstandings all impinged on efficiency and efficacy, but in the end the French response sufficed for his purposes.[32] 'The fever and inundation will make the English [sic] see reason,' he told Clarke.[33] Gratien's division returned from Westphalia by the end of August, but no significant French or German troops were diverted from the Danube, and the British presence on the Dutch coastal islands had no appreciable impact on the peace negotiations now underway.[34]

The picture on the British side of the estuary was considerably different. At enormous expense and effort, Great Britain had placed a substantial army on Dutch soil with a strategically important objective. By late August, however, that army was in the grip of raging fever, and its commanders had concluded that 'no Operations could be undertaken against Antwerp with any Prospect of Success at this advanced Season of the Year, and the Enemy increasing in Strength, and our own Forces diminished by Sickness.'[35] Chatham therefore evacuated South Beveland in early September. The expeditionary force, however, retained its hold on Walcheren pending a decision from London. 'Fortunately, the English [sic] persuaded themselves that Marshal Bernadotte had brought troops with him . . . and did not dare to undertake anything,' noted Bernadotte's chief of staff, 'on the contrary, they evacuated the fort of Batz and limited themselves to protecting Walcheren Island and the mouth of the estuary.'[36] Chatham and part of his army sailed back to Britain on 14 September, leaving 19,000 men on Walcheren, but this force dwindled rapidly.[37] That week, some 7,000 of the 18,000 enlisted men and non-commissioned officers were on the sick list.[38] 'If we remain here, our army will be almost annihilated,' wrote newly commissioned William Keep of the 77th Foot to his father just before he contracted the illness himself. 'It is wretchedly unwholesome and our Regiment increase in sick not less than thirty every day.'[39] Conditions for victims of the fever were utterly miserable, medical personnel and supplies were short, and the army soon ran out of space for the growing numbers of men debilitated by the 'ague'. Although a portion of the force had embarked for home after the evacuation of South Beveland, return to Britain did not necessarily mean an end to misery. Private Wheeler of the 51st related on 15 October from his garrison, 'The Regiment is in a very sickly state, the hospital is full, and two rooms of the barracks each holding 60 men is occupied with convalescents; a great many has died and numbers who have recovered will never be fit for service again.'[40]

The cabinet, however, prompted by the Habsburg court, still saw some advantage to maintaining a presence on Walcheren while the French and Austrians negotiated peace terms. A change of government and associated political turmoil in London during September added an additional layer of complication. Thousands therefore continued to suffer and die until a complete withdrawal was authorised in November. The last British soldier finally departed on 23 December, shortly before the new French commander, Marshal Bessières, was scheduled to launch a counter-attack.

The 'Grand Expedition' thus came to an end after five months of effort and misery at a cost of more than 4,000 dead and 12,000 out of action for an indefinite time to come.[41] All of this expense in blood, health, and treasure achieved nothing. One modern British historian has termed it 'virtually epic in its futility'.[42] Antwerp's ships and naval facilities remained untouched, the estuary was not blocked by obstacles or fortifications, and the invasion came too late to provide any relief to Austria. A little more enterprise and better luck with the weather might have brought a different result. Instead, it only served to vindicate Napoleon's reliance on deception, fortresses, and second-line troops as the principal protection for his lines of communications. 'The slowness of our enemies gave us plenty of time to harden our army and instruct the recruits that were sent to us daily,' wrote a French officer.[43]

This Ridiculous Waste

Britain also undertook several amphibious operations in the Mediterranean. The largest, directed against Joachim Murat's Kingdom of Naples, was by no means as costly in lives or pounds sterling as the Walcheren disaster, but it had even less influence on the Franco-Austrian war. The Austrians had, very belatedly, approached Major General Stuart in Sicily in the hope of gaining British diversions in Italy at the start of the war. There was little time to organise anything substantial before Johann was in retreat across the Julian Alps, but Stuart, in part to quell a near-mutiny among his men and in part to burnish his reputation, eventually decided to launch an expedition against Naples. His armada arrived off the coast with 13,000 men on 24 June, and within a week his sailors and soldiers handily captured two islands in the bay (Ischia and Prochida). They also inflicted several small, but excruciatingly embarrassing defeats on Neapolitan gunboats while Murat watched in fury from the shore.

Having won his worthless prizes, Stuart did not know quite what to do. The King of Sardinia, visiting Italian patriots, the Austrian envoy de la Tour, and some of his own officers entreated him to intervene in Italy on Austria's behalf, but he procrastinated. He could not remain forever on his empty islands, an invasion of mainland Naples would risk much for little gain, and he rightly concluded that a landing force of several thousand men on the western Italian coast could not be sustained without Austrian victories. Very understandably, no one on the British side seems to have given serious consideration to Austrian pleas for a landing in Dalmatia or Croatia. Stuart apparently contemplated some action to respond to the general uproar in Italy when Napoleon had GD Etienne Radet arrest Pope Pius VII on the night of 5/6 July and transport the pontiff to France. News of Wagram, however, squelched that thought. Moreover, Stuart learned that the French had defeated an ancillary British raid at Scilla opposite Messina on 2 July, and this insignificant affair excited his concern for the security of Sicily. Warned as well by Admiral Collingwood that his fleet of transports made a tempting target for the French navy, he departed the waters outside Naples on 26 July. After what one eminent British military historian called 'this ridiculous waste of men, money, and time', Stuart had thus accomplished nothing beyond the humiliation of Murat in sight of his own capital.[44]

British forces in the Mediterranean concluded the year with the successful seizure of several Ionian Islands (Zante, Cephalonia, Ithaca, Cerigo) by Stuart's subordinate, Brigadier General John Oswald, in October just before the Treaty of Schönbrunn was signed. These tidy feats of arms, however, had no bearing on the course of Napoleon's war with Austria.[45]

REBELS IN THE MOUNTAINS: TYROL AND VORARLBERG

Cuxhaven, Walcheren, and Naples were remote threats that Napoleon could contain with minimal attention. The insurgencies in the Tyrol and Vorarlberg, on the other hand, were closer to his lines of communication and endangered his allies. He had remained sharply focused on the strategic priority of defeating the Austrian Hauptarmee from April to July and had therefore treated both problems as 'economy of force' missions. Now, with the armistice signed and Austrian troops withdrawn according to its terms, he endeavoured to erase both of these persistent irritants.

The Vorarlberg and the Tyrol: July–August[46]

Entering its third phase, the Vorarlberg insurgency resolved itself with little intervention from Napoleon. The rebellion here had never burned as brightly as in neighbouring Tyrol and, with Kienmayer gone from central Germany, Württemberg's King Friedrich was free to commit all his resources against it. He was probably all the more keen to do so because a detachment had to be sent to the Nellenburg district from 6 to 16 July to quell unrest that was partly inspired by the Vorarlberg revolt, but more specifically occasioned, as in Mergentheim, by the heavy-handed imposition of new regulations, especially the kingdom's conscription laws and the raising of the local Land-battalion.[47] The Württemberg 'Observation Corps' and its august monarch thus returned to the southern border of Friedrich's realm on 11–13 July. They were just in time to assist in repelling what turned out to be the insurrection's last gasp, a series of unco-ordinated thrusts from the Schussen to Isny between the 14th and 17th. With these efforts defeated, the Vorarlberg insurgency quietly evaporated. King Friedrich went home, leaving Crown Prince Friedrich Wilhelm to march into Bregenz on 6 August as GD Beaumont, leading a Franco-Bavarian force from the Inn valley, crossed the Arlberg Pass to occupy Dornbirn. There was no resistance. The Württembergers, with no interest in making any further exertions on behalf of Bavaria, returned home the following day.[48]

The story in the Tyrol was completely different. For the repression of this rebellion, Napoleon envisaged a three-pronged offensive. Leaving Wrede at Linz, Lefebvre would drive up the Inn valley with the 1st and 3rd Divisions of 7th Corps, while Rouyer, Arco, and Beaumont pushed across the mountains from the north.[49] Rusca would march up the Drava valley from the east, while GD Pasquale Fiorella led a small force of second-line Italian troops up the Adige. In the event, all three failed. Rusca had to give up his two French battalions to join their regiments with the main army, so he marched back to Spittal with barely more than a personal escort for his 'division'. Skilfully avoiding insurgent ambushes, he reached his destination safely on 21 July. Reinforced by six battalions from Severoli, he took control of Sachsenburg from Buol's Austrians on 1 August in compliance with the armistice, and headed for Lienz but soon found that the Tyrolians were by no means subdued. He fought his way into Lienz on the 4th, but feared to stay in this isolated post and retired to Klagenfurt seven days later, leaving strong detachments in Sachsenburg, Tarvis, Spittal, and Villach.

Rusca's setback was minor compared to Lefebvre's repulse. The Bavarian 7th Corps (1st and 3rd Divisions), with Rouyer's multinational German division attached, undertook a second march on Innsbruck in late July. Entering the city on the 30th, Lefebvre sent Rouyer across the Brenner Pass with a strong column, while dispatching a second force to probe further up the Inn. This latter column was to maintain contact with Beaumont, who had turned west for the Vorarlberg after entering the Inn valley via Reutte and the Scharnitz Pass. 'It is one of the worst countries one could see,' wrote a French recruit in the resuscitated 65th Ligne to his parents, 'there are nothing but mountains covered with snow and it is very cold.'[50] August chills and steep mountains notwithstanding, Beaumont trudged on almost unimpeded, while both of Lefebvre's columns met with disaster at the hands of Tyrolians. Rebels captured some 800 Bavarians (II/10th Infantry, two squadrons of 2nd Dragoons) in the upper Inn valley on the 9th, and others, 'more furious than tigers', trapped the 4th Rheinbund in the Eisack valley north of Brixen.[51] The regiment demonstrated great courage, but suffered 948 casualties on 4–5 August before it could be extricated from its painful situation. Remnants of these columns recoiled back to Innsbruck under constant pressure from the insurgents. Attacked south of the city on 13 August in the Fourth Battle of Bergisel, the Bavarians held their own, but Lefebvre was personally demoralised and facing an uncomfortable logistics situation. Seeing no alternative, the marshal ordered a withdrawal, and by

20 August, 7th Corps was once again back in Bavaria and Salzburg. Fiorella, learning of the Bavarian retreat, retired to Dolce.[52]

By late August, therefore, the Tyrol had once again freed itself from French and Bavarian occupation. There had simply not been enough troops to accomplish the daunting task and, with Napoleon still concentrating his attention on the peace process, another pause ensued. The end of the rebellion would have to await the signing of a peace treaty. The emperor, however, did not neglect the Tyrol. In an attempt to mollify the rebels, he instructed Berthier to have Rusca send an officer to the insurgent commanders, offering to restore peace and attend to local grievances if the Tyrolians would return to the Napoleonic fold.[53] This letter, however, was evidently intercepted by the rebels before it reached Rusca and the reconciliation initiative dissipated before it had a chance to develop.[54]

The Tyrol: September–December[55]

Other than minor insurgent raids, late August and early September passed quietly for the French and their allies on the frontiers of the Tyrol. On 29 September, however, GB Luigi Peyri captured Trient with a force of approximately 4,000 men whom he had assembled at Dolce. He probed to Lavis on 2 October, but could not maintain himself in such a vulnerable location and withdrew to the Trient citadel under heavy rebel attack. GD Vial returned to the Tyrol from Venice on the 13th and the two fought a series of skirmishes with the insurgents until the end of the month. The net results of their actions in the Adige valley seem modest, but they cleared the rebels from the eastern shore of Lake Garda and established firm control over both Trient and the western terminus of the Val Sugana. They thereby removed the threat of rebel raids against Verona and laid the foundation for further French operations up the Adige into the heart of the Tyrol.

While Peyri and Vial were busy along the Adige, other troops were active in the eastern and northern portions of the Tyrol. In the east, Rusca had been principally concerned with supplying the fortress of Sachsenburg, but in the north the Bavarians opened their third offensive into their rebellious province. Napoleon had relieved Marshal Lefebvre on 11 October, so the Bavarians were now under the former corps chief of staff, GD Drouet d'Erlon.[56] Working closely with his Bavarian subordinates and local forestry officials, Drouet opened the offensive with a tactical masterpiece, overwhelming rebel outposts in a surprise attack south-west of Salzburg on the night of 16/17 October. The Bavarians entered Innsbruck on 28 October and fought a final Bergisel battle on 1 November, scattering the rebels and securing a firm hold on the middle stretch of the Inn.

This Bavarian offensive was part of Napoleon's grand plan to extinguish the Tyrolian rebellion now that the signing of the Treaty of Schönbrunn (14 October) freed him to concentrate his attention and his troops on the subjugation of the troublesome region. According to his concept, a combined force under Eugene's overall command would push into the Tyrol from three directions: first, the three Bavarian divisions from the north to Innsbruck as related above; second, three Franco-Italian divisions under Baraguey d'Hilliers up the Drava valley from the east to Brixen; and third, Vial's division from the south to Bozen. In all, some 45,000 troops would be involved in the initial operations, with more to be added later. As outlined in a set of 'Instructions for the Viceroy of Italy' written on the same day that the peace treaty was signed, Eugene was to exercise a combination of force and diplomacy to achieve his goal: 'disarm the countryside, subdue it, identify the principal agitators, listen to the grievances of the inhabitants and take steps to satisfy them.'[57] A thoughtful Bavarian artillery officer later observed: 'one must simultaneously flood the entire land in order to conquer it.'[58] Napoleon intended to do just that.

Although Drouet had initiated his attacks in mid-October, Baraguey d'Hilliers did not get his offensive underway until the end of the month. Led by Severoli's division, the main body of the corps began moving up the Drava valley on the 29th, passing over into the Pustertal and reaching Bruneck on 4 November, careful to maintain a fairly secure line of communications back to Villach. Vial complemented this move by advancing to Bozen up the Adige from the south, while Peyri conducted a daring diversionary march over the mountains from Belluno through the Cordevole and Grödner valleys with 900 men to come down to the city from the north. As a consequence of these advances, by 5 November Eugene had completed the first critical step in conquering the Tyrol. The viceroy may have found 'this wretched war' thoroughly distasteful, but he had strong forces at Bozen in the south and Bruneck in the east, while Drouet in the north was moving towards the Brenner from Innsbruck and had captured Telfs on the Inn.[59] The next phase would be to smother the rebellion in its heart—the triangle between Brixen, Sterzing (Vipiteno) and Meran (Merano)—while subduing the upper Inn valley. Eugene's lines of communication, however, especially the valleys connecting Bruneck and Villach, remained vulnerable to new outbreaks of unrest. Guarding these and pacifying the remoter corners of the region north of Lienz and west of Trient would consume a significant percentage of his troops until the end of the year.

Eugene had every reason to describe the combat as 'wretched'. He faced extraordinarily rugged terrain, increasingly bad weather, and significant logistical challenges as winter settled over the Alps. Moreover, his army now included Neapolitans (1st Light Infantry, 1st Chasseurs) as well as French, Italians, Dalmatians, Istrians, and Bavarians—this polyglot composition compounding the countless difficulties inherent in trying to co-ordinate multiple formations across a vast, mountainous, and resource-poor region in winter. Above all, the enemy was a canny population that knew its homeland intimately and fought with the fierce courage of desperation to deal the encroaching Allies painful setbacks (such as the surrender of 1,000 French infantry on 22 November after being surrounded for three days near St Leonhard in Hofer's home valley). Nonetheless, Eugene made slow, inexorable progress as the insurgency dragged towards its conclusion. The French in Meran were greatly encouraged by the arrival of twenty Bavarian chevaulegers on 1 December. The Bavarian cavalrymen not only established another link, albeit tenuous, between 7th Corps and d'Hilliers, they also brought news of the near-complete submission of the Inn valley. Vial could report similar progress in the southern Tyrol, where his small division had encountered almost no resistance since entering the region west of Lake Garda in mid-November. From mid-December, as Eugene progressively strengthened his grip on the Brixen–Bruneck–Lienz area, the insurgency ceased to function in any co-ordinated fashion. Violent resistance continued to flare, but the various branches of the rebellion were isolated from one another as well as from external assistance. As early as mid-November, Bavaria was withdrawing select units from the Tyrol (especially logistically expensive ones that required horses), the Neapolitans departed for Spain in early December, and major reductions began in early January 1810. By the end of that month, the insurrection was finished and Baraguey d'Hilliers redeployed his corps for occupation duties. Starting in late February, even these remaining forces were gradually reduced as Napoleon re-established civil authority and redistributed the various districts of the Tyrol between Bavaria and the Kingdom of Italy.

The campaign in the Tyrol thus came to an end after burning on for six months longer than the war it had accompanied and for three months beyond the signature of the peace treaty. Reviewing its long and tortured course, several interesting points emerge from the welter of marches, counter-marches, ambushes, engagements, and pacifications.

At the higher levels of planning and execution, the fighting in the Tyrol illuminates Napoleon's strategic thinking. First, 1809 is a splendid example of his clear operational vision, his unswerving focus on the crucial objective of the campaign, in this case the destruction of the Austrian Main Army. The insurrection in the Tyrol, though it endangered his communications and threatened to inspire unrest in Germany, was fundamentally secondary. Napoleon repeatedly drew on the troops engaged with the tenacious rebels to bolster his Army of Germany in its struggle with the Habsburg regular forces. Early July, when he withdrew Deroy's Bavarians and even Rusca's tiny division, was the most obvious instance of this strategic focus, but it recurred throughout the war and endured through the peace negotiations as Napoleon attempted to intimidate his Habsburg opponents. Second, the war in the Tyrol is another example of Napoleon's ability to improvise, indeed his *reliance* on improvisation to cope with secondary perils. While his regulars and the best of his allied troops confronted their Austrian counterparts, he was consistently able to conjure up second-line formations to oppose the insurgency. Though the emperor clearly desired a quick eradication of the rebellion, his purposes were adequately served by containing it, and these units sufficed to accomplish the task. At the more tactical or operational levels, the suppression of the Tyrol highlights the enormous expenditure of troops, time, and attention required to overpower a determined though irregular foe in difficult terrain—even when that foe was outnumbered and isolated from any reasonable hope of external assistance. Some 45,000 Allied soldiers were committed for more than two months before the rebellion began to wane indisputably. Nevertheless, the ultimate French success shows that an insurgency could be quelled if there were enough resources, time, and commitment from the senior leadership, especially from Napoleon himself. The Tyrolian campaign of 1809 thus provides an instructive basis for comparison with the French experiences in places such as Spain and Calabria.

From the Tyrolian perspective, the war was a mixture of pride and bitterness. Pride at liberating itself from Bavarian rule more or less on its own and more than once; bitterness at the ultimate failure and especially at the sense of being abandoned by the House of Habsburg. Having extravagantly promised—against Johann's advice—never to conclude a peace that did not ensure the return of the Tyrol to the Habsburg crown, Franz agreed first to an armistice that evicted Austrian troops and then to a treaty that left the region once again at Napoleon's disposal. The Tyrolian insurrection with its colourful folk figures (especially Hofer), its picturesque mountains, and its impassioned struggle, quickly became a touchstone for most German nationalists. As a consequence, much important detail has been lost in subsequent mythologising and hagiography. It is well to remember, therefore, both the accomplishments and the weaknesses (Austro-Tyrolian frictions, intra-Tyrolian disputes) of the Tyrolian rebellion and its place as a significant, but secondary theatre of operations in the scope of the 1809 war.

TWO PATHS TO PEACE

In covering the Tyrolian episode to its conclusion, we have gone somewhat ahead of ourselves in the chronology of 1809. Although events in the Alpine insurgency provide a useful backdrop for the meandering path to peace, we must now return to mid-July and consider briefly how the two parties brought the war to a final close.

The first step on the Austrian side was inconsistent with national and dynastic interests: Franz relieved Charles of command. Peace talks were about to begin and the Austrian negotiators would need a powerful, capable military with a coherent strategy so that the threat of renewed conflict would appear genuine. Yet this was the moment that the Kaiser chose to follow the advice of those at court who had schemed against the Generalissimus for months. He thus removed at one stroke the man who was both the most prominent voice for peace and the only general who was capable of rebuilding the army to present any kind of strategic challenge to Napoleon. Charles took the initiative himself. Sensing the mood at court—the demeaning tone of the letters he received from his elder brother left no doubt—he submitted an offer of resignation on 23 July. It was accepted with unseemly haste and poor grace in a cold imperial note on the 29th. Liechtenstein was appointed in his place with Radetzky as his chief of staff, and Charles rode off to Teschen to commiserate with his adoptive uncle.[60] He would never again hold a major military command.

As this wretched drama played itself out, the Austrian armies, closely followed by the French, adjusted their positions to accord with the terms of the armistice. Disputes arose as the two sides interpreted the terms of the agreement, but these were resolved professionally if not amicably, and the repositioning proceeded with only a modicum of friction.

With the troops settling into new quarters, the Austrian court and the French emperor embarked upon a convoluted series of diplomatic manoeuvres to secure a final peace agreement. These followed two tracks. First, formal negotiations were conducted in Altenburg between Champagny,

Napoleon's foreign minister, and Metternich as Austria's representative.[61] For both sides, however, the Altenburg talks were a means to gain time while sounding out the opposition's demands. On the one hand, the Austrian negotiators were instructed to prolong the talks until at least the end of August so that the army could recover and reorganise in preparation for a renewal of hostilities.[62] On the other, before making a serious proposal to the Austrians, Napoleon was waiting to learn the views of his putative ally, the tsar, on the disposition of territory captured in Austrian Galicia and on the sensitive Polish issue.[63] With this background, it is hardly surprising that the Altenburg conference, which opened on 17 August, yielded few results. 'Neither side had truly decided on peace,' recalled Champagny.[64]

The second track proved more fruitful, though only slightly more beneficial to Austria's interests. This consisted of emissaries sent directly from the Austrian court at Totis (now Tata, south-east of Komorn) to Napoleon at Schönbrunn, bypassing Altenburg and bearing personal communications from the Kaiser to the emperor. The first of these personal missions was prompted by events in Altenburg, where Champagny presented a complete list of French terms to Metternich on 5 September. Napoleon had finally heard from the tsar and, assured of Russian non-interference, he levied demands on the Habsburgs that amounted to some 9 million 'souls' or about one-third of the monarchy's population, in addition to significant monetary compensation.[65] The Austrians were outraged and Kaiser Franz sent FML von Bubna to Vienna on the 8th with an indignant note protesting at the delays at Altenburg generally and the ultimatum specifically. Bubna returned to his sovereign on the 17th with what he thought was good news: Napoleon had eliminated some conditions entirely, reduced the territorial demand by nearly two-thirds, and raised the possibility of a Franco-Austrian alliance. The Habsburg court was temporarily in a bellicose mood, however, and for Franz this new ultimatum was no more acceptable than the first. Bubna, therefore, soon found himself on the road to Vienna again carrying a new letter of protest.

Napoleon, who by now completely dominated the unfortunate Bubna, refused to alter his conditions and the Austrian general rode back to Hungary on the 24th bearing French threats. The next day, after a long and stormy council session in Totis, Liechtenstein was granted plenipotentiary authority to negotiate a peace treaty and, accompanied by Bubna, set off for Vienna with vague instructions to preserve 'every possible portion of the monarchy'.[66] Liechtenstein relished his role as direct intermediary between the two sovereigns, but his mission spelled the end of the Altenburg talks, and Metternich, much vexed at being superseded, departed on 26 September.[67]

Champagny was recalled to Schönbrunn two days later.[68] Liechtenstein remained in Vienna for two weeks, attempting to procure milder peace terms. Completely outflanked by Napoleon and Champagny, however, he was reduced to accepting trivial territorial concessions and a 15 per cent reduction in the indemnity.[69] Overwhelmed by his task and French pressure, he signed a treaty at Napoleon's headquarters in the Schönbrunn Palace on 14 October. The prince saw clearly that his decision would be unwelcome in court, and when he alighted from his carriage upon his return, he told Metternich: 'I bring peace but also my head; the Kaiser will dispose of the one as well as the other as he wishes.'[70] Franz was indeed shocked by the terms of the treaty: among other indignities, Austria's population was reduced by more than 20 per cent (over 3.5 million subjects), it lost its access to the sea, its army was limited to 150,000 men, and it was burdened with an indemnity of 85 million gulden. Nonetheless, Franz had little choice but to ratify the treaty with minimal delay.

Napoleon did not wait for Franz's ratification. Glad to be shed of this unwanted conflict, he left Schönbrunn for Paris on 15 October, the day after the treaty was signed. There is a good likelihood that his speedy departure was accelerated by a troubling incident on 12 October. During a troop review, an 18-year-old German named Friedrich Staps attempted to stab the emperor with a knife. General Rapp intercepted the assailant and Napoleon interviewed him at length later in the day, but emerged baffled from the bizarre interrogation with this calm but single-minded young man. Staps was executed, but his attempt and demeanour clearly made a 'profound impression' on the emperor. Napoleon was already eager to leave and impatient with the sluggish pace of negotiations towards what he saw as an ineluctable outcome. The Staps incident thus seems to have heightened his annoyance and impelled him to reduce the indemnity demand to achieve a faster conclusion to the war. According to Champagny, Napoleon approached him immediately after the attempted assassination and said 'peace will be made … do everything possible to have the peace signed within twenty-four hours.'[71] Champagny achieved this in an all-night session with Liechtenstein on the night of 13/14 October. To Liechtenstein's horror, the French announced the peace that morning with a celebratory cannon salute, even though it had not yet been sanctioned by the Kaiser. While Napoleon's household prepared for an immediate return to France, therefore, the unfortunate prince rode south to report to his master.

Austria's inability to achieve a less painful peace accord can be attributed to a variety of factors, but central to its problem in the negotiations was its failure to reconcile national policy with military capability. Just as in the months prior to the conflict, so now at its ending, the war faction at court fulminated against France and demanded military action, but the military instrument of policy was incapable of meeting the demands placed upon it. The empire's shaky financial situation was another major consideration, but grave deficiencies on the military side—in leadership, planning, and physical capacity—were the fundamental weaknesses. Even late in September, there was no clear national strategy, no operations plan, and no true army commander. Indeed, the putative senior general, Liechtenstein, was entangled in the peace negotiations at the enemy's headquarters. Nominally, the Kaiser was the overall commander, having assumed direct, personal control in one of the letters that led to Charles's offer of resignation in July. In reality, this translated into command by committee with endless meetings, debates, and intrigues as each adviser, qualified or not, endeavoured to have his viewpoint heard or have his grand operations plan come into the Kaiser's hands. 'No centre, no unity, how can this work?' asked a frustrated Joseph in a letter to Johann on 22 August: 'Instead of acting, the Kaiser goes almost daily to watch the exercises of the Insurrection infantry.'[72] Even had a plan been developed and issued, the army was in a poor state of readiness. Logistical shortfalls hampered efforts to re-equip or even feed battered regiments, morale was questionable, sickness was soon rampant in poorly managed encampments (more than 50,000 out of 180,000 men were ill from 'Hungarian fever' in early September), and the majority of senior officers wanted a rapid end to hostilities.[73] Indeed, the desire for peace was widespread and growing. 'Unfortunately', wrote Franz's finance minister, 'one hardly comes upon one individual out of a hundred here who does not prefer the most shameful peace . . . to a resumption of hostilities.'[74]

The external picture was equally bleak. All the feeble and disjointed attempts at rebellion in Germany had failed, and there were no foreign allies to call upon for succour. Russia held itself aloof, Britain's Walcheren expedition had stagnated, and its forces were in retreat in Spain following the Battle of Talavera (28 July). For a time, Prussia represented the one potential bright spot on the horizon. Misinformed initial reports of the armistice led Prussian leaders to conclude that Napoleon, desperately overstretched, had requested the ceasefire and that Austria was in a powerful position. Operating under these false premises, the king agreed to send a new envoy, Oberst Karl Friedrich von dem Knesebeck, to Hungary with plenipotentiary authority. Knesebeck and key government ministers feared that Napoleon and Austria would reach some accommodation at Prussia's expense, Napoleon detaching portions of Austria but compensating the

Habsburgs by granting them Silesia, for example. Prussia was in such a state of anxiety that these outlandish suggestions seemed not only possible but likely. Knesebeck was therefore authorised to pledge active Prussian military support if Austria truly seemed committed to war and if he judged the Austrian army capable. Knesebeck and the Prussian ambassador gradually concluded that neither of these conditions applied. The Habsburg hierarchy was in chaos over the issue of war or peace and was, in any case, utterly incapable of using its large and courageous army to advantage. Furthermore, the truth about the armistice and Austria's precarious military situation soon became clear.[75] Opinion in Königsberg continued to sway with the winds of every rumour and report from the banks of the Danube, but as the weeks rolled by in Totis, it became apparent to all but the most obtuse Habsburg advisers that Prussia would not join the war. Austria remained alone.

Austria's problems were compounded by the continual vacillation of the Kaiser himself. Prone to adopting the opinions of the last person he saw and shifting continually from bold bellicosity to dull resignation, he was incapable of providing the leadership that his monarchy needed in this difficult hour. 'The Kaiser, who still relies on landings, uprisings, etc despite his experiences, secretly wants war,' and several of his closest confidants, including the Kaiserin Maria Ludovica, continued to 'shout for war', but as the days slipped away into autumn, the painful reality became unavoidable.[76] 'The initial object of this war is irrevocably gone,' wrote a passionate Austrian sympathiser to a British diplomat in mid-September, 'prolonging it for a few provinces more or less when all the military chances are evidently and probably against us seems to me to touch on vain delirium.'[77] It took three months to take effect, but pressure from his brothers, his ministers, and his generals finally convinced Franz to accede to peace.

Napoleon was well informed regarding the confusion and indecision at Franz's court, and Austrian threats of war rang hollow. Given these circumstances, the Habsburg Empire was fortunate that he did not choose to push his demands yet further.[78] It was, as Napoleon wrote to the tsar, 'the most advantageous peace they could hope to achieve'.[79]

At the same time, Napoleon could consider himself lucky that Austria was both incapable and ultimately unwilling to prolong the conflict. One of his key goals in this unwanted war was its quick ending. Although it is likely that French arms would have triumphed had fighting begun anew, a drawn-out conflict could have sparked further trouble in Germany, inspired Prussia to join Austria, and exacerbated Napoleon's relations with his truculent Russian 'ally'. Furthermore, war with the Habsburgs was expensive—the Austrian indemnity would not begin to repay the French treasury—and he was faced with domestic difficulties caused by Fouché, his scheming minister of police. An extension of the war was thus an outcome he wanted to avoid if at all possible, and a timely peace was more important than the imposition of more oppressive terms. He did not think it likely that Franz would elect to continue the war but he, unlike his adversary, was prepared for that eventuality. He worked with his accustomed energy to strengthen and train his forces as soon as the armistice was in place. More than 43,000 replacements and reinforcements were already en route as the armies moved to their armistice locations, and by 1 September he had more than 227,000 present for duty in Austria with a further 75,000 in Germany and the Tyrol.[80] 'Kaiser Franz should ask his generals if it is possible to move me from here,' he told Bubna on 20 September. 'You will lose in fourteen days and then still have to agree to my conditions.'[81] With 'calculated imprudence', a French strength report was allowed to fall into Bubna's hands to drive this point home.[82] Napoleon's threats to use force carried weight.

The emperor, however, was pleased not to have to resort to force, and he could look upon the Treaty of Schönbrunn as a satisfactory result, even if the 1809 campaign lacked the stunning victories that had crowned his operations in 1805, 1806, and 1807. While removing Austria as a military threat to his position in central Europe for the immediate future, he had expanded his foothold along the Adriatic, brought Austria into the Continental System, gained enough territory to repay his allies, and secured a large indemnity—albeit inadequate to cover expenses.[83] All this from a war he neither started nor desired. Moreover, there was a good chance of turning Austria into an ally as a counterbalance to wavering Russia, while an alliance of a different sort with an Austrian archduchess might soon bolster his dynasty's legitimacy and provide him with an heir to his throne. He also obtained Austrian recognition of Joseph as King of Spain and Murat as King of Naples. Most important, he had demonstrated anew his dominance of Europe's political-military affairs. In his mind, at the head of an empire founded on military triumph, he had to expunge any perception of defeat or partial victory. This point was so significant to him that he insisted throughout the negotiations that the terms imposed on Austria in 1809 be no less severe than those in the Treaty of Pressburg that ended the war of 1805: Europe must see Wagram as the equivalent of Austerlitz.

The outcome now determined, it is useful to glance back at the course of the conflict through the thematic lens of peace to place the battles and manoeuvres in context and to highlight several key points where war prosecution and war termination interacted. First, the fragile link between the military (Charles) and the political (the court, especially the war faction) on the Austrian side gradually eroded, largely because the two could not agree on how to end the war. The resulting uncertainty, recrimination, intrigue, and confusion weakened the Habsburg war effort and ultimately provided Charles with his opportunity to seek an armistice. Second, Charles's actions throughout the conflict—at least following the April defeats—were informed by his conviction that the monarchy's salvation lay in concluding the earliest possible peace. His increasing concern for how to end the war thus helps explain his decision not to retreat from Znaim and even sheds light on his inactivity after the success at Aspern. Third, the termination of the war was a crucial factor in Napoleon's behaviour as well. Confident that he would triumph in the end, he devoted much attention to the timing of the final act and the terms he planned to demand. Fourth, both men saw in the Znaim armistice an opportunity to achieve their central objectives: for Charles, an immediate peace with the army intact before the war faction dragged the country to ruin; for Napoleon, a peace that was both quick and adequately humiliating to Austria. Finally, the Austrian court's failure to develop a coherent political-military strategy for war termination crippled its efforts to attain a more satisfactory peace. Where Charles and Napoleon seized their fleeting opportunities, Kaiser Franz's advisers clung to illusions and consistently found themselves outmanoeuvred on the battlefield and at the peace table.

In one key respect, however, Napoleon's handling of the negotiations and subsequent distribution of spoils was flawed: his expansion of the Duchy of Warsaw at the expense of Austrian Galicia. Although Russia also received a piece of this dismembered Habsburg province, the duchy's share was four times larger and, to the complete alarm of St Petersburg, it began to take on the shape of the ancient Kingdom of Poland. The Russians were already angered and worried at not being invited to the peace talks, but the expansion of the duchy was perceived as a direct national security threat. By thus deciding to reward the Poles for their support and to chastise the tsar for his hesitancy, Napoleon damaged the Franco-Russian relationship badly, just as Alexander had undermined Napoleon's faith by his ambiguous actions and the blatant pro-Austrianism of his generals. It is hard to see what else Napoleon might have done, considering Russia's peculiar behaviour during the war, but the perceptions that both sides carried away from their 'alliance' in 1809 represented important steps on the road to 1812.

Epilogue

The history of wars is the eternal school of the soldier.

GM Karl von Stutterheim[1]

Following Stutterheim, one might contend that the history of wars is the eternal school of nations. This is not to suggest the promotion of war as the first resort in the solution of human problems, but to understand better a central and enduring component of the interaction among nation states and peoples. Enhanced understanding might contribute to the prevention or mitigation of conflict or lead states to embark upon this course of last resort only upon the direst need. Charles may seem to have been indulging in platitudes when he considered the question of war in the autumn of 1808: 'Of all decisions a monarch is in the position to take, that of war is the one that demands the most consideration; as the misfortunes for humankind and the state that arise therefrom, even in the most fortunate successes, are certain—the result is always uncertain.'[2] Nonetheless, if this was a platitude, it is one to keep well in the forefront of policy thinking. What, then, can we take away from this military-political history of the 1809 war between Napoleonic France and Habsburg Austria? In particular, what were the principal factors leading to its outcome, and where does the war fit in the larger history of the Napoleonic era?

OUTCOMES: LOST BEFORE IT BEGAN

'The campaign of 1809 was lost before it began,' wrote Josef Radetzky as he looked back over his long career of service to the Habsburg state. By the time he wrote his memoirs, Radetzky was a field marshal and one of the most respected military figures in Austrian history. During 1809, as we have seen, he commanded first a brigade, then a division, was promoted to

Feldmarschall-Leutnant in the process, and was appointed (against his wishes) as Liechtenstein's chief of staff when the prince was given command of the Hauptarmee. In that capacity, he drafted a memorandum for Liechtenstein highlighting what he saw as 'the discrepancy between the means and the ends' in Austria's war policy. The old marshal's glum judgement should not mask the very real opportunity open to the Habsburg forces to inflict a serious defeat on Napoleon in the opening phase of the 1809 war, but the odds were against Austria from the start and the opportunity was fleeting. Vienna's policies and misconceptions therefore greatly reduced a slim chance of success that already relied too much on hope and too little on honest assessment. Indeed, the abyss between the monarchy's political intentions and its military capacity set the stage for disaster in 1809 with vague political goals presenting a limited military instrument with an almost insoluble problem.

As discussed in Volume I of this study, the old empire entered into the war on the basis of false premises with a pre-determined outcome (ie, war) that coloured how key leaders interpreted external events such as Napoleon's eviction of the Bourbons in Spain. Having panicked themselves into apocalyptic angst, the war party first pushed the state to adopt urgent defensive measures and then, as Napoleon's intervention in Iberia stumbled in the summer of 1808, transformed the thrust of Habsburg policy into a preventive offensive war with vague, unconstrained aims.[3] Throughout the year leading up to the invasion of Bavaria (April 1808 to April 1809), and on into the months of the armistice, Austrian leaders who favoured war relied on wishful thinking and selected bits of intelligence from dubious sources to promote recourse to arms. Contradictory or inconvenient information was ignored. It was hardly surprising that enthusiastic German or Prussian patriots such as Oberst Goetzen in Silesia or the avowedly anti-French Crown Prince of Bavaria would claim that all Germany was waiting to rise up against Napoleon. Stadion and others, however, expended no effort to listen for other voices; they chose only the vocal few whose impressions bolstered a decision they had already determined to be the Danubian monarchy's only salvation. In other words, rather than analysing their situation and choosing an apposite course of action, they already had a course of action clearly in mind and simply picked up the best intelligence to justify it. Members of the war party thus overestimated favourable factors such as Germany's supposed readiness to rebel, while underestimating the enemy's military forces, leadership, and ability to react. The definition of war aims was equally woolly, almost capricious, leading to vast but vague aspirations of restoring every prince displaced by Napoleon and overturning twenty years of history, without giving any thought to how the interests of potential allies would be accommodated or how Napoleon would be brought to accept such a state of affairs. As a subsequent historian observed, Austria was simply launching itself 'into the void'.[4] Framed in Clausewitzian terms, Austria, at least the war party, did not understand the type of war into which it was about to enter as it faced 'the very God of War himself'. To paraphrase his words, they failed to consider the 'political probabilities' and were 'taking the first step without considering the last'.[5]

The problem with war aims was compounded by the deficiencies of the military instrument when measured against its adversary. This gap specifically led Radetzky to his stark assessment. The army was resilient and courageous, tenaciously standing on the defensive at Aspern, Wagram, Znaim, and many smaller engagements. It was hobbled, however, by a stultifyingly conservative strategic culture that was reflected in serious weaknesses in leadership, particularly at the senior levels, where initiative, energy, and a spirit of accountability were often in short supply. These deficiencies were especially relevant during the opening campaign and the controversy concerning post-Aspern options, but they dogged the army throughout the war. It remained a clumsy offensive tool, difficult to co-ordinate, generally slow on the march (though Hiller going to Vienna and Chasteler in the opening of the Tyrolian invasion demonstrated it could move quickly when properly motivated), and uncomfortable in broken, wooded terrain. Charles, as we have seen, recognised these failings in his corps commanders as they struggled to adapt to their new responsibilities (or simply shied away from them). The Generalissimus himself, however, exhibited many limitations. Although he was a courageous leader who could rally troops in crisis, his thinking remained rooted in the previous century; he was innately cautious, hoarding reserves to cover his retreat rather than employing them to strike a culminating blow, content with tactical, defensive successes, hesitant to take the risks necessary to achieve more substantive victories. 'He never cut himself loose from the ideas and rules of the *ancien regime*,' commented the nineteenth century German military historian, Hans Delbrück. 'He always looks behind him, just as his equestrian statue in Vienna shows him today with unconscious, cruel irony.' Peter Paret broadens the application of Delbrück's analysis: 'A service whose most influential reformer was a conservative contending against soundly entrenched reactionaries could never become fully reconciled to the techniques and to the energy and activity demanded by modern war.'[6]

A debilitating characteristic of many of the Austrian commanders—Charles included—was their tendency to expect the French to pause in the midst of a campaign or series of engagements, to think that Napoleon and his subordinates would halt their operations and allow the Habsburg commanders a few days or more to rest and reassemble the ponderous Austrian machine. Many, like Charles, were overawed by Napoleon from past experience, yet they often seemed surprised by French activity, as if the Habsburg Empire were facing Revolutionary and Napoleonic France for the first time since 1792. In part for these reasons, the defeat in Bavaria hung like an oppressive pall over the army after April: the stunning defeat, the sudden reversal of fortune with Napoleon's arrival, the dashing of many cherished hopes. The army recovered, but even the bright light of Aspern did not entirely dispel the shadow of Regensburg. Fear of the French cavalry was one manifestation of this, leading Austrian commanders to keep their men in masses and squares on the Marchfeld even though this formation was sure to increase casualties under fire of the more numerous French artillery.

These manifold weaknesses of their army, of course, were not unknown to Habsburg leaders at the time. Though ignored by Stadion and others before the war, they daunted Charles in those cases where he considered offensive operations, and generated frustration, even scorn, among senior Habsburg leaders. As Franz told Radetzky on appointing him as Liechtenstein's chief of staff: 'your character guarantees that you will not make stupid mistakes, and if you merely make ordinary mistakes, I am already used to that.'[7] The quality and reputation of the army also had international implications, as both the tsar and the Prussian king held the Habsburg forces in low esteem and were thus unwilling to risk their own armies and crowns as allies to the likely loser. For all of these woes, the Austrian army of 1809 was durable and dogged, earning Napoleon's respect; as he famously told a councillor who expressed scepticism regarding whether Austria should still be counted among Europe's great powers: 'it is obvious, monsieur, that you were not at Wagram.'[8]

The Austrians, of course, also suffered in having the French and their warrior-emperor as their adversaries. The quality of the French troops had declined since the superb armies of Austerlitz and Jena, but the degree of decline is often exaggerated. The number of conscripts in some battalions (especially Oudinot's two divisions) reduced overall capability, and the army as a whole was disadvantaged in the first two months from being hastily assembled as operations were underway and thrown into battle before it was properly integrated. It was, after all, 'l'Armée d'Allemagne', not 'la Grande Armée'. On the other hand, there was a solid core of veterans in most French and German regiments, officers and men were conscious of a long and potent tradition of victory, and leadership at all levels was generally good to excellent, above all Napoleon himself. The soldiers, conscripts as well as veterans, Germans and Italians as well as French, responded to this leadership, demonstrating phenomenal endurance on the march, courage on the battlefield, and skill in manoeuvring. These qualities were the norm, they were expected of anyone serving under French imperial banners. Germans and Italians strove to meet these expectations and their inclusion in the army by no means implied a necessary dilution of combat power. As usual, the keys to combat effectiveness were leadership and training; Napoleon and their own sovereigns provided the motivation. This would change in later years of the empire, especially after 1812, but in 1809 the desire to participate in Napoleon's campaigns, to emulate the French, to fight 'under the eyes of the emperor' was still vivid and real. This complex interaction of leader and led, this mutual trust and reliance, granted Napoleon tremendous flexibility. At the operational level, he could gather forces from enormous distances to concentrate on Lobau Island, and at Wagram two days later, he could shift forces around the tactical battlefield under ferocious enemy fire like a regimental commander on the exercise field.[9] Despite its decline, therefore, in 1809 the French army under Napoleon, with its various allied contingents, retained a significant tactical edge. And that tactical edge had strategic consequences, providing the margin of difference to give the French repeated victories from Abensberg to Znaim. Such victories offered Napoleon realistic options when it came to armistice and peace, and ultimately the quality of his army helped assure him a satisfactory treaty to conclude the war. His opponents were not so fortunate.

Napoleon, like his army, may not have been at the sharp edge of brilliance that had been so evident in earlier stages of his career. He disdained his foe (particularly before Aspern), and displayed a dangerous tendency to underestimate enemy numbers while inflating his own, always rounding friendly numbers up, as it were, while rounding the enemy's down. He occasionally seems to have allowed his legendary focus on detail to lapse, as on the evening of 5 July when he either gave vague orders or failed to oversee the proper execution of his instructions and as a result had to watch his men come roiling back down from the Russbach Heights in bloody disorder. At the same time, the vast scope of the war, with its many interrelated campaigns stretching from the Vistula to the Danube, the Elbe, the Scheldt, and the Po, was well within his strategic grasp, just as he managed more than 180,000 men on the burning plains of the broad Marchfeld in tactics. Nor should the thunder and smoke of the battlefield obscure the organisational, administrative, and technical effort involved in getting an army of 150,000 from Lobau Island onto the Marchfeld at night, in a storm, against opposition in a period of a little more than twelve hours. The Austrian hierarchy (keeping in mind it was a corporate entity, not an individual) could not compete with the French emperor on the strategic level; and Charles, for all of his intelligence, talent, and courage (in coping with the imperial court as well as fighting the French), could avoid calamitous defeat, but could not wrest victory from the combination of Napoleon, his generals, and his army. Nor could the aloof archduke inspire the kind of devotion and zeal routinely displayed by Napoleon's troops of all nations. Despite the erosion evident in parts of the French army, despite the nascent dulling of Napoleon's personal skills, despite Aspern, and despite the less-than-Austerlitz nature of the victory at Wagram, it still took Napoleon only three months to bring the campaign to a close with an undisputed success. The incipient signs of decline, therefore, were not apparent to most of his enemies in 1809. As far as the Austrians were concerned, the terrible French emperor and his impetuous army had once again demonstrated their mastery of the battlefield.

THIS LIMITLESS CONFIDENCE: PROBLEMS TO COME

Looking back from the present day, however, one may discern several factors that help explain why 1809 was Napoleon's last victorious war. In the first place, the decline of French forces and the improvements in his enemies, first evident in 1809, became more pronounced over time. Not just the Austrians (who may have reached their pinnacle of military prowess in 1809), but also the Russians and Prussians gradually enhanced their tactics, training, organisations, and leadership to compete with or exceed the French in almost all areas. In Buat's assessment, France in 1809 was 'touching the point' where it could provide 'men but not soldiers'.[10] This goes too far, but an insightful contemporary officer delivered some penetrating observations that help explicate the downward slide. 'The core of Napoleon's armies, above all the redoubtable class of officers up to the grade of regimental commander, were wiped out in Spain and on the Danube [1809],' wrote the Saxon Ferdinand von Funck. 'A dangerous, growing internal dissolution became ever more noticeable, especially in the Russian campaign.'[11] Furthermore, the relative deterioration of Napoleon's personal skills after 1809 coincided with his adversaries' adoption of cautious strategies to avoid confronting him directly, tackling instead his subordinates to whittle away the army's strength and morale. The war with Austria, especially the repulse at Aspern–Essling, was an important step on this road.[12] The French remained formidable opponents to the end of the empire, but their relative edge diminished conspicuously after 1809.

The second factor concerns logistics and regional infrastructure. With a system of war that relied upon rapid movement, Napoleon could operate with relative ease in Germany and Austria where food and fodder were plentiful and where road networks and rivers, the Danube above all, provided the means to transport supplies and move men with facility. There was also a language dimension to consider: many people in central Europe spoke French or German, languages that were common in the imperial armies (German light horse units were especially valued for this reason). The capacity to procure guides and collect intelligence to a large degree depended on an ability to communicate with the local populace. All of this functioned fairly well in Austria in 1809 (at no little cost in misery to the local people), but shifting the venue of war to other areas posed serious, possibly insurmountable, difficulties. Napoleon had some experience with these problems in Poland in 1807, but they would multiply many times in Russia in 1812, where food and fodder sources were limited, roads were few and poor, rivers ran in the wrong directions, and the ability to simply talk with local people was much restricted.

Third, Napoleon's style of command was to treat nothing as impossible, to expect his subordinates to do their uttermost to accomplish their missions and to reward them richly when they did. In most circumstances, this was a highly desirable quality and, in Napoleon's case, it suffused the army, non-French regiments as well as French, giving troops under his command an impetuosity, vigour, and determination that Prussians, Austrians, and others found enviable. There are, however, limits to this leadership approach and it requires the senior commander to maintain a realistic appreciation of what he is asking of his soldiers and what they might reasonably be expected to accomplish. When the overall commander loses this acuity of judgement, overconfidence sets in, men cannot meet expectations, and combinations fail to produce results. Telling Massena on the Ile du Moulin just before Wagram that 'nothing is impossible with these troops,' Napoleon, like Robert E. Lee before Gettysburg in 1863, seems to have fallen prey to this kind of thinking.[13] This had corrosive consequences, as feelingly expressed by Chef d'Escadron Montesquiou-Fezensac: 'This habit of attempting everything even with the most feeble resources, this spirit of seeing nothing as impossible, this limitless confidence in success that had always been one of our advantages, ended up being fatal to us.'[14]

A fourth feature of Napoleon's standard style of war would also fail when war moved to Germany again in 1813: his method of protecting his rear areas with a combination of second- or third-rate troops and deception. In 1809, as in previous years under the nimbus of victory, this system was adequate. In 1813, it would fail when challenged by increasingly aggressive enemies and restive, if not actively hostile, populations encouraged by the disaster in Russia. Given the exigencies of 1813 on the French side, it is difficult to see what other options Napoleon might have had, but insecurity in his rear areas that year, unlike 1809, would hamper his operations and present a serious drain on the physical and psychological resources of his subordinates and his armies.

PEERING INTO THE FUTURE

In a larger, political-strategic sense, Austria's war of 1809 and its subsequent defeat had several important consequences.[15] In the first place, Austria's obvious military preparations distracted Napoleon from Iberia, indeed, contributed to his leaving Spain in January 1809. Domestic political concerns were the other major—and perhaps preponderant—factor, but the danger of a new war with the Habsburgs clearly weighed heavily on the emperor's mind. The timing is important because Napoleon was then pursuing Lieutenant General Sir John Moore's struggling army through dreadful weather and over rugged terrain into northern Spain. Moore, at the cost of his life, saved his army to be evacuated by the Royal Navy at Corunna despite a lively engagement with Marshal Soult on 16 January. Napoleon was still in Spain at this time, but he had left the army in Soult's hands and was about to depart for Paris. Napoleon's personal involvement in the further pursuit of Moore would not have guaranteed the destruction of Moore's army by any means—the chances of war are far too numerous to justify such a conclusion—but the likelihood of a severe defeat for this valuable British army would certainly have been much higher. The consequences of losing what was in effect the lone major British field force could have been dramatic. London might have reconsidered its commitment to Iberia entirely; at a minimum the army would have been out of action for months longer than was the case in reality. Britain's options for the employment of land forces would thus have narrowed considerably and a true calamity might have led to broader policy changes. The impact on Spanish morale of an indisputable British defeat and subsequent diminution or delay of British commitment might have dampened enthusiasm for resistance when the French invasion was in its relatively early stages. This, in turn, could have opened better opportunities for the French to suppress the insurgency more effectively. Moreover, Napoleon would have had time to set affairs in Spain in better order before turning things over to the hapless Joseph (of course, nothing was predetermined; Napoleon could have failed just as badly in Spain under this scenario as he did in actuality). These speculative exercises have their inherent limits, but this excursion suffices to sketch some possible paths to the future that were cut off by the emperor's departure in mid-January 1809. He never returned.

Second, the results of the war had important repercussions for Austria's internal and external policies. The domestic aspects are beyond the scope of this study, but on the external front, the most fundamental shift was the Habsburg decision to ally themselves with Napoleon.[16] This change was a consequence of Metternich's thinking. Now foreign minister in place of the discredited Stadion, Metternich sought to preserve Austria's great power status against the dual threats of France and Russia by tying the empire to Europe's dominant figure, Napoleon, at least for the near term. The political deal was sealed by Napoleon's marriage to Franz's young daughter, Archduchess Marie Louise, in 1810 (the same woman who had expressed the hope in April 1809 that Napoleon 'would lose his head entirely').[17] Metternich proved remarkably staunch in hewing to his chosen course, maintaining the alliance until the summer of 1813 as Austria rebuilt itself and nourished its future potential.

In Austria's case, it is also worth highlighting something that did not happen: Napoleon did not dismember the empire or remove its crowned head. That is, he allowed the monarchy to survive as a unitary state under Franz I in 1809. This was not a certainty when the war came to a close. In his more vengeful or exasperated moments—especially before Aspern—Napoleon had considered replacing Franz with a more pliant Habsburg such as Ferdinand (then the Grand Duke of Würzburg in the Confederation of the Rhine), or of dividing the monarchy into several smaller kingdoms under a mixture of agreeable Habsburgs or other Napoleonic candidates. One Austrian patriot even suggested that for his own purposes, Napoleon *should* have dismantled the Austrian empire: 'Napoleon's fall did not come about because he went too far, rather because he did not go far enough.'[18] It bears reiterating that Napoleon did not do so partly for military reasons, but

330 ~ THUNDER ON THE DANUBE

primarily from political considerations. On the military front, his army was stretched and stressed after Wagram and a climactic victory, while likely, was not assured within a reasonable time frame (that is, within several days vice dragging the war on for weeks). More important for him, however, was the tsar. Although dissatisfied with Russia's actions in the war, Napoleon knew that Alexander adamantly opposed the destruction of the Austrian state or the eviction of its ruling monarch. The French emperor, with no interest in antagonising Russia at this point, thus imposed conditions on the defeated Habsburgs that were 'harsh but not catastrophic' and permitted the empire to retain a 'political existence', albeit one decidedly subordinate to France.[19]

Third, the war of 1809 brought a deep, perhaps irrevocable, change to Franco-Russian relations. Both sides had grown sceptical about the alliance by mid-1808, and the Erfurt conference only papered over increasing differences, but each was disappointed in its ally's behaviour during the war. Napoleon was disgusted by the sluggish performance of Alexander's armies, the refusal to co-operate with the Poles, the effort to grab Krakow in advance of Poniatowski, and the blatant pro-Austrian partisanship displayed by the Russian officer corps. All of this was true, but overlooked the fact that the Russian advance, despite its torpor and the appalling bonhomie with the Austrians, presented the Habsburgs with a dire threat to their rear that they could not counter. Already worried about the 100,000 Russians along the lower Danube on Austria's southern flank, the encroaching presence of 30,000–40,000 of the tsar's soldiers in Austrian Galicia—however friendly—could only generate anxiety in senior Habsburg circles. In part, Napoleon's ire may have stemmed more from the shattering of his own inflated illusions than from the tsar's faithlessness. That is, during 1808 and early 1809, the French emperor constructed an exaggerated conviction that Russian power would deter Austria from war. When that conviction proved unfounded, or at least less potent than he had imagined, his disappointment was all the more profound.

If the Russian role broadly worked more to Napoleon's advantage than to Austria's, it did not mean that the tsar deserved some great guerdon for this ambivalent involvement. Alexander, on the other hand, not only felt that the reward of Tarnopol and 400,000 new subjects was inadequate, much worse, he and his advisers were gravely alarmed at the expansion of the Duchy of Warsaw. The Polish issue, thrown into sharp relief by the war, compounded the other frictions and dissatisfactions of 1809 against a backdrop of pre-existing mistrust. If not immediately evident to the outside world, the events and impressions created by the 1809 experience thus shifted the Franco-Russian relationship from alliance to 'mutual defiance', paving the way to 1812.[20]

Finally, 1809 helped the major European powers recognise that Napoleon's containment or demise could only be effected by the creation of a sufficiently competent and cohesive coalition. 'The lack of unity in the operations of the powers aligned against France is the principal secret of Napoleon's fortune,' wrote Friedrich Wilhelm III in August that year.[21] Many princes, generals, and ministers, Metternich among them, would have agreed. Napoleon himself told Savary in June 1809 that 'they have all invited one another to my tomb, but they do not dare to meet there.'[22] Recognition of this reality did not mean it was easy to implement. Particularist national and dynastic ambitions, fear of Napoleon, and abiding suspicion of one another meant that only the French cataclysm in Russia would provide an opportunity for the other powers to combine. Even then, unity remained 'more apparent than real' in 1813 and bitter infighting drove fissures in coalition councils through 1814 and 1815.[23] Nonetheless, 1809 was a critical stage in this long, difficult process. Austria in particular, guided by Metternich, seems to have learned this lesson, recognising most importantly that a coalition implied acceptance of limits on Austria's own objectives and actions. Stadion had proposed unconstrained war aims in advance of the 1809 conflict and a vague end-state in which Austria would somehow restore subservient friends to their previous dispensations and distribute favours to those who chose to be its allies. From 1809 onwards, the new Metternich ministry would adopt a more flexible approach, eschewing the *Götterdämmerung* histrionics of its predecessor and accepting compromise as a key element of policies aimed at not only preserving the particularist interests of the Habsburg dynasty and Austrian state (those were certainly not neglected), but of also crafting a new European political system of surprising durability and stability.

All of this, of course, lay in the future. None of it was inevitable, and none of it was obvious as 1809 came to a close. The conclusion of the war opened new opportunities for Napoleon (return to Spain, enhanced legitimacy for his nascent dynasty, a revised European political order) and for the other powers (accommodation, alliance, passive resistance, active combat). The road to Moscow and Leipzig was only one of many paths to the future. All would now depend on how the various monarchs and cabinets chose to exploit or ignore these opportunities. In the end, the other powers would prove willing to change; the Emperor of the French would not.

Appendices

General: orders of battle are always a puzzle and all of the following are necessarily estimated compilations, assembled from official records, regimental histories, personal accounts, and, where necessary, reliable secondary sources. Orders of battle in 1809's ancillary theatres are particularly challenging. Organisational arrangements shifted constantly, new, often ephemeral, units were formed, and details were seldom recorded with the precision we in the twenty-first century might like. Information for the Army of Inner Austria, for example, becomes very murky as its cohesion and organisation weathered defeat and retreat in June. Fractured by combat, its constituent parts seem to scatter across the map like loose marbles. Additional obscurity is generated by the Austrian penchant for multitudinous detachments, the shattering of standard subordination, and the creation of ad hoc 'combined' battalions from disparate second-line troops (depot divisions, remnants of Landwehr, and the like). Even Wagram is difficult. The best Austrian source is a morning report ('Früh-Rapport') of 27 June, as the 4 July report is tantalisingly, but understandably, incomplete. On the French side, the situation is complicated by the arrival of important additional forces right up to the last moment; in other words, after completion of the routine 1 July corps situation reports. The orders of battle here cannot address every detail (absorbing though that might prove), but by providing snapshots at different points in time, it is hoped that the reader will be able to follow these shifting sands to a fair standard of accuracy within reasonable page limits.

Notes:
   a Estimation method: in many cases one has a figure for an entire unit (a regiment, for example), but no precise figures for detachments made from the larger unit.

In these situations I have used the simple expedient of dividing the entire unit's strength to estimate the strength of the detachment. If official records, for instance give a regiment 2,100 men but one battalion of three is detached, the following orders of battle will list 1,400 for the regiment and 700 detached. A 'c.' (*circa*) indicates that this is my estimate.

b   Note that in many cases, the strength figures are the 'best available', but these may not account for all losses or reinforcements. The strengths for Johann's Army of Inner Austria on its march to Wagram, for instance, are based on the 15–30 June 'Früh-Rapport' (the best available source located for this study), but do not account for additions or deletions between the end of June and 5 July. I have tried to provide the requisite detail in notes so that readers may make their own judgements and adjustments.

c   'Baons' = battalions; 'sqdns' = squadrons.

d   See Volumes I and II for other conventions followed in orders of battle.

APPENDIX I

Orders of Battle for the Campaign in Poland: April–June 1809

ORGANISATIONS AT START OF HOSTILITIES

AUSTRIA, 14 APRIL 1809

GdK Erzherzog Ferdinand[1]

	baons /sqdns	present under arms
VII Corps Main Body: GdK Erzherzog Ferdinand		
7th Pioneer Division (two companies)	–	340
Advance guard: GM von Mohr		
Vukassovich Infantry No. 48	3	2,176
I/*1st Siebenbürger-Wallach* Grenz Infantry No. 16	1	1,125
I/*2nd Siebenbürger-Wallach* Grenz Infantry No. 17	1	1,184
Kaiser Hussars No. 1	6	c.780
1 x cavalry battery		
1 x 3-pounder brigade battery		
Division: FML von Mondet		
Brigade: GM von Pflacher		
Davidovich Infantry No. 34	3	2,466
Weidenfeld Infantry No. 37	3	2,072
1 x 6-pounder brigade battery		
Brigade: GM von Trautenberg		
Strauch Infantry No. 24	3	3,293
Baillet Infantry No. 63	3	2,820
1 x 6-pounder brigade battery		

Brigade: GM von Civilart

De Ligne Infantry No. 30	3	3,176
Kottulinsky Infantry No. 41	3	3,382

1 x 6-pounder brigade battery

Division: FML von Schauroth

Brigade: GM von Speth

Somariva Cuirassiers No. 5	6	750
Lothringen Cuirassiers No. 7	6	764

1 x cavalry battery

Brigade: GM von Geringer

Palatinal Hussars No. 12	8	1,023
Artillery:	–	1,090

    2 x 12-pounder position batteries

    2 x 6-pounder position batteries

Infantry: 21,694

Cavalry: 3,317

Guns: 66 (one battery and two howitzers detached to Branowaczky)

Detached

For Czestochowa: GM von Branowaczky

I/*1st Szekler* Grenz Infantry No. 14	1	1,173
I/*2nd Szekler* Grenz Infantry No. 15	1	1,177
Kaiser Chevaulegers No. 1	8	1,042

1 x 3-pounder brigade battery and two howitzers (10 pieces total)

At Okuniew: Maj. von Hoditz

Kaiser Hussars No. 1	2	c.260

At Krakow: Oberst Rakovsky

Szekler Hussars No. 11	8	1,134

Notes:

a Some sources mistakenly give Ferdinand a total of ninety-four guns on 14 April. He certainly had seventy-six as shown here (sixty-six plus ten), however, the remaining eighteen pieces arrived some time after the opening of hostilities: first one 12-pounder position battery and later two cavalry batteries.

b Movements of the *Szekler* Hussars are unclear. The regiment was not with the corps when the war opened and the last elements (one division) did not reach Krakow until 16 April. Thereafter at least three of the four divisions departed for Nowe Miasto and Warsaw.

Sedentary Forces in East Galicia: FML Fürst Hohenlohe-Ingelfingen[2]

FML Graft Merveldt

Czernowitz: 1st Garrison Battalion	1

Brigade: GM von Bicking (Lemberg)

Depot Division/*Strauch* Infantry No. 24	2 companies
Depot Division/*de Ligne* Infantry No. 30	2 companies

Depot Division/*Kottulinsky* Infantry No. 41	2 companies	
Depot Division/*Chasteler* Infantry No. 46	2 companies	
Depot Division/*Beaulieu* Infantry No. 58	2 companies	
Depot Division/*Baillet* Infantry No. 63	2 companies	
Jaroslaw: Depot Division/*Czartoryski* Infantry No. 9	2 companies*	
Sambor: Depot Division/*Bellegarde* Infantry No. 44	2 companies*	
Dukla: 2nd Depot Coy/*Lindenau* Infantry No. 29	1 company	
Zolkiew: Reserve Squadron/*Palatinal* Hussars No. 12	1	
Brigade: GM von Starczynski (Krakow)		
2nd Depot Company/*EH Ludwig* Infantry No. 8	1 company	
2nd Depot Company/*A. Mittrowsky* Infantry No. 10	1 company	
2nd Depot Company/*Zach* Infantry No. 15	1 company	
2nd Depot Company/*J. Mittrowsky* Infantry No. 40	1 company	
2nd Depot Company/*W. Colloredo* Infantry No. 56	1 company	
2nd Depot Company/*J. Colloredo* Infantry No. 57	1 company	
Tarnow: Depot Company/*Manfredini* Infantry No. 12	1 company	
Reserve Squadron/*Kaiser* Chevaulegers No. 1	1	
Brigade: GM von Grosser (Tarnow)		
Zamosc: Depot Division/*Würzburg* Infantry No. 23	2 companies**	
Zamosc: Depot Division/*Reuss-Greitz* Infantry No. 55	2 companies**	
Lublin: Depot Division/*Württemberg* Infantry No. 38	2 companies**	
Brigade: FML von Eggermann (Sandomierz)		
Depot Division/*Stain* Infantry No. 50	2 companies	513
2nd Depot Company/*Schröder* Infantry No. 7	1 company	126
2nd Depot Company/*Koburg* Infantry No. 22	1 company	?
2nd Depot Company/*Kaiser* Infantry No. 1	1 company	?
Rzeszow: Depot Company/*Kaunitz* Infantry No. 20	1 company	263

Approximate totals
Infantry: 7,480 (not including 1st Garrison)[3]
Cavalry: 125
Note: Ten Landwehr battalions en route to garrison Krakow (7,000–8,000 not included above).
* These divisions were captured at Jaroslaw on 24 May.[4]
** These divisions were captured at Zamosc or environs.

DUCHY OF WARSAW, 6 APRIL 1809[5]

Prince Poniatowski

	baons /sqdns	present under arms
Infantry[6]		
1st Infantry	2*	1,642
2nd Infantry	2*	1,742

3rd Infantry	2*	1,927
III/5th Infantry (Czestochowa garrison)	I	585
6th Infantry	2*	1,346
8th Infantry	2*	1,500
12th Infantry	2*	1,102
Cavalry[7]		
1st Chasseurs	3	730
2nd Uhlans	3	800
3rd Uhlans	3	760
5th Chasseurs	3	505
6th Uhlans	3	709
Artillery and Train	–	930
Saxon Detachment: GM von Dyherrn		
Grenadier Battalion *von Einsiedel*	I	501
Grenadier Detachment *von Rechten*	2 companies	257
I/*von Oebschelwitz* Infantry	I	503
Hussar Regiment	2	181
Artillery	–	451

Infantry: 10,520 (9,259 Polish and 1,261 Saxon)
Cavalry: 3,685 (3,504 Polish and 181 Saxon)
Guns: 41 (27 Polish and 14 Saxon)

Notes:

a   Third battalions were being formed for all infantry regiments (indicated by asterisk*).

b   Other Polish units distributed as follows: 5th Infantry (Küstrin, two battalions), 10th Infantry (two battalions in Danzig, one at Stettin), 11th Infantry (Danzig), 4th Chasseurs (Stettin, Küstrin, Glogau, Stralsund).

c   Substantial parts of the Polish cavalry regiments detached: 148 (1st), 49 (2nd), 276 (3rd), 193 (5th), 305 (6th).

d   The Czestochowa garrison also included detachments of 3rd Uhlans and artillery totalling some 215 men.

e   The *Einsiedel* Grenadier Battalion was composed of the grenadier companies of the *König* and *Dyherrn* Infantry Regiments. The *Rechten* detachment consisted of that regiment's two grenadier companies.

GROCHOW, 25–6 APRIL 1809

AUSTRIA

GM von Mohr[8]

	baons /sqdns	present under arms
Advance guard:		
Vukassovich Infantry No. 48	3	c.1,900
I/1st *Wallach* Grenz Infantry No. 16	1	c.1,100
I/2nd *Wallach* Grenz Infantry No. 17	1	c.1,100
Kaiser Hussars No. 1 (includes Maj. von Hoditz)	6	c.780
1 x cavalry battery		
1 x 3-pounder brigade battery		

DUCHY OF WARSAW

Prince Poniatowski[9]

	baons /sqdns	present under arms
1st Column: GB Sokolnicki		
12th Infantry	2	c.1,600
two companies/2nd Infantry	2 companies	c 250
2nd Uhlans	3	c.750
2 x horse artillery pieces		
2nd Column: GB Kamienski		
1st Chasseurs	3	c.750
sqdn/3rd Uhlans	1	c.250
3rd Column: Col. Sierawski		
II/6th Infantry	1	c.800
3rd Uhlans	2	c.500
2 x horse artillery pieces		
Reserve: GD Dabrowski		
5th Chasseurs	3	c.750
6th Uhlans	3	c.750

Notes:

a A company from the Praga garrison apparently joined Sokolnicki in the afternoon.

b An infantry company crossed the Vistula north of Warsaw as a belated diversion on the night of 25/26 April.

THORN, SANDOMIERZ, AND ZAMOSC,
17/18 MAY 1809

AUSTRIA[10]

	baons /sqdns	present under arms
Opposite Thorn: GM von Mohr		
Vukassovich Infantry No. 48	3	
I/*2nd Siebenbürger-Wallach* Grenz Infantry No. 17	1	
Kaiser Chevaulegers No. 1	5	
Kottulinsky Infantry No. 41[11]	2	
1 x cavalry battery		
1 x position battery		
Gabin: EH Ferdinand		
Brigade: GM von Pflacher		
Davidovich Infantry No. 34	3	
Weidenfeld Infantry No. 37	3	
III/*Kottulinsky* Infantry No. 41	1	
1 x 6-pounder brigade battery		
Brigade: GM von Civilart		
De Ligne Infantry No. 30	3	
1 x 6-pounder brigade battery		
Brigade: GM von Speth		
Somariva Cuirassiers No. 5	6	
1 x cavalry battery		
Brigade: GM von Geringer		
Palatinal Hussars No. 12[12]	7	
En route to Sandomierz: FML von Schauroth[13]		
Brigade: GM von Trautenberg		
Strauch Infantry No. 24	3	
III/*Baillet* Infantry No. 63	4 companies	
1 x 6-pounder brigade battery		
I/*1st Szekler* Grenz Infantry No. 14	1	
Lothringen Cuirassiers No. 7	6	
Kaiser Hussars No. 1	6	
Warsaw		
Szekler Hussars No. 11	8	
Patrolling west of Warsaw: Gatterburg		
Kaiser Hussars No. 1	2	
Gora (joined Schauroth)		
Palatinal Hussars No. 12	1	
Nowe Miasto		
III/*Baillet* Infantry No. 63	2 companies	

Czestochowa: Klebelsberg
Kaiser Chevaulegers No. 1	½-sqdn	
I/*2nd Szekler* Grenz Infantry No. 15	2 companies	

En route to Krakow: Gramont
Kaiser Chevaulegers No. 1	2½ sqdns	
I/*2nd Szekler* Grenz Infantry No. 15	4 companies	

Sandomierz: FML von Eggermann
I/*1st Wallach* Grenz Infantry No. 16	3 companies	*c.*550
Kaiser Hussars No. 1	platoon	30
Depot Division/*Stain* Infantry No. 50	2 companies	513
2nd Depot Company/*Kaiser* Infantry No. 1	1 company	?
2nd Depot Company/*Schröder* Infantry No. 7	1 company	126
2nd Depot Company/*Kaunitz* Infantry No. 20	1 company	263
2nd Depot Company/*Koburg* Infantry No. 22	1 company	?

Zamosc: Oberst Pulszky
I/*1st Wallach* Grenz Infantry No. 16	3 companies	567
Kaiser Hussars No. 1	platoon	*c.*30
Depot Division/*Würzburg* Infantry No. 23	2 companies	336
Depot Division/*Württemberg* Infantry No. 38	2 companies	1,283
Depot Division/*Reuss-Greitz* Infantry No. 55[14]	2 companies	*c.*1,000

Notes:
a Hoditz had rejoined the main army.
b Artillery distribution is unclear.

DUCHY OF WARSAW

Prince Poniatowski

	baons /sqdns	present under arms
Ulanow: GD Poniatowski		
1st Infantry	2	*c.*1,600
3rd Infantry (minus voltigeurs)	2	*c.*1,400
8th Infantry (minus voltigeurs)	2	*c.*1,400
grenadiers/III/6th Infantry	1 company	*c.*80
1st Chasseurs	3	*c.*750
3rd Uhlans	2	*c.*500
Approximately seventeen guns		
Sandomierz: GB Sokolnicki		
GB Sokolnicki (left bank):		
I/6th Infantry	1	*c.*800
12th Infantry	2	*c.*1,600
sqdn/6th Uhlans	1	*c.*250
two guns		

GB Rozniecki (right bank):

II/6th Infantry	1	c.800
voltigeurs/8th Infantry	2 companies	c.200
2nd Uhlans	3	c.750
5th Chasseurs	3	c.750
two guns		

Zamosc:

GB Kamienski (arrived 15 May)

sqdn/3rd Uhlans	1	c.250
6th Uhlans	2	c.500

GB Pelletier (arrived 18 May)

2nd Infantry	2	c.1,600
voltigeurs/3rd Infantry	2 companies	c.200
voltigeurs/III/6th Infantry	1 company	c.80
two guns, four howitzers		

Thorn: GB Woyczynski

III/10th Infantry	1	1,103
III/11th Infantry	1	c.700
III/12th Infantry (and depot)	1	1,455
Artillery	–	c.100

Notes:

a All strengths approximate (losses in the first two battalions of 6th Polish Infantry from the bridgehead assault were made up by drafts III/6 before the latter battalion retired to Modlin to reorganise).

b Presence of Grenadiers/III/6 is author's assumption.

c Thorn figures include deductions for losses on 15 May (III/11th and artillery).

FORCE DISPOSITIONS, 5 JUNE 1809

AUSTRIA[15]

	baons /sqdns	present under arms
North of the Pilica: FML Mondet		
Brigade: GM von Mohr		
Vukassovich Infantry No. 48	3	2,927
I/*2nd Siebenbürger-Wallach* Grenz Infantry No. 17	1	994
Kaiser Chevaulegers No. 1	5	563[16]
Kaiser Hussars No. 1 (Gatterburg)	2	c.200
Szekler Hussars No. 11	1	c.140
Palatinal Hussars No. 12	7	c.840
1 x cavalry battery		

Brigade: GM von Civilart		
De Ligne Infantry No. 30	3	3,256
Kottulinsky Infantry No. 41[17]	2	c.2,100
III/*Baillet* Infantry No. 63	2 companies	c.340
1 x 6-pounder brigade battery		
1 x cavalry battery		
3 x position batteries		
'Main body' en route to Sandomierz: GM von Speth (pending Ferdinand's return)		
Brigade: GM von Pflacher		
Davidovich Infantry No. 34	3	3,036
Weidenfeld Infantry No. 37	3	2,803
III/*Kottulinsky* Infantry No. 41	1	c.600
1 x 6-pounder brigade battery		
Brigade: GM von Speth		
Somariva Cuirassiers No. 5	6	689
1 x cavalry battery		
Brigade: GM von Geringer		
Szekler Hussars No. 11	7	c.980
3-pounder half-battery		
Artillery Reserve: 2 x 12-pounder position batteries		
Crossing Vistula at Opatwiec: FML von Schauroth		
Brigade: GM von Trautenberg		
Strauch Infantry No. 24	3	2,915
III/*Baillet* Infantry No. 63	4 companies	c.680
I/*1st Wallach* Grenz Infantry No. 16	3 companies	370
2nd West Galician Volunteers[18]	4 companies	c.380
1 x 6-pounder brigade battery		
I/*1st Szekler* Grenz Infantry No. 14	1	1,141
Lothringen Cuirassiers No. 7	6	769
Kaiser Hussars No. 1	6	654
Palatinal Hussars No. 12 (Szilly)	1	c.120
Field force (Krakow): FML von Eggermann		
Kaiser Chevaulegers No. 1	2½ sqdns	c.170
Reserve Squadron/*Ferdinand* Hussars No. 3	1	?
I/*2nd Szekler* Grenz Infantry No. 15	4 companies	c.760
2nd Depot Company/*Kaiser* Infantry No. 1	1 company	40
2nd Depot Company/*Schröder* Infantry No. 7	1 company	48
2nd Depot Company/*Manfredini* Infantry No. 12	1 company	185
2nd Depot Company/*Kaunitz* Infantry No. 20	1 company	140
2nd Depot Company/*Koburg* Infantry No. 22	1 company	115
Depot Division/*Stain* Infantry No. 50	2 companies	137
GM von Starczynski		
1st Prerau Landwehr	1	863
4th Olmütz Landwehr	1	897
5th Olmütz Landwehr	1	699

Krakow garrison:

Kaiser Chevaulegers No. 1	½-sqdn	*c*.60
Reserve Squadron/*Kaiser* Chevaulegers No. 1	1	?
I/*2nd Szekler* Grenz Infantry No. 15	2 companies	*c*.380
Depot/5th Jägers	–	?
Depot/6th Jägers	–	?
1st Troppau Landwehr	1	829
2nd Prerau Landwehr	1	970
2nd Teschen Landwehr	1	*c*.870
2nd Olmütz Landwehr	1	823
2nd Troppau Landwehr	1	?
1st Teschen Landwehr	1	?
2nd Hradisch Landwehr	1	?

East Galicia: FML Hohenlohe[19]

Brigade: GM von Grosser (Zydaczow)

1st Garrison Battalion	2 companies
Depot Division/*Strauch* Infantry No. 24	2 companies
Depot Division/*de Ligne* Infantry No. 30	2 companies
Depot Division/*Kottulinsky* Infantry No. 41	2 companies
Depot Division/*Chasteler* Infantry No. 46	2 companies
Depot Division/*Beaulieu* Infantry No. 58	2 companies
Depot Division/*Baillet* Infantry No. 63	2 companies
Uhlans	1

Brigade: GM von Kessler (Stanislau)

1st East Galician Volunteers	2 companies
1st Garrison Battalion	1 company
Grenz-Cordon troops	3 companies
Arnauts and Jägers	3 companies
Reserve Sqdn/*Palatinal* Hussars and Bukovina Volunteers	1

Brigade: GM von Bicking (Zaleszczyki)

Grenz-Cordon troops	6 companies
Arnauts and Jägers	3 companies
Reserve Sqdn/*Palatinal* Hussars and Bukovina Volunteers	4

Dukla Pass: 2nd Depot Coy/*Lindenau* Infantry No. 29 — 1 company

Insurrection troops on Hungarian border: GM Hertelendy

Zemplin Insurrection Hussars	4½	641
Abaujvar Infantry No. 19	1	989

Notes:

a   FML Merveldt assumed command of the field forces in East Galicia in early July.

b   Artillery distribution is unclear.

DUCHY OF WARSAW[20]

Prince Poniatowski

	baons /sqdns	present under arms
South of Sandomierz: GD Poniatowski		
1st Infantry	2	
2nd Infantry	1	
8th Infantry	2	
1st Chasseurs	2	
2nd Uhlans	3	
3rd Uhlans	2	
5th Chasseurs	3	
6th Uhlans	2	
Approximately 17 guns		
Sandomierz: GB Sokolnicki		
3rd Infantry	2	
6th Infantry	2	
12th Infantry	2	
sqdn/1st Chasseurs	1	
sqdn/6th Uhlans	1	
Zamosc: battalion/2nd Infantry	1	
Lemberg: sqdn/3rd Uhlans (Chef d'Escadron Strzyzowski)	1	
Forming in Galicia[21]		
Three new 'Franco-Galician' infantry regiments (1st, 5th, 6th)		
Five new 'Franco-Galician' cavalry regiments (2nd, 4th, 5th, 6th, 7th)		
GD Dabrowski		
III/10th Infantry	1	
III/11th Infantry	1	
1st (New) Infantry (3rd Franco-Galician)	2	
2nd (New) Infantry (4th Franco-Galician)	2	
Posen Volunteer Chasseurs	1	
Kalisz Volunteer Chasseurs	1	
1st (New) Cavalry (3rd Franco-Galician Uhlans)	3	
2nd (New) Cavalry (2nd Franco-Galician Hussars)	3	
Artillery: 8 guns		
GB Hauke (*c.*1,600)		
III/12th Infantry	1	
Plock Volunteer Chasseurs	1	
GD Zajaczek		
III/1st Infantry	1	
III/2nd Infantry	1	
III/3rd Infantry	1	
III/6th Infantry	2 companies	

III/8th Infantry	1
Lomza Volunteer Chasseurs	1
1st (New) Cavalry (1st Franco-Galician Uhlans)	3
Artillery: 12 guns	

Notes:

a 'New' infantry and cavalry regiments are those recently formed, but designations of these units had not been settled, so the two '1st New Cavalry Regiments' are not related. Their later titles are shown in parentheses.

b Dabrowski had approximately 7,200 infantry and 1,600 cavalry, not counting Hauke's 1,400.

c Four companies of III/6 were en route to the San.

d Zajaczek had approximately 3,740 infantry and 800 cavalry. Additionally, a new infantry regiment (later 2nd Franco-Galician) was forming in the fortress triangle in Zajaczek's rear.

Russian Forces Available for Poland

General of Infantry Prince Sergey Golitsyn[22]

The following troops entered Galicia in June

	baons /sqdns	present under arms
9th Infantry Division: Lt. Gen. Prince Suvorov		
Brigade: Maj. Gen. Karl Sievers		
10th Jäger Regiment	2	
Sysarev's Cossack Regiment	–	
Novorossiiskii (New Russia) Dragoons	4	
Glukhovskii (Glukhov) Cuirassiers	3	
Brigade: Maj. Gen. Aleksey Sherbatov		
Astrakhanskii (Astrakhan) Grenadier Regiment	2	
Belostokskii (Belostok) Musketeer Regiment	2	
Ryazanskii (Ryazan) Musketeer Regiment	2	
Mariupolskii (Mariupol) Hussars	2	
Artillery: 1 x position battery and 1 x horse artillery battery		
10th Infantry Division: Lt. Gen. Fedor von Löwis		
Brigade: Maj. Gen. Illarion Vasilchikov		
8th Jäger Regiment	2	
Bryanskii (Bryansk) Musketeer Regiment	2	
Akhtyrskii (Akhtyrsk) Hussars	4	
Denisov's Cossack Regiment	–	
1 x horse artillery battery		
Brigade: Maj. Gen. Karl de Lambert		
Kievskii (Kiev) Grenadier Regiment	2	
Yaroslavskii (Yaroslav) Musketeer Regiment	2	
Kurskii (Kursk) Musketeer Regiment	2	

Kharkovskii (Kharkov) Dragoon Regiment	4

18th Infantry Division: Lt. Gen. Andrey Gorchakov (later replaced by Lt. Gen. Vasily Dolgorukov)[23]

Brigade: Maj. Gen. N. Davydov	
32nd Jäger Regiment	2
Yakutskii (Yakutsk) Musketeer Regiment	2
Kostromskoi (Kostroma) Musketeer Regiment	2
Ilovaiski's Cossack Regiment	–
Kaiserov's Cossack Regiment	–
Arzamasskii (Arzamass) Dragoons	2
Serpukhovskii (Serpukhov) Dragoons	2
1 x horse artillery battery	
Brigade: Maj. Gen. I. Khrushchov	
Tambovskii (Tambov) Musketeer Regiment	2
Dneprovskii (Dneprov) Musketeer Regiment	2
Elizavetgradskii (Elisabethgrad) Hussars	4
Aleksandriiskii (Alexandria) Hussars	4
1 x position battery and 1 x horse artillery battery	

1st Cavalry Corps: Lt. Gen. Peter Müller-Zakomelsky

Brigade: Maj. Gen. M. Balk	
Kazanskii (Kazan) Dragoons	4
Rizhskii (Riga) Dragoons	4
1 x horse artillery battery	
Brigade: Maj. Gen. P. Kakhovsky	
Tatar Uhlans Regiment	4
Polish Uhlans	4
Lithuanian Uhlans	4

2nd Cavalry Corps: Lt. Gen. Fedor Korf

Brigade: Maj. Gen. N. Kretov	
Pskov Dragoons	4
Kiev Dragoons	4
1 x horse artillery battery	
Brigade: Maj. Gen. I. Duka	
Military Order Cuirassiers	4
Yekaterinoslavskii (Yekaterinoslavl) Cuirassiers	4
Her Imperial Majesty's Leib-Cuirassier Regiment	4

Total strength: 37,500 (estimate)

Also available to Golitsyn[24]

24th Infantry Division: Lt. Gen. Dmitri Dokhturov	
Brigade: Maj. Gen. A. Laskin	
28th Jäger Regiment	2
Krymskii (Krymsk) Musketeer Regiment	2
Brigade: Maj. Gen. Peter Likhachev	
19th Jäger Regiment	2

Tomskii (Tomsk) Musketeer Regiment	2
Brigade: Maj. Gen. I. Tsybulsky	
Shirvanskii (Shirvan) Musketeer Regiment	2
Ufimskii (Ufa) Musketeer Regiment	2

The following troops may have been available, possibly served as line of communications security inside Russia.

Galitz Musketeer Regiment	2
Ukraine Musketeer Regiment	2
Chernigov Dragoons	4?

Notes:

a Artillery disposition estimated.

b Original Russian correspondence made frequent mention of 7th Division, but this formation did not participate in the campaign.

Orders of Battle for the Campaign in Hungary, 1–13 June 1809

AUSTRIA

Army of Inner Austria, GdK Archduke Johann[25]

(c.1 June > strengths as of 13 June)
(not including Chasteler and I. Gyulai)

	baons /sqdns	present under arms
GM Colloredo[26]		
Brigade: GM Lutz		
Strassaldo Infantry No. 27	3	1,798
St Julien Infantry No. 61	3	1,388
2nd Graz Landwehr[27]	1	458
4th Graz Landwehr	1	414
5th Graz Landwehr	1	466
1st Inner Austrian Volunteers	1 company	140
Brigade: GM Marziani		
I/*Szulin* Grenz Infantry No. 4	1	471
Franz Jellacic Infantry No. 62	2	747
4th Inner Austrian Volunteers	4 companies	257
Maj. Ungerhofer (considered a 'composite Upper Austrian Landwehr' battalion)		
1st Traunviertel Landwehr	–	67
2nd Traunviertel Landwehr	–	103
3rd Traunviertel Landwehr	–	66
2nd Innviertel Landwehr	–	36
2nd Mühlviertel Landwehr	–	288
4th Hausruck Landwehr	–	40
2nd OWW Landwehr (Maj. Clary)[28]	–	110

FML Jellacic
   Brigade: GM Andrassy

EH Josef Hussars No. 2	8	739
Kienmayer and *Liechtenstein* Hussars (reserve squadrons)	–	c.100
Veszprem Insurrection Hussars	6	1,001
Pest Insurrection Hussars	6	776
9th Jägers	–	53

   Brigade: GM Sebottendorf

1st Banal Grenz Infantry No. 10 (eleven companies)	2	1,547
De Vaux Infantry No. 45[29]	1	468
1st Judenburg Landwehr (with remnants of 2nd)	1	273

   Brigade: GM Legisfeld

Esterhazy Infantry No. 32	3	1,152
Warasdin-Kreuz Grenz Infantry No. 5	2	847
1st Bruck Landwehr (remnants)	1	379
Lower Austrian and 1st Salzburg Landwehr (remnants)	–	850

FML Frimont
   Brigade: GM Kleinmayrn

Allvintzi Infantry No. 19	3	2,505
Sallomon Grenadier Battalion (16, 26, 27)	1	423
Van der Mühlen Grenadier Battalion (53, 62)	1	379
Chimani Grenadier Battalion (13, 43)	1	291
Janusch Grenadier Battalion (19, 52, 61)	1	578

   Brigade: GM von Gajoli

Lusignan Infantry No. 16[30]	2	1,615
Ogulin Grenz Infantry No. 3	2	964
Cilli Landwehr (remnants)	1	571

   Brigade: GM von Ettingshausen

III/*Reuss-Greitz* Infantry No. 55	1	154
Brod and *Gradiska* Grenz	1	384
Staff Infantry	–	25
Carniola Grenz-Kordon	–	73
Styria Grenz-Kordon	–	75
8th Pioneer Division	–	69

   Cavalry Brigade: Oberst Besan

Hohenlohe Dragoons No. 2	4	365
Ott Hussars No. 5[31]	6	602
Blankenstein Hussars No. 6[32]	2	278
Hohenzollern Chevaulegers No. 2	1	86
O'Reilly Chevaulegers No. 3	1	84
Reserve Squadron/*Savoy* Dragoons No. 5	1	72

Detached
   Liaison detachment: Maj. Veigl (Radkersburg)

Hohenlohe Dragoons No. 2	1	?

Det/*Ott* Hussars No. 5	–	?
1st and 2nd Marburg Landwehr (remnants)	–	?
company/*St Georg* Grenz (joined in late June)	–	*c.*230
Liaison detachment: Obertlt Lusenszky (Pettau)		
Ott Hussars No. 5	2	?
Liaison detachment: Oberst Attems (in Hungary)		
1st UMB Landwehr (remnants)	1	*c.*460
Warasdin-St Georg Grenz Infantry	1 company	*c.*120
Frimont Hussars Reserve Squadron	1	*c.*80?

Notes:

a   Landwehr formations included fugitives from the disaster at Rottenmann, but Landwehr order of battle is imprecise in many areas, especially regarding Ober Wienerwald remnants.

b   The two battalions of *Reisky* had been sent to I. Gyulai as their depot was in his area.

c   The *Brod/Gradiska* detachment was probably from the regimental Reserve Battalions.

d   Veigl's detachment numbered eighty-five cavalry total (dragoons and hussars, based on his squadron of *Hohenlohe*). Strength, disposition, and origin of the *Warasdin-St Georg* Grenzer is unclear (probably from Reserve Battalion or Land-battalion).

Hungarian Noble Insurrection, FM Archduke Joseph

(c.1 June > strengths of 12 June)[33]

FML von Mecséry		
Pest Insurrection Infantry No. 2	1	1,224
1st Eisenburg Insurrection Infantry No. 5	1	1,191
Komorn Insurrection Infantry No. 7	1	1,148
Szala Insurrection Infantry No. 8	1	1,172
Veszprem Insurrection Infantry No. 9	1	1,207
Bars Insurrection Hussars	4	*c.*560
Eisenburg Insurrection Hussars	4	*c.*730
Ödenburg Insurrection Hussars	2	374
Szala Insurrection Hussars	6	1,071
Sümeg Insurrection Hussars	6	1,150
Entrenched Camp: GM Mesko		
Pressburg Insurrection Infantry No. 1	1	1,191
Neutra Insurrection Infantry No. 3	1	1,311
Neograd Insurrection Infantry No. 4	1	1,221
2nd Eisenburg Insurrection Infantry No. 6	1	1,044
Stuhlweissenburg Insurrection Infantry No. 10	⅓	399
Neograd Insurrection Hussars	4	*c.*730
Bars Insurrection Hussars	2	*c.*280
Eisenburg Insurrection Hussars	2	*c.*360
GM Keglevich		

Pressburg Insurrection Hussars	6	1,038

Artillery: 5 x 6-pounders, 2 x 3-pounders, 3 x howitzers
Arriving at St Istvan (13 June): FML Hadik

Heves Insurrection Hussars	4	c.680
Zemplin Insurrection Hussars	2½	c.500
Arriving at Szöny (13 June): Torontol Insurrection Hussars	6	1,048

Note: two companies of Pest Insurrection Infantry captured on 13 June.

FRENCH ARMY OF ITALY

Viceroy Eugene de Beauharnais[34]

	baons /sqdns	present under arms
Right Wing: GD MacDonald		
Division: GD Broussier		
9th Ligne	3	1,780
84th Ligne	3	2,358
92nd Ligne	4	2,324
6th Hussars	4	515
12 guns	–	
Division: GD Lamarque (GB Alméras, GB Huard)		
18th Léger (III, IV)	2	920
13th Ligne	4	1,997
23rd Ligne (III, IV)	2	634
29th Ligne	4	2,393
12 guns	–	
2nd Dragoon Division: GD Pully (GB Poinsot)		
23rd Dragoons	4	538
28th Dragoons	3	383
29th Dragoons	4	549
4 guns	–	
Präwald; IV/11th Ligne	1	616
Trieste: GB Schilt		
79th Ligne (III, IV)	2	1,110

Note: Three companies of 9th Ligne were escorting prisoners from Laibach.

Centre: GD Grenier[35]		
Division: GD Seras (GB Garreau, GB Roussel)		
IV/1st Léger	1	702
IV/35th Ligne	1	964
IV/42nd Ligne	1	665
53rd Ligne	4	2,211

106th Ligne	4	2,255
9th Chasseurs	4	707
10 guns	–	
Division: GD Durutte		
Brigade: GB Valentin		
22nd Léger (III, IV)	2	684
23rd Léger	4	1,622
60th Ligne (III, IV)	2	724
Brigade: GB Dessaix		
62nd Ligne	4	2,612
102nd Ligne	4	2,101
6th Chasseurs	4	471
6 guns	–	

Left Wing: GD Baraguey d'Hilliers

Division: GD Severoli (GB Bonfanti)		
1st Italian Line	3	2,030
IV/2nd Italian Line	1	618
3rd Italian Line (II, IV)	2	c.650
II/7th Italian Line	1	705
I/Dalmatian Regiment	1	466
112th Ligne	3	1,782
IV/*Napoleon* Dragoons (Italian)	1	259
10 guns	–	
Division: GD Pachtod (GB Abbé) (from 4 June)		
8th Léger (III, IV)	2	1,083
1st Ligne	4	1,792
52nd Ligne	4	2,069
12 guns	–	

Army Reserve

Royal Italian Guard: GD Fontanelli (GB Lecchi, GB Viani)		
Honour Guard (mounted)	1	137
Dragoons	2	339
II/Royal Velites	1	575
Line Infantry of the Guard	2	753
6 guns	–	
1st Dragoon Division: GD Grouchy (GB Guérin)		
7th Dragoons	4	607
30th Dragoons	4	848
Italian Queen's Dragoons	4	629
Light Cavalry: GD Sahuc (GB Debroc)		
8th Chasseurs	4	796
25th Chasseurs	4	484
4 guns	–	

Attached to army headquarters
    IV/24th Dragoons   1   195

Attached Troops
    Baden Brigade: GD Lauriston/GM Harrant

Jäger Battalion Lingg	1	463
1st Infantry Regiment *Grossherzog*	1⅓	975
2nd Infantry Regiment *Erbgrossherzog*	2	1,399
4 guns	–	

    GB Colbert (1,769 for entire brigade)

9th Hussars	4
7th Chasseurs	4
20th Chasseurs	4

    Cavalry Division: GD Montbrun (joined army on 9 June)
        GB Jacquinot (1,566 for entire brigade)

7th Hussars	4
1st Chasseurs	4
2nd Chasseurs	4

Detached in Carinthia
    Division: GD Rusca (GB Julhien, GB Bertoletti)

III/1st Italian Light	1	650
III/2nd Italian Light	1	726
III/4th Italian Line	1	662
Istrian Battalion	1	627
III/67th Ligne	1	891
III/93rd Ligne[36]	1	729
IV/1st Italian Chasseurs *Royal Italian*[37]	1	85
2nd Italian Chasseurs *Prince Royal*[38]	1	168
10 guns	–	

Notes:
a Pachtod took Rusca's place under Baraguey d'Hilliers on 4 June.
b 6th and 9th Chasseurs joined Sahuc on 6 June under GB Debroc.
c Eugene placed Grouchy in command of 1st Dragoon Division and Sahuc's light cavalry division on 7 June.
d Artillery allocations estimated based on early May information.
e Grouchy had commanded a separate detachment consisting of Pachtod (as above) and Sahuc (8th and 25th Chasseurs) until joining the army on 31 May.
f See Table 3 for MacDonald's wing from 5 June.
g Fourth squadron, 28th Dragoons remained in Italy with the regimental depot (from 5 May).

Hungarian Insurrection[39] Mobilisation Structure with Planned Strengths

FM Archduke Joseph, Palatine of Hungary

Brigadiers for each district in parentheses. Except as noted, all infantry are battalions, all cavalry are regiments.

	baons /sqdns	Planned strength	Planned mobilisation dates
District Left of the Danube (Cis-Danube): FZM Davidovich			
(GM Keglevich, GM Mesko)			
Pressburg Infantry No. 1	1	1,129	17–27 May
Pest Infantry No. 2	1	1,224	13 May
Neutra Infantry No. 3	1	1,186	13 May
Neograd Infantry No. 4	1	1,262	15–27 May
Pressburg Insurrection Hussars	6	1,039	11–17 May
Pest Insurrection Hussars**	6	1,056	13 May
Bars Insurrection Hussars	6	858	5–26 May
Neograd Insurrection Hussars**	6	1,074	10–14 May
Infantry: 4,801			
Cavalry: 4,027			
District Right of the Danube (Trans-Danube): FML Mecséry[40]			
(GM Andrassy)			
1st Eisenburg Infantry No. 5**	1	1,191	6 May

2nd Eisenburg Infantry No. 6**	1	1,028	6–10 May
Komorn Infantry No. 7	1	1,148	10–12 May
Szala Infantry No. 8	1	1,176	11–17 May
Veszprem Infantry No. 9	1	1,207	11 May
Stuhlweissenburg Infantry No. 10* 2 companies		490	14–15 May
Sümeg Insurrection Hussars**	6	1,106	11 May
Veszprem Insurrection Hussars*	6	1,007	11 May
Szala Insurrection Hussars*	6	1,071	18 May
Eisenburg Insurrection Hussars*	6	1,098	6–10 May
Oedenburg Insurrection Hussars Division*	2	374	9 May

Infantry: 6,240
Cavalry: 4,656

District Right of the Theiss (Trans-Theiss): FML Duka[41]
(GM Csekonics, GM Vay)

Szatmar Infantry No. 11	1	1,191	15 June
1st Borsod Infantry No. 12	1	760	10 May
Marmaros Infantry No. 13	1	1,071	13 June
Bihar Infantry No. 14	1	545	9 May–13 June
Szabolcs Insurrection Hussars	6	1,135	8 June
Bihar Insurrection Hussars	6	1,055	10–31 May
Torontal Insurrection Hussars	6	1,048	16–21 May
Szatmar Insurrection Hussars	6	1,019	9 May–15 June

Infantry: 3,567
Cavalry: 4,257

District Left of the Theiss (Cis-Theiss): FML Hadik[42]
(GM Hertelendy, GM Luzensky)

Heves Infantry No. 15	1	1,133	20 May
2nd Borsod Infantry No. 16	1	1,191	23 May
Gömör Infantry No. 17	1	1,541	July
Zemplin Infantry No. 18	1	1,137	10–11 May
Abaujvar Infantry No. 19	1	1,200	13–19 May
Zemplin Insurrection Hussars	6	1,234	10–19 May
Heves Insurrection Hussars	6	1,033	17–20 May

Infantry: 6,202
Cavalry: 2,267

En route to Hauptarmee
Cavalry Brigade: GM Kerekes

Primatial Insurrection Hussars	6	1,023	1 May
Neutra Insurrection Hussars	6	1,011	13 May

* Units deployed along the Marcal River by 17 May.
** Units arriving at Raab or on the Marcal by 24 May.

Notes:

a The small Stuhlweissenburg and Ödenburg contingents were organised as 'divisions' of two companies and two squadrons respectively.

b Point of reference for 'this side' (cis-) and 'that side' (trans-) of the rivers was Pest.

c Oberst Gosztonyi of the Pest Hussars was treated as a general in the Trans-Danubian District.

d 1st Borsod and Gömör Infantry had four companies each, all others six.

e Mobilisation dates for the Gömör contingents were very late. Infantry and cavalry appear to have arrived in Pest in mid-July (the cavalry comprised 282 men assigned to the Heves hussars).

Orders of Battle for the Battle of Raab, 14 June 1809

AUSTRIA

GdK Archduke Johann and FM Archduke Joseph[43]

	baons /sqdns	present under arms
Main Army		
Reserve Cavalry Brigade: Oberst Besan (Frimont commanded during battle)		
Hohenlohe Dragoons No. 2	5	365
Blankenstein Hussars No. 6[44]	1?	c.80?
Hohenzollern Chevaulegers No. 2	1	86
O'Reilly Chevaulegers No. 3	1	84
Reserve Squadron/*Savoy* Dragoons No. 5	1	72
Oberst Paszthory (Sümegh)		
Szala Insurrection Hussars	6	1,100
Sümegh Insurrection Hussars	6	1,272
9th Jägers	–	53
Battery: 4 x 3-pounders		
Right Wing: FML Jellacic		
Brigade: GM Sebottendorf		
1st Banal Grenz Infantry No. 10 (11 companies)	2	1,547
De Vaux Infantry No. 45[45]	1	468
1st Salzburg Landwehr (remnants)[46]	–	112
1st Judenburg Landwehr (with remnants of 2nd)	1	273
Staff Infantry	–	25
Carniola Grenz-Kordon	–	73
Styria Grenz-Kordon	–	75

8th Pioneer Division	–	69
Brigade: Oberst Eckhardt (*Esterhazy*)		
Esterhazy Infantry No. 32 (I, III)	2	*c.*770
Oberst Markus (*Veszprem* Infantry)		
Pest Insurrection Infantry No. 2	⅔	657
1st Eisenburg Insurrection Infantry No. 5	1	927
Veszprem Insurrection Infantry No. 9	1	978
Brigade: GM Legisfeld		
1st Bruck Landwehr (remnants)	1	379
UMB Landwehr (remnants)	–	486
OWW Landwehr (remnants)	–	252
Battery: 4 x 3-pounders		
Centre: FML Colloredo		
Brigade: GM Lutz		
Strassaldo Infantry No. 27	3	1,798
St Julien Infantry No. 61	3	1,388
2nd, Graz Landwehr	1	458
4th Graz Landwehr	1	414
5th Graz Landwehr	1	466
1st Inner Austrian Volunteers	1 company	140
Brigade: GM Marziani		
Franz Jellacic Infantry No. 62	2	747
I/*Szulin* Grenz Infantry No. 4[47]	1	471
Maj. Ungerhofer (considered a 'composite Upper Austrian Landwehr' battalion)		
1st Traunviertel Landwehr	–	67
2nd Traunviertel Landwehr	–	103
3rd Traunviertel Landwehr	–	66
2nd Innviertel Landwehr	–	36
2nd Mühlviertel Landwehr	–	288
4th Hausruck Landwehr	–	40
4th Inner Austrian Volunteers	4 companies	257
Oberst Ghilanyi (*Szala* Infantry)		
Komorn Insurrection Infantry No. 7	1	986
Szala Insurrection Infantry No. 8	1	1,094
Artillery: 4 x 6-pounders, 4 x 3-pounders, 2 x howitzers		
Left Wing: FML von Mecséry		
Brigade: GM Andrassy		
EH Josef Hussars No. 2	8	739
Kienmayer and *Liechtenstein* Hussars (reserve squadrons)	–	*c.*100
Veszprem Insurrection Hussars	3	*c.*480
Eisenburg Insurrection Hussars	4	*c.*540
Ödenburg Insurrection Hussars	2	374
Brigade: Oberst Gosztonyi		
Ott Hussars No. 5	6	602
Pest Insurrection Hussars	5	*c.*610

Bars Insurrection Hussars	4	c.480
Brigade: FML Hadik		
Heves Insurrection Hussars	4	c.680
Zemplin Insurrection Hussars[48]	2½	348
Cavalry reinforcements from Mesko (morning of 14 June):		
Eisenburg Insurrection Hussars	2	c.360
Neograd Insurrection Hussars (Jaszkun Division)	1½	c.200
Bars Insurrection Hussars	2	c.280
Reserve: FML Frimont		
Brigade: GM Kleinmayrn		
Allvintzi Infantry No. 19	3	2,505
Sallomon Grenadier Battalion (16, 26, 27)	1	423
Van der Mühlen Grenadier Battalion (53, 62)	1	379
Chimani Grenadier Battalion (13, 43)	1	291
Janusch Grenadier Battalion (19, 52, 61)	1	578
Brigade: GM von Gajoli		
Cilli Landwehr (remnants)	1	571
Lusignan Infantry No. 16[49]	2	1,615
Ogulin Grenz Infantry No. 3	2	964
Brigade: (formerly GM von Ettingshausen)		
III/*Reuss-Greitz* Infantry No. 55	1	154
Composite *Brod* and *Gradiska* Grenz troops	1	384
Detached:[50]		
In rear: reserve artillery (12 guns)		
Szent Marton: Maj. Tittus		
II/*Esterhazy* Infantry No. 32	1	c.380
Pest Insurrection Hussars	1	c.150
Romand: Oberst von Siegenfeld		
Warasdin-Kreuz Grenz Infantry No. 5	2	847
Blankenstein Hussars No. 6	2	278
Veszprem Insurrection Hussars	2	c.320
Two guns		
Kisber: Veszprem Insurrection Hussars[51]	1	c.160
Kleine Schütt: Neograd Insurrection Hussars	2	c.270
Grosse Schütt: Pressburg Insurrection Hussars	2	c.290
Entrenched Camp: GM Mesko (FZM Davidovich with Johann)		
GM Mesko's direct command		
Neutra Insurrection Infantry No. 3	1	1,112
Neograd Insurrection Infantry No. 4	1	956
2nd Eisenburg Insurrection Infantry No. 6	1	918
Stuhlweissenburg Insurrection Infantry No. 10	2 companies	399
Pressburg Insurrection Hussars	4	c.580
Neograd Insurrection Hussars	½	c.70
GM Keglevich		
Pressburg Insurrection Infantry No. 1	1	980

Neograd Insurrection Hussars	2	c.270

Artillery: 5 x 6-pounders, 3 x howitzers, 2 x 3-pounders

Notes:

a It is not clear where the *Kienmayer* (number unknown) and *Liechtenstein* Hussar (91) reserve troopers fought; this assumes they remained with Andrassy as on the previous several days, but they may have been under Besan.

b Landwehr order of battle is imprecise in many areas, especially for Ober dem Wienerwald remnants.

c Health problems forced Ettingshausen to depart the army on 13 June. His former 'brigade' took some casualties during the battle, but disposition and actions are unclear.

Raab Garrison: Oberst Pechy[52]

Vukassovich Infantry Regiment No. 48	–	839 (70)
Franz Karl Infantry Regiment No. 52	–	481 (454)
Johann Jellacic Infantry Regiment No. 58	–	456 (675)
Landwehr	–	70 (451)
Ott Hussar Regiment No. 5	–	42 (36)
Kienmayer Hussar Regiment No. 8	–	44 (29)
Insurrection	–	230 (46)
Other (individuals, small detachments, sick, medical personnel)	–	369 (54)
Other (engineers, artillery, etc)	–	104 (59)
Total		2,635 (1,874)

Note: French report figures shown with Austrian report figures in parentheses.

FRENCH ARMY OF ITALY

Viceroy Eugene de Beauharnais[53]

(Centre, Left, and Right refer to deployments on the battlefield, not army organisation)

	baons /sqdns	present under arms
Right Wing		
GD Grouchy		
1st Dragoon Division: GB Guérin		
7th Dragoons	4	607
30th Dragoons	4	848
Italian *Queen's* Dragoons	4	629
GD Montbrun		
GB Colbert		
9th Hussars	4	486
7th Chasseurs	4	407
20th Chasseurs	4	623

GB Jacquinot		
7th Hussars	4	613
1st Chasseurs	4	474
2nd Chasseurs	4	684
Centre:		
GD Grenier		
Division: GD Seras		
Brigade: GB Moreau		
IV/1st Léger	1	702
IV/35th Ligne	1	964
53rd Ligne	4	2,211
Brigade: GB Roussel		
IV/42nd Ligne	1	665
106th Ligne	4	2,255
10 guns	–	
Division: GD Durutte		
Brigade: GB Valentin		
22nd Léger (III, IV)	2	684
23rd Léger	4	1,622
60th Ligne (III, IV)	2	724
Brigade: GB Dessaix		
62nd Ligne	4	2,612
102nd Ligne	4	2,101
6 guns	–	
GD Baraguey d'Hilliers		
Division: GD Severoli		
Brigade: GB Bonfanti		
IV/2nd Italian Line	1	618
3rd Italian Line (II, IV)	2	c.650
II/7th Italian Line	1	705
I/Dalmatian Regiment	1	466
Brigade: GB Teste		
1st Italian Line	3	2,030
112th Ligne	3	1,782
IV/*Napoleon* Dragoons (Italian)	1	259
10 guns		
Division: GD Pachtod (GB Abbé)		
8th Léger (III, IV)	2	1,083
1st Ligne	4	1,792
52nd Ligne	4	2,069
12 guns		
Left Wing		
Light Cavalry: GD Sahuc		
Brigade: GB Debroc		
6th Chasseurs	4	471

9th Chasseurs	4	707
Brigade: GB Gérard		
8th Chasseurs	4	796
25th Chasseurs	4	484
4 guns	–	
2nd Dragoon Division: GD Pully (GB Poinsot)		
23rd Dragoons	4	c.470
28th Dragoons	3	383
29th Dragoons	4	549
4 guns	–	
Lauriston/Baden Brigade		
Jäger Battalion Lingg	1	463
1st Infantry Regiment *Grossherzog*	1⅓	975
2nd Infantry Regiment *Erbgrossherzog*	2	1,399
4 guns		

Army Reserve

Royal Italian Guard: GD Fontanelli (GB Lecchi, GB Viani)		
Honour Guard (mounted)	1	137
Dragoons	2	339
II/Royal Velites	1	575
Line Infantry of the Guard	2	753
6 guns		
Attached to army headquarters		
IV/24th Dragoons	1	195
Approaching battlefield: GD MacDonald with GD Lamarque's division		
Brigade: GB Alméras		
18th Léger (III, IV)	2	920
13th Ligne	4	1,997
Brigade: GB Huard		
23rd Ligne (III, IV)	2	634
29th Ligne	4	2,393
Attached: 92nd Ligne (I, IV)	2	c. 1,100
12 guns	–	

Note:

a   II/Dalmatian Regiment arrived on the evening of 14 June, too late for the fighting.

b   Artillery allocations are estimated, total French/Italian guns on the field at Raab were approximately fifty-six (not including Lamarque).

c   Two battalions of 92nd Ligne attached to Lamarque from Broussier on 9 June.[54] One company of 23rd Dragoons (c.65) with Broussier.

Orders of Battle for the Campaign in Dalmatia, April–May 1809

AUSTRIA

	baons /sqdns	present under arms
Dalmatian Detachment: GM von Stoichevich[55]		
Licca Grenz Infantry No. 1	2	*c.*2,550
Reserve Battalion/*Licca* Grenz Infantry No. 1	1	*c.*1,270
Reserve Battalion/*Ottocac* Grenz Infantry No. 2	1	*c.*1,290
Reserve Battalion/*Ogulin* Grenz Infantry No. 3	1	*c.*1,295
Reserve Battalion/*Szulin* Grenz Infantry No. 4	1	*c.*1,375
Hohenzollern Chevaulegers No. 2	1	*c.*110
Mounted Serezaner	1	*c.*200
Dalmatian Volunteers	–	?
Artillery:		
1 x 6-pounder position battery		
1 x 3-pounder brigade battery		

Infantry: *c.*7,690 (not including Dalmatian Volunteers)
Cavalry: *c.*310
Guns: 8 x 3-pounders, 4 x 6-pounders, 2 x howitzers
Note: 4th Garrison Battalion (*c.*480) in Zengg also under Stoichevich.

Arriving in Gracac by 1 May:		
Composite Land-battalions		
(from regiments 1, 2, 3, 4 10, 11)	3	*c.*3,000[56]
Arriving in Ottocac on 9 May:		
Reserve Battalions/*Banal* Grenz Regiments 10 and 11	2	*c.*2,500

FRANCE

Army of Dalmatia: GD Marmont[57]

Field Force

1st Division: GD Montrichard		
Brigade: GB Soyez		
5th Ligne	2	1,622
18th Léger	2	1,417
Brigade: GB Launay		
79th Ligne	2	1,575
81st Ligne	2	1,366
2nd Division: GD Clauzel		
Brigade: GB Delzons		
8th Léger	2	1,495
23rd Ligne	2	1,424
Brigade: (GB Deviau remained in Ragusa)		
11th Ligne	3	2,094
Light Cavalry	–	292
(8th Company/3rd Chasseurs and 3rd Company/24th Chasseurs)		

Total infantry: 10,993
Total cavalry: 292
Artillery: 12 guns

Marmont also had approximately 1,000 Dalmatian Pandours (organised in two battalions) to guard his logistics convoys.

Garrisons: GD Poitevin, Comte de Maureillan (in Zara)		
Ragusa: GB Deviau		
60th Ligne	1	c.850
IV/Dalmatian Regiment (part)	–	175
National Guards	2	?
Zara		
60th Ligne	1	c.850
IV/Dalmatian Regiment (part)	–	156
National Guards	1	?
Cattaro		
I/3rd Italian Light Infantry	1	512
I/Chasseurs d'Orient	1	116
National Guards	1	?

Note: Battalions of 60th Ligne were 1st and 2nd, totalling 1,756 present under arms; it is not clear which battalion was in which location.

Orders of Battle for the Northern Tyrol, 10 May 1809

AUSTRIA

	baons /sqdns	present under arms
VIII Corps Detachment: FML Chasteler[58]		
Northern Tyrol		
GM Buol (northern border)		
Obertlt Taxis		
9th Jägers		1 company
Salzburg Jägers		4 companies
III/*de Vaux* Infantry No. 45		3 companies
Hohenzollern Chevaulegers No. 2		½
Tyrolians		14 companies
1 x 6-pounder, 1 x 3-pounder		
Maj. Teimer		
Tyrolians		20 companies
GM Buol		
1st Klagenfurt Landwehr		1
1 x 6-pounder, 1 x 3-pounder		
GM Fenner (Kufstein and towards Salzburg)		
Obertlt Reissenfels (Kufstein area)		
III/*de Vaux* Infantry No. 45		3 companies[59]
O'Reilly Chevaulegers No. 3		1 platoon
Tyrolians		23 companies
2 x 6-pounders		
Obertlt Göldlin		
Koessen		

9th Jägers	1 company
Tyrolians	4 companies
1 x 3-pounder	
Strub Pass	
I/*Hohenlohe-Bartenstein* Infantry No. 26	1 company
Tyrolians	4 companies
2 x 6-pounders	
Luftenstein/Hirschbichl area	
9th Jägers	½ company
Tyrolian Schützen (Oberlt Leis)	2 companies
Tyrolians	3 companies
2 x 3-pounders	
Waidring	
9th Jägers	1/2 company
Hohenzollern Chevaulegers No. 2	1/2
3 x 6-pounders	

FML Chasteler (Innsbruck)

Lusignan Infantry Regiment No. 16 (I, II)	2	
2nd and 3rd Klagenfurt Landwehr	2	
2nd Villach Landwehr	1	
Hohenzollern Chevaulegers No. 2	1½	*c*.90
Ten guns		

Southern Tyrol

GM Marchal (Trient)

Trient/Val Sugana area

9th Jägers	3 companies
Schützen (Maj. Lais)[60]	1 company
Hohenlohe-Bartenstein Infantry No. 26	3
2nd Bruck Landwehr	1
1st Villach Landwehr	1
Hohenzollern Chevaulegers No. 2	1
Brixen	
III/*Lusignan* Infantry No. 16	1

Artillery: 2 x 6-pounder, 1 x howitzer, 4 x 3-pounder

GM Schmidt (Pustertal area)

Johann Jellacic Infantry No. 53	3
2nd Banal Grenz Infantry No. 11	2
Hohenzollern Chevaulegers No. 2	4
6 x 3-pounder	

Detachment: Hptm Kuncz (formerly Zuccheri)

Company/*1st Banal* Grenz Infantry No. 10	1 company
II/*Szulin* Grenz Infantry No. 4	2 companies
I/*EH Franz Karl* Infantry No. 52	1

Maj. Krapf (Sachsenburg)

1st Neustadl Landwehr (towards Taxenbach)	1	?

9th Jägers depot (towards Taxenbach)	–	60
2nd Laibach Landwehr (Tweng)	1	?
3rd Carinthian Cordon Company (Sachsenburg)	1 company	147
1st Neustadl Landwehr (Sachsenburg)	2 companies	282
Artillery, train, sappers (Sachsenburg)	–	53

Note: One company of I/*Hohenlohe-Bartenstein* detached at Strub Pass.

ALLIED

7th Corps: Marshal Lefebvre [61]

Offensive Force
2nd Division: GL von Wrede (advancing through Strub Pass)
    1st Brigade: GM Minucci

6th Light Battalion	1	449
3rd Infantry	2	1,106
13 Infantry	2	1,108

    2nd Brigade: GM Beckers

6th Infantry	2	1,138
7th Infantry	2	1,117

    Attached:

9th Infantry	6 companies	c.1,000
II/14th Infantry	1	c.660

    Cavalry:

3rd Chevaulegers	4	490
4th Chevaulegers	2	c.140

      12 x 6-pounders, 4 x 12-pounders, 8 x howitzers, 1 x 6-pounder attached,
      4 x howitzers attached
3rd Division: GL Deroy (advancing on Kufstein)
    1st Brigade: GM Vincenti

5th Infantry	2	1,286
I/14th Infantry	1	c.660
1st Light	1	696
7th Light	1	470
4th Chevaulegers	2	c.140

      3 x 6-pounders, 1 x howitzer
    Detachment: Chef d'Escadron Montélégier

II/4th Infantry	1	c.700
1st Dragoons	1	c.135

      1 x 6-pounder
Note: Montélégier's detachment had been sent towards Kufstein in late April (see Vol. I).

Garrisons and other forces:
1st Division: GL Kronprinz Ludwig (Salzburg and vicinity)
  1st Brigade: GM Rechberg

1st Infantry	2	1,304
2nd Infantry	2	1,216
2nd Brigade: GM Stengel		
II/4th Infantry	1	c.700
8th Infantry	2	1,328
Attached:		
3rd Light	2 companies	245
Cavalry Brigade		
1st Dragoons	1	c.135
1st Chevaulegers	4	320
2nd Chevaulegers (Lambach)	4	519
2nd Brigade/3rd Division: GM Siebein		
9th Infantry	2 companies	c.350
10th Infantry	2	844
5th Light	1	462
2nd Dragoons	4	425

  Artillery: 11 x 6-pounders, 4 x 12-pounders, 8 x howitzers
  Attached (from 3rd Division): 12 x 6-pounders, 4 x 12-pounders, 4 x howitzers
Kufstein (Maj. Aicher)

Provisional Light Battalion (depots: 1st, 2nd, 5th, 6th Light)	1	471
Fortress artillery	–	98
60 guns		

Oberst Arco (southern Bavaria)

Provisional Battalion (depots: 1st, 2nd, 5th, 7th Inf; 1st, 2nd Light)	1	773
Provisional Squadron (depots: 1st Drgns; 1st, 2nd, 3rd Chevaulegers)	1	204
1st, 2nd, 3rd Gebirgsschützen Divisions and		
Munich Volunteer Schützen	–	c.1,350
2 x 6-pounders	–	26

Note: 555 men of 10th Infantry detached on prisoner escort.

APPENDIX 8

Orders of Battle for Chasteler's Escape, c.1 June 1809

AUSTRIA

	baons /sqdns	present under arms
VIII Corps Detachment: FML Chasteler[62]		
In Drava valley		
9th Jägers	1 company	
2nd *Banal* Grenz	3 companies	
Hohenlohe-Bartenstein Infantry No. 26	2	
Johann Jellacic Infantry No. 53	2	
3rd Inner Austrian Volunteers	1	
Schützen (Maj. Lais)	1 company	
Hohenzollern Chevaulegers No. 2	4½	
1st Villach Landwehr	1	
2nd Bruck Landwehr	1	
1st, 2nd, 3rd Klagenfurt Landwehr	3	
2 x 6-pounders, 5 x 3-pounders, 1 x howitzer		
GM Schmidt (Gail valley)		
2nd *Banal* Grenz	6 companies	
I/*EH Franz Karl* Infantry No. 52	1	
I/*Johann Jellacic* Infantry No. 53	1	
2 x 3-pounders		
Sachsenburg (Maj. Krapf)		
III/*Hohenlohe-Bartenstein* Infantry No. 26	2½ companies	320
Replacement detachment/*J Jellacic* Infantry No. 53	–	296
3rd Carinthian Cordon Company	1 company	100
Cilli Landwehr	–	70
2 x 6-pounders, 1 x howitzer		

ALLIED

Governor of Carinthia: GD Rusca[63]

GB Bertoletti, GB Julhien (wounded)

III/1st Italian Light	I	650
III/2nd Italian Light	I	726
III/4th Italian Line	I	662
Istrian Battalion	I	627
IV/67th Ligne	I	891
IV/93rd Ligne	I	729
IV/1st Italian Chasseurs *Royal Italian*[64]	I	128
2nd Italian Chasseurs *Prince Royal*[65]	I	168
Artillery, train, sappers	—	282
10 guns		

Orders of Battle for the Engagement at Graz, 25–6 June 1809

AUSTRIA

	baons /sqdns	present under arms
IX Corps: FML Ignaz Gyulai[66]		
On west (right) bank of Mur:		
Advance Guard (GM Splenyi)		
Trieste Jägers (Trieste Landwehr)	1 company	66
Ottocac Grenz Infantry No. 2	2 companies	*c.*320
Massal Insurrection Infantry	1	*c.*700–1,200
EH Josef Hussars No. 2	1	*c.*70
Frimont Hussars No. 9	4	*c.*370
Banderial Hussars?	2	*c.*280
Cavalry half-battery and one 3-pounder		
On east (left) bank of Mur: FML Gyulai with 'Corps de Bataille'		
Brigade: GM Kalnassy		
III/*EH Franz Karl* Infantry No. 52	1	928
Simbschen Infantry No. 43	1½	912
St Julien Infantry No. 61 (replacements)	2 companies	428
Land-battalion/*Warasdin-St Georg* Grenz No. 6	2 companies	370
Savoy Dragoons No. 5	2	*c.*150
Banderial Hussars?	2	*c.*280
Brigade: GM Gavassini		
Ottocac Grenz Infantry No. 2	1⅔	*c.*1,600
Szulin Grenz Infantry No. 4[67]	2	1,188
Savoy Dragoons No. 5	2	*c.*150
Banderial Hussars?	2	*c.*280
Cavalry half-battery		

Brigade: GM von Munkacsy

Reserve Battalion/*1st Banal* Grenz No. 10	1	1,061
Reserve Battalion/*2nd Banal* Grenz No. 11	1	880
Banderial Insurrection Infantry	2	1,652

Brigade: GM Kengyel

Personal Insurrection Infantry	2	1,107
Massal Insurrection Infantry	2	*c.*1,400–2,300
Frimont Hussars No. 9	2	*c.*170
Banderial Hussars?	2	*c.*280

Brigade: Oberst Amade

Massal Insurrection Infantry	2	*c.*1,400–2,300
Personal Hussars	3	*c.*530
Savoy Dragoons No. 5	2	*c.*150

Reserve: FML Zach

Brigade: GM Khevenhüller

Reserve Battalion/*Ottocac* Grenz No. 2	1	926
Reserve Battalion/*Szulin* Grenz No. 4	1	895
Land-battalion/*Ottocac* Grenz No. 2	3 companies	415
Warasdin Combined Land-battalion	1	749
4th Combined *Banal* Land-battalion	1	947

Brigade: Oberst Rebrovich

Licca Grenz No. 2No. 1	2	1,865
Reserve Battalion/*Ogulin* Grenz No. 3	1	789

Note: Distribution of Insurrection troops is unclear. There were eight Banderial Hussar squadrons (1,104) total, but two remained in Croatia, leaving six squadrons with approximately 820 around Graz. There should have been four Personal squadrons (total of 669) as there were by 4 July. Designations of the Massal Infantry are not given in source, but 1st Massal totalled 2,366 in three battalions, 2nd Massal 2,232 in two battalions.[68] 4th Massal was on the coast; 3rd Massal still organising.

FRANCE[69]

Division: GD Broussier

9th Ligne	3	1,648
84th Ligne	3	2,015
92nd Ligne (II and III)	2	1,280
6th Hussars	4	515
23rd Dragoons	1 company	67
8 x guns, 4 x howitzers	–	342

In vicinity: GD Marmont with GD Clauzel's 2nd Division

8th Léger	2	1,227
23rd Ligne	2	1,569
11th Ligne	3	1,837

APPENDIX 10

Allied Reserve Forces in Germany, 1 June 1809

	baons /sqdns	present under arms
Corps d'Observation de l'Elbe: Marshal Kellermann[70]		
Cavalry: GB Vaufreland		
6th Provisional Dragoons	4	704
Right Division: GD Rivaud		
Brigade: GB Lameth		
IV/19th Ligne	1	722
IV/25th Ligne	1	654
IV/28th Ligne	1	778
Brigade: GB Taupin		
IV/36th Ligne	1	836
IV/50th Ligne	1	707
IV/75th Ligne	1	848
Left Division: GD Despeaux		
Brigade: GB Clémens		
5th Reserve Demi-Brigade	4	1,444
9th Reserve Demi-Brigade	–	(organising)
Brigade: GB Duverger		
10th Reserve Demi-Brigade	–	(organising)
13th Reserve Demi-Brigade	4	1,553
Under Headquarters: GB Valletaux		
Grenadier and Voltigeur Companies/IV/46th Ligne 2 companies		236
Artillery: 2 x 12-pounders, 8 x 6-pounders, 2 x howitzers	–	294
Independent Formations		
GD Beaumont's Division[71]		
1st Provisional Dragoons	4	569

2nd Provisional Dragoons	4	644
3rd Provisional Dragoons	4	533
4th Provisional Dragoons	4	744
5th Provisional Dragoons	4	581
65th Ligne	1	582
Composite French battalion (*'isolées réunies'*)	1	834
(9th, 17th, 26th Léger; 3rd, 57th, 105th Ligne)		
Bavarian Provisional Battalion (Maj. Pillement)	1	527
(depot troops: 9th, 11th, 13th, 14th Infantry; 3rd, 6th, 7th Light)		
Bavarian Artillery: 1 x 6-pounder		
Württemberg *Franquemont* Infantry	2	1,251
French/Württemberg Artillery: 8 x 6-pounders, 4 x howitzers	–	128

Baden Troops: Oberstleutnant von Cancrin[72]

Hussars	1	63
Guard Grenadier	2 companies	209
Artillery: 2 x 4-pounders	–	22

Württemberg Brigade: GM von Scheler

Prinz Friedrich Infantry	2	c.1,300
Light Infantry and Jäger depots	–	c.200
Guard Horse Grenadiers	2	c.180
Depot cavalry	–	c.50
Artillery: 5 guns		

Bavarian 3rd Division: GL von Deroy

5th Infantry *Preysing*	2	
9th Infantry *Ysenburg*	2	
10th Infantry *Junker*	2	
14th Infantry	2	
5th Light Battalion *Butler*	1	
7th Light Battalion	1	
2nd Dragoons *Thurn und Taxis*	4	
Artillery: two line batteries, one light battery (18 guns)		

Bavarian Brigade: Oberst von Arco

Provisional Infantry Battalion (Hammel)	1	c.750
(depot troops: 1st, 2nd, 5th, 7th, Infantry; 1st, 2nd Light)		
Provisional Cavalry Squadron (Lerchenberg)	1	c.180
(depot troopers: 1st Dragoons; 1st, 2nd, 3rd Chevaulegers)		
1st, 2nd, 3rd Gebirgsschützen Divisions	–	?
Artillery: 2 x 6-pounders	–	18

Kufstein Garrison: Major Aicher

Provisional Light Battalion	1	c.470
(depot troops: 1st, 2nd, 5th, 6th Light)		
Fortress Artillery	–	98
Sixty guns and mortars		

En route to Augsburg

Berg Chasseurs-à-Cheval Regiment	4	815

10th Corps: King Jerome[73]

Westphalian Guard Division: GD Bernterode		
Garde du Corps (mounted)	I	139
Garde-Grenadiers	I	948
Garde-Jäger	I	598
Garde-Chevaulegers	3	306
Jäger-Carabiniers	I	364
Westphalian Line Division:		
1st Infantry	3	1,690
5th Infantry	3	1,583
6th Infantry	3	1,744
1st Cuirassiers	2	263
Westphalian artillery	–	562
Dutch Division: GD Gratien[74]		
Brigade: Maj. Gen. Anthing		
6th Infantry	2	1,056
7th Infantry	2	1,129
Brigade: Maj. Gen. Hasselt		
8th Infantry	2	1,044
9th Infantry	2	1,328
2nd Cuirassiers	3	513
Artillery: 8 x 6-pounders, 4 x howitzers	–	518
Other:		
Col. Chabert		
5th Sapper Battalion	–	53
Det/28th Léger	–	264
Det/27th Ligne	–	101
Det/30th and 65th Ligne	–	146
IV/22nd Ligne	I	366
Magdeburg artillery/train/sappers	–	473
Depot/8th Hussars	–	40
3rd Berg Infantry Regiment	2	1,042
Berg artillery	–	42
In Swedish Pomerania: GB Liébert (Stettin)		
Stettin Garrison		
III/22nd Ligne	I	411
Saxon II/*Dyherrn* Infantry	I	375
Polish II/10th Infantry	I	491
Polish 4th Chasseurs	–	236
French artillery	–	76
Swedish Pomerania: GB Candras		
III/22nd Ligne	–	88
Saxon II/*Dyherrn* Infantry	–	161
Polish II/10th Infantry	–	209
Polish 4th Chasseurs	–	99

7th Rheinbund Regiment (Mecklenburg-Schwerin)	2	1,066
Mecklenburg-Strelitz Battalion	1	301
French artillery	–	100
Küstrin Garrison: Col. Armand		
I/22nd Ligne	1	605
Polish 5th Infantry	2	1,087
Polish 4th Chasseurs	–	89
French artillery	–	96
Glogau Garrison: GB Rheinwald		
II/22nd Ligne	1	527
Saxon *Burgsdorff* Infantry	2	935
Grenadier Companies/Saxon *Prinz Maximilian* Infantry	2 companies	210
Polish 4th Chasseurs	–	119
French artillery	–	96
Danzig Garrison: GB Grabowski		
Polish 10th Infantry (I, III)	2	556
Polish 11th Infantry	3	1,279
Polish artillery	–	73
Saxon *Rechten* Infantry	2	729
Saxon artillery	–	66
French artillery	–	165

Note: Polish 10th and 11th Infantry Regiments had 436 and 679 detached respectively (Posen).

Mobile troops in Saxony: GM von Dyherrn/Oberst von Thielmann

Grenadier Battalion *von Einsiedel*	1	
Composite Battalion *von Wolan*	1	
(Grenadier Companies/*Rechten*, plus two depot companies)		
I/*Oebschelwitz* Infantry	1	
det/*Burgsdorff* Infantry	–	101
Zastrow Cuirassiers	4	
Hussar Regiment	3	
Polenz Chevaulegers	1	
Artillery: two foot batteries (14 guns), 1 x horse battery (8 guns)		
Total: c.2,800		

Erfurt Garrison

Frankfurt battalion	1	556

Danish Brigade: GM von Ewald[75]

Oldenborg Infantry Regiment (I, II)	2	1,351
III/Holsteen Infantry Regiment	1	638
II/Holsteen Skarpskytter-Corps (4th, 5th)	2 companies	171
Hussar Regiment (II, VI)	2	200
Holsteen Cavalry Regiment (det)	–	22
Artillery: 10 x 3-pounders	–	141

Note: the Oldenborg Regiment did not have its grenadier companies.

APPENDIX II

Austrian Forces in Germany, June 1809

	baons /sqdns	present under arms
FML Kienmayer (arrived late June)[76]		
GM Am Ende (Saxony)		
III/*Anton Mittrowsky* Infantry No. 10	1	1,062
III/*Erbach* Infantry No. 42	1	1,308
2nd Leitmeritz Landwehr	1	897
3rd Leitmeritz Landwehr	1	753
4th Leitmeritz Landwehr	1	862
5th Leitmeritz Landwehr	1	816
5th Königgratz Landwehr	1	727
6th Bunzlau Landwehr	1	668
5th Company/1st Jäger Battalion	1 company	157
Merveldt Uhlans No. 1	1	109
Schwarzenberg Uhlans No. 2	1	127
Res Sqdn/*Klenau* Chevaulegers No. 5	1 platoon	20
8 x 3-pounders, 2 x howitzers		
Duke of Brunswick		
Brunswick Hussars[77]	–	c.300
1st and 2nd Brunswick Light Infantry Battalions	2	c.400
2 x 6-pounders, 2 x howitzers		
Hessians		
1st Grenadier Company	1 company	101
Jäger Company	1 company	57
Fusilier Company	1 company	129
Leib Dragoons	–	18
Hussars	–	35

GM Radivojevich (Bayreuth)

Deutsch-Banat Grenz Infantry No. 12	2	1,371
1st and 2nd Tabor Landwehr	2	1,605
4th Königgratz Landwehr	1	732
2nd Chrudim Landwehr	1	488
Merveldt Uhlan Regiment No. 1	1	120
Res Sqdn/*Schwarzenberg* Uhlans No. 2	1 platoon	38
Res Sqdn/*Rosenberg* Chevaulegers No. 3	1 platoon	30
Res Sqdn/*Blankenstein* Hussars No. 6	1 platoon	25
4 x 3-pounders		
Reinforcements: Am Ende (22 June)		
3rd Tschaslau Landwehr	1	?
5th Bunzlau Landwehr	1	?
Reinforcements: Kienmayer (30 June)		
Schwarzenberg Uhlan Regiment No. 2	1	c.120
Reinforcements: Hessians (30 June)		
1st Grenadier Company	–	6
2nd Grenadier Company	1 company	91
Jäger Company	–	20
Fusilier Company	–	21
Leib Dragoons	1	72
Hussars	1	70

Allied Reserve Forces, c.25–30 June 1809

All French unless otherwise indicated.[78]

	baons /sqdns	present under arms
Vorarlberg and Tyrol		
Lake Constance/Vorarlberg[79]		
4th Provisional Dragoons (Col. Grouvel)	4	759
Baden Brigade: Oberst von Stockhorn		
Guard Grenadiers	1	626
Provisional Jäger Battalion	1	361
Hussars	1	65
Light Dragoons (depot)	1	58
Artillery: 2 x 4-pounders	–	26
Württemberg: GL von Phull		
Prinz Friedrich Infantry Regiment	2	c.1,260
Depot/*Kronprinz* Infantry Regiment	–	124
Depot/*Phull* Infantry Regiment	–	112
Depot/*Camrer* Infantry Regiment	–	127
Depot/*Herzog Wilhelm* Infantry Regiment	–	106
Depot/*Neubronn* Fusilier Regiment	–	111
Depot/*König* Jäger Battalion	1 company	100
Depot/*Neuffer* Jäger Battalion	1 company	54
Depot/*Brüsselle* Light Battalion	1 company	113
Depot/*Wolff* Light Battalion	1 company	111
Volunteer Jäger	–	76
Depot Squadron Schlümbach	1	61
Artillery: 1 x 6-pounder, 3 x 3-pounder, 1 x howitzer		

Note: Württemberg Guard in Stuttgart.

Lindau Garrison: Oberstleutnant Lalance

Württemberg *Franquemont* Infantry	3 companies	450
Grenadier Company/65th Ligne	1 company	90
Depot/*Neuffer* Jäger Battalion	–	50
Det/4th Provisional Dragoons	–	40
1 x 6-pounder, 1 x howitzer, 2 x 3-pounders		

Tyrolian border west (approx Iller to Lech): GD Beaumont

Memmingen, Kempten, Kaufbeuren, Oberdorf, Schongau: GB Picard

Composite battalion ('*isolées réunies*')[80]	1	837
2nd Provisional Dragoons	4	592
3rd Provisional Dragoons	4	536
5th Provisional Dragoons (18th Dragoons)	1	217
Bavarian depot battalion (Maj. Pillement)	1	527
Württemberg *Franquemont* Infantry	5 companies	c.820
French Artillery: 4 x 6-pounders, 2 x howitzers	–	87
Württemberg Artillery: 2 x 3-pounders	–	20

Augsburg

Berg Chasseurs-à-Cheval	4	817

GD Lagrange (3rd Division of Junot's corps)

    1st Brigade: GB Vaufreland

65th Ligne (I, II)	2	1,161
Grenadier & Voltigeur Companies/IV/		
46th Ligne (en route)	2 companies	234

    2nd Brigade: GB Ducos

11th Reserve Demi-Brigade (3, 4, 18, 63, 24, 64, 57 Ligne)	3	1,205
12th Reserve Demi-Brigade (7, 17, 9, 10, 21, 28 Léger)	3	1,050

[This brigade was in Alsace and did not join the division (called to Vienna as replacements)]

Tyrolian border east (approx Lech to Saalach):

3rd Bavarian Division: GL Deroy[81]

    1st Brigade: GM Vincenti (Murnau-Habach-Tölz-Tegernsee)

I/5th Infantry	1	572
14th Infantry	2	1,248
7th Light	1	362
2nd Dragoons	1	c.120
one battery		

    Oberst Arco (Kochel)

      Provisional Battalion

(depots: 1st, 2nd, 5th, 7th Inf; 1st, 2nd Light)	1	773

      Provisional Squadron

(depots: 1st Drgns; 1st, 2nd, 3rd Chevaulegers)	1	204
2 x 6-pounders	–	26

    2nd Brigade: GM Siebein (Rosenheim)

9th Infantry	8 companies	c.1,130
10th Infantry	2	1,178

2nd Dragoons	3	c.360
two batteries		
Reichenhall (Oberstleutnant Waible)		
9th Infantry	2 companies	c.280
one gun		
Kufstein Garrison (Maj. Aicher)		
Provisional Light Battalion (depots: 1st, 2nd, 5th, 6th Light)	1	471
Fortress artillery	–	98
60 guns		
Salzburg Garrison (GB Kister)		
II/5th Infantry	1	695
5th Light	1	481

On the Danube in Bavaria: GD Bourcier

Regensburg

GD Delaroche		
1st Provisional Dragoons	4	764

Passau and vicinity

5th Provisional Dragoons (19th, 20th, 21st Dragoons)	3	576
Naval Artificer Battalion	2 companies	270
GD Rouyer		
4th Rheinbund (Saxon Duchies)	3	2,334
5th Rheinbund (Anhalt/Lippe)	2	1,200
(plus 126 detached at Engelhartszell in Austria)		
6th Rheinbund (Reuss/Waldeck/Schwarzburg)	2	473
(plus 459 detached at Eferding in Austria)		
Oberhaus (Passau) Garrison		
Provisional Battalion (depots of 6th, 9th, 10th, 14th Infantry)	1	

Note: 5th Provisional Dragoons had been in Schongau; it is not clear when it went to Passau (before being called north to Nuremberg).

Other

Braunau/Ried: II/*Camrer* (Württemberg)	1	887
Bavarian fortress garrisons (as of 8 July)		
Rosenberg: 10th Infantry depot	1 company	
artillery half-company		
Forchheim: depots of 4th, 8th Inf, 5th Lt	5 companies	
artillery company		
Rothenberg: depots of 5th, 6th Inf, 3rd Lt	3 companies	
artillery half-company		
Erfurt garrison: Frankfurt battalion	1	556

Elbe Observation Corps: GD Junot (Hanau)

Cavalry: GB Vaufreland		
6th Provisional Dragoons	4	839

1st Division: GD Rivaud
 1st Brigade: GB Lameth

IV/19th Ligne	1	762
IV/25th Ligne	1	662
IV/28th Ligne	1	763
2nd Brigade: GB Taupin		
IV/36th Ligne	1	849
IV/50th Ligne	1	738
IV/75th Ligne	1	876
3rd Brigade: GB Valletaux		
IV/13th Léger	1	769
IV/48th Ligne	1	498
IV/108th Ligne	1	706

  [This brigade was in Belgium and did not join the corps during the war]
2nd Division: GD Despeaux
 1st Brigade: GB Clément

5th Reserve Demi-Brigade (12, 14, 34, 88 Ligne)	4	1,610
9th Reserve Demi-Brigade (8, 21, 94, 95, 39, 85 Ligne)	3	1,311
2nd Brigade: GB Duverger		
10th Reserve Demi-Brigade (27, 30, 33, 61, 40, 111 Ligne)	3	855
13th Reserve Demi-Brigade	4	2,410

  (59, 69, 76, 96, 100, 103, 105 Ligne; 6, 16, 24, 25, 26 Léger)
3rd Division: GD Lagrange—see above
Artillery: 2 x 12-pounders, 8 x 6-pounders, 2 x howitzers   –   313

Orders of Battle for the Battle of Wagram, 5–6 July 1809

ORGANISATIONS, MORNING OF 5 JULY

AUSTRIAN HAUPTARMEE[82]

Archduke Charles

	baons /sqdns	present under arms
Advance Guard, FML Nordmann[83]		
Brigade: GM Riese		
Bellegarde Infantry No. 44	3	1,344
2nd UWW Landwehr (Maj. Steinsberg)	1	491
Chasteler Infantry No. 46	3	1,190
1st UWW Landwehr (Maj. Richter)	1	633
Beaulieu Infantry No. 58 (I, III)	2	1,249
3rd UMB Landwehr (Oberstlt Obergfell)	1	568
Brigade battery: 8 x 6-pounder		
Brigade: GM Mayer		
Deutschmeister Infantry No. 4	3	1,533
6th UWW Landwehr (Maj. Hoyos)	1	683
Kerpen Infantry No. 49	3	1,460
5th UWW Landwehr (Maj. Cavriani)	1	544
Brigade battery: 8 x 6-pounder		
Brigade: GM Peter Vécsey		
Wallach-Illyria Grenz Regiment No. 13	1	705
Hessen-Homburg Hussar Regiment No. 4	7¾	942
Cavalry battery: 4 x 6-pounder, 2 x howitzer		

Brigade: GM von Frelich

1st Jäger Battalion (five companies)	1	488
7th Jäger Battalion	1	442
Stipsicz Hussars No. 10	8	815
Primatial Insurrection Hussars	6	771

    Cavalry battery: 4 x 6-pounder, 2 x howitzer
  Artillery Reserve: one position battery (6 guns)
Total infantry: 11,330
Total cavalry: 2,528
Total artillery: 28 guns (likely all 6-pounders), 8 x howitzers
Note: II/*Beaulieu* detached early on 5 July to Marchegg.

I Corps, GdK Bellegarde

Division: FML Fresnel
  Brigade: GM von Stutterheim

2nd Jäger Battalion	1	664
Klenau Chevaulegers No. 5	8	801

    Cavalry battery: 4 x 6-pounders, 2 x howitzers
    Position battery: 4 x 6-pounders, 2 x howitzers
  Brigade: GM Clary

Anton Mittrowsky Infantry No. 10	2	2,421
1st Hradisch Landwehr (Oberstlt Magny)	1	732
Erbach Infantry No. 42	2	2,908

    Brigade battery: 8 x 6-pounders
  Brigade: GM Motzen

Argenteau Infantry No. 35	3	3,382
4th *EH Carl* Legion (Oberstlt Jannek)	1	470

    Brigade battery: 8 x 6-pounders
Division: GM Wacquant (serving as interim commander)
  Brigade: GM Henneberg

Reuss-Plauen Infantry No. 17	3	3,516
Kolowrat Infantry No. 36	3	2,876

    Brigade battery: 8 x 6-pounders
  Brigade: GM Wacquant

Erzherzog Rainer Infantry No. 11	3	2,994
Vogelsang Infantry No. 47	3	2,892

    Position battery: 4 x 6-pounders, 2 x howitzers
  Artillery Reserve:
    Two position batteries: 4 x 12-pounders, 2 x howitzers each
    Position battery: 4 x 6-pounders, 2 x howitzers
Infantry: 22,855
Cavalry: 801
Total artillery: 8 x 12-pounders, 40 x 6-pounders, 12 x howitzers
Note: FML Dedovich joined I Corps on 6 July. Wacquant, Henneberg, and Motzen were
  all wounded on 5 July.

II Corps, FML Hohenzollern
- Division: FML Brady
  - Brigade: GM Paar

Infantry Regiment No. 25 (former *Zedtwitz*)	3	2,217
2nd Znaim Landwehr (Maj. Sterzl)	1	801
Froon Infantry No. 54	3	3,273
3rd Hradisch Landwehr (Maj. Höger)	1	753

  - Brigade battery: 8 x 6-pounders
  - Brigade: GM von Buresch

Zach Infantry No. 15	2	2,035
3rd Brünn Landwehr (Maj. Ségur-Cabanac)	1	913
Josef Colloredo Infantry No. 57	2	3,122
1st Brünn Landwehr (Oberstlt Taafe)	1	750

  - Brigade battery: 8 x 6-pounders
  - Position battery: 4 x 6-pounders, 2 x howitzers
- Division: FML Ulm
  - Brigade: GM von Altstern

Rohan Infantry No. 21	3	3,748

  - Brigade battery: 8 x 6-pounders
  - Brigade: GM Wied-Runkel

D'Aspre Infantry No. 18	3	3,001
Frelich Infantry Regiment No. 28	3	3,485

  - Brigade battery (?): 8 x 6-pounders
  - Position battery: 4 x 6-pounders, 2 x howitzers
- Division: FML Siegenthal
  - Brigade: GM Ignaz vonHardegg

8th Jäger Battalion	1	675
2nd *EH Carl* Legion (Oberstlt Kinsky)	1	883
Vincent Chevaulegers No. 4	6	537

- Artillery Reserve
  - Cavalry battery: 4 x 6-pounders, 2 x howitzers
  - Two position batteries: 4 x 12-pounders, 2 x howitzers each
  - Position battery: 4 x 6-pounders, 2 x howitzers
- Total infantry: 25,656
- Total cavalry: 537
- Total artillery: 8 x 12-pounders, 48 x 6-pounders, 12 x howitzers

III Corps, FML Kolowrat
- Division: FML Vukassovich
  - Brigade: GM Schneller

Lobkowitz Jäger	4 companies	608
Schwarzenberg Uhlans No. 2	6	667

  - Cavalry battery: 4 x 6-pounders, 2 x howitzers
  - Position battery: 4 x 6-pounders, 2 x howitzers
  - Brigade: GM Grill

Schröder Infantry No. 7	3	1,995
Wenzel Colloredo Infantry No. 56	3	2,765
Brigade battery: 8 x 6-pounders		
Brigade: Oberst Wratislaw		
1st and 2nd Combined Prague Landwehr (Oberst Wratislaw)	1	746
1st Beraun Landwehr (Maj. Wrtby)	1	576
2nd Beraun Landwehr (Maj. Klebelsberg)	1	591
Brigade battery: 8 x 3-pounders		
Division: FML St Julien		
Brigade: GM Lilienberg		
Kaiser Infantry No. 1	2	1,736
Manfredini Infantry No. 12	3	2,662
Würzburg Infantry No. 23	2	872
Brigade battery: 8 x 6-pounders		
Brigade: GM Biber		
Kaunitz Infantry No. 20	3	2,469
Württemberg Infantry No. 38	2	909
Brigade battery: 8 x 6-pounders		
Position battery: 4 x 6-pounders, 2 x howitzers		

Artillery Reserve
Two position batteries: 4 x 12-pounders, 2 x howitzers each
Total infantry: 15,929
Total cavalry: 667
Total artillery: 8 x 12-pounders, 36 x 6-pounders, 8 x 3-pounders, 10 x howitzers
Note: 1st and 2nd Battalions of *Schröder* were left in reserve near Stammersdorf when III
Corps advanced; possibly with one additional unidentified battalion.

IV Corps, FML Rosenberg

Division: FML Hohenlohe-Bartenstein		
Brigade: GM Philipp von Hessen-Homburg		
Hiller Infantry No. 2	3	2,717
Sztaray Infantry No. 33	3	2,101
Brigade battery: 8 x 6-pounders		
(Brigade: GM Riese detached to Advance Guard)		
Division: FML Rohan		
(Brigade: GM Mayer detached to Advance Guard)		
Brigade: Oberst Swinburne		
Erzherzog Ludwig Infantry No. 8	3	2,189
1st Iglau Landwehr (Maj. Nesselrode)	1	877
Koburg Infantry No. 22	3	2,001
1st Znaim Landwehr (Maj. Haugwitz)	1	829
Brigade battery: 8 x 6-pounders		
Position battery: 4 x 6-pounders, 2 x howitzers		
Division: FML Radetzky		
Brigade: Oberst Weiss		

Erzherzog Karl Infantry No. 3	3	1,699
4th OMB Landwehr (Oberst Fölseis)	1	578
attached from 1st OMB Landwehr	1 company	123
Stain Infantry No. 50	3	1,652
4th UWW Landwehr (Maj. Gilleis)	1	559
Brigade battery: 8 x 6-pounders		
Brigade: GM Provenchères		
1st *EH Carl* Legion (Maj. Watterich)	1	1,015
2nd Moravian Volunteers (Maj. Vetter)	1	584
Carneville Freikorps (infantry)	1 company	73
Carneville Freikorps (cavalry)	1	48
Erzherzog Ferdinand Hussars No. 3	8	792
Cavalry battery: 4 x 6-pounders, 2 x howitzers		
Position battery: 4 x 6-pounders, 2 x howitzers		
Artillery Reserve		
Two position batteries: 4 x 12-pounders, 2 x howitzers each		
Position battery: 4 x 6-pounders, 2 x howitzers		
Total infantry: 16,997		
Total cavalry: 840		
Total artillery: 8 x 12-pounders, 40 x 6-pounders, 12 x howitzers		

VI Corps, FML Klenau

Division: FML Hohenfeld

Brigade: GM Adler

Klebek Infantry No. 14	2	1,180
1st OWW Landwehr (Maj. Prachma)	1	640
Jordis Infantry No. 59	2⅓	1,110
1st Combined Upper Austrian (Innviertel) Landwehr		
(Maj. Straka)	1	948
3rd *EH Carl* Legion (Maj. Lougier)	1	792
Brigade battery: 8 x 6-pounders		

Division: FML Kottulinsky

Brigade: GM Hoffmeister

Duka Infantry No. 39	3	1,737
Gyulai Infantry No. 60	3	2,194
Brigade battery: 8 x 6-pounders		
Position battery: 4 x 6-pounders, 2 x howitzers		

Brigade: GM Splenyi

Benjovszky Infantry No. 31 (II, III)	2	1,588
Splenyi Infantry No. 51	3	1,514
3rd Vienna Volunteers (Maj. Waldstein)	1	475
4th Vienna Volunteers (Oberstlt Küffel)	1	221
3rd Moravian Volunteers (Maj. Boxberg)	1	927
Brigade battery: 8 x 6-pounders		

Division: FML Vincent

Brigade: GM Mariassy

1st Vienna Volunteers (Maj. St Quentin)	1	575
4th UMB Landwehr (Maj. Colloredo)	1	466

Brigade battery: 8 x 3-pounders

Brigade: GM Walmoden

Liechtenstein Hussars No. 7	8	767
2nd Vienna Volunteers (Oberstlt von Steigentesch)	1	567

Cavalry battery: 4 x 6-pounders, 2 x howitzers

Position battery: 4 x 6-pounders, 2 x howitzers

Brigade: GM August Vécsey

Kienmayer Hussars No. 8	8	639
Warasdin-St Georg Grenz Regiment No. 6	2	937
Brod Grenz Regiment No. 7 (remnants)	2 companies	326

Artillery Reserve

Position battery: 4 x 6-pounders, 2 x howitzers

Total infantry: 16,197

Total cavalry: 1,406

Total artillery: 40 x 6-pounders, 8 x 3-pounders, 8 x howitzers

Note: 2nd Vienna combined with 1st under Mariassy on 6 July.

Reserve Corps, GdK Liechtenstein
Cavalry Reserve

Division: FML Friedrich Hessen-Homburg

Brigade: GM Roussel d'Hurbal

Erzherzog Franz Cuirassiers No. 2	6	493
Herzog Albert Cuirassiers No. 3	6	541

Brigade: GM Lederer

Kronprinz Ferdinand Cuirassiers No. 4	6	563
Hohenzollern Cuirassiers No. 8	6	645

Brigade: GM von Kroyher

Kaiser Cuirassiers No. 1	4	302
Liechtenstein Cuirassiers No. 6	6	504

Division: FML Schwarzenberg

Brigade: GM Theimern

Rosenberg Chevaulegers No. 6	8	973
Knesevich Dragoons No. 3	6	639

Two cavalry batteries: 4 x 6-pounders, 2 x howitzers each

Insurrection: GM Kerekes

Neutra Insurrection Hussars	6	802

Division: FML Nostitz

Brigade: GM Rothkirch

EH Johann Dragoons No. 1	6	631
Riesch Dragoons No. 6	6	671

Cavalry battery: 4 x 6-pounders, 2 x howitzers

Brigade: GM Wartensleben

Blankenstein Hussars No. 6	10	1,164
O'Reilly Chevaulegers No. 3	7	862
Cavalry battery: 4 x 6-pounders, 2 x howitzers		

Total cavalry: 8,790
Total artillery: 16 x 6-pounders, 8 x howitzers
Note: Two squadrons of *Kaiser* Cuirassiers guarding trains.

Grenadier Reserve

Division: FML d'Aspre

Brigade: GM Merville

Scharlach Grenadier Battalion (31, 32, 51)	1	562
Scovaud Grenadier Battalion (4, 49, 63)	1	503
Jambline Grenadier Battalion (14, 45, 59)[84]	1	422
Brzezinski Grenadier Battalion (24, 30, 41)	1	537
Brigade battery: 8 x 6-pounders		

Brigade: GM von Hammer

Kirchenbetter Grenadier Battalion (34, 37, 48)	1	462
Bissingen Grenadier Battalion (3, 50, 58)	1	633
Oklopsia Grenadier Battalion (12, 20, 23)	1	571
Locher Grenadier Battalion (8, 22, 60)	1	612
1st OMB Landwehr (Hptm Marchal)	1	464
Brigade battery: 8 x 6-pounders		

Division: FML Prochaska

Brigade: GM Murray

Frisch Grenadier Battalion (10, 11, 47)	1	620
Georgy Grenadier Battalion (17, 36, 42)	1	555
Portner Grenadier Battalion (40, 44, 46)	1	727
Leiningen Grenadier Battalion (25, 35, 54)	1	801
Brigade: GM Steyrer		
Hahn Grenadier Battalion (2, 33, 39)	1	716
Hromada Grenadier Battalion (1, 29, 38)	1	772
Legrand Grenadier Battalion (9, 55, 56)	1	776
Demontant Grenadier Battalion (7, 18, 21)	1	777
Berger Grenadier Battalion (15, 28, 57)	1	723
Brigade battery: 8 x 6-pounders		

Total infantry: 11,233
Total artillery: 24 x 6-pounders

Army Totals

Infantry: 120,197
Cavalry: 15,569
TOTAL INFANTRY/CAVALRY: 135,766
Guns: 388

Nearby but not engaged on 5 or 6 July: 10,855 infantry/cavalry and 44 guns under FML Reuss (not including an additional 6,000 under Schustekh).

FRENCH ARMY OF GERMANY[85]

Emperor Napoleon

	baons /sqdns	present under arms
Attached to Imperial Headquarters		
Württemberg *Herzog Heinrich* Chevaulegers	–	234
Württemberg I/*Camrer* Infantry	1	477
Company of Guides	–	120
Imperial Guard[86]		
Division (Young Guard): GD Curial		
Brigade: GB Rouget		
Tirailleur-Chasseurs	2	1,287
Tirailleur-Grenadiers	1	1,116
Brigade: GB Dumoustier		
Fusilier-Chasseurs	2	1,120
Fusilier-Grenadiers	2	1,145
5th and 6th Foot Batteries (12 x 6-pounders)		
Division (Old Guard): GD Dorsenne		
GB Gros: Chasseurs	2	1,452
GB Michel: Grenadiers	2	1,203
1st and 2nd Foot Batteries (12 x 6-pounders)		
Cavalry: GD Walther		
Polish Chevaulegers	4	414
Chasseurs-à-Cheval	4	1,046
Dragoons	4	976
Grenadiers-à-Cheval	4	1,001
Elite Gendarmes	2	266
1st through 4th Horse Batteries (24 x 6-pounders)		
Artillery Reserve: 3rd and 4th Foot Batteries (12 x 12-pounders)		
Total infantry: 7,323		
Total cavalry: 1,305		
Total artillery: 48 x 6-pounders, 12 x 12-pounders		
2nd Corps: GD Oudinot[87]		
1st Division: GD Tharreau		
1st Brigade: GB Conroux		
1st Light Demi-Brigade		
IV/6th Léger	1	585
IV/24th Léger	1	451
IV/25th Léger	1	552
3rd Light Demi-Brigade		

Tirailleurs Corses	1	528
IV/9th Léger	1	538
IV/27th Léger	1	612
2nd Brigade: GB Albert		
1st Line Demi-Brigade		
IV/8th Ligne	1	650
IV/24th Ligne	1	435
IV/45th Ligne	1	464
2nd Line Demi-Brigade		
IV/94th Ligne	1	650
IV/95th Ligne	1	537
IV/96th Ligne	1	481
3rd Brigade: GB Jarry		
3rd Line Demi-Brigade		
IV/54th Ligne	1	581
IV/63rd Ligne	1	428
4th Line Demi-Brigade		
IV/4th Ligne	1	518
IV/18th Ligne	1	567
Artillery: one foot and one horse battery		
2nd Division: GD Frère		
1st Brigade: GB Coëhorn		
2nd Light Demi-Brigade		
IV/17th Léger	1	476
IV/28th Léger	1	504
4th Light Demi-Brigade		
IV/16th Léger	1	658
IV/26th Léger	1	539
Tirailleurs du Po	1	543
2nd Brigade: GB Razout		
5th Line Demi-Brigade		
IV/27th Ligne	1	633
IV/39th Ligne	1	458
6th Line Demi-Brigade		
IV/59th Ligne	1	535
IV/69th Ligne	1	634
IV/76th Ligne	1	480
3rd Brigade: GB Ficatier		
7th Line Demi-Brigade		
IV/40th Ligne	1	481
IV/88th Ligne	1	690
8th Line Demi-Brigade		
IV/64th Ligne	1	633
IV/100th Ligne	1	486
Artillery: one foot and one horse battery		

3rd Division: GD Grandjean
  1st Brigade: GB Marion

10th Léger	3	1,846

  2nd Brigade: GB Lorencez

3rd Ligne	3	1,644
57th Ligne	3	1,572

  3rd Brigade: GB Brun

72nd Ligne	3	1,344
105th Ligne	3	1,452

  Artillery: two foot batteries, one horse battery

13th Demi-Brigade d'Elite (Portuguese Legion): GB Carcome Lobo

Infantry	3	1,422
Cavalry	2	229

Light Cavalry Brigade: GB Colbert

9th Hussars	4	617
7th Chasseurs-à-Cheval	3	543
20th Chasseurs-à-Cheval	3	519
Attached: Saxon *Prinz Johann* Chevaulegers	4	524

Corps Artillery: two foot batteries

Total infantry: 25,616
Total cavalry: 2,432
Corps/Divisional Artillery: 4 x 12-pounders, 30 x 6-pounders, 14 x howitzers
Regimental Artillery: 16 x 6-pounders

3rd Corps: Marshal Davout[88]

1st Division: GD Morand
  1st Brigade: GB Guiot de Lacour

13th Léger	3	1,965
17th Ligne	3	2,092

  2nd Brigade: GB L'Huillier

30th Ligne	3	2,053
61st Ligne	3	2,094

2nd Division: GD Friant
  Brigade: GB Gilly

15th Léger	3	1,822
33rd Ligne	3	1,717

  Brigade: GB Barbanègre

48th Ligne	3	1,937

  Brigade: GB Grandeau

108th Ligne	3	1,956
111th Ligne	3	1,878

3rd Division: GD Gudin
  1st Brigade: GB Boyer

7th Léger	3	2,329

  2nd Brigade: GB Leclerc

12th Ligne	3	1,795
21st Ligne	3	1,953
3rd Brigade: GB Duppelin		
25th Ligne	3	1,915
85th Ligne	3	2,130
4th Division: GD Puthod		
1st Brigade: GB Girard		
IV/17th Ligne	1	526
IV/7th Léger	1	280
IV/12th Ligne	1	465
IV/61st Ligne	1	546
IV/65th Ligne	1	275
2nd Brigade: GB Desailly		
IV/21st Ligne	1	632
IV/30th Ligne	1	577
IV/33rd Ligne	1	512
IV/85th Ligne	1	572
IV/111th Ligne	1	624
Light Cavalry Division: GD Montbrun		
Brigade: GB Pajol		
5th Hussars	4	684
11th Chasseurs-à-Cheval	4	674
12th Chasseurs-à-Cheval	4	718
Brigade: GB Jacquinot		
7th Hussars	4	567
1st Chasseurs-à-Cheval	3	325
2nd Chasseurs-à-Cheval	3	359

Total infantry: 32,645
Total cavalry: 3,327
Corps/Divisional Artillery: 8 x 12-pounders, 25 x 6-pounders, 18 x 4-pounders, 2 x 3-pounders (reserve park), 8 x howitzers
Regimental Artillery: 32 x regimental pieces
Attached

1st Dragoon Division: GD Grouchy (GB Debroc)		
7th Dragoons	4	502
30th Dragoons	4	634
Italian *Queen's* Dragoons	4	477
4 or 6 guns		
2nd Dragoon Division: GD Pully (GB Poinsot)		
23rd Dragoons	3	502
28th Dragoons	3	241
29th Dragoons	3	392

Total attached cavalry: 2,748
Note: Pully had 978 men detached in Italy or en route to their regiments, few if any arrived in time for Wagram.

4th Corps: Marshal Massena[89]

1st Division: GD Legrand		
1st Brigade: GB Friedrichs		
26th Léger	3	1,630
18th Ligne	3	1,787
2nd (Baden) Brigade: Oberst von Neuenstein		
1st Baden Infantry *Grossherzog*	1⅓	975
2nd Baden Infantry *Erbgrossherzog*	2	1,399
Jäger Battalion *Lingg*	1	463
2nd Division: GD Carra St-Cyr		
1st Brigade: GB Cosson		
24th Léger	3	1,741
2nd Brigade: GB Dalesme		
4th Ligne	3	1,964
46th Ligne	3	1,953
3rd (Hessian) Brigade: GB Schiner (French) and GM von Nagel (Hesse-Darmstadt)		
Leib-Garde Regiment	2	1,181
Leib-Garde Fusiliers	1	489
Leib Regiment	2	1,167
1st Leib Fusiliers	1	548
3rd Division: GD Molitor		
1st Brigade: GB Leguay		
2nd Ligne	2	1,292
16th Ligne	3	1,399
2nd Brigade: GB Viviès		
37th Ligne	3	1,464
67th Ligne	2	1,184
4th Division: GD Boudet		
1st Brigade: GB Grillot		
3rd Léger	2	1,406
2nd Brigade: GB Valory		
56th Ligne	3	1,590
93rd Ligne	2	1,309
Light Cavalry Division: GD Lasalle		
Brigade: GB Piré		
8th Hussars	3	500
16th Chasseurs	3	441
Brigade: GB Bruyère		
13th Chasseurs	3	485
24th Chasseurs	2	288
Division: GD Marulaz		
3rd Chasseurs	2	329
14th Chasseurs	3	139
19th Chasseurs	3	322

23rd Chasseurs	3	324
Baden Light Dragoons	4	208
Hessian Chevaulegers	3	179

Total infantry: 24,941
Total cavalry: 3,215
French Corps/Divisional artillery: 8 x 12-pounders, 42 x 6-pounders, 11 x howitzers
French Regimental artillery: 17 x regimental pieces
Baden artillery: 8 x 6-pounders, 4 x howitzers
Hessian artillery: 5 x 6-pounders, 1 x howitzer
Note: Four musketeer companies of II/1st Baden Infantry (544) guarding park and baggage; GM Harrant was ill.

9th Corps (Saxon): Marshal Bernadotte[90]

Staff Battalion	1	470
Horse Artillery Battery: 4 x 8-pounders		
Advance Guard: GM von Gutschmid		
Prinz Clemens Chevaulegers	4	462
Hussar Regiment	3	327
Herzog Albrecht Chevaulegers	1	147
1st Division: GL von Zezschwitz		
1st Brigade: GM von Hartitzsch		
combined Leib Grenadier Guard Battalion	1	513
2nd Grenadier Battalion (Major von Bose)	1	529
2nd Infantry Brigade: GM von Zeschau		
König Infantry Battalion	1	899
von Niesemeuschel Infantry Battalion	1	954
Combined Infantry Battalion (Oberstlt von Klengel)	1	805
(from I/*Dyherrn* and II/*von Oebschelwitz*)		
1st Heavy Battery: 4 x 8-pounders, 2 x howitzers		
1st Light Battery: 4 x 8-pounders, 2 x howitzers		
2nd Division: GL von Polenz		
1st Infantry Brigade: GM von Lecoq		
Prinz Clemens Infantry Battalion	1	750
von Low Infantry Battalion	1	837
von Cerrini Infantry Battalion	1	876
2nd Schützen Battalion (Major von Egidy)	1	623
2nd Infantry Brigade: GM von Steindel		
Prinz Anton Infantry Battalion	1	893
Prinz Maximilian Infantry Battalion	1	896
Prinz Friedrich August Infantry Battalion	1	909
Cavalry Brigade: GM von Feilitzsch		
Leib-Garde Cuirassiers	4	572
Gardes du Corps Regiment	2	284
Karabiniers Regiment	2	206
2nd Heavy Battery: 4 x 8-pounders, 2 x howitzers		

2nd Light Battery: 4 x 8-pounders, 2 x howitzers
French Division: GD Dupas
  1st Brigade: GB Gency

5th Léger	2	1,547

2nd Brigade: GB Veau

19th Ligne	3	2,197

Attached

1st Grenadier Battalion (Major von Radeloff)	1	526
1st Schützen Battalion (Major von Metzsch)	1	657

  Artillery: 12 guns
Total infantry: 14,411 (not including Staff Battalion)
Total cavalry: 1,998
Total artillery: 18 x 8-pounders, 8 x howitzers, 12 French pieces

Army of Italy: Viceroy Eugene[91]

Right Wing: GD MacDonald
  Division: GD Lamarque
    1st Brigade: GB Huard

18th Léger (III, IV)	2	894
13th Ligne	3	1,880

2nd Brigade: GB Alméras

23rd Ligne (III, IV)	2	508
29th Ligne	3	1,994
Attached: 92nd Ligne (I, IV)[92]	2	c.1,100

Centre: GD Grenier
  Division: GD Seras (> GB Moreau on 6th)
    1st Brigade: GB Moreau

IV/35th Ligne	1	556
53rd Ligne	3	1,569

2nd Brigade: GB Roussel

IV/42nd Ligne	1	435
106th Ligne	3	1,384

Attached

112th Ligne	3	1,088

Division: GD Durutte
  1st Brigade: (GB Valentin)[93]

23rd Léger	3	1,246
62nd Ligne	4	1,796

2nd Brigade: GB Dessaix

60th Ligne (III, IV)	2	494
102nd Ligne	3	1,675

Royal Italian Guard:
  Cavalry: GB Viani

Honour Guards	1	142
Dragoons	2	324

8th Léger (III, IV)	2	1,062
1st Ligne	3	1,349
2nd Brigade: GB Pastol		
52nd Ligne	3	1,701
Total infantry: 4,112		
Artillery: six guns		

2nd Division/7th Corps (Bavarian): GL von Wrede[101]

1st Brigade: GM Minucci		
6th Light Battalion	1	569
3rd Infantry *Prinz Karl*	2	1,277
13 Infantry	2	1,157
2nd Brigade: GM Beckers		
6th Infantry *Herzog Wilhelm*	2	1,070
7th Infantry *Löwenstein*	2	1,388
Cavalry: GM Preysing		
2nd Chevaulegers *König*	4	474
3rd Chevaulegers *Leiningen*	4	513

Total infantry: 5,461
Total cavalry: 987
Artillery: 4 x 12-pounders, 20 x 6-pounders, 12 x howitzers

Total reinforcements: 22,838 infantry, 1,246 cavalry, 71 guns

Army Totals, 6 July (troops on Lobau Island not included, casualties not deducted)
 Infantry: 145,749
 Cavalry: 26,187
 TOTAL INFANTRY/CAVALRY: 171,939
 Guns: 475

APPENDIX 14

Unengaged Forces Along the Danube during the Battle of Wagram

AUSTRIA

	baons /sqdns	present under arms
Observing Linz: FML Somariva[102]		
In Neumarkt:		
Merveldt Uhlans No. 1	4	476
6th Jäger Battalion	1	497
I/*Peterwardein* Grenz Infantry No. 9	1	248
1st Chrudim Landwehr	1	680
3rd Chrudim Landwehr	1	624
2nd Pilsen Landwehr	1	583
3rd Pilsen Landwehr	1	721
Artillery: 1 x cavalry battery, ½ x 3-pounder brigade battery		
In Hellmonsödt:		
Merveldt Uhlans No. 1	2	197
5th Jäger Battalion	1	578
II/*Peterwardein* Grenz Infantry No. 9	1	712
4th Chrudim Landwehr	1	529
1st Kaurschim Landwehr	1	356
1st Pilsen Landwehr	1	506
2nd Tschaslau Landwehr	1	494
Artillery: ½ x 3-pounder brigade battery		

V Corps, FML Reuss
Division: FML Weissenwolff
  Brigade: GM Neustädter

Reuss-Greitz Infantry No. 55	2	847
3rd Prerau Landwehr (Maj. Bukovsky)	1	794
Czartoryski Infantry No. 9	3	1,390
4th Brünn Landwehr (Maj. Hoffmann)	1	920
Brigade battery: 8 x 6-pounders		

  Brigade: Oberst Pflüger

Lindenau Infantry No. 29	3	2,402
3rd Jäger Battalion	1	770

  Brigade: GM Klebelsberg

Gradiska Grenz Infantry No. 8	2	1,781
4th Jäger Battalion	1	819
EH Carl Uhlans No. 3	8	718
Brigade battery: 8 x 6-pounders		

Artillery Reserve
  Three position batteries

5th Vienna Volunteers (Maj. Salis)	1	414

Division: FML Schustekh
  Brigade: Reinwald

Infantry Regiment No. 40 (formerly *Josef Mittrowsky*)	3	2,006

  Brigade: Hardegg

5th *EH Carl* Legion (Maj. Woracziczky)	1	826
6th *EH Carl* Legion (Maj. Czernin)	1	982
1st Moravian Volunteers (Maj. Seyffert)	1	933
Levenehr Dragoons No. 3	6	280

  Brigade: GM Sinzendorf

2nd Combined Upper/Lower Austrian Landwehr (Maj. Lichtenberg)	1	441
3rd Combined Upper/Lower Austrian Landwehr (Maj. Fürstenberg)	1	535

Army of Inner Austria, Archduke Johann (March Order, 6 July)[103]
Division: FML Frimont
  Advance Guard: GM Eckhardt

EH Josef Hussars No. 2	4	c.205
Warasdin-Kreuz Grenz Infantry No. 5	1	c.690
Esterhazy Infantry No. 32	1	c.530
9th Jäger Battalion	1 company	79
Cavalry half-battery		
Brigade battery		

  Brigade: Oberst Besan

EH Josef Hussars No. 2	4	c.205
Hohenzollern Chevaulegers No. 2	1	35

Hohenlohe Dragoons No. 2	5	337
Savoy Dragoons No. 5	1	59

Division: FML Jellacic
    Brigade: GM Bach

Warasdin-Kreuz Grenz Infantry No. 5[104]	2	c.1,390
Esterhazy Infantry No. 32	2	c.1,060
6 x 3-pounders		

    Brigade: GM de Best

1st Banal Grenz Infantry No. 10	2	1,342
de Vaux Infantry No. 62	1	646

Division: FML Colloredo
    Brigade: GM Devaux

Ogulin Grenz Infantry No. 3	2	801
Allvintzi Infantry No. 19	3	2,165
St Julien Infantry No. 61[105]	1	c.500
4th Graz Landwehr (Maj. Zenone)	1	485
5th Graz Landwehr (Maj. Kottulinsky)	1	470
One battery		

Reserve
    Brigade: GM Lutz

Welsperg Grenadier Battalion (16, 26, 27)	1	417
Zittar Grenadier Battalion (53, 62)	1	270
Chimani Grenadier Battalion (13, 43)	1	253
Gersanich Grenadier Battalion (19, 52, 61)	1	517
Brigade battery: 4 x 6-pounders, 2 x howitzers		

Rear Guard:

Ott Hussars No. 5	8	504
Sümegh Insurrection Hussars	6	915

Artillery Reserve: 2 x 12-pounders, 8 x 6-pounders, 4 x howitzers

Total infantry: 11,615
Total cavalry: 2,260
Artillery: approximately 45 guns

Note: The following had been part of the Komorn garrison, but had likely joined Johann by 5 July:[106]

Hohenlohe-Bartenstein Infantry No. 26 (depot division) 2 companies		206
Franz Jellacic Infantry No. 62	2	869

These would bring his total available infantry on 6 July to 12,690.

Pressburg Garrison: GM Bianchi (6 July)[107]

Lusignan Infantry No. 16	2	723(580)
Strassaldo Infantry No. 27	3	838(756)
I/*Szulin* Grenz Infantry No. 4	3 companies	317(204)
2nd Combined Upper Austrian (Mühlviertel) Lw (Maj. Ungerhofer)	1	385(214)

2nd OWW Landwehr (formerly Maj. Clary)	1	(466)
Pressburg Insurrection Hussars	2	(230)
Marchegg: 3rd UWW Landwehr, 2 guns (Maj. Fuchs)	1	568
Schlosshof: 2nd UMB Landwehr (Maj. Schönborn)	1	671

Notes:

a Figures in parentheses are Bianchi's where different from 30 June 'Früh-Rapport'; 2nd OWW and Insurrection from Bianchi.

b The following was detached from Nordmann early on 5 July to reinforce Marchegg:

II/*Beaulieu* Infantry No. 58	1	c.600

FRANCE

	baons /sqdns	present under arms
Left Wing, Army of Italy: GD Baraguey d'Hilliers		
Vicinity Pressburg: GD Severoli[108]		
1st Brigade: GB Teste		
IV/1st Léger	1	291
IV/2nd Italian Line	1	403
2nd Brigade: GB Julhien		
1st Italian Line	3	1,234
II/7th Italian Line	1	375
Dalmatian Regiment	2	887
Light Cavalry Brigade: GB Thiry		
25th Chasseurs	3	399
1st Provisional Chasseurs	4	662
Württemberg *Herzog Heinrich* Chasseurs	3	304
10 guns		
Raab garrison: GD Narbonne[109]		
3rd Italian Line (II, IV)	2	715
Combined French detachments (eleven different regiments)	–	283
Artillerymen, sappers, miners	–	148
Artillery: 10 x 12-pounders, 4 x 6-pounders, 2 x 3-pounders, 4 x mortars		
Vienna Garrison: GD Andréossy		
Nassau 2nd Rheinbund	2	1,502
Württemberg *Leib* Chevaulegers	2	269
Two other squadrons (255) detached in scattered locations.		
Other		
Wiener Neustadt: 6th Hussars	4	515
Bruck an der Mur: 18th Léger	2	974

Between Melk and Vienna: 8th Corps (Württemberg), GD Vandamme[110]
Cavalry Division: GL Wöllwarth
  Brigade: GM Stettner

König Jäger-zu-Pferd	4	423
Herzog Louis Jäger-zu-Pferd	4	353

Infantry Division:
  Brigade: GM Franquemont

Kronprinz	2	1,230
Herzog Wilhelm	2	1,279

  Brigade: GM Scharffenstein

Phull	2	980
Herzog Wilhelm	2	1,141

  Light Brigade: GM Hügel

Jäger Battalion *König*	1	600
Jäger Battalion *von Neuffer*	1	529
1st Light Battalion *von Wolff*	1	574
2nd Light Battalion *von Brüsselle*	1	610

Artillery:
  Foot Artillery Battery (8 x 6-pounders)
  1st and 2nd Horse Artillery Batteries (4 x 6-pounders, 2 x howitzers each)
Note: Significant numbers detached: *König* (105), *Herzog Louis* (173), *Phull* (223).

Linz: 7th Corps (Bavarian), Marshal Lefebvre[111]
1st Division: GL Kronprinz Ludwig
  1st Brigade: GM Rechberg

1st Infantry Leib	2	1,307
2nd Infantry *Kronprinz*	2	1,210
1st Light Battalion	1	664

  2nd Brigade: GM Stengel

4th Infantry	2	1,212
8th Infantry *Herzog Pius*	2	1,165
3rd Light Battalion	2 companies	242

  Cavalry Brigade

1st Dragoons	2	244
1st Chevaulegers	4	399
4th Chevaulegers	4	429

Artillery: 4 x 12-pounders, 8 x 6-pounders, 12 x howitzers

Orders of Battle for the Battle of Znaim, 10–11 July 1809

AUSTRIAN HAUPTARMEE[112]

Archduke Charles

	baons /sqdns	present under arms
I Corps: GdK Bellegarde		
Division: FML Fresnel		
Brigade: GM Clary		
Anton Mittrowsky Infantry No. 10	2	1,327
1st Hradisch Landwehr (Oberstlt Magny)	1	223
Erbach Infantry No. 42	2	1,574
Brigade: Oberst von Schäffer		
Argenteau Infantry No. 35	3	1,573
4th *EH Carl* Legion (Oberstlt Jannek)	1	?
Division: GM Henneberg		
Brigade: GM Henneberg		
Reuss-Plauen Infantry No. 17	3	1,708
Kolowrat Infantry No. 36	3	1,935
Brigade: Oberst Faber		
Erzherzog Rainer Infantry No. 11	3	1,368
Vogelsang Infantry No. 47	3	1,472
Klenau Chevaulegers No. 5	8	646
Infantry: 11,180		
Cavalry: 646		

Total artillery (Wagram): 8 x 12-pounders, 40 x 6-pounders, 12 x howitzers

Note: The Landwehr battalion is not mentioned in accounts. 4th *EH Carl* Legion effectively destroyed, at most a few dozen men at Znaim.

II Corps: FML Hohenzollern[113]

Division: GM von Buresch
  Brigade: Oberst Quallenberg

Infantry Regiment No. 25 (former *Zedtwitz*)	3	1,038
Froon Infantry No. 54	3	1,970
3rd Hradisch Landwehr (Maj. Höger)	1	?

  Brigade: GM von Buresch

Zach Infantry No. 15	2	1,038
3rd Brünn Landwehr (Maj. Ségur)	1	*
Josef Colloredo Infantry No. 57	2	c.2,000
1st Brünn Landwehr (Oberstlt Taafe)	1	?

Division: FML Ulm
  Brigade: GM von Altstern

Rohan Infantry No. 21	3	1,721

  Brigade: GM Wied-Runkel

d'Aspre Infantry No. 18	3	1,456

Division:

Wallach-Illyria Grenz Regiment No. 13	2	413
Frelich Infantry Regiment No. 28	3	1,335
2nd *EH Carl* Legion (Oberstlt Kinsky)	1	c.500
Vincent Chevaulegers No. 4	6	290

Total infantry: c.11,471
Total cavalry: 290
Total artillery: 8 x 12-pounders, 48 x 6-pounders, 12 x howitzers
Note: GM von Hardegg detached on far left beyond Wittau with 2nd Znaim Landwehr
and a division of cavalry to observe army's flank and make contact with Rosenberg.
  * included with regiment

III Corps: FML Kolowrat[114]

Division: GM Schneller
  Brigade: Oberst Schmuttermaier

Lobkowitz Jäger	4 companies	653
Schwarzenberg Uhlans No. 2	6	535

  Brigade: Oberst Giffling

Schröder Infantry No. 7	3	2,258
Wenzel Colloredo Infantry No. 56	3	2,421

  Brigade: Oberst Wratislaw

1st and 2nd Combined Prague Landwehr (Oberst Wratislaw)	1	436
1st Beraun Landwehr (Maj. Wrtby)	1	492
2nd Beraun Landwehr (Maj. Klebelsberg)	1	473

Division: FML St Julien
  Brigade: GM Reinhard

Kaiser Infantry No. 1	2	1,174
Manfredini Infantry No. 12	3	2,167
Würzburg Infantry No. 23	2	1,124

Brigade: GM Biber

Kaunitz Infantry No. 20	3	2,235
Württemberg Infantry No. 38	2	1,220

Total infantry: *c.*14,653

Total cavalry: 535

Total artillery: 8 x 12-pounders, 36 x 6-pounders, 8 x 3-pounders, 10 x howitzers

V Corps: FML Reuss[115]

Brigade: GM Neustädter

Reuss-Greitz Infantry No. 55	2	1,035
3rd Prerau Landwehr (Maj. Bukovsky)	1	803
Czartoryski Infantry No. 9	3	1,844
4th Brünn Landwehr (Maj. Hoffmann)	1	874

Brigade battery: 8 x 6-pounders

Brigade: Oberst Pflüger

Lindenau Infantry No. 29	3	2,505
5th Vienna Volunteers (Maj. Salis)	1	392

Brigade: GM Klebelsberg

Gradiska Grenz Infantry No. 8	2	1,700
3rd Jäger Battalion	1	822
EH Carl Uhlans No. 3	6	*c.*570
Blankenstein Hussars No. 6	8	*c.*800

Brigade battery: 8 x 6-pounders

Artillery Reserve

Three position batteries

Total infantry: 9,975

Total cavalry: *c.*1,370

Note: This assumes the two squadrons of *Blankenstein* had returned from detachment on 10 July. One squadron of uhlans and 4th Jägers cut off during retreat on 10 July.

VI Corps: FML Klenau[116]

Division: FML Hohenfeld

Brigade: GM Hoffmeister

Duka Infantry No. 39	3	798
Gyulai Infantry No. 60	3	1,769

Brigade: GM Adler

Klebek Infantry No. 14	2	733
1st OWW Landwehr (Maj. Prachma)	1	125
Jordis Infantry No. 59	2⅓	732
1st Combined Upper Austrian (Innviertel) Landwehr (Maj. Straka)	1	533
3rd *EH Carl* Legion (Maj. Lougier)	1	569

Division: FML Kottulinsky

Brigade: GM Splenyi

Benjovszky Infantry No. 31 (II, III)	2	818

Splenyi Infantry No. 51	3	743
3rd Vienna Volunteers (Maj. Waldstein)	1	254
4th Vienna Volunteers (Oberstlt Küffel)	1	89
3rd Moravian Volunteers (Maj. Boxberg)	1	280

Division: FML Vincent
    4th UMB Landwehr (Maj. Colloredo)   1   ?
Brigade: GM Walmoden

Warasdin-St Georg Grenz Regiment No. 6	2	432
Brod Grenz Regiment No. 7 (remnants)	2 companies	252
1st Vienna Volunteers (Maj. St Quentin)	1	260
2nd Vienna Volunteers (Oberstlt von Steigentesch)	1	342
Liechtenstein Hussars No. 7	4	547
Kienmayer Hussars No. 8	4	381

Total infantry: 8,729
Total cavalry: 928
Total artillery: 40 x 6-pounders, 8 x 3-pounders, 8 x howitzers

Reserve Corps: FML Schwarzenberg (GdK Liechtenstein absent)
Cavalry Reserve: FML Schwarzenberg
Division: FML Friedrich Hessen-Homburg
    Brigade: GM Roussel d'Hurbal

Erzherzog Franz Cuirassiers No. 2	6	231
Herzog Albert Cuirassiers No. 3	6	291

    Brigade: GM Lederer

Kronprinz Ferdinand Cuirassiers No. 4	6	389
Hohenzollern Cuirassiers No. 8	6	210

Division: FML Schwarzenberg
    Brigade: GM von Kroyher

Kaiser Cuirassiers No. 1	4	192
Liechtenstein Cuirassiers No. 6	6	351

    Brigade: GM Theimern

Rosenberg Chevaulegers No. 6	8	618
Knesevich Dragoons No. 3	6	471

    Two cavalry batteries: 4 x 6-pounders, 2 x howitzers each
Division: FML Nostitz
    Brigade: GM Rothkirch (not clear if with Schwarz or Nostitz)

EH Johann Dragoons No. 1	6	365
Riesch Dragoons No. 6	6	461

    Cavalry battery: 4 x 6-pounders, 2 x howitzers
    Insurrection Brigade: GM Kerekes

Neutra Insurrection Hussars	6	610
Primatial Insurrection Hussars	4½	346

Total cavalry: 4,535
Total artillery: 16 x 6-pounders, 8 x howitzers
Note: Two squadrons of *Kaiser* Cuirassiers guarding trains.

Grenadier Reserve: FML Prochaska[117]

Brigade: Oberstleutnant Scovaud (former Merville)		1,423
Scharlach Grenadier Battalion (31, 32, 51)	1	
Scovaud Grenadier Battalion (4, 49, 63)	1	
Jambline Grenadier Battalion (14, 45, 59)	1	
Brzezinski Grenadier Battalion (24, 30, 41)	1	
Brigade battery: 8 x 6-pounders		
Brigade: GM von Hammer		2,270
Kirchenbetter Grenadier Battalion (34, 37, 48)	1	
Bissingen Grenadier Battalion (3, 50, 58)	1	
Oklopsia Grenadier Battalion (12, 20, 23)	1	
Locher Grenadier Battalion (8, 22, 60)	1	
Brigade battery: 8 x 6-pounders		
Brigade: GM Murray		2,243
Frisch Grenadier Battalion (10, 11, 47)	1	
Georgy Grenadier Battalion (17, 36, 42)	1	
Portner Grenadier Battalion (40, 44, 46)	1	
Leiningen Grenadier Battalion (25, 35, 54)	1	
Brigade: GM Steyrer		3,329
Hahn Grenadier Battalion (2, 33, 39)	1	
Hromada Grenadier Battalion (1, 29, 38)	1	
Legrand Grenadier Battalion (9, 55, 56)	1	
Demontant Grenadier Battalion (7, 18, 21)	1	
Berger Grenadier Battalion (15, 28, 57)	1	
Brigade battery: 8 x 6-pounders		
Attached to Hammer's brigade:		
1st OMB Landwehr (Hptm Marchal)	1	241
Total infantry: 9,506		
Total artillery: 24 x 6-pounders		

Estimated forces available by midday, 11 July:
Total infantry: c 65,514
Total cavalry: c.8,304
TOTAL: c.73,818

FRENCH ARMY OF GERMANY[118]

Emperor Napoleon

	baons /sqdns	present under arms
Imperial Guard		
Cavalry: GD Walther		c.3,350
Polish Chevaulegers	4	

Chasseurs-à-Cheval	4
Dragoons	4
Grenadiers-à-Cheval	4
Elite Gendarmes	2
1st through 4th Horse Batteries (24 x 6-pounders)	

4th Corps: Marshal Massena[119]

1st Division: GD Legrand		c.4,100
		−4,600
1st Brigade: GB Friedrichs		
26th Léger	3	
18th Ligne	3	
2nd (Baden) Brigade: Oberst von Neuenstein		
1st Baden Infantry *Grossherzog*	1⅓	
2nd Baden Infantry *Erbgrossherzog*	2	
Jäger Battalion *Lingg*	1	
2nd Division: GD Carra St-Cyr		c.4,700
		−5,300
1st Brigade: GB Cosson		
24th Léger	3	
2nd Brigade: GB de Stabenrath		
4th Ligne	3	
46th Ligne	3	
3rd (Hessian) Brigade: GB Schiner/GM von Nagel		
Leib-Garde Regiment	2	
Leib-Garde Fusiliers	1	
Leib Regiment	2	
1st Leib Fusiliers	1	
Light Cavalry Division: GB Piré (former Lasalle)		c.2,000
Brigade: GB Piré		
8th Hussars	3	
16th Chasseurs	3	
Brigade: (former Bruyère)		
13th Chasseurs	3	
Division: (former Marulaz)		
3rd Chasseurs-à-Cheval	2	
14th Chasseurs-à-Cheval	3	
19th Chasseurs-à-Cheval	3	
23rd Chasseurs-à-Cheval	3	
Hessian Chevaulegers	3	
2nd Heavy Cavalry Division: GD St Sulpice[120]		c.1,530
		−1,650
1st Brigade: GB Fiteau		
1st Cuirassiers	4	c.350
5th Cuirassiers	4	c.400

2nd Brigade: GB Guiton

10th Cuirassiers	4	c.420
11th Cuirassiers	4	c.420

Total infantry: c.9,900
Total cavalry: c.3,650
French Corps/Divisional Artillery: 8 x 12-pounders, 30 x 6-pounders, 7 x howitzers
French Regimental Artillery: c.8-10 x regimental pieces
Baden artillery: 8 x 6-pounders, 4 x howitzers
Hessian artillery: 5 x 6-pounders, 1 x howitzer
Notes:

    a 24th Chasseurs and Baden Light Dragoons detached to Krems under Colonel Ameil.

    b 5th Léger and 19th Ligne had not yet joined.

Cavalry Reserve[121]

1st Heavy Cavalry Division: GD Nansouty		2,469
1st Brigade: GB Defrance		
1st Carabiniers	4	394
2nd Carabiniers	4	392
2nd Brigade: GB Doumerc		
2nd Cuirassiers	4	490
9th Cuirassiers	4	439
3rd Brigade: GB St Germain		
3rd Cuirassiers	4	411
12th Cuirassiers	4	343

Total artillery: 10 x 8-pounders, 10 x 4-pounders, 6 x howitzers

Army of Dalmatia: GD Marmont[122]

1st Division: GD Claparède		
1st Brigade: GB Plauzonne		
5th Ligne	2	c.1,200
2nd Brigade: GB Bertrand		
79th Ligne	2	c.1,200
81st Ligne	2	c.990
2nd Division: GD Clauzel		
1st Brigade: GB Delzons		
8th Léger	2	c.1,050
23rd Ligne	2	c.1,350
2nd Brigade: GB Bachelu		
11th Ligne	3	c.1,600
Light Cavalry (8th Company/3rd Chasseurs, 3rd Company/24th Chasseurs)	–	c.200

Total infantry: c.6,740–7,390
Total cavalry: c.200
Total artillery: 4 x 6-pounders, 4 x 3-pounders, 3 x howitzers, 6 x 3-pounder mountain guns

Attached 2nd Division/7th Corps: GM von Minucci (former Wrede)

1st Brigade: GM Minucci		
6th Light Battalion	1	569
3rd Infantry *Prinz Karl*	2	1,277
13 Infantry	2	1,157
2nd Brigade: GM Beckers		
6th Infantry *Herzog Wilhelm*	2	1,070
7th Infantry *Löwenstein*	2	1,388
Cavalry: GM Preysing		
2nd Chevaulegers *König*	4	474
3rd Chevaulegers *Leiningen*	4	513

Total infantry: *c*.4,310–4,840
Total cavalry: *c*.740-870

Attached Light Cavalry Division: GD Montbrun		*c*.3,400
		−4,000
Brigade: GB Pajol		
5th Hussars	4	
11th Chasseurs-à-Cheval	4	
12th Chasseurs-à-Cheval	4	
Brigade: GB Jacquinot		
7th Hussars	4	
1st Chasseurs-à-Cheval	3	
2nd Chasseurs-à-Cheval	3	
Brigade: Col. Gauthrin (former Colbert)		
9th Hussars	4	
20th Chasseurs-à-Cheval	3	

Note: 7th Chasseurs-à-Cheval detached at Laa.

Estimated forces available by midday, 11 July:
Total infantry: *c*.22,130
Total cavalry: *c*.14,530
TOTAL: *c*.36,660

Forces under Viceroy Eugene, 10 July 1809[123]

	baons /sqdns	present under arms
Army of Italy		
Divisions under Marshal MacDonald		
23rd Dragoons	3	549
Division: GD Broussier		
9th Ligne	3	867
84th Ligne	3	1,324
92nd Ligne	4	1,839
Artillery/Engineers:	–	327
Division: GD Lamarque		
1st Brigade: GB Moreau		
18th Léger (III, IV)	2	529
13th Ligne	3	841
23rd Ligne (III, IV)	2	212
2nd Brigade: GB Huard		
29th Ligne	3	883
IV/35th Ligne	1	472
53rd Ligne	3	1,102
Artillery/Engineers:	–	443
Divisions under GD Grenier (wounded)		
Division: GD Durutte		
1st Brigade: (GB Valentin—wounded)		
23rd Léger	3	989
102nd Ligne	3	1,468
2nd Brigade: GB Dessaix		
60th Ligne (III, IV)	2	612
62nd Ligne	4	1,863

Artillery/Engineers:	–	334
Division: GD Pachtod		
1st Brigade: GB Abbé		
8th Léger (III, IV)	2	662
1st Ligne	3	1,199
106th Ligne	3	843
2nd Brigade: GB Pastol		
52nd Ligne	3	1,403
112th Ligne	3	719
Artillery/Engineers:	–	331
Corps of GD Baraguey d'Hilliers		
Division: GD Severoli		
1st Brigade: GB Teste		
IV/1st Léger	1	432
Dalmatian Regiment	2	886
2nd Brigade: GB Julhien		
1st Italian Line (GB Zucchi)	3	1,210
IV/2nd Italian Line	1	327
II/7th Italian Line	1	338
Artillery/Engineers:	–	339
Light Cavalry Brigade: GB Thiry		
25th Chasseurs	3	394
1st Provisional Chasseurs	4	662
Württemberg *Herzog Heinrich* Chasseurs	3	304
Royal Italian Guard: GD Fontanelli		
Cavalry:		
Honour Guards	1	198
Dragoons	2	288
Elite Gendarmes	–	29
Artillery/Engineers:	–	162
Attached: IV/*Napoleon* Dragoons	1	82
Light Cavalry: GB Gérard (GD Sahuc wounded)		
6th Chasseurs	4	490
8th Chasseurs	4	470
9th Chasseurs	3	232
2nd Dragoon Division: GD Pully (GB Poinsot)		
28th Dragoons	3	340
29th Dragoons	3	452
Army headquarters:		
IV/24th Dragoons	1	190
IV/42nd Ligne	1	362
Reserve artillery:	–	169
Raab garrison: GD Narbonne		
3rd Italian Line (II, IV)	2	607
Combined French detachments (eleven different regiments)	–	227

Artillery/Engineers: −   84

Total Infantry: 21,020 (not including Raab garrison, or headquarters troops)

Total Cavalry: 4,490

Notes:

a III and IV/22nd Léger (900) detached escorting prisoners.

b Italian foot guards (GB Lecchi) attached to Imperial Guard.

c 174 Honour Guards and 50 Guard Dragoons at Schönbrunn.

Saxon Contingent: GD Reynier

1st Division: GL von Zezschwitz

Infantry: GM von Zeschau

Staff Battalion	1	216
combined Leib Grenadier Guard Battalion	1	397
1st Grenadier Battalion (Major von Radeloff)	1	257
2nd Grenadier Battalion (Major von Bose)	1	494
3rd Grenadier Battalion (Major von Hake)	1	428
4th Grenadier Battalion (Major von Winkelmann)	1	494
1st Schützen Battalion (Major von Metzsch)	1	398
König Infantry Battalion	1	600
von Niesemeuschel Infantry Battalion	1	719
Combined Infantry Battalion (Oberstlt von Klengel) (from I/*Dyherrn* and II/*von Oebschelwitz*)	1	621
Foot artillery:	−	232

Cavalry: GM von Gutschmid

Prinz Clemens Chevaulegers	4	418
Hussar Regiment	3	191
Herzog Albrecht Chevaulegers	1	144
Gardes du Corps Regiment	2	192
Karabiniers Regiment	2	159

2nd Division: GL von Polenz

Infantry: GM von Steindel

Prinz Clemens Infantry Battalion	1	433
von Low Infantry Battalion	1	539
von Cerrini Infantry Battalion	1	558
2nd Schützen Battalion (Major von Egidy)	1	452
Prinz Anton Infantry Battalion	1	718
Prinz Maximilian Infantry Battalion	1	464
Prinz Friedrich August Infantry Battalion	1	605
Foot artillery:	−	224

Cavalry: GM von Feilitzsch

Leib-Garde Cuirassiers	4	417
Prinz Johann Chevaulegers	4	409
Horse artillery:	−	86

Total infantry: 8,177 (not including Staff Battalion)

Total cavalry: 1,930

VIII Corps (Württemberg): GD Vandamme[124]

Cavalry Division: GL von Wöllwarth
    Brigade: GM von Walsleben

Leib Chevaulegers	4	288/255
Herzog Heinrich Chevaulegers	4	269/234

    Brigade: GM von Stettner

König Jäger-zu-Pferd	4	423/105
Herzog Ludwig Jäger-zu-Pferd	4	353/173

Infantry Division:
    Brigade: GM von Franquemont

Kronprinz Infantry	2	1,230
Herzog Wilhelm Infantry	2	1,279
I/Camrer Infantry	1	477

    Brigade: GM von Scharffenstein

Phull Infantry	2	980/223
Neubronn Infantry	2	1,141/119

    Brigade: GM von Hügel

Jäger Battalion König	1	600
Jäger Battalion von Neuffer	1	529
1st Light Battalion von Wolff	1	574
2nd Light Battalion von Brüsselle	1	610
Artillery:	–	536

Note: Given their mission, many units were distributed in small detachments as shown above (main body/detached); additionally 887 men of II/Camrer at Braunau/Ried.

Orders of Battle for the Walcheren Campaign, July 1809

GREAT BRITAIN

Commander in Chief: Earl of Chatham[125]

	baons /sqdns	present under arms
Army of Walcheren: Lt. Gen. Sir Eyre Coote		
Right Wing: Maj. Gen. Graham		
Detachment/95th Rifles	–	31
68th Light Infantry	2 companies	168
III/1st Foot (Royals)	1	1,078
I/5th Foot	1	1,025
II/35th Foot	1	831
Centre: Lt. Gen. Lord Paget		
Brigade: Brig. Gen. Rottenburg		
Detachment/95th Rifles	–	120
II/68th Light Infantry	1	724
85th Foot	1	676
Brigade: Brig. Gen. Brown		
II/23rd Foot	1	456
I/26th Foot	1	772
I/32nd Foot	1	662
II/81st Foot	1	755
Reserve: Brig. Gen. Houston		
II/14th Foot	1	917
I/51st Foot	1	713
I/82nd Foot	1	1,071

Left Wing: Lt. Gen. Fraser

  Brigade: Maj. Gen. Picton

Detachment/95th Rifles	–	50
I/71st Foot	1	1,066
I/36th Foot	1	813
II/63rd Foot	1	661
77th Foot	1	632
Battalion of Detachments	1	895
II/8th Foot	2 companies	218

Reserve of the Army: Lt. Gen. Sir John Hope

Brigade: Brig. Gen. Disney

I/1st Foot Guards	1	1,463
III/1st Foot Guards	1	1,202
Flank Companies of Guards		
Grenadiers	–	268
Light Infantry	–	267

Brigade: Maj. Gen. Lord Dalhousie

I/4th Foot	1	1,094
II/4th Foot	1	1,022
I/28th Foot	1	719

Brigade: Maj. Gen. Erskine

20th Foot	1	968
I/92nd Foot	1	1,083

2nd Division: Lt. Gen. Lord Huntley

Brigade: Maj. Gen. Dyott

I/6th Foot	1	1,086
I/50th Foot	1	973
I/91st Foot	1	736

Brigade: Brig. Gen. Montresor

I/9th Foot	1	1,064
I/38th Foot	1	912
I/42nd Foot (Black Watch)	1	861

Light Division: Lt. Gen. the Earl of Rosslyn

Brigade: Maj. Gen. Linsingen

2nd Dragoon Guards	6 troops	545
3rd Dragoons	6 troops	572
12th Light Dragoons	6 troops	592
9th Light Dragoons	det	589

Brigade: Maj. Gen. Montresor

II/43rd Foot	1	701
II/52nd Foot	1	499
II/95th Foot	8 companies	907

Brigade (King's German Legion): Col. Baron Alten

1st Light Battalion	1	843
2nd Light Battalion	1	747
2nd Light Dragoons		662

3rd Division: Lt. Gen. Grosvenor
Brigade: Maj. Gen. Leith

II/59th Foot	1	905
II/11th Foot	1	951
I/79th Foot	1	1,091

Brigade: Brig. Gen. Ackland

III/2nd Foot	1	928
I/76th Foot	1	846
II/84th Foot	1	884

KINGDOM OF HOLLAND[126]

	baons /sqdns	present under arms
Troops within the kingdom, 1 July		
Royal Guard		
Adelborsten		209
Carabiniers		196
Grenadiers	2	1,806
Cuirassiers	3	558
Artillery	–	169
Veterans	–	63
Depot/2nd Infantry	–	253
3rd Infantry	2	1,214
Depot/3rd Infantry	–	160
4th Infantry	2	1,525
Depot/4th Infantry	–	59
I/5th Infantry	1	759
Depot/6th Infantry	–	419
Depot/7th Infantry	–	354
Depot/8th Infantry	–	374
Depot/9th Infantry	–	56
3rd Jägers	2	1,083
Depot/3rd Jägers	–	152
Veterans	6 companies	696
Gendarmes	–	296
Depot/Guard Hussars	–	113
Depot/2nd Cuirassiers	–	26

2nd Hussars	3	533
Depot/2nd Hussars	–	101

On Walcheren Island:[127]
Flushing Garrison (French territory): GD Monnet (GB Osten)

1st Colonial Battalion	1	725
Bataillon Déserteurs Français Rentrés (or *Militaires Français Rentrés*)	1	955
I/Irish Regiment	1	441
Prussian Regiment	3	1,607
II/6th Veterans	2 companies	50
Artillery	–	291
Gendarmes	–	4
III/65th Ligne (arrived 1 August)	1	655

Dutch troops: Lt. Gen. Bruce

I/5th Infantry	1	759
3rd Artillery Battalion	–	c.250–300
Town militia	–	1,122

Abbreviations

AG	Archives de la guerre, Service historique de la armée de terre
BKA	Bayerisches Haupstaatsarchiv, Abt. IV, Kriegsarchiv
du Casse, *Eugène*	Eugene de Beauharnais, *Mémoires et Correspondance*, ed. Albert du Casse, Paris: Lévy, 1858–60
Correspondance	Napoleon I, *Correspondance de Napoléon Ier publiée par ordre de l'Empereur Napoléon III*, Paris: Imprimerie Impériale, 1858–70.
GLA	Generallandesarchiv Karlsruhe
HStAS	Hauptstaatsarchiv Stuttgart
Hiller	Manfried Rauchensteiner (ed.), 'Das sechste österr. Armeekorps im Krieg 1809. Nach den Aufzeichnungen des FZM Johann Freiherr v. Hiller (1748–1819)', in *Mitteilungen des österr. Staatsarchivs.*
KAFA	Kriegsarchiv, Alte Feldakten
MOL	Magyar Orszagos Leveltar
Op. J.	*Operations-Journal (in Austrian Kriegsarchiv)*
ÖMZ	*österreichische militärische Zeitschrift* or *Streffleurs österreichische militärische Zeitschrift*
PRO/FO	Public Records Office/Foreign Office
RGVA	Rossiiskii Gosudarstvennii Voenno-Istoricheskii Arkiv
SächsHStA	Sächsisches Hauptstaatsarchiv Dresden
Stadion	Hellmuth Rössler, *Graf Johann Philipp Stadion: Napoleons deutscher Gegenspieler*, Vienna: Herold, 1966.
VPR	*Vneshniaia Politika Rossii*, Moscow, 1965.

Notes

PREFACE

1 Epstein, *Napoleon's Last Victory*; David A. Bell, *The First Total War*, New York: Mariner Books, 2007.
2 See Jeremy Black, 'Why the French Failed: New Work on the Military History of French Imperialism 1792–1815', *European History Quarterly*, vol. 30, no. 1, 2000, pp. 105–15.
3 Brent Nosworthy, 'Introduction' and 'Conclusion', in *Battle Tactics of Napoleon and His Enemies*, London: Constable, 1995.
4 Zehetbauer has made a brilliant and important start, it is to be hoped that others will follow his example.

PROLOGUE

1 Napoleon to Davout, 21 June 1809, *Correspondance*, 15399.
2 Rühle, *Reise mit der Armee*, p. 277.

CHAPTER I: WAR ALONG THE VISTULA

1 This chapter derives in part from John H. Gill, 'From Warsaw to Sandomierz: Contending Strategies and Opening Moves along the Vistula in 1809', in The Consortium on Revolutionary Europe, *Selected Papers 1995*, ed. Bernard A. Cook, Kyle O. Eidahl, Donald D. Horward and Karl A. Roider, Tallahassee: Florida State University, 1995, pp. 310–17.
2 Charles to Ferdinand, 28 March 1809, in Just, *Politik oder Strategie?*, pp. 71–2.
3 In a 22 April letter to Charles, Ferdinand relayed that he had received 'a secret communication' from Goetzen: 'if French or Polish troops enter Prussian territory, he has orders to oppose them energetically' (in Pawlowski, *Historja Wojny*, p. 167).
4 Ibid.
5 Criste, *Erzherzog Karl und die Armee*, p. 30.
6 For a summary of this fighting, see Hausmann/Gill, pp. 42–4.
7 Pelet, vol. III, p. 46.

8   Just, *Politik oder Strategie?*, pp. 22–5 (for example: Ferdinand to Goetzen and to Charles, 8 May 1809).

9   In the opinion of a Polish veteran of the campaign, however, even this amount of cavalry was 'insufficient for the tasks it was charged to accomplish' in a hostile land: outpost/scouting, foraging, and suppressing the local populace (Roman Soltyk, *Relation des Opérations de l'armée aux ordres de Prince Joseph Poniatowski pendant la Campagne de 1809 en Pologne contre les Autrichiens*, Paris: Gaultier-Laguionie, 1841, p. 130).

10 Problems in *Davidovich* were mentioned in Vol. I, p. 62 (Julius Kreipner, *Geschichte des k. und k. Infanterie-Regimentes Nr. 34*, Kaschau: regimental, 1900, p. 407). In *Baillet* Infantry No. 63, 1,990 of the regiment's 2,883 officers and men were new Galician recruits in March 1809—the worst of both worlds: troops that were green and reluctant (Julius Beran, *Die Geschichte des k. u. k. Infanterie-Regiments Freiherr von Merkl Nr. 55*, Vienna: Schneid, 1899). Mondet would later claim that he could hardly rely on *de Ligne* (Mondet to Ferdinand, 1 June 1809, Pawlowski, *Historja Wojny*, p. 348) and Ferdinand suggested withdrawing all of the Galician regiments to fight in Germany (Ferdinand to Franz, 11 May 1809, Pawlowski, *Historja Wojny*, pp. 509–10).

11 Initial plans called for a bridging train to accompany VII Corps, but orders in late March diverted these assets to the Hauptarmee (Brinner, p. 47).

12 Soltyk, pp. 132–4. The only truly permanent bridge was a stone span at Krakow; there were floating bridges at Thorn and Sandomierz. Under Davout's instructions, an expensive bridge on wooden pilings had been constructed to connect Warsaw with Praga, but this had been badly damaged by ice in February; the ruined portion had been replaced by a boat bridge. The boat bridge at Modlin had been removed for the winter. Otherwise, passage of the Vistula was limited to ferries. Just, 'Das Herzogthum Warschau', p. 91.

13 Soltyk, pp. 132–4. Sandomierz, nearly 200 kilometres south of Warsaw by road, was too far away to be useful.

14 Just, 'Das Herzogthum Warschau', p. 91. Pelet refers to Modlin as 'the military capital of the grand duchy' (vol. III, p. 371); see Soltyk, 131–4.

15 Soltyk, p. 133.

16 Just, *Politik oder Strategie?*, pp. 22–5. See also Ferdinand to Charles, 22 April 1809, extract in Pawlowski, *Historja Wojny*, p. 167. See Vol. I of this work.

17 Just, 'Das Herzogthum Warschau', pp. 89–90.

18 Pawlowski, *Historja Wojny*, p. 153.

19 Simon Askenazy, *Le Prince Joseph Poniatowski*, Paris: Plon, 1921 (see especially pp. 214–15); Soltyk's introduction (pp. 1–88). See also Elting, *Swords*, p. 148; and Nigel de Lee, 'Tragic Patriot and Reluctant Bonapartist', in Chandler, *Napoleon's Marshals*, pp. 419–39.

20 Napoleon to Berthier, 5 April 1809, *Correspondance*, no. 15015. Napoleon's misplaced faith in the tsar's promises was still evident as late as the 19th, when he suggested that part of the Polish army might be deployed to Saxony.

21 For Napoleon's early orders concerning the Poles, see Napoleon to Davout, 4 March 1809, *Correspondance*, no. 14848; Davout to Poniatowski, 4 March 1809, Davout, *Correspondance*, vol. II, pp. 388–90; Napoleon to Berthier, 30 March 1809,

Correspondance, no. 14975; and Berthier to Bernadotte, 19 April 1809 (Saski, vol. II, p. 274). The Poles were considered part of the Army of the Rhine in March 1809, so Napoleon's letter of 4 March was sent to that army's commander, Davout, who sent his own instructions to Poniatowski. Bernadotte assumed command of Polish forces in early April.

22 Poniatowski outlined these points quite specifically in a 29 April 1809 letter to Berthier, (Poniatowski, *Correspondance*, vol. II, pp. 112–13).

23 Poniatowski to Davout, 4 February 1809, Poniatowski, *Correspondance*, vol. II, pp. 28–33.

24 Theodor Goethe, *Aus dem Leben eines sächsischen Husaren und aus dessen Feldzügen 1809, 1812 und 1813 in Polen und Russland*, Leipzig: Hinrich, 1853, pp. 32–3; Pelet, vol. III, p. 373.

25 Curiously this plan was the exact opposite of that suggested by Charles in his 28 March instructions. Charles envisaged the entire corps marching through Czestochowa and Piotrkow to Warsaw. Perhaps this is one reason for Ferdinand assigning Branowaczky's detachment to Czestochowa: a sop to Charles. Other reasons, as outlined by Maximilian Ehnl in 'Die Einschliessung von Czestochowa im Jahre 1809', *ÖMZ*, 1910, include prompting Prussia to join the war, suppressing potential unrest, and protecting the Austrian base at Krakow.

26 Ehnl (ibid., pp. 1040–4) excoriates the Austrian leadership for wasting resources in detaching Branowaczky's brigade while ignoring the more important mission of encircling Warsaw from the east.

27 Ferdinand to Charles, 22 April 8 p.m., in Jaromir Formanek, *Geschichte des k. k. Infanterie-Regiments Nr. 41*, Czernowitz: Czopp, 1887, vol. II, p. 23.

28 Two squadrons of hussars under Major Josef Graf Gatterburg crossed at Inowlodz on the left and headed for Rawa, while the third rode on the right towards Osuchow.

29 Welden, p. 314; Johann Baptist Schels, 'Der Feldzug 1809 in Polen', *ÖMZ*, 1844, pp. 293–4.

30 Brusch to Prochaska, 14 April 1809, extract in Pawlowski, *Historja Wojny*, p. 111.

31 For a contemporary analysis, see 'Geschichte des Feldzugs an der Weichsel im Jahre 1809', *Minerva*, vol. I, 1810, pp. 246–7.

32 Poniatowski to Davout, 12 April 1809, Poniatowski, *Correspondance*, vol. II, pp. 90–1; Soltyk, p. 143.

33 Gustav Ritter Amon von Treuenfest, *Geschichte des k. und k. Husaren-Regimentes Kaiser Nr. 1*, Vienna: regimental, 1898, p. 237.

34 Brusch to Prochaska, 17 April 1809, extract in Pawlowski, *Historja Wojny*, p. 138.

35 The skirmish was between *Kaiser* Hussars and Polish uhlans; the Austrians claimed a loss of nine casualties. Rozniecki quoted in Gabriel Zych, *Raszyn 1809*, Warsaw, 1969, p. 59.

36 Much of the following is drawn from John H. Gill, 'The Battle of Raszyn, 19 April 1809', *First Empire*, no. 10, March/April 1993. Note that I incorrectly identified the stream in that article as the Utrata; as noted here, it was actually a tributary of the Utrata called the Mrowa. Some Austrian sources identify it as the 'Rnowa' or 'Utratabach', I have followed the Polish histories here.

37 Most sources place 5th Chasseurs on the field or imply that it was present, but it seems most of the regiment was absent for most of the day (Poniatowski to Saunier, 19 April 1809, in Pawlowski, *Historja Wojny*, p. 149).

38 This figure includes II/6th Infantry (*c*.650 men) and its pair of guns, but does not include 5th Chasseurs as this regiment was absent for most of the day. Adding all of the latter would bring the total to 13,055.

39 Alois Veltzé, *Kriegsbilder aus Polen, Steiermark und Ungarn 1809*, Vienna: Stern, 1910, pp. 11, 17.

40 Mohr had three squadrons of *Kaiser*, one and one-half squadrons of *Palatinal*, *Vukassovich* (minus the four companies on the left), *1st Wallach*, and his 3-pounder battery (580 cavalry, 2,800 infantry, eight guns). Civilart and Pflacher would march after Mohr with Trautenberg bringing up the rear.

41 Mohr to Ferdinand, 19 April 1809, in Pawlowski, *Historja Wojny*, p. 139.

42 Key portions of the disposition are printed in 'Das k. k. Husaren-Regiment Palatinal im Feldzuge 1809', ÖMZ, 1847, pp. 233–4.

43 Gabelkoven's relation of the fighting (dated 29 April 1809) is in Pawlowski, *Historja Wojny*, pp. 507–9.

44 This is the figure from Poniatowski's 'Précis des Opérations' (Fedorowicz, p. 337); a report to the King of Saxony listed 267 dead, 487 wounded, 78 captured, and 169 missing for a total of 1,001 (Pawlowski, '*Historja Wojny*, p. 146), but there were probably many more straggling about in the immediate aftermath of the battle.

45 'Geschichte des Feldzugs an der Weichsel', p. 254. This author and others suggest that the failure at Raszyn led Brusch to seek death in combat at Thorn.

46 The left bank at Warsaw was higher than the right, allowing Austrian guns to dominate the bridgehead fort; on the other hand, howitzers from Praga were in a position to bombard the city and cause considerable destruction, an outcome Ferdinand wanted to avoid (Schels, 'Feldzug 1809 in Polen', p. 61; Ferdinand to Charles, 26 April 1809, in Poniatowski, *Correspondance*, vol. II, pp. 101–2).

47 Ferdinand to Friedrich Wilhelm III, 22 April 1809, Just, *Politik oder Strategie?*, pp. 73–4.

48 Soltyk, pp. 158–9. Poniatowski had recognised the potentially encumbering effect of fortified cities on operations and had used the same verb ('paralyse') in a 4 February letter to Davout (Poniatowski, *Correspondance*, vol. II, p. 30). See also 'Geschichte des Feldzugs an der Weichsel', p. 273.

49 Soltyk, p. 169.

50 Veltzé, *Kriegsbilder aus Polen*, p. 26.

51 Rittmeister von Erben of *Kaiser* Chevaulegers, 26 April, in Cajetan Pizzighelli, *Geschichte des K. u. K. Ulanen-Regiments Kaiser Joseph II. No. 6.*, Vienna: regimental, 1908, p. 67.

52 Theodor Graf Baillet von Latour, *Erinnerungen*, Graz: Kienreich, 1849, p. 61.

53 Ferdinand to Charles, 26 April 1809, in Poniatowski, *Correspondance*, vol. II, pp. 101–2.

54 Mohr shipped over: two Grenz battalions (each *c*.1,100), *Vukassovich* (*c*.1,900 after losses at Raszyn), four *Kaiser* Hussar squadrons (*c*.520), and two batteries to join Hoditz with his division of hussars (*c*.260). The *Kaiser* squadron that had marched

on the army's left had rejoined Mohr on 20 April. The other two squadrons of *Kaiser* Hussars remained on the west bank under Gatterburg.

55 The Praga garrison consisted of some 600 men, mostly young, untrained recruits.

56 The date of this action is variously reported as 25 or 26 April. I have used here the former (25th) as in Pawlowski (*Historja Wojny*, pp. 176–80) and Welden (pp. 322–3); many Polish narratives give the date as 26 April because some fighting occurred on both days; and several Austrian versions place the engagement at Grochow on the 25th, but the skirmish at Radzymin on 26 April.

57 Based on Soltyk, p. 176, using his estimates of 800/battalion and 250/squadron. Note that an additional artillery battery had been formed from guns in fortress arsenals.

58 Zajaczek and Fiszer (Poniatowski's chief of staff) were among those who advised against this move (Gustaw Ochwicz, *Rok 1809*, Posen, 1925, p. 39).

59 Poniatowski, 'Précis des Operations', 28 April 1809, Poniatowski, *Correspondance*, vol. II, pp. 103–11; Paszkowski to Bernadotte, 28 April 1809, in Poniatowski, *Correspondance*, vol. II, pp. 107–10; Soltyk, pp. 177–8; Ochwicz, pp. 42–3.

60 Quoted in Ochwicz, p. 43.

61 In addition to the main columns, an infantry company of I/6 was sent across the Vistula from Modlin to distract the Austrians. The company did not paddle over until the night of 25/26 April, so it was too late to affect the fighting. Some Austrians were sent to investigate, but the company returned safely (Pawlowski, *Historja Wojny*, pp. 175, 180).

62 In addition to Poniatowski's report and other accounts sent to Berthier, Bernadotte, and the Saxon king (in Poniatowski's *Correspondance* and Fedorowicz), sources for this confused fighting include: Alexander Hold, *Geschichte des k. k. 48. Linien-Infanterie-Regimentes*, Vienna: Seidel & Sohn, 1875, pp. 52–4; Mayerhoffer, *Oesterreichs Krieg*, pp. 192–3; Ochwicz, pp. 41–6; Schels, 'Feldzug 1809 in Polen', pp. 65–8; Soltyk, pp. 177–84; Treuenfest, *Husaren-Regimentes Kaiser Nr. 1*, pp. 239–44; Gustav Ritter Amon von Treuenfest, *Geschichte des k. u. k. Infanterie-Regimentes Nr. 46*, Vienna: regimental, 1890, pp. 237–40; Gustav Ritter Amon von Treuenfest, *Geschichte des k. k. Infanterie-Regimentes Nr. 50*, Vienna: Mayer, 1882, pp. 198–200; Welden, pp. 322–3. Austrian losses from KAFA, Kart. 1432/4/16.

63 Poniatowski to Dabrowski, 26 April 1809, in Pawlowski, *Historja Wojny*, p. 180.

64 Soltyk, p. 183. See also 'Geschichte des Feldzugs an der Weichsel', p. 268.

65 Ferdinand to Hüttersthal, 26 April 1809, in Pawlowski, *Historja Wojny*, p. 182.

66 Ferdinand to Branowaczky, 25 April 1809, in Pawlowski, *Historja Wojny*, p. 165.

67 Gramont seems to have picked up the infantry company at Piotrkow en route, so it is included in the total here. The chevaulegers squadron remained in Piotrkow, probing north-west to hamper Polish recruiting.

68 Ehnl, 'Einschliessung', pp. 1044–7; 'Szenen aus dem Leben des k. k. Feldmarschall-Lieutenants Johann Baron Gramont von Linthal', *ÖMZ*, 1847, pp. 211–13.

69 Poniatowski to Berthier, 29 April 1809, Poniatowski, *Correspondance*, vol. II, pp. 112–14.

70 As in many cases during this campaign, it is nearly impossible to sort out the details of the Polish order of battle on any one day. This narrative will therefore focus on the order of battle in combat situations.

71 Paszkowski to Friedrich August, 4 May 1809, Poniatowski, *Correspondance*, vol. II, p. 125.
72 Turno to Sokolnicki, 1 May 1809, midnight, Pawlowski, *Historja Wojny*, p. 190.
73 Poniatowski to Berthier, 3 May 1809, Poniatowski, *Correspondance*, vol. II, pp. 117–18.
74 The assault force was organised in six columns: two voltigeur companies of 8th Infantry and a chasseur squadron; two voltigeur companies of 12th Infantry; two voltigeur companies of 6th Infantry; five grenadier companies (one of 8th, two each of 6th and 12th); fusilier companies of I/6; fusilier companies of II/6. Moreover, some 500 of these (the four fusilier companies of II/6) did not participate in the fighting and were only used to occupy the place after it fell. Though Sokolnicki had some 5,000 infantry and cavalry at hand, therefore, the troops he committed to the assault were only slightly superior to the Austrians in number, approximately 2,000. Figures based on *c*.800 men per battalion (Soltyk, p. 176) and the plan outlined in Sokolnicki's report from Bronislaw Pawlowski, *Dziennik Historyczny I Korespondencja Polowa Generala Michala Sokolnickiego*, Krakow: Nakladem Polskiej Akademji Umiejetnosci, 1931, pp. 18–19.
75 These were the 1st and 2nd Battalions; the 1st and four companies of the 2nd had been in the bridgehead for several days, but the final two companies of II/*Baillet* were not shipped over until around 10 p.m. on 2 May (Beran, pp. 60–1); a hussar platoon may also have been present.
76 Czerwinka's report in Beran, p. 63.
77 Soltyk, p. 196; Sokolnicki's report in Pawlowski, *Dziennik Historyczny*, p. 20.
78 Ochwicz, pp. 49–50; Herzog Albert remarked that Ferdinand's officers blamed 'the dispositions' for this disaster—in other words, Ferdinand himself ('Mémoire sur la Guerre éclatée en 1809', MOL P300/1/100).
79 Ochwicz, pp. 49–50.
80 Poniatowski to Berthier, 3 May 1809, Poniatowski, *Correspondance*, vol. II, pp. 117–18. Key sources for Gora include: Poniatowski's and Paszkowski's correspondence as cited above (including large parts of Ferdinand's report to Charles, 4 May 1809); Ochwicz, pp. 48–50; Sokolnicki's report in Pawlowski, *Dziennik Historyczny*, pp. 18–20; Beran, pp. 60–5 (including parts of Czerwinka's account); Brinner, pp. 97–100; Nahlik, pp. 31–3; Soltyk, pp. 191–9. As Ochwicz points out, there is much disagreement among these on the details, but the general outlines are clear.
81 Soltyk, pp. 187–9. For regular troops, Dabrowski only had 200 depot cavalrymen and some infantry detachments from Thorn. Zajaczek had the third battalions of 1st, 2nd, 3rd, and 8th Infantry as well as the cavalry depots; III/6 (minus its elite companies) was en route from Ostrowek to Serock.
82 Poniatowski to Berthier, 5 May 1809, Poniatowski, *Correspondance*, vol. II, p. 130. Napoleon's instructions in Soltyk, pp. 202–3.
83 Soltyk, p. 211–12; other sources mention only one squadron and place the fight on 4 May.
84 The Poles reported capturing a detachment of 800 to 1,000 Austrian recruits (from *Württemberg*) and a supply convoy during these operations; Austrian sources are largely silent on this.

85 Kamienski: two squadrons of 6th Uhlans and one of 3rd Uhlans (that will play an important role later in the war). Pelletier: 2nd Infantry, voltigeurs of 3rd Infantry (two companies), Voltigeur Company of III/6th Infantry, two cannon, and four howitzers. Although III/6 had returned to Serock after the assault on the Gora bridgehead, the voltigeur and grenadier companies apparently stayed with the army.

86 Poniatowski to Bernadotte, 19 May 1809, Poniatowski, Correspondance, vol. II, p. 139.

87 Sokolnicki had 6th and 12th Infantry, 2nd Uhlans, one squadron of 5th Chasseurs, and four guns.

88 My estimate of Eggermann's strength, given approximately 480 Grenzer, six depot companies (probably over 1,500 men total), thirty hussars, and artillery personnel. Note that Austrian sources routinely give Eggermann a force of only 800, far too low. Soltyk (p. 225) places the number at approximately 3,000.

89 Ehnl, 'Die Berennung und Einnahme der Festung Sandomierz durch die Polen im Jahre 1809', ÖMZ, 1911, pp. 1595, 1600.

90 Rozniecki to Poniatowski, 6 a.m., 18 May 1809, in Pawlowski, Historja Wojny, p. 279.

91 Ferdinand had sent 1st Wallach No. 16 to bolster the recruits in the Sandomierz and Zamosc garrisons (three companies each) when he headed north towards Thorn (see below).

92 Austrian losses and desertions from KAFA, Kart. 1432/5/ad17b2 and b3. The Kaiser, Kaunitz, and Stain depots were gutted, losing 259, 232, and 261 deserters respectively (Stain had an additional sixty-eight listed as missing). Eggermann had a man executed on the spot, but this had no effect on the troops (Ehnl, 'Berennung', p. 1603). See also Sokolnicki to Poniatowski, 20 May 1809, in Pawlowski, Dziennik Historyczny, p. 75–6. The Poles also gained fifteen large-calibre guns.

93 Ibid. and Soltyk, p. 241. Key sources for Sandomierz: Sokolnicki's reports; Soltyk's thorough account (pp. 217–25); Ehnl, 'Berennung'; and Austrian regimental histories.

94 Soltyk, p. 233. Austrian sources condemn the commissioner and thereby lay part of the blame for the town's fall on 'treason'.

95 Austrian killed and wounded numbered thirty-four. This account draws mostly from Soltyk, pp. 229–39.

96 Poniatowski to Berthier, 21 May 1809, Poniatowski, Correspondance, vol. II, pp. 139–40.

97 Poniatowski to Bernadotte, 19 May 1809, ibid., p. 138.

98 Poniatowski to Berthier, 11 May 1809, ibid., p. 134.

99 Schauroth: Weidenfeld, 1st Szekler Grenzer, Szekler Hussars.

100 Ferdinand posted Davidovich and his seven squadrons of Palatinal at the confluence of the Bzura and Vistula to protect his river flank and 'alarm' the Poles on the far bank; II/Davidovich, a squadron, and a cavalry battery were distributed along the left bank almost as far as Plock.

101 Vukassovich, 2nd Wallach, two battalions of Kottulinsky, and five squadrons of Kaiser Chevaulegers.

102 Latour, pp. 62–3.

103 The Polish garrison numbered 3,500 infantry recruits from the third battalions of 10th, 11th, and 12th Regiments and 110 artillerymen. Pawlowski, *Historja Wojny*, pp. 223–8; Soltyk, pp. 208–9. Austrian losses from KAFA, Kart. 1432/5/20.

104 There is some irony here: Austrian sources commonly condemn Davout for bombarding Pressburg in June, but treat Mohr's action as routine procedure. Woyczynski's wonderful reply is in Soltyk, p. 210.

105 Ferdinand to Franz, 11 May 1809, Pawlowski, *Historja Wojny*, pp. 509–10.

106 Ferdinand to Schauroth, 15, 16, and 21 May 1809, from extracts in Pawlowski, *Historja Wojny*, pp. 322–5. Schauroth had *Strauch* and *1st Szekler* along with *Kaiser* Hussars (six squadrons), and *Lothringen* Cuirassiers. En route, he picked up the lone squadron of *Palatinal* Hussars. Four companies of III/*Baillet* joined him near Sandomierz; the other two *Baillet* companies remained at Nowe Miasto.

107 Beran, pp. 65–6.

108 'Tagebuch der Avantgarde des 7ten Armee Corps unter Commando des G. M. Br. Mohr' (hereafter Op. J. 42), KAFA, *Operationsjournale der Hauptarmee und Korps*, Kart. 1385. A raid on Bromberg by one and one-half squadrons and two Grenz companies on 19–20 May was unsuccessful. Three squadrons of *Palatinal* were sent to join Mohr, but were recalled before they arrived: Pizzighelli, *Ulanen-Regiments Kaiser Joseph II. No. 6*, pp. 69–70; 'Palatinal im Feldzuge 1809', ÖMZ, 1847, pp. 240–1. Treuenfest, *Infanterie-Regiments Nr. 46*, pp. (claiming four squadrons at Thorn rather than three).

109 Latour, p. 62.

110 Several skirmishes around the fortress took place in early May, the largest of which (14 May) cost the Austrian forty-one and the Poles twenty casualties.

111 Charles's letter, dated 14 May, reached Ferdinand on 20 or 21 May (Just, *Politik oder Strategie?*, pp. 36–7).

112 Ferdinand to Schauroth, 28 and 29 May 1809, from extracts in Pawlowski, *Historja Wojny*, pp. 336, 337. Herzog Albert commented that he 'never found a solid rationale for the expedition to Thorn' ('Mémoire sur la Guerre éclatée en 1809', MOL P300/1/100).

113 Hauke had III/12th Infantry (*c.*1,000) and Plock Volunteer Chasseurs (*c.*600–800).

114 Though interesting and sometimes involving dozens of casualties, these are too numerous and complex to pursue here.

115 Ferdinand wanted to hold the city until the night of 2/3 May (Ferdinand to Mondet, 31 May 1809), but Mondet felt too threatened and left twenty-four hours earlier (Mondet to Ferdinand, 1 June 1809); corrspondence extracts in Pawlowski, *Historja Wojny*, pp. 346, 348.

116 Number of prisoners is from Soltyk, p. 245. Archival reporting and the regimental mention the incident but give no figures for the two depot divisions (KAFA, Kart. 1482/6/ad17; Branko, p. 187). The haul of prisoners included 104 men from various small detachments.

117 Rozniecki to Poniatowski, 28 May 1809, in Bronislaw Pawlowski, *Z Dziejow Kampanji 1809 Roku w Galicji Wschodniej*, Lwow: University Press, 1928, p. 6.

118 Soltyk, pp. 246–7.

119 This spelling is taken from Pawlowski, other authors spell the name 'Strzyzewski'.

120 Anton Steiner, 'Geschichte der Kriegsbegebenheiten in Ost Galizien', 21 August 1810, KAFA, *Operativen Akten*, Kart. 1388, (French in original).

121 Recall that the depot troops in Zamosc and Jaroslaw had been captured in their entirety (possibly others as well), and that those in Sandomierz had suffered heavily from desertion. Furthermore, the Austrians could no longer recruit for most of their Galician regiments.

122 'Geschichte des Feldzugs an der Weichsel', p. 276.

123 Ferdinand to Charles, 28 May 1809, extract in Pawlowski, *Historja Wojny*, pp. 340–1.

124 Poniatowski to Berthier, 31 May 1809, Poniatowski, *Correspondance*, vol. II, pp. 158–61.

125 Sokolnicki to Poniatowski, 27 May 1809, Pawlowski, *Dziennik Historyczny*, pp. 81–3.

126 See Table 1 and Appendix 1. The 2nd West Galician Volunteer battalion (four companies only, the other two were with Hohenlohe) was apparently left at the crossing site and joined Ferdinand on 9 June.

127 Sokolnicki had been temporarily reinforced by 2nd Uhlans and 5th Chasseurs for this advance (Soltyk, p. 268).

128 Ferdinand had II and III/*Weidenfeld*, *Somariva* Cuirassiers, Szilly's squadron of *Palatinal* and at least three companies of III/*Kottulinsky* (location of the other three unknown); 2nd West Galician Volunteers joined Ferdinand at the crossing site.

129 Rozniecki: 2nd Uhlans, 5th Chasseurs, four companies of 8th Infantry, and four guns (Soltyk, p. 270).

130 Headed for Ulanow were Oberst Johann Ritter Piccard von Grünthal with four companies of *1st Szekler* and a squadron each of *Lothringen* and *Kaiser* Hussars; two more *Lothringen* squadrons joined on 15 June. The detachment for Rozwadow consisted of two *Kaiser* Hussar squadrons under the ubiquitous Major von Hoditz. Just, *Politik oder Strategie?*, p. 40.

131 The 12 June engagement is most commonly known as the 'Battle of Gorzyce', but some accounts refer to it by the name of a village behind the centre of the Polish position: Wrzawy.

132 One squadron of 3rd Uhlans was in Galicia, two companies of III/6th were with Zajaczek.

133 Branowaczky had four squadrons of *Kaiser* Hussars, one squadron each of *Palatinal* Hussars and *Kaiser* Chevaulegers (the latter detached from Eggermann), *1st Szekler* Grenzer, three companies of *1st Wallach* Grenzer, and 2nd West Galician Volunteers (four companies). See Welden (p. 337), but note that Welden mistakenly includes two hussar squadrons that had been detached to the Austrian right flank.

134 Austrian losses from KAFA Kart. 1432/6/10.

135 Latour, p. 65.

136 Soltyk, p. 280; Poniatowski to Napoleon, 10 June 1809, Poniatowski, *Correspondance*, vol. II, pp. 167–9.

137 Fiszer to Sievers and reply, 11 June 1809, Pawlowski, *Historja Wojny*, p. 385; Pazkowski to Friedrich August, 13 June 1809, in Poniatowski, *Correspondance*, vol. II, pp. 170–2; Poniatowski to Suvorov, 13 June 1809, Rossiiskii Gosudarstvennii Voenno-Istoricheskii Arkiv, Fond Voenno-Uchebnii Arkiv (RGVIA/FVUA) 846, opis 16, delo 3375.

138 Soltyk, p. 282.

139 Extract from Geringer's report in Kreipner, p. 418. See also extracts of 16 June 1809 letters between Geringer and Ferdinand in Pawlowski, *Historja Wojny*, pp. 404–5; Latour, pp. 66–7.

140 Ferdinand to Mondet, 4 June 1809, Pawlowski, *Historja Wojny*, p. 349.

141 In/around Rawa: *2nd Wallach*, three squadrons *Kaiser* Chevaulegers, cavalry battery. Gatterburg: two squadrons each of *Kaiser* Hussars and *Kaiser* Chevaulegers, two guns. See regimental histories.

142 Zajaczek to Poniatowski, 7 June 1809, Pawlowski, *Historja Wojny*, p. 373.

143 Op. J. 42.

144 Zajaczek to Poniatowski, 10 June 1809, Pawlowski, *Historja Wojny*, p. 375.

145 Treuenfest, *Husaren-Regimentes Kaiser Nr. 1*, pp. 253–4.

146 Soltyk, pp. 271–3. Soltyk also condemns Zajaczek for retreating towards Pulawy rather than the Pilica where he could have recovered in the forests while protecting Warsaw.

147 Mondet had sent two squadrons of chevaulegers to Konskie; these had skirmishes with Polish troops on 11, 12, 13, and 17 June, most of which did not turn out favourably for the Austrians (Rittmeister Fitzgerald's 17 June report in Pizzighelli, *Ulanen-Regiments Kaiser Joseph II. No. 6*, pp. 74–5).

148 Ferdinand to Mondet, 16 June 1809, Pawlowski, *Historja Wojny*, p. 429.

149 K. Waliszewski, *Le Régne d'Alexandre Ier*, Paris: Plon, 1923, vol. I, p. 286.

150 Just, *Politik oder Strategie?*, pp. 27–8; Caulaincourt to Napoleon, 12 March and 6 June 1809, Mikhaïlowitch, *Relations Diplomatiques*, vol. III, pp. 145, 332–3.

151 Caulaincourt to Napoleon, 22 April 1809, Mikhaïlowitch, *Relations Diplomatiques*, vol. III, pp. 241, 245; Alexander to Golitsyn, 18 May (Julian date: 6 May) 1809, RGVIA/FVUA 3369. Although Alexander had repeatedly stated that his troops would march towards Olmütz in accordance with French desires, the orders only directed Golitsyn to move to the Vistula and await further instructions. With many thanks to Dr Alexander Mikaberidze for providing the archival resources and to Mr Yuri Zhukov for translations.

152 Savary, vol. IV, p. 145.

153 Wolzogen, p. 50.

154 First quote from Caulaincourt to Napoleon, 28 May 1809, Mikhaïlowitch, *Relations Diplomatiques*, vol. III, pp. 331; second quote from Alexander to Golitsyn, 11 June (29 May) 1809, RGVIA/FVUA 846, opis 16, delo 3369.

155 Caulaincourt to Napoleon, 16 April 1809, Mikhaïlowitch, *Relations Diplomatiques*, vol. III, p. 211.

156 Caulaincourt to Napoleon, 22 and 16 April 1809, Mikhaïlowitch, *Relations Diplomatiques*, vol. III, pp. 241, 211; see also Alexander to Napoleon, 20 May 1809: 'Austria, blinded by England, prepared its disasters itself', in Tatistcheff, p. 482.

157 Schwarzenberg's 21 April 1809 letter to Franz in Just, *Politik oder Strategie?*, pp. 69–70. See vol. I of this work, pp. 21–3.

158 Caulaincourt to Napoleon, 26 and 28 May 1809, Mikhaïlowitch, *Relations Diplomatiques*, vol. III, pp. 319, 332–3.

159 Alexander to Golitsyn, 18 May (6 May) 1809, RGVIA/FVUA, 3369 (this is a separate instruction in addition to his operational orders).

160 Alexander to Golitsyn, 29 May (17 May) 1809, RGVIA/FVUA, 3369; Poniatowski to Berthier, 11 May 1809, Poniatowski, *Correspondance*, vol. II, p. 136; Just, *Politik oder Strategie?*, p. 29. This was only the most blatant of several occurrences during May.

161 It is not clear when Dolgorukov personally arrived. Many accounts speak of 'General Lambert's division', so it is likely that Major General Karl de Lambert commanded the division initially and that Dolgorukov only appeared some days or weeks later.

162 Golitsyn to Poniatowski, 10 June 1809 (28 May), RGVIA/FVUA, 3368.

163 Champagny to Caulaincourt, 2 June 1809, in Vandal, vol. II, p. 94.

164 Caulaincourt to Napoleon, 25 June 1809, Mikhaïlowitch, *Relations Diplomatiques*, vol. III, p. 357; Hoditz to Ferdinand, 15 June 1809, Pawlowski, *Historja Wojny*, pp. 362–3.

165 Ferdinand to Charles, 18 June 1809, Pawlowski, *Historja Wojny*, p. 406.

166 Charles to Ferdinand, 23 June 1809, in Just, *Politik oder Strategie?*, pp. 81–2.

167 See Daniel Werenka, 'Der Kriegsruf an die Bukowina im Jahre 1809', *Jahresbericht der gr.-or. Ober-Realschule in Czernowitz*, vol. XXXIX, 1903, pp. 10–11; Johann N. Stöger, *Maximilian Erzherzog von Oesterreich-Este*, Vienna, 1865, pp. 39–40.

168 Ferdinand to Franz, 17 June 1809, and to Charles, 18 June 1809, Pawlowski, *Historja Wojny*, pp. 394, 406.

169 Ferdinand to Franz, 21 June 1809, in Poniatowski, *Correspondance*, vol. II, pp. 172–3.

170 Ferdinand to Charles, 28 June 1809, Pawlowski, *Historja Wojny*, p. 450.

171 Trautenberg: four squadrons *Kaiser* Hussars, *1st Szekler* Grenzer, *1st Wallach* Grenzer (three companies), *Strauch*, all under GM von Branowaczky (Welden, p. 341). Oberst Piccard's detachment (see note above) returned to VII Corps, but Hoditz's two squadrons joined Eggermann on 16 June. On march plans: Ferdinand to Franz, 21 June 1809, in Poniatowski, *Correspondance*, vol. II, pp. 172–3; Ferdinand to Charles, 25 June 1809, Pawlowski, *Historja Wojny*, p. 445–6; Just, *Politik oder Strategie?*, p. 46.

172 Soltyk, p. 295.

173 Poniatowski to Napoleon, 17 June 1809, Poniatowski, *Correspondance*, vol. II, pp. 169–70.

174 Poniatowski to Golitsyn, 23 June 1809, Poniatowski, *Correspondance*, vol. II, pp. 184–6.

175 This was a detachment under Hauptmann Anton Steiner; he brought one and one-half squadrons of Zemplin Insurrection Hussars from Dukla Pass and was joined by a platoon of *Ferdinand* Hussars, a company of *2nd Szekler*, and two guns from Eggermann (Steiner, p. 13).

176 Poniatowski to Napoleon, 27 June 1809, Poniatowski, *Correspondance*, vol. II, pp. 188–9.

177 Soltyk, p. 327.

178 Soltyk, pp. 325–9; Welden, pp. 348–9.

179 Ferdinand to Charles, 2 July, KAFA, Kart. 1461/7/21 3/4.

CHAPTER 2: ON HUNGARY'S ENDLESS PLAINS

1 Grouchy had the light cavalry, at least two infantry battalions, and a battery; GD Pachtod's division was still in Mahrenburg. MacDonald had Broussier and Pully (two regiments) in Marburg; Lamarque had one dragoon regiment as well as his infantry.

2 Austrian strength figures from Welden, pp. 11–12.

3 'Operations-Journal der I. Ö. Armee' (hereafter Op. J. 52), KAFA, *Operationsjournale der Hauptarmee und Korps*, Kart. 1386.

4 The skirmish at Frohnleiten involved a squadron of 6th Chasseurs and a voltigeur company on the French side, for the Austrians: a detachment of 9th Jägers, a division of *1st Banal*, three platoons of *Ott* Hussars, and two guns.

5 Grouchy sent an unspecified detachment from Mahrenburg directly towards Graz; its timely arrival helped unhinge and unnerve the Austrian defenders.

6 Also part of Andrassy's command were three companies of Pest Infantry No. 2 and two Insurrection cavalry batteries in Türje.

7 'Ordre de Bataille des kais. königl. Inneroesterreichischen Armee', 25 June 1809, KAFA, *Italien (Erzherzog Johann)*, Kart. 1404/6/169.

8 Charles to Johann, 1 June 1809, Zwiedineck-Südenhorst, *Erzherzog Johann im Feldzuge von 1809*, p. 52; Wimpffen memorandum, 29 May 1809, Moriz Edlen von Angeli, 'Wagram: Novelle zur Geschichte des Kriges von 1809', *Mittheilungen des K. und K. Kriegs-Archivs*, Vienna, 1881, pp. 44–7.

9 Op. J. 52, notation for 8 June (by which time Johann was on the march for Tuskevar).

10 Johann to Maria Ludovica, undated (probably 6 June), Zwiedineck-Südenhorst, *Erzherzog Johann im Feldzuge von 1809*, p. 38.

11 Johann, *Feldzugserzählungen*, p. 149.

12 Ibid.

13 Johann to Franz, 6 June 1809, Zwiedineck-Südenhorst, *Erzherzog Johann im Feldzuge von 1809*, p. 65 (emphasis in original).

14 First quotation: Johann to Joseph, 6 June 1809, Domanovszky, *Palatin Josefs Schriften*, vol. IV, p. 65; second quotation: Johann, 'Lebensbeschreibung', in Zwiedineck-Südenhorst, *Erzherzog Johann im Feldzuge von 1809*, p. 226.

15 Joseph, diary entries for 9 and 10 June, in Sandor Domanovszky (ed.), *Jozsef Nador Elete es Iratai*, Budapest, 1925–44, vol. III, pp. 482–6.

16 Johann, *Feldzugserzählungen*, p. 154. On Johann's thoughts of insubordination, see Joseph's diary entry for 10 June, Domanovszky, *Jozsef Nador*, vol. III, p. 487.

17 With thanks to Dr Jozsef Zachar for his thorough and insightful presentation 'Die Insurrektion des Königreichs Ungarn', given at the 'Napoleon und Graz 1809' symposium, June 2004. See also his 'Die Insurrektion des Königreichs Ungarn'; Tomas Laszlo Vizi, 'Die politische Rolle des ungarischen Adels im Zeitalter der französischen Kriege'; and Balazs Lazar, 'Die Schlacht bei Raab (Györ)', all in *Zusammenfassung der Beiträge zum Napoleon Symposium 'Feldzug 1809'*, Vienna: Delta Druckproduktionen, 2009, pp. 93–100, 112–19, 219–24.

18 1st Borsod and Gömör Infantry had only four companies each. See Appendix 4.

19 Several of the Insurrection staff officers complained about this decision, for example 'Authentische Darstellung des Ungrundes der Beschuldigungen, die in der Druckschrift: Vertheidigung des Brückenkopfes vor Pressburg, enthalten sind', *Europäische Annalen*, vol. I, 1814, p. 68.

20 Major Ernst Gideon von Maretich, 'Geschichte des Feldzugs 1809 in Ungarn nebst Relation der Schlacht am 14. Juni', 30 April 1810, KAFA, *Operationsjournale der Hauptarmee und Korps*, Kart. 1388.

21 Lipsky, KAFA, *Operationsjournale der Hauptarmee und Korps*, Kart. 1388, p. 16; Kisfaludy manuscript.

22 Oberst Eugen Graf Haugwitz, 'Darstellung der Kriegseriegnisse bei der ungarischen Insurrection vom Monat April angefangen bis 24. August 1809', 19 August 1810, KAFA, *Operationsjournale der Hauptarmee und Korps*, Kart. 1388.

23 Demuth manuscript.

24 Ibid.

25 Joseph's diary entry for 7 June, Domanovszky, *Jozsef Nador*, vol. III, p. 476.

26 Haugwitz manuscript.

27 Joseph to Franz, 5 June 1809, cited in Kisfaludy manuscript. See also Gomez to Nugent, 11 June 1809, KAFA, *Italien (Erzherzog Johann)*, Kart. 1404/6/70; and Joseph's diary entries for late May and early June, Domanovszky, *Jozsef Nador*, vol. III, pp. 468–90.

28 Haugwitz manuscript.

29 One anonymous officer assessed that the Insurrection cavalry needed six months to prepare for combat ('Uebersicht der Operationen der ungarischen Insurrection-Armee im Jahr 1809', *Europäische Annalen*, vol. V, 1814, p. 144). Herzog Albert offered a very similar analysis regarding the Insurrection as he travelled from Vienna to Hungary in mid-May ('Mémoire sur la Guerre éclatée en 1809', MOL P300/1/100).

30 'Authentische Darstellung', p. 67; Lipsky manuscript.

31 These were: 2nd Eisenburg No. 6 and Komorn No. 7; Eisenburg Hussars and two squadrons of Neograd Hussars. The other four Neograd squadrons were on the Kleine Schütt (though this regiment's movements are unclear).

32 These were: 1st Eisenburg No. 1, Szala No. 8, Veszprem No. 9, and Stuhlweissenburg No. 10 (the latter only two companies); three companies of Pest Infantry No. 2; Szala and Sümeg Hussar Regiments; Ödenburg Hussar Division.

33 These two cavalry regiments, uniformly assessed as the best in the Insurrection at that time, became the objects of considerable squabbling between Johann and Joseph, as the former was desperate for any sort of cavalry while the latter objected to the loss of the only units he felt he could trust for even minimal action.

34 These were: Pressburg No. 1, Neutra No. 3, Neograd No. 4; Pressburg and Bars Hussars.

35 He departed Pest on the 1st. Joseph's diary entry for 1 June, Domanovszky, *Jozsef Nador*, vol. III, p. 468; and *Palatin Josephs Schriften*, vol. IV, pp. 57–62.

36 Joseph to Franz, 4 June 1809, Domanovszky, *Palatin Josephs Schriften*, vol. IV, pp. 60–1.

37 Napoleon to Eugene, 4 June 1809, *Correspondance*, no. 15923.

38 Grouchy, with 9th Chasseurs supported by a squadron of *Queen's* Dragoons, overcame an Austrian security detachment under Oberstleutnant Leopold von Geramb of *Joseph* Hussars north of Steinamanger on 7 June. As in so many cases in this campaign, the Austrian forces present are unclear: certainly a squadron or division each of *Joseph* Hussars and some Insurrection cavalry (likely a division of Pest Hussars); and possibly 230–260 *Gradiska* and *St Georg* Grenzer and a division of *Blankenstein* Hussars. Geramb withdrew to Hidveg.

39 Meier, p. 51.

40 Haugwitz manuscript, KAFA. See also Ferdi Irmfried Wöber, *1809: Das Gefecht bei Pápa*, Vienna: Delta Druckproduktionen, 2005, p. 3. The Grenzer were apparently from the *Brod* and *Gradiska* Reserve Battalions (F. Vanicek, *Specialgeschichte der Militärgrenze*, Vienna: Kaiserlich-Königlich Hof- und Staatsdruckerei, 1875).

41 This ride is related in some detail in Jean Nicolas Curély, *Itinéraire d'un Cavalier Léger de la Grande Armée*, Paris: Librairie des Deux Empires, 1999, pp. 230–2; and Antoine Fortune de Brack, *Avant-Postes de Cavalerie Légère*, Paris: Aux Trois Hussards, 1984, p. 188. Eugene reported the results that night: Eugene to Napoleon, 6 June 1809, du Casse, *Eugène*, vol. V, p. 357–8. Though perhaps embellished over the years and sometimes misleadingly labelled a 'ride around the Austrian army', Curély and his men at least rode into and through Austrian lines, successfully performing a difficult mission with no casualties. Note that Curély names Fürstenfeld as the target of his reconnaissance, but this seems very unlikely given the distance to that town and the fact that Johann's headquarters was in Körmend.

42 Eugene to Clarke, 9 June 1809, du Casse, *Eugène*, vol. V, p. 358.

43 Montbrun to Berthier, du Casse, *Eugène*, vol. V, p. 347.

44 Austrian forces at Karako on 11 June are unclear. Gosztonyi apparently had at least one division of his regiment (Pest Hussars), the 230–260 *Gradiska/St Georg* Grenzer, and probably two guns; he may have had two divisions of Pest. Andrassy brought up two squadrons of Veszprem Hussars, a division of *Joseph* Hussars, a division of *Blankenstein* Hussars, a cavalry half-battery, and two 3-pounders. Austrian losses came to some 300 men (Ferdi Irmfried Wöber, *1809 The Battle of Raab*, Vienna: Delta Druckproduktionen, 2003, p. 13).

45 Charles to Johann, 9 June 1809, in Domanovszky, *Palatin Josephs Schriften*, vol. IV, pp. 71–2.

46 Johann to Stadion and to Maria Ludovica, 21 June 1809, in Zwiedineck-Südenhorst, *Erzherzog Johann im Feldzuge von 1809*, pp. 109–16.

47 Franz to Johann, 9 June 1809, 'Haupt-Operations-Journal der K. K. Inneroesterreichischen Armee' (hereafter Op. J. 54), KAFA, *Operationsjournale der Hauptarmee und Korps*, Kart. 1386. It is worth stressing the blunt and imperative nature of this brief missive.

48 Chef de Bataillon Jean Gougeon of 92nd Ligne conducted a reconnaissance to Ilz from Graz with his battalion, a squadron of 6th Hussars, and one 3-pounder on 1 June and established himself near Gleisdorf. Poinsot arrived four days later with six dragoon squadrons (23rd Dragoons and half of 29th), four more battalions (including another of 92nd Ligne), and a second 3-pounder. The hussars returned to Broussier.

49 The 6th Hussars left Graz on 4 June to conduct a probe to Marburg, but had to turn back to Ehrenhausen in the face of superior forces; the regiment returned to Graz on 8 June.

50 These troops (Pest No. 2, Komorn No. 7, Veszprem No. 9, one division of Bars Hussars, two divisions of Eisenburg Hussars, and a cavalry battery) joined other Insurrection elements already deployed along the Raab: 1st Eisenburg No. 5, Szala No. 8, and the Ödenburg Hussar Division. The Pest, Veszprem, Szala, and Sümegh Hussars were to march in with Johann's troops (Kisfaludy and Lipsky manuscripts).

51 Op. J. 52.

52 MacDonald's presence in Vasarhely on the 11th caused Johann to fear for his communications. He therefore detached the *Warasdin-Kreuz* Grenzer (Siegenfeld's regiment), the two *Blankenstein* Hussar squadrons, three squadrons of Veszprem Hussars, and two guns to shield the approach to Komorn (Siegenfeld report, 12 June 1809, KAFA, Kart. 1404/6/81).

53 Ettingshausen's memoirs in Zwiedineck-Südenhorst, *Erzherzog Johann im Feldzuge von 1809*, pp. 79–80.

54 Jozsef Magyarasz, *Historia Domus*, 1809, cited in Wöber, *Pápa*, p. 15.

55 Vaudoncourt, vol. I, p. 341.

56 Ibid., Vaudoncourt was present at the engagement.

57 *Journal des Großherzoglich Badischen General-Staab*, GLA 48/4286.

58 Meier, p. 51.

59 Diary of resident Karoly Francsics cited in Wöber, *Pápa*, p. 19.

60 Ettingshausen's memoirs, in Zwiedineck-Südenhorst, *Erzherzog Johann im Feldzuge von 1809*, p. 80.

61 Vaudoncourt, vol. I, p. 341.

62 *Journal des Großherzoglich Badischen General-Staab*, GLA 48/4286.

63 Csaba D. Veress, *Napoleon Hadai Magyar-Oragon 1809*, Budapest: Zrinyi Katonai Kiado, 1987, p. 116. With many thanks to Herr Wöber and Ms Anita Széphegyi for translation assistance.

64 Johann later dismissed the fighting at Papa with the words 'the losses were insignificant' (Johann, *Feldzugserzählungen*, p. 157).

65 Eugene to Napoleon, 12 June 1809, du Casse, *Eugène*, vol. V, p. 372. In addition to this report, for the French side, see Grouchy's 17 June summary (Grouchy, pp. 32–3); Vaudoncourt, vol. I, pp. 338–43; Vignolle, 'Armée d'Italie: Journal Historique de la Campagne de 1809', AG, MR734. On the Austrian side: Kisfaludy manuscript; Veress, pp. 110–18; Zwiedineck-Südenhorst, *Erzherzog Johann im Feldzuge von 1809*, pp. 78–80. Note that Veress, while often useful, grossly overestimates French strength and misrepresents French orders of battle. He cites, for example, fictitious designations such as '5th Corps' in the Army of Italy; Napoleon did not use the numbers one, five, or six at all (certainly not for Eugene's subordinate formations) in this war and no such designation appears in any of the French documentation.

66 Joseph, diary entry for 12 June, Domanovszky, *Jozsef Nador*, vol. III, pp. 492–3. I have used 'relat[tively]' to indicate where the actual entry reads 'zieml' for 'ziemlich'. Other Insurrection officers also noted the bedraggled appearance of Johann's men

('Operationen der ungarischen Insurrection-Armee', vol. V, p. 154). Comment on cheers from Beckers manuscript.

67 Joseph, diary entry for 12 June, Domanovszky, *Jozsef Nador*, vol. III, pp. 492–3.

68 Johann to Charles, 16 June 1809, in Zwiedineck-Südenhorst, *Erzherzog Johann im Feldzuge von 1809*, pp. 86–7; Beckers manuscript.

69 Demuth manuscript.

70 Joseph, diary entry for 12 June, Domanovszky, *Jozsef Nador*, vol. III, p. 492; Demuth manuscript; Kisfaludy and Beckers manuscripts; Haugwitz manuscript. Curiously, Ettingshausen, who was to command Johann's rear guard, was told that the army would march at midnight on 12/13 June and that he should follow at 3 a.m.; given the timing, he must have received his instructions from Johann within an hour or so of Joseph's departure from Tet (Ettingshausen's memoirs, in Zwiedineck-Südenhorst, *Erzherzog Johann im Feldzuge von 1809*, pp. 80–1).

71 The brothers may have had harsh words at their parting. A local citizen claimed to have overheard a quarrel concerning the question of command and the prospect of battle at Raab. While not impossible, this does not comport with the generally intimate tone of their correspondence during the preceding several days (the incident is cited in Wöber, *Raab*, p. 20).

72 Kisfaludy and Beckers manuscripts.

73 Haugwitz manuscript. Johann skims over this period in his recollections. In fairness to Johann and Nugent, it is important to keep in mind that the most thorough accounts come from Insurrection officers writing immediately after the war (spring 1810); these men may have had reason to stress or colour certain aspects of events. See also Kisfaludy manuscript and 'Operationen der ungarischen Insurrection-Armee'.

74 Ettingshausen initially placed one battalion of Grenzer in a square garden south of Menfo and the Insurrection troops near the village, but he soon decided that this was too exposed and withdrew the Grenzer to the heights and the Insurrection troops (minus one division of hussars) behind Menfo.

75 Ettingshausen's memoirs, in Zwiedineck-Südenhorst, *Erzherzog Johann im Feldzuge von 1809*, pp. 81–3.

76 Kisfaludy manuscript. Troops disposed themselves as follows: Frimont and the regular cavalry near the 'Rotes Kreuz' shrine, Jellacic and Colloredo around Szabadhegy towards Kismegyer; of the Insurrection that had been at Tet with Mecséry, part was outside Raab (Pest, 1st Eisenburg, Komorn, and Veszprem Infantry; Szala Hussars and two squadrons of Sümegh), the remainder were south of Kismegyer (Pest Hussars, four squadrons each of Veszprem and Bars, Ödenburg Division); it is not clear where the Eisenburg Hussars were (Veress, pp. 120–1).

77 Quoted in Veress, p. 123.

78 Actual dispositions on the French side are unclear; what follows is my best guess from Vaudoncourt, vol. I, pp. 342–7; du Casse, *Eugène*, vol. V, pp. 268–71; and the Vignolle manuscript.

79 Joseph, diary entry for 13 June, Domanovszky, *Jozsef Nador*, vol. III, p. 497.

80 Austrian sources for actions on 13 June include 'Relation über die Schlacht bei Raab am 14. Juny 1809' (written by Maretich), KAFA, Kart. 1388; Kisfaludy and Haugwitz manuscripts; Johann to Charles, 16 June 1809, Zwiedineck-Südenhorst,

Erzherzog Johann im Feldzuge von 1809, p. 87; Johann, *Feldzugserzählungen*, p. 167; Veress, pp. 121–7; Wöber, *Raab*, pp. 20–3.

81 Austrian losses were 600 to 700, according to 'Operationen der ungarischen Insurrection-Armee'; Wöber gives 400 for Insurrection losses, *Raab*, p. 21. French sources give total killed as forty-one men, from which one may extrapolate 120 to 150 wounded for a total of approximately 200; du Casse states 300 (*Eugène*, vol. V, p. 270). According to some Austrians, Lauriston 'admitted' during the ceasefire that one of 'his' chasseur regiments (ie Colbert) had lost 281 men on 13 June and was unfit for combat the following day; it is not clear that Lauriston was present, and there is no mention of such a calamity in the French sources. Note that Austrian archival sources combine losses for 13 and 14 June, making it impossible to separate casualties by day.

82 Demuth manuscript.

83 Lipsky manuscript and 'Operationen der ungarischen Insurrection-Armee', vol. VI, p. 259.

84 All quotations from Eugene to Napoleon, 13 June 1809, du Casse, *Eugène*, vol. V, p. 374–6.

85 'Operationen der ungarischen Insurrection-Armee', vol. VI, p. 258.

86 Veress, pp. 124–6. Zwiedineck-Südenhorst attempts to exculpate Johann regarding the failure to occupy the Csanak Heights (claiming that Johann feared the Csanak position could be easily outflanked), but his argument is not persuasive (*Erzherzog Johann im Feldzuge von 1809*, pp. 83–4). Also Haugwitz and Kisfaludy manuscripts.

87 Joseph, diary entry for 13 June, Domanovszky, *Jozsef Nador*, vol. III, p. 498.

88 Ibid., p. 495. The full letter is Franz to Joseph, 11 June 1809, in Domanovszky, *Palatin Joseph Schriftens*, vol. IV, pp. 76–7.

89 Charles to Johann, 11 June 1809, Op. J. 54.

90 'Impervious to reason' is from a work of fiction: Jack Vance, *The Book of Dreams*, New York: Daw, 1981, p. 228.

91 Johann, *Feldzugserzählungen*, pp. 163–4.

92 Quoted in Veress, p. 125.

93 Quoted in Veress, p. 126.

94 Routier, p. 85.

95 Many French accounts state that the Austrians benefited from low berms or retaining walls in the area between Szabadhegy and Kismegyer. Hauptmann Schmutz of 2nd Graz made similar observations (Franz Ilwof, 'Karl Schmutz: Sein Leben und Wirken', *Mittheilungen des historischen Vereins für Steiermark*, vol. XXXVIII, 1890, p. 198).

96 Johann's 'Tagesbericht', 15 June 1809, in Zwiedineck-Südenhorst, *Erzherzog Johann im Feldzuge von 1809*, pp. 84; Op. J. 52.

97 Ilwof, p. 202; Carl von Hummel, *Landwehrmänner der eheren Mark 1809*, Vienna: Stern, 1907, p. 13.

98 Austrian sources vary greatly on the exact location, identity, and composition of the various detachments; see Appendix 5.

99 Joseph, diary entry for 14 June, Domanovszky, *Jozsef Nador*, vol. III, pp. 498–9.

100 Haugwitz manuscript.

101 Vaudoncourt, vol. I, p. 351.
102 Pierre Auvray, 'Souvenirs Militaires', *Carnet de la Sabretache*, March 1914, p. 158; Barat, p. 30. See also Teste, p. 600.
103 Based on French strength returns for 25 May after the Battle of St Michael; note that these figures are probably high as there would have been some march attrition in the three weeks between the two battles in addition to some losses during the fighting from 9 to 13 June.
104 Vaudoncourt, vol. I, pp. 352–3.
105 This total does not include the Insurrection squadrons on the Schütt Islands.
106 Some of the Landwehr would soon prove quite doughty, but their numbers were roughly balanced by the completely new recruits present in many regular units. The Insurrection 'on the field' does not include Mesko or the other detachments. Two depot companies joined *Strassaldo* in St Gotthard, *Esterhazy* had recently added 400 (Seeliger, p. 158), and *Franz Jellacic* had, according to its regimental history (Bichmann, p. 103), incorporated 840 recruits during the halt in Körmend (though this is difficult to reconcile with the total of 747 on the field at Raab).
107 Auvray, p. 158; Routier, p. 86.
108 The Austrians consisted of one squadron of *Ott* and several of Insurrection hussars.
109 Hauptmann Karl Schmutz of the garrison is quite specific in describing his men firing on Italian *Queen's* Dragoons and causing severe casualties (Ilwof, p. 201). While not impossible, it seems more likely the victim was 9th Hussars (Schmutz makes other errors). See also Hummel, p. 12; Amon von Treuenfest, 'Das zweite Grazer Landwehr-Bataillon 1809', *ÖMZ*, 1889.
110 Hummel, p. 10.
111 Carlo Zucchi, *Memoirie del Generale Carlo Zucchi*, Milan: Guigoni, 1861, p. 32.
112 Vaudoncourt, vol. I, p. 359.
113 Quoted in Veress, p. 146.
114 Noël, p. 69.
115 Rittmeister Tamas Dessewffy, quoted in Veress, p. 147.
116 Quoted in Veress, p. 152.
117 Vaudoncourt, vol. I, p. 362.
118 'Operationen der ungarischen Insurrection-Armee', vol. VI, p. 267.
119 Joseph, diary entry for 14 June, Domanovszky, *Jozsef Nador*, vol. III, pp. 502–3.
120 Demuth manuscript.
121 Rittmeister Karoly Hertelendy, quoted in Veress, pp. 152–3.
122 J. W. Ridler, 'Der Ruckzug des Generals Mesko nach der Schlacht bey Raab', *Archiv für Geographie, Historie, Staats- und Kriegskunst*, 1–3 November 1813; also printed in *Taschenbuch für die vaterländische Geschichte*, vol. III, 1813.
123 These included Johann, Haugwitz, Demuth, Maretich (in the 'Relation'), Herzog Albert; Zucchi, p. 32.
124 Chevillet, letter of 15 June 1809, p. 261.
125 Henckens, p. 79. The 8th had begged the 25th for support, but the latter refused without specific orders from Sahuc; Sahuc delayed for some thirty minutes. This incident apparently occasioned much debate among the French after the battle. See Grouchy, p. 35; Teste, p. 601.

126 Hertelendy, in Veress, p. 153.
127 Haugwitz manuscript. Curély, who had no use for Montbrun, blamed that general for lack of enterprise (pp. 234–5).
128 Eugene may have had second thoughts as well: Eugene to Clarke, 15 June 1809, du Casse, *Eugène*, vol. V, p. 384.
129 Auvray, p. 159; Hertelendy, in Veress, p. 154.
130 French casualties from Vaudoncourt, vol. I, p. 366. Austrian regular/Landwehr casualties from 'Verzeichniss der am 13ten und 14ten Juny 809 in der Action bey Raab Verlust' (with supplements); Insurrection losses from reports submitted by Davidovich and Mecséry on 18 June, KAFA, Kart. 1458.
131 Among many examples, Johann excoriated the Insurrection in a 16 June letter to Charles describing the battle, in Zwiedineck-Südenhorst, *Erzherzog Johann im Feldzuge von 1809*, pp. 87–90. The editor of this work, Zwiedineck-Südenhorst, is acidic in his analysis (pp. 96–100). For explanatory notes from the Insurrection viewpoint, see extracts from the operations journal in Domanovszky, *Palatin Josephs Schriften*, vol. IV, p. 89 and the various manuscripts cited in this chapter.
132 Joseph to Charles, 16 June 1809, Domanovszky, *Palatin Josephs Schriften*, vol. IV, p. 83.
133 Johann, *Feldzugserzählungen*, p. 163.
134 Joseph, diary entry for 14 June, Domanovszky, *Jozsef Nador*, vol. III, p. 503.
135 Vaudoncourt, vol. I, p. 367.
136 There are small hints (nothing more) that Johann might have been disappointed with Nugent: for example, in his *Feldzugserzählungen* (p. 167), where he complains that the attack at Raab had to be postponed to 15 June because 'nothing had been prepared'.
137 Eugene to Napoleon, 16 June 1809, du Casse, *Eugène*, vol. V, pp. 377–8.
138 Mayerhoffer, p. 125. Zwiedineck-Südenhorst argues it was insignificant (*Erzherzog Johann im Feldzuge von 1809*, p. 101).
139 Vaudoncourt, vol. I, p. 367.
140 Ibid.
141 'Nineteenth Bulletin of the Army of Germany', 16 June 1809 *Correspondance*, no. 15356; the 16 June order of the day is in Albert, *Historique du 98e Régiment d'Infanterie*, AG, manuscript, 1892.
142 Napoleon to Eugene, 16 June 1809, *Correspondance*, no. 15358. The Nineteenth Bulletin was also dated 16 June (*Correspondance*, no. 15356), as were the letters to Josephine and Auguste (*Correspondance*, nos. 15354–5).
143 Joseph, diary entry for 14 June, Domanovszky, *Jozsef Nador*, vol. III, p. 503.
144 Ferdi Irmfried Wöber, *1809: Die Zeit nach der Schlacht bei Raab*, Vienna: Delta Druckproduktionen, 2006, pp. 18–19; Veress pp. 160–1.
145 These were 1st Borsod No 12 (1,072), 2nd Borsod No 16 (662), Zemplin No 18 (1,247), and one company of Abaujvar No 19 (185). Refugees from Raab included Ödenburg (198), Bars (120), Neograd (80), Heves (50), Veszprem (35), Zemplin (18), and Eisenburg (10) Hussars. FM Allvintzi report, 17 June 1809, in Istvan Bodnar, 'A Györi Csata 1809 Junius 14-en', *Hadtortenelmi Kozlemenyek*, 1897, p. 504. Haugwitz avers the brigade was ordered to return to Pest, others claim it turned about on meeting the fugitives.

146 Joseph, diary entry for 16 June, Domanovszky, *Jozsef Nador*, vol. III, p. 505.

147 Quotations from Johann, *Feldzugserzählungen*, pp. 174–5.

148 Johann to Maria Ludovica, 21 June 1809, extracts in Franz Xaver Krones, *Zur Geschichte Österreichs im Zeitalter der französischen Kriege und der Restauration*, Gotha: Perthes, 1886, pp, 113–14.

149 Confidential letter from Charles to Bianchi, 23 June 1809, in Heller, *Bianchi*, p. 258.

150 Mesko to Joseph, 14 June 1809, cited in Wöber, *Die Zeit*, p. 23.

151 Ridler, 'Ruckzug'; Ferdinand Voith (Mesko's General Staff Corps officer), 'Mesko Tabornok Visszavonulasarol 1809-ben', *Hadtorteneti Kozlemenyek*, 1894.

152 Brack, p. 283.

153 Frimont with twelve squadrons from the Szala, Sümegh, and Eisenburg regiments, the regular dragoons, and six guns (Veress, p. 179; Gustav Ritter Amon von Treuenfest, *Geschichte des k. und k. Husaren-Regimentes Kaiser Nr. 15*, Vienna: regimental, 1894, p. 199); a weak Insurrection battalion may have been on hand as well. Curély, pp. 236–40; Ledru, pp. 118–19.

154 Joseph had the following complete regiments: Veszprem (550), Eisenburg (669), Sümegh (915), Szala (869), Torontol (1,028); as well as Neograd (one division, 250), Pressburg (three and one-half squadrons, 400); two cavalry batteries, one howitzer, three 6-pounders. In Komorn were the Bars (four squadrons, 739), Heves, (four squadrons, 335), Zemplin (two and one-half squadrons, 356), Neograd (one squadron, 170), and Ödenburg (division, 142) Hussars; 1st Eisenburg (553), Komorn (445), Szala (682), Veszprem (375) Infantry, and fourteen 3-pounders. From 'Stand der Insurrections-Truppen den 23ten Juni 1809', KAFA, *Siebenbürgische Insurrektion, Ungarische Insurrektion*, Kart. 1395. It appears that the following infantry had also arrived in Komorn by 23 June: 1st Borsod No. 12, 2nd Borsod No. 16 (together 1,933), and Bihar No. 14 (400).

155 Johann left the following in the Komorn bridgehead to form the garrison along with several depot companies that were already in place: *Franz Jellacic, Lusignan, I/Szulin*, 1st Inner Austrian Volunteers, as well as the remaining Bruck, Cilli, Judenburg, and Salzburg Landwehr (KAFA, Kart. 1404/6/169). By the end of the month, *Lusignan, I/Szulin* had joined Bianchi at Pressburg (the location of *Franz Jellacic* at that point is unclear).

156 Franz to Charles and Charles's reply with Franz's marginalia, 23 June 1809, KAFA, *Hauptarmee VI(B)*, Kart. 1460/6/464–5.

157 For Lasalle, see Robinet, *Lasalle* pp. 89–170.

158 These were: 3rd Chasseurs (329), 14th Chasseurs (139), 19th Chasseurs (322), Baden Light Dragoons (208), Hessian Chevaulegers (179). Strengths as of 30 June (AG, C2/510). Marulaz had neither artillery nor infantry.

159 Marulaz, pp. 341–3.

160 In K. C. Peeters, *Soldaten van Napoleon*, Antwerp: De Vlijt, 1955, p. 80.

161 Marulaz, 'Journal Historique', AG, C2/93.

162 Joseph to Franz, 16 June 1809, Domanovszky, *Palatin Josephs Schriften*, vol. IV, p. 79.

163 Quote from Joseph's 27 June diary entry, Domanovszky, *Jozsef Nador*, vol. III, p. 532. It is not clear how many Grenz battalions Johann left with Joseph; there were at least two (*1st Banal*) and possibly as many as four (adding one or two from *Ogulin*).

164 Napoleon to Eugene, 28 June 1809, *Correspondance*, no. 15456.

165 Johann, *Feldzugserzählungen*, p. 180. Johann, if acerbic, was correct: the initial orders for the bridgehead project were issued on 3 May and did not envisage offensive operations; these were confirmed when Prochaska visited the site on 11 May. See 'Authentische Darstellung', *Europäische Annalen*, vol. I, 1814, pp. 60–4 (this piece seems to have been written in self-justification by the responsible engineer officer, then-Hauptmann Paul Cholich).

166 The presence of French cavalry precluded work from 14 to 20 May.

167 Lasalle to Davout, 30 May 1809, a.m., Robinet, *Lasalle*, p. 41.

168 Buat, vol. II, pp. 35–6; Napoleon to Davout, 31 May 1809, *Correspondance*, no. 15283.

169 The 7th Léger and 25th Ligne joined the division in this general area on 4 June.

170 Quote from Bianchi in his *Vertheidigung des Brückenkopfes vor Pressburg im Jahre 1809*, Pressburg, 1811, p. 10.

171 Largest losses on the Allied side were 436 from 12th Ligne and 125–175 Hessians. The French claimed to have taken 300–400 prisoners. Allied casualties from French and Hessian regimental histories and Davout to Napoleon, 3 June 1809, Mazade, vol. III, pp. 5–7; Austrian losses from Karl Schikofsky, 'Die Vertheidigung des Brückenkopfes von Pressburg im Jahre 1809', *Organ der militär-wissenschaftlichen Vereine*, vol. XLVI, 1893, p. 186.

172 Sources sometimes refer to the French position as Wieselburg instead of Ungarisch-Altenburg. The two towns were adjacent to one another (they now form the combined community of Mosonmagyarovar) and, for purposes of clarity, only Altenburg is shown on the maps.

173 While Lasalle was at Raab, Gudin moved temporarily to Ungarisch-Altenburg to be in a position to support Eugene as needed.

174 The Austrian raiding party consisted of 450 men of Stain and 150 of 3rd UMB Landwehr. The Allied response included an intrepid counter-attack by the Hessian light infantry (229) from Ybbs and Melk who were marching to join their comrades. The Austrians lost at least seventy-two men (Hessian sources say 150 were captured alone) and captured forty-eight French. Weiss's brigade (*EH Carl*, Stain, 3rd UMB, 4th UWW, 6-pounder brigade battery) deployed between Pressburg and Theben with *EH Carl* at Marchegg. Bianchi, pp. 37–8; Schikofsky, pp. 194–6; Gill, *Eagles*, p. 237.

175 One Landwehr battalion from Weiss's brigade remained at Marchegg with the two guns, and another stayed at Schlosshof, but both were placed under Rosenberg. Op. J. 52.

176 The *Banal* Grenz battalions that had been left with Joseph were also called to Pressburg.

177 Rabbi Moshe Sofer, *Pressburg under Siege*, New York: CIS, 1991, p. 66.

178 Many Austrians expressed outrage at the bombardment (Johann depicting it as 'malicious arson', Bianchi called it 'a counterpart to Copenhagen'), and Charles protested to Napoleon.

179 The *St Julien* battalion numbered only 380 men, the two Grenz companies totalled 480 (Schikofsky, p. 204).

180 Davout's report of 30 June, Mazade, vol. III, pp. 75–7; Hervieu, *Historique du 21e Régiment d'Infanterie*; Schikofsky, p. 204 (gives total Austrian casualties as 140).

CHAPTER 3: THE SOUTHERN FLANKS

1 Napoleon referred to it as 'the best corps of my army', probably as a means of prodding Marmont (Napoleon to Marmont, 28 June 1809, *Correspondance*, no. 15453).

2 Artur Khuepach, *Geschichte der K. K. Kriegsmarine während der Jahre 1802 bis 1814*, Vienna: Staatsdruckerei, 1942, vol. II, pp. 213–14, 234.

3 Johann, *Feldzugserzählungen*, p. 34.

4 Although officially designated 'Landbataillone', these often appear as 'Landwehr' in contemporary reports.

5 Napoleon to Eugene, 14 January 1809, *Correspondance*, no. 14705.

6 Napoleon to Eugene, 13 and 14 January, 1 and 8 March 1809, *Correspondance*, nos. 14698, 14705, 14829, 14874. Eugene transmitted these instructions to Marmont, see his letters of 27 January, and 8, 14, 20 March 1809 in Marmont, vol. III, pp. 189–97.

7 Marmont, vol. III, p. 136.

8 Report of Pierre Laurent Jean Baptiste David, 4 May 1809, cited in Paul Pisani, *La Dalmatie de 1797 à 1815*, Paris: Picard, 1893, p. 313.

9 Emil von Woinovich, *Kämpfe in der Lika, in Kroatien und Dalmatien*, Vienna: Stern, 1906, p. 20. Grenz desertion as a theme appears repeatedly in contemporary Habsburg writings about Croatia: for example, Johann, *Feldzugserzählungen*, pp. 142–3.

10 Johann to Stoichevich, 1 April 1809, KAFA, *Truppenkorps gegen Dalmatien (Stoichevich)*, Kart. 1399.

11 Johann Baptist Schels, 'Der Feldzug 1809 in Dalmatien', *ÖMZ*, 1837, p. 294.

12 Johann, *Feldzugserzählungen*, pp. 82, 100.

13 I have followed the dates given in Woinovich, *Dalmatien* and Pisani, *Dalmatie*; but note that an early piece on this campaign gives the date of attack as 27 April (Schels, 'Dalmatien').

14 Pisani, p. 310; Schels and Woinovich do not mention this latter column.

15 Marmont, vol. III, p. 136.

16 Marmont gives a slightly different timeline, but the results are the same (vol. III, pp. 139–40).

17 Klobusiczky to Johann, 10 May 1809, KAFA, *9. Korps (Gyulay in Italien)*, Kart. 1439. The Insurrection troops were under Major Peharnik.

18 Khuepach, p. 235.

19 These two battalions had been sent to Ottocac by mistake (they were supposed to reinforce Kengyel) and Gyulai quickly recalled them, but Stoichevich decided to hold onto them (Woinovich, *Lika*, p. 30).

20 Schels, 'Dalmatien', p. 304.

21 Marc Desboeufs, *Souvenirs du Capitaine Desboeufs*, Paris: Picard, 1901, p. 100.

22 Hrabovsky stated that detachment of fugitives came to 'around seven companies' (Woinovich says nine): [Hrabovsky] 'Journal des Truppen Corps gegen Dalmatien' (Op. J. 63), KAFA, Kart. 1387.

23 Quoted in Woinovich, *Lika*, p. 47.

24 The French forces involved on 17 May are not clear. Montrichard's division seems to have played little part and some elements of Clauzel's may have been off to the right

trying to outflank the Austrian position. Note that Marmont's claim of 300 casualties is for both 16 and 17 May and is probably understated (Woinovich, *Lika*, p. 50).

25 The progress of the war meant that the garrison battalion's employment south of Spalato was unrealistic, while Rebrovic's urgent situation called for reinforcement. The two Banal Reserve Battalions were the ones mistakenly sent to Ottocac on 9 May.

26 Desboeufs, p. 100.

27 The commander of 79th Ligne mentions in his memoirs that a powerful storm delayed the advance by two hours (until 9 a.m.): Roch Godart, *Mémoires*, Paris: Flammarion, 1895, p. 125.

28 II/81st was guarding the trains and wounded (evidently near Medak) and spent much of its day fending off armed peasantry in fairly hot combat (Desboeufs, p. 101).

29 Marmont, vol. III, p. 148.

30 Marmont to Napoleon, 29 May 1809, ibid., p. 205.

31 The role of 23rd Ligne during this battle is unclear but evidently limited; it may have been assigned to watch the Jadova valley to preclude interference by the Austrian troops at Ploca.

32 Desboeufs, p. 101.

33 Woinovich, *Lika*, p. 61.

34 Both quotations from a report by Marmont's chief of staff in Pisani, p. 317.

35 Woinovich, *Lika*, p. 61. It is not clear where the other Austrian guns were.

36 Woinovich (*Lika*, p. 64) gives French losses on these two days alone as 1,581, but Pisani's research puts losses for the entire month of May at 1,953 (p. 318).

37 Launay is also known as Jean Marie Auguste 'Baron Auly de Launey' and 'Delaunay'.

38 Johann, *Feldzugserzählungen*, pp. 142–3. The *Licca* Grenz Regiment was down to 205 men as of 29 May ('Operations Journal des 9ten Armee Corps Von Anfang der Feindseligkeiten' (Op. J. 59), KAFA, *Operationsjournale der Hauptarmee und Korps*, Kart. 1387).

39 Hauptmann Gerstorf, 'Relation des Feldzugs gegen Dalmatien 1809' (Op. J. 65), 19 February 1810, KAFA, Kart. 1387.

40 Auguste Garnier, *Notice sur le Général Delzons*, Paris: Belin, 1863, p. 116.

41 Both quotes from Marmont, vol. III, pp. 153–4.

42 Op. J. 63.

43 Kengyel had eleven and one-half companies of Banderial infantry, five companies of Personal infantry, and four companies of Massal infantry, along with one squadron each of Banderial and Personal hussars (Op. J. 59).

44 Woinovich, *Lika*, p. 77.

45 Godart, p. 129.

46 First quotation: Desboeufs, p. 101. Second quotation: Marmont, vol. III, p. 155. Marmont to Eugene, 28 May 1809, in Marmont, vol. III, p. 202.

47 As shown on Map 22, Hauptmann Zuccheri's command (now under Kuncz), marched via San Stefano, while another detachment under Major Lachovsky of *Hohenzollern* headed up the Cordevole valley.

48 The leaders were Count Rudolfo Paravicini and a former Austrian officer named Corrado (or Scipio) Juvalta. Vaudoncourt gives Polfranceschi 200 men; Hormayr

says there were 1,200. Some of these were mounted gendarmes. Hormayr, *Das Heer von Innerösterreich*, pp. 261–5; Vaudoncourt, vol. I, p. 322; Cesare Cantù, *Storia della Citta e della Diocesi di Como*, Como: Ostinelli, 1831, pp. 458–61, and his *Della Indipendenza Italiana Cronistoria*, Turin: Unione Tipografico, 1872, pp. 402–4. Carlo Bullo, 'Dei Movimenti Insurrezionali del Veneto sotto il Dominio Napoleonico', *Nuovo Archivio Veneto*, vol. XVII, 1899 (quotation from Bullo); Gellio Cassi, 'L'Alta Lombardia durante l'insurrezione tirolese nel 1809', *Rassegna Storica del Risorgimento*, vol. XVIII, 1931; Vincenzo Marchesi, 'La Guerra Intorno a Venezia nel 1809', *Rivista Storica del Risogimento Italiano*, vol. I, 1895; Giuseppe Romegialli, *Storia della Valtellina*, Sondrio: Cagnoletto, 1839, vol. IV, pp. 530–49.

49 Some Austrian sources give the departure date of the first detachment as 3 May, this account follows the timing in Ferdinand Hirn's detailed study (*Vorarlbergs Erhebung im Jahre 1809*, Bregenz: Teutsch, 1909, pp. 89, 93, 128): the first detachment reaching Feldkirch on 25 April, the second arriving in Bludenz on 12 May.

50 On Jellacic, see Vol. II, pp. 290–91. The fortress commandant's journal describes the garrison observing the fighting in the distance: Anton Peternader, *Tirols Landes-Vertheidigung nebst interessanten Biografien und Skizzen merkwürdiger Tiroler Landesvertheidiger*, Innsbruck: Witting, 1853, pp. 5–26.

51 Berthier to Lefebvre, 6 May 1809, 8.30 p.m., Saski, vol. III, pp. 175–6.

52 Berthier to Beaumont, 4 May 1809, Saski, vol. III, pp. 159–61.

53 Schemfil, p. 64. Other Austrian sources give Chasteler only 2,876 men of all arms (eg Rudolf Bartsch, *Der Volkskrieg in Tirol*, Vienna: Stern, 1905, p. 50). Chasteler's cavalry only numbered some 90 troopers (Alexander Theimer, *Geschichte des k.k. siebenten Uhlanen-Regiments*, Vienna: Sommer, 1869, p. 237).

54 The presence of four Landwehr battalions (and detaching 1st Klagenfurt at Rattenberg) is from Major Veyder's operations journal, September 1810, 'Journal des VIII Armee-Corps der Kriegsbegebenheiten in Tirol im Jahre 1809' (hereafter Op. J. 46), KAFA, *Operationsjournale der Hauptarmee und Korps*, Kart. 1386: Chasteler must have called upon the latter battalion from Buol's reserve in Seefeld.

55 Reissenfels seems to have had two companies, a gun, and his platoon of chevaulegers; another company and a gun had been left near Kufstein. Veyder's operations journal (Op. J. 46) gives the strength of Reissenfels's battalion as 600 men. The presence of two companies at Wörgl is my estimate. Some sources mistakenly place a company of *De Vaux* at the Strub Pass; in fact, it was a company of *Hohenlohe-Bartenstein*.

56 Three Landwehr battalions (1st and 2nd Judenburg, 1st Bruck) had been at Saalfelden to link Jellacic with Chasteler. Recalled in early May, their remnants ended up joining the Army of Inner Austria. Their place was taken by a few Tyrolian companies.

57 Op. J. 46.

58 Chasteler to Hormayr, 12 May 1809, Hormayr, *Das Heer von Innerösreich*, p. 284.

59 Op. J. 46. Wrede's strength estimate from 20 May figures with casualties for 13 May added in; Wrede had another 1,000 men in six companies of 9th Infantry, but these were dedicated to Luftenstein Pass.

60 Hormayr, quoted in Schemfil, pp. 66–7.

61 Op. J. 46.

62 Volders's cloister diary, in Ludwig Rapp (ed.), *Schicksale des Servitenklosters bei Volders in Tirol*, Brixen: Weger, 1886, pp. 22–3.

448 ~ NOTES TO PAGES 124–8

63 'Operationsjournal von jenen Theil des VIIIt Armee Corps welches unter FML Chasteler nach Tyrol rückte' (hereafter Op. J. 45), KAFA, *Operationsjournale der Hauptarmee und Korps*, Kart. 1385.

64 Austrian losses taken from Veyder's operations journal (Op. J. 46) with my own estimate of dead and wounded (based on Bavarian losses). Many Austrian sources give total Habsburg losses as 600, but Veyder was quite specific in listing 607 as 'going into true prisoner of war status'. Bavarian casualties from Max Leyh, *Die Feldzüge des Königlich Bayerischen Heeres unter Max I. Joseph von 1805 bis 1815*, Munich: Schick, 1935, p. 147.

65 Johann's 'Denkwürdigkeiten', quoted in Viktor Theiss, *Leben und Wirken Erzherzog Johanns*, Graz: Historische Landeskommission, 1963, vol. II, p. 297.

66 Hausmann, p. 84.

67 Op. J. 46.

68 Ibid.

69 Joseph von Anders, 'Geschichtliche Skizze der Kriegsereignisse in Tirol im Jahre 1809', *ÖMZ*, 1833-4, p. 276.

70 Josef Rapp, *Tirol im Jahre 1809*, Innsbruck: Rauch, 1852, p. 294.

71 It is also worth noting that there were serious frictions and suspicions among different groups of Tyrolians, particularly between townspeople and mountain dwellers. This often resulted in abuse of Tyrolians by Tyrolians.

72 Buol's after-action report, published in [Joseph Hormayr], *Das Land Tyrol und der Tyrolerkrieg von 1809*, Leipzig: Brockhaus, 1845, p. 369. Fenner had a similar experience, Johann G. Mayr, *Der Mann von Rinn*, Innsbruck: Ostermann, 1851, pp. 69–70.

73 Mändler, p. 29; 'Ueber das Betragen der königlich-baierischen Truppen im Inn-Kreise', *Europäische Annalen*, vol. IX, 1809, p. 291; Wilhelm G. Becker, *Andreas Hofer und der Freiheitskampf in Tyrol 1809*, Leipzig: Teubner, 1841, vol. II, pp. 101–2.

74 Hausmann, p. 84.

75 Josef Deifl, *Infanterist Deifl. Ein Tagebuch aus napoleonischer Zeit*, ed. Eugen von Frauenholz, Munich: Beck, 1939, p. 23.

76 Weinbach to Hompesch, 13 May 1809, in J. Hirn, *Tirols Erhebung*, pp. 404–5. Hormayr uses almost exactly the same formulation (*Land Tyrol*, p. 290).

77 These and other bewildering notes are printed in Hormayr, *Das Heer von Inneröstreich*, pp. 298–302.

78 Order of the Day, 5 May 1809, in the 23rd Bulletin of the Army of Germany, 28 June 1809, *Correspondance*, no. 15464. Napoleon was also angered by the treatment of Bavarian officials in captured Tyrol. Austrians viewed this order with great indignation and Franz issued a reciprocal threat; his letter to Charles is dated 25 May in *Interessante Beyträge zu einer Geschichte der Ereignisse in Tirol von 10. April 1809 bis zum 20. Februar 1810*, Munich, 1810. This correspondence also appeared in the 6 July 1809 number of the *Journal de l'Empire*.

79 Josef Egger, *Geschichte des Tirols von den ältesten Zeiten bis in die Neuzeit*, Innsbuck: Wagner, 1880, p. 613.

80 Berthier to Lefebvre, 17 May 1809, Saski, vol. III, p. 308.

81 Lefebvre to Max Joseph, 21 May 1809, Camille Sauzey, *Nos Alliés les Bavarois*, Paris: Teissedre, 1988, p. 141.

82 Napoleon to Bernadotte, 24 May 1809, *Correspondance*, no. 15250. See also Robinet de Cléry, *En Tyrol*, pp. 68–79.

83 Sobriquet for Wrede from a Tyrolian leader quoted in Leyh, pp. 156–7.

84 Gill, *Eagles*, pp. 339–43. On 25 May, there were approximately 1,200 Austrians and 6,400 Tyrolians against 3,000 Bavarians; the numbers increased to some 12,000 Tyrolians and 1,350 Austrians versus 5,600 Bavarians on 29 May. See Gedeon Freiherr Maretich von Riv-Alpon, *Die zweite und dritte Berg Isel-Schlacht*, Innsbruck: Wagner, 1895; Werner Köfler, *Die Kämpfe am Bergisel 1809*, Vienna: Bundesverlag, 1983. The 13 April surrender is considered here the first Berg Isel 'battle'.

85 Best accounts are Hermann Sallagar, 'Die Kämpfe um Sachsenburg, am Plöckenpasse, im Drautale und bei Klagenfurt 1809', *Carinthia I*, no. 2–5, 1909; Anders, *ÖMZ*, 1833, pp. 155–6. Herta Ogris ('Die Kriegesereignisse in Kärnten 1809', dissertation, University of Vienna, May 1941, pp. 88–91) erroneously states that Rusca advanced to Sachsenburg as early as 22 May with most of his division. French summary accounts only speak of one notable engagement (27 May).

86 The first reinforcement, two *2nd Banal* companies and two *Szulin* companies (200) under Hauptmann Kuncz, arrived on 23 May (Zuccheri's old *1st Banal* company had been left behind north-east of San Stefano di Cadore). The two II/*Szulin* companies, trapped north of the Möll river dispersed into the mountains and finally made their way, much reduced, to Pettau to join Ignaz Gyulai. The second tranche of reinforcements, arriving on the night of 25/26 May, included: two more *2nd Banal* companies, a company of 9th Jägers (100), three companies of III/*Hohenlohe-Bartenstein* (427), and two 6-pounders.

87 Sallagar, 'Sachsenburg', p. 160.

88 Addobbati, pp. 14–17. Sallagar ('Sachsenburg', pp. 157–9) states that the Dalmatians were being 'escorted' by two companies and that only the Dalmatians marched on to Villach. Austrian sources give the column a strength of 600–700 men. The defenders were two companies of Tyrolians ('who dispersed entirely') and two companies of *J Jellacic* (who lost 91 men!): Ogris, p. 92; *Geschichte des K. K. 53. Infanterie-Regimentes*, pp. 174–5.

89 This is the figure given in the Army of Italy's 25 May 'Situation Sommaire'; Rusca told Marmont that he had only 3,400 men, 'officers included' (Rusca to Marmont, 5 June 1809, Marmont, vol. III, p. 279).

90 Rusca to Marmont, 4 June 1809, Marmont, vol. III, p. 277.

91 This was a Schützen company of 2nd Klagenfurt Landwehr commanded by Major Anton von Lais (also spelled Laïs, Leis, or Leiss).

92 Joseph Hamberger, 'Die französischen Invasion in Kärnten i. J. 1809', Part II, *Jahresbericht der Staats-Oberrealschule zu Klagenfurt*, 1894, p. 6.

93 Chasteler to Allvintzi, 12 June 1809, KAFA, *8. Korps (Chasteler Tirol)*, Kart. 1437; the 'Früh-Rapport' for 1–13 June, however, gives Chasteler a total of only 4,105 infantry and 337 chevaulegers (KAFA, *Italien (Erzherzog Johann)*, Kart. 1404).

94 Johann, *Feldzugserzählungen*, pp. 158–9.

95 Anders, *ÖMZ*, 1833, p. 300.

96 Vignolle, 'Italie'. An Austrian source gives French/Italian losses as 630 (Hamberger, p. 8). For this engagement, see Sallagar, 'Sachsenburg', pp. 165–76; Anton Marx, 'Das Gefecht am Kalvarienberg bei Klagenfurt, am 6. Juni 1809', *ÖMZ*, 1836; Chasteler to

Johann, 9 June 1809, Zwiedineck-Südenhorst (ed.), 'Zur Geschichte des Krieges von 1809 in Steiermark'; Vaudoncourt, vol. I, pp. 375–7; Austrian and French regimentals.

97 In his memoirs, Marmont defends himself against severe criticism for not marching to Rusca's assistance, (vol. III, pp. 212–15): uncertain of the enemy's intentions, he sent Clauzel's division to Krainburg (Kranj) on 4 June and Montrichard's to Oberlaibach (Vrhnika) on the 6th.

98 'Gott weiss wo' from 'Brigade Eintheilung', 12 June 1809, KAFA, 8. Korps (Chasteler Tirol), Kart. 1437.

99 Buol's after-action report in Hormayr, Land Tyrol, p. 372.

100 Dutaillis was French commandant in Munich, quote in Robinet de Cléry, En Tyrol, pp. 80–1; see Gill, Eagles, pp. 344–5.

101 Vaudoncourt, vol. I, p. 326; and Journal des Sciences Militaires, vol. II, 1826, p. 288. Levié probably had some 1,000 infantry (II and IV/3rd Line); Austrian sources also credit him with 60–170 cavalry and three guns for a total of over 1,700 men. The Tyrolians probably numbered at least 1,300. Buol had marched south to assist Leiningen with a battalion, thirty horse, and four guns, but turned around on learning of Levié's repulse and was not engaged.

102 Hormayr, Innerösotreich, pp. 358–64.

103 Johann to Ignaz Gyulai, 11 May 1809, Krieg 1809, vol. II, pp. 479–80.

104 It is difficult to pin down exactly what troops were in Laibach, but the following seem to have been present: one battalion of Simbschen (1,207: seems to have been mostly recruits), four companies of II/Szulin (526), one cordon company (74), and a composite Laibach Landwehr battalion (possibly 500); 'Operations Journal des 9ten Armee Corps' (Op. J. 60), KAFA, Operationsjournale der Hauptarmee und Korps, Kart. 1387. This represents additional information acquired after the publication of Vol. II, see p. 284 of that volume.

105 From Op. J. 60, with the exception that I have used the figures from the 1–13 June 'Früh-Rapport' for the cavalry (467 for Frimont rather than 1,110; 577 for Savoy rather than 727); the operations journal also lists Hohenlohe Dragoons as 835, which seems far too strong. Another source gives much lower numbers: Ottocac Grenzer (800), Franz Karl (456), Simbschen (1,400), Frimont Hussars (450), Savoy Dragoons (360) according to a IX Corps officer (almost certainly writing on Gyulai's behalf): 'Ueber die Operationen des Grafen Gyulai, als Rechtfertigung gegen die Beschuldigungen des Verf. Der "Darstellung der Schlachten auf dem Marchfelde"', Europäischen Annalen, vol. 8, 1811, p. 97. Note that the Hohenlohe Dragoons are not included here; they marched off on 25 May to rejoin Johann, but would have added another 450 to 500 horse at this point.

106 Diary of Zagreb Bishop Maximilian Vrhovac, entry for 25 May, Maksimilijan Vrhovac, Dnevnik, Zagreb: Zavod za Hrvatsku povijest, Filozofskag fakultete u Zagrebu, 1987, p. 528. With thanks to Vlado Brnardic.

107 Ibid., entry for 22 May, pp. 526–8.

108 Johann, Feldzugserzählungen, pp. 142–3; Op. J. 59.

109 Report submitted by Zach and Munkascy, 30 May 1809, in 'Ueber die Operationen', p. 98.

110 Op. J. 59.

111 FML Zach brought the remnants of six or seven battalions back from Präwald, joining Gyulai at Auersperg (Turjak) on 19 May: 1st and 2nd Trieste, 1st and 2nd Adelsberg, 2nd Görz, 2nd Neustadl, and one and one-half unspecified Laibach (Op. J. 52). These, however, numbered only 1,200–1,500 men and most soon disintegrated.

112 Gyulai to Johann, 15 June 1809, Zwiedineck-Südenhorst (ed.), 'Zur Geschichte des Krieges von 1809 in Steiermark'.

113 Friedrich von Seidel, 'Die Operazionen des von dem Banus von Kroazien, Feldmarschall-Lieutenant Grafen Ignaz Gyulai befehligten östreichischen neunten Armeekorps in Feldzuge 1809', ÖMZ, 1837, p. 233.

114 V. Levec, (ed.), 'Ein Tagebuch aus dem Jahre 1809', *Mittheilungen des historischen Vereines für Steiermark*, vol. XLVI, 1898, p. 79.

115 On the likelihood that the French efforts were more 'demonstrations' than serious 'assaults', see Tepperberg's excellent booklet, pp. 20–7. See also fine essay by Leopold Toifl, 'Belagerung und Zerstörung des Grazer Schlossberges im Jahr 1809', *Zusammenfassung der Beiträge zum Napoleon Symposium 'Feldzug 1809'*, Vienna: Delta Druckproduktionen, 2009, pp. 106–11.

116 Historian Alois Veltzé pointedly criticises Gyulai's lack of initiative: 'Der Grazer Schlossberg 1809', *Mitteilungen des K. und K. Kriegsarchivs*, vol. V, 1907.

117 Hackher's journal and correspondence are in Josef Scheiger, 'Quellen und Beiträge zur Geschichte der Vertheidigung des Schlossberges von Graz im Jahre 1809', *Mittheilungen des historischen Vereines für Steiermark*, vol. XIV, 1866.

118 Broussier's journal, AG, C4/10.

119 Ibid. Gyulai's operations journal recorded that the Massal troops were 'completely demoralised' (Op. J. 59).

120 Marmont, vol. III, p. 222.

121 Berthier to Marmont, 7, 14, 19, and 28 June (two letters) 1809, *Correspondance*, nos. 15312, 15349, 15381, 15453, and 15454. Other Berthier letters are in Marmont, vol. III, pp. 285–90.

122 Napoleon to Eugene, 28 June 1809, *Correspondance*, no. 15455.

123 Broussier's journal, AG, C4/10. The bridge is just north of Gösting at a hamlet called Weinzödl.

124 Around this time, the 2nd Battalion's Voltigeur Company and part of its 4th Fusilier Company became separated from the main body and had to retire to the bridge (leaving Gambin's overall strength at something less than 1,200).

125 Lacorde, pp. 80–1.

126 Op. J. 59.

127 Journal of Franz Wastel (Scheiger, 'Quellen', p. 130).

128 Ibid.

129 Jérome-Etienne Besse, 'Mémoires', *Revue de l'Agenais et des Anciennes Provinces du Sud-Ouest*, 1892, p. 316.

130 Seventeen hours of combat action from 11 p.m. 25 June until 4 p.m. 26 June. Of course, the men had been on the move since 8 p.m. on the 25th. Claims for the amount of time Gambin defended his position range from fourteen to nineteen hours.

131 Léon Loÿ, *La Campagne de Styrie en 1809*, Paris: Chapelot, 1908, p. 70.

132 Napoleon to Eugene, 28 June 1809, *Correspondance*, no. 15456.

133 Such rewards are often exaggerated and Napoleon never elaborated on how the ratio was obtained (nor is it likely that much deep calculation was involved in the midst of the war), but the following is a possible explanation. Taking just the forces on the east bank of the Mur (not counting the fortress garrison or Zach's reserve): Gyulai totalled some 14,400 against 1,340 French (10:1). Forces actually engaged (as per Tepperberg's table) on the Austrian side totalled 9,000–10,000 or approximately 7:1; their attacks, of course, were spread out over the day. Adding Clauzel and the rest of Broussier on the French side and Splenyi for the Austrians to consider all of the forces available to both sides by the end of the day yields approximately 22,000 Austrians against 10,100 French (give or take a few hundred French depending on what cavalry Marmont had along), for an overall ratio of 2:1.

134 Op. J. 59; Seidel, pp. 248–9.

135 Op. J. 59.

136 Johann, *Feldzugserzählungen*, pp. 186–8. Marmont, on the other hand, proved incapable of arresting or disturbing Gyulai's retreat (Loÿ, *Styrie*, pp. 80–1).

137 Wastel in Scheiger, 'Quellen', p. 131.

138 Levec, p. 86.

139 In addition to those cited above, key sources include: Gyulai to Johann, 30 June 1809, Zwiedineck-Südenhorst, (ed.), 'Zur Geschichte des Krieges von 1809 in Steiermark'; Pelet, vol. IV, pp. 122–8; Léon Loÿ, *Historiques du 84e Régiment d'Infanterie de Ligne 'Un Contre Dix'*, Lille: Danel, 1905, pp. 161–9.

140 Johann to Chasteler, 18 and 26 June 1809, KAFA, *8. Korps (Chasteler Tirol)*, Kart. 1437.

141 'Der Überfall auf Laibach, am 27. Juni 1809', ÖMZ, 1843.

CHAPTER 4: A MONTH OF PREPARATION

1 Skall, p. 232. A written prompt followed on the 25th (Helmut Hertenberger, 'Die Schlacht bei Wagram', dissertation, University of Vienna, 1950, p. 40).

2 Rauchensteiner, *Hiller*, pp. 155–62; Rauchensteiner, ed., 'Hiller', pp. 190–3.

3 Extracts from reports/orders in Hertenberger, pp. 19–26; Binder, *Krieg Napoleons*, vol. II, pp. 235–40.

4 [Charles], 'Warum benutzten die Oesterreicher den Sieg von Aspern nicht zu einer offensiven Operation auf das rechte Donauufer?', Pest, 1811; Charles, 'Denkschrift', vol. VI, p. 341; Major Ferdinand von Löben, 'Bericht eines Augenzeuges über die Schlacht von Deutsch-Wagram', KAFA, Kart. 1461. Many contemporaries found these excuses embarrassing or incomprehensible, for example, the anonymous authors of 'Marginalien zur Relation über die Schlacht bey Wagram', *Europäische Annalen*, vol. II, 1810 (also *Minerva*, no. 2, 1810); 'Ueber die Benutzung der in der Schlacht von Aspern erfochtenen Vortheile und über den Waffenstillstand von Znaym', *Pallas*, vol. IV, 1810; 'Darstellung der Schlachten auf dem Marchfelde', *Europäische Annalen*, vols VII, VIII, X, 1810; *Authentischer Bericht über die Schlacht bei Wagram am 5ten und 6ten July 1809: Von einem Augenzeugen*, Hanover: Hahn, 1813, pp. 8–9; 'Einige Bemerkungen über die Disposition zur Schlacht bei Wagram', *Zeitschrift für Kunst, Wissenschaft und Geschichte des Krieges*, vol. XVIII, 1830, p. 75.

5 Damas, entries for 12 and 16 June, pp. 114–15.

6 Joseph to Johann, 8 June 1809, Domanovszky, *Palatin Josephs Schriften*, vol. IV, p. 66; and Johann to Stadion, 21 June 1809, Zwiedineck-Südenhorst, *Erzherzog Johann im Feldzuge von 1809*, p. 112; also Theiss, vol. II, p. 320.

7 Maria Ludovica to Johann, 6 and 28 June 1809, Zwiedineck-Südenhorst, *Erzherzog Johann im Feldzuge von 1809*, pp. 114–17; see also Eduard Wertheimer, *Die drei ersten Frauen des Kaisers Franz*, Leipzig: Duncker & Humblot, 1893, pp. 88–92.

8 Kübeck, p. 270 (the remark is from early May but provides a sense of the atmosphere at court).

9 Stadion to Hudelist, in Criste, *Carl*, vol. III, pp. 173–4.

10 Stadion was not alone in mistrusting the army—the Kaiser and many in the court had doubts, Theiss, vol. II, p. 307; Bathurst to Canning, no. 37, 1 July 1809, PRO/FO 7/88.

11 Quotations from a Stadion memorandum of late June, Criste, *Carl*, vol. III, pp. 179–83.

12 Franz to Alexander, 24 June 1809, Just, *Politik oder Strategie?*, p. 82.

13 That is, in modern Romania; see Rössler, *Oesterreichs Kampf*, vol. II, p. 36. Stadion feared the 'annihilation of Austria' should Turkey make peace and the tsar yield to 'the persuasions of Buonaparte' (Bathurst to Canning, no. 39, 1 July 1809, PRO/FO 7/88).

14 Stadion to Starhemberg, 21 June 1809, Fedorowicz, pp. 392–3; Adair to Collingwood, 4 August 1809, Adair, pp. 179–84.

15 Stadion to Starhemberg, 21 June 1809 (separate letter from the preceding), Fedorowicz, pp. 393–4.

16 Stadion to Wessenberg, 9 June 1809, [Josef Freiherr Hormayr], *Lebensbilder aus dem Befreiungskriege*, Jena: Frommann, 1844, vol. II. pp. 47–53; Ludwig Häusser, *Deutsche Geschichte*, Berlin: Weidmann, 1856, vol. III, pp. 461–2 (following notes of Major Georg von Valentini, who accompanied Orange); Bathurst to Canning, no. 26, 1 June 1809, PRO/FO 7/88.

17 Stadion to Charles, 30 May 1809, in Ludwig Eberle, 'Die Mission des Obersten Steigentesch nach Königsberg im Jahre 1809', *Mitteilungen des K. und K. Kriegsarchivs*, vol. V, 1907, p. 346.

18 Gaede concludes (pp. 117–18) that the prince went too far; similarly Alfred Stern in *Abhandlungen und Aktenstücke zur Geschichte der preussischen Reformzeit*, Leipzig: Duncker & Humblot, 1885, p. 67. Eberle (p. 343), following Paul Bailleu, disagrees. Bailleu argues that the prince's correspondence demonstrates Friedrich Wilhelm III's clear decision for war in mid-May 1809: 'Zur Geschichte des Jahres 1809', *Historische Zeitschrift*, vol. XLVIII, 1900, p. 458. The prince certainly thought Friedrich Wilhelm had 'finally taken the most positive determination to join himself to the cause of Austria' (Orange to van Heerdt, 14 May 1809, H. T. Colenbrander, *Gedenkstukken der Gemeene Geschiednenis van Nederland*, The Hague: Nijhoff, 1909, vol. V, pp. 791–2).

19 Ludwig von Ompteda, *Politischer Nachlass*, Jena: Frommann, 1869, vol. I, p. 426; Gaede, p. 119.

20 Eberle, p. 379. See also Max Duncker, 'Friedrich Wilhelm III. im Jahre 1809', *Preussische Jahrbücher*, vol. XLI, 1878, pp. 151–3; John H. Gill, 'I Fear Our Ruin is Very Near: Prussian Foreign Policy during the Franco-Austrian War of 1809', in

The Consortium on Revolutionary Europe, *Selected Papers 2002*, ed. Bernard Cook, Susan V. Nicassio, Michael F. Pavkovic, and Karl A. Roider, Tallahassee: Florida State University, 2002; Bathurst to Canning, no. 41, 5 July 1809, PRO/FO 7/88.

21 Charles to Albert, 23 June 1809, Criste, *Carl*, vol. III, p. 489.

22 Charles to Albert, 28 May 1809, ibid., p. 483.

23 Charles to Albert, 23 June 1809, ibid., p. 489. Rothenberg avers that Charles 'lapsed into lethargy and remained passive' (*Last Victory*, p. 131).

24 Wimpffen, 'Beweggrunde zum Uebergang über die Donau', 20 June 1809, Pawlowski, *Historja Wojny*, pp. 440–1; Charles to Albert, 27 June 1809, Criste, *Carl*, vol. III, p. 490.

25 Franz to Ferdinand, 23 June 1809, Pawlowski, *Historja Wojny*, pp. 444–5.

26 Charles to Ferdinand, 23 June 1809, Just, *Politik oder Strategie?*, pp. 81–2.

27 Franz to Ferdinand, 23 June 1809, Pawlowski, *Historja Wojny*, pp. 443–5; Charles to Ferdinand, 23 June 1809, Just, *Politik oder Strategie?*, pp. 81–2. Schwarzenberg returned from St Petersburg in late June with reassuring words (eg the tsar tacitly wished for Austrian success, the Russian generals favoured Austria), but anxiety remained prominent in the Habsburg court (Bathurst to Canning, nos. 36 and 39, 30 June and 1 July 1809, PRO/FO 7/88; Alexander Horn to Canning, 22 June 1809, Fedorowicz, p. 397).

28 Stadion to Charles, 22 June 1809, Pawlowski, *Historja Wojny*, p. 442.

29 Franz to Charles, 2 July 1809, KAFA, *Deutschland, Hauptarmee VII(A)*, Kart. 1461/7/39; and Stadion to Wimpffen, 2 July 1809, Pawlowski, *Historja Wojny*, pp. 451–3.

30 Ibid.

31 Charles to Albert, undated (3 July from content/context), Criste, *Carl*, vol. III, p. 491.

32 Champagny to Caulaincourt, 2 June 1809, (to be burned after reading), in Driault, pp. 430–1.

33 Savary, vol. IV, p. 145; also Vandal, pp. 93–100.

34 Napoleon apparently attempted to instil worries in the Austrian court with references such as 'the French await the approach of the Russian army' that appeared in the press (*Journal de l'Empire*, 26 and 27 June 1809) and in army bulletins (no. XVII, 8 June 1809, *Correspondence*, 15316); it is not clear that these had any influence on Austrian strategy.

35 Hertenberger, pp. 41–8.

36 In a 29 May memorandum, Wimpffen outlined a plan for crossing on the night of 6/7 June (Angeli, 'Wagram', pp. 44–7). Valentini offers a detailed excursion on crossings, advocating Tulln as best, pp. 126–50.

37 'Warum benutzten die Oesterreicher den Sieg von Aspern nicht', p. 11.

38 Charles, memo for the Kaiser, 23 June 1809, in Criste, *Carl*, vol. III, p. 177.

39 Charles to Albert, 7 June 1809, Criste, *Carl*, vol. III, p. 486.

40 This reminds one of Ulysses S. Grant's remarks about Robert E. Lee in 1864: 'Oh, I am heartily tired of hearing about what Lee is going to do. Some of you seem to think he is suddenly going to turn a double somersault, and land on our rear and both of our flanks at the same time' (Horace Porter, *Campaigning with Grant*, Secaucus: Blue and Grey Press, 1981, p. 70). Contemporaries (especially Charles's

enemies at court) also noted both the lack of confidence in the army's offensive capacity and 'the ascendant Buonaparte has gained over the mind of the Arch Duke' (Bathurst to Canning, nos. 20 and 37, 23 May and 1 July 1809, PRO/FO 7/88).

41 Charles to Albert, 23 and 27 June 1809, Criste, *Carl*, vol. III, pp. 489–90. These letters were written during a new debate over strategy in which Charles—probably relying on his imperial brother's indecisiveness—requested specific orders to cross, but laced his request with such dire warnings that Franz and his immediate advisers would be likely to deliberate indefinitely (as indeed they did); see Criste, *Carl*, vol. III, pp. 177–84.

42 Charles, memo for the Kaiser, 27 June 1809, in Criste, *Carl*, vol. III, p. 184.

43 [Johann Jacob Otto August Rühle von Lilienstern] 'Gedanken über die beiden Schlachten auf dem Marchfelde bei Wien', *Pallas*, vol. XI, 1809, p. 613. Among many other instances: Castellane, vol. II, p. 57; Dumas, vol. II, p. 196; Löwenstern, vol. I, p. 115; Pelleport, p. 276.

44 This figure was over and above the seven battalions of volunteers that had fought at Aspern and remained with the army: 1st through 4th Vienna Volunteers, 2nd and 3rd Moravian Volunteers, 2nd *EH Carl* Legion.

45 'Bemerkungen eines Officiers vom österreichischen Generalstabe zu der in Pesth, im Druck erschienenen Relation über die Schlacht bei Teutsch-Wagram', *Pallas*, vol. III, 1810, pp. 250–1. This author and others also criticise Charles for not bringing heavy guns from the Bohemian fortresses to reinforce the defences. See also Rothenberg, *Last Victory*, pp. 148–9.

46 Instructions of 5 and 7 June 1809 in *Beiträge zur Geschichte des österreichischen Heerwesens*, Vienna: Seidel & Sohn, 1872, vol. I, pp. 224–7.

47 Charles to Albert, 27 June 1809, Criste, *Carl*, vol. III, p. 490.

48 'Marginalien', p. 236; Rothenberg, *Last Victory*, p. 143.

49 Koch, *Massena*, vol. VI, p. 280.

50 Victor Abel de Salle (or Desalle), 'Les Souvenirs du Général Baron de Salle', *La Revue de Paris*, vol. I, 1895, p. 411.

51 Although some sources claim this was emplaced, it proved too awkward to use (Koch, vol. VI, p. 278; Thiers, vol. X, p. 408).

52 [Rittmeister Czettritz und Neuhaus], 'Erinnerungen eines Kavallerie-Offiziers', *Zeitschrift für Kunst, Wissenschaft und Geschichte des Krieges*, vol. 46, 1839, pp. 242–3. Bavarian artilleryman Reichold also described the bridge as 'elegant' (p. 114), and states that it was painted red (see also Rühle von Lilienstern in Kircheisen, *Feldzugserinnerungen*, p. 110).

53 Löwenstern, vol. I, pp. 119–20.

54 In this flotilla, and in all of the boat, bridge, and related construction projects, the emperor made extensive use of two special battalions: 44th Naval Battalion (44e bataillon de le flottille) and the Battalion of Naval Artificers (bataillon d'ouvriers militaires de la marine). They arrived in Strasbourg in late April and reached Vienna on 24 and 26 May respectively. Organised by a decree of 17 March, the 44th had 1,103 men in nine companies on 20 June; the Naval Artificers, 786 men in six companies on the same date (516 in Vienna, 270 in two companies at Passau). Capt. S., 'Les Marins de la Flottille et les Ouvriers Militaires de la Marine pendant la Campagne de 1809 en Autriche', *Carnet de la Sabretache*, 1895.

55 Twenty-Fourth Bulletin, 3 July 1809, *Correspondance*, 15487. At least one near-contemporary commentator regarded the accomplishment as 'ten times more significant than Caesar's' ('Ueber das Passieren von Flüssen', *Zeitschrift für Kunst, Wissenschaft und Geschichte des Krieges*, vol. VII, 1841, pp. 193–4.

56 More bridges would be added to this list on 30 June and 2 to 3 July before the crossing, and on the 5th as the operation was in progress. For details, see Buat, vol. II, pp. 108–25; 'Ponts Militaires', in Gachot, pp. 412–20; F.-G. Hourtoulle, *Wagram: The Apogee of the Empire*, Paris: Histoire & Collections, 2002, pp. 10–17; Howard Douglas, *An Essay on the Principles and Construction of Military Bridges and the Passage of Rivers in Military Operations*, London: Boone, 1832 (extract on the Napoleon Series website: www.napoleon-series.org); Alexandre Frédéric Drieu, *Le Guide du Pontonnier*, Paris: Levrault, 1820, pp. 61–9 (including descriptions of the 'infernal machines' that the Austrians launched into the river).

57 Rühle von Lilienstern, 'Gedanken über die beiden Schlachten', p. 482.

58 Of these, 20,401 arrived between 22 May and 12 June, the remainder between 12 June and 4 July (Buat, vol. II, p. 16). An additional 3,900 were assigned to the reserve command at Augsburg.

59 Boulart, p. 219.

60 Dumas, vol. II, p. 197.

61 Berthier to Songis, 25 May 1809, and the 9 June decree are in Martin de Brettes, 'Canons dans l'Infanterie', *Spectateur Militaire*, vol. 43, 1888, pp. 217–18. It is important to note, as Binder points out (*Krieg Napoleons*, vol. II, p. 366), that regimental guns were the fastest way to address the numerical superiority in artillery that the French had experienced at Aspern; raising new artillery batteries would have taken much longer and absorbed more resources.

62 This was seventeen (2nd Corps), thirty-two (3rd), and seventeen (4th), rather than the seventy-eight that should have been on hand to fulfil Napoleon's directive (twenty-four, thirty, and twenty-four respectively). The Armies of Italy and Dalmatia were also to acquire regimental guns, as was Dupas, but this could not be accomplished prior to Wagram. See Buat, vol. II, pp. 27–9; Alain Pigeard, 'L'Artillerie Régimentaire sous le Premier Empire', *Tradition*, no. 154, March 2000.

63 Savary, vol. IV, p. 147; Löwenstern, vol. I, p. 120.

64 Guillaume Joseph Roux Peyrusse, *1809–1815: Mémorial et Archives*, Carcassone: Labau, 1869, p. 21.

65 In Général V., 'Les Vues de Napoléon Ier sur l'Organisation des Ponts Militaires', *Carnet de la Sabretache*, 1895, p. 103.

66 Christian Friedrich Frenzel, *Erinnerungen eines sächsischen Infanteristen an die napoleonischen Kriege*, ed. Sebastien Schaar, Dresden: Thelem, 2008, p. 85 (with thanks to Thomas Hemmann).

67 For the actions of the various German contingents during June, see Gill, *Eagles*, chs 2, 3, 6, 7, and 8.

68 Parts of the following section were presented to the Consortium on Revolutionary Europe annual conference in 2000 (Gill, 'Imaginary Numbers').

69 Kellermann's situation, 1 June 1809, AG, C2/508.

70 Beaumont to Berthier, 12 May 1809, Saski, vol. III, pp. 254–5; Napoleon to Berthier, 9 May 1809, *Correspondance*, 15178; Beaumont's situation, 2 June 1809, AG, C2/510.

NOTES TO PAGES 162–6 ~ 457

71 Gottlieb Hufeland, *Erinnerungen aus meinem Aufenthalt in Danzig in den Jahren 1808 bis 1812*, Königsberg: Nicolovtus, 1815, pp. 71–3.

72 Kellermann to Clarke, 16 June 1809 in Buat, vol. II, p. 12.

73 Napoleon to Jerome, 25 February 1809, *Correspondance*, no. 14809.

74 The *Journal de l'Empire*, for instance, featured frequent stories on reserve formations (eg, 12, 24, 27 June).

75 Steigentesch to Stadion, 16 and 19 June 1809, Stern, *Abhandlungen*, pp. 75, 82. Dörnberg reported to Charles that Jerome was to command 30,000–40,000 men in central Germany (Carl Scherer, 'Zur Geschichte des Dörnbergischen Aufstandes im Jahre 1809', *Historische Zeitschrift*, vol. XVIII, 1900, p. 263). According to the 27 June entry in the army's operations journal (largely compiled after the war), the Austrians had at least one intelligence report that the French were intentionally exaggerating Kellermann's strength ('Operations Journal der Haupt-Armee vom 24ten Juny bis 6ten July' (Op. J. 1e), KAFA, *Operationsjournale der Hauptarmee und Korps*, Kart. 1381).

76 Rudolf von Katte, 'Der Streifzug des Friedrich Karl von Katte auf Magdeburg im April 1809', *Geschichts-Blätter für Stadt und Land Magdeburg*, vols 70–1, 1935/1936, p. 17.

77 Heinrich Wesemann, *Kannonier des Kaisers*, Cologne: Verlag Wissenschaft und Politik, 1971, pp. 17–18. There were probably two brief skirmishes with the rebels: first with the 'advance guard', then with the 'main body'; the Westphalian cavalry had orders only to strike with the flats of their swords. See Friedrich Baumann, *Skizzen aus den Jugendjahren eines Veteranen*, Berlin: Reinhardt, 1845, pp. 61–7; Jacques Alexandre François Allix de Vaux, 'Souvenirs Militaires et Politiques', *Journal des Sciences Militaires*, vol. XIX, 1830, p. 54.

78 Gill, *Eagles*, pp. 424–7; Dörnberg, 'Dörnberg und der Aufstand in Hessen', in Friedrich Bülau, *Geheime Geschichten und Rätselhafte Menschen*, Leipzig: Brockhaus, 1854, vol. V, pp. 409–20; Arthur Kleinschmidt, *Geschichte des Königreichs Westfalen*, Kassel: Mamecher, 1970, pp. 234–48; Karl Lyncker, *Geschichte der Insurrectionen wider das westphälische Gouvernement*, Kassel: Bertram, 1857, pp. 104–26; H. Martin, 'Zur Ehrenrettung Sigmund Peter Martins', *Zeitschrift des Vereins für hessische Geschichte und Landeskunde*, vol. XVIII, 1893, pp. 455–517; Scherer, pp. 258–63.

79 August von Voss, 'Zur Geschichte des Schillschen Zuges im Jahre 1809', manuscript, 1854, pp. 6–7; from notes kindly provided by Dr Sam Mustafa. See also recollections of one of his officers in Karl Rudolf von Ollech, 'Carl Friedrich Wilhelm von Reyher', *Beiheft zum Militär-Wochenblatt*, Berlin: Mittler & Sohn, 1861–76, vol. I, p. 22.

80 Schill's peroration is rendered many ways; this is from Georg Bärsch, in Christian Binder von Krieglstein, *Ferdinand von Schill*, Berlin: Voss, 1902, p. 135.

81 Binder, *Schill*, p. 143. The details of the Prussian government's response are beyond the scope of this work, see Gaede and the superb recent study of Schill's escapade by Sam A. Mustafa: *The Long Ride of Major von Schill*, Plymouth: Rowman & Littlefield, 2008.

82 Julius von Wickede, *Ein Deutsches Reiterleben*, Berlin: Duncker, 1861, p. 63.

83 C. von Scriba, 'Der Zug Schills nach Stralsund', in Kircheisen, *Feldzugserinnerungen*, p. 366; also Neigebauer, 'Schills Zug nach Stralsund und sein Ende', p. 308; Mustafa, pp. 101–3.

84 The hapless defenders were the Mecklenburg-Schwerin Garrison Company of sixty-five men.

85 The defending force at Damgarten was II/7th Rheinbund, the invalids of III/7th Rheinbund, two guns, and fifty constabulary hussars; in all some 700–800 men (Gill, *Eagles*, pp. 474–5). The French in Stralsund were an artillery company of approximately fifty men, almost all of whom were butchered in a street battle that probably resulted from a misunderstanding (Binder, *Schill*, pp. 179–81).

86 Schill to Charles, 30 May 1809, in Rudolf Bartsch, *Die Schill'schen Offiziere*, Vienna: Stern, 1909, pp. 79–86; Mustafa, pp. 106–9.

87 Jerome to Kellermann 5 May 1809, Albert du Casse, *Mémoires et Correspondance du Roi Jérome et de la Reine Catherine*, Paris: Dentu, 1863, vol. IV, pp. 42–3. Jerome remained nervous about Prussia's 'perplexing' behaviour (to Napoleon, 4 June 1809, ibid., p. 110); Allix, p. 55. The question of Prussian official involvement with Schill remains tantalisingly unanswered; for the best modern treatment, see Mustafa, ch. 3.

88 Sample correspondence: Jerome to Napoleon, 4 and 5 May 1809, and Kellermann to Clarke, 7 and 8 May 1809, du Casse, *Jérome*, vol. IV, pp. 38–44; Clarke to Napoleon, 8 May 1809, Saski, vol. III, pp. 311–12.

89 Napoleon to Clarke, 17 May 1809, and Berthier to Kellermann, 17 May 1809, Saski, vol. III, pp. 312–13.

90 Napoleon to Berthier, 19 May 1809, *Correspondance*, no. 15231.

91 E. van Löben-Sels, *Bijdragen tot de Krigsgeschiedenes van Napoleon Bonaparte*, The Hague, 1839, vol. II, pp. 522–3. According to this source, the Westphalian force was supposed to consist of two infantry regiments, a 'lancer' regiment (doubtless the Guard Chevaulegers), and a half-battery, but it is not clear if any or all these were present; they certainly played little role in capturing Dömitz on the 24th.

92 King Frederik VI to Düring, 21 May 1809 (two letters), *Meddelelser fra Krigsarkiverne*, Copenhagen: Hegel, 1890, vol. IV, pp. 356–7 (GL Düring was the Danish commander in Holstein).

93 'Beiträge zur Geschichte des Schillschen Zuges durch Nord-Deutschland', *Minerva*, March–April 1810. Schill left approximately 418 men in Dömitz: 50 infantry, 100 unarmed recruits, 200 pikemen, 10 Jägers, 18 uhlans, 40 gunners (Johann C. L. Haken, *Ferdinand von Schill*, Leipzig: Brockhaus, 1824, vol. II, p. 106). The Dutch captured some thirty to fifty (mostly pikemen, it seems) when they took the fortress.

94 From the unpublished memoirs of Jan-Willem van Wetering, courteously provided by Bas de Groot.

95 Ewald to Frederik VI, 31 May 1809, *Meddelelser fra Krigsarkiverne*, vol. IV, pp. 361–2; see also F. L. von Bardenfleth, *Stormen paa Stralsund*, Copenhagen: Reitzel, 1846, pp. 98–113, 154–61.

96 Gratien to Bourienne, 31 May 1809, du Casse, *Jérome*, vol. IV, p. 109.

97 Ollech/Reyher, p. 22.

98 Additional sources: P. B. Krieger Thomsen, 'Schills Tog till Stralsund (1809)', *Krigshistorisk Tidsskrift*, no. 1, 1968 (I am grateful to Col. Thomsen for providing

an English translation of this excellent article); Louis Bonaparte, *Documens Historiques et Réflexions sur le Gouvernement de la Hollande*, Gand: Houdin, 1820, vol. III, pp. 103–8; J. Bosscha, *Neerlands Heldendaden te land*, Leeuwarden, 1873, pp. 261–76; Gérard A. Geerts, *Samenwerking en Confrontatie*, Amsterdam: Bataafsche Leeuw, 2002, pp. 112–14; Marco van der Hoeven, *Van de Weser tot de Weichsel*, Amsterdam: Bataafsche Leeuw, 1994, pp. 57–64; Victor de Stuers, 'Voor 80 Jaren: De Hollanders te Straalsund', *Haagsche Stemmen*, no. 41, 8 June 1889; Victor de Stuers, 'Een Episode uit de Bestorming van Stralsund', *Eigen Haard*, 1899; du Casse, *Jérome*, vol. IV, pp. 1–30.

99 Charles to Albert, undated, Criste, *Carl*, vol. III, p. 491; Charles, 'Denkschrift', p. 343.

100 Riesch to Am Ende, 29 May 1809, [Oskar Criste], 'Die Streifzüge der Österreicher in Sachsen und Franken im Feldzuge 1809', *Organ der militär-wissenschaftlichen Vereine*, vol. LVII, 1898, pp. 340–1.

101 Wickede, vol. II, p. 91.

102 Ibid., pp. 84–7.

103 Both Am Ende quotations from report cited in Criste, 'Streifzüge', pp. 347–8. For problems with the Hessians, see also Premierleutnant Dechend, 'Das hessische Freicorps im Jahre 1809', *Jahrbücher für die deutsche Armee und Marine*, vol. 54, 1885, pp. 129–3; Willi Varges, 'Die Theilnahme des Kurfürsten Wilhelm I. von Hessen am Oesterreichischen Kriege 1809', *Zeitschrift des Vereins für hessische Geschichte und Landeskunde*, vol. XVI, 1891; and his 'Die kurhessische Legion im Jahre 1809', *Zeitschrift des Vereins für hessische Geschichte und Landeskunde*, vol. XXI, 1896.

104 Wickede, vol. II, p. 92; Friedrich Ludwig Wachholtz, *Aus dem Tagebuche des Generals Fr. L. von Wachholtz*, Braunschweig: Vieweg, 1843, p. 234.

105 'Journal der Operation des kais. österreichischen Truppen-Corps under dem Generalmajor von Am Ende vom 12ten bis 22ten July 1809', *Europäische Annalen*, vol. VI, 1810, p. 271.

106 Rössler, *Oesterreichs Kampf*, vol. II, p. 24.

107 Am Ende's descendants emphasise the constraints in their forebear's orders to excuse his timorous behaviour (Christian Gottlob Ernst Am Ende, *Feldmarschall-Lieutenant Carl Friedrich Am Ende besonders sein Feldzug in Sachsen 1809*, Vienna: Braumüller, 1878). Most of Brunswick's officers blamed Am Ende exclusively, Heyde faults Riesch as well (G. von der Heyde, *Der Feldzug des Herzoglich-Braunschweigischen Korps im Jahre 1809*, Berlin: Mittler, 1819, pp. 13–18).

108 He reached Wilsdruff on the 20th. Although Dyherrn was senior in rank, Thielmann truly commanded the little brigade even before Dyherrn was withdrawn on 23 June to reorganise the troops returning from Austria.

109 Albrecht Graf von Holtzendorff, *Beiträge zu der Biographie des Generals Freiherrn von Thielmann*, Leipzig: Rauck, 1830, pp. 25–32; Gustav von Kortzfleisch, *Geschichte des Herzoglich Braunschweigischen Infanterie-Regiments*, Braunschweig: Limbach, 1896; Gill, *Eagles*, pp. 434–6. The Brunswickers, organising around Nachod, had marched into Zittau on 21 May.

110 Riesch, reacting to reports from Brunswick, berated Am Ende for his lack of celerity, but the latter replied that 'no rapid movements can be made with the barefoot Landwehr' (Criste, 'Streifzüge', pp. 348–9).

111 Charles to Brunswick, 18 June 1809, Louis Ferdinand Spehr, *Friedrich Wilhelm Herzog von Braunschweig-Lüneburg-Oels*, Braunschweig: Meyer, 1848, p. 116.

112 Combined advance guard: Brunswick contingent (minus 100 Jägers, fifty hussars at Wilsdruff), four companies of III/*Mittrowsky*, company of 1st Jägers, *Schwarzenberg* squadron, Hessian cavalry. On the duke's frustration, see *An Account of the Operations of the Corps under the Duke of Brunswick*, London: Stockdale, 1810, p. 12, among many others.

113 Dresden: 5th Königgrätz, 6th Bunzlau, *Klenau* platoon, Hessian infantry (3rd Tschaslau arrived on 22 June); a Brunswick Schützen company and an uhlan squadron were being organised in Dresden. Wilsdruff: one hundred Brunswick Jägers, fifty hussars. Freiberg: two companies of *Mittrowsky*, a *Merveldt* platoon (later joined by 5th Bunzlau).

114 Holtzendorff, *Thielmann*, p. 52.

115 E. G. M. Freiherr von Friesen, *Dresden im Kriegsjahre 1809*, Dresden: Baensch, 1983, pp. 43–4.

116 The 1st Westphalian and 2nd Dutch under GB Jean Bongars.

117 *Baireuther Kriegs-Blätter*, no. 1, 13 June 1809.

118 Criste, 'Streifzüge', p. 351.

119 Völderndorff, p. 214. Austrians: II/*Deutsch-Banat* Grenz battalion, 4th Königgratz, seventy uhlans, and two 3-pounders. Michanovich's and Radivojevich's reports, 29 June 1809, KAFA, Kart. 1460/6/570–1; Criste, 'Streifzüge', pp. 352–3; Johann Paul Priem, *Geschichte der Stadt Nürnberg*, Nuremberg: Zeiser, 1875, pp. 326–31.

120 Delaroche, with only 1st Provisional Dragoons, some 227 Bavarian depot troops (3rd Light, 5th and 6th Infantry), and a lone gun, was badly outnumbered; another 300 men from the depot of 8th Infantry did not arrive in time to contribute (Gill, *Eagles*, p. 347).

121 Radivojevich to Riesch, 21 June 1809, in Hertenberger, p. 31; Eduard Deuerling, *Das Fürstentum Bayreuth unter französischer Herrschaft und sein Übergang an Bayern 1806–1810*, Erlangen: Palm & Enke, 1932, pp. 56–72. Nostitz had made initial attempts to raise this legion in late April, but had to flee the principality after Regensburg, barely evading Bernadotte's advance guard near Asch as he made his way to Bohemia with a few adherents (the 'legion' soon dwindled to seventy-one men); see Anton Ernstberger, *Die deutschen Freikorps 1809 in Böhmen*, Prague: Volk und Reich Verlag, 1942, pp. 306–12.

122 Bezzel, 'Grenzschutze', pp. 82–5, 163–4.

123 GB Boyer (Junot's chief of staff), report of 8 July 1809; Junot to Berthier, 8 July 1809, both AG, C2/93.

124 Rosenhyan: platoon of *Schwarzenberg* Uhlans (26), 1st and 2nd Prachin Landwehr (1,399), 1st and 2nd Klattau Landwehr (1,651), 3rd Klattau Landwehr (746), 1st and 2nd Budweis Landwehr (1,116), 3rd Budweis Landwehr (581); strengths as of 6 May. From *Krieg*, vol. IV, Appendices XII and XIV.

125 Napoleon to Berthier, 17 June 1809, *Correspondance*, no. 15436; Beaumont, 'Situation', 30 June 1809, AG, C2/510. By the end of the month, Bourcier had been placed under Lefebvre's orders (Napoleon to Bourcier, 26 June 1809, *Correspondance*, no, 15445).

126 Berthier to Junot, 20 June 1809, Buat, vol. II, p. 13.

127 Troops were *Hohenzollern* Chevaulegers, one company of *Lusignan*, 4th Company of 9th Jägers. These figures come from Ferdinand Hirn, *Vorarlbergs Erhebung im Jahre 1809*, Bregenz: Teutsch, 1909, pp. 89–134; Theimer, p. 243; Cajetan Pizzighelli, *Auszug aus der Geschichte des k. u. k. Feldjäger-Bataillons Nr. 9*, Graz: battalion, 1890, pp. 12–14. Johann Gunz ('Der Krieg der Vorarlberger im Jahr 1809', *Militair-Wochenblatt*, June–July 1820) gives variant numbers: 180 infantry, fourteen dragoons, five hussars, and thirty Jäger arriving on 14 May; 120 infantry arriving on 15 May (many escaped prisoners of war re-armed in Innsbruck).

128 F. Hirn, *Vorarlberg*, p. 126.

129 Friedrich to Napoleon, 11 May 1809, August von Schlossberger, *Politische und militärische Correspondenz König Friedrich von Württemberg mit Kaiser Napoleon I.*, Stuttgart: Kohlhammer, 1889, p. 162.

130 Gill, *Eagles*, p. 162.

131 These forces totalled nine battalions, six carabinier companies, thirty dragoons, and some artillery. M. Feldmann and H. G. Wirtz, *Histoire Militaire de la Suisse*, Berne: Kuhn, 1921, pp. 134–5; Johann Wieland, *Geschichte der Kriegsbegebenheiten in Helvetien und Rhätien*, Basel: Schweighaus, 1868, pp. 252–71.

132 Friedrich to Napoleon, 20 May 1809, Schlossberger, p. 167.

133 Max Josef to Berthier, 3 June 1809, Robinet de Cléry, *En Tyrol*, pp. 48–9.

134 Gill, *Eagles*, p. 162.

135 Scheler: I/*Prinz Friedrich*, depots of the light infantry and Jäger battalions (200 men), the two Guard Horse Grenadier squadrons, fifty depot cavalrymen, five guns. These arrived at Lake Constance on 18 May; II/*Prinz Friedrich* joined shortly thereafter.

136 Oberstleutnant Ludwig von Cancrin with Hussar depot squadron (sixty-three men), two Guard Grenadier companies (209 men), two 4-pounders with twenty-two artillery and train personnel.

137 F. von der Wengen, *Der Feldzug der Grossherzoglich Badischen Truppen unter Oberst Freiherrn Karl v. Stockhorn gegen die Vorarlberger und Tiroler 1809*, Heidelberg: Winter, 1910, pp. 67, 77–8, 88.

138 Picard had 500 French dragoons, 100 French infantry, Major Pillement's Bavarian depot battalion, *Franquemont*, some local militia, and about five guns (four Württemberg, one Bavarian).

139 Marie-Antoine de Reiset, *Souvenirs*, Paris: Lévy, 1899, pp. 63–9. In Eichstätt, Reiset had picked up a company of Hohenzollern troops (181 men) on its way to join the 2nd Rheinbund; these men and one of Reiset's squadrons under his personal leadership engaged at Pfeffertshofen; another squadron later captured most of the remaining Austrians (Gill, *Eagles*, p. 396). The brush with the Bavarian depot troops occurred near Geislingen an der Steige when seventy men of the 1st Infantry's depot attempted to surprise the Austrians (Gill, *Eagles*, p. 377; F. Hirn, *Vorarlberg*, pp. 155–7).

140 Reiset, pp. 57–8.

141 F. Hirn, *Vorarlberg*, p. 243.

142 Ibid., pp. 146–7.

143 Depot companies of *Kronprinz*, *Phull*, *Herzog Wilhelm*, *Camrer*, and (probably), *Franquemont*, a depot squadron (ninety troopers under Rittmeister Schlümbach),

and two small companies of volunteer foresters; the two Guard Horse Grenadier squadrons returned to Stuttgart (Gill, *Eagles*, p. 177).

144 Baden: Guard Grenadiers (644 men, arrived 12 June), Provisional Jäger Battalion (362 men, arrived 15 June), Light Dragoon depot squadron (fifty-eight men, arrived 18 June); the Baden contingent now came under Oberst Karl Freiherr von Stockhorn. The French troops were apparently the 1st Conscript-Grenadiers of the Guard (1,640); it is not clear if the 1st Conscript-Chasseurs (1,680) were also made available.

145 Picard, worried about his right flank, had withdrawn to Landsberg on 5 June, only to return to Kempten by the 7th.

146 Both sides employed small flotillas on Lake Constance, but these tended to be evanescent creations and none played a major role in the war: Gerhard Wanner, *Kriegsschauplatz Bodensee 1799/1800 und 1809*, Vienna: Bundesverlag, 1987, pp. 42–50.

147 *Die Württemberger in Mergentheim*, 1818; Albert Pfister, *König Friedrich von Württemberg und seine Zeit*, Stuttgart: Kohlhammer, 1888, pp. 192–5. The troops involved were: *Prinz Friedrich*, Land-Battalion Stuttgart, Land-Battalion Ludwigsburg, two Guard cavalry squadrons, four guns. See also M. Erzberger, *Die Säkularisation in Württemberg*, Stuttgart: Deutsches Volksblatt, 1902, pp. 327–31.

148 Willi Varges, 'Der Marburger Aufstand des Jahres 1809', *Zeitschrift des Vereins für hessische Geschichte und Landeskunde*, vol. XVII, 1892.

149 Napoleon to Friedrich, 24 June 1809, *Correspondance*, no. 15432.

CHAPTER 5: WAGRAM

1 Charles, 23 June memorandum for the Kaiser, Criste, *Carl*, vol. III, pp. 176–7.

2 This chapter relies heavily on archival materials. On the Austrian side, these include the 'Relations' of the major commands (KAFA, Kart. 1461), the Hauptarmee's operations journal (Op. J. 1e and 1f), and several subordinate journals. Michael Wenzel has provided enormous assistance in this regard. On the French side, the following items were used from AG, C2/93: reports of 2nd Corps, 3rd Corps, 4th Corps, Friant, Molitor (MR662), Marulaz, Dupas, MacDonald, 1st Dragoon Division, 3rd Heavy Cavalry Division, Guard artillery, and letters from Bernadotte. There are also several letters written to Pelet in the 1820s and a manuscript by then-Colonel Campi (MR661). Bavarian accounts are from BKA/B445; Baden mostly from GLA 48/4286; Hessian records were destroyed during the Second World War.

3 Napoleon to Davout and Eugene, 29 June 1809, *Correspondance*, nos. 15465, 15466.

4 Buat, vol. II, pp. 140–1.

5 Gueheneuc, AG/MR1843. The journal of the Advance Guard agreed that the French crossing was very rapid: 'Journal der Avantgarde der Haupt-Armee unter FML Nordmann', (Op. J. 70), KAFA, *Operationsjournale der Hauptarmee und Korps*, Kart. 1387.

6 Pelet, vol. IV, p. 148.

7 Napoleon to Eugene, 30 June, 10 p.m., and 1 July 1809, 5 a.m., *Correspondance*, nos. 15478–9.

8 Napoleon to Eugene, 1 July 1809, 5 a.m., *Correspondance*, no. 15479.
9 Hoen, *Wagram*, p. 8.
10 II and III Corps behind Aspern and Essling, IV Corps near Wittau, the remainder between Raasdorf and Breitenlee.
11 Charles to Albert, undated [3 July from content], Criste, *Carl*, vol. III, p. 491.
12 On fears about the latter two places as late as 2 July, see Valentini, p. 168; persistent worries about Nussdorf and vicinity are evident in the disposition issued on the night of 5/6 July.
13 Franz to Charles, 2 July 1809, KAFA, Kart. 1461/7/39.
14 Napoleon to Eugene, 2 July 1809, 3 a.m., *Correspondance*, no. 15480.
15 The defenders are variously given as ten or a hundred *Wallach-Illyria* Grenzer, but they had the support of numerous infantry and artillery on the Austrian shore.
16 Heller, vol. II, p. 136. Efforts to create a smoke screen by burning green wood failed (de Salle, p. 412).
17 Pelet, vol. IV, p. 151.
18 The bridge from the Mühl-Haufen to the Marchfeld seems to have been constructed on the afternoon of 4 July (Koch, *Massena*, vol. VI, p. 409; 'Operations Journal der Haupt-Armee vom 24ten Juny bis 6ten July' (hereafter Op. J. 1e), KAFA, Kart. 1381).
19 Pelet, vol. IV, p. 151.
20 Op. J. 1e.
21 Charles, 'Denkschrift', pp. 343–5; 'Beitrag', pp. 376–7.
22 Disposition, 5 June 1809, Angeli, 'Wagram', pp. 50–2.
23 Charles to Johann, 5 July 1809, 5.30 a.m., Zwiedineck-Südenhorst, *Erzherzog Johann im Feldzuge von 1809*, p. 138.
24 Op. J. 1e; 'Disposition', 3 July 1809, 9 a.m. This section also draws heavily on Binder, *Krieg Napoleons*, vol. II, pp. 296–300; and Hoen, *Wagram*, pp. 19–24.
25 Franz to Charles, 3 July 1809, KAFA, Kart. 1461/7/62.
26 Unsigned orders to Rosenberg, Hiller, Bellegarde, Hohenzollern, and Reuss, 4 July 1809, KAFA, Kart. 1461/7/77–82.
27 Binder claims they were generated by news from Kienmayer (*Krieg Napoleons*, vol. II, pp. 303–4); Criste avers the pressure came from the court (*Carl*, vol. III, p. 198).
28 Binder, *Krieg Napoleons*, vol. II, pp. 299–301; Criste, *Carl*, vol. III, pp. 194–5; 'Vague' from Wimpffen to Franz, 17 August 1809, Criste, *Carl*, vol. III, p. 504.
29 FML d'Aspre to an unnamed friend, 4–5 July 1809, 'Lettres Interceptées 1809', *Carnet de la Sabretache*, 1895.
30 Napoleon to Davout, 29 June 1809, *Correspondance*, no. 15465.
31 Carl Pilzecker, 'Scenen aus dem Feldzuge der Sachsen in Oesterreich, und zwar vor, während und nach der Schlacht bei Deutsch-Wagram; vom 2. bis mit dem 27. Juli 1809', *Sachsenzeitung*, no. 233 ff., August–September 1830, p. 1118.
32 Dumas to Berthier, 4 July 1809, Buat, vol. II, pp. 156–7.
33 Charles to Hiller, 4 July 1809, 9 a.m., KAFA, Kart. 1422/7/43.
34 Charles to Johann, 4 July 1809, 7 p.m., Angeli, 'Wagram', pp. 91–2.
35 Lasalle brought with him his small Hessian detachment; it rejoined 4th Corps. The Hessians from Ybbs had linked up with their countrymen near Pressburg as the latter were marching north from Raab.
36 Rühle von Lilienstern, *Reise*, p. 273.

37 Paulin, p. 202.
38 Pelet, vol. IV, pp. 153–4.
39 Ludwig Ferdinand Bucher, 'Erlebnisse aus dem Jahre 1809', *Miscellanea Napoleonica*, 1895, pp. 69–70; Schaller, p. 74.
40 Peeters, pp. 83–4; compare Chevillet, pp. 282–3.
41 Napoleon to Davout, 29 June 1809, *Correspondance*, no. 15465.
42 Orders to Bernadotte, 3 July 1809, AG, C2/93.
43 Pilzecker, p. 1118.
44 Schaller, pp. 73–4. Wrede proudly reported to his king that, as of 3 July, he had had only three sick and a few stragglers despite the gruelling march (Wrede to Max Josef, 3 July 1809, BKA/B445).
45 Barat, p. 77; Espinchal, p. 262.
46 Bucher, pp. 75–9.
47 Henckens, p. 85
48 Hertenberger states (p. 62) that Charles seldom left his headquarters. This may be too harsh, but the archduke's level of activity certainly pales in comparison with Napoleon's.
49 Marmont, vol. III, p. 225.
50 Berthezène, p. 247; also Wilhelm, p. 91.
51 Paulin, p. 197.
52 Berthezène, pp. 248–9.
53 Orders to Baraguey d'Hilliers and Thiry, 3 July 1809, AG, C2/93.
54 Rusca had remained in Klagenfurt with the exception of a brief foray to Tarvis on 30 June with the two French battalions and the Istrians; this was a successful attempt to intimidate GM Schmidt and thereby curb Austrian probes towards the French line of communications. Rusca returned to Klagenfurt on 1 July.
55 A contemporary Austrian criticism of Charles for failing to bring in more forces is 'Einige Bemerkungen', pp. 77–8.
56 Johann to Charles, 30 June (two letters); Charles to Johann, 30 June, 1 and 2 July 1809, Zwiedineck-Südenhorst, *Erzherzog Johann im Feldzuge von 1809*, pp. 128–33.
57 'Disposition', 3 July 1809, Op. J. 1e.
58 Rauchensteiner, *Hiller*, pp. 159–64.
59 Charles to Hiller, 2 July 1809, KAFA, Kart. 1422. For derision of same: Rauchensteiner, *Wagram*, p. 8; Friedrich Anton Heller von Hellwald, *Der Feldzug des Jahres 1809 in Süddeutschland*, Vienna: Gerold, 1864, vol. II, pp. 64–5; 'Einige Bemerkungen', p. 76.
60 Op. J. 1e.
61 Schwarzenberg to his wife, 4 July 1809, *Briefe*, p. 173.
62 'Ordre pour le Passage du Danube', 2 July 1809, 11 p.m., *Correspondance*, no. 15481; Buat, vol. II, pp. 167–72; Pelet, vol. III, pp. 483–8. The Lobau troops were disposed as follows: one Baden battalion and the Neuchâtel battalion in the Mühlau bridgehead, the other Baden battalion with half on the Stadtler Islands and the other half in reserve, one of Oudinot's battalions in a bridgehead to be constructed on the north bank where Oudinot crossed, the other French battalion and a Saxon battalion in the Lobau bridgeheads for the principal bridges, the final Saxon battalion in reserve.

63 Jomini complains that the orders forced Davout to cross behind Oudinot and might thereby have caused 'a dreadful scene of confusion' (*Art of War*, pp. 243–4). This seems a callow manner of attacking his enemy, Berthier, whom he faults for this putative error. There were actually several points at which the advancing corps would cross one another, and it seems self-evident that Napoleon, his Major General, and everyone else involved was fully aware and completely untroubled. The fact that there were no major problems with the crossing further diminishes Jomini's cavil. Neither Davout, nor Friant, nor Oudinot make any mention of serious disruptions in their after-action reports. See discussion in Petre, pp. 400–1; Buat, vol. II, p. 192.

64 This and previous quotation from Pilzecker, p. 1118.

65 Frenzel, p. 88.

66 Op. J. 70.

67 Lejeune, pp. 314–15.

68 As with any event in this era, times can only be estimated. This section broadly follows Buat; Austrian operations journals generally give earlier times for specific incidents (attack on Enzersdorf starting at 8 vice 9, for example). The storm apparently began around nightfall (*c*.7.30 p.m. at that time of year), the Hauptarmee's journal states between 8 and 9 p.m. Note that the Austrians reported hearing three cannon shots from Lobau at 8 and three more at 9, each time followed by 'drums, trumpets, and music' (Op. J. 1e); none of the French sources mention such a tintamarre.

69 Some of the French troops wore white cloth brassards for identification purposes (Chlapowski, p. 174).

70 Approximate timings: French right flank guns opened fire after Baste made contact (9.30 p.m.), Austrian Advance Guard pieces replied (weakly, it seems, and with little effect); Austrian VI Corps artillery opened fire as ordered at 11 p.m., to which French guns on the left flank answered.

71 C.-H. Lejeune, p. 523.

72 D'Aspre, 4/5 July 1809 letter, *Carnet*, pp. 354–8; Stadion from Skall, p. 242.

73 Czettritz und Neuhaus, p. 49.

74 Op. J. 70.

75 Rühle, p. 278; and [Ferdinand von Larisch], 'Meine zweite Campagne (Aus dem Tagebuche eines Verstorbenen)', *Bautzener Nachrichten*, vols. 21–5, 1883.

76 Pelet, vol. IV, pp. 172–3.

77 Larisch, 'Meine zweite Campagne'.

78 Bühle, pp. 9–10.

79 Nicholas Louis Planat de la Faye, *Vie de Planat de la Faye*, Paris: Ollendorff, 1895, pp. 57–8; Reichold, p. 112.

80 Aspre, letter of 5 July 1809, pp. 354–8.

81 Frenzel, p. 88. Similar phrases in Abbeel, p. 87; Lejeune, p. 315, Pilzecker, p. 1119; Baden brigade journal, GLA/4287.

82 Rühle, p. 277.

83 Lejeune, p. 315; similarly, Thielen on the Austrian side, p. 60.

84 Löwenstern, p. 120.

85 Berthezène, p. 249.

86 Pelleport, p. 280; Savary, vol. IV, p. 161.

87   Bühle, p. 8.
88   Pierre Marbotin to his mother, 10 July 1809, 'Deux Lettres de 1809', *Carnet de la Sabretache*, 1909, p. 517.
89   Lejeune, p. 315.
90   Paulin, p. 203; de Salle, p. 417. Another story relates that Napoleon personally observed the launching of the one-piece bridge and famously gave the responsible officer five minutes to complete his work: C. A. Haillot, *Essai d'une Instruction sur le Passage des Rivières*, Paris: Corréard, 1835, pp. 197–9; Jean Jacques Basilien de Gassendi, *Aide-Mémoire a l'Usage des Officiers d'Artillerie*, Paris: Maginel, Anselin et Pochard, 1819, vol. II, pp. 1185–7. As Paulin and de Salle were on the spot and intimately involved in bridging operations, I tend to grant veracity to their accounts.
91   Completion times respectively: 11.30 a.m., 2 p.m., 5 p.m. Buat, vol. II, pp. 190–1.
92   Older French sources, following the 25th Bulletin, often refer to the 5 July action as the 'Battle of Enzersdorf'.
93   Op. J. 1e.
94   Baste to Berthier, 14 July 1809, AG, C2/93. Some sources (eg Petre, p. 348) state that Baste landed a force of 200 sailors on Rohrhaufen (or Rohrworth), but this is not mentioned in the captain's detailed report. Baste's other two gunboats, *Arcole* and *Lodi*, sailed north of the *estacade* to annoy Austrian posts with cannon fire and perform important service in sinking or diverting the mills, boats, and other debris with which the Austrians attempted to damage the French bridges.
95   Other sources give the time required as four or eight minutes. See above for versions of this bridge's construction. One famous commentator criticised the bridge for being too narrow: J. G. von Hoyer, *Handbuch der Pontonnier-Wissenschaften*, Leipzig: Barth, 1830, vol. II, p. 98–100.
96   Bühle, p. 7.
97   Quoted in Heinrich Sittig, *Geschichte des k. u. k. Feldjäger-Bataillons Nr. 1*, Reichelberg: Stiepel, 1908, p. 49.
98   Ibid. p. 51.
99   2nd Corps, 'Rapport des Journées des 5 et 6 Juillet 1809', 8 July 1809, AG, C2/93.
100 It is not clear how long the mixed Jäger detachment resisted. Oudinot's report and the Hauptarmee's journal pass over the fight very quickly (as does François Pils, *Journal de Marche du Grenadier Pils*, Paris: Ollendorff, 1895, pp. 76–7), but Reiche states in his personal account that the officers finally capitulated at 2.30 p.m. See also Kandelsdorfer, *Feld-Jäger-Bataillons Nr. 7*, pp. 46–7.
101 Timing from Buat, vol. II, pp. 193–4; other sources give 8 or 9 a.m. for the fall of Enzersdorf. Austrian forces from Branko, pp. 177–8; Hermannsthal, p. 250; *Chasteler* Infantry 'Relation', KAFA. The Advance Guard's operations journal does not mention the *Chasteler* battalion.
102 Meier, p. 57.
103 Valentini, p. 173.
104 Advance Guard, 'Relation über die in der Schlacht vom 4. auf den 5. und am Tage des 5. von der Avantgarde mit dem Rechten Flügel der feindlichen Armee bestandenen Gefechte', KAFA, Kart. 1461.
105 Nordmann to Klenau and Charles, 5 July 1809, 10 a.m., KAFA, Kart. 1461.

106 Op. J. 70: this states the Advance Guard was 'at the level of the Esslinger Hof' (Schafflerhof), approximately half-way between Enzersdorf and Raasdorf; Nordmann had evacuated Redoubt No. VIII, but had it re-occupied when the French did not advance at once.

107 'Relation der feindlichen Vorfälle bei dem 6. Armee-Korps vom 30. Juni bis inklusiv 9. July 809', KAFA, Kart. 1461.

108 The idea that Charles intentionally kept his left very weak to 'lure' Napoleon over the Danube crops up occasionally in the literature ('Anmerkungen über die im 8ten und 10ten Stück der europäischen Annalen Jahrgang 1810 enthaltene Darstellung der Schlachten auf dem Marchfelde', Europäische Annalen, vol. VIII, 1811), but does not seem well grounded in evidence. The position of Beaulieu, facing almost due west in entrenchments that ran north–south between Redoubts VIII and IX, for example, clearly indicates an Austrian expectation that the French would debouch from the Mühlau; Charles had to order traverses to be thrown up at the last minute along this line (night of 2/3 July, Op. J. 70). Similarly, Charles to Klenau, 5 July 1809, 6 a.m., gives no hint that the left had been made intentionally weak to seduce Napoleon into attacking there (KAFA, Kart. 1461).

109 Klenau to Charles, 5 July 1809, 6 and 8 a.m., KAFA, Kart. 1461.

110 Nordmann to Charles, 5 July 1809, 10 a.m., (apparently shortly after the previous 10 a.m. message), KAFA, Kart. 1461.

111 Op. J. 1e; 'Relations' of IV Corps and Cavalry Reserve, KAFA, Kart. 1461.

112 'Relations' of the Cavalry Reserve (quotation), Advance Guard, and Riesch Dragoons, KAFA, Kart. 1461.

113 Hoen, Wagram, pp. 39–40; Hertenberger, p. 108; Valentini. p. 176. Charles did send a note to Franz at 9.30, stating, 'I do not doubt it will come to a battle today' (Binder, Krieg Napoleons, vol. II, p. 316), but in his subsequent orders he only alerted IV Corps to be available to support Liechtenstein—hardly the action of someone expecting a decisive battle on 5 July. One is left to conclude that his use of the word 'battle' (Schlacht) only suggested some initial sparring before the main event.

114 Charles to Johann, 4 July, 7 p.m. and 5 July 1809, 5.30 a.m., Zwiedineck-Südenhorst, Erzherzog Johann im Feldzuge von 1809, pp. 136–8.

115 Op. J. 1e.

116 Rühle von Lilienstern, 'Gedanken über die beiden Schlachten', p. 646; Valentini, p. 204.

117 Op. J. 1e; Pelet, vol. IV, pp. 188–9; Petre, p. 358. The spots where cavalry could cross without a bridge were few and difficult. It is not clear how much water was in the Russbach on 5 and 6 July 1809. It seems likely the water would have been high after the deluge the night of the 4th (as Dupas states in his report), but some sources describe it as low and slow, so it may be that the water level dropped significantly in the heat of the 5th and 6th. Whether a gush or a trickle, however, it formed an important hindrance to military movement.

118 Rühle von Lilienstern, 'Gedanken über die beiden Schlachten', pp. 478–9.

119 The square stone tower was subsequently destroyed and replaced by the round structure visible to visitors today.

120 Some of the Austrian troops built their huts by excavating shallow pits to protect themselves from the wind and covered these with branches or other material.

121 Auguste François Marcel Comte de Ségur-Cabanac, *Journal*, Vienna: Stern, 1910, p. 110, courtesy of Ferdi Wöber.

122 Lejeune, vol. I, p. 316; also Chevalier, p. 115. Counting 2nd (minus Colbert), 3rd, 4th, and 9th Corps, along with the Army of Italy and the Guard. Note that this figure does *not* include artillery or other arms.

123 Nagel's report to his grand duke, quoted in Carl Röder von Diersburg, *Geschichte des 1. Grossherzoglich Hessischen Infanterie- (Leibgarde-) Regiments Nr 115*, Berlin: Mittler, 1899, p. 159.

124 Pils, p. 77.

125 Davout, 'Opérations du 3e Corps dans la Campagne d'Allemagne en 1809', AG/MR667.

126 There may have been more guns in the lead: Friant stated that thirty guns preceded his division's advance, but perhaps these covered the entire corps front ('Précis Historique des Différents Affaires ou la 2e Division du 3e Corps etc.', AG/MR660). Some Austrian sources state that Davout 'stormed' Glinzendorf; there is no indication of such an action in Davout's thorough report.

127 Letter of 15 July 1809, Coudreux, p. 158.

128 Carl August Schneider, 'Erinnerungen aus dem Feldzuge 1809 in Oesterreich', manuscript, SächsHStA, Geheimes Kriegs-Kollegium, D4137. Schneider noted that the Saxons 'were not accustomed to such rhodomontade' and believed they might truly miss the battle!

129 Dupas, 'Rapport des 4, 5, 6 et 7 Juillet 1809', 7 July 1809, AG, C2/93. Bernadotte reported that two Saxon battalions had been involved as well (Bernadotte to Napoleon, 7 July 1809, AG, C2/93).

130 Gill, *Eagles*, pp. 295–7; quote from Grueber, p. 81. This is the famous incident in which two regiments with same proprietor (*Inhaber*) encountered one another: the Saxon *Herzog Albrecht* Chevaulegers and the Austrian *Herzog Albert* Cuirassiers (the varying orthography is another curiosity of the era). Contrary to subsequent mythology, however, the two regiments did not charge one another, and the weak Saxon squadron certainly did not overthrow the Austrian regiment; at most they were both involved in the same general melee. Two other points of interest: (1) Duke Albert of Sachsen-Teschen was Archduke Charles's adoptive uncle; and (2) participants immediately noted this peculiar aspect of the engagement.

131 Exner, p. 50. The identity of the Austrian infantry is unclear. Bernadotte reported the capture of a flag from *Chasteler* (Bernadotte to Napoleon, 7 July 1809, AG, C2/93), but Hoen believes it was three companies of *Beaulieu* (p. 43).

132 4th Corps, 'Relation', KAFA, Kart. 1461. Additionally, several hundred hussars were on the Russbach Heights.

133 Pelet, vol. IV, pp. 185–6; Savary, vol. IV, pp. 163–4.

134 Note that Pelet (vol. IV, pp. 185–7), reflecting the 25th Bulletin (*Correspondance*, no. 15505) offers a different explication: that Napoleon wanted to dislodge Charles from the strong Russbach position and inflict severe harm on the Hauptarmee before it was fully united (that is, while part was on the Bisamberg and Johann still at Pressburg). Dumas's account, statements in Davout's report, and especially

the loose conduct of the attack suggest that in this case Pelet is incorrect. See Buat, vol. II, p. 219.

135 Savary, vol. IV, pp. 164–5.

136 Dumas, vol. II, p. 201.

137 Reille's report, AG, C2/93. In his memoirs, MacDonald states that Napoleon personally gave Eugene verbal orders to attack and that he, MacDonald, attempted in vain to have Eugene dispute these instructions (vol. I, pp. 332–5); no other source offers this version of events.

138 From a work of fiction, Jack Vance, *Servants of the Wankh*, New York: DAW, 1979, p. 30.

139 Veigl, p. 99.

140 Castillon, p. 345.

141 Berthezène, p. 252. This portrayal draws heavily on his account. Note that one battalion of 19th Ligne and the 1st Company of the *Metzsch* Schützen from Dupas were also involved at Baumersdorf (Exner, p. 58).

142 For example, Pelet, vol. IV, p. 189.

143 Quote from Op. J. 1e (the Austrians feared that loss of Baumersdorf would ease French access to the heights as the slope behind the hamlet was gentle). Participation of II/*d'Aspre* from Padewieth, p. 181; III/former *Zedtwitz* and a battalion of *Froon* may also have fought near Baumersdorf (*Geschichte des k. k. 25. Infanterie-Regiments*, p. 440; Neuwirth, p. 231).

144 Oudinot's report, AG, C2/93. Note that he kept his artillery 'à la prolonge' during the night.

145 Berthezène, p. 252.

146 Losses were 199 of 675 (8th Jägers 'Relation', KAFA).

147 Jaromir Hirtenfeld, *Der Militär-Maria-Theresien-Orden und seine Mitglieder*, Vienna: Staatsdruckerei, 1857, vol. II, p. 892. The Hauptarmee's journal has 10th Léger's attack raging at the same time as the MacDonald/Dupas assault, but ending sooner (Op. J. 1e).

148 Dupas's report, AG, C2/93.

149 Note that some sources mention a small footbridge somewhere between Baumersdorf and Wagram that both Dupas and Lamarque used (not in Dupas's or MacDonald's reports).

150 MacDonald's report, AG, C2/93.

151 Brandner, pp. 91–2.

152 Dupas's report, AG, C2/93.

153 I Corps 'Relation', KAFA, Kart. 1461; Op. J. 1e.

154 Valentini, p. 181. This incident caused Charles to castigate *Argenteau* publicly in an army order on 7 July (in Kurt Peball, 'Zum Kriegsbild der österreichischen Armee und seiner geschichtlichen Bedeutung in den Kriegen gegen die französische Revolution und Napoleon I. in den Jahren von 1792 bis 1815', in Wolfgang von Groote and Klaus-Jürgen Müller (eds), *Napoleon I. und das Militärwesen seiner Zeit*, Freiburg: Rombach, 1968, pp. 166–7).

155 Schneider manuscript, SächsHStA, D4137.

156 MacDonald's report, AG, C2/93. MacDonald stated that his men had captured 2,000–3,000 Austrians and five standards, but lost all of these (one standard

excepted) in the ensuing retreat and confusion. Dupas likewise claimed the capture of a standard and the surrender of several hundred Austrians. Even if these figures are exaggerated, it is clear that many Habsburg units were momentarily stunned and sought escape in surrender.

157 Hoen, p. 52.

158 It is not clear how Sahuc got across the Russbach; Vignolle's history (AG/MR734) states he crossed between Baumersdorf and Markgrafneusiedl. Vignolle claims that part of the Army of Italy's artillery also got across the stream.

159 The *Hessen-Homburg* squadrons had ended up behind II Corps 'by accident' after the Advance Guard's disjointed retreat (II Corps, 'Relation', KAFA, Kart. 1461).

160 Letter of 10 August 1809, Chevillet, p. 291.

161 The sequence depicted here is partly from Valentini, an eyewitness (p. 182), but the confused struggle is very difficult to disentangle in detail: Hoen places the *Vincent* attack somewhat later in the engagement (pp. 53–4). Charles's anger is from the 7 July order in Peball (Groote/Müller, p. 167).

162 Dupas's report, AG, C2/93. Dupas does not identify the division as Seras (Buat unilaterally added this detail), but this seems clear from the relative casualties suffered by Seras and Durutte. Seras's wounding may have contributed to the disorder, but it is not clear when he was hit.

163 Vignolle, AG/MR734.

164 Letter of 10 August 1809, Chevillet, p. 289.

165 Vaudoncourt, vol. I, p. 408.

166 5th Léger, and 19th, 29th and 62nd Ligne. Austrian claims to have captured a general seem invalid.

167 Dupas's report, AG, C2/93. Contrary to Pelet's insinuation (vol. IV, p. 191), Dupas did not mean that the Saxon grenadiers had deserted or defected; he praised the Schützen specifically.

168 Hoen, p. 55.

169 *Histoire du 29e Régiment d'Infanterie*, manuscript, AG, 1886.

170 Davout's campaign history, AG/MR667. The sardonic, I-told-you-so tone of much of this official report is remarkable.

171 Friant's 'Précis Historique', AG/MR660.

172 Initially 2,300 men in town (*Reuss-Plauen*) covered by 660 Jägers, with 1,200 on their right and another 1,150 in immediate reserve (III/*Reuss-Plauen*).

173 Lecoq's disordered battalions were assembled on the right of Steindel's brigade near Aderklaa (Exner, p. 54).

174 'Kriegstagebuch 1809/12 meines Grossvaters', SächsHStA, D4098

175 Subordination of Egidy's battalion at this point is not clear; I have followed Albrecht von Holtzendorff, *Geschichte der Königlich Sächsischen Leichten Infanterie*, Leipzig: Geisecke, 1860.

176 The regimental history mentions the volunteers (*Geschichte des k. k. Infanterie-Regimentes Oskar II. Friedrich No. 10*, Vienna: regimental, 1888, p. 251), but reverses the battalion numbers; I have followed GM Clary's 'Relation' (17 July 1809, KAFA).

177 Barton, *Bernadotte*, pp. 217–21.

178 For an extended critique of this action, see Gill, *Eagles*, p. 301.

NOTES TO PAGES 224–8 ~ 471

179 With 5,500 men (counting *Zach*, one battalion of *J. Colloredo*, 100 Jägers, two battalions of *Hiller*, and the *Vincent* Chevaulegers)—not to mention a significant terrain advantage—the Austrians had a superiority of 3:1 over 10th Léger's 1,800 (another 1,650 Landwehr and 2,000 Habsburg regulars were also immediately available).

180 Dupas's report, AG, C2/93; MacDonald offered similar praise to the troops.

181 Criste, *Carl*, vol. III, 207.

182 Davout's report, AG, C2/93.

183 Paulin, pp. 204–5.

184 Noël, p. 73; Tascher, p. 232.

185 Boulart, p. 223.

186 Criste, *Carl*, vol. III, pp. 207, 232–4.

187 'Marginalien', p. 252.

188 Charles, 'Denkschrift', p. 346; Binder, *Krieg Napoleons*, vol. II, pp. 329–32; Hoen, pp. 59–61. Two other considerations may have influenced thinking at headquarters: the recently experienced vulnerability of the Russbach position and, conversely, a sense of confidence derived from repelling the French assault.

189 The disposition called for Kolowrat to command Klenau as well as his own corps, but there is no evidence that this occurred in practice.

190 He received the *Hohenzollern* Cuirassiers as a reinforcement.

191 Charles to Johann, 6 July 1809, 2 a.m., Zwiedineck-Südenhorst, *Erzherzog Johann im Feldzuge von 1809*, pp. 139–40.

192 Op. J. 1e.

193 Rauchensteiner, *Wagram*, pp. 28, 35; 'Einige Bemerkungen', pp. 151–2.

194 Charles, 'Denkschrift', p. 347.

195 Many sources list the 'reserve' as three battalions, I have only been able to verify I and II/*Schröder* (regimental 'Relation'); perhaps one of the Landwehr battalions was left behind as well.

196 The absence of a reserve, highly uncharacteristic for Charles, leads some commentators to conclude that the archduke was indisposed during the night and that the 'Disposition' stemmed from the minds of Wimpffen and Grünne (Heller, vol. II, pp. 188–91). At a minimum, some observers question Charles's role in its drafting (Binder, *Krieg Napoleons*, vol. II, pp. 333–4; Criste, *Carl*, vol. III, pp. 232–4). Rauchensteiner and Rothenberg disagree (*Wagram*, p. 24; *Adversaries*, p. 167); Hoen (pp. 61–2) is probably correct in asserting that Charles provided the general concept, but left the details to his staff—of course, as things turned out, there were several dangerous devils in those details.

197 Rauchensteiner cites this as evidence that Charles was considering his retreat options from the start (*Wagram*, p. 32).

198 Timings from Binder, *Krieg Napoleons*, vol. II, p. 333; the anonymous author of 'Anmerkungen' (who may have been Grünne) argues unpersuasively that there was adequate time to deliver orders and set the corps in motion (pp. 139–40).

199 Radetzky, 'Erinnerungen', p. 67. Note that he gives the arrival time of the disposition as midnight; I have used the time given in the 'Relation' (2 a.m.).

200 Pelet, vol. IV, p. 198; Binder, *Krieg Napoleons*, vol. II, pp. 338–9.

201 Dumas, p. 202; Pelet, vol. IV, p. 204.

202 Pelet, vol. IV, p. 198.

203 Pelet, vol. IV, p. 197.

204 From excellent discussion in Buat, vol. II, pp. 230–4.

205 Larisch, 'Meine zweite Campagne'; Frèche, p. 122; also Chevalier, p. 116.

206 Chlapowski, p. 178; Parquin, p. 101.

207 *Chasteler, Beaulieu, Bellegarde.* The remnants of 1st and 7th Jägers seem to have remained behind as well (five weak companies); the *Wallach-Illyria* Grenzer seem to have disappeared.

208 IV Corps, 'Relation'. The advance may have proceeded in a somewhat disorderly fashion as Charles criticised the corps after the battle.

209 Letter of 17 July 1809, Coudreux, p. 160.

210 Varnhagen, p. 87.

211 IV Corps, 'Relation' (all quotations); 'Bericht über die Cavallerie des linken Flügels in der Schlacht am 6. July', Nostitz, KAFA, Kart. 1461. The Austrian cavalry, pre-empted by French horse, could not get past Leopoldsdorf.

212 Davout's report; and Arrighi to Berthier, 7 July 1809, both AG, C2/93.

213 According to Pelet, Nansouty's battery also remained with Davout. The owning unit of the seven 12-pounders is not clear.

214 Davout's report, AG, C2/93.

215 Savary, vol. IV, p. 171. The officer may have been Dumas rather than Reille.

216 Dedovich's journal, KAFA, Kart. 1387. Dedovich stated that *Vogelsang* was 'only some 600 men strong' that morning. GM Clary also remained with this portion of I Corps.

217 Campi, account of Aspern and Wagram, AG, C2/93.

218 Pelet, vol. IV, p. 208.

219 Hoen, pp. 70–1; Marulaz's report, AG, C2/93; Buat places this combat slightly later (vol. II. pp. 255–6). Galloping to the cuirassiers, Liechtenstein supposedly jumped his horse over a sunken road along which a column of grenadiers was marching.

220 Gachot, p. 265.

221 I Corps, 'Relation', KAFA, Kart. 1461.

222 Boyeldieu, p. 497.

223 Marbot, vol. II, p. 376; Baden war diary, GLA/48/4286.

224 Buat identifies the cavalry as Nansouty (vol. II, p. 251), but it seems much more likely it was St Sulpice.

225 'Rapport Historique des Opérations de la Division du Général Molitor', 12 November 1809, AG/MR662. Austrian sources do not acknowledge Molitor capturing the town, so perhaps he only took part of it and only for a short time.

226 Baden war diary, GLA/48/4286.

227 Zech/Porbeck, p. 166.

228 Wilhelm, p. 93.

229 Boudet's report, 7 July 1809, in Koch, vol. VI, pp. 42–3. Boudet had 93rd Ligne in Aspern, 3rd Léger just to the north, and 56th Ligne in support of the twelve guns, apparently forward of Aspern towards Hirschstetten.

230 Ludwig Graf von Wallmoden-Gimborn, 'Notes sur la Bataille du 5 et 6 Juillet 1809', AG, C2/93.

231 According to Gachot (pp. 268–9), 56th Ligne fell back to the bridgehead, the other two regiments towards Essling.

232 VI Corps, 'Relation', KAFA, Kart. 1461.

233 Reichold, pp. 114–15.

234 Madroux, 'Floret', p. 189.

235 Ibid. Arrival timing from 3rd Bavarian Chevaulegers, 'Relation', BKA/B445.

236 Girault, p 185.

237 Davout's report, AG, C2/93. Many witnesses report that Napoleon was magisterially unconcerned about Klenau's progress. See also Buat, vol. II, p. 258.

238 Buat, vol. II, p. 257.

239 Valentini, p. 198. Prussian Major Georg Valentini had come to Wagram as the Prince of Orange's aide-de-camp.

240 The cavalry's role is unclear; the probability that some may have been on hand in the afternoon is a change from *Eagles*, p. 304.

241 Contrary to Marbot's tale, Napoleon did not relieve Bernadotte of command on the field of battle; that would not happen until the afternoon of 9 July (Berthier to Bernadotte, 9 July 1809, AG, C2/93), and the marshal was still with the army at Znaim (Louis Bertrand Pierre Brun, *Les Cahiers du Général Brun*, Paris: Plon, 1953, pp. 92–3).

242 Boulart, p. 224. In general, see Emile François Litre, 'La Grande Batterie de la Garde a Wagram', *Revue d'Artillerie*, vol. LXVI, 1895; Alain Pigeard, 'L'Artillerie à Pied de la Garde', *Tradition*, no. 237, May–June 2008, p. 13.

243 Drouot to Pelet, 31 January 1824, AG, C2/93.

244 Czettritz, p. 57.

245 Valentini, p. 192.

246 'Relations' of the Cavalry Reserve and Grenadier Corps, KAFA, Kart. 1461.

247 Boulart, p. 225.

248 Coignet, p. 183.

249 Capitaine Marin in Litre, *Les Régiments*, p. 65.

250 Czettritz, p. 57.

251 Coignet, p. 183. Pelet writes that the *Georgy* Grenadiers were overthrown during these charges, but the battalion's casualties for this period do not reflect a major defeat and Austrian sources relate only that *Frisch* wavered for a time.

252 Savary, vol. IV, p. 174 (first quotation); Chlapowski, p. 184 (second quotation); Pelet, vol. IV, pp. 220–1; Marbot, vol. II, pp. 377–8; Löwenstern, vol. I, pp. 127–8; Broussier's journal, AG, C2/93.

253 'Feldzug der zweiten Division', p. 633.

254 St Sulpice initially rode on the right flank (towards the Austrians), but was punished by Austrian artillery fire and shifted to the other side of Massena's infantry.

255 Gueheneuc, AG/MR1843; Campi, AG, C2/93; Pelleport, pp. 283–5.

256 Baden war diary, GLA/48/4286.

257 Pelet, vol. IV p. 221; Dumas, vol. II, pp. 204–5; Marbot, vol. I, pp. 377–8; Koch, *Massena*, vol. VI, pp. 322–3; Paulin, p. 208; Wilhelm, pp. 93–4. There are several versions of what Napoleon said; this is from Pelet. Marbot and Wilhelm of Baden claim to have received instructions from Napoleon around this time; both may be right.

258　It was apparently around this time, shortly after noon, that Napoleon stretched himself out on a mantle on the ground, in the shadow of some drums and took a brief nap (Paulin, p. 209; Brun, pp. 90–1).

259　I/30th Ligne was attached to Montbrun (Dupuy, pp. 129–31). It seems reasonable to speculate that the entire regiment was held on the far right as insurance against Johann (Hoen, *Wagram*, p. 87).

260　Davout's and Friant's reports, AG, C2/93.

261　According to Bonneval (pp. 31–2) Napoleon directed an officer to find Davout and 'tell him of my surprise that with his well-known vigour and energy he still finds himself lagging behind the rest of my line'. The emperor specifically selected Chef de Bataillon Jean Charles Pernet for this mission as Pernet, who had a reputation as something of a blockhead, would be sure to deliver the message literally and thus excite Davout's pride.

262　All three brigade commanders had been promoted after Aspern. Rosenberg reinforced the troops on the northern edge of town with 1st Iglau.

263　IV Corps, 'Relation', KAFA, Kart. 1461.

264　Report of 1st Dragoon Division, 8 July 1809, AG, C2/93.

265　Montbrun's report (extract) in Margon, p. 111.

266　This and previous quote, Dupuy, pp. 129–31.

267　Letter of 17 July 1809, Coudreux, p. 160.

268　Bertrand, pp. 83–4.

269　Arrighi's report, 8 July 1809, AG, C2/93.

270　Radetzky, 'Erinnerungen', p. 68.

271　Ségur-Cabanac, p. 111; Victor de Ségur-Cabanac, *Histoire de la Maison de Ségur*, Brünn, 1908, p. 241.

272　Varnhagen, p. 93.

273　Valentini, p. 198.

274　*Victoires, Conquêtes, et Désastres, Revers et Guerres Civiles des Français, de 1792 à 1815*, Paris: Panckoucke, 1820, vol. XIX, p. 209.

275　MacDonald's report famously states that he had only 8,000 men at hand. However, close reading suggests that this figure refers to *his* divisions only (Broussier and Lamarque). He seems to have considered Seras as 'extra', a separate reserve; he certainly did not regard Seras as part of his initial 'square' (just as earlier in the report he did not seem to count Pachtod as part of his '7,000–8,000 men'). Furthermore, this figure tallies with the likely strengths of the available divisions. Broussier had at least some 4,000; and Lamarque, with about 6,300 on the morning of the 5th, would have had at least 4,000 even if his losses in the evening attack came to 37 per cent (more probably he lost 25 to 30 per cent). Seras, assuming a similar percentage of losses on the 5th, would have had 3,500–3,700 on 6 July.

276　This arrangement is from MacDonald's and Broussier's reports (AG, C2/93). According to Pelet, Lamarque reported that his battalions were arrayed in columns of battalions one behind the other (vol. IV, p. 222).

277　MacDonald's report makes particular mention of the carabiniers. Some authors (eg Buat) dispute this statement, but it is hard to imagine MacDonald erring on this point (his report was written immediately after the battle). He was clearly concerned that his rear was open and wanted to close it off as he advanced (but he was not trying to replicate in every degree a tactical infantry square). It seems likely that the cavalry did not hold this unusual post for long, being soon called upon to support the advance with charges.

278 See Rothenberg, *Last Victory*, pp. 191–4; Schneid, *Italian Campaigns*, pp. 97–9; Robert M. Epstein, 'The Army of Italy at the Battle of Wagram: Turning Point of the Napoleonic Wars', in The Consortium on Revolutionary Europe, *Proceedings 1989*, ed. Donald D. Horward and John C. Horgan, Tallahassee: Florida State University, 1990, pp. 226–34. Jean Colin (*Les Transformations de la Guerre*, Paris: Flammarion, 1926, pp. 22, 111) highlights the uniqueness of MacDonald's square and praises its tactical flexibility (though he had derided it in an earlier work: *La Tacticque et la Discipline dans les Armées de la Révolution*, Paris: Chapelot, 1902, p. LXVI). Chandler (p. 728) specifically states that poor infantry dictated MacDonald's formation; Petre, (pp. 361–8) discusses the supposed decline in French troop quality in general. Furthermore, as Rothenberg and Schneid have noted, its size may have made it appear more fearsome to the Austrians.

279 Pelet, vol. IV, p. 223.
280 Savary, vol. IV, pp. 177–8.
281 Broussier's journal, AG, C2/93.
282 Lacorde, pp. 83–4.
283 Quotations, unless otherwise indicated, are from MacDonald's report (AG, C2/93) or his memoirs (vol. I, pp. 335–43, including an 8 July letter to his grandfather, pp. 349–52). Among many other commentaries, see Joseph Rogniat, *Considérations sur l'Art de la Guerre*, Paris: Anselin and Pochard, 1820, p. 384.
284 Savary, vol. IV, pp. 178–9.
285 Buat, vol. II, p. 268; Reille's report, AG, C2/93.
286 Location from Op. J. 1e, but some dispositions carry the location Breitenlee.
287 Op. J. 1e.
288 Baden war diary, GLA/48/4286.
289 Riedl, p. 69.
290 VI Corps, 'Relation', KAFA, Kart. 1461.
291 Regimental 'Relation' cited in Mayer, p. 329.
292 Robinet, *Lasalle*, pp. 191–9.
293 Unlike most of the Army of Italy's divisions (who had contributed their artillery to the grand battery), Durutte had six pieces that had been damaged but returned to service (Vignolle, 'Italie', AG/MR1843).
294 The strength of MacDonald's command at this point is difficult to determine. MacDonald stated he was reduced to only some 1,500 men. As before, this may be exaggerated or may refer only to Lamarque and Broussier, or possibly solely to Broussier (Gachot so asserts without explication). Broussier claimed to have only a 'battalion' of 300–400 left. On the other hand, Seras reported that 'the Army of Italy passed Süssenbrunn with more than 4,000 men' (in Gachot, p. 280); James R. Arnold, *Napoleon Conquers Austria*, London: Arms and Armour, 1995, p. 147.
295 Völderndorff, vol. II, p. 247. As Heilmann points out (*Wrede*, p. 159), there are several versions of Napoleon's remarks to Wrede.
296 Reille's report, AG, C2/93 (giving the time as 3.30); Buat, vol. II, pp. 272–3.
297 Davout's report, AG, C2/93.

298 Tascher, p. 234.
299 Friant's report, AG, C2/93.
300 Veigl, p. 99.
301 Oudinot's report, AG, C2/93; Valentini, p. 203.
302 II Corps, 'Relation', KAFA, Kart. 1461.
303 Barat, pp. 77–8; Bernard, *Carnet*, pp. 458–9 (quotes from these two participants); Noël, pp. 74–5.
304 Hoen, *Wagram*, pp. 98–9; II Corps, 'Relation', regimental histories; quotes from Parquin, p. 102.
305 Löwenstern, vol. I, pp. 133–4.
306 As mentioned above, Davout had detached at least I/30th Ligne—probably the entire regiment—to Montbrun in the morning. It seems likely that this battalion (or the regiment) was ensconced in Leopoldsdorf and other villages; it is also likely that some quantity of French cavalry was on hand.
307 Johann, *Feldzugserzählungen*, pp. 194–7 (first quotation); Johann to Franz, 7 July 1809, Zwiedineck-Südenhorst, *Erzherzog Johann im Feldzuge von 1809*, pp. 146–8 (second quotation).
308 Marmont ('horrible'), vol. III, p. 241; Paulin, pp. 210–1; Roguet, p. 71.
309 Savary, an 'intelligence officer' of sorts himself, was mystified that the Austrians, in their own country, 'could remain ignorant of our dispositions to the point that the army at Pressburg was not recalled' (vol. IV, p. 159).
310 Bianchi, quoted in Heller, vol. II, pp. 156–7.
311 Demuth, who believed Johann could have marched eight hours earlier, related in Criste, *Carl*, vol. III, pp. 243–5.
312 [Ludwig de Traux] 'Bermerkungen über die im 2ten und 3ten Stück der europäische Annalen enthaltenen Marginalien zur Relation über die Schlacht bei Wagram', *Europäische Annalen*, vol. V, 1810.
313 Related in Criste, *Carl*, vol. III, pp. 243–5.
314 That was certainly Radetzky's judgement, Bibl, *Radetzky*, p. 98.
315 In addition to the sources already cited, the following relate to the 'Johann question': Johann's writings (*Feldzugserzählungen* and Zwiedineck-Südenhorst); Oskar Regele, 'Erzherzog Johann und die Schlacht bei Wagram', *Kulturnachrichten der Marktgemeinde Deutsch-Wagram*, January 1962; Kurt Simon, *Erzherzog Johann bei Wagram*, Berlin, 1900; Pelet, vol. IV, pp. 161–3; Theiss, pp. 320–7, 387.
316 Parteger to his father, 1 August 1809, in Emile Fairon and Herni Heuse, *Lettres des Grognards*, Liege: Bénard, 1936, p. 109; Coëhorn to his wife, 8 July 1809, pp. 194–5; Pelet, vol. IV, pp. 166–7; Charles to Albert, 9 July 1809, Criste, *Carl*, vol. III, p. 493; Charles to Zichy, 21 July 1809, *Ausgewählte Schriften*, vol. VI, p. 306; Jacquin, p. 72.
317 Calculations rely on KAFA materials (principally 'Summarischer Ausweis A des von den verschiedenen k. k. Armee-Corps in der Schlacht bei Wagram am 5. u. 6. July 1809 erlittenen Verlusten' and 'Summarischer Ausweis des in den verschiedenen Affairen vom 29ten Juny bis incls. 11ten July 809 erlittenen Verlusten'); AG materials (corps reports cited previously, loss reports from 3rd Corps, 1st Dragoons, 1st and 3rd Heavy Cavalry, Guard); Hoen, *Wagram*, pp. 109–10; Binder, *Krieg Napoleons*, vol. II, pp. 368–76; Buat, vol. II, pp. 306–11; Exner, p. 104; GLA/48/4283 and 4286; Gill, *Eagles*, pp. 241–2; *Relation über die Schlacht bei Deutsch-Wagram*, Pest, 1809.

318 Tascher, p. 235; Noël, p. 76; Bucher's diary in Exner, pp. 122–3. For a vivid account of Vienna under French occupation, see Robert Ouvrard, *1809: Les Français à Vienne*, Paris: Nouveau Monde, 2009.

319 Lauthonnye, p. 405. Valentini, an eyewitness, remarked that in some cases artillery seemed to replace skirmishing (pp. 192–3). A later commentator opined that the previous system of nurturing battles by feeding in forces over time through the use of skirmish lines was 'entirely missing' at Wagram; instead there was 'more artillery employment and battle of masses' (W. H. Harder, 'Gebrauch der Artillerie vor dem Feinde', *Zeitschrift für Kunst, Wissenschft und Geschichte des Krieges*, vol. VI, 1833, p. 242),

320 Lariboisière to Songis, 8 July 1809, A. Abaut, 'Lariboisière', *Revue d'Artillerie*, vol. XXXV, 1889–90, pp. 11–12.

321 Charles to Albert, 9 July 1809, Criste, *Carl*, vol. III, p. 493.

322 *Relation über die Schlacht bei Deutsch-Wagram*, p. 23; Abaut, p. 12.

323 Wallmoden, 'Notes sur la bataille', AG, C2/93.

324 Ibid.

325 Buat, vol. II, pp. 300–1; Epstein *Modern War*, p. 173.

326 Noël, p. 75.

327 Berthezène, p. 260.

328 Hans Holtzheimer, 'Erzherzog Karl bei Wagram', dissertation, University of Berlin, 1904, p. 7.

329 Marmont, vol. III, p. 241. Marmont was a skilled soldier and an informed observer, but it is well to keep his disaffection with Napoleon in mind.

330 Dumas, vol. II, p. 207

331 Bonneval, pp. 33–4; Chlapowski, pp. 192–3; Noël, p. 75; Paulin, p. 211; Méneval, vol. II, p. 583.

332 Paulin, p. 209. Similarly: Lejeune, vol. I, p. 319; Castellane, p. 63.

333 Godart, p. 132.

334 Coëhorn to his wife, 8 July 1809, pp. 194–5; Desboeufs, p. 111.

335 Savary, vol. IV, pp. 182–3; Charles to Albert, 9 July 1809, Criste, *Carl*, vol. III, p. 494.

336 Drouot to a friend, 21 July 1809, 'Nouvelles Lettres du Général Drouot', *Carnet de la Sabretache*, 1897, p. 402; Marmont, vol. III, p. 244.

CHAPTER 6: ZNAIM

1 Ségur-Cabanac, p. 111.

2 Napoleon to Cambacérès, 7 July 1809, *Correspondance*, no. 15492.

3 Binder, *Krieg Napoleons*, vol. II, pp. 356–8; Marbot, vol. I, pp. 378–9.

4 Buat, vol. II, p. 318.

5 MacDonald, letter of 8 July, *Memoirs*, vol. I, pp. 349–50.

6 Berthier to Bernadotte, 9 July 1809, 5 p.m., AG, C2/93.

7 The *Hohenzollern* history says the entire regiment only counted 150 mounted, combat-ready men and that only one squadron went with Altstern (Eduard Freiherr

von Tomaschek, *Geschichte des k. k. Dragoner-Regiments No. 8*, Vienna: Hof- und Staatsdruckerei, 1889, pp. 306–7). Altstern may have had a cavalry battery as well.

8 Rosenberg had received verbal orders on the night of 6/7 July to continually cover the left flank of the army' (Heller, vol. II, p. 245). The troops from II Corps consisted of most of *Frelich* with stragglers and broken bits of several other regiments, all under Oberst Karl Johann Freiherr von Mecséry.

9 Op. J. 1f; Peball (Groote/Müller), p. 167.

10 Op. J. 39; Op. J. 1f.

11 Zwiedineck-Südenhorst, *Erzherzog Johann im Feldzuge von 1809*, p. 149.

12 Charles to Franz, 7 July 1809, Binder, *Krieg Napoleons*, vol. II, p. 382.

13 Charles to Albert, 9 July 1809, Criste, *Carl*, vol. III, p. 493.

14 Austrian casualties from regimentals (595 from *Benjovszky* alone); the Badeners lost 145; French records only show aggregate losses from 1 to 15 July (Gachot gives 315 total, but does not note if this includes Baden troops, p. 297).

15 Marmont to Berthier, 9 July, 10 a.m., Buat, vol. II, p. 334.

16 Commander's report in Capitaine Allenou, *Historique du 7eme Régiment de Dragons*, manuscript, AG, 1890.

17 Rössler, *Oesterreichs Kampf*, vol. II, pp. 42–5; Criste, *Carl*, vol. III, pp. 261–2.

18 Criste, *Carl*, vol. III, pp. 250–8.

19 Charles gave Hohenzollern leeway to cross the Thaya and test the enemy's strength. As Bornemann points out (pp. 46–7) this could have placed Marmont in a very dicey situation, but Hohenzollern, uninterested in such responsibility (Binder, *Krieg Napoleons*, vol. II, p. 391), simply marched along the south bank of the river (Op. J. 10).

20 Napoleon to Davout, 10 July 1809, 8.30 a.m., *Correspondance*, no. 15510.

21 Op. J. 1f.

22 Charles to Albert, 13 July 1809, Criste, *Carl*, vol. III, p. 494.

23 Op. J. 1f.

24 Napoleon was ill with a fever on 9 July (Savary, vol. IV, pp. 188–95).

25 Indeed, Johann's greatest value to the Habsburg cause may have been as a 'force in being', that is, maintaining himself as a *potential* threat rather than exposing himself to possible destruction in a chancy engagement.

26 Source material for Znaim and the pursuit includes Marmont's report (AG, C2/93), Minucci's report (BKA/445), the Hauptarmee's operations journal (Op. J. 1f), 'Relations' and/or operations journals of key Austrian formations, and the campaign accounts already widely used in this study (Buat, Pelet, Binder, Criste, Heller, etc). Additional references include: Ernst von Kwiatkowski, *Die Kämpfe bei Schöngrabern und Ober-Hollabrunn 1805, 1809*, Vienna, 1908; Julius Wisnar, 'Die Schlacht bei Znaim', *Jahresbericht des k. k. Gymnasiums Znaim*, 1910; Josef Krenstetter, 'Die Folgen der Schlacht bei Wagram in militärischer Hinsicht', dissertation, University of Vienna, 1959; Karl Bornemann, *Napoleon bei Znaim*, Geislingen/Steige: Südmährischen Landschaftrat, 1975.

27 Some sources describe two bridges for this highway: one carrying the highway from the south bank to an island, the other span crossing from the island to the north bank.

28 There were some partly completed earthworks just south of Znaim intended to protect the highway, but they were rudimentary and did not play a major in the fighting.

29 South of the Thaya were *Knesevich*, *Rosenberg*, and the two Insurrection regiments.

30 A lone battery took the French and Bavarians under fire and some skirmishers appeared on the bank, but the battery was soon silenced and II/7 Bavarian Infantry drove off the skirmishers (Minucci, 'Relation', BKA/445; Op. J. 10). Neither Marmont's report nor Minucci's make any mention of troops being sent south of the river, but some Austrian accounts speak of at least some minimal fighting.

31 Bellegarde's rear guard (a division of III/*Reuss-Plauen* and three squadrons of *Klenau*) joined Henneberg; somehow a division each of former *Zedtwitz* and 2nd Jägers also showed up to help the grenadiers.

32 III Corps operations journals, Op. J. 12, 16, 18.

33 Grenadier Corps, 'Relation', KAFA, Kart. 1462. The *Zedtwitz* division was also caught up in this scurry.

34 BKA/445.

35 Marmont to Berthier, 10 July 1809, evening, Koch, vol. VI, p. 440.

36 Marmont, vol. III, p. 249.

37 Marmont to Berthier, 10 July 1809, evening, Koch, vol. VI, p. 440; paraphrase from Buat, vol. II, p. 351.

38 Zech/Porbeck, p. 182.

39 Pelet, vol. IV, p. 263.

40 'Rückzug des abgeschnittenen 4. Jäger-Bataillons, im Jahre 1809', ÖMZ, 1843. Gachot gives 415 French casualties for the day (p. 299).

41 Op. J. 1f. That night, Nostitz returned to the Cavalry Reserve, Altstern to II Corps, and Henneberg to I Corps along with two regiments that had retreated from Wagram under Hohenzollern (*Vogelsang* and *Argenteau*).

42 V Corps, 'Relation', KAFA, Kart. 1462. Reuss specifically praised the Landwehr's endurance under this trial.

43 Grenadier Corps, 'Relation', KAFA, Kart. 1462. Note that where the grenadiers performed well, their attached Landwehr battalion seems to have dissolved, losing only one man wounded while ninety-three went missing.

44 V Corps, 'Relation', KAFA, Kart. 1462.

45 Unterleutnant Philipp le Beau, 2nd Baden Infantry, diary extract courteously provided by Reinhard Franz Kaufmann and published in his 'Die Schlacht bei Znaim veränderte die Landkarte Europas', *Zusammenfassung der Beiträge zum Napoleon Symposium 'Feldzug 1809'*, Vienna: Delta Druckproduktionen, 2009, p. 75.

46 Meier, p. 64. The generals were de Stabenrath and Lazowski; Austrian accounts often claim that Massena was almost captured; this is almost certainly an exaggeration.

47 It is difficult to sort out the sequence of this counter-charge and the exact regiments that participated in it. This account (based on Marbot, Wilhelm, Zech/Porbeck, Koch, Pelet, regimental histories, and 'Feldzug der zweiten Division') proceeds from the assumption that 1st Cuirassiers were on the north (left) bank of the Thaya (Wilhelm took orders to them), but were slow to get into action owing to mud and poor ground; Guiton's brigade, led by the 10th, came across the bridge (as seen by Marbot) and hit the grenadiers from that direction.

48 'Feldzug der zweiten Division', p. 636.

49 Austrian operations journals uniformly state that there was very little action on their left wing during the 11th. Buat, however, portrays Montbrun pushing back the Austrian left.

50 Gueheneuc, AG/MR1843.

51 Espinchal, p. 277; near same phrase in Meier, p. 64.

52 This section draws on John H. Gill, 'From Wagram to Schönbrunn: War and Peace in 1809', in The Consortium on Revolutionary Europe, *Selected Papers 1998*, ed. Kyle Eidahl and Donald D. Horward, Tallahassee: Florida State University, 1998.

53 Some 7,300 Austrians (*Lindenau, Gradiska,* 5th Vienna, two grenadier brigades) against Legrand's 4,100–4,600.

54 Franz to Charles and Liechtenstein, 8 July 1809, Criste, *Liechtenstein,* p. 133.

55 Charles to Albert, 13 July 1809, Criste, *Carl,* vol. III, p. 494.

56 Savary, vol. IV, p. 198.

57 Orange to Heerdt, 12–13 July 1809, Colenbrander, pp. 804–5.

58 Napoleon indirectly confirmed Charles's assessment, telling a Russian emissary: 'I negotiate with Austria because she still has an army in the field.' Alexander to Rumiantsev, 16 August 1809, *VPR,* vol. V, pp. 130–1; and Caulaincourt to Napoleon, 19 August 1809, Mikhaïlowitch, *Relations Diplomatiques,* vol. IV, p. 46.

59 'Welche Ursachen bewogen den österreichischen Feldherrn zu dem Waffenstillstand von Znaym und war er vortheilhaft für Oesterreichs Interesse?', Pest, 1811. Johann likewise believed the armistice 'saved the exhausted army', *Feldzugserzählungen,* p. 207.

60 Charles to Franz, 13 July 1809, and to Albert, 19 July 1809, Criste, *Carl,* vol. III, pp. 268–74, 496. Binder suggests that leaving the army vulnerable was a way of forcing the Kaiser to negotiate (*Krieg Napoleons,* vol. II, pp. 415–17).

61 Charles to Albert, 9 and 18/19 July 1809, Criste, *Carl,* vol. III, pp. 492–6; Zichy to Franz, 15 July 1809, Criste, *Liechtenstein,* p. 138.

62 Koch, vol. VI, p. 341.

63 Franz to Charles, 9 July 1809, Charles to Franz, 13 July 1809, and Charles to Albert, 23 July 1809, Criste, *Carl,* vol. III, pp. 266, 268–74, 497; Gustav Just, *Der Friede von Schönbrunn,* Vienna: Stern, 1909, pp. 22–3.

64 Rough estimate of 24,750 for Davout, 16,500 for Oudinot, 4,000 for Molitor, and 8,500 for the French and Italian Foot Guards. Arrighi probably had 1,200–1,400 combatants. These would also bring a subsbtantial quantity of artillery.

65 'Ueber die Benutzung der in der Schlacht von Aspern erfochtenen Vortheile und über den Waffenstillstand von Znaym', *Pallas,* vol. I, 1810, pp. 412–33; Savary, vol. IV, p. 196; Dumas, vol. II, p. 208.

66 As it did; Charles modified his initial instructions so that much of the army remained at Znaim through the night (Op. J. 1f).

67 Buat's military interpretation is thorough, but too narrow (vol. II, pp. 365–73). For dangers posed by Russia and Prussia, as well as the influence of English action and the Spanish situation, see Lefebvre, vol. IV, pp. 267–78.

68 Chandler suggests that Napoleon may have been simply growing tired of war (pp. 733–4).

69 Pelet, vol. IV, p. 278.

70 Pelet, vol. IV, pp. 277–8; Berthezène, pp. 259–60. Observation regarding the horse grenadiers and sabres from an excised portion of Larrey's memoirs printed in Triare, p. 64.

71 Baraguey d'Hilliers to Eugene, 9 July 1809, AG, C2/93; Bianchi, pp. 86–92.

72 Bianchi, pp. 100–4; Gutschmid's report (extract), AG, C2/93; Gill, *Eagles*, pp. 309–10. II/*Beaulieu* had been detached from the Advance Guard to cover the bridgehead at Marchegg on 5 July.

73 Charles to Albert, 18 July 1809, Criste, *Carl*, vol. III, p. 495.

74 Chasteler left Szent Groth on 8 July and made his way by a roundabout route to Tet by the 15th; Mesko had already departed on 2 July, marching behind Lake Balaton and via Ofen to reach Komorn on the 18th. Johann was not with his army; having been summoned to the Kaiser, he arrived in Komorn on 18 July, and rejoined his men on the 20th with news of the armistice. Op. J. 52, Op. J. 46, and Op. J. 47.

75 Andrassy: 2nd, 5th, 9th, 15th Infantry battalions, Szala Hussars, six guns (Haugwitz manuscript).

76 Anders, ÖMZ, pp. 252–6. Villach was occupied on 3 July. Another detachment (600) went to Malborghetto, but was turned back by the garrison on 8 July.

77 Vignolle, 'Italie'; Rusca to Berthier, 11 July 1809, Buat, vol. II, pp. 317–18.

CHAPTER 7: INSURGENTS, INVASIONS, AND PEACE

1 Op. J. 1f.

2 Austrian operations journal in Just, *Politik oder Strategie?*, p. 54; Mondet to Ferdinand, 14 July 1809, 10 p.m., in Poniatowski, *Correspondance*, vol. II, pp. 219–20.

3 Poniatowski to Napoleon, 14–15 July 1809, Poniatowski, *Correspondance*, vol. II, pp. 216–28.

4 Soltyk, pp. 329–35. Bicking had 800 Kordonisten and other more-or-less regular, if second-line, infantry, 300 Bukovina Jägers and volunteers, 200 'Arnauts' (these may have been detached before the encirclement), 40 Bukovina mounted Jägers, and 50 from the *Palatinal* Hussars depot, plus a 6-pounder and two 3-pounders. He may have had only 600 infantry by the time of his surrender. The Poles kept the guns, but parolled the troops, escorting them back to Czernowitz. Statement by Merveldt, KAFA, Kart. 1430. See also Jaroslaw Dudzinski, 'Dzialania Piotr Stryzewskiego w Galicji Wschodniej w Czasia Wojny Polsko-Ausrtiackiej w 1809 Roku' at http://napoleon.gery.pl/bitwy/strzyzewski.php. With thanks to Andrzej Kosim for translation. On the Bukovina troops, see Werenka, pp. 7–13.

5 Ferdinand to Charles, 9 July 1809, KAFA, Kart. 1430. The Russians, on the other hand, saw the Franco-Austrian war as an opportunity to prosecute their conflict with the Turks without interference ('Uebersicht der Kriegsbegebenheiten zwischen Russland und der Pforte an der unteren Donau, vom Jahre 1806 bis 1812', ÖMZ, 1829; Alexander Mikhailovsky-Danilevsky, *Russo-Turkish War of 1806–1812*, trans. Alexander Mikaberidze, West Chester: Nafziger, 2002).

6 Vignolle, 'Italie'; Khuepach, p. 226–36; Collingwood to Mulgrave, 15 July 1809, *Collingwood*, pp. 403–4; Mackesy, pp. 322–4. L'Espine had 800 Insurrection, some 200 from various regiments, 120 Banderial hussars, two 3-pounders, and two

6-pounders; the revived 'Istrian Landwehr' (Khuepach's phrase; he presumably meant Trieste Landwehr) was also supposed to participate. Schilt had III and IV/79th Ligne and 310 reinforcements drawn from Italy.

7   Two weak battalions of *Reisky, Licca* Reserve Battalion, two companies of Dalmatian Volunteers, three *Licca* Land-companies, one squadron of *Hohenzollern*, one squadron of Serezaner, seven guns (Op. J. 63).

8   Woinovich, pp. 79–83; Pisani, pp. 321–6. A two-hour sea 'battle' between Italian and Austrian trabakels and other coastal vessels occurred on 30 July outside Zara, but no losses were incurred. Both sides complained that the other violated terms of the accord during August.

9   Sources include: Junot's July reports (AG, C2/93); Kienmayer's and Radivojevich's reports (KAFA, Kart. 1461) along with Op. J. 1f; Gill, *Eagles*, chs 7, 8, 9. A study of Gefrees by the author appeared in *First Empire*, no. 12, July/August 1993 with addendum in no. 15, February/March 1994.

10   Kienmayer to Charles, Op. J. 1f.

11   Johann C. Gross, *Erinnerungen aus den Kriegsjahren*, Leipzig: Voss, 1850, pp. 27–8.

12   'Journal der Operationen des kaiserl. Österreichischen Truppen-Corps', pp. 262–75.

13   The duke's words have several versions, this is from Gustav von Kortzfleisch, *Des Herzogs Friedrich Wilhelm von Braunschweig Zug durch Norddeutschalnd im Jahre 1809*, Berlin: Mittler, 1894, pp. 8–9. This section is largely drawn from *Eagles*, ch 9.

14   Arwed Richter, 'Das hamburgische Amt Ritzebüttel und die Elbmündung in den Jahren 1795–1814', Cuxhaven, 1895, pp. 49–51; William Laird Clowes, *The Royal Navy*, London: Sampson Low, Marston and Company, 1900, vol. V, p. 442; H. Lüders, *Europas Palingenesie*, Leipzig and Altenburg: Richter, 1810, vol. III, pp. 280–1.

15   Jerome to Napoleon 17, 18, and 27 July 1809, *Mémoires et Correspondance*, vol. IV, pp. 276–8.

16   Friedrich Thimme, *Die innere Zustände des Kurfürstentums Hannover unter der französisch-westfälischen Herrschaft*, Hanover: Hahn, 1893, vol. I, pp. 442–6.

17   John W. Fortescue, *A History of the British Army*, London: Macmillan, 1912, vol. VII, p. 56.

18   Christopher D. Hall, *British Strategy in the Napoleonic War 1803–15*, Manchester: Manchester University Press, 1992, pp. 176–7; Muir, p. 89.

19   Hall, p. 177.

20   Muir, pp. 89–90.

21   Fortescue, vol. VII, pp. 56–8. As Jeremy Black points out, the size of the expedition highlights the importance that Britain attached to maritime security threats (*Britain as a Military Power*, London: UCL Press, 1999, p. 9). See also Peter Hicks, 'Maintaining the Contest with Bonaparte: Britain in 1809', *Zusammenfassung der Beiträge zum Napoleon Symposium 'Feldzug 1809'*, Vienna: Delta Druckproduktionen, 2009, pp. 80–7.

22   The French commandant, GD Louis Claude Monnet, was subjected to military investigations for surrendering his post too readily. Similarly, Dutch Lt. Gen. Edward Bruce was charged with abandoning Fort Batz (Bath or Bat) for no reason (François Dumonceau, *Mémoires*, Brussels: Brepols, 1958, vol. I, pp. 378–80). On the other hand, a Dutch observer was astonished that Monnet's uninspiring collection

of troops held out for more than two weeks (S. van Hoeck, 'Die Engländer auf Seeland im Jahre 1809', *Europäische Annalen*, 1812, p. 52).

23   Bond, p. 90.

24   Martin R. Howard, 'Walcheren 1809: A Medical Catastrophe', *British Medical Journal*, December 1999; John Lynch, 'The Lessons of Walchren Fever, 1809', *Military Medicine*, March 2009.

25   Louis to Kraijenhoff, 5 July 1809, Cornelis Rudolphus Theodorus Kraijenhoff, *Bijdragen tot de vaterlandsche Geschiedenis van de belangrijke Jaren 1809 en 1810*, Nijmegen: Vieweg & Zoon, 1831, pp. 35–7; Theo Fleischman, *L'Expedition Anglaise sur le Continent en 1809*, Paris: Renaissance du Livre, 1973, pp. 23–6.

26   Jacobus Antonius Tellegen, *Gedane Veldtogten, bekomene Wonden*, Oosterbeek: G. Tellegen, 2005, p. 43.

27   Albert de Rocca, *Mémoires sur la Guerre des Français en Espagne*, Paris: Gide, 1817, pp. 334, 346.

28   Bond, pp. 78–80.

29   Bernadotte and Clarke angered Napoleon by allowing information to be published that undermined his efforts at deception: Napoleon to Clarke, 18 September 1809, in J. Lorette, 'L'Alerte de Walcheren et la Défense d'Anvers (1809)', *Revue Internationale d'Histoire Militaire*, no. 20. 1959.

30   Army 'Situations', AG, C2/512; André l'Huillier, 'Les Armées de la Tête des Flandres et d'Anvers (Août–Septembre 1809)', 1972, available at www.histoire-empire.org/1809.

31   Rocca, pp. 332, 336.

32   Louis was also coping with some low-level unrest in his kingdom, some from disturbances that preceded the invasion and other outbursts after the landing; some resulting from the same species of rumours that flew around Germany: 60,000 British troops marching on Amsterdam, for example! I am indebted to Dr Johan Joor for calling my attention to these internal problems. For a thorough study, see his *De Adelaar en het Lam*, Amsterdam: De Bataafsche Leeuw, 2000, pp. 467–70.

33   Napoleon to Clarke, 9 August 1809, *Correspondance*, no. 15630.

34   Napoleon was pleased that the British invasion gave him an excuse to form an army in the north as that would be 'necessary' to the negotiations (ibid.). He did authorise Clarke to retain some of the replacements slated for the main army (Napoleon to Clarke, 7 August 1809, *Correspondance*, no. 15620). The Dutch division, now under Hasselt, reached the Antwerp theatre at the end of August (J. W. van Sypesteijn, *Geschiednis van het Regiment Rijdende Artillerie*, Zaltbommel, 1852, p. 116). For Dutch actions, see J. C. C. Tonnet, 'De Landing in Zeeland in 1809', *De Militaire Spectator*, 1909.

35   Strachan to Pole, 27 August 1809; Chatham's statement, 15 October 1809, *A Collection of Papers Relating to the Expedition to the Scheldt, Presented to Parliament in 1810*, London: Strahan, 1811, pp. 462–4, 759.

36   Etienne, Baron d'Hastrel, 'Mémoires du Général Baron d'Hastrel', *Carnet de la Sabretache*, 1934, p. 369.

37   Muir, p. 103.

38   Fortescue, vol. VII, pp. 88–9.

39 William Thornton Keep to his father, 28 August 1809, Ian Fletcher (ed.), *In the Service of the King*, Staplehurst: Spellmount, 1997, pp. 55–6.

40 William Wheeler, letter of 15 October 1809, *Letters of Private Wheeler*, Boston: Houghton Mifflin, 1952, p. 32.

41 Bond, p. 159.

42 Charles Esdaille, *Napoleon's Wars*, London: Allen Lane, 2008, p. 394.

43 Rocca, p. 347.

44 Fortescue, vol. VII, p. 302.

45 For all of these operations, see (in addition to Fortescue), Bunbury, pp. 237–53; Collingwood to Stuart, 15 July 1809, *Collingwood*, pp. 395–8; Mackesy, pp. 328–34.

46 This section is largely drawn from Gill, *Eagles*, especially chs 4, 7, 8. Some of this information appeared in the first part of an article in *The Age of Napoleon*.

47 Paul Sauer, *Napoleons Adler über Württemberg, Baden und Hohenzollern*, Stuttgart: Kohlhammer, 1987, pp. 130–1; Gill, *Eagles*, p. 177, n. 112.

48 Five companies of *Franquemont* and two guns remained attached to Beaumont's division until mid-August (Gill, *Eagles*, pp. 167–8).

49 For actions of Lefebvre and Somariva in June–July, see *Eagles*, pp. 107–10, 117.

50 Jean-Pierre Haimart to his parents, 8 September 1809, 'Lettres d'un Conscrit de 1809', *Nouvelle Revue de Champagne et de Brie*, 1924, p. 218.

51 Lefebvre to Napoleon, 12 August 1809, in Derrécagaix, *Tyrol*, pp. 251–2.

52 The Italian troops were probably Levié's. It is not clear whether Fiorella actually accompanied the advancing column or remained in Verona (Zanoli, p. 100).

53 Napoleon to Berthier, 29 August 1809, *Correspondance*, 15725; Robinet de Cléry, *En Tyrol*, pp. 115–16.

54 Vaudoncourt, vol. II, pp. 10–11; J. Hirn, p. 700.

55 This section is largely drawn from Gill, *Eagles*, especially chs 4, 7, 8.

56 For Lefebvre's relief and Franco-Bavarian tensions, see *Eagles*, ch. 7.

57 'Instruction pour le Vice-Roi d'Italie', 14 October 1809, *Correspondance*, no. 15945.

58 C. Baur, *Der Krieg in Tirol während des Feldzugs 1809*, Munich: Baur, 1812, p. 150.

59 Eugene to Auguste, 10 November 1809, du Casse, *Eugène*, vol. VI, p. 113.

60 Criste, *Carl*, vol. III, pp. 267–77.

61 Although he was *de facto* head of the Foreign Affairs Ministry, Metternich had no official position at this point and thus went by the catch-all title 'Minister of State'.

62 The Kaiser's instructions for Metternich in *Memoirs of Prince Metternich*, New York: Scribner's, 1880, vol. II, pp. 367–8; see also Just, *Friede*, p. 45; and Johann, *Feldzugserzählungen*, p. 208.

63 Champagny to Napoleon, 8 September 1809, in Wertheimer, vol. II, p. 401. Also Enno Kraehe, *Metternich's German Policy*, Princeton: Princeton University Press, 1963, pp. 92–6; and Vandal, vol. II, pp. 119–29.

64 Champagny, p. 113.

65 The tsar's answer was vague, but it was enough for Napoleon to clarify his position in the peace talks. Vandal, vol. II, pp. 133–40; Just, *Schönbrunn*, pp. 51–2.

66 Franz's instructions in Criste, *Liechtenstein*, p. 145. A Prussian representative at Franz's court reported of Liechtenstein that 'he has a passion to be charged with negotiations for which he has neither the talent nor the knowledge' (Wertheimer, vol. II, p. 418).

67 Kraehe, pp. 114–16; Wertheimer, *Geschichte*, vol. II, p. 420; Alan Palmer, *Metternich*, New York: Harper & Row, 1972, p. 71.

68 Rössler, *Österreichs Kampf*, vol. II, pp. 59–79.

69 Napoleon reduced the demand from 100 million to 75 million gulden, but Champagny, on his own initiative, told Liechtenstein that 85 million was the lowest acceptable amount.

70 Criste, *Liechtenstein*, pp. 147–8.

71 Both quotations from Champagny, p. 116. See also Rapp, pp. 141–8; Lefebvre, vol. IV, pp. 342–4.

72 Joseph to Johann, 22 August 1809; things were no better on 20 September, Domanovszky, *Palatin Josephs Schriften*, vol. IV, pp. 112, 119.

73 Beer, pp. 430–50. Ferdinand von Strantz, 'Rückzug des kaiserlich–königlich östreichischen VII. Armeekorps aus Polen im Jahre 1809', *Zeitschrift für Kunst, Wissenschaft und Geschichte des Krieges*, vol. XXVI, 1832, pp. 1–10. Sickness figures from 'Früh-Rapport' summary for 5 September 1809, KAFA, Kart. 1389.

74 Odonell to Stadion, 20 September 1809, Wertheimer, vol. II, p. 413.

75 Gaede, pp. 139–60.

76 Joseph to Johann, 22 August 1809, Domanovszky, *Palatin Josephs Schriften*, vol. IV, p. 112.

77 Friedrich Gentz to Adair, 16 September 1809, in Clemens von Klinkowström, *Aus der alten Registratur der Staatskanzlei*, Vienna: Braumüller, 1870, p. 40; also letters to Liechtenstein and Bubna in Criste, *Liechtenstein*, pp. 145–6, 227–8.

78 Such as forcing Franz's abdication or eradicating the entire dynasty.

79 Napoleon to Alexander, 10 October 1809, *Correspondence*, no. 15926. Champagny recorded that 'he [Napoleon] could not be dissatisfied with the treaty', Champagny, p. 119. On St Helena, Napoleon regretted his decision, Marie-Joseph Las Cases, *Memoirs of the Life, Exile, and Conversations of the Emperor Napoleon*, New York, 1890, vol. II, p. 109.

80 'Situation du Armée d'Allemagne, comparé au 15. juin et au 15. juillet' and 'Situation de l'Armée au 1er Septembre 1809', AG, C2/520.

81 Kircheisen, *Gespräche Napoleons*, vol. II, p. 79.

82 Buat, vol. II, p. 387.

83 Ibid., p. 393.

EPILOGUE

1 Stutterheim, p. XVI.

2 Charles, *Ausgewählte Schriften*, vol. VI, p. 300.

3 Schroeder offers a different interpretation, seeing the war as an effort to 'revive a sphere' that would permit other states to 'live in tolerable security and independence with a still dominant Napoleonic France' (Paul W. Schroeder, 'Preventive War to Restore Order and Stabilize the International System', paper presented at the International Studies Association annual meeting, 26 March 2008, www.allacademic.com).

4 Beer, '. . . ins Ziellose verrannte', p. 311.

5 Clausewitz, pp. 583–4.

6   Delbrück was piercingly trenchant in his criticism of Charles. This sentence combines quotations from two of his works: 'Erzherzog Carl', in *Erinnerungen, Aufsätze und Reden*, Berlin: Stilke, 1902, p. 603, and *The Dawn of Modern Warfare*, Lincoln: University of Nebraska Press, 1990, vol. IV, p. 436; second quotation: Peter Paret, *Yorck and the Era of Prussian Reform*, Princeton: Princeton University Press, 1966, p. 199. See also Rothenberg, *Adversaries*, pp. 103, 124; *Last Victory*, pp. 42–7, 82, 215; and a fine, balanced summary by Lee W. Eysturlid, *The Formative Influences, Theories, and Campaigns of the Archduke Carl of Austria*, Westport: Greenwood, 2000.

7   Radetzky, 'Erinnerungen', p. 69.

8   Said to Jean Gérard Lacuée, Comte de Cessac, January 1810, Albert Beugnot, *Mémoires*, Paris: Dentu, 1868, vol. I, p. 425. Jomini later quoted Napoleon as saying 'of all my enemies, the Austrians at Essling and at Wagram seem to me the most respectable' (as told to Eugen of Württemberg, related in his *Memoiren*, Frankfurt an der Oder: Haarnecker, 1862, vol. I, p. 233).

9   Pelet, vol. IV, p. 166.

10 Buat, vol. II, p. 397.

11 Karl Wilhelm Ferdinand von Funck, *In Russland und Sachsen 1812–1815*, Dresden: Heinrich, 1935, p. 307. Funck concluded by noting that 'because of the high degree of intelligence among the common French soldiers, the lack of officers was not visible as quickly as it would have been in other armies.'

12 Thierry Lentz, 'L'Empire napoléonien dans la Tourmente', *Zusammenfassung der Beiträge zum Napoleon Symposium 'Feldzug 1809'*, Vienna: Delta Druckproduktionen, 2009, pp. 13–19.

13 Some of Lee's statements in this regard are strikingly similar to Napoleon's.

14 Montesquiou-Fezensac, p. 129.

15 In addition to the points outlined below, it is interesting to note that 1809 was a 'year of emergence' for the Rheinbund armies as they assumed a front-line role in many of the war's major battles, particularly per force of circumstances, during the opening campaign.

16 Schroeder describes this as a 'turning point' and highlights that this Franco-Austrian alliance meant only Russia and Great Britain were left to oppose Napoleon from 1810 to 1813, *Transformation*, p. 370.

17 See Vol. II, p. 35.

18 Hormayr, *Lebensbilder*, vol. I, p. 223. On St Helena, Napoleon remarked 'I committed a great fault after the Battle of Wagram in not reducing the power of Austria still more' (Las Cases, vol. II, part 3, pp. 103–4).

19 The phrase 'harsh but not catastrophic' is from Englund, p. 347. 'Political existence' from Friedrich Wilhelm III's statement before the war (vol. I, p. 17). It is worth noting that Napoleon never called upon Prussia to provide the 12,000 men it had agreed to supply under the 1808 agreement.

20 Mikhaïlowitch, *Alexandre*, p. 65.

21 Friedrich Wilhelm III to the Prince of Orange, 23 August 1809, Colenbrander, vol. V, p. 813. For similar comments from Metternich to Franz in August, see Wilhelm Oncken, *Das Zeitalter der Revolution, des Kaiserreiches und der Befreiungskriege*, Berlin: Grote, 1886, p. 441.

22 Savary, vol. IV, p. 145.

23 Philip G. Dwyer, 'Self-Interest versus the Common Cause: Austria, Prussia, and Russia against Napoleon', *Journal of Strategic Studies*, vol. XXXI, no. 4, August 2008, p. 624; Schroeder, *Transformation*, p. 362. Dwyer points out that what he terms the 'eastern empires' faced an especially thorny challenge in trying to reconcile popular participation in war with fundamental monarchical principles.

APPENDICES

1 From Just, 'Herzogtum Warschau'. Artillery distribution from Edmund Finke, *Geschichte des k. u. k. ungarischen Infanterie-Regimentes Nr. 37 Erzherzog Joseph*, Vienna: St Norbertus, 1896, p. 680.

2 This list of units, strengths, and locations is taken from Angeli, vol. IV, pp. 589–90. Note, however, that Angeli overlooked the 1st Garrison Battalion, so it is not clear if his strength figure includes this battalion.

3 At full strength, a garrison battalion should have had six companies with 1,114 men.

4 KAFA, 1429/6/303 and 1482/6/ad17.

5 Figures are best estimates from the following sources. Polish strengths from Soltyk, p. 119 (except 5th Infantry); Poniatowski's 6 April report gives slightly different numbers (10,058 total). Saxon strengths are from Poniatowski's report (as it is more detailed); Soltyk, followed by Exner, gives the Saxons a total of 1,619 infantry. See also Just, 'Das Herzogthum Warschau', pp. 121–3.

6 Some sources show Polish forces organised into divisions (or legions) at the start of the war, but the army was in such a state of flux in March/April 1809 that these notional orders of battle were not operationally relevant; they are thus omitted here.

7 Polish cavalry regiments each had three squadrons.

8 Schels, 'Feldzug 1809 in Polen'.

9 Soltyk, pp. 176–9 (identity of voltigeurs from Ochwicz, p. 43, stating that there were two companies).

10 Sources include: Latour, 'Geschichte der Operationen des VIIten Armee Korps im Herzogtum Warschau und in Galizien unter Kommando Seiner Königlichen Hoheit des Erzherzogs Ferdinand im Jahre 1809' (Op. J. 40), 9 March 1810, KAFA, *Operationsjournale der Hauptarmee und Korps*, Kart. 1385.

11 It is likely that there were two 3rd Battalion companies here (for a total of fourteen), leaving only four with 3rd Battalion.

12 Three squadrons of *Palatinal* Hussars joined Mohr temporarily sometime after 19 May.

13 According to Latour (Op. J. 40), Schauroth also had a squadron of *Kaiser* Chevaulegers; this may have been a concept, but it does not appear that it was implemented.

14 Strength derived by subtracting known figures from overall garrison strength of 2,600 given in Emil Kipa, *Pod Zamosciem w Roku 1809*, Zamosc: Pomaranski, n.d., p. 6.

15 Organisation from Welden, ch. 5. Strengths from the end of May ('Stand- und Dienstabelle für den Monat Mai 1809', 24 June 1809, KAFA, 1482/5/27; Romberg to Ferdinand, 2 June 1809, 1482/6/3).

16 This is the figure in the monthly report of May for the entire regiment, but this likely only applied to the largest element of the regiment.

17 As noted above, this was apparently fourteen companies, the first two battalions, plus two companies from the 3rd.

18 There were three Galician *Freikorps* battalions, 1st and 3rd were designated 'East Galician', the 2nd 'West Galician'. This battalion had been part of the Warsaw garrison (KAFA, Kart. 1385).

19 Austrian authorities considered many depot troops unreliable and removed some to Hungary to stem desertion (Steiner, p. 7). Those that remained seem to have been formed into two composite battalions.

20 Soltyk, pp. 259–67.

21 These units were designated as 'Franco-Galician' in an attempt to cater to Russian anxiety about an enlarged Polish military.

22 Basic order of battle is from Just, 'Politik', pp. 76–7, and Welden, pp. 35–6 with confirmation and clarifications supplied by Dr Alex Mikaberidze utilising RGVIA/FVUA, 3360 and 3365a; also Alexander to Golitsyn, 9 (21) April 1809, RGVIA/FVUA, 3369. Dr Mikaberidze has been enormously thorough, thoughtful, and generous with his time. Additional thanks go to the helpful Alexander Zhmodikov and Robert Goetz. Spellings of Russian names adopted from Alexander Mikaberidze, *The Russian Officer Corps in the Revolutionary and Napoleonic Wars 1792–1815*, New York: Savas Beatie, 2005. Strength estimate based on: 2,000/infantry regiment, 1,400/Jäger regiment, 125–50/cavalry squadron, 500/Cossack regiment (pulk).

23 There are convincing indications that Lambert commanded this division during June after Gorchakov's departure and before Dolgorukov's arrival.

24 Some Austrian sources mention the 25th rather than the 24th Division.

25 Welden, p. 13; Zwiedineck-Südenhorst, *Erzherzog Johann im Feldzuge von 1809*, appendix.

26 Colloredo-Mannsfeld promoted to FML on 17 June.

27 The 1st and 3rd Graz Battalions, large portions of which had been captured at Laibach, had been dissolved and remaining troops absorbed into the other three battalions (Hummel, p. 9).

28 Probably included remnants of 3rd, and 4th Battalions; possibly 1st as well.

29 Johann listed as two battalions, but regimental history states its remnants were consolidated into one.

30 Though listed as two battalions, the *Lusignan* detachment apparently consisted of fugitives from the Tyrol and the men of the depot division that joined Johann in Graz.

31 The other two squadrons of *Ott* were in Pettau.

32 Like several other hussar regiments, *Blankenstein* formed a fifth division (two squadrons) during the war. This division apparently achieved organisation early enough to join Johann's army in early June (possibly along with the reserve squadron); transferred to the Hauptarmee prior to Wagram.

33　Strengths from Kiss, pp. 142–3 as of 12 June. These were the figures presented to Nugent by Joseph's chief of staff and probably represented 'effectives', including sick, detached, etc.

34　Sources: Army of Italy, 'Situation Sommaire', 25 May, in Army of Germany, 'Livret de Situation', 1 June 1809, AG, C2/675; Pelet, vol. IV. The Fourth Battalions of 9th and 84th Ligne had been sent back to Italy for fortress and line of communications duties. At some point in June, the squadron of 1st Italian Chasseurs may have joined the main body of Eugene's army.

35　Losses for 25 May Battle of St Michael apparently subtracted.

36　French sources differ as to whether these battalions of the 67th and 93rd were Third or Fourth Battalions; I have opted here to use 3rd as in both regimental histories and Army of Italy returns.

37　Location of this squadron in June is uncertain. All of the Army of Italy's official situation reports from 25 June through 1 August place it with Rusca's division; however, some viable sources (eg Zanoli, p. 98) place it at Wagram. If it spent time with the main body, the dates are not known.

38　The 'Situation' lists this as one squadron, but it is possible this was both III and IV.

39　Demuth manuscript; brigadiers from Stutterheim.

40　Mecséry took command of this district after the death of FML Peter Freiherr Ott on 10 May.

41　An additional cavalry regiment was formed from Arad in October (Wrede, vol. V, chart XXII).

42　Hadik was promoted to FML on 16 May 1809.

43　Zweidineck-Südenhorst, *Erzherzog Johann im Feldzuge von 1809*, appendix, with elaborations and Insurrection strengths from Veress (pp. 133–4). Kiss (pp. 142–3) gives higher Insurrection strengths; these were the figures provided to Johann by the Insurrection staff on 12 June and are shown in Appendix 3. I have used Veress figures for Raab because they match those in Insurrection after-action reports (KAFA) and seem to represent troops 'present under arms' rather than total 'effectives' (the latter would include sick, detached, etc); providing both sets is intended to inform readers. See also Istvan Nagy-Luttenberger, 'Einteilung und Stärke der Armee von Innerösterreich im Feldzug von Ungarn', *Zusammenfassung der Beiträge zum Napoleon Symposium 'Feldzug 1809'*, Vienna: Delta Druckproduktionen, 2009, pp. 200–5.

44　A division of *Blankenstein* was under Siegenfeld at Romand on 14 June. It is possible, but unconfirmed, that the *Blankenstein* Reserve Squadron was present on the right flank with the other depot cavalry. The regiment recorded no casualties in the battle.

45　Johann listed as two battalions, but regimental history states its remnants were consolidated into one.

46　Included remnants of other Salzburg battalions.

47　This battalion is absent (usually assumed to be detached with Siegenfeld) in most orders of battle. Its subordination during the battle is unclear (probably Marziani), but the 163 casualties it suffered attest to its presence on the field ('Verzeichniss der am 13ten und 14ten Juny 809 in der Action bey Raab Verlust', KAFA).

48　Joseph specifically gave this strength figure in a 20 June note to Franz (KAFA).

49 Though listed as two battalions, the *Lusignan* detachment apparently consisted of fugitives from the Tyrol and the men of the depot division that joined Johann in Graz.

50 This deployment of detachments adapted from the operations journal, the 'Relation über die Schlacht bei Raab am 14ten Juni 1809', KAFA (though the former states that 300 Insurrection cavalry were attached to Tittus); also Beckers manuscript and Kiss, vol. I, pp. 146, 158. It is possible the Pest squadron from Szent Marton rejoined the left wing prior to the battle. Note that sources vary widely (Kisfaludy: Pest squadron with Siegenfeld, one squadron each of Veszprem at Kisber and Romand). Doubtless owing to its weakness, many sources refer to the *Warasdin-Kreuz* Grenzer as a 'battalion'.

51 This squadron had been under Siegenfeld.

52 French figures: Vignolle, 24 June 1809 letter, *Armée d'Italie*, AG, C4/10; Austrian figures: 'Tagebuch der Vertheidigung der Festung Raab', KAFA, *Operationsjournale der Hauptarme und Korps*, Kart. 1388. One of the biggest discrepancies is the 800 men from *Vukassovich*; as this large number agrees with the regimental history (Hold, p. 68), it seems that the French figures are more accurate.

53 Sources: Army of Italy, 'Situation Sommaire', 25 May, in AG, C2/675. Strengths, therefore, do *not* account for losses on 5–13 June. Colbert's and Jacquinot's brigades from Bowden/Tarbox, p. 154 (Pelet, vol. IV, gives the brigades total strengths of 1,769 and 1,566 respectively). Baden troops from Lauriston report of 13 June 1809, AG, C2/510. At some point in June, the squadron of 1st Italian Chasseurs may have joined the main body of Eugene's army; it is not clear that it was present at Raab. Note that Veress grossly overestimates French strength (adding Pajol to Montbrun, arming Eugene with far too many artillery pieces, etc). He also misrepresents French orders of battle (perhaps following Welden's mistaken lead), citing, for example, fictitious designations such a '6th Corps' in the Army of Italy; Napoleon did not assign numbers to Eugene's subordinate formations and no such designations appear in any French documentation.

54 Réthoré, p. 246. The regimental lists these battalions as II and III, but I have used here the designations from the 25 June 'Situation' (I, IV).

55 Woinovich, *Kämpfe an der Lika*, p. 10.

56 This figure is a guess based on a low estimate of 150 men per company plus 300 Serezaner. At full strength, the total for the three Land-battalions plus 360 Serezaner (sixty per regiment) could have been as high as 4,500.

57 'Situation', 15 April 1809, AG, C6/15; guns from Marmont, vol. III, p. 133.

58 Anders, *ÖMZ*, 1833, pp. 263–5, 272.

59 Reissenfels certainly had at least two companies; I estimate he had three. Austrian sources often speak of these three as a 'battalion', and Veyder states that they totalled 600 men (Op. J. 46). Tyrolian companies varied widely, but may be estimated at 100 per company.

60 Comprised of Schützen detached from Klagenfurt Landwehr.

61 Strengths as for 20 May (Saski, vol. III), Wrede's division would have been approximately 500 men stronger on 12 May (deducting 459 casualties from 12 to 19 May); Bezzel, 'Grenzschutze', p. 173.

62 'Aufstellung', c.1 June 1809, KAFA, *8. Korps (Chasteler Tirol)*, Kart. 1437.

63 Army of Italy, 'Situation Sommaire', 25 May, in AG, C2/675.

64 Location of this squadron in June is uncertain; see Appendix 5.

65 The 'Situation' lists this as one squadron, but it is possible this was both III and IV. The next 'Situation' (25 June) gives this detachment only 58 officers and men.

66 Gyulai's organisational structure changed frequently and is poorly recorded. This estimate is based on: basic organisation from Tepperberg, pp. 64–6, with variations from June–July 'Früh-Rapports' (strengths from 'Früh-Rapport von 16ten bis Ultimo Juny 809'), KAFA, Kart. 1404; 'Brigade Eintheilung' schemes of 10 June and 4 July, Op. J. 59; and Wengen, 13. Dragoner-Regiments, p. 627.

67 Though listed as two battalions in the 'Früh-Rapport', this was actually one and one-half, as half of 1st Battalion was at Pressburg.

68 Note that this assumes that the formation of 1st Massal into three battalions occurred before July: 16–30 June 'Früh-Rapport' shows the regiment with two battalions; 1–15 July report shows three.

69 For Broussier: 'Situation Sommaire', 25 June 1809, AG, C2/509; for 6th Hussars (forgotten in the 'Situation'), I have simply brought forward the previous 515. For Marmont: 'Situation', 15 June 1809, AG, C6/15. It is not clear how many guns Clauzel had, nor what, if any, of Marmont's total 259 cavalry were on hand (the 'Situation' lists a detachment of 135 men from 6th Hussars with Marmont, but it unclear when this attachment was made). Note that Broussier's journal claims he only had some 3,500 men.

70 'Situation', 1 June 1809, AG, C2/510.

71 'Situation', 2 June 1809, AG, C2/510. In Napoleon's original concept, this division was to include 3rd Berg Infantry and the Baden Hussars, but the Berg regiment went to Jerome and the weak Baden squadron stayed near Lake Constance.

72 Wengen, Badischen Truppen, p. 50.

73 10th Corps, 'Situation', 31 May 1809, AG, C2/509.

74 Shown with his French rank (rather than Lt. Gen.) as he was a Frenchman in Dutch service and better known under this rank.

75 J. von Raeder, Danmarks Krigs- og Politiske Historie, Copenhagen: Reitzel, 1852, vol. III, pp. 450–1; Bardenfleth, p. 100.

76 'Operations Journal des gegen Sachsen und Bayreuth operierenden Corps unter G.d.C. Bron Kienmayer 1809', KAFA, Operationsjournale der Hauptarmee und Korps, Kart. 1388; Dechend, p. 252. Strengths for the Brunswick troops at this early stage are unclear; the number given (from Austrian records) probably indicates the total that initially marched into Saxony.

77 Theoretically, this regiment was composed of eight squadrons.

78 Compiled from: 'Livret de Situation', 1 June 1809, AG, C2/675; 'Livret de Situation', 15 July 1809, AG, C2/676; Junot, 'Situation Journalier', 27 June 1809, AG, C2/508; Beaumont, 'Situation', 30 June 1809, AG, C2/510; Beaumont, 'Etat et l'Emplacement des Postes et Cantonnements', undated [June], AG, C2/510; 'Position der vereinigten Truppen unter dem Commando des General Lieuts. Von Phull', 20 June 1809, HStAS, E270aBü110; Bezzel, 'Grenzschutz', pp. 125–9; Gerneth/Kiesling, pp. 247–51; Wengen, Badischen Truppen, p. 111.

79 Accounts of the campaign against the Vorarlbergers often mention French 'Guard grenadiers'. Such statements are imprecise, probably deriving from two order of

battle features. First, the company in Lindau was a grenadier company of 65th Ligne. Second, the 1st Conscript Grenadiers (1,640) and 1st Conscript Chasseurs (1,680) of the Guard were en route to Augsburg from Strasbourg in early June 1809; it seems that at least the grenadiers (and possibly both) were temporarily diverted to the Vorarlberg front for a week (approximately 11–17 June) before continuing their march ('Livret de Situation', 1 June 1809, AG, C2/675; F. Hirn, *Vorarlberg*, p. 225).

80 Composed of detachments from 9th, 17th, 26th Léger and 3rd, 57th, 105th Ligne (AG, C2/510).

81 Third Division strengths from 15 July 'Situation', AG, C2/507.

82 From 'Früh-Rapports' of 27 June (I, III, IV, V) and 4 July (II, VI, Reserve), KAFA, *Operationsjournale der Hauptarmee und Korps*, Kart. 1389. Names of Landwehr and volunteer commanders included as other sources often use names rather than numbers as references.

83 The *Schlegelberg* Vienna Jägerfreikorps (one company, fifty-seven men) was apparently in Gaunersdorf.

84 According to the regimental history (Grois, p. 237), Hauptmann Hieronimus Jambline assumed command of this battalion before Wagram, but Austrian reports still list it as Puteany through Znaim.

85 Note on artillery: number and distribution of guns/howitzers is unclear, complicated by the inclusion of regimental pieces in June. Numbers in this appendix are taken from corps 'Situations' (which give only corps totals, not distribution); from the 15 July 'Livret' (C2/676), or from Buat, vol. II, pp. 159–66.

86 Imperial Guard, 'Situation', 12 June, AG, C2/505; guns from Litre, pp. 57–9.

87 2nd Corps, 'Situation', 1 July, AG, C2/506 (number of batteries from 15 July 'Situation').

88 3rd Corps 'Situation', 1 July, AG, C2/506; Jacquinot: Cavalry Reserve 'Situation Sommaire', 1 July, AG, C2/510; Montbrun: 30 June report, AG, C2/510; dragoons: Army of Italy, 'Situation Sommaire', 25 June, AG, C2/509.

89 4th Corps 'Situation', 1 July, AG, C2/507; Baden: Lauriston report, 13 June, AG, C2/510; Hessians: Lasalle, 30 June report, AG, C2/510; Lasalle: Cavalry Reserve, 'Situation Sommaire', 1 July, AG, C2/510. Grillot's position as a brigade commander is my assumption (Fririon had become corps chief of staff). Note: all Bavarian troops with Wrede, none assigned to 4th Corps.

90 9th Corps report, 20 June, and 9th Corps 'Situation', 15 June, AG, C2/508. Organisation reflects changes made up to 5 July (Gill, *Eagles*, p. 294). The Saxons had nine howitzers; it is not clear if one was assigned to the putative horse battery or if it was with the corps park. See vol. I, Appendix 2 for grenadier battalion composition. Staff Battalion remained on the south bank with the baggage.

91 Army of Italy, 'Situation Sommaire', 25 June, AG, C2/509; artillery from Buat, vol. II, pp. 162–3; *Historique du 112e Régiment*, p. 50.

92 These two battalions did not rejoin Broussier until 10 July.

93 Though still listed as brigade commander, Valentin had been badly wounded at Raab and likely was not at Wagram.

94 Presence of this squadron at Wagram is uncertain; it seems likely that it was based on: Buat, vol. II, p. 163; Jean-Pierre Perconte, *Les Chasseurs à Cheval Italiens 1800–1814*, Lyon: Perconte, 2008, p. 190; Zanoli, p. 98. However, all of the Army of

Italy's official situation reports from 25 June through 1 August place it with Rusca's division.

95 Assumes three 6-pounders and one howitzer with Grouchy.

96 'Situation Sommaire' 1 July, AG, C2/510.

97 Some sources put St Germain in command of 2nd Division at Wagram. However, St Germain did not replace St Sulpice until after Znaim; newly promoted GB Sigismond Frédéric Berckheim took St Germain's place. See regimental histories of 1st, 3rd, 5th, and 12th Cuirassiers.

98 Detachment of IV/21st Léger based on regimental (Bouvier) and Martinien, IV/103rd Ligne on Martinien (lack of losses). By approximately 24 June, Lobau artillery consisted of thirty 6-pounders, eighteen 12-pounders, eighteen 18-pounders, ten howitzers, and ten mortars. Napoleon ordered a reinforcement of nine 6-pounders, four 12-pounders, six 18-pounders, and eight mortars for a total of 113 pieces, but four of these (unspecified) did not arrive, leaving the number on hand at 109 (Buat, vol. II, pp. 130–3).

99 Excludes other troops previously noted, assumes six guns for the dragoons, assumes six guns for Pachtod.

100 Army of Dalmatia, 'Situation' 1 July, AG, C2/509. Although Marmont (vol. III, p. 218) states he brought his artillery to twenty-four guns while in Laibach, figures from the 1 and 15 July 'Situations' are used here.

101 7th Corps, 'Situation', 2 July, AG, C2/507.

102 'Journal über den Marsch und militärischen Operationen des unter F.M.L. Marquis Sommariva gestandene Arrièrgarde von 27. April bis 21 September 1809' (Op. J. 68), and 'Journal über alle Vorfallenheiten, welche sich bey dem Detachement des Herrn Feldmarschallieutnent marquis Sommariva in Laufe des Feldzugs von 809 zutragen' (Op. J. 69), KAFA, Operationsjournale der Hauptarmee und Korps, Kart. 1387.

103 Strengths from 'Früh-Rapport 15-Ultimo Juny', KAFA, 1404/6/169 (except Sümegh Hussars, 23 June, KAFA, Kart. 1381). Structure from Johann, Feldzugserzählungen, pp. 193–4; Zwiedineck-Südenhorst, Erzherzog Johann im Feldzuge von 1809, p. 140.

104 From hints in Austrian records, it seems that the regiment's Reserve Battalion joined in late June, thus the total of three battalions under Johann.

105 Per the regimental history (Donnersberg, p. 82): the regiment was combined into a single battalion of 500 after the Alte Au engagement of 29–30 June; marched as shown on 5–6 July.

106 This conclusion because they are listed in the 15–30 June 'Früh-Rapport', while none of the Komorn garrison are mentioned. Lusignan and I/Szulin had also come from Komorn.

107 Bianchi, pp. 85, 99.

108 'Situation des Troupes Composant l'Aile Gauche de l'Armée d' Italie', 5 July, AG, C4/10.

109 'Situation', 2 July, AG, C3/4.

110 Württemberg troops, 'Situation', 1 July, AG, C2/508.

111 7th Corps, 'Situation', 1 July, AG, C2/507.

112 The Austrian order of battle changed almost daily, this is a best estimate. Basic structure from Heller, vol. II, pp. 264–6 with modifications from official 'Relations', regimental histories, and other accounts. Strength figures are from 7–10 July

returns (KAFA, Kart. 1461). Units that were effectively destroyed at Wagram are not shown (eg 1st Jägers); units that had not submitted strength returns are shown with a question mark or my estimate. Artillery shown based on 1 July returns (thus aggregated at corps level), many pieces were likely damaged and unavailable on 11 July.

113 Strength returns incomplete, estimates shown with 'c.' include 10 per cent march attrition.

114 Strength returns for III Corps are in some cases *higher* than before Wagram; this seems unlikely, but data is presented here with that caveat.

115 Structure from V Corps, 'Relation', 17 July, KAFA, Kart. 1462. Strengths do not show losses for 10 July.

116 The figure for *Gyulai* seems unusually high and may be an error of transcription.

117 Grenadier Corps, 'Relation', 17 July, KAFA, Kart. 1462.

118 Estimate based on July 'Situations', memoirs, and regimental histories. I have deducted 10 to 20 per cent march attrition. Artillery is estimated based on 1 July availabilities, some pieces were probably damaged or still en route on 11 July.

119 Strength estimate based on comparison of 1 July and 15 July strengths (considering officers losses and actions 7–10 July); further deductions for ten to twenty per cent march attrition.

120 Strength estimate based on assumption of twenty men lost per officer casualty deducted from 1 July strength; further deductions for 10 to 20 per cent march attrition. Officer-to-men loss ratios for the other two heavy divisions varied from 1:10 to 1:20 approximately.

121 1st Heavy Cavalry Division, 'Situation', approximately 8 July, AG, C2/93.

122 As the three infantry divisions had almost no casualties between 4 and 9 July, estimated strengths are based on simple deduction of 10 (shown) to 20 per cent march attrition rounded down.

123 Army of Italy, 'Situation Sommaire', 10 July, AG, C2/509.

124 Report of 1 July, HStAS, E289aBü93.

125 Strengths for July: Gordon Bond, *The Grand Expedition*, Athens, GA: University of Georgia Press, 1979, pp. 167–71.

126 From Kraijenhoff, courteously provided by Geert van Uythoven.

127 Compiled from Bond, p. 173; Pierre Jacques Osten, 'Rapport Circonstancé', *Spectateur Militaire*, vol. XXI, 1836, p. 285; and T. van Gent, *De Engelse invasie van Walcheren in 1809*, Amsterdam: Bataafsche Leeuw, 2001, p. 86.

Bibliography

To know what remains from the old historians, to know all that we have lost, to distinguish the original fragments from supplements written by good or bad commentators, is in itself almost a science, or at least an important object of study. Thus the knowledge and the selection of good historians, good memoirs, and true chronicles of the times is a useful and genuine knowledge.

Napoleon, 'Observations sur un projet d'établissement d'une école spéciale de littérature et d'histoire au collége de France', 17 April 1807, *Correspondance*, no. 12416.

Covering all three volumes, this bibliography includes the works listed in the summary bibliographies in Volumes I and II. Some of the following materials were used extensively, while others were merely scanned, but, for the reader's benefit, it seemed important to list both. Additionally, it is hoped that this will serve as a comprehensive thematic bibliography of the 1809 war for future researchers. There are doubtless lacunae in this list, but it should establish a solid foundation for further investigations into this conflict. See notes for specific citations from the archival materials.

ARCHIVAL MATERIAL

Austria: branches of the Oesterreichisches Staatsarchiv, Vienna
    Haus-, Hof- und Staatsarchiv (HHStA),
    Kriegsarchiv, alte Feldakten (KAFA),
    Nachlässe und Sammlungen (Nachl.)

France
    Archives des Affaires Étrangères, *Correspondance politique: Autriche* (AE), Paris
    Archives de la Guerre (AG), Vincennes
    Archives Nationales (AN), Paris

496 ~ BIBLIOGRAPHY

Germany
Bayerisches Haupstaatsarchiv, Abt. IV—Kriegsarchiv (BKA), Munich
Generallandesarchiv (GLA), Karlsruhe
Sächsisches Hauptstaatsarchiv (SächsHStA), Dresden
Hauptstaatsarchiv Stuttgart (HStAS)

Hungary
Magyar Orszagos Leveltar (MOL), Budapest

Russia
Rossiiskii Gosudarstvennii Voenno-Istoricheskii Arkiv (thanks to Dr Alexander
Mikaberidze)

United Kingdom
Public Record Office, Foreign Office files (PRO/FO), Kew

United States
National Archives (NA), Washington, DC

BIBLIOGRAPHIES, DICTIONARIES, ENCYCLOPEDIAS

Hirtenfeld, Jaromir, *Der Militär-Maria-Theresien-Orden und seine Mitglieder*, Vienna:
Staatsdruckerei, 1857.
Kudrna, Leopold and Digby Smith, 'Biographical Dictionary of All the Austrian
Generals during the French Revolutionary and Napoleonic Wars 1792–1815', at
www.napoleon-series.org.
Martinien, Aristide, *Tableaux par Corps et par Batailles des Officiers Tués et Blessés
pendant les Guerres de l'Empire (1805–1815)*, Paris: Editions Militaires
Européennes, 1984.
Palmer, Alan, *An Encyclopaedia of Napoleon's Europe*, New York: St Martin's Press,
1984.
Pigeard, Alain, *Les Etoiles de Napoléon*, Entremont-le-Vieux: Quator, 1996.
—— *Les Campagnes Napoléoniennes*, Entremont-le-Vieux: Quator, 1998.
Quintin, Danielle and Bernard, *Dictionnaire des Colonels de Napoléon*, Paris: SPM,
1996.
Schmidt-Brentano, Antonio, *Kaiserliche und k. k. Generale (1618–1815)*, Vienna:
Österreichisches Staatsarchiv, 2006.
—— *Die k. k. bzw. k. u. k. Generalität 1816–1918*, Vienna: Österreichisches Staatsarchiv,
2007.
Schröder, Bernd Philipp, *Die Generalität der deutschen Mittelstaaten 1815–1870*,
Osnabrück: Biblio Verlag, 1984.
Six, Georges, *Dictionnaire Biographique des Généraux & Amiraux Français de la
Révolution et de l'Empire*, Paris: Manutention a Mayenne, 1989.

Tulard, Jean, *Nouvelle Bibliographie Critique des Mémoires sur l'Époque Napoléonienne Écrits ou Traduits en Français*, Paris: Droz, 1991.
—— *Dictionnaire Napoléon*, Paris: Fayard, 1987.
Wurzbach, Constant von, *Biographisches Lexikon des Kaiserthums Oesterreich*, Vienna: Zamarski, 1856–91.

MEMOIRS, CORRESPONDENCE, BIOGRAPHIES

Abaut, A., 'Lariboisière', *Revue d'Artillerie*, vol. XXXV, 1889–90.
Abbeel, Joseph, *L'Odyssée d'un Carabinier à Cheval*, ed. Rene H. Willems, Brussels: Meyere, 1969.
Adair, Sir Robert, *The Negotiations for the Peace in the Dardenelles in 1808–9*, London: Longman, Brown, Green, and Longman, 1845.
Allix de Vaux, Jacques Alexandre François, 'Souvenirs Militaires et Politiques', *Journal des Sciences Militaires*, vol. XIX, 1830.
Ameil, Auguste Jean Joseph Gabriel, *Notes et Documents provenant des Archives du Général Baron Ameil*, Paris: Teissedre, 1997.
Am Ende, Christian Gottlob Ernst, *Feldmarschall-Lieutenant Carl Friedrich Am Ende besonders sein Feldzug in Sachsen 1809*, Vienna: Braumüller, 1878.
'Anmerkungen über die im 8ten und 10ten Stück der europäischen Annalen Jahrgang 1810 enthaltene Darstellung der Schlachten auf dem Marchfelde', *Europäische Annalen*, vol. VIII, 1811.
Angeli, Moriz Edlen von, *Erzherzog Carl von Oesterreich als Feldherr und Heeresorganisator*, Vienna: Braumüller, 1897.
Anthouard de Vraincourt, Charles Nicholas comte d', 'Notes et Documents provenant des Archives du Général de Division d'Anthouard', *Carnet de la Sabretache*, 1906.
Arneth, Alfred Ritter von, *Johann Freiherr von Wessenberg*, Vienna: Braumüller, 1898.
Askenazy, Simon, *Le Prince Joseph Poniatowski*, Paris: Plon, 1921.
Aubriet, M. A., *Politische und militärische Lebensgeschichte des Fürsten Eugen*, Speyer: Kolb, 1826.
Augustin-Thierry, A., *Masséna*, Paris: Albin Michel, 1947.
Authentischer Bericht über die Schlacht bei Wagram am 5ten und 6ten July 1809: Von einem Augenzeugen, Hanover: Hahn, 1813.
'Authentische Darstellung des Ungrundes der Beschuldigungen, die in der Druckschrift: Vertheidigung des Brückenkopfes vor Pressburg, enthalten sind', *Europäische Annalen*, vol. I, 1814.
Auvray, Pierre, 'Souvenirs Militaires', *Carnet de la Sabretache*, March 1914.
Bailleu, Paul (ed.), *Briefwechsel König Friedrich Wilhelm's III und der Königin Luise mit Kaiser Alexander I.*, Publikationen aus den Preussischen Staatsarchiven, vol. 75, Leipzig: Hirzel, 1900.
Bangofsky, Georges, 'Les Étapes de Georges Bangofsky', *Mémoires de l'Académie de Stanislas*, vol. I, 1903–4.

Barat, Jean-Claude, 'Les Mémoires du Commandant J.-C. Barat', *Revue du Nivernais*, vol. XIII, 1908–9.

Barton, Sir Dunbar Plunket, *Bernadotte and Napoleon 1799–1810*, London: Murray, 1921.

—— *The Amazing Career of Bernadotte*, London: Murray, 1929.

Baumann, Friedrich, *Skizzen aus den Jugendjahren eines Veteranen*, Berlin: Reinhardt, 1845.

Bausset, Louis François Joseph de, *Private Memoirs of the Court of Napoleon*, Philadelphia: Carey, Lea & Carey, 1828.

'Beiträge zur Geschichte des österreichischen Heerwesens 1809', *Oesterreichische Militärische Zeitschrift*, vol. III, 1869; also as *Beiträge zur Geschichte des österreichischen Heerwesens*, Vienna: Seidel & Sohn, 1872.

Bellot de Kergorre, Alexandre, *Journal d'un Commissaire des Guerres pendant le Premier Empire (1806–1821)*, Paris: La Vouivre, 1997.

'Bemerkungen eines Officiers vom österreichischen Generalstabe zu der in Pesth, im Druck erschienenen Relation über die Schlacht bei Teutsch-Wagram', *Pallas*, vol. III, 1810.

'Bemerkungen über den gegenwärtigen Feldzug', *Minerva*, June 1809.

Béniton, Etienne, *A la Conquête de l'Europe: Souvenirs d'un Soldat de l'Empire*, Paris: Editions du Grenadier, 2002.

'Bericht eines Augenzeugen über die Schlacht bei Deutsch-Wagram', *Minerva*, vol. IV, 1809.

Berthezène, Pierre, *Souvenirs Militaires de la République et de l'Empire*, Paris: Dumaine, 1855.

Bertrand, Henri Gatien, *Cahiers de Sainte-Hélène*, Paris: Flammarion, 1949.

Besse, Jérome-Etienne, 'Mémoires', *Revue de l'Agenais et des Anciennes Provinces du Sud-Ouest*, vol. XIX, 1892.

Bessières, Albert, *Le Bayard de la Grande Armée: Le Maréchal Bessières*, Paris: Charles-Lavauzelle, 1941.

Beugnot, Albert, *Mémoires*, Paris: Dentu, 1868.

Bial, Jean-Pierre, *Souvenirs des Guerres de la Révolution et de l'Empire*, Paris: Pensée Latine, 1927.

Bibl, Viktor, *Der Zerfall Oesterreichs: Kaiser Franz und seine Erbe*, Vienna: Rikola, 1922.

—— *Radetzky: Soldat und Feldherr*, Vienna: Günther, 1955.

—— *Kaiser Franz*, Vienna: Günther, 1958.

Blasendorf, G., 'Fünfzig Briefe Blücher's', *Historische Zeitschrift*, vol. 54, 1885.

Blocqueville, Adélaïde-Louise d'Eckmühl, Marquise de, *Le Maréchal Davout Prince d'Eckmühl*, Paris: Didier, 1879.

Bonaparte, Louis, *Documens Historiques et Réflexions sur le Gouvernement de la Hollande*, Gand: Houdin, 1820.

Bonnefons, André, *Un Allié de Napoléon, Frédéric-Auguste Premier Roi de Saxe et Grand-Duc de Varsovie*, Paris: Perrin, 1902.

Bonnéry, Jean-Louis, *Ledru des Essarts: Un Grand Patriote Sarthois Méconnu*, Le Mans: Imprimerie Maine Libre, 1988.

Borcke, Johann von, *Kriegerleben des Johann von Borcke 1806–1815*, ed. Stanislaus von Leszczynski, Berlin: Mittler & Sohn, 1888.

Boulart, Jean François, *Mémoires Militaires*, Paris: Librairie Illustrée, 1892 (reprinted Paris: Tallandier, 1992).

Boyeldieu, Louis Léger, 'Itinéraire et Notes Historiques du 4e Régiment de Ligne', in Léon Charles Emile Auguste Loÿ, 'Le Général de Division Baron Boyeldieu', *Carnet de la Sabretache*, August 1914–May 1919.

Brack, Antoine Fortune de, *Avant-Postes de Cavalerie Légère*, Paris: Aux Trois Hussards, 1984.

Bro, Louis, *Mémoires*, Paris: Plon, 1914.

Buhle, Carl, *Erinnerungen aus den Feldzügen von 1809 bis 1816*, Bautzen: Schlüssel, 1844.

Bunbury, Sir Henry, *A Narrative of Military Transactions in the Mediterranean 1805–1810*, London: Boone, 1851.

Brandner, F. A., *Aus dem Tagebuch eines österreichischen Soldaten im Jahre 1809*, Lobau: J. Breyer, n.d.

Brun, Louis Bertrand Pierre, *Les Cahiers du Général Brun*, Paris: Plon, 1953.

[Bruyère, Jean Pierre Joseph], 'Notices Historiques et Topographiques sur les Marches et Combats des Troupes aux Ordres du Général Bruyère en 1809', *Carnet de la Sabretache*, 1909.

Bucher, Ludwig Ferdinand, 'Erlebnisse aus dem Jahre 1809', *Miscellanea Napoleonica*, 1895.

Cambacérès, Jean-Jacques-Régis, *Mémoires Inédits*, Paris: Perrin, 1999.

Castellane, Espirit Victor Elisabeth Boniface de, *Journal du Maréchal de Castellane*, Paris: Plon, 1895.

Castillon, Jean François Antoine Marie, 'Mémorial Militaire', *Carnet de la Sabretache*, 1902.

Castex, Bernard Pierre, 'Quatre Lettres du Colonel Castex', *Carnet de la Sabretache*, 1903.

Caulaincourt, Armand de, *Memoirs of General de Caulaincourt*, London: Cassell, 1935.

Chandler, David G. (ed.), *Napoleon's Marshals*, New York: Macmillan, 1987.

Charles, Archduke of Austria, *Ausgewählte Schriften*, Vienna: Braumüller, 1893–4.

[Charles], *Warum benutzten die Oesterreicher den Sieg von Aspern nicht zu einer offensiven Operation auf das rechte Donauufer?*, Pest, 1811.

Chlapowski, Dezydery (Désiré), *Mémoires sur les Guerres de Napoléon 1806–1813*, Paris: Plon, 1908.

Chenier, L.-J. Gabriel de, *Histoire de la Vie Politique, Militaire et Administrative du Maréchal Davout*, Paris: Cosse, Marchal et Cie, 1866.

Chevalier, Jean Michel, *Souvenirs des Guerres Napoléoniennes*, Paris: Hachette, 1970.

Chevillet, Jacques, *Ma Vie Militaire*, Paris: Hachette, 1906.

Coignet, Jean-Roche, *The Note-Books of Captain Coignet*, London: Greenhill, 1989.

Cole, Hubert, *Fouché: The Unprincipled Patriot*, New York: McCall, 1971.

Colenbrander, H. T., *Gedenkstukken der Gemeene Geschiedenis van Nederland*, The Hague: Nijhoff, 1909.

—— *Willem I Koning der Nederlanden*, Amsterdam: Meulenhoff, 1921.

Collingwood, Lord Cuthbert, *Selection from the Public and Private Correspondence of Vice-Admiral Lord Collingwood Interspersed with Memoirs of His Life*, ed. G. L. Newnham Collingwood, New York: Carvill, 1829.

Comeau de Charry, Baron Sébastien Joseph de, *Souvenirs des Guerres d'Allemagne pendant la Révolution et l'Empire*, Paris: Plon, 1900.

Cooper, Duff, *Talleyrand*, London: Cape, 1939.

Corti, Count Egon César, *Ludwig I of Bavaria*, London: Thornton Butterworth, 1938.

Coudreux, Alexander, *Lettres du Commandant Coudreux a Son Frère 1804–1815*, ed. Gustave Schlumberger, Paris: Plon, 1908.

Criste, Oskar, *Feldmarschall Johannes Fürst von Liechtenstein*, Vienna: Seidel & Sohn, 1905.

—— *Erzherzog Karl und die Armee*, vol. V of *Das Kriegsjahr 1809 in Einzeldarstellungen*, ed. Emil von Woinovich and Alois Veltzé, Vienna: Stern, 1906.

—— *Erzherzog Carl von Oesterreich: Ein Lebensbild*, Vienna: Braumüller, 1912.

Crossard, Jean Baptiste Baron de, *Mémoires Militaires et Historiques*, Paris: Migneret, 1829.

Curély, Jean Nicolas, *Itinéraire d'un Cavalier Léger de la Grande Armée*, Paris: Librairie des Deux Empires, 1999.

[Czetteritz und Neuhaus, von], 'Erinnerungen eines Kavallerie-Offiziers', *Zeitschrift für Kunst, Wissenschaft und Geschichte des Krieges*, 1838–9.

Damas, Roger de, *Mémoires*, Paris: Plon, 1912–14.

Dard, Emile, *Napoleon and Talleyrand*, London: Philip Allan, 1937.

'Darstellung der Schlachten auf dem Marchfelds', *Europäische Annalen*, vols VII, VIII, X, 1810.

Davout, Marshal Louis-Nicolas, *Correspondance de Maréchal Davout*, ed. Charles de Mazade, Paris: Plon, 1885.

Deifl, Josef, *Infanterist Deifl. Ein Tagebuch aus napoleonischer Zeit*, ed. Eugen von Frauenholz, Munich: Beck, 1939.

Delmarche, Joachim, *Les Soirées du Grenadier Delmarche*, Philippeville: Musée de Cerfontaine, 1980.

Denmark, General Staff, *Meddelelser fra Krigsarkiverne*, Copenhagen: Hegel, 1890.

Derrécagaix, Victor Bernard, *Le Maréchal Berthier*, Paris: Chapelot, 1905.

Desboeufs, Marc, *Souvenirs du Capitaine Desboeufs*, Paris: Picard, 1901.

Desplat, Christian, 'Bernadotte—Soldat und Feldherr', in *Jean Baptiste Bernadotte: Bürger—Marschall—König*, exhibition catalogue, Boras: Kulturreferat Schloss Mainau, 1998.

Dieffenbach, L. Ferdinand, *Karl Ludwig Schulmeister*, Leipzig: Webel, 1879.

Doher, Marcel, *Charles de La Bédoyère*, Paris: Peyronnet, 1963.

Dormann, Hasso, *Feldmarschall Fürst Wrede*, Munich: Süddeutscher Verlag, 1982.

Dorsch, Paul (ed.), *Kriegszüge der Württemberger im 19. Jahrhundert*, Calw: Vereinsbuchhandlung, 1913.

Douay, Abel and Gérard Hertault, *Schulmeister*, Paris: Nouveau Monde, 2002.

Drimmel, Heinrich, *Kaiser Franz*, Vienna: Amalthea, 1981.

Drujon de Beaulieu, 'Mémoires', in Alain Pigeard (ed.), *Mémoires d'Empire*, Annecy: Quator, 1997.

Drouet, Comte d'Erlon, Jean Baptiste, *Le Maréchal Drouet, Comte d'Erlon: Vie Militaire*, Paris: Barba, 1844.

Dubouloz-Dupas, Ferdinand and André Folliet, *Le Général Dupas*, Paris: Chapelot, 1899.

Du Casse, Albert, *Mémoires et correspondance politique et militaire du Prince Eugène*, Paris: Lévy, 1858–60.

—— *Mémoires et Correspondance du Roi Jérome et de la Reine Catherine*, Paris: Dentu, 1861–8.

—— *Le Général Vandamme et sa Correspondance*, Paris: Didier, 1870.

—— *Les Rois Frères de Napoléon Ier*, Paris: Baillière, 1883.

Dumas, Count Mathieu, *Memoirs of his Own Time*, Philadelphia: Lea & Blanchard, 1839.

Dumonceau, François, *Mémoires*, Brussels: Brepols, 1958.

Dupuy, Victor, *Souvenirs Militaires*, Paris: Lévy, 1892.

Duriau, François, *Carnet de Route*, extract from *Mémoires de la Société Dunkerquoise*, 1907.

Eissen, Georges Geoffrey, letter to his father, in Paul Schmid, 'La Défense et la Capitulation de Ratisbonne', *Carnet de la Sabretache*, June 1909.

Englund, Steven, *Napoleon: A Political Life*, New York: Scribner, 2004.

Epstein, Robert M., *Prince Eugene at War*, Arlington, Texas: Empire Press, 1984.

Ernouf, Alfred Auguste, *Maret Duc de Bassano*, Paris: Perrin, 1884.

Espinchal, Hippolyte d', *Souvenirs Militaires*, Paris: Ollendorf, 1901.

Eysturlid, Lee W., *The Formative Influences, Theories, and Campaigns of the Archduke Carl of Austria*, Westport: Greenwood, 2000.

Fairon, Emile and Herni Heuse, *Lettres des Grognards*, Liege: Bénard, 1936.

Faré, Charles A., *Lettres d'un Jeune Officier a sa Mère*, Paris: Delgrave, 1889.

Fezensac, Raymond-Aimery-Philippe-Joseph de Montesquiou, *Souvenirs Militaires de 1804 à 1814*, Paris: Dumaine, 1870.

Flahaut, Jean, *Charles-Louis Cadet de Gassicourt: Bâtard Royal, Pharmacien de l'Empereur*, Paris: Teissedre, 2001.

Fouché, Joseph, *Memoirs Relating to Fouché*, New York: Sturgis & Walton, 1912.

Frèche, Louis, *Mémoire de mes Campagnes (1803–1809)*, ed. Fernand Beaucour, Levallois: Centre d'Etudes Napoléoniennes, 1994.

Frenzel, Christian Friedrich, *Erinnerungen eines sächsischen Infanteristen an die napoleonischen Kriege*, ed. Sebastien Schaar, Dresden: Thelem, 2008.

Friant, Jean François, *Vie Militaire du Lieutenant-Général Comte Friant*, Paris: Dentu, 1857.

Funck, Karl Wilhelm Ferdinand von, *In the Wake of Napoleon, Being the Memoirs (1807–1809) of Ferdinand von Funck, Lieutenant-General of the Saxon Army and Adjutant-General to the King of Saxony*, ed. Oakley Williams, London: Lane, 1931.

—— *In Russland und Sachsen 1812–1815*, Dresden: Heinrich, 1935.

Gachot, Edouard, *1809 Napoléon en Allemagne*, vol. VI of *Histoire Militaire de Massena*, Paris: Plon, 1913.

Gallaher, John G., *The Iron Marshal*, Carbondale and Evansville: Southern Illinois University Press, 1976.

—— *Napoleon's Irish Legion*, Carbondale and Evansville: Southern Illinois University Press, 1993.

—— *Napoleon's Enfant Terrible: General Dominique Vandamme*, Norman: University of Oklahoma Press, 2008.

Gallavresi, Giuseppe and Victor Sallier de La Tour de Cordon, *Le Maréchal Sallier de La Tour*, vol. VIII of *Biblioteca di Storia Italiana Recente*, Turin: Bocca, 1917.

Garnier, Auguste, *Notice sur le Général Delzons*, Paris: Belin, 1863.

Gassicourt, Charles Louis Cadet de, *Voyage en Autriche, en Moravie et en Bavière fait a la suite de l'Armée Française pendant la Campagne de 1809*, Paris: L'Huillier, 1818.

'Das Gefecht bei Linz am 17. Mai 1809', *Zeitschrift für Kunst, Wissenschaft und Geschichte des Krieges*, vol. IV, 1828.

Germain, Pierre, J.-B. *Drouët d'Erlon, Maréchal de France*, Paris: Lanore, 1985.

Gersdorff, General-Lieutenant von, 'Zwei Schreiben veranlasst durch eine Stelle in den *Notes et mélanges, redigis par le Comte Montholon*', *Militair-Wochenblatt*, no. 353, 29 March 1823.

Girault, Philippe Réne, *Mes Campagnes sous la Révolution et l'Empire*, Paris: Le Sycomore, 1983.

Goergler, Laurent, *Georges Mouton Comte de Lobau*, Drulingen: Scheuer, 1998.

Goethe, Theodor, *Aus dem Leben eines sächsischen Husaren und aus dessen Feldzügen 1809, 1812 und 1813 in Polen und Russland*, Leipzig: Hinrich, 1853.

Gonneville, Aymar Oliver Le Harivel de, *Recollections of Colonel de Gonneville*, Felling: Worley, 1988 (reprint of 1875 edition).

Granier, Herman (ed.), *Berichte aus der Berliner Franzosenzeit 1807–1809*, vol. 88 of *Publikationen aus den Preussischen Staatsarchiven*, Leipzig: Hirzel, 1913.

Griewank, Karl, *Gneisenau: Ein Leben in Briefen*, Leipzig: Koehler & Amelang, 1939.

Gross, Johann C. *Erinnerungen aus den Kriegsjahren*, Leipzig: Voss, 1850.

Grouchy, Emmanuel, *Mémoires*, Paris: Dentu, 1873.

Grueber, Karl Johann Ritter von, *Lebenserinnerungen eines Reiteroffiziers vor Hundert Jahren*, Vienna: Seidel & Sohn, 1906.

Grunwald, Constantin de, 'La Fin d'une Ambassade: Metternich à Paris en 1808–1809', *Revue de Paris*, 1 and 15 October 1937.

Gueulluy, Marie Théodore, comte de Rumigny, *Souvenirs*, Paris: Émile-Paul, 1921.

Guglia, Eugen, *Kaiserin Maria Ludovica*, Vienna: Graeser, 1894.

Haimart, Jean-Pierre, 'Lettres d'un Conscrit de 1809', *Nouvelle Revue de Champagne et de Brie*, vol. II, 1924.

Hastrel, Etienne, Baron d', 'Mémoires du Général Baron d'Hastrel', *Carnet de la Sabretache*, 1934.

Hausmann, Cynthia Joy and John H. Gill (eds), *A Soldier for Napoleon: The Campaigns of Franz Joseph Hausmann, 7th Bavarian Infantry*, London: Greenhill, 1998.

Heilmann, Johann von, *Leben des Grafen Bernhard Erasmus v. Deroy*, Augsburg: Rieger, 1855.

—— *Feldmarschall Fürst Wrede*, Leipzig: Duncker & Humblot, 1881.

Helfert, Joseph Alexander Freiherr von, *Maria Louise, Erzherzogin von Oesterreich, Kaiserin von Frankreich*, Vienna: Braumüller, 1873.

—— *Königin Karolina von Neapel und Sicilien im Kampf gegen die französische Weltherrschaft 1790–1814*, Vienna: Braumüller, 1878.

Heller von Hellwald, Friedrich Anton, *Friedrich Freiherr von Bianchi*, Vienna: Sommer, 1857.

Henckens, J. L., *Mémoires*, La Haye: Nijhoff, 1910.

Herre, Johann Gottlob, *Erinnerungen des Schlossaufsehers—aus den Feldzügen der Jahre 1806, 1809, 1813, 1814 und 1815*, Mergentheim, 1847.

Hertenberger, Helmut and Franz Wiltschek, *Erzherzog Karl: Der Sieger von Aspern*, Graz: Styria, 1983.

Hoeck, S. van, 'Die Engländer auf Seeland im Jahre 1809', *Europäische Annalen*, vol. I, 1812.

Holler, Gerd, . . . *für Kaiser und Vaterland: Offizier in der alten Armee*, Vienna: Amalthea, 1990.

Horward, Donald D., 'Massena: Napoleon's Great Competitor', in The Consortium on Revolutionary Europe, *Selected Papers 1997*, ed. Kyle O. Eidahl, Donald D. Horward and John Severn, Tallahassee: Florida State University, 1997.

Hourtoulle, F. G., *Davout le Terrible*, Paris: Maloine, 1975.

—— *Le Général Comte Charles Lasalle 1775–1809*, Paris: Copernic, 1979.

Hufeland, Gottlieb, *Erinnerungen aus meinem Aufenthalt in Danzig in den Jahren 1808 bis 1812*, Königsberg: Nicolovtus, 1815.

Ilwof, Franz, 'Karl Schmutz: Sein Leben und Wirken', *Mittheilungen des historischen Vereins für Steiermark*, vol. XXXVIII, 1890.

Jacquin, François-Joseph, *Carnet de Route d'un Grognard de la Révolution et de l'Empire*, Paris: Clavreuil, 1960.

Johann, Archduke of Austria, *Erzherzog Johanns 'Feldzugserzählung' 1809*, ed. Alois Veltzé, *Supplement zu den Mitteilungen des K. und K. Kriegsarchivs*, Vienna: Seidel & Sohn, 1909.

—— 'Gedrängtes Journale zur Uebersicht der Ereignisse bei der Armee unter höchsten Befehlen Sr. kaiserlichen Hoheit des Erzherzogs Johann in dem Feldzug vom Jahre 1809', ed. Alois Veltzé, *Mitteilungen des K. und K. Kriegsarchivs*, vol. V, 1907.

Joseph, Archduke of Austria, *Jozsef Nador Elete es Iratai*, ed. Sandor Domanovszky, Budapest, 1929–44 (vols I–III); *Palatin Josephs Schriften*, Budapest, 1991 (vol. IV).

Jouan, Jacques, 'Souvenirs du Général Jouan', *Miscellanea Napoleonica*, serie III–IV, 1898.

Kaisenberg, Moritz von (ed.), *König Jérome Napoleon, Ein Zeit- und Lebensbild*, Leipzig: Schmidt und Günther, 1899.

Kaufmann, Reinhard Franz, 'Die Schlacht bei Znaim veränderte die Landkarte Europas', *Zusammenfassung der Beiträge zum Napoleon Symposium 'Feldzug 1809'*, Vienna: Delta Druckproduktionen, 2009.

Keep, William Thornton, *In the Service of the King*, ed. Ian Fletcher, Staplehurst: Spellmount, 1997.

Kerchenawe, Hugo and Alois Veltzé, *Feldmarschall Karl Fürst zu Schwarzenberg*, Vienna: Gerlach & Wiedling, 1913.

Kircheisen, Friedrich M., *Gespräche Napoleons*, Stuttgart: Lutz, 1912.

—— *Jovial King: Napoleon's Youngest Brother*, London: Elkin Mathews & Marrot, 1932.

—— (ed.), *Feldzugserinnerungen aus dem Kriegsjahre 1809*, Hamburg: Gutenberg, 1909.

Klaeber, Hans, *Marschall Bernadotte Kronprinz von Schweden*, Gotha: Perthes, 1910.

Klessmann, Eckart (ed.), *Deutschland unter Napoleon in Augenzeugenberichten*, Düsseldorf: Rauch, 1965.

Koch, Jean Baptiste, *Mémoires d'André Massena*, Paris: Bonnot, 1967 (reprint of 1850 edition).

Kraijenhoff, Cornelis Rudolphus Theodorus, *Bijdragen tot de vaterlandsche Geschiedenis van de belangrijke Jaren 1809 en 1810*, Nijmegen: Vieweg & Zoon, 1831.

Kübeck von Kübau, Carl Friedrich Freiherr, *Tagebücher*, Vienna: Gerold, 1909.

Kummer, August, *Erinnerungen aus dem Leben eines Veteranen der Königlich Sächsischen Armee*, Dresden: Meinhold & Söhne, n.d.

Lacorde, Jean-Louis, *Lieutenant Lacorde: Journal Historique*, Paris: Clavreuil, 1992.

Lacour-Gayet, Georges, *Talleyrand*, Paris: Payot, 1930.

[Larisch, Ferdinand von], 'Meine zweite Campagne (Aus dem Tagebuche eines Verstorbenen)', *Bautzener Nachrichten*, nos. 21–5, 1883.

Larrey, Dominique Jean, *Mémoires de Chirugie Militaire et Campagnes de D. J. Larrey*, Paris: Smith, 1812.

—— *Memoirs of Baron Larrey*, Felling: Worley, 1997 (reprint of 1862 edition).

Las Cases, Emmanuel, *Journal of the Private Life and Conversations of the Emperor Napoleon at Saint Helena*, London: Colburn, 1823.

Latour, Theodor Graf Baillet von, *Erinnerungen*, Graz: Kienreich, 1849.

Laurillard-Fallot, Salomon Louis, *Souvenirs d'un Médecin Hollandais sous les Aigles Françaises*, Paris: La Vouivre, 1997.

Lehmann, Max, *Scharnhorst*, Leipzig: Hirzel, 1887.

Lejeune, Charles Henri, 'Souvenirs', *Carnet de la Sabretache*, 1910.

Lejeune, Louis-François, *Memoirs of Baron Lejeune*, Felling: Worley, reprint, 1987.

Levec, V. (ed.), 'Ein Tagebuch aus dem Jahre 1809', *Mittheilungen des historischen Vereines für Steiermark*, vol. XLVI, 1898.

Ligne, Prince Charles Joseph de, *Fragments de l'Histoire de Ma Vie*, ed. Félicien Leuridant, Paris: Plon, 1928.

Lorencez, Guillaume de Latrille, Comte de, 'Etat Raisonné de Mes Services', *Le Carnet Historique & Littéraire*, vol. X, 1901.

Löwenstern, Vladimir Ivanovich Baron, *Mémoires du Général-Major Russe Baron de Löwenstern*, ed. M. H. Weil, Paris: Fontemoing, 1903.

Luvaas, Jay (ed.), *Napoleon on the Art of War*, New York: The Free Press, 1999.

MacDonald, Etienne Jacques, *Recollections of Marshal MacDonald*, London: Bentley & Son, 1892 (reprinted Felling: Worley, 1987).

Madroux, Ludwig von, 'August von Floret', *Archiv für Offiziere aller Waffen*, vol. II, 1846.

Magenschab, Hans, *Erzherzog Johann*, Graz: Styria, 1981.

Mändler, Friedrich, *Erinnerungen aus meinen Feldzügen*, ed. Franz J. A. Schneidawind, Nuremberg: Lotzbeck, 1854.

Marbot, Jean-Baptiste-Antoine-Marcelin, *The Memoirs of Baron de Marbot*, trans. Arthur J. Butler, London: Longmans, Green, and Co., 1905.

Marbotin, Pierre, 'Deux Lettres de 1809', *Carnet de la Sabretache*, 1909.

'Marginalien zur Relation über die Schlacht bey Wagram: Eingesendet von einem Offizier des k. k. östreichischen Generalstaabs', *Europäische Annalen*, vol. II, 1810.

Marmont, Marshal Auguste-Frédéric-Louis Viesse de, *Mémoires du Maréchal Duc de Raguse*, Paris: Perrotin, 1857.

Marshall-Cornwall, James, *Marshal Massena*, London: Oxford University Press, 1965.

Meibom, Heinrich Friedrich von, *Aus napoleonischer Zeit*, Leipzig: Koehler & Amelang, n.d.

Meier, Wilhelm, *Erinnerungen aus den Feldzügen 1806 bis 1815*, Karsruhe: Müller, 1854.

Méneval, Napoléon Joseph Ernest Baron de, *Le Général Baron de Coëhorn: Un Bayard Alsacien*, Paris: Fischbacher, 1912.

Metternich-Winneburg, Prince Clemens Lothar Wenzel von, *Memoirs of Prince Metternich*, New York: Scribner's, 1880.

—— *Memoirs of Prince Metternich*, New York: Fertig, 1970.

Meynert, Hermann, *Kaiser Franz I.*, Vienna: Hölder, 1872.

Mikhaïlowitch, Grand Duke Nicolas (ed.), *Les Relations Diplomatiques de la Russie et de la France d'après les Rapports des Ambassadeurs d'Alexandre et de Napoléon*, St Petersburg, 1905.

—— *L'Empereur Alexandre Ier*, St Petersburg, 1912.

Muller, Paul, *L'Espionnage Miliaire sous Napoléon*, Paris: Berger-Levrault, 1896.

Napoléon I, *Correspondance de Napoléon Ier publiée par ordre de l'Empereur Napoléon III*, Paris: Imprimerie Impériale, 1858–70.

—— *Supplément a la Correspondance de Napoléon Ier*, Paris: Dentu, 1887.

—— *Lettres Inédites de Napoléon Ier*, ed. Léon Lecestre, Paris: Plon, 1897.

—— *Lettres Inédites de Napoléon Ier*, ed. Léonce de Brotonne, Paris: Champion, 1898.

—— *Dernières Lettres Inédites de Napoléon Ier*, ed. Léonce de Brotonne, Paris: Champion, 1903.

—— *Unpublished Correspondence of Napoleon I Preserved in the War Archives*, ed. Ernest Picard and Louis Tuetey, New York: Duffield, 1913.

—— *Inédits Napoléoniens*, ed. Arthur Chuquet, Paris: de Boccard, 1914–19.

'Nouvelles Lettres du Général Drouot', *Carnet de la Sabretache*, 1897.

Ollech, Karl Rudolf von, 'Carl Friedrich Wilhelm von Reyher', Beiheft zum Militär-Wochenblatt, Berlin: Mittler & Sohn, 1861–76.

Ommen, Heinrich, Die Kriegsführung des Erzherzogs Carl, Vaduz: Kraus Reprints, 1965.

Ompteda, Ludwig von, Politischer Nachlass, Jena: Frommann, 1869.

Osten, Pierre Jacques, 'Rapport Circonstancé', Spectateur Militaire, vol. XXI, 1836.

Pahl, Johann Gottfried von, Denkwürdigkeiten aus meinem Leben und aus meiner Zeit, Tübingen, 1840.

Pajol, Comte Charles Pierre Victor, Pajol: Général en Chef, Paris: Didot, 1874.

Palmer, Alan, Alexander I: Tsar of War and Peace, New York: Harper & Row, 1974.

—— Bernadotte: Napoleon's Marshal, Sweden's King, London: Murray, 1990.

Parquin, Denis Charles, Napoleon's Army: The Military Memoirs of Charles Parquin, London: Greenhill, 1987.

Pasquier, Etienne-Denis, Memoirs of Chancellor Pasquier, New York: Scribner's Sons, 1893.

Paulin, Jules Antoine, Les Souvenirs du Général Baron Paulin, Paris: Plon, 1895.

Peeters, K. C., Soldaten van Napoleon, Antwerp: De Vlijt, 1955.

Pelleport, Pierre, Souvenirs Militares et Intimes, Paris: Didier, 1857.

Pertz, Georg Heinrich, Das Leben des Ministers Freiherrn vom Stein, Berlin: Reimer, 1851.

—— Das Leben des Feldmarschalls Grafen Neithardt von Gneisenau, Berlin: Reimer, 1864.

Peter, Benedikt, Wachtmeister Peter, Stuttgart: Steinkopf, 1980.

Peyrusse, Guillaume Joseph Roux, 1809–1815: Mémorial et Archives, Carcassone: Labau, 1869.

Pfister, Albert von, König Friedrich von Württemberg und seine Zeit, Stuttgart: Kohlhammer, 1888.

Picard, Ernest (ed.), Préceptes et Jugements de Napoléon, Paris: Berger-Levrault, 1913.

Pils, François, Journal de Marche du Grenadier Pils, Paris: Ollendorff, 1895.

Pingaud, Léonce, Bernadotte et Napoléon 1797–1814, Paris: Plon, 1933.

Pirquet, Pierre-Martin, Journal de Campagne, Liege: Société des Bibliophiles, 1970.

Planat de la Faye, Nicholas Louis, Vie de Planat de la Faye, Paris: Ollendorff, 1895.

Poiron, Jean-Pierre, 'Antoine-François Morandini, Chevalier d'Eccataye (1766–1831)', at www.histoire-empire.org/persos/morandini/morandini.

Poniatowski, Joseph, Correspondance du Prince Joseph Poniatowski avec la France, Posen, 1921–3.

Pouget, François Réné, Souvenirs de Guerre du Général Baron Pouget, ed. Mme de Boisdeffre, Paris: Plon, 1895.

'Prise de Ratisbonne', Carnet de la Sabretache, 1895.

Rabel, André, Le Maréchal Bessières, Paris: Librarie des Deux Empires, 2004.

Rapp, Jean, Memoirs of General Count Rapp, London: Colburn, 1823 (reprinted Cambridge: Ken Trotman, 1985).

Rapp, Josef, Tirol im Jahre 1809, Innsbruck: Rauch, 1852.

Rapp, Ludwig (ed.), *Schicksale des Servitenklosters bei Volders in Tirol*, Brixen: Weger, 1886.

Rauchensteiner, Manfried, *Kaiser Franz und Erzherzog Karl*, Vienna: Verlag für Geschichte und Politik, 1972.

—— *Feldzeugmeister Johann Freiherr von Hiller*, Vienna: Notring, 1972.

—— 'Das sechste österr. Armeekorps im Krieg 1809', *Mitteilungen des österr. Staatsarchivs*, vol. XVII/XVIII, Vienna, 1964–5.

Regele, Oskar, *Feldmarschall Radetzky: Leben, Leistung, Erbe*, Munich: Herold, 1957.

[Regnier, Ferdinand], 'Auszug aus dem Tagebuch eines k. bayerischen Stabsoffiziers', *Archiv für Offiziere aller Waffen*, vol. II, 1844.

Reichold, N., *Soldaten-Sohn und das Kriegsleben von 1805 bis 1815*, Munich, 1851.

Reiset, Marie-Antoine de, *Souvenirs*, Paris: Lévy, 1899.

Reithofer, Franz D., *Die Kriegsereignisse in Landshut am 16. und 21. April 1809 als die ersten in diesem Kriegsjahre*, Leipzig: Baumgartner, 1810.

Riancey, Henry de, *Le Général Comte de Coutard*, Paris: Dentu, 1857.

Richardson, Robert G., *Larrey: Surgeon to Napoleon's Imperial Guard*, London: John Murray, 1974.

Rivollet, Georges, *Général de Bataille Charles Antoine Louis Morand, Comte de l'Empire (1771–1835), Généraux Friant et Gudin du 3e Corps d'Armée*, Paris: Peyronnet, 1963.

Robinaux, Pierre, *Journal de Route du Capitaine Robinaux*, ed. Gustave Schlumberger, Paris: Plon-Nourrit, 1908.

Robinet de Cléry, Gabriel Adrien, *D'Essling à Wagram: Lasalle*, Paris: Berger-Levrault, 1891.

Rocca, Albert de, *Mémoires sur la Guerre des Français en Espagne*, Paris: Gide, 1817.

Roguet, François, *Mémoires Militaires*, Paris: Dumaine, 1865.

Roos, Heinrich von, *Mit Napoleon in Russland*, Stuttgart: Lutz, 1911.

Rössler, Hellmuth, *Graf Johann Philipp Stadion: Napoleons deutscher Gegenspieler*, Vienna: Herold, 1966.

Rothenberg, Gunther E., 'The Case of Archduke Charles', in The Consortium on Revolutionary Europe, *Proceedings 1983*, ed. Clarence B. Davis, Athens, GA: Consortium on Revolutionary Europe, 1985.

Routier, Léon-Michel, *Récits d'un Soldat de la République et de l'Empire*, Paris: Editions du Grenadier, 2001.

Rühle von Lilienstern, Johann Jacob Otto August, *Reise mit der Armee im Jahre 1809*, Rudolstadt: Hof- Buch- und Kunsthandlung, 1810.

—— 'Gedanken über die beiden Schlachten auf dem Marchfelde bei Wien', *Pallas*, vol. XI, 1809.

Russia, Ministerstvo Inostrannykh del, *Vneshniaia Politika Rossii XIX i nachala XX veka: dokumenti rossiiskogo Ministersva Inostrannykh del*, Moscow, 1965.

Salle (or Desalle), Victor Abel de, 'Les Souvenirs du Général Baron de Salle', *La Revue de Paris*, vol. I, 1895.

Savary, Anne-Jean-Marie-René, *Mémoires du Duc de Rovigo*, Paris: Bossange, 1828.

Schaller, Christian, *Fragmente aus dem Feldzuge gegen Oestreich im Jahr 1809*, Augsburg: Bürglen, 1810.

Schauroth, Wilhelm Freiherr von, *Im Rheinbund-Regiment der Herzoglich Sächsischen Kontingente Koburg-Hildburghausen-Gotha-Weimar während der Feldzüge in Tirol, Spanien und Russland 1809–1813*, Berlin: Mittler & Sohn, 1905.

Scheltens, Colonel, *Souvenirs d'un Grognard Belge*, Brussels: Dessart, n.d.

Schlossberger, August von (ed.), *Politische und Militärische Correspondenz König Friedrichs von Württemberg mit Kaiser Napoleon I. 1805–1813*, Stuttgart: Kohlhammer, 1889.

Schlotheim, Capitain von, *Berichte von den Schlachten auf dem Marchfelde bey Wien, Gross-Aspern und Deutsch-Wagram von einem Augenzeugen*, Gotha, 1809.

Schmaltz, Christian von, 'Aus dem Leben des Generalmajors von Schmaltz mit besonderer Berücksichtigung des Zuges nach Griechenland', *Darstellungen aus der Bayerischen Kriegs- und Heeresgeschichte*, vol. XX, 1911.

Schmidt, Alois, *Karl Freiherr von Scheibler*, Bonn: Georgi, 1908.

Schnierer, Johann, *Aus der Franzosenzeit, Innviertler Volksbücher*, vols 4 and 5, Braunau: Stampfl, n.d.

Schwarzenberg, Carl Fürst zu, *Briefe des Feldmarschalls Fürst zu Schwarzenberg an seine Frau*, Vienna: Gerlach & Wiedling, 1913.

Ségur, Philippe-Paul, *Histoire et Mémoires*, Paris: Didot, 1873.

Ségur-Cabanac, Auguste François Marcel Comte de, *Journal*, Vienna: Stern, 1910.

Ségur-Cabanac, Victor de. *Histoire de la Maison de Ségur*, Brünn, 1908.

Skall, Johann Baptist, 'Feldzugsreise des Kaisers Franz I. von Oesterreich im Jahre 1809', ed. Hauptmann Sommeregger, *Mitteilungen des K. und K. Kriegsarchivs*, vol. 5, 1907.

Smola, Karl Freiherr von, *Das Leben des Feldmarschalls Heinrich Grafen von Bellegarde*, Vienna: Heubner, 1847.

Sommerock, H., 'Kriegserlebnisse im Jahre 1805 und 1809 bei Landshut und insbesondere zu Berg ob Landshut', *Verhandlungen des Historischen Vereins für Neiderbayern*, vol. 47, 1911.

Spehr, Louis Ferdinand, *Friedrich Wilhelm Herzog von Braunschweig-Lüneburg-Oels*, Braunschweig: Meyer, 1848.

Stamm-Kuhlmann, Thomas, *König in Preussens grosser Zeit: Friedrich Wilhelm III., der Melancholiker auf dem Thron*, Berlin: Siedler, 1992.

Stendahl [Henri Beyle], *To the Happy Few: Selected Letters of Stendahl*, trans. Norman Cameron, New York: Grove Press, 1952.

Stöger, Johann N., *Maximilian Erzherzog von Oesterreich-Este*, Vienna, 1865.

Stoll, Franz Xaver, 'Kriegsberichte aus den Jahren 1800 und 1809, was sich in der Stadt und im Landgerichte Abensberg ereignet', ed. J. Schuegraf, *Verhandlungen des Historischen Vereins für Niederbayern*, vol. 7, 1860.

Strantz, Karl Friedrich Ferdinand von, 'Rückzug des kaiserlich–königlich österreichischen VII. Armeekorps aus Polen im Jahre 1809', *Zeitschrift für Kunst, Wissenschaft und Geschichte des Krieges*, vol. XXVI, 1832.

Szymanowski, Joseph, *Mémoires*, Paris: Lavauzelle, 1900.

'Tagebuch eines bayerischen Artillerieoffiziers aus dem Jahre 1809', *Das Bayernland*, Munich, 1908.

Tascher, Maurice de, *Journal de Campagne d'un Cousin de l'Imperatrice (1806–1813)*, Paris: Plon, 1933.

Tellegen, Jacobus Antonius, *Gedane Veldtogten, bekomene Wonden*, Oosterbeek: G. Tellegen, 2005.

Teste, François, 'Souvenirs du Général Baron Teste', *Carnet de la Sabretache*, 1911.

Theiss, Viktor, *Leben und Wirken Erzherzog Johanns*, Graz: Historische Landeskommission, 1963.

Thielen, Maximilian Ritter von, *Erinnerungen aus dem Kriegerleben eines 82jährigen Veteranen der österreichischen Armee*, Vienna: Braumüller, 1863.

Thomas, Charles Antoine, *Les Grands Cavaliers du Premier Empire*, Paris: Berger-Levrault, 1890–1909.

Triare, Paul, *Dominique Larrey*, Tours: Mame, 1902.

'Ueber die Benutzung der in der Schlacht von Aspern erfochtenen Vortheile und über den Waffenstillstand von Znaym', *Pallas*, vol. IV, 1810.

'Uebersicht der Operationen der ungarischen Insurrection-Armee im Jahr 1809', *Europäische Annalen*, vol. 5, 1814.

V., Général (ed.), 'Les Vues de Napoléon Ier sur l'Organisation des Ponts Militaires', *Carnet de la Sabretache*, 1895.

Varnhagen von Ense, Karl August, *Denkwürdigkeiten des eigenen Lebens*, Leipzig: Brockhaus, 1843.

—— *Sketches of German Life and Scenes from the War of Liberation in Germany*, London: Murray, 1847.

Vaudoncourt, Frédéric Guillaume de, *Histoire politique et militaire du Prince Eugène Napoléon*, Paris: Mongie, 1828.

Veigl, Josef, 'Erinnerungen eines Veteranen aus dem Jahre 1809', *Oesterreichische militärische Zeitschrift*, vol. II, 1860.

Veling, Pierre Guillaume (ed.), *Nos Alliés Allemands*, Paris: Frères, 1909.

Vigier, Henri, *Davout Maréchal de l'Empire*, Paris: Ollendorf, 1898.

Voith, Ferdinand, 'Mesko Tabornok Visszavonulasarol 1809-ben', *Hadtorteneti Kozlemenyek*, 1894.

Voss, August von, 'Zur Geschichte des Schillschen Zuges im Jahre 1809', manuscript, 1854 (courtesy of Sam A. Mustafa).

Vrhovac, Maksimilijan, *Dnevnik*, Zagreb: Zavod za Hrvatsku povijest, Filozofskag fakultete u Zagrebu, 1987 (courtesy of Vlado Brnardic).

Wachholtz, Friedrich Ludwig, *Aus dem Tagebuche des Generals Fr. L. von Wachholtz*, Braunschweig: Vieweg, 1843.

Walter, Jakob, *A German Conscript with Napoleon*, ed. and trans. Otto Springer, Lawrence: University of Kansas, 1938.

Watson, S. J., *By Command of the Emperor: A Life of Marshal Berthier*, Cambridge: Trotman reprint, 1988.

Wencker-Wildberg, Friedrich, *Bernadotte: A Biography*, trans. Kenneth Kirkness, London: Jarrolds, 1936.

Wertheimer, Eduard, 'Berichte des Grafen Friedrich Lothar Stadion ueber die Beziehungen zwischen Oesterreich und Baiern (1807–1809)', *Archiv für Oesterreichische Geschichte*, vol. 63, 1882.

Wesemann, Heinrich, *Kannonier des Kaisers*, Cologne: Verlag Wissenschaft und Politik, 1971.

Wheatcroft, Andrew, *The Habsburgs*, London: Viking, 1995.

Wheeler, William, *Letters of Private Wheeler*, Boston: Houghton Mifflin, 1952.

Wickede, Julius von, *Ein Deutsches Reiterleben*, Berlin: Duncker, 1861.

Wilhelm von Baden, Markgraf, *Denkwürdigkeiten des Markgrafen Wilhelm von Baden*, ed. Karl Obser, Heidelberg: Winter, 1906.

Wirth, Joseph, *Le Maréchal Lefèbvre Duc de Dantzig (1755–1820)*, Paris: Perrin, 1904.

Wolzogen, Ludwig von, *Memoiren des königlich preussischen Generals der Infanterie Ludwig von Wolzogen*, Leipzig: Wigand, 1851.

Würdinger, Josef, 'Das Leben des königl. bayerischen Generallieutenants Maxim. Grafen v. Preysing-Moos', *Verhandlungen des Historischen Vereins für Niederbayern*, vol. 9, 1863.

Württemberg, Eugen von. *Memoiren*, Frankfurt an der Oder: Harnecker, 1862.

Württemberger in Mergentheim, Die, 1818.

Zimmermann, P., *Erinnerungen aus den Feldzügen des bergischen Truppen in Spanien und Russland*, Düsseldorf: Stahl, 1840.

Zucchi, Carlo, *Memoirie del Generale Carlo Zucchi*, Milan: Guigoni, 1861.

Zwiedineck-Südenhorst, Hans von (ed.), *Erzherzog Johann von Oesterreich im Feldzuge von 1809*, Graz: Styria, 1892.

GENERAL WORKS

Ableitinger, Alfred, 'Zur Geschichte der steierischen Landwehr von 1808/09', in *Die steierische Landwehr Einst und Jetzt*, Graz: Landeszeughaus, 1977.

Abriss von der Schlacht bei Esling und Gross-Aspern am 21. und 22. May 1809, Weimar: Geographisches Institut, 1810.

An Account of the Operations of the Corps under the Duke of Brunswick from the Time of Formation in Bohemia to the Embarkation for England, London: Stockdale, 1810.

Anders, Joseph von, 'Geschichtliche Skizze der Kriegsereignisse in Tirol im Jahre 1809', *ÖMZ*, 1833–4.

Adam, Alfons, 'Das Treffen bei Ebelsberg am 3. Mai 1809', *Linzer Tages-Post*, 6 May 1906.

Altmann, Karl, 'Die Franzosen in Türnitz 1809', and 'Die Franzosen in Annaberg 1805 und 1809', *Blätter des Vereines für Landeskunde von Niederösterreich*, Vienna, 1901.

Angeli, Moriz Edlen von, 'Wagram: Novelle zur Geschichte des Kriges von 1809', *Mittheilungen des K. und K. Kriegs-Archivs*, Vienna, 1881.

'Die Armee Napoleon I. im Jahre 1809', *Mittheilungen des k. k. Kriegs-Archivs*, Vienna, 1881.

Arnold, James R., *Crisis on the Danube*, New York: Paragon House, 1990.

—— *Napoleon Conquers Austria*, London: Arms and Armour, 1995.

B., T., 'Die Gefechte zwischen Riedau und Neumarkt-Kallham am 1. und 2. Mai 1809', *Linzer Volksblatt*, 17 May 1914.

Baden und Württemberg im Napoleonischen Zeitalter, Stuttgart: Cantz, 1987.

Bailleu, Paul, 'Zur Geschichte des Jahres 1809', *Historische Zeitschrift*, vol. XLVIII, 1900.

Balagny, Dominique E. P., *Campagne de l'Empereur Napoléon en Espagne (1808–1809)*, Paris: Berger-Levrault, 1902–7.

Bardenfleth, F. L. von, *Stormen paa Stralsund*, Copenhagen: Reitzel, 1846.

Bartholdy, J. L., *Der Krieg der Tyroler Landleute im Jahre 1809*, Berlin: Hitzig, 1814.

Bartsch, Rudolf, *Der Volkskrieg in Tirol 1809*, vol. II of *Das Kriegsjahr 1809 in Einzeldarstellungen*, ed. Alois Veltzé, Vienna: Stern, 1905.

—— *Die Schill'schen Offiziere*, vol. VII of *Das Kriegsjahr 1809 in Einzeldarstellungen*, ed. Alois Veltzé, Vienna: Stern, 1909.

Baur, C., *Der Krieg in Tirol während des Feldzugs 1809*, Munich: Baur, 1812.

Bavaria, Generalstabssektion des königlichen bayerischen Generalquartiermeisterstabes, 'Der Feldzug von 1809 in Bayern', manuscript, Bayerisches Kriegsarchiv, 1865.

Bechtolsheim, Anton Freiherr von, '"Activité, Activité, Vitesse!" Operativer Gegenangriff aus der Versammlung', *Wehrwissenschaftlicher Rundschau*, 1959.

Becker, Wilhelm G., *Andreas Hofer und der Freiheitskampf in Tyrol 1809*, Leipzig: Teubner, 1841.

Beer, Adolf, *Zehn Jahre österreichischer Politik 1801–1810*, Leipzig: Brockhaus, 1877.

'Beiträge zur Geschichte des Schillischen Zuges durch Nord-Deutschland von einem Augenzeugen', *Minerva*, March–April 1810.

Bell, David A., *The First Total War*, New York: Mariner Books, 2007.

Beobachtungen und historische Sammlung wichtiger Ereignisse aus dem Kriege zwischen Frankreich, dessen Verbündeten und Oesterreich im Jahr 1809, Weimar: Landes-Industrie Comptoir, 1809.

'Bericht des k. k. General-Majors Graf Bubna, ddo. 11. October 1808, an dem Generalisimuss Erzherzog Carl über die Zusammenkunft mit dem königl. preussischen Obersten Graf Goetzen in der Ottendorfer Mühle', *Mittheilungen des K. K. Kriegs-Archivs*, 1882.

'Berichtigung zweier in dem württembergischen Jahrbuche erzählten Anekdoten', *Oesterreichische militärische Zeitschrift*, vol. 7, 1818.

Bertin, Georges, 'Combat d'Amstetten', *Carnet de la Sabretache*, 1901.

[Bianchi, Friedrich Freiherr von], *Vertheidigung des Brückenkopfes vor Pressburg, im Jahre 1809*, Pressburg, 1811.

Binder von Krieglstein, Christian Freiherr, *Der Krieg Napoleons gegen Oesterreich 1809*, ed. Maximilian Ritter von Hoen, Berlin: Voss, 1906 (review: Alexander Kirchhammer, 'Regensburg 1809', *Danzers Armee-Zeitung*, vols 50 and 51, 1903).

—— *Ferdinand von Schill*, Berlin: Voss, 1902.

Bismark, Friedrich Wilhelm Graf von, *Bismark's Ideen*, part I of the *Reuter-Bibliothek*, Karlsruhe: Müller, 1825.

—— *Ideen-Taktik der Reuterei*, Karlsruhe: Müller, 1829.

Bittard des Portes, René, 'Les Préliminaires de l'Entrevue d'Erfurt', *Revue d'Histoire Diplomatique*, 1890.

Black, Jeremy, *Britain as a Military Power*, London: UCL Press, 1999.

—— 'Why the French Failed: New Work on the Military History of French Imperialism 1792–1815', *European History Quarterly*, vol. 30, no. 1, 2000.

Blackburn, Christopher, 'Prince Poniatowski Finds an Army: Galician Attitudes in 1809', in The Consortium on Revolutionary Europe, *Proceedings 1992*, ed. Gordon C. Bond and John W. Rooney, Tallahassee: Florida State University, 1993.

Bleibtreu, Carl, *Aspern und Wagram in neuer Beleuchtung*, Vienna, Seidel & Sohn, 1902.

—— *Die Grosse Armee*, Stuttgart: Krabbe, 1907.

Bodnar, Istvan, 'A Györi Csata 1809 Junius 14-en', *Hadtortenelmi Kozlemenyek*, 1897.

Bond, Gordon C., *The Grand Expedition*, Athens, GA: University of Georgia Press, 1979.

Bonnal, Henry, *La Manœuvre de Landshut*, Paris: Chapelot, 1905.

Bornemann, Karl, *Napoleon bei Znaim*, Geislingen an der Steige: Verlag des Südmährischen Landschaftsrates, 1975.

Bosscha, J., *Neerlands Heldendaden te Land*, Leeuwarden, 1873.

Botzenhart, Manfred, *Metternichs Pariser Botschafterzeit*, Münster: Aschendorff, 1967.

Boué, Gilles, *Essling: Napoleon's First Defeat?*, Paris: Histoire & Collections, 2008.

Bourgoing, Jean de, *1809*, Vienna: Bergland, 1959.

Bowden, Scott and Charles Tarbox, *Armies on the Danube 1809*, Arlington: Empire Games Press, 1980 (revised and expanded edition, 1989).

Bran, Friedrich Alexander, 'Fortgesetzte Bemerkungen über den gegenwärtigen Krieg', *Minerva*, July 1809.

Bremen, Walter von, 'Die Tage von Regensburg', *Beiheft zum Militär-Wochenblatt*, Berlin, 1891.

Brettes, Martin de, 'Canons dans l'Infanterie', *Spectateur Militaire*, vol. 43, 1888.

Broers, Michael, *Europe Under Napoleon 1799–1815*, London: Arnold, 1996.

Buat, Edmond Alfonse Léon, *1809 De Ratisbonne à Znaïm*, Paris: Chapelot, 1909.

—— 'Vingt-Quatre Heures au Grand Quartier Général de l'Armée d'Allemagne (2–3 Mai 1809)', *Journal des Sciences Militaires*, vol. LXXXIV, Paris, 1908.

—— 'Massena à Ebersberg (3 Mai 1809)', *Journal des Sciences Militaires*, vol. LXXXIV, Paris, 1908.

Buckland, Charles S. B., *Metternich and the British Government from 1809 to 1813*, London: Macmillan, 1932.

Bülau, Friedrich, *Geheime Geschichten und Rätselhafte Menschen*, Leipzig: Brockhaus, 1854.

Bullo, Carlo, 'Dei Movimenti Insurrezionali del Veneto sotto il Dominio Napoleonico', *Nuovo Archivio Veneto*, vol. XVII, 1899.

Camon, Hubert, *La Manoeuvre de Wagram*, Paris: Berger-Levrault, 1926.

—— *La Guerre Napoléonienne: Précis des Campagnes*, Paris: Teissèdre, 1999.

Canitz, F. R. von and C. W. E. von Dallwitz, *Nachrichten und Betrachtungen über die Thaten und Schicksale der Reuterei*, Berlin and Posen: Mittler, 1824.

Cantù, Cesare, *Storia della Citta e della Diocesi di Como*, Como: Ostinelli, 1831.

—— *Della Indipendenza Italiana Cronistoria*, Turin: Unione Tipografico, 1872.

Casareto, Marco, *L'Esercito Austriaco 1805/15: Fanteria*, Milan: Editrice Militare Italiana, 1987.

Cassi, Gellio, 'Napoléon et la Défense de l'Italie sur la Piave', *Revue des Etudes Napoléoniennes*, vol. XIX, July–December 1922.

—— 'L'Alta Lombardia durante l'insurrezione tirolese nel 1809', *Rassegna Storica del Risorgimento*, vol. XVIII, 1931.

Castle, Ian, *Aspern and Wagram 1809: Mighty Clash of Empires*, Osprey Campaign Series 33, London: Osprey, 1994.

—— *Eggmühl 1809*, Osprey Campaign Series 56, London: Osprey, 1998.

Chandler, David G., *The Campaigns of Napoleon*, New York: Macmillan, 1966.

Christoph, Franz, 'Die Isar-Uebergänge der Oesterreicher bei Landshut am 16. und 21. April 1809', *Verhandlungen des Historischen Vereins für Niederbayern*.

Clercq, M. de, *Recueil des Traités de la France*, Paris: Amyot, 1864.

Clowes, William Laird, *The Royal Navy*, London: Sampson Low, Marston and Company, 1900.

Colin, Jean, *La Tacticque et la Discipline dans les Armées de la Révolution*, Paris: Chapelot, 1902,

—— *Les Transformations de la Guerre*, Paris: Flammarion, 1926.

A Collection of Papers Relating to the Expedition to the Scheldt, Presented to Parliament in 1810, London: Strahan, 1811.

Connelly, Owen, *Blundering to Glory: Napoleon's Military Campaigns*, Wilmington: SR Books, 1987.

Craig, Gordon A., 'Command and Staff Problems in the Austrian Army, 1740–1866', in Gorgon A. Craig, *War, Politics, and Diplomacy*, New York: Praeger, 1966.

Criste, Oskar, 'Die Offensiv-Operationen des Erzherzogs Johann in Italien im Jahre 1809', *Organ der militär-wissenschaftlichen Vereine*, vol. LVI, 1898.

—— 'Die Streifzüge der Österreicher in Sachsen und Franken im Feldzuge 1809', *Organ der militär-wissenschaftlichen Vereine*, vol. LVII, 1898.

Crociani, Piero, Virgilio Ilari, and Ciro Paoletti, *Storia Militare del Regno Italico 1802–1814*, Rome: Ufficio Storico Dello SME, 2003.

Darstellung des Feldzugs vom Jahr 1809 von einem Augenzeugen, (no further information), 1811.

Dechend, Premier-Lieutenant, 'Das hessische Freicorps im Jahre 1809', *Jahrbücher für die deutsche Armee und Marine*, vol. 54, 1885.

Decker, Carl von, 'Besuch der Insel Lobau und der Schlachtfelder von Aspern (Eslingen) und Wagram im Sommer 1835', *Zeitschrift für Kunst, Wissenschaft und Geschichte des Krieges*, vol. I, 1836–7.

Delbrück, Hans, *Erinnerungen, Aufsätze und Reden*, Berlin: Stilke, 1902.

—— *The Dawn of Modern Warfare*, Lincoln: University of Nebraska Press, 1990.

Derrécagaix, Victor Bernard, *Nos Campagnes au Tyrol*, Paris: Chapelot, 1910.

Deuerling, Eduard, *Das Fürstentum Bayreuth unter französischer Herrschaft und sein Übergang an Bayern 1806–1810*, Erlangen: Palm & Enke, 1932.

Dimitz, August, *Geschichte Krains*, Laibach: Kleinmayer & Bamberg, 1876.

Driault, Edouard, *Tilsit*, Paris: Alcan, 1917.

Drieu, Alexandre Frédéric, *Le Guide du Pontonnier*, Paris: Levrault, 1820.

Dunan, Marcel, *Napoléon et l'Allemagne*, Paris: Plon, 1942.

Duncker, Maximilian Wolfgang, *Aus der Zeit Friedrichs des Grossen und Friedrich Wilhelms III*, Leipzig: Duncker & Humblot, 1876.

—— 'Friedrich Wilhelm III. im Jahre 1809', *Preussischer Jahrbücher*, vol. 41, 1878.

Durieux, J., 'Soldats d'Essling et de Wagram', *Carnet de la Sabretache*, 1909.

Dwyer, Philip G., 'Self-Interest versus the Common Cause: Austria, Prussia, and Russia against Napoleon', *Journal of Strategic Studies*, vol. XXXI, no. 4, August 2008.

Eberle, Ludwig, 'Die Mission des Obersten Steigentesch nach Königsberg im Jahre 1809', *Mitteilungen des K. und K. Kriegsarchivs*, vol. V, 1907.

Egger, Josef, *Geschichte des Tirols von den ältesten Zeiten bis in die Neuzeit*, Innsbuck: Wagner, 1880.

Ehnl, Maximilian, 'Die Einschliessung von Czestochowa im Jahre 1809', *ÖMZ*, 1910.

—— 'Die Berennung und Einnahme der Festung Sandomierz durch die Polen im Jahre 1809', *ÖMZ*, 1911.

'Einige Bemerkungen über die Disposition zur Schlacht bei Wagram', *Zeitschrift für Kunst, Wissenschaft und Geschichte des Krieges*, vol. XVIII, 1830.

Elting, John R., *Swords Around a Throne*, New York: The Free Press, 1988.

Engel, Friedrich, *Geschichte der oberösterreichischen Landwehr*, Linz: Akad. Pressverein, 1910.

Epstein, Robert M., 'The Army of Italy at the Battle of Wagram: Turning Point of the Napoleonic Wars', *The Consortium on Revolutionary Europe, Proceedings 1989*, ed. Donald D. Howard and John C. Horgan, Talahassee: Florida State University, 1990.

—— *Napoleon's Last Victory and the Emergence of Modern War*, Lawrence: University of Kansas Press, 1994.

Esdaille, Charles, *Napoleon's Wars*, London: Allen Lane, 2008.

Erinnerungsblätter an die Schlacht bei Ebelsberg am 3. Mai 1809, Ebelsberg, 1930.

Ernstberger, Anton, 'Oesterreich und der preussische Tugendbund 1809', *Zeitschrift fuer sudetendeutsche Geschichte*, vol. III, 1939.

—— *Die deutschen Freikorps 1809 in Böhmen*, Prague: Volk und Reich Verlag, 1942.

Erzberger, M., *Die Säkularisation in Württemberg*, Stuttgart: Deutsches Volksblatt, 1902.

Esposito, Vincent J. and John R. Elting, *A Military History and Atlas of the Napoleonic Wars*, New York: Praeger, 1968.

Fedorowicz, Wladyslaw de, *1809 Campagne de Pologne*, Paris: Plon, 1911.

Feldmann, M. and H. G. Wirtz, *Histoire Militaire de la Suisse*, Berne: Kuhn, 1921.

Feldzug Frankreich und seiner Verbündeten gegen Oesterreich im Jahre 1809, Der, Meissen: Goedsche, 1810.

Ferry, Edmond, *La Marche sur Vienna*, Paris: Chapelot, 1909.

Fircks, G. von, 'Ausgezeichneter Muth der Heldenjünglinge Herrmann und Hensel bei der Vertheidigung der Blockhäuser auf dem Predill und zu Malborghetto, am 17ten Mai 1809', *Militair-Wochenblatt*, no. 88, 28 February 1818.

Fleischman, T., *L'Expedition Anglaise sur le Continent en 1809*, Paris: Renaissance du Livre, 1973.

Fortescue, John W., *A History of the British Army*, London: Macmillan, 1912.

Fournier, August, 'Zur Geschichte des Tugendbundes', *Historische Studien und Skizzen*, 1st Series, 1885.

—— 'Oesterreichs Kriegsziele im Jahre 1809', *Beiträge zur neueren Geschichte Oesterreichs*, vol. IV, December 1908.

France, Ecole Supérieure de Guerre, 'Campagne de 1809', 1931.

Frasca, Francesco, 'La battaglia del Piave nella napoleonica campagna del 1809', *Informazione della Difesa*, no. 2, 2002.

Freytag-Loringhoven, Hugo Friedrich Philipp Johann Freiherr von, *Napoleonische Initiaitive 1809 und 1814*, Berlin: Mittler & Sohn, 1896.

—— 'Die Armeen des ersten Kaiserreichs', *Vierteljahrsheft für Truppenführung und Heereskunde*, vol. V, 1908.

Friesen, E. G. M. Freiherr von, *Dresden im Kriegsjahre 1809*, Dresden: Baensch, 1893.

Fuchs, Karl, *Oesterreichs Befreiungskrieg*, Regensburg: Manz, 1908.

Fugier, André, *La Révolution Française et l'Empire Napoléonien*, Paris: Hachette, 1954.

Gaede, Udo, *Preussens Stellung zur Kriegsfrage im Jahre 1809*, Hanover: Hahn, 1897.

Garros, Louis, *Quel Roman que ma vie! Itinéraire de Napoléon Bonaparte*, Paris: Éditions de l'Encyclopédie Française, 1947 (new edition with revisions by Jean Tulard published as: *Itinéraire de Napoléon au Jour le Jour*, Paris: Tallandier, 1992; re-issued 1998).

Gassendi, Jean Jacques Basilien de, *Aide-Mémoire a l'Usage des Officiers d'Artillerie*, Paris: Maginel, Anselin et Pochard, 1819.

Gates, David, *The Spanish Ulcer*, New York: W. W. Norton, 1986.

'Gedanken über die beiden Schlachten auf dem Marchfelde bei Wien', *Pallas*, vol. 2, 1809.

Geerts, Gérard A., *Samenwerking en Confrontatie*, Amsterdam: Bataafsche Leeuw, 2002.

'Die Gefechte zwischen Riedau und Neumarkt-Kallham am 1. und 2. Mai 1809', *Linzer Volksblatt*, May 1914.

Gerster, Raimund, *Napoleon und Regensburg 1809*, Regensburg, 1909.

'Geschichte des Feldzugs an der Weichsel im Jahre 1809', *Minerva*, vol. 1, 1810.

Gill, John H. *With Eagles to Glory: Napoleon and his German Allies in the 1809 Campaign*, London: Greenhill, 1992.

—— 'The Battle of Raszyn, 19 April 1809', *First Empire*, no. 10, March/April 1993.

—— 'The Battle of Neumarkt, 24 April 1809', *First Empire*, no. 11, May/June 1993.

—— 'Vignettes of 1809: The Engagement at Gefrees, 8 July', *First Empire*, no. 12, July/ August 1993, addendum in no. 15, February/March 1994.

—— 'What Do They Intend? Austrian War Aims in 1809', in The Consortium on Revolutionary Europe, *Selected Papers 1996*, ed. Charles Crouch, Kyle O. Eidahl, and Donald D. Horward, Tallahassee: Florida State University, 1996.

—— 'The Strategic Setting in 1809: Intelligence and Operational Decisions on the Road to War', in The Consortium on Revolutionary Europe, *Selected Papers 1997*, ed. Kyle O. Eidahl, Donald D. Horward, and John Severn, Tallahassee: Florida State University, 1997.

—— 'From Wagram to Schönbrunn: War and Peace in 1809', in The Consortium on Revolutionary Europe, *Selected Papers 1998*, ed. Kyle O. Eidahl and Donald D. Horward, Tallahassee: Florida State University, 1998.

—— 'Impossible Numbers: Solving Rear Area Security Problems in 1809', in The Consortium on Revolutionary Europe, *Selected Papers 2000*, ed. Donald D. Horward, Michael F. Pavkovic, and John Severn, Tallahassee: Florida State University, 2000. Note that the title given here is a misprint: it should read 'Imaginary Numbers'.

—— 'I Fear Our Ruin is Very Near: Prussian Foreign Policy During the Franco-Austrian War of 1809', in The Consortium on Revolutionary Europe, *Selected Papers 2002*, ed. Bernard Cook, Susan V. Nicassio, Michael F. Pavkovic, and Karl A. Roider, Tallahassee: Florida State University, 2002.

—— 'Decision in Bavaria: The Austrian Invasion of 1809', in Jonathan North (ed.), *The Napoleon Options*, London: Greenhill, 2000.

—— 'Les armées de la Confédération du Rhin en Hongrie, en 1809', trans. Robert Ouvrard, *Histoire du Consulat et du Premier Empire*, June 2004, at www.histoire-empire.org/1809/raab/confederation.htm.

Glaser, Hubert (ed.), *Krone und Verfassung. König Max I. Joseph und der neue Staat*, vol. III, part 1 of *Wittelsbach und Bayern*, Munich: Hirmer, 1980.

Goetz, Robert, 'Russian Naval Forces in the Mediterranean: 1805–1809', at www. napoleon-series.org.

Gorchkov, Dmitri, 'La Cavalerie Légère de Montbrun á Wagram, le 6 Juillet 1809', *Tradition*, nos. 242–4, March–August 2009.

Gregory, Desmond, *Sicily: The Insecure Base*, Rutherford: Fairleigh Dickinson University Press, 1988.

Groote, Wolfgang von and Klaus-Jürgen Müller (eds), *Napoleon I. und das Militärwesen seiner Zeit*, Freiburg: Rombach, 1968.

Gruber, Max, *Bruneck und das westliche Pustertal im Jahre 1809*, Schlern-Schriften 86, Innsbruck: Wagner, 1952.

Gunz, Johann, 'Der Krieg der Vorarlberger im Jahr 1809', *Militair-Wochenblatt*, vols 206, 210, 211, and 212, 3 June–15 July 1820.

H., M., 'Ueber die Verwendung der Kavallerie in den Schlachten und Gefechten des Feldzuges 1809 in Süd-Deutschland', *Neue Militärische Blätter*, vol. LIV, Berlin, 1899.

Haillot, C. A., *Essai d'une Instruction sur le Passage des Rivières*, Paris: Corréard, 1835.

Haken, Johann C. L., *Ferdinand von Schill*, Leipzig: Brockhaus, 1824.

Hall, Christopher D., *British Strategy in the Napoleonic War 1803–15*, Manchester: Manchester University Press, 1992.

Hamberger, Joseph, 'Die französischen Invasion in Kärnten i. J. 1809', *Jahresbericht der Staats-Oberrealschule zu Klagenfurt*, 1889, 1892, 1894, 1896.

Harder, W. H., 'Gebrauch der Artillerie vor dem Feinde', *Zeitschrift für Kunst, Wissenschft und Geschichte des Krieges*, vol. VI, 1833.

Harford, Lee, 'Defending the Fatherland: The Operations of the Bavarian Army During the Ratisbon Cycle', in *The Consortium on Revolutionary Europe, Proceedings 1992*, ed. Gordon C. Bond and John W. Rooney, Tallahassee: Florida State University, 1993.

Hassel, Paul, *Geschichte der Preussischen Politik*, vol. 6 of *Publikationen aus den Preussischen Staatsarchiven*, Leipzig: Hirzel, 1881.

Häusser, Ludwig, *Deutsche Geschichte*, Berlin: Weidmann, 1856.

[Heilmann, Johann von], 'Das "Bayerische Corps der grossen Armee" im Aprilfeldzuge von 1809', *Jahrbücher für die deutsche Armee und Marine*, vol. XXI, 1876.

—— 'Der Feldzug von 1809 in Tirol, im salzburgischen und an der bayerischen Südgrenze', *Jahrbücher für die deutsche Armee und Marine*, vols 68 and 69, 1888, vol. 88, 1893.

Heller von Hellwald, Friedrich Anton, *Der Feldzug des Jahres 1809 in Süddeutschland*, Vienna: Gerold, 1864.

Hertenberger, Helmut, 'Die Schlacht bei Wagram', dissertation, University of Vienna, 1950.

Heyde, G. von der, *Der Feldzug des Herzoglich-Braunschweigischen Korps im Jahre 1809*, Berlin: Mittler, 1819.

Hicks, Peter, 'Maintaining the Contest with Bonaparte: Britain in 1809', *Zusammenfassung der Beiträge zum Napoleon Symposium 'Feldzug 1809'*, Vienna: Delta Druckproduktionen, 2009.

Hiederer, Johann, 'Die Schreckentage von Stadtamhof im April 1809', Regensburg: Habbel, 1899.

Hirn, Ferdinand, *Vorarlbergs Erhebung im Jahre 1809*, Bregenz: Teutsch, 1909.

Hirn, Josef, *Tirols Erhebung im Jahre 1809*, Innsbruck: Haymon, 1983.

Hoen, Maximilian Ritter von, *Aspern*, vol. 3 of *Das Kriegsjahr 1809 in Einzeldarstellungen*, ed. Alois Veltzé, Vienna: Stern, 1906.

—— *Wagram*, vol. 8 of *Das Kriegsjahr 1809 in Einzeldarstellungen*, ed. Alois Veltzé, Vienna: Stern, 1909.

—— '1809. Ein Gedenkblatt zur Jahrhundertfeier des großen Krieges', *Streffleurs militärische Zeitschrift*, vol. 1, January 1909.

Hoeven, Marco van der, *Van de Weser tot de Weichsel*, Amsterdam: Bataafsche Leeuw, 1994.

Höfler, Edmund, *Der Feldzug des Jahres 1809 in Deutschland und Tirol*, Augsburg: Rieger, 1858.

Hollins, David, *Austrian Auxiliary Troops 1792–1816*, London: Osprey, 1996.

—— *Austrian Grenadiers and Infantry 1788–1816*, London: Osprey, 1998.

—— *Austrian Commanders of the Napoleonic Wars*, London: Osprey, 2004.

Holtzendorff, Albrecht Graf von, *Beiträge zu der Biographie des Generals Freiherrn von Thielmann*, Leipzig: Rauck, 1830.

Holtzheimer, Hans, 'Erzherzog Karl bei Wagram', dissertation, University of Berlin, 1904.

[Hormayr, Josef Freiherr], *Das Heer von Innerösterreich unter den Befehlen des Erzherzogs Johann im Kriege von 1809 in Italien, Tyrol und Ungarn*, Leipzig and Altenburg: Brockhaus, 1817.

—— 'Tyrolensia', *Taschenbuch für vaterländische Geschichte*, vol. XXIX, 1840.

—— *Lebensbilder aus dem Befreiungskriege*, Jena: Frommann, 1844.

—— *Das Land Tyrol und der Tyrolerkrieg von 1809*, Leipzig: Brockhaus, 1845.

Howard, Martin R., 'Walcheren 1809: A Medical Catastrophe', *British Medical Journal*, 18 December 1999.

Hoyer, J. G. von, *Handbuch der Pontonnier-Wissenschaften*, Leipzig: Barth, 1830.

Hutter, Herman, 'Die Operationen Napoleons in den Tagen vom 16. bis 24. April 1809', *Neue Militärische Blätter*, vol. XX, 1882.

Interessante Beyträge zu einer Geschichte der Ereignisse in Tirol von 10. April 1809 bis zum 20. Februar 1810, Munich, 1810.

James, William, *The Naval History of Great Britain*, London: Bentley & Son, 1878.

Janitsch, Aemilian, *Kriegsvorfälle zwischen Oesterreich und Frankreich im Jahr 1809*, vol. IV of *Merkwürdige Geschichte des Kriegsvorfälle neuester Zeit*, Vienna: Gruaffer, 1812.

Johnson, David, *Napoleon's Cavalry and its Leaders*, New York: Holmes & Meier, 1978.

—— *The French Cavalry 1792–1815*, London: Belmont, 1989.

Jomini, Antoine Henri, *Life of Napoleon*, West Point: US Military Academy, 1939.

—— *The Art of War*, Westport: Greenwood, n.d. (reprint of 1862 edition).

Joor, Johan, *De Adelaar en het Lam*, Amsterdam: De Bataafsche Leeuw, 2000.

'Journal der Operation des kais. österreichischen Truppen-Corps under dem Generalmajor von Am Ende vom 12ten bis 22ten July 1809', *Europäische Annalen*, vol. VI, 1810.

Junkelmann, Marcus, *Napoleon und Bayern*, Regensburg: Pustet, 1985.

Just, Gustav, 'Das Herzogthum Warschau von seinen Anfängen bis zum Kampf mit Oesterreich 1809', *Mitteilungen des K. und K. Kriegsarchivs*, vol. IV, 1906.

—— *Politik oder Strategie? Kritische Studien über den Warschauer Feldzug Oesterreichs und die Haltung Russlands 1809*, Vienna: Seidel & Sohn, 1909.

—— *Der Friede von Schönbrunn*, vol. 9 of *Das Kriegsjahr 1809 in Einzeldarstellungen*, ed. Alois Veltzé, Vienna: Stern, 1909.

Katte, Rudolf von, 'Der Streifzug des Friedrich Karl von Katte auf Magdeburg im April 1809', *Geschichts-Blätter für Stadt und Land Magdeburg*, vols 70–1, 1935–6.

Kerchnawe, Hugo, *Bei Linz und Ebelsberg Anno Neun*, Vienna: Stern, 1910.

Khuepach, Artur, *Geschichte des K. K. Kriegsmarine während der Jahre 1802 bis 1814*, vol. II, Vienna: Staatsdruckerei, 1942.

Kipa, Emil, *Pod Zamosciem w Roku 1809*, Zamosc: Pomaranski, n.d.

Kirchhammer, Alexander, 'Aspern', *Beilage des Fremden-Blatt*, vol. 148, 31 May 1902.

—— 'Zur offiziellen "Relazion" über die Schlacht von Aspern 1809', *Beilage des Fremden-Blatt*, vols 176, 183, 204, 213, 239, 259, 273, 334, 28 June–6 December 1902.

—— 'Etwas mehr über die Schlacht von Aspern', *Beilage des Fremden-Blatt*, 20 December 1902 and 3 January 1903.

—— *Das Gefecht in der Schwarzen Lacken-Au am 13. Mai 1809*, Vienna: Seidel & Sohn, 1903 (expanded special extract from *Danzer's Armee-Zeitung*, 28 May 1903).

Kirschmaier, Fritz, *Die Gefechte an der Pontzlatzer Brücke 1703 und 1809*, Militärhistorische Schriftenreihe 48, Vienna: Bundesverlag, 1983.

Kissinger, Henry A., *A World Restored*, Boston: Houghton Mifflin, 1957.

Kleinschmidt, Arthur, *Bayern und Hessen 1799–1816*, Berlin: Räde, 1900.

Klier, Franz Augustin, *Oesterreichs letzter Krieg im Jahre 1809*, Munich: Lentner, 1810.

Klinkowström, Clemens von, *Aus der alten Registratur der Staatskanzlei*, Vienna: Braumüller, 1870.

Koch, Hannsjoachim W., *Die Befreiungskriege 1807–1815*, Berg: Türmer, 1987.

Köfler, Werner, *Die Kämpfe am Pass Lueg im Jahre 1809*, Militärhistorische Schriftenreihe 41, Vienna: Bundesverlag, 1980.

—— *Die Kämpfe am Bergisel 1809*, Militärhistorische Schriftenreihe 20, Vienna: Bundesverlag, 1983.

Kortzfleisch, Gustav von, *Des Herzogs Friedrich Wilhelm von Braunschweig Zug durch Norddeutschland im Jahre 1809*, Krefeld: Olmes, 1973 (reprint of 1894 edition).

Kosáry, Domokos, *Napoléon et la Hongrie*, Budapest: Akademiai Kiado, 1979.

Kraehe, Enno E., *Metternich's German Policy*, Princeton: Princeton University Press, 1963.

Krieg 1809, prepared by the staff of the k. und k. Kriegsarchiv as part of the series *Kriege unter der Regierung des Kaisers Franz*, Vienna: Seidel & Sohn, 1907–10.

Krones, Franz Xaver, *Zur Geschichte Österreichs im Zeitalter der französischen Kriege und der Restauration*, Gotha: Perthes, 1886.

Kukiel, M., 'Bitwa pod Raszynem', *Bellona*, Warsaw, 1918.

Kulturverein Schloss Ebelsberg, *Das Gefecht bei Ebelsberg am 3. Mai 1809*, museum catalogue, Ebelsberg, 1989.

Kurz, Franz, *Geschichte der Landwehr in Oesterreich ob der Enns*, Linz: Haslinger, 1811.

Laborde, Alexandre de, *Précis Historique de la Guerre entre la France et l'Autriche en 1809*, Paris: Didot, 1822.

Lachouque, Henri, *Napoleon's Battles*, London: George Allen & Unwin, 1964.

Langsam, Walter C., *The Napoleonic Wars and German Nationalism in Austria*, New York: Columbia University Press, 1930.

Lanyi, Ladislas, 'Napoléon et les Hongrois', *Annales Historiques de la Révolution Française*, vol. 141, October–December 1955.

Larisch, August von, *Das Kriegsjahr 1809*, Kötzchenbroda: Trapp, 1899.

Lazar, Balazs, 'Die Schlacht bei Raab (Györ)', *Zusammenfassung der Beiträge zum Napoleon Symposium 'Feldzug 1809'*, Vienna: Delta Druckproduktionen, 2009.

Ledru, A., *Montbrun 1809*, Paris: Fournier, 1913.

Lefebvre, Armand and Eduard Lefebvre de Béhaine, *Histoire des Cabinets de l'Europe pendant le Consulat et l'Empire*, Paris: Amyot, 1867–8.

Lentz, Thierry, 'L'Empire napoléonien dans la Tourmente', *Zusammenfassung der Beiträge zum Napoleon Symposium 'Feldzug 1809'*, Vienna: Delta Druckproduktionen, 2009.

'Lettres Interceptées 1809', *Carnet de la Sabretache*, 1895.

L'Huillier, André, 'Les Armées de la Tête des Flandres et d'Anvers (Août–Septembre 1809)', 1972, at www.histoire-empire.org/1809.

Litre, Emile François, 'La Grande Batterie de la Garde a Wagram', *Revue d'Artillerie*, vol. LXVI, 1895.

Litschel, Rudolf W., *Das Gefecht bei Ebelsberg am 3. Mai 1809*, Militärhistorische Schriftenreihe 9, Vienna: Bundesverlag, 1968.

Litten, Neil, 'The Battle of Linz 17th May 1809', no further information.

Löben-Sels, E. van, *Bijdragen tot de Krigsgeschiedenes van Napoleon Bonaparte*, The Hague, 1839.

Lorette, J., 'L'Alerte de Walcheren et la Défense d'Anvers (1809)', *Revue Internationale d'Histoire Militaire*, vol. 20, 1959.

Loÿ, Léon C. E. A., *La campagne de Styrie en 1809*, Paris: Chapelot, 1908.

Lüders, H., *Europa's Palingenesie*, part I, *Oesterreichs Kriegsgeschichte im Jahre Achtzehnhundertneun*, Leipzig and Altenburg: Richter, 1810.

Lyncker, Karl, *Geschichte der Insurrectionen wider das westphälische Gouvernement*, Kassel: Bertram, 1857.

Lütgendorf, Kasimir Freiherr von, *Die Kämpfe in Südtirol*, Vienna: Seidel & Sohn, 1911.

Madelin, Louis, *Histoire du Consulat et de l'Empire*, Paris: Hachette, 1944.

Mackesy, Piers, *The War in the Mediterranean 1803–1810*, Westport: Greenwood, 1981.

Marchesi, Vincenzo, 'La Guerra Intorno a Venezia nel 1809', *Rivista Storica del Risogimento Italiano*, vol. I, 1895.

Maretich von Riv-Alpon, Gedeon Freiherr, 'Die Gefechte in der Umgebung von Salzburg in den Jahren 1800, 1805 und 1809', *Streffleur's Oesterreichische Militärische Zeitschrift*, January and February 1893.

—— *Die zweite und dritte Berg Isel-Schlacht*, Innsbruck: Wagner, 1895.

—— 'Josef Struber und die Kämpfe in der Umgebung des Passes Lueg im Jahre 1809', *Mittheilungen der Gesellschaft für Salzburger Landeskunde*, vol. XXXVII, 1897.

—— *Die vierte Berg Isel-Schlacht am 13. August 1809*, Innsbruck: Wagner, 1899.

'Les Marins de la Flottille et les Ouvriers Militaires de la Marine pendant la Campagne de 1809 en Autriche', *Carnet de la Sabretache*, 1895.

Martens, Fedor, *Recueil des Traités et Conventions conclus par la Russie avec les Puissances Etrangères*, St Petersburg, 1876–1908.

Martens, Karl von, *Geschichte der innerhalb der gegenwärtigen Gränzen des Königreichs Württemberg vorgefallenen kriegerischen Ereignisse vom Jahr 15 vor Christi Geburt bis zum Friedensschlusse 1815*, Stuttgart: Königliche Hofbuchdruckerei, 1847.

Martin, H., 'Zur Ehrenrettung Sigmund Peter Martins', *Zeitschrift des Vereins für hessische Geschichte und Landeskunde*, vol. XVIII, 1893.

Marx, Anton, 'Das Gefecht am Kalvarienberg bei Klagenfurt, am 6. Juni 1809', ÖMZ, 1836.

Mayr, Johann G., *Der Mann von Rinn*, Innsbruck: Ostermann, 1851.

Mayerhoffer von Vedropolje, Eberhard, *Oesterreichs Krieg mit Napoleon I*, Vienna: Seidel & Sohn, 1904.

—— 'Die französische "Armee in Deutschland" bei Ausbruch des Krieges im Jahre 1809', *Organ der militär-wissenschaftliche Vereine*, vol. LXV, 1902.

—— '1809. Aufmarsch des Heeres Napoleon I.', *Organ der Militärwissenschaftlichen Vereine*, vol. LXVII, 1903.

—— '1809: Die Konzentrierungsbewegungen der Armee Napoleon I. in der Zeit vom 10. bis 17. April', *Organ der Militärwissenschaftlichen Vereine*, vol. LXIX, 1904.

Menge, August, *Die Schlacht von Aspern am 21. und 22. Mai 1809*, Berlin: Stilke, 1900.

Mikaberidze, Alexander, *The Russian Officer Corps in the Revolutionary and Napoleonic Wars, 1792-1815*, New York: Savas Beattie, 2005.

Mikhailovsky-Danilevsky, Alexander, *Russo-Turkish War of 1806-1812*, trans. Alexander Mikaberidze, West Chester: Nafziger, 2002.

Molières, Michel, *La Campagne de 1809: Les Opérations du 20 au 23 Avril*, Paris: Le Livre Chez Vous, 2003.

—— *Napoléon en Autriche: La Campagne de 1809: Les Opérations du 24 Avril au 12 Juillet*, Paris: Le Livre Chez Vous, 2004.

Morel, Lieutenant, 'Insurrection au Tyrol en 1809', AG, Manuscrits, MR736.

Mortonval [pseudonym for Alexandre-Fursy Guesdon], *Die Feldzüge in Teutschland*, Leipzig: Leske, 1831.

Mowat, R. B., *The Diplomacy of Napoleon*, London: Arnold, 1924.

Muir, Rory, *Britain and the Defeat of Napoleon 1807–1815*, New Haven: Yale University Press, 1996.

Müller, W., *Relation of the Operations and Battles of the Austrian and French Armies in the Year 1809*, Cambridge: Ken Trotman, 1986 (reprint of 1810 edition).

Münchow-Pohl, Bernd von, *Zwischen Reform und Krieg: Untersuchungen zur Bewusstseinlage in Preussen 1809–1812*, Göttingen: Vandenhoeck & Ruprecht, 1987.

Mustafa, Sam A., *The Long Ride of Major von Schill*, Plymouth: Rowman & Littlefield, 2008.

Nagy-Luttenberger, Istvan, 'Einteilung und Stärke der Armee von Innerösterreich im Feldzug von Ungarn', *Zusammenfassung der Beiträge zum Napoleon Symposium 'Feldzug 1809'*, Vienna: Delta Druckproduktionen, 2009.

Nüschler, Conrad, 'Rückblick auf die kriegerischen Ereignisse in Tirol im Jahre 1809', *Organ der militär-wissenschaftlichen Vereine*, vol. XIX, 1879.

Ochwicz, Gustaw, *Rok 1809*, Posen, 1925.

Ogris, Herta, 'Die Kriegesereignisse in Kärnten 1809', dissertation, University of Vienna, May 1941.

Oman, Sir Charles, *A History of the Peninsular War*, London: Greenhill, 1995–7.

Oncken, Wilhelm, *Oesterreich und Preussen im Befreiungskriege*, Berlin: Grote, 1879.

—— *Das Zeitalter der Revolution, des Kaiserreiches und der Befreiungskriege*, Berlin: Grote, 1886.

Otto, Friedrich, 'Schlacht bei Landshut am 21. April 1809', *Verhandlungen des Historischen Vereins für Niederbayern*, vol. 33, 1897.

—— 'Gefecht zwischen Hausen und Teugn am 19. April 1809', *Verhandlungen des Historischen Vereins für Niederbayern*, date not available.

Ouvrard, Robert, *1809: Les Français à Vienne*, Paris: Nouveau Monde, 2009.

P., A. von, 'Die Lobau im Jahre 1809', *Oesterreichische militärische Zeitschrift*, vol. III, 1893.

[Pahl, Johann Gottfried von, writing as 'Alethinos'], *Der Krieg in Deutschland im Jahre 1809 und dessen Resultate politisch und militärisch betrachtet*, Munich: Lentner, 1810.

Paret, Peter, *Yorck and the Era of Prussian Reform*, Princeton: Princeton University Press, 1966.

—— (ed.), *Makers of Modern Strategy*, Princeton: Princeton University Press, 1986.

Parker, Harold T., *Three Napoleonic Battles*, Durham, NC: Duke University Press, 1983.

Pawlowski, Bronislaw, *Z Dziejow Kampanji 1809 Roku w Galicji Wschodniej*, Lwow: University Press, 1928.

—— *Dziennik Historyczny I Korespondencja Polowa Generala Michala Sokolnickiego*, Krakow: Nakladem Polskiej Akademji Umiejetnosci, 1931.

—— *Historja Wojny Polsko-Austrajackiej 1809 Roku*, Warsaw, 1935.

Pelet, Jean-Jacques, *Mémoires sur la guerre de 1809 en Allemagne*, Paris: Roret, 1824–6.

Pergler, Adolf, *Selbst- und Landesverteidigung der vereinten Pinzgauer und Tiroler in den Jahren 1800, 1805 und 1809 an den Pässen Botenbühel, Strub und Luftenstein*, Lofer, 1906.

Peternader, Anton, *Tirols Landes-Vertheidigung nebst interessanten Biografien und Skizzen merkwürdiger Tiroler Landesvertheidiger*, Innsbruck: Witting, 1853.

[Petit], *Histoire des Campagnes de l'Empereur Napoléon dans la Bavière et l'Autriche en 1805, dans la Prusse et la Pologne en 1806 et 1807, dans la Bavière et l'Autriche en 1809*, Paris: Piquet, 1843.

Petre, Francis Loraine, *Napoleon and the Archduke Charles*, London: John Lane, 1909.

Pfalz, Anton, *Die Marchfeldschlachten von Aspern und Deutsch-Wagram im Jahre 1809*, Korneuburg: Kühkopf, 1900.

Pfau, Franz, 'Die Vertheidigung und der Fall des Blockhauses auf dem Predil, im Jahre 1809', *ÖMZ*, 1843.

Philipp, Lt. Col. de, *Le Service d'Etat-Major pendant les Guerres du Premier Empire*, Paris: Teissèdre, 2002.

Picard, L., *La Cavalerie dans les Guerres de la Révolution et de l'Empire*, Paris: Teissedre, 2000.

Pigeard, Alain, 'L'Artillerie Régimentaire sous le Premier Empire', *Tradition*, no. 154, March 2000.

—— 'L'Artillerie à Pied de la Garde', *Tradition*, no. 237, May–June 2008.

Pingaud, Albert, 'Napoléon et la Défense de l'Italie sur la Piave', *Revue des Études Napoléoniennes*, vol. XIX, July–December 1922.

Pisani, Paul, *La Dalmatie de 1797 à 1815*, Paris: Picard, 1893.

Plischnack, Alfred, *Vive l'Empereur, weil's sein muss*, Vienna: Amalthea, 1999.

Das preussische Heer der Befreiungskriege, Berlin: Mittler & Sohn, 1912 (reprinted Bad Honnef: LTG Verlag, 1982).

Priem, Johann Paul, *Geschichte der Stadt Nürnberg*, Nuremberg: Zeiser, 1875.

Pritz, Franz Xaver, *Geschichte des Landes ob der Enns von der ältesten bis zur neuesten Zeit*, Linz: Haslinger, 1847.

'Quellen über die Kriegs-Geschichte der württemb. Truppen von 1792 an', *Jahrbücher für vaterländische Geschichte Geographie, Statistik und Topographie*, vol. I, 1853.

Raeder, J. von, *Danmarks Krigs- og Politiske Historie*, Copenhagen: Reitzel, 1847–52.

Rambaud, Alfred, *L'Allemagne sous Napoléon Ier (1804–1811)*, Paris: Perrin, 1897.

Rapp, Ludwig, *Schicksale des Servitenklosters bei Volders in Tirol in den Kriegsjahren 1703, 1805 und 1809*, Brixen: Weger, 1886.

Rassow, Peter, 'Die Wirkung der Erhebung Spaniens auf die deutsche Erhebung gegen Napoleon I', *Historische Zeitschrift*, vol. 167, 1943.

Rauchensteiner, Manfried, *Die Schlacht bei Deutsch Wagram am 5. und 6. Juli 1809*, Militärhistorische Schriftenreihe 36, Vienna: Bundesverlag, 1977.

—— *Die Schlacht von Aspern am 21. und 22. Mai 1809*, Militärhistorische Schriftenreihe 11, Vienna: Bundesverlag, 1986.

—— (ed.) *Clausewitz, Jomini, Erzherzog Carl: eine geistige Trilogie des 19. Jahrhunderts und ihre Bedeutung für die Gegenwart*, Vienna: Bundesverlag, 1988.

—— 'Sieger und Besiegte: Die österreichische Generalität 1809', *Zusammenfassung der Beiträge zum Napoleon Symposium 'Feldzug 1809'*, Vienna: Delta Druckproduktionen, 2009.

Regnault, Jean, *Les Aigles Impériales et le Drapeau Tricolore 1804–1815*, Paris: Peyronnet, 1967.

Reichel, Rudolf, 'Mittheilungen aus einem Gerichtsprotokolle des Marktes Deutsch-Feistritz', *Mittheilungen des historischen Vereines für Steiermark*, vol. XXXVIII, 1890.

Renémont, C. de [pseudonym for Auguste Clément Gérome], *Campagne de 1809*, Paris: Charles-Lavauzelle, 1903.

Die Reorganisation der Preussischen Armee nach dem Tilsiter Frieden, Berlin: Mittler & Sohn, 1857.

Reschounig, Friedrich, 'Das Jahr 1809 im Urtheile der Zeitgenossen', dissertation, University of Vienna, 1939.

Revue de Cavalerie, March 1899.

Richter, Arwed, *Das hamburgische Amt Ritzebüttel und die Elbmündung in den Jahren 1795–1814*, Cuxhaven, 1895.

Ridler, J. W., 'Rückerinnerung an Österreichische Helden', *Archiv für Geographie, Historie, Staats- und Kriegskunst*, nos. 45 and 46, April 1811.

—— 'Die Thermopylen der kärnischen Alpen', *Archiv für Geographie, Historie, Staats- und Kriegskunst*, no. 51, April 1811.

—— 'Die Erstürmung des Forts von Malborghetto 1809', *ÖMZ*, 1813.

—— 'Der Ruckzug des Generals Mesko nach der Schlacht bey Raab', *Archiv für Geographie, Historie, Staats- und Kriegskunst*, nos. 131 and 132, November 1813; also published in *Taschenbuch für die vaterländische Geschichte*, vol. III, 1813.

Robinet de Cléry, Gabriel Adrien, *En Tyrol*, Paris: Olldendorff, 1897.

Rogniat, Joseph, *Considérations sur l'Art de la Guerre*, Paris: Anselin and Pochard, 1820.

Romegialli, Giuseppe, *Storia della Valtellina*, Sondrio: Cagnoletto, 1839.

Rössler, Hellmuth, *Oesterreichs Kampf um Deutschlands Befreiung*, Hamburg: Hanseatische Verlagsanstalt, 1940.

Rothenberg, Gunther E., *The Military Border in Croatia 1740–1881*, Chicago: University of Chicago Press, 1966.

—— *Napoleon's Great Adversaries: The Archduke Charles and the Austrian Army 1792–1814*, Bloomington: Indian University Press, 1982.

—— *The Emperor's Last Victory: Napoleon and the Battle of Wagram*, London: Weidenfeld & Nicolson, 2004.

R. [Rothenburg], F. R. von, *Die Waffenthaten der Oesterreicher im Jahre 1809*, Vienna: Hirschfeld, 1838.

Sallagar, Hermann, 'Die Verteidigung der Position von Präwald im Jahre 1809', *ÖMZ*, vol. VI, 1908.

—— 'Die Kämpfe um Sachsenburg, am Plöckenpasse, im Drautale und bei Klagenfurt 1809', *Carinthia I*, nos. 2–5, 1909.

Sapherson, C. A., *A Year at War 1809*, Leeds: Raider Books, 1986.

Saski, Charles, *Campagne de 1809 en Allemagne et en Autriche*, Paris: Berger-Levrault, 1899–1902.

Schieger, Josef, 'Quellen und Beiträge zur Geschichte der Vertheidigung des Schlossberges von Graz im Jahre 1809', *Mittheilungen des historischen Vereines für Steiermark*, vol. XIV, 1866.

Schels, Johann Baptist, 'Der Feldzug 1809 in Dalmatien', *ÖMZ*, 1837.

—— 'Überfall auf eine französische Kolonne bei Wolfsbach, am 15. Mai 1809', *ÖMZ*, 1843.

—— 'Die Schlacht bei Aspern am 21. und 22. Mai 1809', *ÖMZ*, 1843.

—— 'Der Feldzug 1809 in Italien', *ÖMZ*, 1844.

—— 'Der Feldzug 1809 in Polen', *ÖMZ*, 1844.

—— 'Das Gefecht an der Isar bei Landshut am 16. April 1809', *ÖMZ*, 1845.

—— 'Das Treffen bei Neumarkt an der Roth am 24. April 1809', *ÖMZ*, 1846.

Schemfil, Viktor, 'Das k. k. Tiroler Korps im Kriege 1809', *Tiroler Heimat*, vol. XXIII, 1959.

Scherer, Carl, 'Zur Geschichte des Dörnbergischen Aufstandes im Jahre 1809', *Historische Zeitschrift*, vol. XVIII, 1900.

Schikofsky, Karl, 'Die Vertheidigung des Brückenkopfes von Pressburg im Jahre 1809', *Organ der militär-wissenschaftlichen Vereine*, vol. XLVI, 1893.

Schimmer, Karl August, *Die Französischen Invasionen in Oesterreich und die Franzosen in Wien in den Jahren 1805 und 1809*, Vienna: Dirnböck, 1846.

Die Schlacht bei Ebelsberg, Linz: Mareis, 1902.

Schlagintweit, Maximilian, 'Kufsteins Kriegsjahre (1504, 1703, 1809)', *Darstellungen aus der Bayerischen Kriegs- und Heeresgeschichte*, vol. XII, 1903.

Schneid, Frederick C., *Soldiers of Napoleon's Kingdom of Italy*, Boulder: Westview, 1995.

—— *Napoleon's Italian Campaigns 1805–1815*, Westport: Praeger, 2002.

Schneidawind, Franz J. A., *Der Krieg Oersterreich's gegen Frankreich, dessen Alliirte und den Rheinbund im Jahre 1809*, Schaffhausen: Hurter, 1842.

—— *Der Feldzug des Herzogs Friedrich Wilhelm von Braunschweig und seines schwarzen Corps im Jahre 1809*, Darmstadt: Leske, 1851.

Schroeder, Paul W., *The Transformation of European Politics*, Oxford: Clarendon Press, 1994.

—— 'Preventive War to Restore Order and Stabilize the International System', paper presented at the International Studies Association annual meeting, 26 March 2008, www.allacademic.com.

Ségur, Philippe Paul Comte de, *Histoires et Mémoires*, Paris: Didot, 1873.

Seidel, Friedrich von, 'Die Operazionen des von dem Banus von Kroazien, Feldmarschall-Lieutnant Grafen Ignaz Gyulai befehligten östreichischen neunten Armeekorps im Feldzuge 1809', *ÖMZ*, 1837.

Sherwig, John M., *Guineas and Gunpowder*, Cambridge, MA: Harvard University Press, 1969.

Soltyk, Roman, *Relation des Opérations de l'Armée aux Ordres du Prince Joseph Poniatowski pendant la Campagne de 1809 en Pologne contre les Autrichiens*, Paris: Gauthier-Laguione, 1841.

Smekal, Gustav, *Die Schlacht bei Aspern und Esslingen 21. und 22. Mai 1809*, Vienna: Seidel & Sohn, 1899.

Stark, Nicolaus, *Erinnerungs-Blätter an die Schlachttage bei Abensberg*, Abensberg, 1908 (with thanks to the town museum of Abensberg).

Staudenrauss, Alois, *Chronik der Stadt Landshut in Bayern*, Landshut: Thomann, 1832.

Steiner, Herta, 'Das Urteil Napoleons I. über Oesterreich', dissertation, University of Vienna, 1946.

Steinkellner, Franz, *Die Franzosenzeit im Bezirk Amstetten*, Amstetten-Ludwigsdorf, 1968.

Stern, Alfred, *Abhandlungen und Aktenstücke zur Geschichte der preussischen Reformzeit 1807–1815*, Leipzig: Duncker & Humblot, 1885.

—— 'Gneisenau's Reise nach London im Jahre 1809 und ihre Vorgeschichte', *Historische Zeitschrift*, vol. 85, 1900.

Strobl, Ad, *Aspern und Wagram*, Vienna: Seidel & Sohn, 1897.

Stuers, Victor de, 'Voor 80 Jaren: De Hollanders te Straalsund', *Haagsche Stemmen*, no. 41, 8 June 1889.

—— 'Een Episode uit de Bestorming van Stralsund', *Eigen Haard*, 1899.

[Stutterheim, Karl Freiherr von], *La Guerre de l'An 1809 entre l'Autriche et la France*, Vienna: Strauss, 1811; published in German as *Der Krieg von 1809 zwischen Oesterreich und Frankreich*, Vienna: Strauss, 1811.

—— 'Der Feldzug 1809 zwischen Oesterreich und Frankreich nach Stutterheim', ÖMZ, 1849.

'Taktische Betrachtungen über die Schlacht bei Sacile am 16. April 1809', ÖMZ, 1861.

Tatistcheff, Serge, *Alexandre Ier et Napoléon d'après leur Correspondance Inédite*, Paris: Perrin, 1891.

Tepperberg, Christoph, *Die Kämpfe um den Grazer Schlossberg 1809*, Vienna: Bundesverlag, 1987.

Thiers, Adolphe, *Histoire du Consulat et de l'Empire*, Paris: Paulin, 1845–69.

Thimme, Friedrich, *Die innere Zustände des Kurfürstentums Hannover unter der französisch-westfälischen Herrschaft*, Hanover: Hahn, 1893.

—— 'Die hannoverschen Aufstandspläne im Jahre 1809 und England', *Zeitschrift des Historischen Vereins für Niedersachsen*, 1897.

—— 'Zu den Erhebungsplänen der preussischen Patrioten im Sommer 1808', *Historische Zeitschrift*, vol. 86, 1901.

Thiry, Jean, *Wagram*, Paris: Berger-Levrault, 1966.

Thomsen, P. B. Krieger, 'Schills Tog til Stralsund (1809)', *Krigshistorisk Tidsskrift*, no. 1, 1968.

Thonhauser, Josef, *Osttirol im Jahre 1809*, Schlern-Schriften 253, Innsbruck: Wagner, 1968.

Thoumas, Charles A., *Les Grands Cavaliers du Premier Empire*, Paris: Berger-Levrault, 1890.

Toifl, Leopold, 'Belagerung und Zerstörung des Grazer Schlossberges im Jahr 1809', *Zusammenfassung der Beiträge zum Napoleon Symposium 'Feldzug 1809'*, Vienna: Delta Druckproduktionen, 2009.

Tonnet, J. C. C., 'De Landing in Zeeland in 1809', *De Militaire Spectator*, 1909–10.

Tranie, Jean and Juan Carlos Carmigniani, *Napoléon et l'Autriche——La Campagne de 1809*, Paris: Copernic, 1979.

[Traux, Ludwig de], 'Bermerkungen über die im 2ten und 3ten Stück der europäische Annalen enthaltenen Marginalien zur Relation über die Schlacht bei Wagram', *Europäische Annalen*, vol. V, 1810.

'Das Treffen von Ebelsberg am 3. Mai 1809', ÖMZ, vol. 7, 1832.

Turotti, Felice, *Storia dell'Armi Italiane dal 1796 al 1814*, Milan: Boniotti, 1856.

U., J. A., *Der Feldzug Frankreichs und seiner Verbündeten gegen Oesterreich im Jahre 1809*, Meissen: Goedsche, 1810.

'Der Überfall auf Laibach, am 27. Juni 1809', ÖMZ, 1843.

'Ueber das Passieren von Flüssen', *Zeitschrift für Kunst, Wissenschaft und Geschichte des Krieges*, vol. VII, 1841.

'Ueber den Volkskrieg mit Bezug auf den Tyroler Krieg 1809', *Militair-Wochenblatt*, no. 107, 11 July 1818.

'Ueber die Operationen des Grafen Gyulai, als Rechtfertigung gegen die Beschuldigungen des Verf. Der "Darstellung der Schlachten auf dem Marchfelde"', *Europäischen Annalen*, vol. 8, 1811.

'Uebersicht der Kriegsbegebenheiten zwischen Russland und der Pforte an der unteren Donau, vom Jahre 1806 bis 1812', ÖMZ, 1829.

Unger, L. A., *Histoire Critique des Exploits et Vicissitudes de la Cavallerie*, Paris: Corréard, 1848.

Valentini, Georg Freiherr von, *Versuch einer Geschichte des Feldzugs von 1809 an der Donau*, 2nd edn, Berlin: Nikolai, 1818.

Vandal, Albert, *Napoléon et Alexandre Ier*, Paris: Plon, 1918.

Van Gent, T., *De Engelse invasie van Walcheren in 1809*, Amsterdam: Bataafsche Leeuw, 2001.

Van Hattem, Mark, 'In the Name of a New Austria: Archduke Johann's Programme for Army Reform 1805–1809', *Zusammenfassung der Beiträge zum Napoleon Symposium 'Feldzug 1809'*, Vienna: Delta Druckproduktionen, 2009.

Vann, James Allen, 'Habsburg Policy and the Austrian War of 1809', *Central European History*, vol. VII, no. 4, December 1974.

Varges, Willi, 'Die Theilnahme des Kurfürsten Wilhelm I. von Hessen am Oesterreichischen Kriege 1809', *Zeitschrift des Vereins für hessische Geschichte und Landeskunde*, vol. XVI, 1891.

—— 'Der Marburger Aufstand des Jahres 1809', *Zeitschrift des Vereins für hessische Geschichte und Landeskunde*, vol. XVII, 1892.

—— 'Die kurhessische Legion im Jahre 1809', *Zeitschrift des Vereins für hessische Geschichte und Landeskunde*, vol. XXI, 1896.

Vaupel, Rudolf (ed.), *Das Preussische Heer von Tilsiter Frieden bis zur Befreiung*, part 2 of *Die Reorganisation des Preussischen Staates unter Stein und Hardenberg*, vol. 94 of *Publikationen aus den Preussischen Staatsarchiven*, Leipzig: Hirzel, 1938.

Veltzé, Alois, 'Aus den Tagen von Pordenone und Sacile', *Mitteilungen des K. und K. Kriegsarchivs*, 1904.

—— *Österreichs Thermopylen 1809*, Vienna: Stern, 1905.

—— 'Die Schlacht an der Piave', *Mitteilungen des K. und K. Kriegsarchivs*, vol. IV, 1906.

—— 'Der Grazer Schlossberg 1809', *Mitteilungen des K. und K. Kriegsarchivs*, vol. V, 1907.

—— *Kriegsbilder aus Polen, Steiermark und Ungarn*, volume XI of *Das Kriegsjahr 1809 in Einzeldarstellungen*, Vienna: Stern, 1910.

Veress, Csaba D., *Napoleon Hadai Magyar-Oragon 1809*, Budapest: Zrinyi Katonai Kiado, 1987.

'Die Vertheidigung der Blockhäuser Malborghet und Predil im Jahre 1809', *Mittheilungen über Gegenstände des Artillerie- und Geniewesens*, vol. XXXII, 1901.

Victoires, Conquêtes, et Désastres, Revers et Guerres Civiles des Français, de 1792 à 1815, Paris: Panckoucke, 1820.

Vignolle, Martin, 'Historique de la Campagne de 1809 (Armée d'Italie)', *Revue Militaire*, no. 16, July 1900.

Vizi, Tomas Laszlo, 'Die politische Rolle des ungarischen Adels im Zeitalter der französischen Kriege', *Zusammenfassung der Beiträge zum Napoleon Symposium 'Feldzug 1809'*, Vienna: Delta Druckproduktionen, 2009.

Wachtel, Wilhelm, 'Die Division Jellacic im Mai 1809', *Mitteilungen des K. und K. Kriegsarchivs*, vol. VIII, 1911.

Wagner, Anton H., *Das Gefecht bei St. Michael-Loeben am 25. Mai 1809*, Vienna: Bundesverlag, 1984.

Wanner, Gerhard, *Kriegsschauplatz Bodensee 1799/1800 und 1809*, Vienna: Bundesverlag, 1987.

Welden, Ludwig Freiherr von, *Der Krieg von 1809 zwischen Oesterreich und Frankreich von Anfang Mai bis zum Friedensschlusse*, Vienna: Gerold, 1872.

Werenka, Daniel, 'Der Kriegsruf an die Bukowina im Jahre 1809', *Jahresbericht der gr.-or. Ober-Realschule in Czernowitz*, vol. XXXIX, 1903.

Wertheimer, Eduard, *Geschichte Oesterreichs und Ungarns im ersten Jahrzehnt des 19. Jahrhunderts*, Leipzig: Duncker & Humblot, 1890.

—— 'Zur Geschichte Wiens im Jahre 1809', *Archiv für österreichische Geschichte*, vol. 47, 1889.

—— *Die drei ersten Frauen des Kaisers Franz*, Leipzig: Duncker & Humblot, 1893.

Whitcomb, Edwards A., *Napoleon's Diplomatic Service*, Durham, NC: Duke University Press, 1979.

White, D. Fedotoff, 'The Russian Navy in Trieste', *American Slavic and East European Review*, vol. VI, nos. 18–19, December 1947.

Wieland, Johann, *Geschichte der Kriegsbegebenheiten in Helvetien und Rhätien*, Basel: Schweighaus, 1868.

Will, Cornelius, 'Beiträge zur Geschichte des französisch-österreichischen Kriegs im Jahre 1809', *Verhandlungen des Historischen Vereins für Oberpfalz und Regensburg*, vol. XXXI, 1875.

—— 'Archivalische Beiträge zur Geschichte der Erstürmung von Regensburg am 23. April 1809 und deren Folgen', *Verhandlungen des Historischen Vereins für Oberpfalz und Regensburg*, vol. 47, 1895.

Wisnar, Julius, 'Die Schlacht bei Znaim im Jahre 1809', *Jahresbericht des k. k. Gymnasiums in Znaim für das Schuljahr 1909 1910*, Znaim: Lenk, 1910.

Wöber, Ferdi Irmfried, *1809: Schlacht bei Aspern und Essling*, Vienna: Lang & Gratzenberger, 1992.

—— *1809: The Battle of Raab*, Vienna: Delta Druckproduktionen, 2003.

—— *1809: Das Gefecht um Pápa*, Vienna: Delta Druckproduktionen, 2005.

—— *1809: Die Zeit nach der Schlacht bei Raab*, Vienna: Delta Druckproduktionen, 2006.

Woinovich, Emil von, *Kämpfe in der Lika in Kroatien und Dalmatien 1809*, vol. 6 of *Das Kriegsjahr 1809 in Einzeldarstellungen*, ed. Alois Veltzé, Vienna: Stern, 1906.

Wolf-Schneider von Arno, Oskar Freiherr, 'Radetzky in Oberösterreich', *Linzer Tages-Post*, no. 4, 1933.

Xylander, Rudolf von, 'Zum Gedächtnis des Feldzugs 1809 in Bayern', *Darstellungen aus der Bayerischen Kriegs- und Heeresgeschichte*, vol. 18, 1909.

Yorck von Wartenburg, Maximilian Count, *Napoleon as a General*, Carlisle, PA: US Army War College, 1983.

Zachar, Jozsef, 'Die Insurrektion des Königreichs Ungarn', unpublished paper presented at the 'Napoleon und Graz 1809' symposium, June 2004.

—— 'Die Insurrektion des Königreichs Ungarn' *Zusammenfassung der Beiträge zum Napoleon Symposium 'Feldzug 1809'*, Vienna: Delta Druckproduktionen, 2009.

Zanoli, Alessandro, *Sulla Milizia Cisalpino-Italiana cenni Storico-Statistici dal 1796 al 1814*, Milan, 1845.

Zehetbauer, Ernst, *Landwehr gegen Napoleon: Oesterreichs erste Miliz und der Nationalkrieg von 1809*, Vienna: öbv & hpt, 1999.

Zelle, 'Welche Truppentheile Napleon's fochten bei Aspern', *Allgemeine Militär-Zeitung*, vols 47–8, November 1901.

Zschokke, Heinrich, *Der Krieg Oesterreichs gegen Frankreich und den rheinischen Bund im Jahre 1809*, Aarau: Remigius, 1810.

Zwiedineck-Südenhorst, Hans von, 'Zur Geschichte des Krieges von 1809 in Steiermark', *Beiträge zur Kunde steiermärkischer Geschichtsquellen*, vol. 23, 1891.

—— 'Das Gefecht bei St Michael und die Operationen des Erzherzogs Johann in Steiermark 1809', *Mittheilungen des Instituts für österreichische Geschichtsforschung*, vol. 1, 1891.

—— 'Die Brigade Thierry im Gefechte von Abensberg am 19. und 20. April 1809', *Mittheilungen des Instituts für österreichische Geschichtsforschung*, vol. V, 1896.

—— 'Die Ostalpen in den Franzosenkriegen', *Zeitschrift des Deutschen und Oesterreichischen Alpenvereins*, vol. XXIX, 1899.

Zych, Gabriel, *Raszyn 1809*, Warsaw, 1969.

AUSTRIAN UNIT HISTORIES: INFANTRY, INSURRECTION, AND LANDWEHR

Amon von Treuenfest, Gustav Ritter, *Geschichte des k. k. Infanterie-Regiments Nr. 20*, Vienna: Mayer, 1878.

—— *Geschichte des Kaiserlich Königlich Infanterie-Regiments Hoch und Deutschmeister*, Vienna, 1879.

—— *Geschichte des k. k. Infanterie-Regiments Nr. 47*, Vienna: Mayer, 1882.

—— *Geschichte des k. k. Infanterie-Regimentes Nr. 50*, Vienna: Mayer, 1882.

—— 'Die Fahne des k. k. 2. böhmischen Legions-Bataillons Erzherzog Carl', *Oesterreichische militärische Zeitschrift*, vol. III, 1883.

—— 'Das zweite Grazer Landwehr-Bataillon 1809', *ÖMZ*, 1889.

—— *Geschichte des k. u. k. Infanterie-Regimentes Nr. 46*, Vienna: regimental, 1890.

—— *Geschichte des kaiserl. und königl. Kärnthnerischen Infanterie-Regiments Feldmarschall Graf von Khevenhüller Nr. 7*, Vienna: St Norbertus, 1891.

Auspitz, Leopold, *Das Infanterie-Regiment Freiherr von Hess Nr. 49*, Teschen: Prochaska, 1889.

Bach, Franz, *Otocaner Regiments-Geschichte*, Karlstadt: Prettner, n.d.

Baxa, Jakob, *Geschichte des k. u. k. Feldjägerbataillons No. 8 1808–1918*, Klagenfurt: Kameradschaftsbundes ehemaliger Achterjäger, 1974.

Beran, Julius, *Die Geschichte des k. und k. Infanterie-Regiments Freiherr von Merkl Nr. 55*, Vienna: regimental, 1899.

Bichmann, Wilhelm, *Chronik des k. k. Infanterie-Regiments Nr. 62*, Vienna: Mayer, 1880.

Blazekovics, Karl von and Julius Pössl, *Geschichte des k. u. k. Infanterie-Regiments Nr. 31*, regimental, 1909.

Branko, Franz von, *Geschichte des k. k. Infanterie-Regimentes Nr. 44*, Vienna: kaiserlichköniglich Hof- und Staatsdruckerei, 1875.

Dengler, Friedrich, *Kurzgefasste Geschichte des kaiserlichen und königlichen Infanterie-Regiments Rupprecht Prinz von Bayern Nr. 43*, Vienna: Stern, 1908.

Donnersberg, August Hofmann von, *Geschichte des k. u. k. Infanterie-Regimentes Nr. 61*, Vienna: Kreisel & Gröger, 1892.

Ebhardt, Ferdinand, *Geschichte des k. k. 33. Infanterie-Regiments*, Ung. Weisskirchen: Wunder, 1888.

Faust, F., *Geschichte des k. k. Infanterie-Regiments von Plüschau, nun Prinz Leopold beider Sicilien*, Vienna, 1841.

Finke, Edmund, *Geschichte des k. u. k. ungarischen Infanterie-Regimentes Nr. 37 Erzherzog Joseph*, Vienna: St Norbertus, 1896.

Formanek, Jaromir, *Geschichte des k. k. Infanterie-Regiments Nr. 41*, Czernowitz: Czopp, 1887.

Geschichte des k. k. Infanterie-Regimentes Oskar II. Friedrich No. 10, Vienna: regimental, 1888.

Geschichte des k. und k. Infanterieregiments Markgraf von Baden No. 23, Budapest: regimental, 1911.

Geschichte des k. k. 25. Infanterie-Regiments, Prague: regimental, 1875.

Geschichte des k. k. Infanterie-Regiments Leopold II., König der Belgier Nr. 27, Vienna: Mayer, 1882.

Geschichte des kaiserlichen und königlichen Infanterie-Regimentes Freiherr von Mollinary Nr. 38, Budapest: regimental, 1892.

Geschichte des k. k. 53. Infanterie-Regimentes, Tulln, 1881.

Geschichte des k. und k. Infanterie-Regiments Erzherzog Ludwig Salvator Nr. 58, Vienna: regimental, 1904.

Grois, Victor, *Geschichte des k. k. Infanterie-Regiments Nr. 14*, Linz: Feichtinger, 1876.

Hailig von Hailingen, Emil Ritter, *Geschichte des k. und k. Infanterie-Regiments Nr. 30*, Lvov: regimental, n.d.

Hermann and Kesch, *Geschichte des k. und k. 52. Linien-Infanerie-Regiments*, Vienna: Hof- und Staatsdruckerei, 1871.

Hermannsthal, Friedrich von, *Geschichte des Tyroler Feld- und Land-, später 46. Linien-Infanterie-Regiments*, Krakow: Czas., 1859.

Hödl, Rudolf von, *Geschichte des k. und k. Infanterieregimentes Nr. 29*, Temesvár: regimental, 1906.

Hold, Alexander, *Geschichte des k. k. 48. Linien-Infanterie-Regimentes*, Vienna: Seidel & Sohn, 1875.

Hubka von Czernczitz, Gustav Ritter, *Geschichte des k. und k. Infanterie-Regiments Graf Lacy No. 22,* Zara, 1902.

Hummel, Carl von, *Landwehrmänner der ehernen Mark 1809,* Vienna: Stern, 1907.

Janota, Robert, *Geschichte des k. und k. Infanterie-Regimentes Graf Daun Nr. 56,* Teschen: Prochaska, 1889.

Johann, Erzherzog von Oesterreich, *Geschichte des K. K. Linien-Infanterie-Regiments Erzherzog Wilhelm No. 12,* Vienna: Seidel & Sohn, 1877.

Kandelsdorfer, Karl, *Geschichte des K. und K. Feld-Jäger-Bataillons Nr. 7,* Bruck an der Mur: battalion, 1896.

—— *Geschichte des k. u. k. Feld-Jäger-Bataillons Nr. 3,* Vienna: Vergani, 1899.

Kisfaludy, Alexander (Sandor), 'Auszug aus der Geschichte der Insurrection des Adels von Ungarn im Jahre 1809 und 1810', manuscript, Országos Szechényi Könyvtár.

Knorz, Justus, *Geschichte des k. k. Infanterie-Regiments Erzherzog Rainer Nr. 59,* Salzburg: regimental, n.d.

Kreipner, Julius, *Geschichte des k. und k. Infanterie-Regimentes Nr. 34,* Kaschau: regimental, 1900.

Kussan, Paul, *Kurzgefasste Geschichte des Oguliner dritten National-Grenz-Infanterie-Regiments,* Vienna: Sommer, 1852.

Maendl, Maximilian, *Geschichte des k. und k. Infanterie-Regiments Nr. 51,* Klausenburg: regimental, 1899.

Mandel, Friedrich, *Geschichte des k. u. k. Infanterie-Regiments Guidobaldo Graf von Starhemberg Nr. 13,* Krakow: regimental, 1893.

May, Josef, *Geschichte des kaiserlich und königlich Infanterie-Regimentes No. 35,* Pilsen: Maasch, 1901.

Mayer, Ferdinand, *Geschichte des k. k. Infanterie-Regimentes Nr. 39,* Vienna: kaiserlichen-königlichen Hof- und Staatsdruckerei, 1875.

Nahlik, Johann Edlen von, *Geschichte des kais. kön. 55. Infanterie-Regimentes,* Brünn: Winiker, 1863.

Netoliczka, August, *Geschichte des k. k. 9. Infanterie-Regiments,* Comorn: Siegler, 1866.

Neuwirth, Victor Ritter von, *Geschichte des K. u. K. Infanterie-Regimentes Alt-Starhemberg Nr. 54,* Olmütz: Hölzel, 1894.

Oesterreichische militärische Zeitschrift:

Waida, Hauptmann, 'Geschichte des 21. Linien-Infanterieregiments Prinz Victor Rohan (dermalen Albert Graf Guilay) im Feldzug 1809', 1819.

'Geschichte des k. k. 49. Linien-Infanterie-Regiments Baron Kerpen in den Feldzügen von 1809, 1813, 1814 und 1815', 1821.

'Geschichte des kaiserlichen-österreichischen 7. Linien-Infanterie-Regiments Grossherzog Toskano', no. 8, 1824.

'Aus der Geschichte des k. k. Grenz-Infanterie-Regiments Szuliner Nr. 4', 1846.

'Aus der Geschichte der beiden k. k. Grenz-Infanterie-Regimenter Siebenbürger Wallachen Nr. 16 und 17', 1847.

'Episoden aus der Geschichte des k. k. 49. Infanterie-Regiments Baron Hess', 1861.

'Rückzug des abgeschnittenen 4. Jäger-Bataillons, im Jahre 1809', 1843.

Padewieth, Mansuet, *Geschichte des kaiserl. königl. 18. Linien-Infanterie-Regimentes*, Vienna: Hof- und Staatsdruckerei, 1859.

Pillersdorf, Albert Freiherr, *Das 57. Infanterie-Regiment*, Vienna: Sommer, 1857.

Pizzighelli, Cajetan, *Geschichte des k. k. Infanterie-Regimentes Kaiser Franz Josef No. 1*, Troppau: regimental, 1881.

—— *Auszug aus der Geschichte des k. u. k. Feldjäger-Bataillons Nr. 9*, Graz: battalion, 1890.

—— *Geschichte des k. u. k. Feldjäger-Bataillons Nr. 9*, Kötschach: battalion, 1911.

Posselt, Oskar, *Geschichte des k. und k. Infanterieregiments Ritter v. Pino Nr. 40*, Rzeszow: Gerold, 1913.

Rona, Ludwig, *Geschichte des k. u. k. Infanterie-Regimentes Adolf Grossherzog von Luxemburg, Herzog zu Nassau Nr. 15*, Prague: Bellmann, 1901.

Schmarda, Carl, *Kurzgefasste Geschichte des k. und k. Otocaner Infanterieregimentes Graf Jellacic Nr. 79*, Agram: regimental, 1898.

Schmedes, Emil, *Geschichte des k. k. 28. Infanterie-Regimentes*, Vienna: Seidel & Sohn, 1878.

Schneider, Michael, *Geschichte des k. u. k. Infanterieregiments Nr. 63*, Bistritz: regimental, 1906.

Schweigerd, C. A., *Geschichte des k. und k. Linien-Infanterie-Regimentes No. 8*, Vienna: Wallishauser, 1857.

Seeliger, Emil, *Geschichte des kaiserlichen und königlichen Infanterie-Regiments Nr. 32*, Budapest, 1900.

Sittig, Heinrich, *Geschichte des k. u. k. Feldjäger-Bataillons Nr. 1*, Reichelberg: Stiepel, 1908.

Stanka, Julius, *Geschichte des K. und K. Infanterie-Regimentes Erzherzog Carl Nr. 3*, Vienna: regimental, 1894.

Strobl von Ravelsberg, Ferdinand, *Die Landwehr Anno Neun*, vol. 10 of *Das Kriegsjahr 1809 in Einzeldarstellungen*, ed. Alois Veltzé, Vienna: Stern, 1909.

—— 'Die kärntnerische Landwehr', *Carinthia I*, nos. 2–5, 1909.

Sypniewski, Alfred Ritter von, *Geschichte des k. und k. Infanterie-Regimentes Feldmarschall Carl Joseph Graf Clerfayt de Croix*, Jaroslau: regimental, 1894.

Virtsolog, Coloman Rupprecht von, *Geschichte des k. k. 60. Linien-Infanterie-Regimentes*, Vienna: k. k. Hof- und Staatsdruckerei, 1871.

AUSTRIAN UNIT HISTORIES: CAVALRY AND OTHER

Amon von Treuenfest, Gustav Ritter, *Geschichte des k. k. Huszaren-Regimentes Alexander Freiherr v. Koller Nr. 8*, Vienna: Mayer, 1880.

—— *Geschichte des k. k. Dragoner-Regimentes Feldmarschall Alfred Fürst zu Windisch-Graetz Nr. 14*, Vienna: Brzewzowsky, 1886.

—— *Geschichte des kaiserl. und königl. Husaren-Regimentes Nr. 10*, Vienna: regimental, 1892.

—— *Geschichte des k. und k. Husaren-Regimentes Kaiser Nr. 1*, Vienna: regimental, 1898.

—— *Geschichte des k. u. k. Husaren-Regiments Nr. 4*, Vienna: regimental, 1903.

Brinner, Wilhelm, *Geschichte des k. k. Pionnier-Regimentes*, Vienna: Seidel & Sohn, 1878.

Dolleczek, Anton, *Geschichte der Oesterreichischen Artillerie*, Vienna: Kreisel & Gröger, 1887.

Geschichte des k. k. achten Uhlanen-Regimentes, Vienna: Hof- und Staatsdruckerei, 1860.

Geschichte des k. und k. Dragoner-Regiments Graf Paar Nr. 2, Olmütz, 1895.

Jedina, Karl Anton Ritter von, *Geschichte des kaiserlich königlich österreichischen ersten Uhlanen-Regimentes*, Vienna: Schmid, 1845.

Kielmansegg, Oswald Graf, *Schwarzenberg Uhlanen 1790–1887*, Tarnow, 1887.

Oesterreichische militärische Zeitschrift:

'Das Kürassier-Regiment Kronprinz Ferdinand in der Schlacht bei Wagram am 5. und 6. Juli 1809', 1844.

'Kronprinz Kürassiere im Treffen bei Regensburg am 23. April 1809', 1844.

'Kriegsszenen aus der Geschichte des k. k. Husaren-Regiments Nr. 10', 1846.

'Kriegsszenen aus der Geschichte des Chevauleger-Regiments Graf Wrbna Nr. 6', 1846.

'Szenen aus der Geschichte des k. k. Kürassier-Regiments Graf Ignaz Hardegg Nr. 8', 1847.

'Das k. k. Husaren-Regiment Palatinal im Feldzuge 1809', 1847.

Ow, Josef Baron, *Geschichte des kaiserl. königl. Erzherzog Ferdinand dritten Husaren-Regiments*, Sarvos Patak: regimental, 1843.

Pizzighelli, Cajetan, *Geschichte des k. u. k. Husaren-Regimentes Wilhelm II. König von Württemberg Nr. 6*, Rzeszów: regimental, 1897.

—— *Geschichte des K. und K. Dragoner-Regimentes Johannes Josef Fürst von und zu Liechtenstein Nr. 10*, Vienna: regimental, 1903.

—— *Geschichte des K. u. K. Ulanen-Regiments Kaiser Joseph II. No. 6.*, Vienna: regimental, 1908.

—— *Geschichte des k. u. k. Dragoner-Regimentes Friedrich August, König von Sachsen Nr. 3*, Vienna, 1925.

Riedl von Riedenau, Erich Freiherr, *Geschichte des k. und k. Uhlanen-Regimentes Erzherzog Karl Nr. 3*, Vienna: Hof- und Staatsdruckerei, 1901.

Schwarzbach, Moriz, *Gedenkblätter aus der Geschichte des k. k. 3. Dragoner-Regimentes*, Vienna: Hof- und Staatsdruckerei, 1868.

Semek, Major, 'Die Artillerie im Jahre 1809', *Mittheilungen des K. und K. Kriegsarchivs*, vol. III, 1904.

Strack, J., *Geschichte des Sechsten Dragoner-Regimentes*, Vienna: Hof- und Staatsdruckerei, 1856.

Strobl von Ravelsberg, Ferdinand, *Geschichte des k. und k. 12. Dragoner-Regiments*, Vienna: regimental, 1890.

534 ~ BIBLIOGRAPHY

Tomaschek, Eduard Freiherr von, *Geschichte des k. k. Dragoner-Regiments No. 8*, Vienna: Hof- und Staatsdruckerei, 1889.

Theimer, Alexander, *Geschichte des k.k. siebenten Uhlanen-Regiments*, Vienna: Sommer, 1869.

Thürheim, Andreas Graf, *Geschichte des k. k. achten Uhlanen-Regimentes*, Vienna: Hof- und Staatsdruckerei, 1860.

—— *Die Reiter-Regimenter der k. k. österreichischen Armee*, Vienna: Geitler, 1866.

Treuenfest, Gustav Ritter Amon von, *Geschichte des k. und k. Husaren-Regimentes Kaiser Nr. 1*, Vienna: regimental, 1898.

—— *Geschichte des k. und k. Husaren-Regimentes Kaiser Nr. 15*, Vienna: regimental, 1894.

Wengen, Friedrich von der, *Geschichte des K. und K. Oesterreichischen 13. Dragoner-Regiments*, Brandeis: regimental, 1879.

Wrede, Alfons Freiherr von, *Geschichte des K. u. K. mährischen Dragoner-Regimentes Albrecht Prinz von Preussen*, Brunn: Rohrer, 1906.

FRENCH UNIT HISTORIES: INFANTRY

Adam, A., *Historique du 111e Régiment d'Infanterie*, Bastia: Ollangnier, 1890.

Albert, Lieutenant, 'Historique du 98e Régiment d'Infanterie', manuscript, AG, 1892.

Arvers, Paul, *Historique du 82e Régiment d'Infanterie de Ligne*, Paris: Lahure, 1876.

Belhomme, Victor Louis Jean François, *Historique du 90e Régiment d'Infanterie de Ligne ex-15e Léger*, Paris: Tanera, 1875.

Bissey, Lafond and Durand, *Historique du 65e Régiment d'Infanterie de Ligne*, Nantes: regimental, 1888.

Bourgue, Marius Pierre Alphonse, *Historique du 3e Régiment d'Infanterie*, Paris: Charles-Lavauzelle, 1894.

Boutié, François André Adrien, *Historique du 59e d'Infanterie*, 1888.

Bouvier, J.-B., *Historique du 96e Régiment d'Infanterie*, Lyon: Storck, 1892.

Buresi, Dominique, *Les Corses au Combat sous Trois Drapeaux 1792–1815*, Ajaccio: Editions DCL, 2003.

Coste, Emile Louis François Désiré, *Historique du 40e Régiment d'Infanterie de Ligne*, Paris: Chamerot, 1887.

Cruyplants, Eugène, *Histoire Illustrée d'un Corps Belge au Service de la République et de l'Empire: La 112e Demi-Brigade*, Brussels: Spineux, 1902.

Dehon Dahlmann, Georges Fernand, *Historique du 12e Régiment d'Infanterie de Ligne*, Paris: Tanera, 1877.

Dollin du Fresnel, Henri Victor comte, *Un Régiment à travers l'Histoire: Le 76e, ex-1er Léger*, Paris: Flammarion, 1894.

Duneau, Simon, *Historique du 48e Régiment d'Infanterie*, Paris: Rouff, 1878.

Duplessis, R., *Combat de Pordenone 15 Avril 1809: Une Page de l'Histoire du 35me Régiment d'Infanterie*, Belfort: Devillers, 1907.

Duroisel, Capitaine, *Résumé de l'Histoire du 93e Régiment d'Infanterie*, La Roche-sur-Lyon: Ivonnet, 1891.

Edme, Capitaine, 'Historique du 105e Régiment d'Infanterie', manuscript, AG, 1894.

Espérandieu, Emile, *Histoire Abrégée des Campagnes du 61me Régiment d'Infanterie*, Marseille: Aubertin, 1897.

Estrabaut, A., *Le Livre d'Or du 8e Régiment d'Infanterie*, Paris: Charles-Lavuzelle, 1891.

Fallou, L., *La Garde Impériale*, Paris: La Giberne, 1901.

Fraguier, Capitaine Adjutant-Major de, *Historique du 25e Régiment de Ligne*, manuscript, AG, 1886.

Froidevaux, Capitaine, 'Notice Historique sur le 30e Régiment d'Infanterie et les Régiments qui l'ont précédé', manuscript, AG, 1887.

Gaillard and Fleuriot, *Historique du 62e Régiment d'Infanterie*, Paris: Berger-Levrault, 1899.

Grosselin and André, 'Historique du 100e Régiment d'Infanterie', manuscript, AG, 1896.

Gueheneuc, Charles Louis Joseph Olivier, 'Historique du 26e Léger pendant la Campagne de 1809', manuscript, AG, MR1843, August 1810.

Hervieu, E., 'Historique du 21e Régiment d'Infanterie de Ligne', manuscript, AG, 1876.

'Histoire du 29e Régiment d'Infanterie', manuscript, AG, 1886.

Historique du 65e Régiment d'Infanterie de Ligne, Paris: Tanera, 1875.

'Historique du 72e Régiment d'Infanterie', manuscript, AG, 1878.

Historique du 85e Régiment d'Infanterie, Paris: Charles-Lavauzelle, 1888.

'Historique du 99e Régiment d'Infanterie de Ligne', manuscript, AG, 1889.

Historique du 112e Régiment d'Infanterie de Ligne, Paris: Dutemple, 1875.

Historique Sommaire du 39e Régiment d'Infanterie, Rouen: regimental, 1889.

Itier, Jean Baptiste Fulbert Arthur and Lieutenant Favatier, *Historique du 57e Régiment d'Infanterie*, Libourne, 1890.

Lalande d'Obee, Lieutenant de, 'Historique du 108e R. I. (Ancien Régiment de l'Ile de France) des origines à 1890', manuscript, AG, 1890.

Lemaitre, Capitaine Adjutant-Major, 'Historique du 56e Régiment d'Infanterie de Ligne', manuscript, AG, 1869.

Loÿ, Léon, *Historiques du 84e Régiment d'Infanterie de Ligne 'Un Contre Dix,' du 9e Régiment d'Infanterie Légère 'l'Incomparable,' et du 4e Régiment de Voltigeurs de la Garde*, Lille: Danel, 1905.

Masse, P., *Le 19e Régiment d'Infanterie à travers l'Histoire 1597–1923*, Paris: Morlaix, 1923.

Molard, J., *Historique du 63e Régiment d'Infanterie*, Paris: Berger-Levrault, 1887.

Noret, Chef de Bataillon, 'Historique du 2e Régiment d'Infanterie de Ligne', manuscript, AG, 1875.

Pagès Xartart, Capitaine, 'Historique du 17e Régiment d'Infanterie de Ligne', manuscript, AG, 1894.

536 ~ BIBLIOGRAPHY

Pigeard, Alain, 'Le 17e Léger sous le Premier Empire', *Tradition*, no. 234, November–December 2007.

Pitot, Georges Edmond, *Historique du 83e Régiment d'Infanterie*, Toulouse: Privat, 1891.

Poitevin, Maurice Alexandre, *Historique du 16e Régiment d'Infanterie*, Paris: Baudoin, 1888.

Réthoré, Lieutenant, *Historique du 92e Régiment d'Infanterie*, Paris: Charles-Lavuzelle, 1889.

Rondol, G. and V. Jannesson, 'Historique du 35e Régiment d'Infanterie de Ligne', manuscript, AG, 1893.

Sage, E., 'Historique du 85e Régiment d'Infanterie de Ligne et du 10e Régiment d'Infanterie Légère', manuscript, AG, 1877.

'67e Régiment d'Infanterie: Historique du Corps', manuscript, AG, 1891.

Sommervogel, Lieutenant, 'Historique du 33eme Régiment d'Infanterie', manuscript, AG, 1891.

Thuy, Lt. Brasier de, *1er Régiment d'Infanterie*, Cambrai: Deligne et Lenglet, 1889.

Vassias, Jules G., *Historique du 69e Régiment d'Infanterie*, Paris: Chapelot, 1913.

FRENCH UNIT HISTORIES: CAVALRY AND OTHER

Albert, A., *Manuscrit des Carabiniers*, Paris: Bruno Sepulchre, 1989.

Allenou, Capitaine, 'Historique du 7eme Régiment de Dragons', manuscript, AG, 1890.

Amonville, Capitaine d', *Le 8e Cuirassiers*, Paris: Lahure, 1892.

Aubier, Lieutenant, *Un Régiment de Cavalerie Légère*, Paris: Berger-Levrault, 1888.

Bonie, A., 'Historique du 3e Régiment de Chasseurs', manuscript, AG, 1875–6.

Bouchard, S., *Historique du 28e Régiment de Dragons*, Paris: Berger-Levrault, 1893.

Brye, P. de, *Historique du 6e Régiment de Cuirassiers*, n.p., 1839.

Castillon de Saint-Victor, Marie Emilien de, *Historique du 5e Régiment de Hussards*, Paris: Lobert/Person, 1889.

'Le Centenaire des Cuirassiers', *Carnet de la Sabretache*, 1904.

Champvallier, H. de, 'Historique du 9eme Régiment de Chasseurs à Cheval', manuscript, AG, 1890.

Chavane, J., *Histoire du 11e Cuirassiers*, Paris: Charavay, 1889.

Chevillotte, Lieutenant, 'Historique du 16eme Chasseurs à Cheval', manuscript, AG, 1887.

Cosse-Brissac, René de, *Historique du 7e Régiment de Dragons*, Paris: Leroy, 1909.

Dezaunay, Capitaine, *Historique du 1er Régiment de Cuirassiers*, Angers: Lachèse & Dolbeau, 1889.

Dupont, Marcel, *Guides de Bonaparte et Chasseurs à Cheval de la Garde*, Paris: Les Éditions Militaires Illustrées, 1946.

Dupuy, Raoul, *Historique du 12e Chasseurs de 1788 à 1891*, Paris: Person, 1891.

Fontenaille, H. de, 'Histoire Militaire: 5eme de Cuirassiers', manuscript, AG, 1890.

Hache, Edouard, *Historique du 23e Régiment de Dragons*, Paris: Hachette, 1890.

Histoire du 1er Régiment de Cuirassiers, Angers: Lachese & Dolbeau, 1889.

Histoire du 4e Régiment de Cuirassiers, Paris: Lahure, 1897.

'Histoire Militaire: 5eme de Cuirassiers', manuscript, AG, n.d.

Historique du 7e Régiment de Chasseurs, Valence: Céas, 1891.

'Historique du 19e Chasseurs à Cheval', manuscript, AG, 1878.

'Historique du 10e Régiment de Cuirassiers', manuscript, AG, 1892.

Historique du 2me Régiment d'Artillerie, Grenoble: Dauphinoise, 1899.

Ivry, Ogier d', *Historique du 9e Régiment de Hussards*, Valence: Céas, 1891.

Juzancourt, G. de, *Historique du 7e Régiment de Cuirassiers*, Paris: Berger-Levrault, 1887.

Lamotte, Charles H. P. P., *Historique du 8e Régiment de Hussards*, Valence: Ceas, 1891.

Litre, Emile François, *Les Régiments d'Artillerie à Pied de la Garde, le Régiment Monté de la Garde et le 23e Régiment d'Artillerie*, Paris: Plon, 1895.

Louvat, Captaine, *Historique du 7eme Hussards*, Paris: Pairault, 1889.

Maumené, Capitaine, *Historique du 3e Régiment de Cuirassiers*, Paris: Boussod, Valadon et Cie, 1893.

Moine de Margon, Gabriel M. J. R., *Historique du 8e Régiment de Chasseurs*, Verdun: Renvé-Lallemant, 1889.

—— *Historique du 11e Régiment de Chasseurs*, Vesoul: Bon, 1896.

Oré, Delphin Charles, *1er Régiment de Chasseurs*, Chateaudun: Laussedat, 1903.

Place, R. de, *Historique du 12e Cuirassiers*, Paris: Lahure, 1889.

Quinemont, Commandant de, 'Historique du 2e Régiment de Chasseurs à Cheval', manuscript, AG, 1888.

Rembowski, Alexandre, *Sources Documentaires concernant l'Histoire du Régiment des Chevau-légers de la Garde Napoléon I*, Warsaw: Rubieszweski and Wrotnowski, 1899.

Rothwiller, Antoine Enrst, *Histoire du Deuxième Régiment de Cuirassiers*, Paris: Plon, 1877.

S., Capt., 'Les Marins de la Flottille et les Ouvriers Militaires de la Marine pendant la Campagne de 1809 en Autriche', *Carnet de la Sabretache*, 1895.

Voisin, C., *Historique du 6me Hussards*, Libourne: Maleville, 1888.

BADEN AND HESSIAN UNIT HISTORIES (4TH CORPS)

Abriss der Grossherzoglich Hessischen Kriegs- und Truppen-Geschichte 1567–1871, Darmstadt and Leipzig: Zernin, 1886.

Barsewisch, Theophil von, *Geschichte des Grossherzoglich Badischen Leib-Grenadier-Regiments 1803–1870*, Karlsruhe: Müller, 1893.

Beck, Fritz, Karl von Hahn and Heinrich von Hahn, *Geschichte des Grossherzoglichen Artilleriekorps 1. Grossherzoglich Hessischen Feldartillerie-Regiments Nr. 25 und seiner Stämme*, Berlin: Mittler & Sohn, 1912.

Bigge, Wilhelm, *Geschichte des Infanterie-Regiments Kaiser Wilhelm (2. Grossherzoglich Hessisches) Nr. 116*, Berlin: Mittler & Sohn, 1903.

Bray, Graf von, *Geschichte des 1. Badischen Leib-Dragoner-Regiments Nr. 20 und dessen Stammregiments des Badischen Dragoner-Regiments von Freystedt von 1803 bis zur Gegenwart*, Berlin: Mittler & Sohn, 1909.

Caspary, Ernst, *Geschichte des dritten Grossherzoglich Hessischen Infanterie-Regiments (Leib-Regiments) Nr. 117*, Darmstadt: Lange, 1877.

'Feldzug der 2ten Division 4ten Armeecorps der Armee von Teutschland im Jahr 1809', *Pallas*, vol. II, 1810.

Ferber, Alexander, *Geschichte des 1. Badischen Feldartillerie-Regiments Nr. 14*, Karlsruhe: Müller, 1906.

Haffner, J. D., *Geschichtliche Darstellung des Grossherzoglich Badischen Armee-Corps*, Karlsruhe: Malsch und Vogel, 1840.

Kattrein, Ludwig, *Ein Jahrhundert deutscher Truppengeschichte dargestellt an derjenigen des Grossh. Hessischen Kontingents 1806–1906*, Darmstadt: Schlapp, 1907.

Keim, August, *Geschichte des Infanterie-Leibregiments Grossherzogin (3. Grossherzogl. Hessisches) Nr. 117*, Berlin: Bath, 1903.

Klingelhöffer, Friedrich, *Geschichte des 2. Grossherzoglich Hessischen Infanterie-Regiments (Grossherzog) Nr. 116*, Berlin: Mittler & Sohn, 1888.

Kösterus, Martin, *Geschichtliche Darstellung der Entwicklung der Militär-Verfassung der Hessen-Darmstädtischen Truppen seit Phillip dem Grossmüthigen bis auf unsere Tage. Nebst den Feldzügen welchen dieselben von 1792 bis 1815 beigewohnt haben*, Darmstadt: Brill, 1840.

Legde, Adolf, *Geschichte des 2. Badischen Dragoner-Regiments Nr. 21*, Berlin: Mittler & Sohn, 1893.

Rau, Ferdinand, *Geschichte des 1. Badischen Leib-Dragoner Regiments Nr. 20 und dessen Stamm-Regiments von Freystedt von 1803 bis zur Gegenwart*, Berlin: Mittler & Sohn, 1878.

Renschler, Adolph, 'Die badischen Husaren', manuscript, Wehrgeschichtliches Museum, Rastatt, 1978,.

Röder von Diersburg, Carl Christian Freiherr von, *Geschichte des 1. Grossherzoglich Hessischen Infanterie- (Leibgarde-) Regiments Nr. 115*, ed. Fritz Beck, Berlin: Mittler & Sohn, 1899.

Söllner, Gerhard, *Für Badens Ehre: Die Geschichte der Badischen Armee*, Karlsruhe: Info Verlagsgesellschaft, 1995–2001.

Theilnahme der Grossherz. Hess. Truppen an dem Kriege zwischen Oestreich und Frankreich im Jahre 1809, Darmstadt: Auw, 1850 (written in October 1809).

Walz, Hauptmann, *Geschichte des Linien-Infanterie-Regiments Grossherzog Nr. 1.*, manuscript, Wehrgeschichtliches Museum, Rastatt, 1843–4.

Wengen, Freiherr von der, *Der Feldzug der Grossherzoglich Badischen Truppen unter Oberst Freiherrn Karl v. Stockhorn gegen die Vorarlberger und Tiroler 1809*, Heidelberg: Winter, 1910.

Wenz zu Niederlahnstein, Rolf von, Heinrich Hentz, and Otto Abt, *Dreihundert Jahre Leibgarde Regiment (1. grossherzoglich Hessisches) Nr. 115*, Darmstadt: Kichler, 1929.

Zech, Karl von and Friedrich von Porbeck, *Geschichte der Badischen Truppen 1809 im Feldzug der Französischen Hauptarmee gegen Oesterreich*, ed. Rudolf von Freydorf, Heidelberg: Winter, 1909.

Zimmermann, Karl von, *Geschichte des 1. Grossherzoglich Hessischen Dragoner-Regiments (Garde-Dragoner-Regiments) Nr. 23*, Darmstadt: Bergsträsser, 1878.

BAVARIAN UNIT HISTORIES (7TH CORPS)

Auvera, Alfred, *Geschichte des Kgl. Bayer. 7. Infanterie-Regiments Prinz Leopold von Bayern*, Bayreuth: Ellwanger, 1898.

Berg, Franz, *Geschichte des königl. Bayer. 4. Jäger-Bataillons*, Landshut: Rietsch, 1887.

Bezzel, Oskar, 'Die Massnahmen Bayerns zum Grenzschutze im Feldzuge 1809', *Darstellungen aus der Bayerischen Kriegs- und Heeresgeschichte*, vol. 14, 1905.

—— *Das K. B. 4. Infanterie-Regiment König Wilhelm von Württemberg vom Jahre 1806–1906*, Munich: Lindauer, 1906.

—— *Geschichte des Königlich Bayerischen Heeres unter Max I. Joseph von 1806 (1804) bis 1825*, vol. VI, part 1 of *Geschichte des Bayerischen Heeres*, Munich: Schick, 1933.

Buxbaum, Emil, *Das königlich Bayerische 3. Chevaulegers-Regiment 'Herzog Maximilian' 1724 bis 1884*, Munich: Oldenbourg, 1884.

Dauer, Joseph, *Das königlich Bayerische 10. Infanterie-Regiment Prinz Ludwig*, Ingolstadt: Ganghofer, 1901.

Döderlein, Alfred, *Geschichte des Königlich Bayerischen 8. Infanterie-Regiments (Pranckh)*, Landshut: Rietsch, 1898.

Fabrice, Friedrich von, 'Nochmals die bayerische Reiter-Brigade Seydewitz bei Eggmühl', *Jahrbücher für die deutsche Armee und Marine*, vol. 65, October–December 1887.

—— *Das Königlich Bayerischen 6. Infanterie-Regiment Kaiser Wilhelm, König von Preussen*, Munich: Oldenbourg, 1896.

Füchtbauer, Heinrich, 'Geschichte der Stammtruppen des K. B. 14. Infanterie-Regiments', part I of *Festschrift zur Jahrhundertfeier des k. b. 14. Infanterie-Regiments Hartmann*, Nuremberg: Stich, 1914.

Gerneth, Hans and Bernhard Kiessling, *Geschichte des Königlich Bayerischen 5. Infanterie-Regiments*, Berlin: Mittler & Sohn, 1893.

Grosch, Feodor, Eduard Hagen, and Albert Schenk, *Geschichte des K. B. 12. Infanterie-Regiments Prinz Arnulf und seiner Stammabteilungen*, Munich, 1914.

H., M., *Kurze Darstellung der Geschichte des Königlich Bayerischen 4. Chevaulegers-Regiments 'König' von 1744 bis zur Gegenwart*, Berlin: Mittler & Sohn, 1895.

Heinze, Emil, *Geschichte des Kgl. Bayer. 6. Chevaulegers-Regiments 'Prinz Albrecht von Preussen'*, Leipzig: Klinkhardt, 1898.

Hutter, Herman, *Das Königlich Bayerische 1. Chevaulegers-Regiment 'Kaiser Alexander von Russland' 1682 bis 1882*, Munich: Oldenbourg, 1885.

J., M., 'Die bayerische Reiter-Brigade Seydewitz bei Eggmühl', *Jahrbücher für die deutsche Armee und Marine*, vol. 63, April–June 1887.

Käuffer, Karl, *Geschichte des königlich bayerischen 9. Infanterie-Regiments Wrede*, Würzburg: Ballhorn und Craner, 1895.

Kneussl, Paul, *Geschichte des K. bayer. 2. (vormals 3.) Jäger-Bataillons*, Würzburg: Stürtz, 1899.

'Kriegsscenen aus der Geschichte des königlich bayerischen Infanterie-Regiments Prinz Karl (Nro. 3.) in den Jahren 1807 und 1809', *Archiv für Offiziere aller Waffen*, vol. II, 1848.

Leyh, Max, *Die Feldzüge des Königlich Bayerischen Heeres unter Max I. Joseph von 1805 bis 1815*, vol. VI, part 2 of *Geschichte des Bayerischen Heeres*, Munich: Schick, 1935.

Lipowsky, *Bürger-Militär-Almanach für das Königreich Bayern 1809*, Munich: Fleischmann, 1809.

Madroux, Ludwig von, 'Die bayerische Kavallerie-Brigade Seydewitz in der Schlacht von Eggmühl (22. April 1809)', *Archiv für Offiziere aller Waffen*, vol. 2, 1845.

Münich, Friedrich, *Geschichte der Entwicklung der bayerischen Armee seit zwei Jahrhunderten*, Munich: Lindauer, 1864.

Obpacher, Josef, *Das k. b. 2. Chevaulegers-Regiment Taxis*, Munich: Bayerisches Kriegsarchiv, 1926.

Paulus, G., 'Bayerische Kriegsvorbereitungen, Mobilmachung und Einleitung zum Feldzuge 1809', *Darstellungen aus der Bayerischen Kriegs- und Heeresgeschichte*, vol. 2, 1893.

Pfeffer, Joseph, *Geschichte des K. bayer. 15. Infanterie-Regiments König Friedrich August von Sachsen von 1722 bis 1907*, Neuburg a. Donau: Griessmayer, 1907.

[Prielmeyer, Max von], *Geschichte des k. b. I. Infanterie-Regiments König*, Munich: Huttler, 1881.

Rattelmüller, Paul E., *Das Bayerische Bürgermilitär*, Munich: Süddeutscher Verlag, 1969.

Reichert, Moritz Ritter von, *Das Königlich Bayerische 2. Infanterie-Regiment 'Kronprinz'*, Munich: Oldenbourg, 1913.

Röder, Fritz, *Geschichte des bisherigen K. B. 4. Jäger-Bataillons und seiner Stamm-Abteilungen*, Landshut: Rietsch, 1890.

Ruith, Max, *Das k. bayerische 10. Infanterie-Regiment 'Prinz Ludwig'*, Ingolstadt: Ganghofer, 1882.

—— *Das K. Bayer. 12. Infanterie-Regiment 'Prinz Arnulf'*, Ulm: Ebner, 1902.

Ruith, Max and Emil Ball, *Kurze Geschichte des K. B. 3. Infanterie-Regiments Prinz Karl von Bayern*, Ingolstadt, 1890.

Schmelzing, Julius, *Darstellung der mobilen Legionen oder der Nationalgarde IIter Klasse im Königreich Bayern aus den Gesetzes-Quellen*, Nuremberg: Zeh, 1818.

Schubert, Franz and Hans Vara, *Geschichte des K. B. 13. Infanterie-Regiments*, Munich: Lindauer, 1906.

Sichlern, Oskar von, *Geschichte des königlich bayerischen 5. Chevaulegers-Regiments 'Prinz Otto'*, Munich: regimental, 1876.

Uebe, Kurt, *Die Stimmungsumschwung in der Bayerischen Armee gegenüber den Franzosen 1806–1812*, Munich: Beck, 1939.

Völderndorff und Waradein, Eduard Freiherr von, *Kriegsgeschichte von Bayern unter König Maximilian Joseph I.*, Munich, 1826.

Wolf, Gustav, *Der Eilmarsch Wredes von Linz bis Wagram*, Innsbruck: Wagner, 1909.

Xylander, Rudolf Ritter von, *Geschichte des 1. Feldartillerie-Regiments Prinz-Regent Luitpold*, Berlin: Mittler & Sohn, 1909.

Zechmayer, Georg, *Geschichte des Königlich bayerischen 14. Infanterie-Regiments und seiner Stammtruppen*, Nuremberg, 1885.

Zoellner, Eugen, *Geschichte des K. B. 11. Infanterie-Regiments 'von der Tann' 1805–1905*, Munich: Lindauer, 1905.

SAXON UNIT HISTORIES (9TH CORPS)

Bucher, H., 'Die Theilnahme der sächsischen Truppen an den Kriegsereignissen vor hundert Jahren', *Dresdener Anzeiger*, nos. 185 and 186, 6–7 July 1909.

Exner, Moritz, *Die Antheilnahme der Königlich Sächsischen Armee am Feldzuge gegen Oesterreich und die kriegerischen Ereignisse in Sachsen im Jahre 1809*, Dresden: Baensch, 1894.

Friedel, Hauptmann, *Geschichte des 7. Infanterie-Regiments 'König Georg' Nr. 106*, Leipzig: Jacobsen, n.d.

Friesen, Edwin Freiherr von, *Versuch einer Geschichte des Königlich Sächsischen II. Reiterregiments*, Dresden: Heinrich, 1861.

Geschichte des Königl. Sächs. Königs-Husaren-Regiments No. 18, Leipzig: Baumert & Ronge, 1901.

Geschichte des Königlich Sächsischen 3. Infanterie-Regiments Nr. 102 'Prinz-Regent Luitpold von Bayern' 1709–1909, Berlin: Mittler & Sohn, 1909.

Geschichte des Königl. Sächs. Schützen-Regiments 'Prinz Georg' No. 108, Leipzig: Jacobsen, n.d.

Herrman, Pfarrer Heinrich, *Geschichte des Königlich Sächsischen Leibgrenadier-Regiments Nr. 100*, Zittau: Mönch, n.d.

Holtzendorff, Albrecht von, *Geschichte der Königlich Sächsischen Leichten Infanterie von Ihrer Errichtung bis zum 1. October 1859*, Leipzig: Geisecke & Devrient, 1860.

Kretschmar, A. von, *Geschichte der kurfürstlich und königlich Sächsischen Feld-Artillerie von 1620–1820*, Berlin: Mittler & Sohn, 1876.

Larrass, Johannes Anton, *Geschichte des Königlich Sächsischen 6. Infanterie-Regiments Nr. 105 und seine Vorgeschichte 1701 bis 1887*, Strasbourg: Kayser, 1887.

Lichterfeld, M. S. von, *Regiments-Geschichte des Königlich Sächsischen Garde-Reiter-Regiments*, Berlin: Vobach, 1904.

Lommatzsch, Carl, *Geschichte des 4. Infanterie-Regiments Nr. 103*, Dresden: Heinrich, 1909.

Pilzecker, Carl, 'Scenen aus dem Feldzuge der Sachsen in Oesterreich, und zwar vor, während und nach der Schlacht bei Deutsch-Wagram; vom 2. bis mit den 27. Juli 1809', *Sachsenzeitung*, no. 233 ff., August–September 1830.

'Die sächsischen Husaren im Feldzuge von 1809 in Oestreich', *Zeitschrift für Kunst, Wissenschaft und Geschichte des Krieges*, no. 7, 1847.

'Das 2. sächsische Schützenbataillon in der Schlacht bei Wagram am 5. Juli 1809', *Sachsen-Post*, 14 July 1909.

Schimpff, Georg von, *Geschichte des Kgl. Sächs. Garde-Reiter-Regiments*, Dresden: Baensch, 1880.

Schimpff, Hans von, *Geschichte der beiden Königlich Sächsischen Grenadier-Regimenter: Erstes (Leib-) Grenadier-Regiment Nr. 100 und Zweites Grenadier-Regiment Nr. 101, Kaiser Wilhelm, König von Preussen*, Dresden: Höckner, 1877.

Schönberg, Georg von, *Geschichte des Königl. Sächsischen 7. Infanterie-Regiments 'Prinz Georg' Nr. 106*, Leipzig: Brockhaus, 1890.

Schuster, O. and F. A. Francke, *Geschichte der Sächsischen Armee von deren Errichtung bis auf die neueste Zeit*, Leipzig: Duncker & Humblot, 1885.

Süssmilch Gen. Hörnig, Moritz von, *Geschichte des 2. Königl. Sächs. Husaren-Regiments 'Kronprinz Friedrich Wilhelm des Deutschen Reichs und von Preussen' Nr. 19*, Leipzig: Brockhaus, 1882.

Treitschke, Eduard von, 'Die königl. sächsischen Truppen in der Schlacht bei Wagram, am 5. und 6. Juli 1809', *Zeitschrift für Kunst, Wissenschaft und Geschichte des Krieges*, vol. 34, 1838.

Verlohren, Heinrich A., *Stammregister und Chronik der Kur- und Königlich Sächsischen Armee von 1670 bis zum Beginn des Zwanzigsten Jahrhunderts*, Leipzig: Beck, 1910.

Werlhof, Generalmajor von, 'Bernadotte und die Sachsen bei Wagram 5. und 6. Juli 1809', *Beiheft zum Militär-Wochenblatt*, vol. 1, 1911.

WÜRTTEMBERG UNIT HISTORIES (8TH CORPS)

Duvernoy, Hauptmann, *Württembergischen Heeresgeschichte*, Berlin: Eisenschmidt, 1893.

Felder, R. M., *Der schwarze Jäger oder Württembergs Krieger in den Jahren 1805–1816*, Cannstatt: Ruckhäberle, 1839.

Geschichte des 3. Württ. Infanterie-Regiments No. 121 1716–1891, Stuttgart: Kohlhammer, 1891.

Geschichte des Ulanen-Regiments 'König Karl' (1. Württembergisches) Nr. 19., n.d.

Gessler, Karl, Ulysses Tognarelli, and Theodor Strobl, *Geschichte des 2. Württembergischen Feldartillerie-Regiments Nr. 29*, Stuttgart: regimental, 1892.

Gleich, Wilhelm, *Die ersten 100 Jahre des Ulanen-Regiments König Wilhelm I. (2. Württemb.) Nr. 20.*, Stuttgart: Uhland, n.d.

Greisinger, Theodor, *Geschichte des Ulanenregiments 'König Karl' (1. Württembergischen) Nr. 19 von seiner Gründung 1683 bis zur Gegenwart*, Stuttgart: Deutsche Verlags-Anstalt, 1883.

Fromm, Ferdinand, *Geschichte des Infanterie-Regiments König Wilhelm I (6. Württ.) Nr. 124.*, Weingarten: regimental, 1901.

Köberle, Rudolf, *Geschichte des 4. Württemb. Infanterie-Regiments Nr. 122 von seiner Gründung 1806 bis 1874*, Ludwigsburg: regimental, 1881.

Kraft, Heinz, *Die Württemberger in den Napoleonischen Kriegen*, Stuttgart: Kohlhammer, 1953.

'Die leichte württembergische Brigade Hügel in dem Gefechte bei Linz, im Jahre 1809', *Archiv für Offiziere aller Waffen*, vol. 3, 1847.

Marx, Karl, *Geschichte des Infanterie-Regiments Kaiser Friedrich, König von Preussen (7. Württembergischen) Nr. 125. 1809–1895*, Berlin: Mittler & Sohn, 1895.

Muff, Karl and Adolf Wencher, *Geschichte des Grenadier-Regiments König Karl (5. Württembergischen) Nr. 123.*, Stuttgart: Metzler, 1889.

Müller, Herbert, *Füsilier-Regiment Kaiser Franz Joseph von Oesterreich, König von Ungarn (4. Württemb.) Nr. 122.*, 'Die Achselklappe' Sammlung kurzer Regimentsgeschichten 6, Stuttgart: Uhland, n.d.

—— *Geschichte des 4. Württembergischen Infanterie-Regiments No. 122 Kaiser Franz Joseph von Oesterreich, König von Ungarn 1806–1906*, Heilbronn: Scheuerlen, 1906.

Neubronner, Oberleutnant von, *Geschichte des Dragoner-Regiments König (2. Württ.) Nr. 26.*, Stuttgart: regimental, n.d.

Niethammer, Georg von, *Geschichte des Grenadierregiments Königin Olga*, Stuttgart: Kohlhammer, 1886.

Nübling, Oberleutnant, *Geschichte des Grenadier-Regiments König Karl (5. Württembergischen) Nr. 123.*, Berlin: Eisenschmidt, 1911.

Petermann, Hermann, *Geschichte des Infanterieregiments Kaiser Wilhelm König von Preussen (2. Württ.) Nr. 120.*, Stuttgart: Kohlhammer, 1890.

Pfaff, Karl, *Geschichte des Militärwesens in Württemberg von der ältesten bis auf unsere Zeit*, Stuttgart: Schweizerbart, 1842.

Pfister, Albert von, *Infanterie-Regiment 'König Wilhelm I.' (6. Württ.) Nr. 124.*, 'Die Achselklappe' Sammlung kurzer Regimentsgeschichten 7, Stuttgart: Moritz, n.d.

—— *Denkwüdigkeiten aus der württembergischen Kriegsgeschichte des 18. und 19. Jahrhunderts im Anschluss an die Geschichte des 8. Infanterieregiments*, Stuttgart: Grüninger, 1868.

—— *Geschichte des 1. württ. Infanterieregiments*, Stuttgart: Kirn, 1875.

—— *Das Infanterieregiment Kaiser Wilhelm, König von Preussen (2. Württ.) No. 120.*, Stuttgart: Metzler, 1881.

[Roessler], *Tagebücher aus den zehen Feldzügen der Württemberger unter der Regierung König Friedrichs*, Ludwigsburg: Nast, 1820.

Spiess, Karl and Hans Ritter, *Geschichte des Dragoner-Regiments Königin Olga (1. Württ.) Nr. 25.*, Ludwigsburg: regimental, n.d.

Stadlinger, Leo Ignaz von, *Geschichte des Württembergischen Kriegswesens*, Stuttgart: Guttenberg, 1856.

Starklof, Richard, *Geschichte des Königlich Württembergischen Zweiten Reiter-Regiments ehemaligen Jäger-Regiments zu Pferde Herzog Louis*, Darmstadt and Leipzig: Zernin, 1862.

—— *Geschichte des Königlich Württembergischen vierten Reiterregiments Königin Olga 1805–1866*, Stuttgart: Aue, 1867.

Strack von Weisenbach, Hauptmann, *Geschichte der Königlich Württembergischen Artillerie*, Stuttgart: Kohlhammer, 1882.

Wacker, Peter, 'Der württembergische Feldzug gegen die Vorarlberger 1809', *Die Zinnfigur*, vol. 8, 1959.

OTHER GERMAN UNIT HISTORIES

Ardenne, Freiherr Armand von, *Bergische Lanziers, Westfälische Husaren Nr. 11*, Berlin: Mittler & Sohn, 1877.

Eck, Hans von, *Geschichte des 2. Westfälischen Husaren-Regiments Nr. 11 und seiner Stammtruppen von 1807–1893*, Mainz: Militär-Verlagsanstalt, 1893.

Fiebig, Rittmeister, 'Das 4., 5. und 6. Rheinbund-Regiment', *Zeitschrift für Heeres- und Uniformkunde*, vols 64/66, April 1934.

Gärtner, Markus and Edmund Wagner, *Westfälisches Militär*, Beckum: Deutsche Gesellschaft für Heereskunde, 1990.

Helmes, Hermann, 'Die Würzburger Truppen vor hundert Jahren', *Archiv des historischen Vereins von Unterfranken und Aschaffenburg*, no. 55, 1913.

Herrmann, Friedrich, 'Bergische Reiter', *Zeitschrift für Heereskunde*, no. 287, January–February 1980.

Hewig, W., 'Die Armee des Königreichs Westfalen 1808–13', *Zeitschrift für Heeres- und Uniformkunde*, nos. 142/143, May/July 1955, nos. 144/145, September/November 1955, and nos. 146/147, January/March 1956.

Jacobs, Gustav, *Geschichte der Feldzüge und Schicksale der Gotha-Altenburgischen Krieger in den Jahren 1807–1815*, Altenburg: Gleich, 1835.

Kopp, Walter, *Würzburger Wehr*, vol. 22 of *Mainfränkische Studien*, Würzburg: Freunde der Mainfränkische Kunst und Geschichte, 1979.

Kortzfleisch, Gustav von, *Geschichte des Herzoglich Braunschweigischen Infanterie-Regiments und seiner Stammtruppen 1809–1867*, Braunschweig: Limbach, 1896.

Küster, Hans, *Geschichte des Anhaltischen Infanterie-Regiments Nr. 93*, Berlin: Mittler & Sohn, 1893.

Lünsmann, Fritz, *Die Armee des Königreichs Westfalen 1807–1813*, Berlin: Leddihn, 1935.

Neff, Wilhelm, *Geschichte des Infanterie-Regiments von Goeben (2. Rheinischen) Nr. 28*, Berlin: Mittler & Sohn, 1890.

Oesterhaus, Wilhelm, *Geschichte der Fürstlich Lippischen Truppen in den Jahren 1807–1815*, Detmold: Meyer, 1907.

Pivka, Otto von [Digby Smith], *Napoleon's German Allies (1): Westfalia and Kleve-Berg*, London: Osprey, 1975.

—— *Napoleon's German Allies (2): Nassau and Oldenburg*, London: Osprey, 1976.

—— *Napoleon's German Allies (3): Saxony*, London: Osprey, 1979.

—— *Napoleon's German Allies (4): Bavaria*, London: Osprey, 1980.

—— *Napoleon's German Allies (5): Hessen-Darmstadt & Hessen-Kassel*, London: Osprey, 1982.

Sauzey, Camille, *Les Allemands sous les Aigles Françaises*, Paris: Terana, 1987–8.

Schneidawind, Franz J. A., *Das Regiment der Herzoge von Sachsen in den blutigen Tagen des 4. und 5. August 1809 bei Ober- und Unter-Au in dem Kriege in Tirol*, Aschaffenburg: Wailandt, 1852.

Seebach, Ludwig Freiherr von, *Geschichte der Feldzüge des Herzoglich Sachsen-Weimarischen Scharfschützenbataillons im Jahr 1806 und des Infanterieregiments der Herzöge von Sachsen in den Jahren 1807, 1809, 1810 und 1811*, Weimar: Voigt, 1838.

Thomas, J., *Un Régiment Rhénan sous Napoléon Premier*, Liege: Vaillant-Carmanne, 1928.

OTHER FRENCH ALLIES

Addobbati, Simeone, *Il Reggimento Reale Dalmata*, Zara: Artale, 1899.

Boppe, Paul, *La Légion Portugaise 1807–1813*, Paris: Berger-Levrault, 1897.

Brnardic, Vladimir, *Napoleon's Balkan Troops*, Oxford: Osprey, 2004.

Chelminski, Jan V. and A. Malibran, *L'Armée du Duché de Varsovie*, Paris: Leroy, 1913.

Nafziger, George, Mariusz T. Wesolowski, and Tom Devoe, *Poles and Saxons of the Napoleonic Wars*, Chicago: The Emperor's Press, 1991.

Perconte, Jean-Pierre, *Les Chasseurs à Cheval Italiens 1800–1814*, Lyon: Perconte, 2008.

Pivka, Otto von [Digby Smith], *Napoleon's Polish Troops*, New York: Hippocrene, 1974.

Sypesteijn, J. W. van, *Geschiednis van het Regiment Rijdende Artillerie*, Zaltbommel, 1852.

Errata

ERRATA FOR VOLUME II: ASPERN

Page	Correction/Clarification
38	Bergheim is four kilometres north-west of Salzburg.
39	Neumarkt am Wallersee is shown as 'Neumrkt' on Map 5.
50–1	The 'Raab' here is a village in Upper Austria, not to be confused with the town/fortress in Hungary (see Map 4).
82	The Berg unit that was to join Beaumont was the 3rd Infantry.
111–12	Sedlitz and Oberplan are on Map 14.
121	The unnamed town on Map 18 is Harbach.
233	Fortogna is on the Piave approximately twelve kilometres north of Belluno.
266	Sacco is a suburb of San Daniele, where the Reisky unit symbol is shown on Map 38.
290	Source for the quotation about Jellacic is Johann's memoirs from an extract in Zwiedineck-Südenhorst, 'Das Gefecht bei St Michael', p. 45.
291–4	Ettingshausen (not Ettinghausen).
300	Map 48: Insurrection commander should be Davidovich (not Duka).
344	Appendix 10: Johann's rank should be GdK (not FML).
353	Appendix 10: Should be GB Deviau (not Devian) under Marmont; note that he remained in Ragusa and did not march with the army.
368	Clarification: one squadron of 28th Dragoons had been detached on 5 May.
371	Clarification: the three Klagenfurt battalions had not been ordered to return.
408/Note 14	Clarification: the troops under Hertelendy were four and one-half squadrons of Zemplin Hussars and five companies of Abaujvar Infantry No 19, approximately 1,600 men.

Index

('>' indicates a promotion during 1809)